SOUTH BIRMINGHAM COLLEGE

089892

SOUTH & CITY COLLEGE BIRMINGHAM
LIBRARY SERVICES
Hall Green Campus
Tel: 0121 694 6312

Book No: *089 892*

This book is due for return on or before the last date shown below:-

2 4 OCT 2014

D1513663

PENGUIN BOOKS

VISHNU'S C...

Maria Misra is Lecturer in Modern History at Oxford University and Fellow of Keble College. She presented the television series *An Indian Affair*, broadcast on Channel Four, and is the author of *Business, Race and Politics in British India*.

MARIA MISRA

Vishnu's Crowded Temple
India since the Great Rebellion

PENGUIN BOOKS

PENGUIN BOOKS

Published by the Penguin Group
Penguin Books Ltd, 80 Strand, London WC2R ORL, England
Penguin Group (USA) Inc., 375 Hudson Street, New York, New York 10014, USA
Penguin Group (Canada), 90 Eglinton Avenue East, Suite 700, Toronto, Ontario, Canada M4P 2Y3
(a division of Pearson Penguin Canada Inc.)
Penguin Ireland, 25 St Stephen's Green, Dublin 2, Ireland
(a division of Penguin Books Ltd)
Penguin Group (Australia), 250 Camberwell Road, Camberwell, Victoria 3124, Australia
(a division of Pearson Australia Group Pty Ltd)
Penguin Books India Pvt Ltd, 11 Community Centre, Panchsheel Park, New Delhi – 110 017, India
Penguin Group (NZ), 67 Apollo Drive, Rosedale, North Shore 0632, New Zealand
(a division of Pearson New Zealand Ltd)
Penguin Books (South Africa) (Pty) Ltd, 24 Sturdee Avenue, Rosebank, Johannesburg 2196, South Africa

Penguin Books Ltd, Registered Offices: 80 Strand, London WC2R ORL, England

www.penguin.com

First published by Allen Lane 2007
Published in Penguin Books 2008
1

Copyright © Maria Misra, 2007
All rights reserved

The moral right of the author has been asserted

Typeset by Rowland Phototypesetting Ltd, Bury St Edmunds, Suffolk
Printed in England by Clays Ltd, St Ives plc

Except in the United States of America, this book is sold subject
to the condition that it shall not, by way of trade or otherwise, be lent,
re-sold, hired out, or otherwise circulated without the publisher's
prior consent in any form of binding or cover other than that in
which it is published and without a similar condition including this
condition being imposed on the subsequent purchaser

978-0-140-28531-4

www.greenpenguin.co.uk

Penguin Books is committed to a sustainable future
for our business, our readers and our planet.
The book in your hands is made from paper
certified by the Forest Stewardship Council.

To my father,
Manmohan Nath Misra, 1926–2006

Contents

SOUTH BIRMINGHAM COLLEGE

954 MIS

089892   03/09/08

LIBRARY HALL GREEN

List of Illustrations

Photographic acknowledgements are given in parentheses.

Acknowledgements

I would like to thank the Oxford History Faculty and the Warden and Fellows of Keble College for their support for this project. I am also very grateful to Dr David Washbrook and the filmmaker Partha Chatterjee, who read the manuscript and offered invaluable help, saving me from embarrassing errors. I have spent many happy weeks at the Indian International Centre in New Delhi discussing Indian politics and history with its invariably lively and friendly denizens, especially Robbi Chatterji. During my visits to India, politicians Mani Shankar Aiyar, Ambika Soni, Jairam Ramesh, Dr Swamy Subramanian, Arun Jaitley and Sushma Swaraj generously gave up their time to talk to me.

I would also like to thank Charlotte Ridings for her care with copyediting, Amanda Russell for all her help with the pictures and Richard Duguid for overseeing production. I have benefited greatly from the help and encouragement of Gill Coleridge and Andrew Wylie, and I would particularly like to thank Simon Winder at Penguin for his super-human patience, good humour and shrewd advice.

My greatest debt by far is to David Priestland, who is now (not altogether by choice) unusually well informed about Indian history.

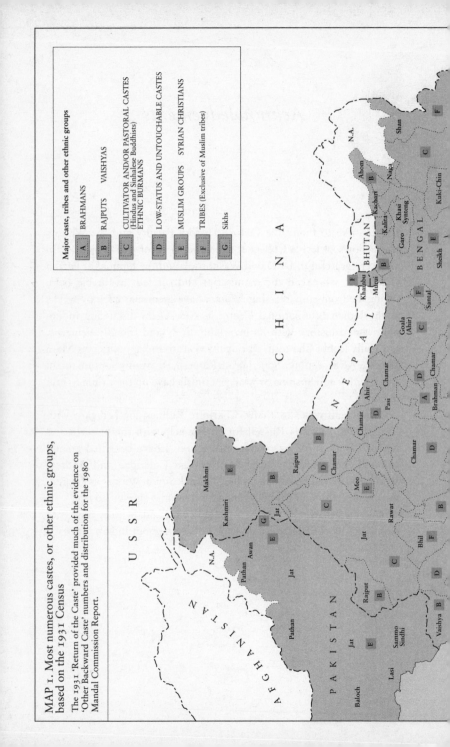

MAP 1. Most numerous castes, or other ethnic groups, based on the 1931 Census

The 1931 'Return of the Caste' provided much of the evidence on 'Other Backward Caste' numbers and distribution for the 1980 Mandal Commission Report.

Major caste, tribes and other ethnic groups

A   BRAHMANS
B   RAJPUTS   VAISHYAS
C   CULTIVATOR AND/OR PASTORAL CASTES
    (Hindus and Sinhalese Buddhists)
    ETHNIC BURMANS
D   LOW-STATUS AND UNTOUCHABLE CASTES
E   MUSLIM GROUPS   SYRIAN CHRISTIANS
F   TRIBES (Exclusive of Muslim tribes)
G   Sikhs

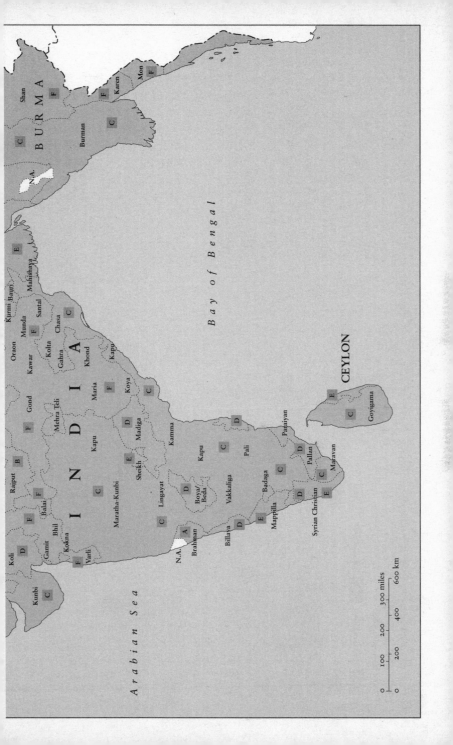

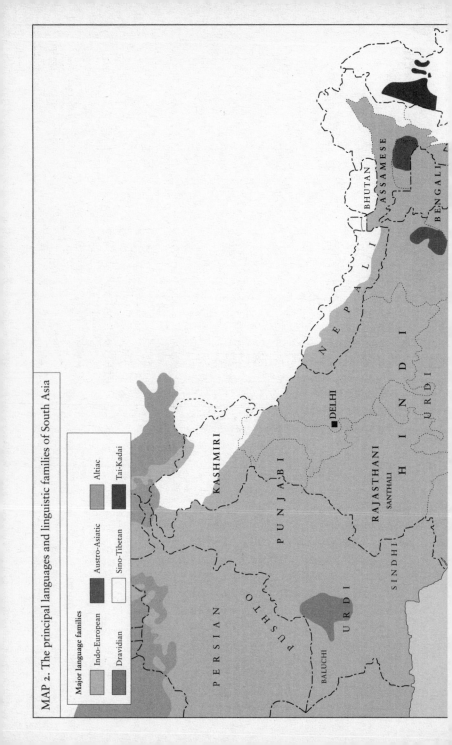

MAP 2. The principal languages and linguistic families of South Asia

Major language families

Indo-European

Dravidian

Altaic

Austro-Asiatic

Sino-Tibetan

Tai-Kadai

PERSIAN

PUSHTO

BALUCHI

URDI

SINDHI

KASHMIRI

PUNJABI

RAJASTHANI

SANTHALI

HINDI

URDI

■ DELHI

NEPALI

BHUTAN

ASSAMESE

BENGALI

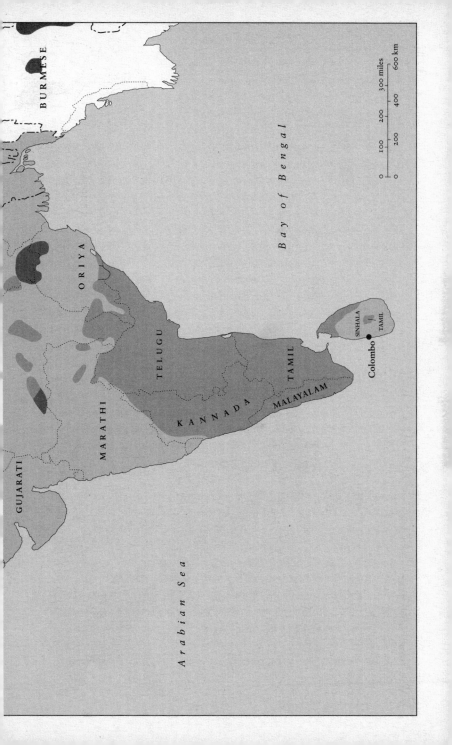

BURMESE

Bay of Bengal

ORIYA

TELUGU

MARATHI

KANNADA

GUJARATI

MALAYALAM

TAMIL

SINHALA

TAMIL

Colombo

Arabian Sea

0   100   200   300 miles
0   200   400   600 km

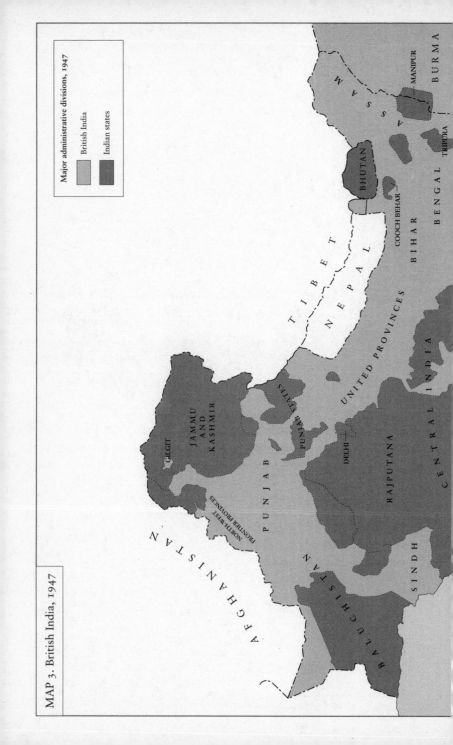

MAP 3. British India, 1947

Major administrative divisions, 1947

British India

Indian states

AFGHANISTAN

TIBET

NEPAL

BHUTAN

ASSAM

MANIPUR

BURMA

TRIPERA

BENGAL

COOCH BEHAR

BIHAR

UNITED PROVINCES

CENTRAL INDIA

RAJPUTANA

DELHI

PUNJAB STATES

PUNJAB

JAMMU AND KASHMIR

GILGIT

NORTH-WEST FRONTIER PROVINCE

SINDH

BALUCHISTAN

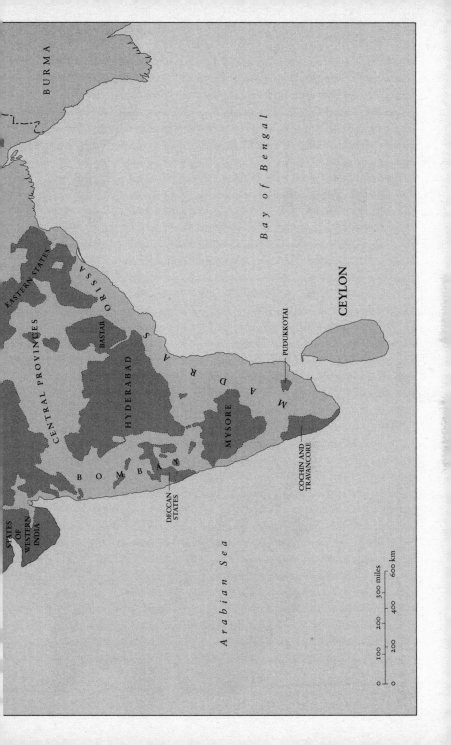

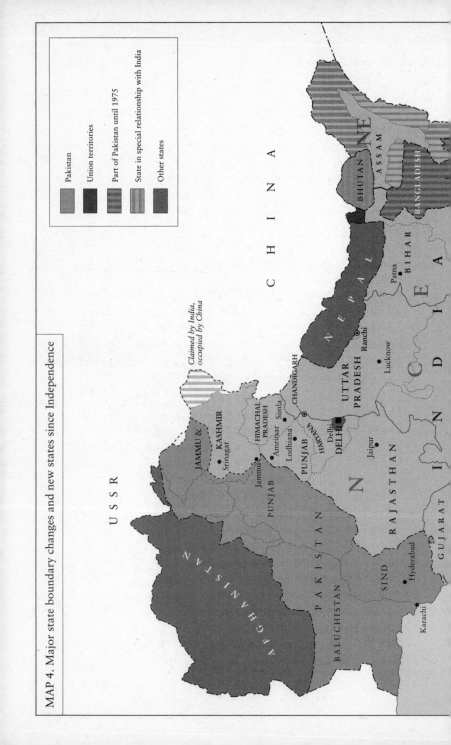

MAP 4. Major state boundary changes and new states since Independence

Legend:
- Pakistan
- Union territories
- Part of Pakistan until 1975
- State in special relationship with India
- Other states

Claimed by India, occupied by China

USSR

AFGHANISTAN

PAKISTAN

BALUCHISTAN

SIND

Karachi

Hyderabad

PUNJAB

JAMMU & KASHMIR

Srinagar

Jammu

HIMACHAL PRADESH

Simla

Amritsar

Ludhiana

PUNJAB

HARYANA

CHANDIGARH

Delhi

DELHI

Jaipur

RAJASTHAN

GUJARAT

CHINA

NEPAL

BHUTAN

ASSAM

BANGLADESH

BIHAR

Patna

Ranchi

UTTAR PRADESH

Lucknow

I N D I A

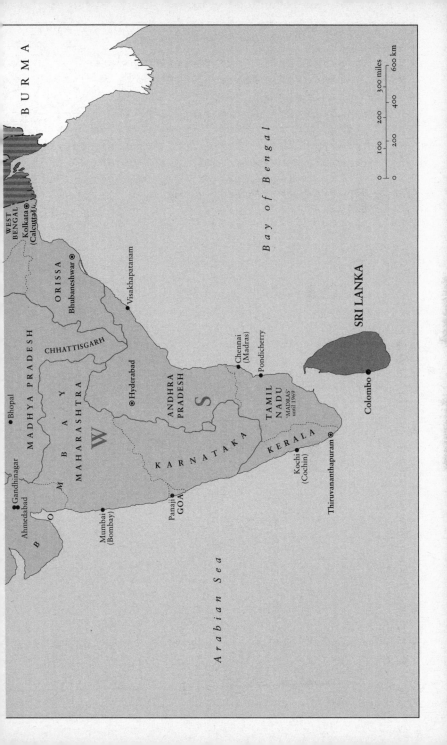

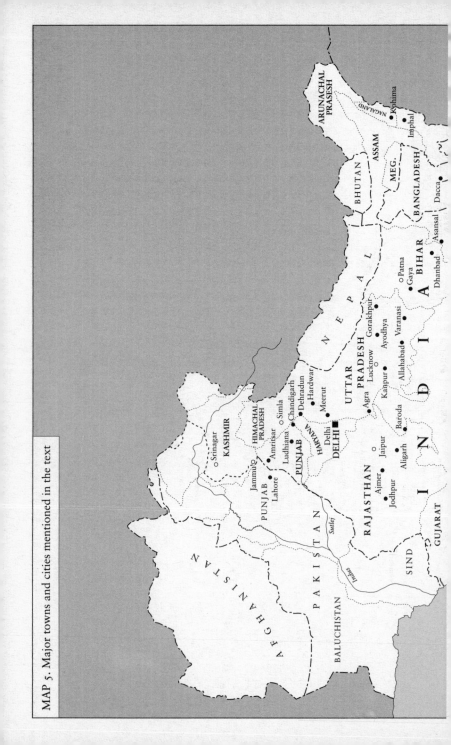

MAP 5. Major towns and cities mentioned in the text

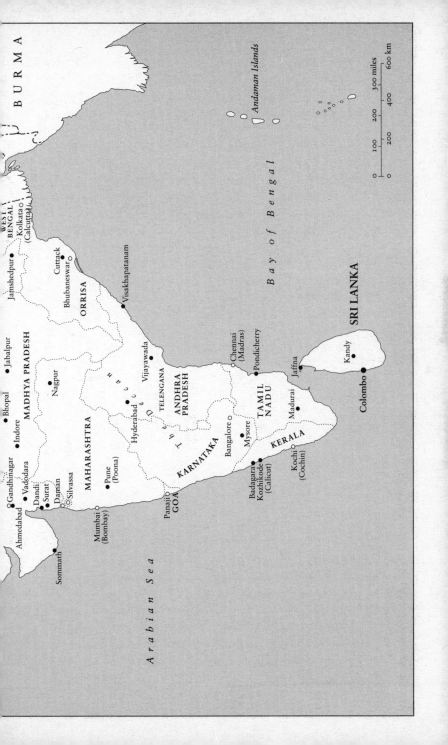

Introduction

In the district of Thrissur in the old southern princely state of Travancore, now known as Kerala, is the town of Guruvayur, home to the Guruvayur temple. The seventeenth-century temple is dedicated to the god Vishnu – the Preserver of the Universe – one of the great trinity of Hindu deities. Guruvayur is an important pilgrimage centre held to be particularly auspicious for those desiring children. Its history, however, has been a tumultuous one: in 1716 it was looted and torched by the Dutch, and though swiftly rebuilt it was taken again in 1766, this time falling into the hands of the Muslim warlord Haider Ali. After another brief recovery, the temple was stormed by Tipu Sultan, an ally of the French who, by coincidence, chose 1789, the year of the French Revolution, to mount his assault. However, it was a later generation of revolutionaries who became the temple's most formidable adversaries. In 1931 a campaign was launched by members of the untouchable castes (dalits) demanding entry to the temple, which had hitherto been the preserve of only the highest castes. The 'temple-entry' movement, true to its revolutionary forebears, adopted the aggressive strategies of mass chanting, gate-storming and menacing encirclements of high-caste worshippers. The campaign was closely associated with E. V. Ramaswami Naicker, a low-caste intellectual who had recently formed the 'Self-Respect' movement – an organization which sought to mould the lowest castes into a grand unity founded on Enlightenment notions of rationalism and equality in opposition both to the old, hierarchical and Brahman-dominated order, and to the main party of Indian nationalism, the Indian National Congress. Congress, Naicker argued, was in reality a Brahman-dominated claque devoted to the preservation of high-caste privilege and hierarchy.

Soon, however, the commander-in-chief of Congress – 'Mahatma' Gandhi – descended on Guruvayur bringing his own idiosyncratic ideas concerning the accommodation of low-caste groups within elite institutions. Violent self-assertion and forced entry were not in his rulebook. Temple-entry could only proceed with the willing consent of the high castes, their agreement to be won by reincorporating the 'fallen' low castes into the great hierarchy of the Hindu fold, not by overthrowing it. He forbad gate-storming and Brahman baiting, insisting that respect be given to the sensitivities of those Brahmans who found 'in their conscience the presence of untouchables objectionable'. A roster restricting untouchable entry to certain times of the day, after which the temple would be ritually purified, was his first proposal, and one immediately rebuffed as insulting. He then suggested a referendum of all temple-goers. But though 70 per cent of voters gave their approval, Gandhi was still unhappy, insisting that no temple gates should be opened until the remaining 30 per cent agreed. The 'temple-entry' campaign, and with it the brief unity of low and high-caste reformers, collapsed in disarray.

Four years later, however, the low castes seemed triumphant; the Maharaja of Travancore declared every public temple in his state open to all and very soon afterwards similar proclamations were made throughout India. But though Naicker had won a legal victory, low castes continued to be excluded. Indeed the Guruvayur temple doors did not, in fact, open to them until independence, and its inner sanctum remained forbidden to dalits. Moreover, even after independence low castes were barred from many temples by harassment and the threat of violence.

The struggle over the Guruvayur temple encapsulates some of the principal dynamics of modern Indian history: the enduring tension between hierarchy and equality, between difference and commonality, and between the conflicting views of how to integrate and 'modernize' India. While radicals wanted the entire temple of India, including the inner sanctum of power, thrown open to all on equal terms regardless of caste status or other religious considerations, others insisted that democracy and modernity were perfectly compatible with venerable rankings and religiously sanctioned notions of difference. Most states have had to adapt old aristocratic hierarchies to the demands of modern egalitarian politics. For some the adaptation has come about through violent rupture. In Russia and China *ancien régimes* were swept away in revolution and civil war, while World War II destroyed old elites in much of the rest of Asia. Elsewhere, however, such elites have been notably adept at maintaining status hierarchies. Britain, whose privileged groups successfully adapted to change and were never defeated in war, retains much of its old 'class' culture, even if the old aristocracy has lost formal power. India is closer to the British model, although India's distinctive and protean caste system has been even more resilient than British 'class'. So while India has escaped revolutionary turmoil, one consequence has been that it retains features of an old society of orders within a democratic system. Though India is a democracy, and one bound by the rule of law, it is also a place where an individual's status, and his or her treatment by others and by the state, is still determined to a significant degree by supposedly traditional identities of caste and religion. While some justify this as a happy continuity with ancient notions of organic hierarchy, others celebrate such differences as a form of 'post-modern' multi-cultural democracy.

It is the remarkable coexistence of ideas of formal equality and democracy with notions of hierarchy and difference that helps to explain the distinctiveness of modern India. It is a creative, vibrant and attractive society. By comparison to the increasingly homogenized cultures of the west, the subcontinent is an oasis of diversity. Its films, music, architecture and even dress are a unique hybrid of many regional forms, only partially overlaid with a veneer of 'westernization'. India has also resisted the more malign homogenizing hand of modernizing nationalist governments or communist regimes, and with it the often brutal strategies of statist 'development' and cultural integration. Unlike Russia or Cambodia, India has witnessed no state-initiated slaughter of 'enemy classes', and, unlike China, the independent state has not unleashed famine on millions as the result of ill-conceived economic 'leaps forward'. Its democracy is vibrant, its elections great public *tamashas* (festivals), its politicians spectacles in themselves – if not always edifying ones. But the peculiar cohabitation of democracy with the lack of integration and persistent hierarchy also underpins various striking characteristics: the persistence of caste rankings, the increasing separation of its religious communities, grotesque inequalities and ubiquitous violence. And, in particular, people's loyalty to caste and community rather than to the nation has led them to view the state as a source of enrichment for their particular group, rather than as an agent for the common good. India's poor education system and underdeveloped infrastructure, both serious obstacles to economic development, have been among the most obviously malignant consequences.

The purpose of this book is to show how this peculiar form of modernity emerged. The history of India presented here is by no means a simple linear lyric but, like the struggle over the Guruvayur temple, a complex fugue of theme and counter-theme. At times Gandhi's arcadian hierarchies harmonized uneasily with the paeans to progress of his apprentice, Jawaharlal Nehru (later India's first Prime Minister); at others the radical chants of Naicker and the low castes became a deafening cacophony intended to drown the more chauvinistically high-caste and nationalistic anthems of the Hindu right. Nor is the history of India exclusively Indian, but rather the complex counterpoint of the indigenous with the western, as the brisk British imperial march encountered, and was, to a degree, subsumed by the more elegiac and elegant *rags* of Indian tradition. And ultimately this complex polyphony, despite endless exceptions, initiatives and threats, has produced something like a honeycomb society composed of elaborately tiered cells framed within the body of an enduring democracy.

This analysis of India's evolution departs from other mainstream interpretations, which fall broadly into liberal, Marxist and 'subaltern' historical schools. Liberal accounts of India's progress, common in the western press, tell a story of triumphant westernization. British legacies of democracy and free markets were, they argue, grafted on to Indian nationalism and bore fruit in the shape of India's democratic republic. This welcome transfusion of western practice is now, finally and happily, being transposed to the economic sphere as India abandons its 'planned' economy and embraces the free market and globalization. The demands of a free market economy, these commentators insist, will make old hierarchies moribund.

Marxist approaches, more common among academic writers, have taken a less optimistic view. They too detect important legacies and continuities from the British Raj, but their gaze falls not on the virtuous bequest of democracy but on the deeply rooted social and economic inequalities of modern India. These, they argue, were the inevitable consequence of the Raj's strategy of collaborating with elites, which entrenched certain social classes in their power and privileges. Independence did not, therefore, mark so much a radical break with the old colonial enterprise, as a re-staffing of its executive board. Underlying economic and social structures were undisturbed, but now the main exploiters of poor Indians were rich Indians, not rich white people.

In the 1980s a new approach to India's history emerged, known as 'subalternism'. This school, much in vogue among the elite Indian intelligentsia, also detected divisions and inequalities of power among Indians, and also attributed them to the baleful influence of the Raj. But for them the crucial division was not economic but cultural. Imperialism had created a breed of 'brown Englishmen', Indian in name but alien in spirit. This hybrid elite had imbibed the westernizing and cosmopolitan mores of their erstwhile British masters and now sought to impose a wholly ersatz 'modernity' on India's 'subaltern' or non-elite classes. The result, they claimed, was a bifurcated India, of lofty and arrogant elites lording it over the common man and woman, who disliked 'modernity' and harked after a more authentic and bucolic communitarian nation.

These approaches are not without insight: liberals are right to emphasize India's surprisingly resilient democracy; Marxists clearly have a point when they draw attention to its egregious material inequalities; and the subalternists have identified, if perhaps exaggerated, an important cultural rupture between the mass of Indians and their leaders. All of them, however, neglect the persuasive and persistent influence of hierarchical assumptions in all spheres of life – economic, cultural, social, religious and political. Liberal writers tend to exaggerate the British Raj's commitment to equality and modernization; they also assume that because the formal institutions of democracy are present in India – the parliaments, elections and so forth – then so too is its cultural substance. But democracy in India often operates rather differently to the way it works in western Europe. And for many Indians democracy is a mechanism for furthering group advantage, not for the pursuit of ideology or individual interest. It is for this reason that the most bizarre political partnerships can emerge – communists allying with market liberalizers, centralizers with regionalists or untouchable parties in coalition with high-caste chauvinists. Marxists also project western preconceptions on to a resolutely non-western entity, and in so doing they exaggerate the simple polarization between haves and have-nots, the unity of the elite, and its ability to manipulate political and economic life to its own ends. India is too extravagantly multi-tiered for such simple oppositions, and its very resistance to the homogenizing impress of class identities has also made a nation-wide revolution virtually inconceivable. Subalternists similarly exaggerate polarization, this time cultural, between elites and masses, as this relationship, from the Gandhian era onwards, has been one of dialogue, not dictatorship. Meanwhile, romanticized notions of idyllic communitarian rural life call to mind more the fantasies of Raj administrators than the realities of India's status-riven villages. Most of the arcadian and utopian yearnings for 'community' that have periodically decorated the Indian political landscape have originated among India's elites, not its masses. Meanwhile the enthusiastic participation of 'subaltern' Indians in the rituals of electoral politics suggests that this aspect of modernity at least commands their consent. Moreover, subaltern historians have rather underplayed the evident desire of many 'subaltern' Indians themselves to conform to the culture and mores of their 'betters' by means of 'sanskritization' – the emulation of high-caste customs.

The history of India recounted in this book is, then, not a tale of straightforward liberal westernization, nor of a struggle between all-powerful elites and the hopelessly subordinated poor, but of its complex and halting evolution into a very particular kind of modern nation. It begins with the British. The role of the British on the Indian historical stage should not be exaggerated: the subcontinent is too vast and too ancient, and the British presence too brief and microscopic for them to be seen as its leading players. However, while their political and economic power was always highly circumscribed, their interventions in shaping the culture and identity of Indians at a particular point in the nation's unfolding drama were not without significance. When the British became dominant in India its society was very fluid. Castes, though they certainly existed, were not the frozen and hierarchical entities they later became. In much of India the thousands of local *jatis* – loose and open-ended agglomerations similar to kinship networks, clans, militias or even occupational guilds – were more important than the strict four-tiered graded structure of priest, warrior, merchant and peasant – the *varna* system – now understood as the 'caste system'. *Jatis* could and did, under the patronage of the Mughals, and later of regional kings, move up and down the *varnashrama* ladder. And in parts of so-called 'tribal' India – the forest and mountain peoples – caste was unknown. The British officials of the East India Company who governed parts of India from the late eighteenth century until the Great Rebellion* of 1857, hoped to ground their authority on indigenous laws and customs, and sought information on these among the country's literate classes. Among Hindus, literate groups tended to be Brahmans; and throughout the seventeenth and eighteenth centuries Brahman elites had been involved in disputes with 'kingly' warriors and land controllers about who possessed higher status. British enquiries into these matters were seized upon by Brahman literati as an opportunity to settle these controversies to their own advantage. They duly reported that the ancient laws of Hinduism reflected a religiously authorized hierarchy, with the priestly Brahmans at the top, above the warrior and kingly castes, or Ksatriyas, who were in turn above the merchants or Vaishyas, with the rest, the Shudras, beneath them. And beyond the pale of the Hindu fold were the dalits. This order, they claimed, was based on a divinely ordained Hindu cosmology according to which individuals were born or re-born into the caste they merited by virtue of their dutiful action (*dharma*) in a previous life.

---

*The rising of much of north India against the British in 1857 has traditionally been called the 'Great Mutiny', and it did indeed begin with a mutiny of sepoys – Indian troops in the army. However it spread far beyond its military origins, and is now frequently referred to as the 'Great Rebellion', or even as the 'First War of Indian Independence'.

This account of the meaning of caste, while not wholly untrue, was highly partial. It was an idealized vision harking back to ancient 'Vedic' times, and only in the northern Gangetic plain did anything like it exist. Elsewhere power arose from land control and military dominance, not divine cosmologies. In much of southern and western India great landlords did not wear the sacred thread betokening the 'twice-born' status of the higher castes, and were, therefore, technically, Shudras, the lowest caste. Brahmans, meanwhile, were few and far between, and though some were wealthy and powerful, many were rather lowly temple priests. Even in the Gangetic plain itself, influential Brahmans had long-since adopted bureaucratic rather than priestly roles, and many powerful Brahmans owed their social position more to the possession of land than to ritual purity. Nevertheless the British concluded that caste and religion, not land-ownership and martial prowess, were the informing principle of Indian social organization.

This was rather as if seventeenth-century Europe had been colonized by a phalanx of Indian scholar-bureaucrats who decided to run Britain according to the highly idealized notion that power and status flowed from a medieval three-estates system (prayers–fighters–toilers). Informed by eager prelates, these Indian colonizers would have been convinced that the clergy enjoyed higher status than land magnates and generals, and that those bearing the surname Tanner or Gardener lay beyond the pale of civilized society. And, to press the analogy, they would also have learnt that Catholics and Protestants constituted such profoundly estranged ethnic groups that they required entirely separate sets of laws to govern them. Further, in segregating Britons into the 'loyal' and 'disloyal', these subcontinental empire-builders would have drafted only Celts, Highlanders and Catholics into the imperial army, while dismissing lowland Protestant Englishmen as hopelessly feeble and effeminate.

Doubtless if caste had remained only a matter of nomenclature this would have made little difference. But it did not, and especially after the Rebellion of 1857 the British, through their censuses, their property laws, recruitment to the army, quotas for jobs and universities and, later, their electoral schemes, created positive incentives for Indians to seek a particular caste status or fixed religious identity for themselves and deny it to others. The ancient Vedic idea of a four-tiered, rigidly structured hierarchy, along with the belief that Hindus and Muslims were incorrigibly antagonistic, was turned, unwittingly by the British, and more wittingly by their Indian collaborators, into a reality fixed in concrete. More generally, the British colonial system, frail and ragged at its edges, depended heavily on Indian allies, princes and great landlords as well as Brahmans, to govern and tended, therefore, to embrace, not challenge, pre-existing forms of rule. The effect was to cultivate vested interests devoted to the preservation of supposedly traditional identities and hierarchies and to rigidify patterns of power and status that had been highly flexible in the late eighteenth and early nineteenth centuries.

British power was also Janus-faced, however. While its institutions and collaborator strategies entrenched hierarchy, its liberal rhetoric and the egalitarian message of Christian missionaries broadcast a very different message. Before the First World War the Raj raised its colonial temple upon foundations of hierarchy – of race, caste and religion. But thereafter, challenged by the nationalists, the Raj assumed the mask of democracy, and attempted to outmanoeuvre its opponents with high rhetoric and limited reform. But as fast as the British built their temple, expanding and reshuffling its congregation, they triggered a complex set of reactions and counter-reactions as Indians themselves, no slouches where power and status-jockeying were concerned, manipulated the contradictory messages of fixed hierarchy and radical equality, of centralization and regionalism, of veneration for tradition and love of modernity. The result was a rainbow of regional patriotisms and religious revivals that began, along with the Indian National Congress, to parley with the British over the terms of entry to the temple, and which, during the Second World War, effectively stormed the temple itself. However beneath these elite-led machinations more radically egalitarian movements had erupted in the south and the west, among the low castes and dalits. These movements disputed the doctrines of hierarchy on which the colonial temple had been erected, demanding, like Naicker, a more genuinely revolutionary re-ordering of power.

Yet India's modern history is not merely about storming, but also about building the temple. India's rulers and elites have pursued a variety of grand projects of integration and modernization, some egalitarian and liberal in a recognizably 'western' sense, others seeking a more nuanced form of modernity, one compatible with gradation of status, old practices of social deference and systematic inequality. Among the former were the British Utilitarians of the 1820s, who thought that society could be revolutionized by the imposition of 'rational' laws; Naicker, who sought equality in the displacement of caste by ethnicity; and Nehru, for whom the gods of science, technology and planning were more than a match for the old Hindu deities. More recently the advocates of liberalization have dreamt of an India integrated by information technology and software systems into a bright new age of cyber-equality. Opposing them have been the votaries of hierarchy, who have, with some success, attempted to both 'modernize' and integrate society while maintaining the caste and religious rankings of the old order. Among these hybrid visions have been the curious elision of liberalism and 'tradition' practised by the post-mutiny Raj, Gandhi's arcadian dream of folding the four-caste order into a modern democracy and, latterly, the ill-starred efforts of high-caste Hindu nationalists to promote an economic revolution while, at the same time, holding back the low-caste social revolution it beckoned.

This book, then, is a three-act drama. Chapters 1 and 2 narrate the building of the Raj before the First World War and the diverse and complex response of Indians to this curious edifice. Chapters 3, 4 and 5 examine the crisis of the imperial system; British efforts to reshape their temple and broaden its congregation; and the determination of Indian nationalists to evict the western clerisy and install their own temple priests. The last third of the book tells the story of the Nehruvian and Hindu nationalist projects to create a more integrated India, each in turn thwarted by successive stormings of the temple by, respectively, populist neo-Gandhian farmer lobbies of the 1960s and 1970s, and the 'silent revolution' of the lower castes and dalits in the 1980s and 1990s.

India is a unified, democratic nation, but its history demonstrates the immense difficulties involved in shaping a cohesive society from ancient, highly diverse, multi-lingual and fissiparous materials; materials that, moreover, have already been partially assembled according to a western colonial design. And while India has developed its own very particular brand of modernity, the disputes and controversies over the nature of this subcontinental temple continue – both figuratively and literally. In the city of Tiruchirappalli in the southern state of Tamil Nadu is another Vishnu temple, the Srirangam temple. Indeed this is probably the most revered Vishnu temple and the largest religious complex in all India. It boasts twenty-one *gopurams* (towers), and is surrounded by seven concentric walls within which a statue of Vishnu reclines on a great serpent. The government of Tamil Nadu, led by the Dravida Munnetra Kazhagam (DMK) party – the principal legatee of E. V. Ramaswami Naicker's 'Self-Respect' movement – has recently erected a statue of their illustrious forebear Naicker (also known as Periyar 'the wise one') in front of Srinangam's greatest *gopuram*. From his plinth Periyar, icon of rationalism, glares provocatively at a temple edifice festooned with the galaxy of gods and deities that he so detested. This gesture has had its intended effect. Outraged high-caste Hindus have 'beheaded' Periyar and, in retaliation, several godly statues across the state have been defaced, precipitating yet another round in the seemingly endless struggle to control Vishnu's crowded temple.

I

Tropical Gothic

On 1 January 1877 Queen Victoria was made Empress of India. To mark the occasion an Imperial Assemblage was held, not in Calcutta, the first city of British India, but in the capital of the old Mughal emperors, Delhi. The preparations began a year earlier. A vast area of land a few miles north of Old Delhi was chosen and its unlucky inhabitants, thousands of villagers, were summarily evicted. In their place, in an arc stretching for over 5 miles, 8000 tents, of varying degrees of luxury, were erected. Though each encampment was carefully calibrated to reflect the precise status of its occupant, the most up-to-date sanitation had been provided for all. In this city of palanquins and marquees resided the delegations of princes, aristocrats, officials and their various retinues, which included 85,000 camp followers and their attendant animals. At 10 a.m. on the appointed day the assemblage officially began. Two hundred and fifty elephants, one hundred and fifty horses, forty-five camels, several hundred spear-bearing sepoys, armed horsemen and thousands of caparisoned bearers trooped behind the procession of over ten thousand dignitaries as it made its way towards the ceremonial amphitheatre. At exactly noon, after a roar of guns and a display of firecrackers, a fanfare of six trumpeters announced the arrival of the Viceroy, Lord Lytton, who, to the strains of Wagner's *Tannhäuser*, strode across the parade ground before installing himself on a throne set atop a large elevated dais. From there he loftily surveyed the ranks of princes, nobles, gentry and other Indian worthies banked in ascending tiers before him. The seating had been arranged according to strict rules of precedence. Closest to the Viceroy were the greatest princes: the Gaekwad of Baroda, the Nizam of Hyderabad and the Maharaja of Kashmir;

behind them the thirty or so slightly less important princes, and behind them the hundreds of princelings. Next came the great aristocratic landowners and wealthy merchants, and finally the lesser gentry and other native gentlemen at the back. Once enthroned, the Viceroy mused on the 'providential' nature of the British Raj, its intention to bring 'progressive prosperity' and its place as worthy successor to the 'House of Tamerlaine' (India's erstwhile Mughal emperors), before he grandly proclaimed Queen Victoria's accession as 'Kaiser-I-Hind' (Emperor of India). This was a curious Indo-Germanic soubriquet considered the least likely of all possible titles to be mispronounced by Indians.

Awesome though it was, such pomp did not impress all observers. Some regarded it as vulgar: 'they have stuck tin shields and battleaxes all over the place. Never was there such a brummagem ornament, or more atrocious taste', sneered one critic. Others mocked the newly minted princely coats of arms, a flurry of rampant boars, elephants, camels and gryphons fashioned for the occasion by a Hungarian professor of heraldry assisted by a team of Bengali bureaucrats. To many the entire spectacle evoked not so much generations of imperial dynasts as a circus. Certainly the entire event was the apotheosis of colonial kitsch, but while the symbolism may have been confused, the message was clear. The Imperial Assemblage announced, as a later viceroy, Lord Curzon, would aptly observe, that the Raj had 'stepped into the shoes of the Great Mogul'. With its flamboyant combination of the bogusly baronial and the ostentatiously oriental, the Imperial Assemblage of 1877, along with the great imperial *durbars* of 1902 and 1911, were intended to suggest a fusion of eastern and western traditions. Far from being mere alien interlopers, the British wished to be seen as the apex of a great subcontinental chain of being, topped by the Queen Empress and passing seamlessly down through British officialdom, the Indian princes and gentry, native gentlemen and respectable townspersons to the millions of loyal peasant subjects at the bottom. The Imperial Assemblage demonstrated that the British were now presiding over an ancient, ordered hierarchy.

The Great Assemblage was in many ways a microcosm of the Victorian Raj, its methods and its ideas. Like the assemblage, the Raj was eclectic, ersatz and ramshackle. For, despite much talk of providence, up-lift, progress and the mighty powers of its mandarin officials, the Raj was neither an enlightened despotism, nor a slick bureaucratic machine, but a pragmatic partnership. Its partners, or collaborators, were selected according to ease of assimilation and effectiveness, and they were richly rewarded with local power, autonomy and prestige. But the system, as the Assemblage so dramatically illustrated, depended on exquisite calibrations of status and difference, otherwise Indians, recognizing some greater unity of purpose and identity, might combine against their alien overlords. Though these gradations were vaguely justified as reflecting antiquity and 'authenticity' (the 'real India' or 'natural leaders'), in reality the criteria for partnership were loyalty and usefulness.

If India were a temple, under the Raj it was one in which worshippers were carefully scrutinized for their similitude to the presiding deity, the British. For after the Rebellion of 1857–8 the ideological underpinnings of imperialism acquired an evolutionary flavour: those 'closest' to the British were imagined as not merely useful, but also as similar to the British, be it in culture, values, race or class, while those found awkward, recalcitrant, critical or oppositional were dismissed as 'different'. But, as the diverse array of styles, uniforms and rituals incorporated into the Imperial Assemblage made abundantly clear, the Raj, far from defending an ageless and unchanging hierarchical order, was actually manufacturing it. And, while the objectives of economic development and administrative modernity eluded the British imperium, its ability to shape Indian self-perception and catalyse endlessly proliferating identities proved as impressive as its flair for the spectacular.

Yet, only forty years earlier, all had been very different. Far from seeing India as a living museum of traditions to be categorized, ranked and preserved at all costs, the subcontinent was imagined as a great laboratory in which to conduct experiments with the future. After the consolidation of British supremacy with the final defeat of the Marathas in 1818, thoughts turned to what should be done with this vast newly acquired land. For some the mere maintenance of power, along with the generation of revenue, was sufficient justification for the British presence. But for others the project was far more ambitious: to turn India into a showpiece of British powers of development.

Far from preserving what they found there, these innovators were determined that India should be blasted out of its 'oriental' torpor, its 'state of ecstatic dreaming', into modernity. And since modernity was clearly English, it followed that India should be anglicized.

By the 1820s and 1830s a new breed of professional administrators had replaced the amateur administration of soldiers that characterized the early years of East India Company rule. Utilitarian in outlook, these administrators were notorious in England for their hostility to the past and anything that stood in the way of progress. Old ideas, old practices, old laws and old elites had to be swept aside to make way for the modern. Frustrated in their more sweeping ambitions to transform Britain, they saw in India the perfect opportunity. Here, it seemed, was a society even more mired in the past than medieval England had been, a dusty attic of aimless aristocrats, scheming priests and immiserated peasants. This was the perfect site for a mammoth experiment with modernity. Utilitarians believed passionately in the power of ideas to transform human consciousness and, through that, the world. Indians, they insisted, were the captives of pre-Enlightenment mentalities, but they could be easily transformed by the spirit of reason. India's so-called learning would crumble before the might of western knowledge; India's mind would be reshaped by English education; her institutions would be remodelled. Laws would be codified, trade would be freed. Even religion would be reformed. The superstitious priest-craft of Brahmans and the fanatical passions of the Islamic *ulema* (clerics) would yield to a sober and rational religion, if not outright Christian conversion. The parasitical aristocracy, princes and landed gentry would also be swept aside, while the down-trodden peasantry would be transformed into independent yeoman farmers, sons of the soil, under whose tutelage the parched scrub of agrarian India would give way to edenic plenty.

The anglicizing project was not without its enemies, and in parts of the subcontinent Company officials continued to advocate government sympathetic to Indian tradition. The 'orientalists', as they were known, men like Thomas Munro in the south and Mountstuart Elphinstone in the west, were moved by both a romantic attachment to the past and the view that institutions and cultures which represented the accretion of generations of wisdom should not be lightly cast aside. For them change was desirable, but radical change was not. India's princes and landlords, its patterns of cultivation, even its religious cultures, were worthy of respect; Indian progress had to rest on these ancient foundations.

By the early decades of the nineteenth century, therefore, two very different schools of thought had developed among the British; both prized progress, but the utilitarians saw progress as westernization and denied that India's past could offer anything of value to its future. The orientalists believed that progress needed to be founded on Indian tradition. The subsequent history of the British in India was, to a great extent, the history of the contest between these two schools.

Between 1820 and 1850 the westernizers had the upper hand. The will to transform in this era was very powerful, if not always entirely successful. Their sweeping project of social engineering suggested breathtaking confidence, if not hubris, and much of it never came to pass. Ambitious hopes were frustrated by Indian intransigence, untrustworthy intermediaries, penny-pinching and the many expedient compromises of everyday reality. Nevertheless, despite these disappointments, what was envisaged (and to some extent achieved) seemed little short of revolutionary. The structure of landholding was transformed by the introduction of notions of individual property rights. Railways were laid and telegraphs erected. Wars against cultural 'backwardness' were waged as evangelicals joined with utilitarians to impose 'progress'. The 'horrific excrescences' of Indian religion, both real and imagined, were targeted and supposedly purged. *Sati* (widow burning) was outlawed and several widows were snatched from funeral pyres; the marauding menace of ritualistic garrotting, *thugee*, was suppressed. The impact of western ideas on the Indian intelligentsia, however, was far from imaginary. The new learning, partly purveyed by the Company's schools and colleges, was shaping an Indian elite which, if not exactly 'English in taste, in opinions, in morals and in intellect', as the utilitarian-inspired reforming official Thomas Macaulay had hoped, was certainly radically different from anything seen before. Therefore why, after thirty years of rational progress, did the British in India turn with such relish to the renovation of tradition? The simple and not entirely simplistic answer is the Indian Rebellion of 1857, during which the British were forcibly reminded how very far they were from establishing Macaulay's ideal of an 'imperishable empire'.

In the dusty north Indian city of Kanpur, in a neglected churchyard, looms a large stone angel. The angel had originally presided over the Bibighar compound, an exclusively 'white' domain built as a shrine to British heroes of the 'mutiny' and forbidden to all Indians. On 15 August 1947, Independence Day, a group of revellers broke into the compound and assaulted the celestial entity, leaving it noseless. The statue was swiftly relocated to its present resting place and a statue of Tantia Topi, a great Indian hero of the rebellion, put in its place – symbolic recompense for events of ninety years earlier. On 10 May 1857, a group of sepoys from the Bengal Army, then stationed in the north-western provincial town of Meerut, mutinied and delivered something infinitely worse than a bloody nose to the face of British imperial power. After marching on Delhi to restore the last Mughal emperor, the ailing octogenarian Bahadur Shah, to the Peacock throne, the mutineers, accompanied by thousands of disaffected townsmen, peasants and gentry, proceeded to extinguish British power across much of north India in little over a month. The sepoys – the Indian troops in the British army – threw off their uniforms and rode around in buggies looted from the fleeing British. Government buildings were ransacked and tax records burnt, telegraph wires were ripped down and post offices – symbolic outposts of British culture – were torched. In Kanpur, cockpit of the rebellion, convoys of soldiers and townsmen set fire to the magistrate's office, stole the land records, plundered the treasury and made off with the government's bullocks and elephants. But this was more than just opportunistic looting; other aspects of the rebellion carried a distinct whiff of liberation and revenge. British prisoners faced a hail of abuse, British women were made to grind corn – a deliberately humiliating task – and *Vhiktoria rani* (Queen Victoria) was denounced as a 'polluting bitch'. Throughout northern India, rumours that British power was faltering met with scenes of riotous joy; children were showered with sweets and dancers took to the streets as a carnival atmosphere reigned in many towns.

According to swiftly manufactured Raj mythology, the causes of the

Rebellion were to be found in the entrenched religious superstitions of the Indian sepoys. Orders to grease the cartridges for their new Enfield rifles with cow and pork grease had, it was said, affronted the religious sensibilities of Hindu and Muslim alike; the mutiny was a spasm of mass religious 'irrationality'. But there was more to it than that. For many peasants and their sepoy cousins the rebellion was less a fit of petty religious pique than a violent rejection of an alien culture and, surprisingly, many who had benefited from British land reform measures joined the revolt in support of their dispossessed landlords. This was less a mere irrational reflex, more a roar of rage against a regime which, regardless of local sensibilities, had reordered social status, meddled with property, and seemed hell-bent on destroying the moral economy of urban and rural life. The rhetoric and songs of the rebels, as well as the more considered writings and speeches of some of their leaders, suggest minds not sunk in mystical torpor but sharply attuned to British hypocrisy instead. What informs their rhetoric is not narrow sectarian concerns or the issue of what kind of grease should lubricate gun cartridges, but a broader sense of patriotism and the need to defend a virtuous order being defiled by the British who, while delivering lectures on piety and morality, swilled beer, cavorted with loose women and engaged in nothing more lofty than the single-minded pursuit of money.

The after-shock of the Rebellion was if anything even more influential than the event itself. It soon became a defining myth, a history-changing moment. In the immediate aftermath came anger and revenge. The perhaps inappropriately named journal *The Friend of India*, was typical: 'We shall drive the rebels before us and leave nothing in our rear, but lines of burning villages and the hanging bodies of felons, swinging to every breeze.' Histories poured from the presses almost immediately and readers could be both appalled and thrilled by lurid descriptions of English women 'hacked to death by dusky ruffians'. It was a literature steeped in haemorrhagic metaphors: 'Pavements were thickly caked with blood' or 'clotted gore lay ankle deep'. Memories of the Rebellion continued to haunt the work of Kipling and other writers for decades to come, poisoning relations between the British and Indians for several generations.

The British never entirely agreed on the causes and meaning of the Rebellion. For many officials it was clearly caused by religious meddling. For missionaries themselves the opposite was more obviously true: the Rebellion was 'a national chastisement', God's punishment for not evangelizing enough. As the evangelical missionary Alexander Duff averred, 'he has delivered us, provided we realize the great object of our covenant – the subversion of Satan's empire'. Others detected a conspiracy of Muslim fanatics and, as we shall see, this view did much to shape future British policy towards Muslims in India. But the most influential interpretation was the view that the rebellion had been precipitated by excessive westernization. The evidence for this lay, it was thought, in the behaviour of the many peasant beneficiaries of British land reform in north India. For, instead of rallying to the side of their liberators, the British, the peasants had treacherously aligned with their erstwhile oppressors, the old Indian landed classes or *taluqdars*. The only conclusion to be drawn was that these people were incorrigible dependants, unwilling to take advantage of the liberty bestowed on them. According to Governor General Canning: 'They do not value these rights. They [view] the Talooqdari system as the ancient, indigenous and cherished system of the country.' It seemed to the British that this was proof that Indians could not be made into 'modern' individuals. Here was a group that appeared to defy Enlightenment predictions about the pursuit of freedom and instead seemed determined to defend hierarchy. The Indian peasant and soldier seemed addicted to subservience, always seeking their 'natural' leaders. For the British the lesson was clear: the project of modernizing India should be jettisoned, or at least radically modified to take account of this native love of traditional authority. However, given the highly fluid conditions of the time, it was rather unclear exactly what India's traditions were or who embodied them. History would provide the answers; and history, both Indian and European, was ransacked for models, examples and precedents.

Bombay is a gothic city, literally so, for no other city in the British Empire can boast so many monuments to late nineteenth-century medieval revivalism. The greatest of these Puginesque extravaganzas is F. W. Stephen's magnificent railway station, Victoria Terminus. An edifice of startling flamboyance, it was begun in 1878 and took almost a decade to build. Fundamentally neo-gothic in conception, it is richly embellished with a forest of Indian-inspired ornamentation, described by a contemporary as 'a free treatment of Early Gothic with an Oriental feeling'. Tigers, elephants and lotuses dance across its façades, while the open galleries, balconies and verandas adorning its frontage all imitate the Mughal style. Curiously, in the midst of this fabulous confection of old-fashioned eastern and western architectural motifs, and towering over its central dome, is a fourteen-foot-high statue: 'Progress'.

The Victoria Terminus was a marked departure from earlier British building styles in India. During the Company era European classicism had dominated, embodying universal values of order and proportion, a style deemed particularly apt for a modernizing imperialism. With the reversal of the confident utilitarian policies that followed the rebellion it became clear that a new architecture was needed, one that would demonstrate the government's new-found respect for Indian culture and tradition, and might even hint that the British themselves were in some way the heirs of India's traditional rulers. The Indo-Saracenic style, of which Victoria Terminus was a precursor, was the hallmark of the Raj. Like the *durbars*, it attempted to meld Indian and British traditions together, although, in reality, this style was an oriental façade cloaking a fundamentally western framework. This was architecture with a peculiar message – progress, for India, would lie in emulating Britain's past.

In the 1860s and 1870s medieval-mania swept the British Isles. Pugin summoned up gothic fantasies at Westminster, Ruskin lamented the lost age of the artisan, and in many Oxbridge senior common rooms medieval history became the last word in modern studies. But the most striking manifestation of the mock-medieval was in India. The new Raj was the midwife to the birth of this curious hybrid of eastern and western forms. Its chief ideologist was Henry Somers Maine, a Cambridge academic, historian and law minister of the Viceroy's Council between 1862 and 1869, while Lord Lytton (Viceroy between 1876 and 1880), poet, romantic and favourite of the Queen Empress, was its most active practitioner. Maine exerted a formative influence on the early post-mutiny period because his tenure coincided with a rather lacklustre collection of viceroys.

Originally a scholar of Anglo-Saxon law, Maine had become fascinated with the evolutionary history of European medieval institutions.
Drawing on the German theory that Sanskrit was a precursor of Greek
and Latin and that therefore Indians and Europeans must share a
common ancestry, he concluded that India was the missing link
between the classical and medieval ages. India, he insisted, was a living
museum of Europe's distant past, a 'great repository of verifiable
phenomena of ancient usage and ancient judicial thought'. In 1863
Maine published the results of his enquiries into this subcontinental
museum. *The Indian Village Community* argued that the Indian village was the remote ancestor of the feudal manor, similar to Germanic
village communities of the early Middle Ages. Indian villages, Maine
argued, were based on communal ownership of the land among the
clan; ideas of individual ownership and contract had not yet emerged.
There were notions of rank and hierarchy, but since the clan leader's
authority was based on kinship and blood and not 'contract', it didn't
amount to genuine sovereignty. And so the British could not be
accused of having usurped the legitimate authority of the country's
kings. Maine's work helped build a new orthodoxy, that India was
roughly at the same point that Britain had been in the early Middle
Ages. As one contemporary official enthused, 'barring oriental scenery
and decorations, the whole feeling of this country is medieval; the
Rajput *noblesse* caracoles along with sword and shield; the small
people crowd round with rags and rusty arms; the king and his
principal chiefs are lords of the country, and the peasant is at their
mercy.' It followed that the best way forward would be for the British
to 'restore' this aristocracy and govern with its collaboration.

Lytton was delighted by the fortuitous discovery that India was an
old prototype of Europe. Under his auspices princely India came
increasingly to resemble a vast feudal theme park, where India's hereditary elite were transfigured into a picturesque feudal-cum-Mughal
aristocracy. A College of Arms was established in Calcutta to create
an Indian peerage and to design coats of arms for the most senior
princes. And, as was seen at the Imperial Assemblage, wild boars,
lions rampant and various Hindu gods and goddesses jostled for space
on the resulting banners and entablatures. Lytton also envisaged an
Indian privy council, and, scorning the ineffably middle-class Indian

Civil Service (ICS), established the Statutory Civil Service, a failed experiment in aristo-bureaucratic administration staffed by the sons of rajas.

The project of bringing western progress to the east had not been entirely abandoned, even if the radical utilitarian strategy of pre-mutiny days had. A conscious hostility to social levelling (coinciding with Disraelian Conservatism in Britain), combined with the assumption that Indians preferred 'feudal' rule, was justification enough for a determined policy of revitalizing supposed 'tradition'. And so, para-doxically, this oriental 'feudalism' was entwined with the economics of laissez-faire liberalism. 'A system which recognizes the legitimacy and advantages of capital and of baronial landlordism' was lauded as the high road to development, infinitely preferable to 'a system which tends to reduce the entire population to the dreary ever-sinking level of a demi-pauperised peasant proprietary'. This was a pointed refer-ence to the policies of the unlamented utilitarians who had promoted the policy of giving property rights to the peasantry. For the neo-medievalists the best way to set India back on the road to stability and prosperity was by encouraging the remnants of its proto-feudal past, the 'natural leaders' as Maine dubbed them. But having identi-fied the past as the future, the British now had the difficult task of identifying who the avatars of India's past actually were.

The British hoped to find 'natural leaders' who would be both loyal and economically dynamic, and who would command sufficient respect among Indians to keep the peace and preside over local admin-istration. However, it proved difficult to find candidates who fitted these ambitious desiderata. Part of the problem was that, contrary to Maine's assertions, Indian notions of rulership and authority were very different from western ones. Pre-colonial India was a society of shared and fluid sovereignty, not of long-established dynasties or rigid hierarchies. There were 'big kings', like the Mughal emperors, who aspired to overlordship across great swathes of territory. But there were also hundreds of 'little kings', warrior chiefs, patriarchs of domi-nant clans, peasant brotherhoods and so forth, who effectively governed regions and localities. These bosses were not generally her-editary but rose and fell rather swiftly according to military prowess and their ability to deliver land, peace and security to their followers.

As Mughal power waned in the eighteenth century new regional strongmen emerged, among them Tipu Sultan, Ranjit Singh and the Maratha Peshwas. Such men had at one time looked set to transcend the role of local boss to become real state builders. But these potential big kings had all been swept away by the Company by 1818, and the purges after 1857 swept away any remaining threats. Though the British had ambitions to displace all local and regional authority, the sheer cost of a modern penetrative bureaucracy, the difficulties of raising revenue to finance it, and the alarming experience of the Rebellion, had deterred them. After 1857, in north India especially, the task was to identify reliable sources of local authority who could act as collaborators. This enterprise was, however, presented as the restoration of the old aristocracy.

Early in March 1858, about a year after the first outbreak of the Rebellion, the Governor General, Lord Canning, issued a general proclamation confiscating all but five of the landed estates of Oudh – but with the proviso that estates would be restored to those who, whatever their past, 'now lent hearty support to the British Government in re-establishing order'. It was a crafty manoeuvre. Though Canning's advisers had pleaded with him simply to reverse the order of 1856 and restore the landlords *tout court*, Canning reasoned that this would be to 'reward rebellion', because, as everyone knew, 'when dealing with an oriental people' one must first manifest power, and only then 'display your clemency'. Canning's judgement was right. As word spread that the British were promising very generous terms to any *taluqdar* who submitted, previously rebellious landlords flocked into the British camp. In the end only 14 of the 220 *taluqdars* lost their land. The best stratagem, as Canning recognized, was to start with an apparently clean slate and then reward loyalty. Loyalty became the informing principle of British policy from thenceforth. Tradition and heredity could be counterfeited, only loyalty was the true currency.

The British hoped that these restored, or in some cases newly fashioned, aristocrats would be seen as 'natural leaders', command popular legitimacy and be useful mediating agents of British power. These loyal liegemen were 'invaluable to us [possessing] a sympathy with and a hold over the feelings and hearts of the common herd'. The loyal *taluqdars* now found – as the Imperial Assemblage made symbolically manifest – that they had been 'incorporated' into the Raj. The most senior were made deputy magistrates, with powers to settle tax disputes and try petty criminal cases. By 1862 there were nearly fifty *taluqdars* with these administrative powers. This could be seen, in effect, as throwing modernization into reverse. While before the rebellion the British had striven, albeit unsuccessfully, to centralize and professionalize administration, they now chose to rely on 'traditional' networks of administration. 'It is of immense benefit to the people,' one official argued, 'that their disputes be settled in a paternalist fashion, by their feudal superiors, rather than in an alien court.' This was, of course, to overlook the fact that as interested parties, the *taluqdars* might not be wholly impartial administrators of land or revenue policy. The *taluqdars* now had direct access to British District Officers, who were ordered to show them the greatest respect and consideration. As Canning observed, 'Much, very much, of the unpopularity of our rule is attributable to that principle of equality, which renders every man liable to be sued and summoned into a public court by any mean man who may choose to offend the dignity of his superior.' The *taluqdars*, along with other great landlords in India, would now be exempted from this inconvenience.

The restored landlords were joined by other 'natural leaders' selected by the British to share in the exercise of local power. *Raises* (rich urban landlords) and wealthy merchants in the cities also gained magisterial powers and tax privileges. And in the 1880s and 1890s these 'natural leaders' were invited to join the new consultative councils set up in the major towns and regions of India to 'advise' on policy and give vent to 'native opinion'. These were the ruling partnerships that characterized the two-thirds of the subcontinent that was officially 'British India'. Through the remainder of the country, princely India, British power was even more dilute.

Within twenty years, however, it was clear that the system of 'natural rulers' wasn't working as intended. Parts of rural India were in a state of subterranean, chronic rebellion, which periodically burst forth into dramatic peasant and 'tribal' uprisings, while in the cities the native gentlemen found their authority constantly challenged by groups not included in the charmed circle of 'natural leaders'. This was partly a problem of legitimacy. While some 'natural leaders' could boast genuine pedigree, many were of a much more recent vintage, and even Canning admitted that many *taluqdars* were 'distinguished neither by birth, good service or connection with the soil', and had obtained their position largely by 'usurpation and fraud . . . a coarse looking lot'. Nevertheless, Canning was determined to restore the gentry across the whole of the subcontinent. In the United Provinces (modern Uttar Pradesh) the old aristocracy had evaporated in the 1830s and the British were forced to advertise for suitable replacements; only 57 suitable candidates presented themselves, 13 of whom were European. Elsewhere a gentry class was cobbled together from whatever was to hand. A motley array of ambitious village headmen was elevated in the Punjab, the British having removed the original landlords in the 1840s. In the newly created Central Provinces a group of erstwhile revenue collectors under the Mughals, the *Malguzars*, suddenly found they owned all the land on which they had once only collected taxes. Meanwhile, Baluchi tribal chiefs (the Bhutto clan among them) were catapulted into the higher echelons of the nobility in Sindh. Most of these self-fashioned princes' claims to legitimacy were as fragile as those of the British themselves.

The absence of an aristocratic lineage was not necessarily a bad thing. Indians were not, unlike Europeans, overly concerned with the bloodlines of their rulers but more interested in their efficacy. Lack of antiquity could be obscured by good government. Indian princes and major landlords had been granted substantial autonomy over how they spent the revenues from their estates, and for a while British officials hoped to mould the 'natural leaders' into a credible governing class, both loyal to their imperial overlords and attentive to the needs of the people. The driving force behind this enterprise was a certain Colonel Walter, sometime Resident in the Bharatpur princely state, who in 1869 urged the British authorities to

establish an Eton in India [complete with] a staff of thoroughly educated English gentlemen, not mere bookworms, but men fond of fieldsports and outdoors exercise . . . The pupils, or rather their guardians, the tutors, should be allowed ample funds from the coffers of the state. Holidays should be spent in constant travel in Europe . . . with an occasional visit to their own homes.

Walter insisted that the motive was to both 'perpetuate their dynasties' and make the alumni 'worthy feudatories of the Crown of England'. The first of the Indian Etons, Mayo College, was established in Ajmer (in modern Rajasthan) in 1875. Set in extensive grounds it was a palatial architectural extravaganza of gothic and Indo-Saracenic styles, from whence, it was hoped, a progressive oriental nobility would emerge. Other establishments – Rajkumar College and Aitchison College – soon followed.

Each school adopted a rather daunting curriculum: English literature, English and Indian history, physical and general geography, arithmetic, algebra, Euclidean geometry, Sanskrit and Persian, Hindi and Urdu. Lessons in drawing, dancing and verse recitation were also considered necessary to complete the education of a young Anglo-Oriental gentleman. All of this was overseen by a corps of gentlemanly English tutors, well away from the influence of unsuitable mothers.

But, neither the careful elocution of Wordsworth's lyrics, nor hours of landscape sketching seemed able to transform these highly privileged parvenus into a duty-bound *noblesse*. Typical was the dashing Maharaja Bhupinder Singh of Patiala, the ruler of 5,500 square miles of prime real estate in eastern Punjab. He had been sent to Aitchison College for four years and had also been trained in the principles of modern administration. However, he turned out to be an incorrigible rake who neglected the rigours of sound administration for a life of hunting, wrestling, poker and protracted trips to Europe. Another disappointment was the Maharaja of Pudukkotai, a small but important southern state, who was lengthily and expensively educated at Mayo. Carefully groomed for service as an enlightened monarch by teams of dedicated British officials, he abdicated in 1914 in order to marry an Australian showgirl he had met while on his European tour.

Those that remained to govern their kingdoms did not, on the whole, make edifying rulers. Rack-renting, extortion through forced labour or, in the spirit of modernity, forced levies to buy motor cars all became features of modern kingship in India. This economic rapacity was compounded by the failure to become modern constitutionalists. Hardly any of the princely states introduced even consultative, let alone representative, councils into their polities, and as late as the 1930s the majority were still being run as petty tyrannies. Awadh British Indian Association, a body of *taluqdars* founded in 1871, turned out to be resolutely antediluvian. Elections were disdained, and offices became virtually hereditary. Rather than the vanguard of a new era of constitutionalism, it became a troublesome and vociferous lobby devoted entirely to the defence of its own interests.

Not only were the princes and *taluqdars* frustratingly resistant to 'improvement', but many also seemed predisposed to squander awesome quantities of time and money on luxury and litigation. By the later nineteenth century many of the newly created gentry estates and princely states were mired in debt. Several ruling houses ruined themselves in lengthy court battles over property and succession. Cadet branches of the family would launch speculative cases against the succession of minors or women. Other families had an unfortunate tendency to divide their lands between all the surviving sons, creating tiny, unviable estates. Both princes and landlords spent lavishly on sumptuous lifestyles, extravagant gift-giving, festivals and religious endowments that the British regarded as frivolous.

Neglecting the duties of welfare and social integration that they traditionally had observed, India's princes became ever more obsessed with the minutiae of status, squabbling endlessly about ceremonial protocols and precedence. The gun salutes of the imperial *durbars* were the cause of the most intense status anxieties because the number of salutes a state received effectively marked its relative standing to all the others. These had originally been assigned according to degrees of service rendered during the Rebellion and did not, therefore, reflect relative size, wealth or importance. The King-Emperor had 101, the Viceroy 31, 113 princes received between 9 and 21 and the rest, about 500 of them, received none. The discrepancy between salute status and real status was potentially explosive when states ranging from France-sized Hyderabad to the half-square-mile state of Vejanoness enjoyed exactly the same 'salutage'. Heraldic ostentation also became a minor obsession: princes offered to buy their own ceremonial swords and *khalat* (brocade mantles) for the presentation, fearful that those proffered by the notoriously stingy British would be humiliatingly meagre.

The failure of the strategy to create a progressive aristocracy was nowhere more starkly evident than in Oudh, the storm centre of the Rebellion and the region where the restoration of 'traditional' elites was most assiduously pursued. A few years before the rebellion, in 1850, the Nawab of Oudh, Wajid Ali Shah, had built a stately pleasure dome after the manner of Kubla Khan. Costing over Rs. 80,000, the Kaiserbagh palace of Lucknow was expressly designed to accommodate the Nawab's large collection of concubines. Florid, ostentatious and costly, the Kaiserbagh symbolized for the British all that was most corrupt and depraved about Nawabi culture. And so, after the Rebellion had been suppressed, it is perhaps not entirely surprising that the palace was commandeered for more salubrious purposes. The remaining concubines were expelled and in their stead the British installed the British Indian Association of newly restored *taluqdars*. The intention was that it should become a proto-parliament. The *taluqdars* would meet there, in the manner of feudal barons or, perhaps, progressive whiggish landlords, to discuss edifying matters of estate improvement and constitutional reform. However, by the 1880s many apartments had been transformed into bijou urban residences for the arriviste *taluqdars*. Addicted to luxury, pleasure and the sensual arts, they had swiftly restored the concubines to their erstwhile home and, far from becoming the sober-minded reforming gentry of British hopes, the *taluqdars* had mutated into an embarrassing clique of parasitical spendthrifts.

By 1900 India was changing rapidly. It was not a frozen museum of tradition bound by immemorial custom, and the restored princes and rural gentry did not hold the authority or sway over the rest of the population anticipated by the British. For many, their kingly pretensions had been emptied of meaning and they wore only hollow crowns. Despite the autonomy they enjoyed under the British, it was, nevertheless, evident that they depended less on local legitimacy for their powers than on British favour. Moreover, the British had overestimated the authority of 'big kings' and underestimated that of little ones – local bosses, rich peasants, clan patriarchs, and newly emergent urban groups who enjoyed no preferment in the regime of 'natural leaders'.

Below the layer of 'natural leaders' lay what the British increasingly liked to believe was the 'real' India. This was the India of the peasant, the 300,000 village 'republics', living in placid, self-sufficient, egalitarian, almost communistic harmony. Certainly by the last quarter of the nineteenth century this bucolic idyll was, at least partially, a reality. India was indeed a predominantly and overwhelmingly peasant society, though not, *pace* official stereotypes, an egalitarian one. However this rustic 'traditional' India, like its newly minted ancient aristocracy, was, to a great extent, a British creation. By the last third of the nineteenth century, after sixty years of dismantling the cities, courts and armies of the Mughal successor regimes, of forcibly settling migrant and 'wandering' peoples, of felling forests and jungles, of reclaiming wasteland and dispersing the inflated clerisies of the great temples, of ruralizing the artisans, spinners and weavers who lost their livelihoods to the ubiquitous imports of Manchester cottons, the British had indeed peasantized India. Across parts of western and southern India the power and dominance of better-off peasants had been recognized in the 1820s and 1830s, by the introduction of the *ryotwari* settlement. Under the terms of this land reform the British hoped to make the actual tillers of the fields the owners of the land, and thus transform them into successful commercial farmers.

In some parts of India this did indeed happen. However, the impact of private ownership, the profit motive and the productivity-boosting effects of new technology were considerably weaker than the British had hoped: by 1914 the countryside consisted of pockets of affluence amidst a sea of dire poverty. The tiny, uneconomic plots that characterized much of peasant landholding, were not consolidated by market forces into larger and more efficient farms, but proliferated into ever fragmenting atoms. The railways and canal irrigation systems built under British auspices boosted the incomes of only a few, while even the more antediluvian technologies of the bullock and the cart remained the preserve of the relatively privileged. By the 1890s, it was calculated that much of the peasantry across India was in heavy debt, many carrying obligations that stretched across several generations and bonded them almost as serfs to their rich farmer creditors. The consequence was that agricultural productivity beyond the well-irrigated regions producing exportable wheat, cotton, jute and oil-seeds, stagnated. While the British tended to blame the custom-bound peasantry themselves for this stubborn failure to 'modernize' and develop, the truth was that the market forces that should, theoretically, have driven the feckless and hide-bound out of business and rewarded the enterprising, were being blunted by the British themselves.

Neither profitability nor bankruptcy received their due reward. The market was shackled by a ponderous and expensive legal system, and land was anything but freely tradable. Though the *ryotwari* system theoretically recognized sole proprietorship and the right to buy and sell one's land freely, in reality the British preferred to bolster not the individual, but corporate peasant identities, or brotherhoods – the *biradaris* of the northern provinces or the *mirsadars* of Maharashtra. These often made it impossible for the lone farmer to buy or sell his land without the consent of his confrères. Moreover, after a series of peasant rebellions during the 1880s and 1890s, the British passed a series of acts designed to protect weak farmers and poor peasants from outsider 'money-lenders' and made it illegal for peasants to sell their land to those not deemed to be members of 'agricultural castes'. This legislation had the unfortunate and unintended results of making credit more expensive, discouraging merchant groups from investing in the countryside, and protecting the indigent and inefficient from the iron hand of the market and bankruptcy. The alternative to allowing the market to impose efficiency and force the unproductive from the land was greater intervention by the state. But while the British recognized the problems of bonded labour, share-cropping and land fragmentation, they lacked the power or the revenues to deal with them directly, having allowed rural authority to devolve on local collaborators.

Why were the British so chary of either allowing the free market to transform the Indian countryside, or, alternatively, of employing more direct state power to do it themselves? Both ideology and pragmatism, happily congruent, offer explanations. Many British officials seem sincerely to have believed that India was naturally a self-sufficient 'peasant' society, despite the evidence of only a few decades earlier that it was instead an urbanized, commercial and artisanal economy, in which many villages, far from being self-sufficient, were closely intermeshed through trading networks. The immiseration of the rural poor was attributed to fecklessness and rapacious money-lending. Convinced that the villages were republics of egalitarian virtue, it was not until after the First World War that the intense stratification, the exploitation of poor peasants by the rich and the need for massive injections of capital were recognized – by which time the Raj was both too indigent and politically beleaguered to do much about it.

More pragmatically, it was far from clear where poor peasants displaced from their tiny plots would go. Rural industry was declining rather than thriving, and though there were pockets of modern industry in Calcutta, Bombay and Ahmedabad, agriculture still accounted for over 75 per cent of employment in India. Also, the countryside desperately needed capital; rural productivity rates were among the lowest in Asia, for which the solution was rural industry, more irrigation, more bullocks, more carts, better seed and so forth. British capital had indeed flowed into the country to build the railways, assured of healthy, government-guaranteed dividends, but was otherwise conspicuous by its absence. To develop the Indian countryside the British would have needed to abandon their chosen collaborators, the 'natural leaders', and seek partners instead among the very groups excluded from this magic circle and with whom they enjoyed increasingly fractious relations: commercial men (merchants, traders and money-lenders) and the educated middle classes.

The holders of capital, the merchant usurers, were discouraged from pursuing business by preferential legislation that protected peasants from the consequences of debt default. State-led development would have required the construction of a more modern administrative machine than the tiny ICS was able to muster, the jettisoning of old collaborators with their local autonomies and far greater reliance on India's growing educated middle classes. Unsurprisingly both the merchants and the educated middle classes had, by the last quarter of the nineteenth century, adopted a highly critical stance towards British policies and were beginning to present themselves as the 'true' agents of Indian prosperity. This contributed to British perceptions, inchoate, but inhibiting nevertheless, that the imperial state simply lacked the legitimacy essential for the imposition of a major restructuring of the economy. In such circumstances it seemed simply easier, cheaper and safer to protect 'traditional' India from the depredations of modern capitalism or the attentions of a modernizing bureaucracy.

This is not to say that the British gained no economic rewards from 'traditional' India. A settled peasantry was easy to tax, and though tax revenues may have been unusually low, they were sufficient to finance the Indian army, which was increasingly used to project and protect British interests in the Middle and Far East and Africa. Moreover, the British did not entirely neglect modern infrastructural investment when it suited their purposes. As every schoolchild knows, the British built hundreds of thousands of miles of railways and canals in India. These served two important purposes. The railways made India easier to secure while also linking the commercially prosperous areas of farming to the cities and ports from where their commodities could be exported. The canals, largely constructed in the Punjab and western United Provinces; from whence the greatest proportion of the Indian army was recruited, served both to enrich their recruiting grounds and ensure placid sepoys, while also, like the railways, generating great productivity gains in areas where export crops were grown.

The British hoped that modern technology in and of itself might have a solvent effect on the ingrained 'traditionalism' of the peasant that they both fostered and deplored. This was particularly true of the railways – imagined by many British as almost a god itself. On inaugurating the great Bhore Ghat Incline, a massive piece of rail engineering that connected the city of Bombay with the interior in April 1863, the governor of Bombay Presidency, Sir Bartle Frere, marvelled at the technological and logistical feats accomplished in its construction:

were I to tell you that the bulk of so many pyramids was contained in the earthwork and masonry of embankments – that it would take many times all the bridges in London to equal the viaducts – or were I to compare the bulk of the stone quarried with the breakwaters of Plymouth or Portland – I could give you but an imperfect idea ... Nor could any description give to the uninitiated a notion of the difficulties you have had to overcome. Military men who know what it is to organize and feed an army of 10,000 men, may have some notion of the difficulties of organizing, feeding, and working a multitude of labourers averaging for years together 25,000 men, and rising to the enormous number of 42,000; but most of us must be content with the impression we have this day derived, and it is I am sure an impression which can never be effaced, of that which I believe may, without exaggeration, be described as the greatest work of its kind in the whole world.

The impress of the railways would not, Frere believed, be confined to the landscape, but would also reshape popular mentalities: 'in future ages the works of our Indian engineers on these Ghauts will take the place of their demigods'. This was a view of railways advanced by Kipling in his highly metaphorical short story, 'The Bridge-Builders'. In 'The Bridge-Builders' a group of British engineers are attempting to construct a railway crossing (the Kashi Bridge) across the Ganges near Banaras (Varanasi), the holiest city of Hinduism, where, reputedly, heaven meets earth. The story dwells on the driving willpower of the British, conquering all manner of 'backward' forces: epidemics, caste wars and the superstitions of native workers. But the greatest challenge comes from a fearsome flood that threatens to wash the bridge away. For the Indian workmen the flood is clearly a portent of the wrath of 'Mother Gunga', the river goddess, enraged at attempts to 'chain' her. During the flood the chief British engineer, half crazy with anxiety, experiences an opium-induced hallucination in which he overhears a 'parliament' of Hindu gods called by 'Mother Gunga' to settle the fate of the bridge. Strangely, the godly consensus is to save the bridge, though Shiva and Krishna, its defenders, prize it for very different reasons. For Shiva the railway, far from 'chaining' the gods, will enhance their power by bringing more pilgrims: 'Kali knows that she has held her chiefest festivals among the pilgrimages that are fed by the fire-carriage [railway] . . . Before the fire-carriage came it was a heavy toil. The fire-carriages have served thee well, Mother of Death.' Krishna, presumably speaking for Kipling, also advocates saving the bridge, but, more fatalistically, predicts that this demonstration of the power of western technology will soon wean the god-struck from their superstitions and set them on the iron-road to scientific rationality. Shiva, it transpired, in reality if not in fiction, was right. Doubtless Indians were impressed by the technology of the iron-road, and many would become trained engineers themselves, but for the multitude the most conspicuous role for the 'fire-carriage' lay in promoting religious life.

Though Indians had always made pilgrimages in their hundreds of thousands, rail travel enabled them to make more, and more quickly. The British had deplored these journeys as emblems of mass irrationality. And while Lord Dalhousie had insisted in 1853 that the principal objectives of the railways were greater military efficiency, the creation of markets for British goods and channels for the extraction of exportable commodities, they were quickly turned to peregrinational profit. By the early 1880s the construction of a railway line had more than doubled the pilgrim traffic to Gaya in Bihar, and railways reduced the journey time from Calcutta to the Jagannath temple at Puri from 26 days to 12 hours. In 1913 a government committee discovered that numbers attending festivals such as the *Rath Yatra* had soared. Some muttered that the ease of pilgrimage now had turned the event into something akin to tourism, with pilgrims jostled and harassed by *panda* priests-turned tour-touts. Gandhi himself, no friend of the railways, though a frequent user, sourly observed that while 'good travels at a snail's pace . . . evil has wings'. The pious hopes of Frere and Kipling were thus frustrated. The coffers of the Brahmans and other religious professionals were not emptied by the iron progress of rationality and railways, but filled to overflowing.

Pilgrimage was only one aspect of the burgeoning of Indian religious life under the Raj, for, like feudalism and aristocracy, British officials regarded religion in India as a fixed identity, and one that informed all aspects of social and political affairs; and by their policies they did much to make it so. By the eve of the First World War many Indians, who had previously viewed their primary identities as a complex mixture of culture, locale and kinship, increasingly viewed the central division in their society as religious in a way that had not been the case only a century earlier.

Mohurram commemorates the martyrdom of Husain, the grandson of Mohammed, in seventh-century Persia, and was commemorated in nineteenth-century India in a ten-day festival of immense importance to many Indian Muslims. The festival had its solemn moments and sermons were held, but there was also music and dancing. In nineteenth-century Bombay Mohurram was the occasion for a marathon festival, the centrepiece of which was a fourteen-hour procession of as many as two hundred *tazias*, bamboo models of the tombs of the martyrs. These tinsel-covered towers (some were twenty feet high) were borne through the city's streets, accompanied by dancing, drum beating and displays of self-flagellation. Beginning in the central market place, the processants toured the main streets, the various mosques and then wended their way through the smaller alleys, so that the women and the sick would not be denied a sighting, ending with the ritual immersion of the *tazias* in the river. Theologically Mohurram is a Shia festival, but for much of the nineteenth century participants included not just Shia, but also Sunnis (who constituted the majority of India's Muslims) and perhaps most surprisingly, Hindus. Indeed Hindus contributed their own *tazias*, along with drumming bands and wrestling troupes to march alongside the Muslim procession. Donning the green clothes of Muslim mourning or even appearing as *fakirs* (Islamic holy men), thousands of Hindus would wail, chant and mourn the martyrdom of Husain.

Mohurram was not the only great religious festival of India which, while ostensibly the preserve of one of the great religious communities, was also celebrated by the other. The *Ramlila*, or the play of Ram, was commonly based on a sixteenth-century version of the Story of Ram, the ideal Hindu king, whose wife and kingdom are stolen by the evil god Ravanna and then restored after epic battles. In the early nineteenth century the annual staging of the play became immensely popular across north India. *Ramlila* became particularly associated with Banaras, a city then sacred to Hindus and Muslims alike, and many Muslims would participate in this most Hindu of commemorations. For ten days Banaras resembled a vast film set, as life-size replicas of *Ramlila*'s principal scenes were erected. Of the tens of thousands of spectators who would attend from neighbouring regions, many were *Julahas* or Muslim weavers. This guild-like community joined all the processions, made elaborate decorations and even sold souvenirs to visiting pilgrims, and it became traditional for the actors playing the various gods and demons to visit *Julaha* homes for refreshments and gift-giving.

So, although Hindus and Muslims in the towns of late eighteenth- and early nineteenth-century India were in no doubt that they belonged to different religions, they had, nevertheless, developed a syncretic *mélange* of festivals, rituals and observances which tended to blur confessional identity into grand spectacles of religions passion. Neither Hinduism nor Islam as yet constituted monolithic identities. Pre-colonial Hinduism was highly fragmented and localized. Broad divisions might be drawn between a 'high' form based on texts like the Rig Veda or the Laws of Manu and a 'popular' or folk form which focused on ritual sacrifice, personal devotion (*bhakti*) and the worship of local gods. The north was also distinct from the south in its much greater veneration of Brahmans and the hierarchical caste system. Lacking an orthodoxy which might define the faith of its followers, Hinduism was more a set of sects, beliefs and practices which were essentially localized and part of a much broader social order.

Islam, which accounted for around 20 per cent of the population, was more obviously distinctive, founded, as it was, on veneration for a single 'revealed' text. But within South Asian Islam there were many divisions. Regionally distinct groups had their particular heritage and traditions. Most of India's Muslims were Sunni but with pockets of Shias in the north and south-west. In the north, the large Muslim populations of the Punjab and the North Western Provinces were related to the Central Asian invaders of the twelfth century; in Bengal, Muslims were a poor group and supposedly the descendants of converts; and on the south-west coast of Malabar they had originally been Arab traders. Descent itself was an important marker of prestige, and rigid distinctions were drawn between Muslims of Arab or Persian descent, the *ashraf*, and indigenous Muslims. Significantly, differences developed between those who followed the faith in its textual or high form, and those who practised a more localized and popular version. The former, mostly townspeople, adopted the strict moral codes of the mosque and *madrasa* (religious school); the rural majority, however, followed a brand of folk Islam which was less concerned with texts than with the worship of charismatic saints or *sufis*. *Sufi* cults, with their semi-magical and healing gifts, had an appeal that reached far beyond Muslims and deep into rural Hinduism. While no one would suggest that pre-British India was a paradise of religious unity, and certainly there were cases of religious rioting and violence, these were sporadic and localized. There was not yet any sense that India was divided into two rigidly separate and opposed religious communities.

The very presence of the British, however, exerted a powerful cultural influence on the self-perception and practices of India's religious communities, though their attitudes to Hinduism and Islam shifted radically over time. One might perhaps say that an early British enthusiasm for Hinduism later made way for sustained ridicule and denigration, while the trajectory of official opinion towards Islam was rather the reverse. These shifting perceptions reflected not only intellectual fashion, but also changing strategies and calculations towards collaborators and power relationships. The British increasingly saw the two religions as great monolithic communities, the majority Hindus and the minority Muslims, which needed to be balanced. Moreover, they projected their own preoccupation with religion as the crucial organizing category of social and political life on to Indians themselves.

Under British auspices a very particular form of Hinduism, 'Brahmanical' or priestly Hinduism, became dominant. The somewhat unlikely cause of this was a combination of British scholarship and statecraft. The British engagement with Hinduism began in the eighteenth century with the so-called orientalists and, in particular, the scholar-officials William Jones and Nathaniel Holhead. Conservative by temperament, these men were determined that India should be governed according to her own traditions, but they tended to view these traditions through a European lens. As Enlightenment scholars they sought textual authority for tradition and deprecated custom and practice as 'inauthentic'. In the ancient Laws of Manu, the Puranas and the Smriti, texts used by orthodox Brahmanical sects, they believed they had found the 'real' Hinduism. Moreover, in the early days of Company rule the British tended to rely very heavily on Brahmans, the literate classes, for both interpretation of customary law and for administrative assistance. Inevitably, the consequence of this approach was to elevate one brand of Hinduism above all the others. The British and their Brahman collaborators campaigned to turn a loose agglomeration of multifarious sects, customs and mores into a monolithic religion of the book. In south India especially this meant effacing a very different tradition of Hinduism characterized by personal devotion, in which caste and priesthood were much less prominent. Local gods and goddesses, rituals and sacrifices were officially disapproved and Brahman priests, the equivalent of church-wardens in British eyes, were imposed on previously Brahman-free temples. In north India the desire to emulate the textual religions of Christianity and, to a degree, Islam, had, by the late nineteenth century, produced highly influential and increasingly politicized reform movements.

But British attitudes to Hinduism and the power of Brahmans soon changed. By the 1820s and 1830s the utilitarian school, which strongly disapproved of 'tradition' (and especially its oriental varieties), was more dominant among Company officials, many of whom concurred with James Mill's notorious judgement that Hinduism was 'built upon enormous and tormenting superstitions with minds enchained more intolerably than bodies . . . paying court to the divine . . . [with] a great variety of grotesque and frivolous ceremonies'. These hostile views of Hinduism were bolstered by an influx of evangelical Christians the ranks of Company officials at this time. With its cults, priests and multitudes of popular deities, which in their gaudiness and profusion reminded evangelicals of European saints, Hinduism, they concluded, was a particularly insidious and decadent relation of Catholicism. The denigration continued in the mid-nineteenth-century, driven not by the evangelical dogmatists but by the rise of a philosophical rationalism that stressed the hopelessly unscientific mindset of Hinduism. Hegel mused on the supposedly dreamlike state of ecstatic imaginings inhabited by the Hindu, and in the mid-nineteenth century the Hindu was depicted by him as passive and weak, lost in 'a vast swamp . . . a tangled jungle of disorderly superstitions'. By the late nineteenth century the British view of Hindus, especially Brahmans, had petrified into an unflattering stereotype: they were idle herbivores, harmless, unmanly and rather contemptible.

As a monotheistic religion of the book the British felt more comfortable with Islam and its puritanical aesthetic than with the polytheistic profusion of Hinduism. The coming of Company rule had, of course, marked a great loss of cultural prestige for Muslims who, under Mughal rule, had previously been the dominant group. The British were, however, careful to woo notables and clerics. *Muftis* (Islamic lawyers) were employed to translate and assist the British in the newly created courts, and were encouraged to develop a new hybrid of

Anglo-Muslim law which conceded substantial autonomy in the regulation of many aspects of everyday life. Like the early elevation of Brahmanical Hinduism this involved, to an extent, the promotion of text-based Islam at the expense of customary local practice. Moreover, the shock of the British takeover in India provoked one of Islam's periodic radical reform movements in the country. Islam's weakness, radicals reasoned, had been caused by decadent syncretic practices and it had to be purged of its Hindu accretions if it was ever to be strong again. Polytheism, saintly intercession, pilgrimages, and consultations with Brahmans and astrologers had to be stamped out. A striking manifestation of this was a movement led by Syed Ahmad of Bareilly, who created a military brotherhood in alliance with the Pathans of the North West Frontier to wage holy war or *jihad* against the Sikhs and the British in the 1840s. Naturally this kind of radical Islam was alarming to the British, and coupled with the shock of 1857 briefly dented their otherwise cautious approach to Islam.

In the immediate aftermath of the Rebellion British attitudes to Muslims darkened. Despite lack of evidence, it soon became the received wisdom that the rebellion was proof of a Muslim anti-British conspiracy. A rich tradition of stereotyping dating back to the Crusades had been reawakened, and to many it now seemed obvious that Muslims were somehow obliged to be disloyal. The British frightened themselves with lurid visions of hoards of fanatical zealots armed with sword and Quran, primed to launch a *jihad* at any time. The new Viceroy, Lord John Lawrence, felt that 'something in their religion makes warriors of them' and imparts 'an active, vindictive and fanatic spirit'. Suddenly the activities of the Muslim reformers seemed terribly sinister: 'a network of conspiracy has spread itself out . . . the bleak mountains which rise beyond the Punjab, united by a chain of treason depots with the tropical swamps through which the Ganges merges into the sea'.

At first the British sought vengeance, sending punitive expeditions to the North West Frontier and purging Muslims from positions of power and influence in government and the army. But by the 1870s Muslims were to be rehabilitated as friends of the Raj. This striking volte-face, like so much in British India, can be traced to a combination of intellectual fashion and pragmatic calculation. In

1871 W. W. Hunter, yet another scholar-official, published his intriguingly titled *Are India Musulmans Bound by their Religion to Rebel Against the Queen?* Hunter insisted that they were not. His widely read tome offered a more nuanced analysis of Indian Muslims and presented a careful taxonomy of the subcontinent's different forms of Islam. The aggressive and frightening Wahhabis (the expansionist and *jihad*-prone sect common to the North West Frontier) were firmly distinguished from the more moderate votaries of establishment Islam. While the former were depicted as fanatical puritan dissenters appealing to the dispossessed, the latter were portrayed as an Indian version of the Anglicans. The establishment Muslims were reasonable and worldly gentlemen, 'men of inert convictions and some property, who say their prayers, decorously attend the mosque and think very little about the [religious] matter'. Wahhabism, it turned out, not only unnerved the British, it upset better-off Muslims too. Hunter's thesis was influential because it told the British what they wanted to hear. Hindus were becoming increasingly involved in oppositional politics, as will be seen in the next chapter, and the British believed that Muslims would be useful allies against them.

From the early 1870s the British gave more affluent Muslims various educational benefits, bureaucratic preferments and, ultimately, special electoral privileges within the slowly democratizing Indian constitution. In the 1880s the British introduced consultative councils into the towns and cities in an effort to bolster their collaborator networks and imbue them with broader legitimacy. The idea was that 'native' gentlemen and country gentry would have to stand for election among their peers, and it was hoped that these bodies would be training grounds in modern administration. The introduction of representative politics, however limited, raised the question of how the British would balance what they increasingly saw as the distinct 'communities' of Muslims and Hindus on these councils. In the wake of Hunter's persuasive hypothesis that Muslims were not only a minority but also an 'oppressed' one, the British were sympathetic to representations from certain Muslim groups that they required special protection from the dynamic and domineering ambitions of the Hindu majority. The irony of this was that the very Muslim groups so privileged were among the wealthiest and best educated elites in British India.

However, the notion that these rather unrepresentative and well-favoured Muslims somehow spoke for all the Muslims of India soon came to be accepted fact.

The British decision to favour Muslims was part of a more fundamental change in their understanding of India after the Rebellion: they now increasingly saw it as a society defined and determined by religious identity and difference. While the causes of the uprising went far deeper than the issue of pork fat or cow grease, for the British the Mutiny proved beyond doubt that Indians were a religion-soaked people. The first sign of this heightened sensitivity to religion came in official record-keeping. Soon any kind of popular altercation, whatever its real causes, tended, in official discourse, to be ascribed to religious conflict. This phenomenon produced some extraordinary rewriting of history. For example, the notorious rioting that enveloped Banaras in 1809, had, according to contemporary Company accounts, been a relatively unimportant affair: a petty dispute over land use had spilt over into violence, but no one was killed and Hindu and Muslim leaders had intervened to calm the passions of the young rioters. The substance of the dispute was later settled by negotiation and, far from poisoning relations, the very next year Hindus and Muslims co-operated in a revenue tax strike against the Company state. But by 1900 this episode had become the subject of several rewritings, according to which it had erupted as the result of Muslims insulting Hindu monuments during Mohurram, thousands had died and community relations had never healed. The case of the Banaras riot was now regularly invoked in government inquiries as proof of the ferocious and irrational enmity that had always existed between the two 'communities'.

Throughout the 1880s and 1890s a series of such wildly inaccurate histories of India and its religious communities poured from the pens of British writers. Particular groups were singled out for calumny. The Muslim weavers or *Julahas* of north India acquired a reputation for mindless fanaticism rivalled only by the fearsome warrior brotherhoods of the North West Frontier, while Emperor Aurangzeb, the last of the Great Moguls, was routinely depicted as a vindictive Islamic zealot whose fanaticism had destroyed the Mughal Empire (Aurangzeb had reintroduced a special tax on non-Muslims). Moreover, histories of India written at this time began to project the then popular periodization of European development – the classical eras, the dark ages, enlightenment – on to India. A 'classical' Hindu golden age was now said to have collapsed into the 'dark ages' of Muslim dominance, only to revive under the 'enlightened' rule of the British. While the ponderings of historians may seem trivial, in the following century the question of Aurangzeb's tyranny or the relative cultural achievements of the Hindu Guptas and the Muslim Delhi sultanates became the stuff of both elite and popular Indian histories, novels, plays and folklore.

Paradoxically, now convinced that India was a land of warring religions, the British decided that the best way to govern was to abjure any involvement in the religious life of their Indian subjects whatsoever. This approach lay at the heart of Queen Victoria's Proclamation of 1858:

While firmly relying ourselves on the truth of Christianity, and acknowledging with gratitude the solace of religion, we disclaim alike the right and desire to impose our convictions on any of our subjects. We declare it be our royal will and pleasure that none be in any wise favoured, none molested or disquieted, by reason of their religious faith or observances, but that all shall enjoy the equal and impartial protection of the law; and we do strictly charge and enjoin all those who may be in authority under us that they shall abstain from all interference with the religious belief or worship of any of our subjects on pain of our highest displeasure.

So, unlike the Company state, which, like the pre-colonial Mughal and Hindu states had actively managed religious affairs, the Raj withdrew from all dealings with religious rituals, processions and temples. Religion, it was now argued, was part of the 'private' sphere and no business of the state – unless it became a public order matter. However, consigning religion to the private sphere when the British and their hand-picked collaborators had so completely colonized the public one was to prove an impossible task. The implications of such a policy in late nineteenth-century India would be momentous. This was a dynamic and fluid society; economic, social and cultural changes were throwing up new men who needed some outlet for their political aspirations and some public acknowledgement of their newly acquired prestige. If they could not achieve this in the conventional public sphere of the Raj-controlled city councils or the regional boards, or socializing with the District Officer, then they would seek it elsewhere. The most obvious alternative arenas for power and status were the very mosques and temples that the British had so scrupulously vacated. Evidence for the increasing politicization of religion began to mount in the 1880s, as relatively minor flare-ups over issues like music playing in front of mosques or cow-killing became occasions for major riots and organized protests. Religious festivals, processions and *melas* (fairs) also increasingly became causes of violence and community polarization.

Just as the idea of religion as a great divide came to be reified under the Raj, so also did equally dubious British notions about the fissiparous roles of caste and racial identities in the subcontinent. Both scholarly and official writing in the post-Rebellion period was obsessively preoccupied with what the British regarded as the peculiarly decentralized and cellular nature of Indian society. The British might have debated the nature of the fragments, but all agreed that India was in pieces, a poorly made jigsaw nation which could never be put together. In truth India was by the mid-nineteenth century a highly disrupted society. The glue holding it together in the Mughal era had dissolved long since, and fifty years of British rule had produced great disruption. In response society and culture had become decentralized, but this was a temporary state which the British mistook for age-old permanence. To explain this puzzling cellularity the British reached for concepts like caste, tribe and race, which they believed captured the essence of India. For some scholar-officials it was a society of ancient village republics; for others a congeries of sturdy peasant brotherhoods and ancient feudal nobilities. And for a few it was an arena of warring races held in uneasy equilibrium through the sheer willpower of the British, the conquering race. But, whatever the nature of the fragmentation, the implication was clear: India was not a nation. As Herbert Risley observed, 'anarchy is the peculiar peril of a society that is organized on this basis. So long as [this] persists, it is difficult to see how the sentiment of unity and solidarity can penetrate.' J. D. Baines, Chief Census Commissioner in 1891, put it more bluntly:

It is well to begin by clearing out of the way the notion that in the Indian population there is any cohesive element that is implied in the term nationality. There is, indeed, an influence peculiar to the country, but it is adverse to nationality, and tends rather towards detachment without independence . . . it is that of an excessive devotion to hereditary attributes, a process which ends in the formation of a practically unlimited number of self-centred and mutually repellent groups.

And yet, ironically, it was the British who did more than anyone to make these fluid and often fleeting identities into hard, permanent realities. This was most apparent in attitudes to caste.

British fascination with caste began early. In the eighteenth century it already occupied substantial terrain in the British imagination. Castes were sometimes seen as akin to the estates order of early modern Europe: a social pyramid ranked by occupation, with lowly barbers and washerwomen at the bottom, rising towards an elite of nobles and clerics at the apex. For others, it was an institution entirely peculiar to India: a malign mosaic presided over by a tyranny of priests who had usurped the rightful power of kings. Between these two extremes lay a host of conflicting interpretations of the phenomenon. Castes, some asserted, were just regional clans; others claimed that they resembled medieval guilds or corporations; for others they denoted religious sects. Class and tribe were also suggested as possible analogues. This diversity of views probably came closer to the truth of caste than the rigid definitions of the later nineteenth century. In fact caste, as it manifested itself towards the end of the nineteenth century, seems to have been a conflation of two distinct Indian categories: *Jati* and *Varna*. *Jati* are perhaps best understood as regional kinship groups or clans, of which there were thousands. *Varna*, however, is a religiously sanctioned moral system of four hierarchically arranged orders. According to the creation myth found in the Rig Veda, these orders were created from the dismemberment of the body of the original cosmic man Purusha. From his head sprang the Brahmans, or priests; from his arms the Ksatriyas or warrior aristocrats; from his trunk the Vaishyas or merchants; and from his feet the peasants and labourers, the Shudras. Other Hindu scriptures supplied further guidance as to the roles and relationships between these four orders. The Brahmans were the intellectual and priestly elite; the Ksatriyas exercised secular power. Finally, a group emerged below the Shudras, whose work was so polluting that they became literally untouchable – the ordure collectors, sweepers, barbers and corpse-keepers. According to the Brahmanical versions of Hinduism, a strict hierarchy operates between these orders. The so-called 'clean' or 'twice-born' castes of Vaishyas, Ksatriyas and Brahmans must maintain a rigid separation from the dalits and some of the more lowly Shudras. This extreme inequality is justified by the notion of rebirth. Those who conduct their lives well are reborn as high caste. Therefore high caste status is a sign of virtue and low caste is indicative of past sin.

Before the arrival of the British this rigidly hierarchical system based on notions of purity and pollution seems to have had little, if any, significance, and a variety of systems of status differentiation held sway. The most significant were *jatis*, which were essentially local groupings that bundled together a variety of relationships, ranging from kinship to clan, from occupation to corporation or guild. *Varna*, in the sense of a four-part moral order fixed at birth, played little role in ordering *jati* relationships. Indeed, far from being fixed into a particular *varna* group at birth, *jati* status was fluid. Great swathes of the population – tribal groups, forest dwellers and nomads – had little, if any conception of caste at all. In South India, Bengal, the Punjab and much of the central Deccan plain, caste was a pretty vague notion too. Even where something approximating to modern notions of caste hierarchy did hold sway, as in the Gangetic heartlands of eastern United Provinces, the pollution barrier was not rigid, and Brahmans were by no means unchallenged in their pre-eminence. In so far as any extreme pollution barrier existed at all it seems only to have applied to small groups of village servants, who under the traditional *jajmani* (patron-client) system, were required to perform all the waste removal and funerary services of their particular village.

For the pre-colonial rulers of India caste meant something very different from the rigidly hierarchical structure we think of today. Ksatriyas, not Brahmans, were at the top of the hierarchy, and Ksatriya kings were able to manipulate caste to maintain political stability and foster social integration. For both the Mughals and their successors, the Muslim Nawabs and the Hindu upstart kings of the eighteenth century, ordering *jati* status was a matter of statecraft. The notion that Brahmans should decide who had status was unthinkable, after all most of the post-Mughal kings were (in ritual terms) rather lowly. Shivaji, for example, the great seventeenth-century Maratha warlord, was technically a Shudra – the lowest of the low. But Shivaji viewed caste as just another political tool, something he could manage for his own benefit. Shivaji thus became part of an intriguing pre-colonial phenomenon: the born-again high caste king. One particularly inventive 'king' sprang forth from a huge hollow wooden cow in a flamboyant display of symbolic playfulness. Indeed many of the parvenu dynasts of the period designed elaborate and highly dubious ceremonies from which they were 'reborn' as warrior Ksatriyas.

Unsurprisingly then the British also sought to manipulate caste, but with their academic and textualist approach, they tended, initially at least, to promote the ascendancy of Brahmans. Desperately in need of collaborators to help them consolidate their fragile grip on India in the early nineteenth century, Brahmans and the Vaishyas or merchant castes were ideal allies. They were literate and could help staff Company courts and revenue-gathering bureaucracies. Revenue collection was the overriding priority of the Company and its Brahman allies assisted the British in cutting a swathe through much of south India, up through the Deccan and into Maharashtra, reordering existing traditions of loose land entitlements into more easily taxable rigid owner-tenant distinctions, and giving land to the 'higher' caste groups at the expense of the supposedly 'lower'. This was then justified as the restoration of a pure *varna* order. Moreover, British dominance could be legitimized by association with these virtuous Brahmans, so similar in many ways to the Victorian British with their conspicuous piety and fear of spicy food (strict Brahmans eschew onions, garlic and spices), which meshed well with the mores of their new rulers. Ksatriyas, by contrast, with their exultation of war and display, seemed, initially, less biddable.

Needless to say, this process created great insecurity and anxiety among the rural populations, for whom *varna* status had been relatively unimportant. Now, however, status distinctions mattered and the best way of making good one's own claim to status (and therefore land) was to insist on one's caste superiority to others. Thus throughout the economically turbulent 1820s, 1830s and 1840s many better-off peasants assiduously worked to present themselves as high caste and began piously aping the lifestyle of the Brahmans. In this frenzied struggle for status, temples were endowed, pilgrimages were made, and far more attention was paid to marriage arrangements and the correct treatment of widows (all signs of 'clean' caste status) than had been the case hitherto. At the same time poorer peasants, tribal peoples and nomads came to be labelled low caste or dalit for the first time.

The casteization of Indian society was not simply a by-product of taxation policy or the machinations of wily Brahmans. An enthusiasm for the application of science to government also drove the craze to classify and order society. The greatest manifestation of this modern scientific urge towards 'governmentality' was the decennial census. Begun in 1871 these massive 'fact' gathering jamborees were spectacular, if misconceived, enterprises; every inch of the subcontinent would be visited, every town, village and hut investigated, and every hapless inhabitant interrogated. While European censuses sought principally to establish who could be taxed and by how much, the Indian census was more metaphysical than fiscal in its ambitions. The Raj wanted to understand its subjects, to know them completely – their religions, their sectarian affiliations, who they married, what they ate and so on. In sum, the census was supposed to capture the vast diversity of India in a single, statistical snapshot – literally so in many cases, for great photogravures accompanied each report, ordering Indians by colour, shape and physiognomy into album after album of so much subcontinental exotica. The intention was to create a database of loyalty, a ready-reckoner of reliability. Serendipitously, the post-Rebellion moment coincided with the birth of many new sciences closely connected with state and nation-building. Statistics, ethnology and anthropology were all corralled into service as the Raj sought to scientize the government of India. From the 1860s onwards the bewilderingly diverse and still rather amateur gazetteers, surveys and agency reports of Company rule were spun together into a great web of intellectual and administrative understanding that would capture the demoralizing diversity of Indian social and cultural life into a few digestible paragraphs.

The reality was very different. The first census did not go well and it took two years to complete. It was run by a skeleton force of white officials attempting to regulate an army of Indian enumerators, half a million in all, chosen from among the better sort of Indian. This regiment of fact-gatherers toured the countryside generating alarm. Bizarre rumours swiftly spread about the government's intentions. Some said that Queen Victoria had ordered that two virgins from every village be shipped to Windsor to fan her while she slept. Others were convinced that it was all a ruse designed to get Englishmen into the harems and zenanas of the natives. More plausible was the belief that the census heralded conscription for a war against the Russians. Panic wasn't the only problem. The data, when it was collated, was a bewildering profusion of information of dubious worth. No uniform definitions were applied to caste; it appeared that there were 107 different varieties of Brahman in Banaras alone, 85 per cent of the population of Bihar, Oudh and the Punjab were apparently Rajputs (warrior aristocrats), while Bengal turned out to be a caste-free zone. Similarly, the notion of *varna* produced some improbable results: one category alone included an implausible mix of market owners, military pensioners, eunuchs and brothel-keepers. The Madras census commissioner was forced to conclude that caste 'is a subject upon which no two divisions, or sub-divisions of the people themselves are agreed, and upon which European authorities who have paid any attention to it differ hopelessly.'

Undeterred by this depressing confusion, the census officials pressed on, and a second and third campaign for knowledge were launched in 1881 and 1891. These censuses were notable for their attempts to systematize the profusion of castes, hitherto seen as phenomena with purely local meaning, into national entities. This impulse to turn castes into mega-castes had clear administrative purposes. If the myriad of local *jatis* could be understood as somehow linked to one another horizontally and embodying certain characteristics then this would make it easy to predict who was criminally inclined, or to decide which peasants deserved permanent land rights, without going to the time-consuming bother of judging each individual on his own merits. Enumerators were told to look for caste groups of 100,000 or more, and they claimed to have found 207 of them. But there is some doubt about this since, frustrated by proliferation of sub-groups, many took matters into their own hands and invented caste titles into which the inconvenient sub-castes were then collapsed. This raises the uncomfortable possibility that many of what are now thought of as ancient traditional castes were invented by impatient enumerators a little over a hundred years ago.

The most elaborate innovation, however, came between 1901 and 1911. This was the era when race science was at its most fashionable and strenuous efforts were made to yoke caste, race and social rank into a kind of periodic table of scientifically verifiable status. The most popular version of this theory held that at some point the subcontinent had been invaded by a race of superior fair-skinned beings from Central Asia – the Aryans. The Aryans, it was surmised, were the ancestors of the white European 'races', but in India it was not clear what had happened to them. Some officials maintained that they had become degenerate, either by interbreeding with people of lower stock or by vegetarianism, or some combination of the two. But one important official thought differently. Herbert H. Risley, the official most closely associated with the racialization of caste, was first posted to Bengal in the early 1870s as assistant director of statistics. While there he amassed several tons of data purporting to prove striking physical differences between various castes and tribes. India, with its strict caste rules governing who could marry whom, had, unlike Europe, preserved pure racial types across the centuries. Here, it seemed, was a great zoo of pure racial types where modish theories could be put to the test. Employing the new sub-science of anthropometry, a technique of measuring various aspects of the physique to discover racial differences, Risley hoped to reveal that Indians were actually several distinct races – Aryan, Kolarian, Dravidian, Lohitic, Tibetan and so on (although the British could never decide whether there were six or sixteen discrete races in India) – each with their particular qualities and shortcomings. He also believed that castes were really racial groupings and caste ranking would be found to coincide with racial prestige. The 'advanced' Brahmans and Ksatriyas were at the top of this merged caste-race hierarchy, and the 'lowly' dalits at the bottom.

Physiognomy came to be seen as an index of status. Risley was particularly preoccupied with noses and he found justification for it in ancient Indian wisdom:

No one can have glanced at the literature . . . and in particular at the Vedic accounts of the Aryan advance, without being struck by the frequent references to . . . noses. So impressed were the Aryans with the shortcomings of their enemies' noses that they often spoke of them as the 'noseless ones'. In taking their nose then as the starting point of the present analysis, we may claim to be following at once the most ancient and the most modern authorities on the subject of racial physiognomy.

Risley was as good as his word, and in the course of collecting the returns for the 1901 census the nose caliper made its first appearance as an instrument of government. Throughout 1901 British census officials and their Indian underlings toured the length and breadth of the subcontinent measuring the length of every typical nose and dividing it by the width of every representative nostril to arrive at the nasal ratio. It was a thankless task. The calipers were unwieldy, mistakes were made and some individuals, when measured by different hands, turned out to have several different nasal ratios. Many officials demurred at Risley's pronouncements concerning the relationship between race and nostril width, and at his insistence that no person with a nasal ratio greater than 0.75 was suitable for government employment (although this suggestion never became policy). Nevertheless the task was eventually accomplished and the census produced an authoritative account of the relative standing of every caste in India. Thus, in the course of thirty years, the untidy and haphazard jumble that characterized *jati* relations and made it so difficult to tell who was at the top of the pecking order had been reorganized into a neat, hierarchical pyramid.

This data gathering was not merely a sign of idle curiosity. It was very directly linked to power. From this data recruits to the army were selected, and in the 1880s detailed Caste Handbooks were issued to recruiting officers. These gave detailed, scientific accounts of the physical, mental and moral capacities of India's various martial 'races', that is, those deemed especially suitable for military service. The hill tribes of the Dogras and Afridis were supposedly ideal soldiers. With their 'distinctly European appearance', they were, the

British surmised, the likely descendants of Alexander's Greek soldiers, kept pure by strict caste marriage rules. The Bengalis, on the other hand, were regarded as uniquely unsuited to the martial life (though they had constituted the larger part of the Indian army at the time of the Rebellion). Deemed excessively effeminate, physically degenerate and incorrigibly dishonest, Bengalis were barred from the Indian army. One extraordinary effect of this categorizing was the remarkable spread of Sikhism in the Punjab. Sikhism was a brand of reformist Hinduism that had developed in the Punjab in the seventeenth century, but by the nineteenth century it had developed many sects and subsects of its own. The Sikhs came to be regarded by the British as the ideal 'martial race' – but only 'pure' Sikhs. The British worried that many Sikhs were being contaminated by unorthodox and depraved Hindu practices. To counteract this they insisted that all Sikh military recruits must be baptized, keep their hair uncut, carry ceremonial daggers and bangles and adopt the name of Singh. As one recruiting sergeant noted, 'it is the British officer who has kept Sikhism up to its old standard'. The advantages and prestige that accrued to members of the army meant that soon many Hindu families in the Punjab changed their name to Singh in order to maximize their sons' chances of military preferment.

Other beneficiaries of these new classifications were the members of the village councils or *panchayats*, charged with tax collection, and the 'native gentlemen' who were appointed by the British to higher consultative assemblies. Membership of both was overwhelmingly determined by high caste status. Others, however, lost out from these new caste classifications. Unfortunates who acquired the label criminal tribe could be imprisoned merely on suspicion of a tendency to illegal activity. The first Criminal Tribes Act was passed in 1871 at the time of the first census. The British now defined certain groups as officially 'dangerous' classes – people like the Todas and the Bangas who were handed over to the Salvation Army for redemption, but ended up as poorly paid workers in cigarette factories. Some officials had their personal *bêtes noires* inserted into the governmental lists of pariahs. One insisted that eunuchs be included in the criminal castes, convinced that they were in charge of 'an organized system of sodomitical prostitution', devoted to kidnapping and castrating children, though their real crime was cross-dressing. By far the largest group of losers were those who came to be labelled 'dalit'. There is a great deal to be said for the view that untouchability was an institution initially confined to some locales, but under the Raj it became consolidated across India, especially in the burgeoning urban metropolises of the late nineteenth century. Expanding towns and cities sucked in great swathes of urban poor. These groups worked almost exclusively as waste clearers or in the dirtiest and most dangerous jobs in the factories and on the railways. The British, anxious to control these groups whom they saw as potentially criminal, helped propagate the belief that people of this type were a caste of dalits and only suited to these kinds of jobs. Working as servants on the railways or in big western hotels they were often given uniforms and badges to identify them as such.

Much of this colonial 'science' was absurd, but it had a real effect on society because there were powerful reasons for Indians to internalize these formal caste divisions. The census and other British classificatory schemes gave scientific credibility to the idea that India was composed of elaborate hierarchies and that some groups were better than others – more intelligent, more honest, more manly and more modern. These distinctions, now supposedly empirically verified, flowed through the Raj's administrative channels and were soon used to determine highly political questions such as the allocation of land, representative rights, martial honour, bureaucratic office and higher education; and, of course, who should be denied all of these boons. However, the most profound legacy of this urge to catalogue and control was on the way Indians thought (and, to an extent, still think) about themselves. A symbiotic relationship developed between British ideas and Indian realities, between British stereotypes and Indian self-perceptions. No sooner had the British proposed that a type existed than the 'type' sprang forth to claim its rights, contest its disabilities or demand the stigmatization of others. Indians soon learnt that the British only responded to claims grounded in caste, tribe or religion.

Crucially too, Indians soon realized that the British could be manipulated; census classifications, like any paper asset, were negotiable. Brahmans had always been the preferred informants on caste.

But soon after the initiation of the censuses other castes, especially lowly ones, became so vocal and well-organized that it was impossible to ignore them. The more creative began to fabricate elaborate genealogies and folk histories which purported to show that they were of royal descent. In the Madras districts of Tiruneveli and Kanyakumari, a locally powerful clan of hooch brewers known as the *shatras*, unhappy with their lowly Shudra branding in the 1871 census, began agitating for promotion. During the survey for the 1891 census, the chief commissioner received a hefty volume entitled *A Short Account of the Tamil Xatras, the Original but Downtrodden Royal Race of Southern India*, in which evidence of their ancient royal status was detailed. Another local caste, the Pullys of Madras, also contested their lowly ranking, claiming rather imaginatively that they were descended from the 'shepherd kings of Egypt'. On this occasion the British were unmoved. The district magistrate responded, 'no doubt they have abandoned their hereditary occupation and have won for themselves by frugality and industry respectable positions ... but sympathy will not be increased by unreasonable and unfounded pretensions'. Risley's efforts to list castes by social rank greatly intensified this casteism. In villages census officials would be importuned by delegates of the various local *jatis* and alternately harangued and cajoled into promoting their *varna* status and demoting that of the neighbouring village. Others were besieged with lobbyists and petitioners, and by the early twentieth century caste *sabhas* or societies had mushroomed throughout the subcontinent to lobby the state for proper recognition. The resulting competition between groups for rank, honour and status would shape the future development of Indian society more profoundly than the thousands of miles of railway gouged into the landscape.

Under the Raj competition for rank in the census's classificatory schema became embroiled with issues of political and social privilege, but this was not the only reason that caste became a central feature of Indian life. Caste, although traditional, had acquired a modern and scientific carapace. Moreover, the British – supposed heralds of modernity – lived according to caste-like rules themselves. Indian elites eager to embrace modernity were quick to emulate them. To a casual observer it might seem that British power was founded on race, and that there was a simple dichotomy between white and black. But it was much more complicated than that. Just as Indians were minutely segregated by caste, community and complexion, so also was white society. Raj-era fiction extolling the racial cohesion and powerful social bonds between whites was just that – fiction. The reality of life behind the white lines, among the cantonments and high up in the hill stations, was one of exquisitely calibrated snobbery. In many ways the exclusions and resentments that this bred in white society were simply a reflection of what was happening in India as a whole. Behind the frozen façade of grandeur and stability was a barely contained ferment of frustration and bitterness.

After the Rebellion some argued that the British needed to pull together. The opening of the Suez Canal had made the passage to India easier, and the increasing numbers of whites who now ran tea gardens, business houses or practised law and medicine might, it was thought, form the core of a settler group. Throughout the 1860s there was even talk of 'settling' India with destitute Scots and Irish, shipped out to colonize the hills and provide a citizen militia to hold back any future oriental uprising. Few of these schemes came to anything, and the one that did – the unfortunately named Hope Town built ten miles from Darjeeling – collapsed after a few years amid government indifference. Nevertheless, the numbers of British people living in India grew substantially, from the paltry 30,000 of the early nineteenth century to about 250,000 on the eve of the First World War. But it was still a tiny group, spread across about a dozen major towns and cities, and acutely conscious of their own internal differences. White society was minutely graded according to real or imagined class differences. At the very bottom were white soldiers and other working-class groups. Poor whites were regarded as a menace and were liable to be shipped back to Britain at the state's expense; others might end up in one of several mental asylums built in the 1860s and 1870s to deal with the 'morally insane' – a broad category that included women who had 'relations' with Indian men, and those suffering from the mysterious Raj affliction 'Punjab head'. Above them hovered the serried ranks of the petty bourgeoisie, the railway engineers, shopkeepers and shipping clerks. Close to the top were the wealthy merchants, expatriate company managers (box-wallahs) and the professional middle class – the lawyers and doctors. But while these groups were riven with petty jealousies, they were united in their antagonism towards the 'official' British – the government and particularly the prestigious mandarinate of the Indian Civil Service. This division between official and non-official white society was a social canyon rarely crossed. Wits would joke that whites were more caste-ridden than Indians. Each group socialized and married narrowly. This was shown most starkly in the variety and profusion of clubs that developed to cater for each individual social strata. The Tollygunge club of Calcutta would admit only top-notch officials and army top-brass, the Byculla club of Bombay was exclusively for businessmen, while the Colonial club of Madras would accept accounts clerks but vetoed ship engineers.

Gradations within white society were perhaps most starkly evident in the craze for hill-station living that developed after the Rebellion. At first glance this withdrawal to the hills might seem confirmation that this was an essentially racialized society. Here, surely, was a form of Olympian apartheid, with the whites dwelling god-like seven thousand feet above the Indians below. Again the reality was more complex. Initially established as sanatoria in the early ninteenth century, the hill stations mushroomed from twenty to over sixty in the years after the Rebellion. Soon the annual relocation of the Raj from plains to hills began. The Viceroy and 500 government staff moved to Simla, the Government of the North West Provinces moved to Nainital; the Government of Madras to Ooty and that of Bombay to Mahabaleshwar. The cost of managing this form of peripatetic government was enormous. Profusions of clock towers, bandstands, mock-Tudor mansions, Swiss chalet hotels and gothic post offices began to litter the foothills of the Himalayas. Prodigious quantities of cash and manpower were needed to haul the Raj and its paraphernalia from the lowlands to the highlands. Fifteen thousand Indians were required to move the Viceroy and his entourage alone. One official insisted on having his grand piano carried up to Mussoorie by 24 unfortunate porters. Once in the hills the British government and military command tended to linger there for increasingly long sojourns – anything from four to eleven months of the year. Though justified on grounds of health and efficiency, this elaborate ritual served to put physical as well as social distance between 'official' British India and the noisome elements of both white 'non-official' and Indian middle-class society that increasingly sought to hold it to account.

Needless to say, the non-officials left in the plains complained bitterly about the expense, the showiness and the distance this placed between them and the government. But of course this was precisely the point. The Raj panjandrums intended to distance themselves, not so much from Indians, but from hoi polloi of any colour. And a development that absolutely infuriated the less well-off non-officials, for whom Kipling was chief spokesman, was the appearance of several Indian princes in the hill stations, not only living in the flashiest houses, but also hob-nobbing with the cream of the Raj. By 1885 thirteen princes owned the thirty-four 'best' houses in Simla, in which they hosted lavish and well-attended parties for British officials and other wealthy whites. One official commented that they 'were brought more and more into social intercourse into the higher European community', and compared them to 'noblemen coming up to town for the season'.

Some officials doubtless disliked this inter-racial familiarity, but it seems to have been an established feature of official life. Princes were one thing of course, but what was disturbing to the less exalted whites and to some officials was the increasing infiltration of hill stations by wealthy, but less elevated Indians. The popularity of the hill stations as models of modern elite leisure made them irresistibly attractive to newly wealthy and westernized Indians, and soon advance parties of India's own burgeoning middle classes began to promenade in the streets of Ooty and Simla. The contest for the hill stations was a minor prelude to the later contest for India itself. Just as the increasingly assertive and self-consciously modern Indian middle classes challenged British claims to exclusive power, so by the late 1890s they began to encroach on the symbolic redoubts of power. Guidebooks appeared written in the Indian vernaculars which detailed the benefits of hill-station life that the British also sought: a respite from the inferno of the plains, proven therapeutic benefits, especially efficacious in cases of diarrhoea. As one explained, 'the voice of silence from afar will whisper into your ears and your fancy will lift you up on its wings and carry you to a region of heavenly ecstasy conjuring up the unspeakable sense of the infinite glory of the Great Unseen Hand behind'.

But as the Indian middle classes progressed up the mountains of the Raj they would have met the British coming back down. Distressed by this non-aristocratic Indian invasion of their sacred places, the British quit and went back down to the plains. From 1902 the numbers of European visitors to Simla began to decline. By 1908 many of the European bungalows in Ooty stood vacant, and by 1919 Simla's property prices were plunging. Nineteen hundred and two was also the year of the last *durbar*. Lord Curzon's extravagant spectacle had been designed to show that nothing had changed since Viceroy Lytton's day, but, as the Indian invasion of the mountains showed, everything was in flux. While the British tried to fix India in the Edwardian aspic of *durbar* hierarchy, the fissile and dynamic mass of Indian society refused to be still.

2

Babel-Mahal

Hindu temples in nineteenth-century South India were rather like pre-Reformation monasteries – not merely places of worship, but axes of local economic, political and social life. The managers of these institutions were hardly mere 'churchwardens' (as the British imagined them), but petty potentates and arbiters of social prestige: they were, literally, the temple gatekeepers, empowered to determine which castes had the right of temple entry and which were forbidden. Before the British, temples were often run by a surprising motley of groups and individuals. Men of quite lowly caste status often presided, sometimes even Christians and, in one case, a major Hindu temple, it was alleged, was in the hands of a prosperous Muslim pimp. The main qualification for this prestigious position was wealth. However, with the arrival of the British the sole requirement became caste, and the priestly Brahmans achieved a social pre-eminence that they had never previously enjoyed. In the late nineteenth century, however, a series of assaults were mounted on Brahman power. In 1897 a small party of fifteen Nadars (a mid-ranking caste) entered the great Minakshi temple in the Tiruneveli district. They were thrown out and subsequently sued by the temple's Brahman board of control for compensatory damages to cover the cost of 'purification rituals'. These were necessary, it was said, because the Nadars, not being 'Aryan' castes, had defiled the sacred space. Major riots followed, and within ten years the Nadars were reclassified as 'Aryan' Ksatriyas by the government and went on to usurp their Brahman enemies as keepers of the temple. Soon, however, these recently resurgent middle castes were fighting off similar challenges to their dominance by even lower castes. In 1924 a small party of *paraiyars* (dalits) entered the Vaikom temple in Travancore, against the wishes of the mid-caste managers. Although initially sponsored by the Indian National Congress (the principal organization of the nationalist movement), the leader of this low-caste protest, E. V. Ramaswami Naicker, subsequently denounced the nationalist cause as a high-caste conspiracy, declaring that true freedom and unity for India would only be achieved 'with the destruction of the Indian National Congress, Hinduism, Caste, and Brahmanism'.

The tale of the temples is an exemplar of the larger story of late nineteenth-century India: the ascendancy of the Brahmans and the subsequent challenge from a myriad other groups. To begin with the British relied on the high castes as useful and literate amanuenses, but they also brutally mocked and disparaged them. Although they initially accepted these barbs and resolved to emulate the west by 'reforming' their own society, by the late nineteenth century the educated high-caste elites had moved to embrace a pungently Hindu-flavoured cultural reawakening or revival. This revivalism often manifested itself as the aggressive assertion of high caste, especially Brahman superiority, over other Indians. But cultural reaction did not stop there. Rather in the manner of atomic fission, just as British arrogance triggered high-caste bombast, this in turn became the catalyst for middle-caste assertion, which then produced radical resistance among the poorest and most excluded. And so, just as the idea of a unified Indian nationalist movement made its debut in the form of the Indian National Congress, the putative nation was splitting into fragments.

In the early nineteenth century the relationship between India and Britain seemed, to many Indians, more akin to a joint venture than an empire. Between 1820 and 1870 a generation of the Indian elite flourished in the great presidency cities, convinced that the British were the very models of progress, earnest coaches for an intensive course in 'modernization', keen to help manage the promotion of India's hidebound culture into the premier division of world civilizations. On occasion this enthusiasm for the occident could be extreme. In the early 1820s it became briefly fashionable among groups of high-caste college students to ride around Calcutta in a horse and trap flinging sacred cow bones into the homes of the devout, hurling insults at Hinduism and proclaiming their determination henceforth to adopt western manners. Most educated responses, though more sober and considered, were still warmly disposed towards a judicious dose of cultural westernization. But by the 1870s disillusionment with the promise of western-style progress had set in. Some now questioned their earlier rejection of Indian culture, and even those who remained attached to the notion of cultural reform were forced to admit that the Raj was a disappointing ally, apparently more wedded to Indian tradition than the most antediluvian guru.

This was hardly surprising, as the Indian appetite for western learning had always outpaced the British inclination to feed it. From the early 1800s young high-caste men from the rural hinterlands of Calcutta, Bombay and Madras were pressed by ambitious families to obtain the latest passport to prestige – knowledge of the English language. Years were spent grappling with 'Word Book', 'Spelling Book' and other dispiriting primers in village schools, where fees (from Rs. 4–16 per month) were exorbitant sums for the time. As early as 1817, Bengali Brahmans had established an English academy, later Presidency College in Calcutta, part of India's first University, and by the 1850s Calcutta was heaving with ambitious rustics from the old priestly castes pursuing positions in the new colonial clerisy – the lower rungs of the Indian Civil Service. By the 1880s the craze for English learning had bitten so deep that even a 'BA (failed)' was worth having; the British noted, rather sourly, that Bengal was essentially 'an oligarchy of caste tempered by matriculation'. Much the same could have been said of Madras and Bombay.

The passage from a life steeped in rural tradition to the career of a Victorian 'native gentleman' entailed, unsurprisingly, major cultural crises. Many became convinced that there was something deeply wrong with Indian, and especially Hindu, culture, which made it incompatible with rational 'modernity'; so much so that their writings can seem drenched in self-hatred. The Cambridge-trained lawyer (and early president of Congress) W. C. Bonnerjee denounced Hinduism as 'inert, torpid, degenerate, dreaming, in thrall to outmoded ideas, lacking in energy and initiative and doomed to subordination'. For many of these cultural critics the greatest problem was a fundamental lack of unity, which seemed to flow from great flaws marbling Indian civilization: the oppressive inequality of the caste system, the other-worldliness of Hindu religion, its chaotic individualism and lack of independent and critical intellectual traditions. Even early nationalists were pessimistic, as the Bengali politician Surendranath Bannerjea grimly observed: 'If we are deficient in one quality more than another, it is the instinct and habit of co-operation.' Meanwhile Bonnerjee, writing from England in 1865, proclaimed:

I have come to hate all the demoralizing practices of our countrymen and I write this letter an entirely altered man – altered in appearance, altered in costume, altered in language, altered in habits, altered in ways of thought – in short altered and altered for the better in everything. I should say in all things which have contributed towards the making of our nation the most hateful of all others in the world.

The answer, such critics concluded, was a complete rejection of Hinduism, or at least a root and branch reform of it. Many felt that the only answer was a wholly new civilization and religion that would bridge cultural difference with a harmonious blend of eastern and western ideas. The earliest and most famous of these syntheses was the Brahmo Samaj of Bengal, established in 1828 to amalgamate elements of Hinduism and Christianity into a seamless modern belief system. After the Mutiny its most notable exponent was Keshub Chandra Sen, a western-educated official from Calcutta, whose passion for anglicizing Indian practice had been spurred by a visit to England in 1870. While there he had mingled with a galaxy of intellectual and social luminaries – two queens (of Britain and Holland), William Gladstone, John Stuart Mill, Charles Dickens – and lectured at the Jewish Metropolitan Tabernacle in Newington Butts, south London. He returned to the subcontinent engrossed by 'The Early Years of the Prince Consort' (a gift from Queen Victoria) and, perhaps inspired by this, established a heroic variety of voluntary improvement societies: the Indian Reform Association for the Social and Moral Reformation of Indians, the Native Ladies' Normal School and the Society for the Suppression of Public Obscenity were just some of his many projects. From his religious musings Keshub concocted a new global theology, propounded in his 'New Dispensation' of 1869:

A Church Universal ... repository of all ancient wisdom and the receptacle of all modern sciences, which recognizes in all prophets and saints harmony, in all scriptures unity ... and always magnifies unity and peace, which harmonizes reason and faith, yoga and *bhakti*, asceticism and social duty, and which will make of all nations and sects one kingdom and one family in the fullness of time.

A new liturgy swiftly followed. A 'eucharistic' ritual was performed at Brahmo meetings, involving rice and water rather than the Christian bread and wine. And an Apostles' Durbar or assembly was founded – an order of lay Brahmo monks who preached sermons on 'sin' and 'spiritual triumph' across India. Many of Keshub's campaigns concerned social reform and women's rights, and culminated in vigorous attacks on polygamy and child marriage.

Not all the westernizers were as ambitious as Keshub. Eschewing the challenge of total spiritual reinvention, they confined themselves to the propagation of modern science. The 'scientific' method was invoked as the solution to all problems, social, economic, political and moral. Having escaped the mysteries of the Vedas, they became enchanted by the prophets of modernity – Comte, Bacon and Mill – and their hymns to empirical positivism. They also saw the British as the bearers of the greatest gifts of modernity: technology, rationalism, the English language, railways, property rights, notions of citizenship and public service. To this highly intellectual generation, British rule was a historical necessity, and imperialism was less a sentence of shaming subordination than a providential learning opportunity. The British might be rather haughty and distant, but they were excellent teachers and even early Congress meetings resounded with extravagant praise for the Raj from men who regarded themselves as nationalist, such as B. N. Dhar:

I thank God that I am a British subject, and feel no hesitation in saying that the government of India by England – faulty as it is in many respects and greatly as it needs to be reformed – is still the greatest gift of Providence to my race! For England is the only country that knows how to govern those who cannot govern themselves.

This class and generation had, of course, generally done quite well for itself. Adept at manipulating the achievements of modernity, it had swiftly mastered English, absorbed the new law and secured prestigious positions in the Raj hierarchy, from which it could view fellow Indians with benign condescension. But these westernizers were by no means brainwashed yes-men. They remained (or became) patriots and their advocacy of empire was strictly conditional. So long as the Raj was a force for intellectual renewal and cultural regeneration they would support it. However, by the 1870s the British seemed much less of a good thing. This high noon of ebullient western progressivism was soon eclipsed by shadows of economic stagnation, urban crisis, racist reaction and stalled political reform.

The first brake on the journey of progress came in the form of famine. Between 1874 and 1879 major famines were the scourge of western and southern India. While estimates of the death toll varied from between ten and twenty million, all agreed that official policy was, at least in part, responsible; food handouts were discouraged on the grounds they would disrupt the free market mechanism. The horror of these events provoked serious intellectual reflection. The British began to develop a more humane famine code, and among Indian intellectuals the famines provoked the first serious questioning of colonial economics. The Bengali official R. C. Dutt and the Parsi nationalist and sometime Liberal MP Dadabhai Naoroji, led the intellectual assault against laissez-faire markets and the intransigent dogmas of Raj economics. Their tirades mixed argument, analysis and invective in what soon became the foundation of the nationalist economic critique of colonialism. So Naoroji's 1876 pamphlet, 'The Poverty of India', marshalled a battery of statistics to show that British rule was systematically draining wealth from the country. Indian goods were being exported too cheaply, while taxpayers shouldered the exorbitant bill for (white) administrative salaries and the swanky India Office in London. More tellingly, the nationalist economists grimly noted the coincidence of Lytton's great Imperial Assemblage (costing £500,000), a new forward policy in Afghanistan (£2 million) in addition to a military budget of £17 million (or 40 per cent of Indian Revenue), with the catastrophe of the famines. The British may have heeded their Roman imperial predecessors in the ample provision of circuses, but they had neglected the essential counterpart – bread.

British administrative failings were not confined to the countryside, but extended even more glaringly into the cities and towns. The crisis on the land had set off a great wave of migration into the cities and the populations of India's cities had increased exponentially since the 1850s. The leading cities of Calcutta, Bombay and Madras had grown rapidly. Outside this presidency triangle expansion was even more striking as new industrial towns appeared at Kanpur and Ahmedabad, and even the old commercial and administrative cities of Delhi, Poona, Lucknow and Bangalore expanded. Throughout the subcontinent, small-town India was proliferating, from Ludhiana in the Punjab to Badagara in modern Kesala. Little provision was made to house the newly bloated populations of the cities, with *bustis* (slum houses) thrown up haphazardly by private developers to accommodate them. In the 1850s and 1860s, funds for civic improvement tended to concentrate on the *saheb para* or white town. In Lucknow the British corporation was responsible for replacing closed with open sewers in the 'black town', while installing the most up-to-date sanitary facilities in their own quarters. Such obvious favouritism caused fury and Indians lobbied hard for more municipal representation, which came in 1871. New groups of western-educated elites emerged to fill these municipal posts. New journals began to represent householder interests, such as the *Amrita Bazar Patrika* and the *Bengalee*.

But municipal councils, like most state entities, were chronically short of funds. The British businessmen and professionals who had run the cities and towns before 1871 bitterly resented sharing power with 'natives'; wealthy urban Indians proved reluctant taxpayers; and both sides squabbled endlessly over who should foot the bill for the removal of 'night soil'. Little was done to improve matters despite the alarming conclusion of a team of German sanitary inspectors, who found that the 'huge open cess pools ... seething and festering in the sun' (and now commonplace in Indian towns) were 'filling the surrounding atmosphere with poisonous exhalations'. Officialdom confined itself to exaggerated marvelling at the aversion of Indians to modern health care, and to castigating the relatively powerless Indian municipal authorities for their fecklessness. Kipling's tale 'City of Dreadful Night' captures the British attitude in perhaps its most extreme form, depicting an Indian-run city mired in filth and disease, while failing to mention that it was the British who had introduced open drains into India in the first place. Under such racially charged and penny-pinching governance, the cities lurched from one health and sanitation crisis to another, with cholera epidemics in the 1880s and an outbreak of bubonic plague between 1896 and 1900 that killed over eight million people. The famine conditions in the countryside and the epidemics in the cities prompted Indians to embark on social investigations of their own. In Maharashtra the Poona *Sarvajanik Sabha* (a society of educated Brahman professional men) set up a sub-committee to collect statistics on famine and peasant destitution, while Surendranath Bannerjea's Indian Association (composed of graduates and professionals), with branches throughout the towns of Bengal, presented themselves as peasant tribunes and agitated for greater Indian involvement in municipal government.

While economic pessimism had undoubtedly quickened these early political organizations, what most vexed their educated, propertied and largely urban members was the egregious racism of the Raj, which had, by the early 1880s, become impossible for even the most stoical to ignore. For a decade there had been rumbling discontent with the government's hypocritical ICS recruitment policy. This officially colour-blind approach had produced a grand total of 6 Indians in high-level posts out of 1000. This was unsurprising as the obstacles to aspirant Indians were formidable. ICS entrance exams were held in England and demanded a portfolio of intellectual, social and cultural skills that only those educated at elite institutions in Britain could possibly hope to muster. In addition to these hurdles, successful candidates had to demonstrate accomplished horsemanship – a qualification that abruptly halted the rise of the brilliant mathematician Ananda Mohan Bose, even though he had passed all the exams and gained the top first at Cambridge. Even those who did manage to clear these hurdles, equestrian or otherwise, could not be assured of a successful official career. Several were posted to heart-sink districts, or their prospects stalled mysteriously at the lowly sub-divisional or deputy magistrate rank; others were simply dismissed for rather minor transgressions. No Indians were to be found in the officer corps of the army, while the managing elite of British-run firms was a wholly

Indian-free zone. Moreover, well-educated and westernized Indians were lampooned as *babus*, originally an honorific title but in British mouths meant to suggest a pretentious 'jumped-up native' trying to imitate a western gentleman.

For those lower down the pecking order racism was more brutal. There was a grim succession of cases of the murder, beating or rape of Indians by British men, few of which came to court or, if they did, were summarily dismissed. Several cases concerned *punkah wallahs* who failed to pull the *punkahs* (fans) with sufficient energy to cool their sweaty English masters. In the early 1900s one notorious case involved a cook in the army who was brutally dispatched when he declined to act as regimental procurer. Between 1880 and 1900 there were 30 cases of British soldiers accused of serious robbery or rape, and 81 shooting 'accidents'. Railway travel seems to have been a particularly incendiary issue, since the democracy of the ticket meant that white and Indian often rubbed shoulders in the first class compartment. One notorious incident involved a minor raja forced by two British 'gentleman', returning from a snipe shoot, to clean their boots. Another British official described humiliating experience of racism as he rode the railway disguised as a *sadhu* (wandering holy-man).

The straw that broke the *babus'* back was the bizarre Ilbert Controversy of 1883. This concerned the relatively mild proposal by the colonial law minister that in future Europeans in *mofussil* (up-country) districts should no longer enjoy the right not to be tried by an Indian judge (Europeans in the cities were already subject to the jurisdiction of Indian high court judges). This proposal produced a 'white mutiny' among the English planters, factory managers, professional men and many officials, who summoned up lurid images, reminiscent of the Rebellion, of white women at the mercy of Indian men, implying that the reform was tantamount to rape. Meetings of enraged Europeans were held throughout India, culminating in a mass meeting in Calcutta where a plot was hatched to kidnap and deport the liberal Viceroy, Lord Ripon, who had supported the Bill. The government was forced to retreat and offer a compromise, whereby no white defendant could be required to appear before a jury which was less than 50 per cent white. The uproar, pungent rhetoric and official climb-down enraged Indian opinion. It was impossible not to conclude from this episode that British claims to colour-blind justice were a sham. The race issue poisoned relations irremediably and brought about the crystallization of nationalist group activity that had been gathering in Indian cities throughout the 1870s.

By the mid 1880s a turning point had been reached in Indian elite political life. Across the country a critical mass of urban associations with rural links, various business organizations and many kinds of professional and interest groups began to extend cautious feelers to one another. Furthermore, a persuasively coherent economic critique of the Raj had emerged and, in the Ilbert Controversy, there was both an insulting provocation and also a compelling example of the influence that could be wielded over the Raj by a well-organized pressure group. Thus the Indian National Congress was born.

Despite its subsequent flair for heroic myth-making, the Indian nationalist movement, launched in December 1885 when 72 self-appointed delegates met at Bombay, did not get off to a terribly promising start. Its principal founding member was an Englishman, the ex-ICS officer and sometime mystic Allan Octavian Hume: a 'tall and erect figure, with beady squinty eyes and a walrus mustache that covered his mouth'. Hume had left the service under something of a cloud, with senior Raj officials suggesting he was 'the greatest liar who ever came to India', 'cleverish, a little cracked, vain [and] unscrupulous' with 'tactless and cantankerous habits'. But elite Indian opinion did not agree, and the Indian paper *Amrita Bazar Patrika* lauded him as a 'pure and unblemished' character. Hume certainly had some eccentricities. He was initially drawn into the orbit of Indian politics through an association with the Theosophical Society, a body founded by a Russian émigré, Madame Blavatsky, and a Yankee soldier of dubious provenance, Colonel Olcott, to foster spiritual understanding between east and west. Hume had attended several of their séances, during which a certain *mahatma* (great soul) – Koot Hoomi Lal Singh, supposedly a rebel leader from 1857 – had spoken from beyond the grave, urging Hume to take up the standard of Indian political reform. Hume's commitment to the cause remained undented by the scandalous revelation that the bellicose *mahatma* was none other than the mysterious Madame Blavatsky herself.

In its first twenty years the nationalist movement was barely national and hardly moved. Modelling itself on the Irish Home Rule movement, these early nationalists politely lobbied for greater Indian involvement in government and greater representation in the civil service, while protesting trenchant loyalty to the British Empire. This paradox was conceded by one of its first presidents, the disgraced ICS officer Surendranath Bannerjea: 'the peculiar character of the struggle is that we are fighting with Englishmen for the preservation of English principles . . . while [they are] apparently resolved to fall back upon Oriental methods'. In short, the early Congress sought to make India more 'British'. Its success was hindered by more than just lily-livered ideology, for the rancorous personal rivalry and factionalism of its early years suggested that many supposed nationalists harboured antipathies for one another infinitely more bitter than those directed at the British. During the 1890s, squabbles over the funds of the Deccan Education Society rent the Congress in western India asunder; in the Punjab not two but three rival factions had emerged within only ten years; and in Calcutta Surendranath Bannerjea and Motilal Ghose, its two principals, loathed one another so intensely that three separate defamation suits were exchanged in 1898 alone. The *Bengalee* newspaper observed sourly that the intra-nationalist abuse surrounding contests for seats on the Calcutta Corporation was 'a spectacle more nauseating than putrid human flesh'.

Another obstacle to the emergence of fellow-feeling was regional parochialism. And although the annual general meetings of Congress, the 'germ of a native parliament', were designed to promote friendship and familiarity among like-minded men from across the subcontinent, brotherly love did not blossom. Delegates from different regions refused to live or dine together. At the Lahore session in 1893, the Maharashtrian politician Tilak opted to board with his fellow Maharashtrians, Gokhale and Ranade, even though they were his political enemies, rather than muck-in with ideological allies from Bengal. Caste further complicated regional chauvinism: southern Indian Brahmans were especially fussy, refusing to eat with non-Brahmans, even when these putative dining partners were wealthy aristocrats. Problems of social integration could also have more material causes. These early annual gatherings were dominated by an extraordinary generation of successful, wealthy and often highly anglicized lawyers. Many travelled with vast retinues of servants on private trains hired to shuttle them from one session to another. Notoriously, but probably apocryphally, Motilal Nehru (father of future Prime Minister Jawaharlal Nehru) had his English shirts laundered in Paris, while the dandified Manmohan Ghose, according to the radical Aurobindo Ghose, 'though a Hindu by religion dresses like a European from top to toe and shaves his mustache like a eunuch'. These extravagant manifestations of cultural displacement caught the beady eye of one particular delegate to the 1901 session – a certain M. K. Gandhi, who noted these billiard playing, horse-riding, spats-wearing antics with distaste.

For its first twenty years the INC did little other than meet for eight-day annual jamborees and speechifying sessions every December. The highlight of these meetings were the presidential speeches, notable in the early years both for their encomiums to the British and their length – Pandit Madan Mohan Malaviya apparently spoke for two and a half hours in 1909, apologizing at the end for his brevity. As well he might, given that six years earlier Bannerjea's speech had taken six weeks to write and four hours to deliver. These speeches were almost invariably in English and this, more than anything else, was emblematic of the most striking feature of early nationalism – its remoteness from the vast majority of other Indians. The British, well aware of this gulf, dismissed the nationalists as a 'microscopic minority' of metropolitan mendicants irrelevant to the Indian masses; even one of the movement's early leaders, Bal Gangadhar Tilak, admitted that, '[we are] unlikely to achieve any success . . . if we just croak once a year like a frog'. However, the politely croaking frog was soon to join in an unrehearsed chorus with the more raucous politics of cultural revivalism.

In the late 1870s the cream of Calcutta society, its best and brightest graduates, lawyers, teachers and journalists were gripped by the cult of Ramakrishna Paramahamsa. Beyond the elite, among the dejected petty-bureaucracy and despised clerks of Bengal, this semi-literate *pujari* (lowly temple priest) was hailed as a new messiah, though he was more the personification of a mass identity crisis. This eccentric individual, a devotee of the demon goddess Kali at a temple in north Calcutta, preached an extravagantly anti-rational creed to these sons of colonial enlightenment, urging them to find fulfilment in what he termed the 'madness of religion'. Ramakrishna seems to have enjoyed a prolonged period of assumed insanity himself, during which he 'trained' with assorted gurus (male and female) of diverse persuasions to perfect his soul. Having achieved perfection he appeared before a startled Calcutta public as a beacon of spirituality and cast an unflattering light on the modern Bengalis' anglicized lives, their obsession with self-improvement, self-discipline, municipal affairs, drains, office work, clock-time, punctuality, progress and, indeed, reason itself. He preached a religion of ecstatic infantilism, invoking the life of a five-year-old boy as the ideal. He also dabbled in gender-bending, dressing as a woman, flirting with his (largely) male votaries, sitting teasingly on their laps and even, allegedly, menstruating. Ramakrishna's extraordinary popularity can only be interpreted as indicative of a massive rejection of the west and its values. The Brahmo Samaj luminary Keshub Chandra Sen underwent a stunning reconversion after meeting him in 1875. Renouncing his previous westernizing reformism, including his opposition to child brides, Keshub married off his nine-year-old daughter to the Maharaja of Cooch Behar.

The Ramakrishna cult was a particularly striking example of a phenomenon manifest across north India: an urge to recover self-esteem and assert cultural parity with the west through a revivified (and to a great extent reinvented) Hindu tradition. These various movements may be loosely described as *sangathan* ('self-strengthening'), typical of Asian nationalism from the 1870s onwards, with notable examples in China and Japan. Unlike Congress these self-strengthening movements challenged imperial power on the field of culture, questioning its claims to superior rationality and its monopoly on progress. All aspects of 'modernity', it was now claimed, could be found within the Indian tradition itself. Cultural borrowing (as preached by the westernizers of Congress) was not just unnecessary, but a terrible admission of weakness. An early sign of this change of mood was the ridicule now heaped on those who 'mimicked' western habits. Indeed, the contempt of British officials towards the anglicized *babu* paled in comparison with the *babu*'s loathing of himself. The Bengali guru Swami Vivekananda complained, 'we have become real earthworms, crawling at the feet of everyone who dares put his foot on us'. But *babu* self-loathing was perhaps most acutely delineated by the novelist Bankimchandra Chattopadhyay.

Bankim had achieved high office in the Bengal bureaucracy and early in his career had flirted with the lifestyle of a Victorian 'native gentleman' – immersed in the novels of Walter Scott and Wilkie Collins, wielding a knife and fork and even acquiring a harmonium. However, he later came to reject what he saw as unthinking westerniz-ation with a scorching disdain, evident in his satirical *Ingrajstotra* (Hymn to the Englishman), which purported to be a lost passage from the holy *Mahabharata*:

Babus are invincible in speech, fluent in foreign languages and hate their own . . . The word babu has many meanings: those Englishmen who rule India in the age of Kali [darkness] understand it to mean just a common clerk . . . But I wish to celebrate the qualities of those who are proper babus . . . Like [the god] Visnu they have ten incarnations; clerk, teacher, brahmo samajist, broker, doctor, lawyer, judge, landlord, newspaper editor and idler . . . He who uses one word in his head, ten when he speaks, a hundred when he writes and thousands when he quarrels is a babu . . . He who drinks water at his own home, alcohol at his friend's . . . takes abuse from a prostitute and kicks from his employer is a babu . . . O great creator, the people whose virtues I sing now believe that by chewing pan [a mild intoxicant], lying in bed all day, speaking English and smoking tobacco they will regenerate their country.

In his Kamalakanta stories (1885) Bankim detailed the adventures of Kamalakanta Chakravarti, a Don Quixote-like Bengali: a homeless, jobless, drug-addicted parasite. In a series of stories *babu*-like traits are relentlessly pilloried by the apparently insane Kamalakanta. In one he converses with an exceedingly articulate cockatoo, which squawks the pro-western clichés of respectable babudom with arrest-ing accuracy, but shrieks 'platitude' at the end of each homily in a gesture of rather brutal self-commentary. When Kamalakanta spots an ant colony under its perch, the loquacious bird corrects him:

True, these creatures are very small like ants; they look like ants too, but they're not really ants. They are called Bengalis . . . They live on stray drops of milk falling from my perch; and still they have the nerve to say I'm not good to them!

Bankim bemoaned the feebleness of high-caste Bengali culture and longed for a hero. His ideal appears to have been the self-disciplined Hindu-devout far removed from the western-mimicking *babu* – a soldier-monk rigorously trained physically, spiritually and mentally to promote Hindu culture. In his *Krishna Charita* (Life of Krishna, 1892) he reinterpreted the bucolic and erotic child-god Krishna as a heroic warrior-politician, a battling saviour figure. Meanwhile *Anandamath* (Monastery of Bliss, 1882), his most famous novel, concerns an imagined regiment of spiritual soldiers rescuing 'Mother India' from the ravages of foreign invaders. Bankim was not alone in these yearnings, and soon his fictional army of soldier-monks crusading for a revived Hinduism became a reality.

A longing for martial valour and the aggressive assertion of Hindu masculinity became widespread among high-caste young men in late nineteenth-century India. Underpinning this striking preoccupation with 'manliness' were the decades of British disparagement of Bengali virility to which *babus* had been subjected. That these taunts had hit home was proven by the popular ditty:

> Behold the mighty Englishman!
> He rules the Indian small;
> Because, being a meat-eater,
> He is five cubits tall!

Annoyance at British ridicule of their diminutive stature, lack of athleticism, feeble physiques and vegetarianism was indicated in the mid 1880s. Yet another Russian scare on the North West Frontier had created a minor panic and brought calls from the Indian press, especially in Bengal, for the creation of a Reserve Force of 'native gentlemen'. The demand was insultingly rebuffed by the colonial government, for though the Raj was certainly partial to the martial, it made it brutally clear that upper-caste native gentlemen were just too puny for military service – 'soft-bodied little people' as one official put it. It now seemed to many Indians that the British were deliberately emasculating high-caste men by preventing them from enlisting. British insults precipitated a counter-reaction and the notion of physical self-strengthening elided with ideas of national assertion. Even Congress delegates berated the government for 'degrading our nature [and] converting a race of soldiers and heroes into a timid flock of quill-driving sheep'. Soon many young Hindu men became obsessed, quite literally, with self-strengthening.

In Bombay the elites took to cricket; in Calcutta there was an early preference for football, which would, they were informed by the revered Bengali guru, Swami Vivekananda, bring them closer to God than reading the *Bhagavad Gita*. But cricket and football were, of course, foreign sports and therefore not really ideal vehicles for fashioning a nationalist physique. The key to physical revival had to be a specifically Indian exercise, and so the cult of wrestling emerged in the 1890s and 1900s. Wrestling was presented as a form of training unique to India, not merely a sport or martial art, but a spiritual practice. Wrestling had been closely associated with venerable religious traditions, especially the *maths* (monastries) of Banaras and other towns of north India. Moreover, wrestling had its own theological text, the sixteenth-century *Mallapurana*, which contained lengthy disquisitions on ideal physiques, massage techniques and complex regimens; it also insisted that excellence in wrestling was a mark of 'purity of birth'. Several early nationalist radicals, like Tilak and Lajpat Rai, were enthusiastic practitioners of the art, while the less athletic, such as Motilal Nehru, exhorted India's youth to take it up as a path to national reform; he also accompanied the champion wrestler Gulam to an international bout in Paris. Even the stern founder of Banaras Hindu University, Madan Mohan Malaviya, insisted that *akharas* (traditional gymnasiums) be set up in every locality as part of an All India Central Athletic Association to foster national 'happiness and harmony'. *Akharas* proliferated throughout the towns and cities of north and west India; wall-hung portraits of great Indian warriors of the past, such as Shivaji and Baji Rao, gazed down approvingly on the boxing, wrestling, sword and *lathi* (truncheon) training below.

Akharas were not new, but the patrons of the 1890s were: for the first time high-caste, English-educated students began training there, mixing with those from more lowly backgrounds. The spread of this cult of physicality was especially edifying for lower-caste peasant Shudras and urban artisans, to whom it represented an opportunity to reassert their supposedly lost warrior past and increase their status. The cult reached its peak around the figure of the great wrestler Gama. Gama had impressed a maharaja patron as a youth with his phenomenal capacity for *bethaks* (deep knee bends). In 1910 his fame had reached England and he was invited by the John Bull Society to compete in world wrestling championships in London. Having won, he returned to India a national hero. Much was made of Gama's diet, which apparently consisted exclusively of milk, ghee (clarified butter) and almonds, all consumed in awesome quantities. This, it was asserted, was the proper diet of a manly conquering race.

Late nineteenth-century India, like *fin-de-siècle* Europe, was gripped by race fever. High-caste Hindu imaginations were fired by the work of German orientalist Max Müller. Müller was obsessed with the implications of the common ancestry of Indo-European languages, which proved, he argued, the existence of an 'Aryan' or 'noble' master-race in the past, from whom Europeans and high-caste Hindus must be descended. He embarked on lengthy expositions of the great achievements of these 'Aryans', paying close attention to the wisdom of their 'Bible', the Vedas. These pure 'Aryans' had created the greatest civilization in history, the ancient 'golden age' of Vedic Hinduism. In Madame Blavatsky's Theosophical Society these ideas found an effective popularizer. Originally founded in New York in 1875, it pooh-poohed the hegemony of 'scientific materialism', urging closer attention to 'occult manifestations'. *Isis Unveiled*, Madame Blavatsky's *magnum opus*, was an example of this occult wisdom, which, she insisted, had been revealed to her by the Great White Brotherhood of *mahatmas* living in Tibet. These claims were met with some scepticism and in 1882 the Society and its founders moved to India, 'the fountainhead of true religion'. Soon India was awash with books, societies and speakers trumpeting 'pure' Vedic Hinduism as the most elevated civilization on earth; all modern science and technology, it seemed, had been prefigured in the civilization of the Vedic golden age. Young men assiduously adopted the paraphernalia of 'traditional'

Hindu identity: fasting, growing pig-tails and ostentatiously displaying the sacred thread of high-caste Hinduness. There was, however, a gloomy denouement to this tale of ancient glory – decline. The Vedic age had passed, apparently, because the pure Aryans had intermarried with lower races, weakened the stock and now India was a subject race. To recover former glory meant exercising proper control over reproduction, so that only 'manly' types were bred.

Women were clearly central to this project and so the fashioning and preservation of the ideal 'high-caste Hindu woman' came to preoccupy cultural revivalists just as much as the alleged problem of Hindu men's effeminacy. For the revivalists the greatest threat to the virtue of the high-caste Hindu woman, and thus to the destiny of the race, was westernization and social reform. The westernized founders of Congress were among the greatest proponents of the 'up-lift' of women. They wanted to see them educated and they challenged traditional high-caste practices such as child marriage and the ban on the remarriage of widows (many Indian women were widowed in their teens). But this kind of reform, many revivalists claimed, was the high road to immorality and decadence. A worrying example of the dangers of the educated woman was Tarabhai Shinde, who had mastered Sanskrit and produced *A Comparison between Men and Women* (1882), in which she criticized what she saw as the gross accretion of male power under colonial rule, men's poor treatment of women, their vanity and their religious hypocrisy. While revivalists were willing to countenance some education for women, particularly if it would make them more effective mothers of manly sons, it seemed that the education proffered by social reformers was actually undermining 'proper' womanly duties. Bankim, having once been a proponent of equal treatment for women, performed a complete U-turn after he noticed a new menace to Hindu well-being – the 'westernized' or *babu*-woman:

[Her] foremost vice is laziness. The old-type of woman was very hardworking and was highly skilled at housework; the new woman is a great babu . . . The whole burden of housework is left to hired maids . . . A woman who comes to earth to loll in bed and read novels . . . may be marginally superior to an animal, but her womanhood is worthless. We counsel such women to rid the earth of their useless weight by applying ropes to their necks.

Like Bankim, many feared that high-caste women, infected with the consumerism and materialism of the west, had turned into lax and greedy harridans, bullying their 'effeminate' husbands into ever more humiliating employment in pursuit of money to feed their debased desires. To many men this was unbearable. Surely it was enough that one was humiliated by the British without being rendered impotent in one's own home.

It is in this context that the extraordinary politicization of gender in the 1890s becomes comprehensible. The issue which most notoriously exercised revivalist passions was that of child marriage and early consummation. In July 1890 Hari Mohan Maity, aged 35, was tried at the Sessions Court in Calcutta for causing the death by brutal sexual intercourse of his bride Phulmoni, aged 11. There had been several similar cases in recent years where the plaintiff had either been acquitted or found guilty only of causing 'bodily harm', since it was not an offence to have sex with a girl under twelve if she was your wife. As a result of Indian reformist and westernizing pressure, the government introduced an Age of Consent Bill in 1891, which classified intercourse with a girl under the age of twelve as rape, even if she was your wife. The storm of opposition to the bill shocked reformed Indian opinion and revealed the links emerging between cultural revivalism and resurgent nationalism.

Revivalist opponents argued that the bill was an outrageous and unprecedented colonial interference in private life and tradition, yet only thirty years before, in 1860, a similar bill raising the age of consent to ten had aroused little comment. Revivalists cited Vedic texts, arguing that ancient rights were being violated in a blatant attempt to import 'the gross sexual vices of Europe into India' and undermine the Hindu race. The *Bangabasi* journal predicted that once the bill was passed Bengal would be plagued by 'females in groups hurrying from door to door begging males to gratify their lust'. Raj officials did not help matters by confirming a racial dimension to the policy, suggesting that early consummation was a particular problem in Bengal where 'effeminacy' was producing all manner of sexual irregularities, such as 'physical deterioration, mental imperfection, moral debility' and possibly even 'homosexuality'. They drew a marked distinction between the 'effeminate' Bengalis and the 'manly races' who allegedly delayed consummation. As one official noted, 'no one who has seen a Punjabi regiment march past, or watched the sturdy Jat women lift their heavy water jars at the village well, could have any misgivings about the effect of the marriage system on the physique of the race'. The 'effeminate' Bengali, however, was unable to control himself, was addicted to masturbation (the cause, apparently, for the high incidence of diabetes), and couldn't stand up for himself against the 'old dames' who took a particular delight in promoting sexual congress between the very young.

While reformers insisted that ancient texts supported their position for a higher age of consent, the real argument was not about ancient practice, but about the rights of modern men over modern women. *Bangabasi*, a leading opponent of the bill, insisted that Hindu men were being reduced to the status of sepoys, 'forbidden from visiting their women without the permission of the government'. Mass meetings were held in Calcutta and Poona, and a circus-like open-air protest on the Calcutta *maidan* (central park) in February 1891 drew the largest crowds ever seen at such events, aroused by the cry of 'religion in danger' propagated by local religious associations and the press. *Bangabasi* saw its circulation surge to 20,000 against the pro-bill *Sanjivani*'s 4000, while the weekly *Amrita Bazar Patrika* was converted to a daily to feed the appetite of anti-bill readers. The Bill eventually passed but its impact on popular politics had been noted: challenges to cultural and religious 'tradition' elicited a much more passionate and socially diverse response than Congress's croakings about constitutional reform. The manipulation of such issues was obviously a very effective way of building a broader and deeper constituency for nationalist politics. This analysis was confirmed when the frustrated fury attending the passage of the bill helped to fuel the rage over another cultural issue which had been gently simmering for the previous twenty years – cow protection.

The unlikely, and bony, figure of the Indian cow became the symbolic embodiment of Hindu preoccupations with 'self-strengthening'. The cow had, of course, long been central to Indian life, for reasons the old Mysorean rhyme, *Gau Mater's* (Mother Cow's) *Song*, made plain:

Living, I yield milk, butter and curd, to sustain mankind,
My dung is used as fuel,
Also to wash the floor and wall;
Or burnt, becomes the sacred ash on foreheads.
When dead, of my skin are sandals made,
Or the bellows at the blacksmith's furnace;
Of my bones are buttons made . . .
But of what use are you, O Man?

But for Hindu revivalists the centrality of 'Mother Cow' to cultural and national regeneration was increasingly asserted. The cow, they insisted, was sacred – to die holding a cow's tail would, reputedly, grant a short-cut across the river of death – while the cow's products were plentiful and could help revitalize the economy. Moreover, milk and ghee were crucial nutriments for the fitness of the race – sufficient consumption would empower pious vegetarian Hindus to compete with any meat-eater. But the cow was also victimized (like Hindus) by Muslims, who murdered her in brutal sacrifices, and by the British (whose national dish was roast beef). British refusal to ban cow sacrifices was thus seen as proof of their contempt for Hindu sensibilities. During the 1870s Hindu revivalists began to assert themselves, *gaurakshini sabhas* (cow protection societies) appeared across north India devoted to rescuing vagrant cows who wandered the streets unkempt, eating garbage and exposing themselves to the Muslim butcher's knife. Reclaimed cows were settled in *gaushalas* (cow refuges). Charitable networks developed throughout north Indian towns and villages and small donations of rice (*chukris*) were taken from individual families, pooled and then resold to fund *gaushalas*. Petitions (in some cases of up to 350,000 signatures) appeared demanding a government ban on cow slaughter and law suits challenging the right to sacrifice cows were brought. By the late 1880s *gaurakshini sabhas* had become more militant, intercepting cows on their way to slaughterhouses and cattle fairs and spiriting them away to safe houses.

Initially cow protection was most popular with members of farmer and merchant castes, for whom such ostentatious displays of piety were a means of gaining social respect and status. But soon the societies attracted a variety of high-caste, socially conservative Hindus, both rural and urban – landholders, shopkeepers, lawyers and wandering *sadhus* – and spread to the rest of north and central India. And by the 1890s the issue of cow protection and nationalism had become interlinked. In the Punjab, support for Congress and cow protection often overlapped, while in Allahabad a wealthy merchant and ally of the leading north Indian Congressman Madan Mohan Malaviya made generous donations to the Swami Ram cow-shed fund. Supporters from more educated groups tended to stress the 'rational' economic arguments for protecting cows. Scientific studies appeared showing that cows in India were unusually sickly and produced too little milk. This was supposedly a serious problem because a shortage of dairy stuffs, the Hindus' main source of protein, was leading to the degeneration of the race, now prey to epidemic and disease. There was also the question of efficiency: a dead cow could feed only twenty people, but a live one with her six offspring could, it was said, feed over 100,000 in a single day. Moreover, poor cow husbandry was a likely cause of famine. Lack of cow manure was damaging the fertility of the soil; as the famous revivalist Swami Dayananda Saraswati opined, 'soon natives will have to live on grass, dust and the leaves of trees'. The more superstitious saw famines, epidemics and droughts as divine retribution for cow neglect.

In 1893 the movement became decidedly more aggressive and anti-Muslim. There were signs that frustration at the failure to block the Age of Consent Bill was fuelling greater efforts to get legislative protection for cows. Large public meetings were held (sometimes of 10,000 or more) in towns like Nagpur, Hardwar and Banares, where beef-eaters were denounced as sub-human. Donations to cow funds became compulsory and cow-shaped collecting tins appeared in many post offices, shops and markets. Melodramas were staged to illustrate the pitiful plight of the cows secretly abducted by Muslims and then sacrificed at Bakr-Id festivals. Inflammatory pamphlets depicting a human figure with a pig's head trying to kill a cow whose body was composed of various Hindu deities were distributed. Special cow tribunals, imitating British courts, were established to try Hindus who sold cattle to the British or Muslims. One case concerned Gao Maharani (Cow Empress) versus Sita Ram Ahir of Haldi, the latter charged with 'impounding a cow in the government pound' and sentenced to 'twelve days' out-casting and a fine of eight cows'.

Antagonized Muslims, insisting on their religious and civil liberties, retaliated by slaughtering more cows in more provocative ways. The British, who were the largest consumers of beef in India, cited the principle of religious neutrality promulgated after the Rebellion and refused to intervene. In April 1893 cow protection riots broke out between Hindus and Muslims in the UP town of Mau. It was the most serious violence of its kind for seventy years and it took three days to reimpose government control. The rioting swiftly spread – as the result of press coverage – to other towns in Bihar and Oudh, and as far as Bombay city and Rangoon. Altogether 107 people were killed in 45 separate communal riots. Surprisingly, perhaps, the apparatus of the cow protection movements swiftly collapsed after this outbreak of violence. Many Indians were clearly repelled by the open aggression and, since there was no chance of securing legislative intervention, judged that the issue simply wasn't worth more bloodshed. However, the phenomenon had a wider significance. It showed what a powerful, integrative symbol the cow could be, appealing both to 'traditional' and 'modern' concerns, linking the urban with the rural and the educated with the unlettered. Like the Age of Consent controversy, it encompassed issues of cultural pride and the reinforcement (or reinvention) of tradition in a manner that could be presented as modern, 'rational' and national. Crucially, both the Age of Consent controversy and the cow protection movement had greatly assisted the creation of a wider sense of community, an achievement that had so far eluded Congress. But this was a sense of community arising from largely high-caste Hindu values, and it raised troubling questions about the nature of both 'Hinduness' itself and Indian 'national' identity more broadly.

The individual most responsible for turning the loosely co-ordinated cow protection movements into a well-organized popular pressure group was a wandering holy-man, or *sanyasi*, known as Dayananda Saraswati. Dayananda's ambitions, however, extended far beyond the recuperation of old cows: he wanted to redefine Hinduism. Born and raised as a strictly orthodox Brahman in the princely state of Kathiawar, legend has it that the sight of a mouse nibbling holy offerings in his local temple had left the young Dayananda with deep spiritual doubts, his search for enlightenment had led him to embrace *Sannyasa* (renunciation) at the age of 22, and in his subsequent wanderings he had encountered a blind Gujarati ascetic who told him he must reform Hinduism and return it to its ancient roots. But Dayananda's more conspicuous inspiration was not eastern asceticism but western scholarship, and, influenced by the writings of the German Sanskritist Max Müller, he concluded that 'real' Hinduism reposed in the ancient Vedic texts. The beliefs and practices not traceable to the Vedas he held responsible for Hinduism's supposedly decadent and 'effeminate' state, and he set out, Martin Luther-like, to purge it of 'false' practices. These included polytheism, idol worship, casteism, child marriage, priestcraft, death rituals, food laws, pilgrimages and horoscopes – virtually the entire corpus of popular, and some elite, Hindu beliefs. A purged and strengthened Hinduism would, he insisted, soon triumph over its predatory competitors, Islam and Christianity.

Dayananda's views, particularly his hostility to caste, were not popular with the orthodox, and several attempts were made to assassinate the energetic reformer. However, his message found a receptive audience in 1870s' Punjab (a province where Hindu reformism had deep roots), where his somewhat inflammatory oratorical style provoked a Hindu 'bonfire of the vanities', as temple idols were hurled into rivers or smashed at bazaars. Unlike earlier Hindu reformers such as the Brahmo Samajists, Dayananda denied that all religions were inherently equal, insisting that Vedic Hinduism was superior to all and should be actively proselytized like Islam and Christianity. His new sect, the Arya Samaj (Noble Society), set up schools, colleges and seminaries to train missionaries and preachers, who, in the manner of the Salvation Army, would march, sing and preach in markets and other public places. Its journal, *The Regenerator of the Aryavarta*, carried blistering attacks on Christian missionaries: 'they are prepared to use every foul and unchristian means to convert the people to Christianity . . . [there must be a] counter force to counteract this pernicious and unhealthy influence', it declared. Arya Samajists worried, especially, that Christian conversions among low caste, dalit and poor Muslim groups would weaken the power of Hindus in north India.

Despite Dayananda's strictures against ritual, after his death the Arya Samajists developed *shuddhi* (reconversion and purification) ceremonies to counter Christian proselytism. By the 1890s a set of conversion rituals had become standard: the convert's head was shaved, they were 'purified' by drinking water mixed with cow dung, and, for a fee of Rs.5, blessed by a *pujari* or priest. The 'conversion' climaxed with investiture with the sacred thread (a sign of high caste) and all attendees then celebrated with a sherbet drink. Arya Samajists had much success in reconverting low castes and poorer groups, in part because of their conscious emulation of the social work of Christian missionaries. Converts were organized into model villages where Arya volunteers dug wells for them, helped with housing and medical care and offered basic education. The movement was phenomenally successful, with over 20,000 members by 1900 and over half a million by 1920, spread across north India in the towns and villages of the Punjab, parts of the United Provinces and Maharashtra. Although many of its members were low-caste converts, it was also strong among relatively high-caste trading and peasant communities too. Its popularity is not difficult to understand: it offered social mobility, status and self-respect. Many of the trading and peasant castes sought western education for their sons, but were reluctant to send them to mission schools. They wanted to be treated with greater respect by the highest castes, but they also wanted to feel that they were part of the 'modern' world of rationality and science, without wholly abandoning their cultural roots. The Arya Samajists offered such an education (even to women), without any attendant spiritual dangers. They offered a 'purified' and 'rational' Hinduism that was based on venerable texts, not 'superstition', and they had a seductively ambiguous attitude to caste, promising to both 'reform' and preserve it. An example of its 'rational' appeal comes from Munshi Ram (Swami Shraddhanand), a leading Arya Samaj ideologue, who recalled his childhood frustration with petty and time-wasting Hindu ritual:

At the time of answering the call of nature, the child had to fully undress himself, even during the cold months. Only after getting himself cleaned with a bath, could he dress again. Even the touch of the drains cost him a bath. If in his wanderings, he came to touch any water, he had to take a bath and wash again.

Ram was high caste, but many more followers were from aspiring middle castes, including peasants and *banias* (traders). The great attraction of the Arya Samaj was that while it kept the ladder of caste in place, it promised to help the middling sorts move up a few rungs. Dayananda argued that just as there were 'false' non-Vedic texts, so also were there false Brahmans. Brahman-hood had to be earned; even the lowest could be a Brahman if he became 'learned, and of good habits'. However, he did not want to repel those who already enjoyed high-caste status, so, while there was always the possibility of 'rising' in this hierarchy, there was fairly little chance of falling. Birth Brahmans would retain their status as long as they acquired education. This was an inspired solution to the problem of integrating upper and middling castes into a common sense of community: middle groups could always hope to rise, while those at the top could now feel that they had 'earned' their elite position through virtuous action. Meanwhile Shudra converts tended to retain their low-caste status once in the Arya Samaj, while the dalits were generally ignored entirely.

The reformed Hinduism of the Arya Samaj was therefore likely to be a compelling model of a more integrated Hindu identity (at least in northern India), appealing to many lower castes groups while preserving and justifying the power and status of high castes. Someone who saw the political potential of this new sense of Hindu community was the Maharashtrian political leader, Bal Gangadhar Tilak. A Brahman with ancestors among the Peshwas (the famous Brahman prime ministers who had governed seventeenth- and eighteenth-century Maharashtra) he was always convinced that Brahmans were India's natural leaders. Intellectually able, though moody and 'difficult', as a youth (like Gandhi after him) he disliked his 'puny' physique and at college embarked on a regimen of physical exercise, wrestling and swimming, and cultivated a 'manly' moustache. He became an effective journalist and, though a member of Congress, was increasingly repelled by its 'mendicant' strategies and impatient with those who argued that political reform should wait upon social reform. While socially reformist in his own views (his own wife and daughters were educated and were not married until adulthood), he perceived that such progressivism would alienate a broader, less westernized constituency and seized on the Age of Consent Bill controversy as a means to connect with less educated and more religiously orthodox groups.

Like Dayananda he was alert to the success of other religions in building a sense of unified community. In particular, Tilak noted with disapproval the immense popularity of the Shia Muslim Mohurram festival throughout Maharashtra, not only with Muslims but with Hindus too. Hinduism in Maharashtra was, he decided, woefully divided – by caste, region and sect – and in 1893 he began a campaign to prevent Hindu musicians and dancers from performing at Mohurram festivals. His nationalist paper, *Kesari* (Lion), berated them thus:

> Oh! Why have you abandoned Hinduism today?
> How have you forgotten Ganapati, Shiva and Maruti [Hindu deities]?
> What boon has Allah conferred on you
> That you have become Musalmans today?
> The cow is our mother, do not forget her!

He formulated the notion of a purely Hindu public event that would compete with Mohurram in colour and excitement and allow Hindus publicly to assert their community identity. He explained that he wanted an Olympic-style festival that would bring better-off Hindus into contact with the common people, and skilfully transformed the purely domestic rituals of devotion to the elephant-headed god Ganapati (Ganesh), into a public carnival where 'all Hindus of high and low classes will stand together [as] a joint national community'. Ganapati, with his diverse appeal across the various communities of Maharashtra, seemed an ideal unifying symbol for Hindus. As the god of learning and wisdom, he was a tutelary deity to the Brahmans, as the son of Shiva he was venerated by Ksatriyas, while as the plump and jolly elephant-headed hedonist associated with fertility cults he would, it was hoped, exert an earthy plebeian magnetism. In 1894 the first Ganapati festival was held in Tilak's hometown of Poona. This novel event turned out to be strongly reminiscent of Mohurram. Huge wooden and papier mâché Ganeshes were modelled (paid for by subscriptions – each set of streets competing to fund the most flamboyant Ganapati), and once enthroned in their *tazia*-style floats they were paraded through Poona for ten successive days (like Mohurram), accompanied by marching choirs of students and schoolboys running into their hundreds. Dressed as Shivaji's soldiers, these largely high-caste marching bands brandished bamboo *lathis* and, along with hymns of praise to Ganesh, sang songs of a more political hue, castigating Hindus for attending Muslim rituals or mocking various moderate Congress leaders regarded as enemies of Tilak. On the tenth day (just like Mohurram), all the Ganeshes assembled for a final mass parade before being ritually immersed in the nearby river.

The Ganapati procession was an instant and runaway success, and in 1894 the Poona parade attracted 25,000 participants and 50,000 spectators. By 1905 the Ganesh cult had seized the Deccan and 72 towns, including Bombay, held Ganapati festivals, thus instilling Hindus, regardless of background, with a powerful sense of their own distinctness as a community; few Hindus now participated in Mohurram. The success of Ganapati also offered a vivid demonstration of how cultural 'tradition' could become infused with very contemporary political concerns. Both Tilak and Dayananda were inspired vintners, shrewdly decanting the new wine of modern politics and mass organization into the old bottles of Hindu tradition. Their innovations, along with all the other manifestations of 'self-strengthening', were potent symbols for mobilizing a broad swathe of north Indian society, appealing to its ambitions for social status, stoking its resentment of British cultural denigration, and arousing and channelling anger at perceived 'favouritism' towards Muslims. However, there was an obvious problem: an Indian national identity fashioned around notions of high-caste Hindu triumphalism and the stigmatization of Muslims, and relatively indifferent to the grievances and sensibilities of lower castes and Indians from other regions, was always likely to alienate more people than it attracted. The patient, constitutional politics of the moderate Congressmen may have seemed anaemic and passionless, but they were also potentially universal and inclusive; the politics of Hindu revivalism were emotive and rousing, violent and divisive. Yet despite the conflicts between them, soon they would be uncomfortably yoked together.

In a precedent that was to become something of a pattern in Indian politics, the divisions and disunities of the revivalist and reformist nationalists were temporarily healed by a gross miscalculation on the part of the British. The external irritant that quickened the pearl of nationalist unity at the turn of the century was the new Viceroy, Lord Curzon, who succeeded where all Indian politicians had failed and united the nationalists. Curzon had arrived with much fanfare as the self-proclaimed scourge of administrative sclerosis. He regarded the ICS as the graveyard of efficiency – 'round and round, like the diurnal revolution of the earth, went the file, stately, solemn, sure and slow', he complained – though despite his reforms, when he left in 1905 spending on office stationery alone had doubled, while file circulation had not accelerated. It was not Curzon's intention, however, to pinch pennies where the martial or ornamental spheres of government were concerned. Prodigious sums were expended on the Viceroy's *durbar* of 1902, and vertiginous military budgets continued to climb as he pursued a 'forward' policy against the phantom Russian bogey in Tibet; meanwhile plague and cholera swept the country. He further incensed Indian sensitivities with a new excise tax on Indian cotton exports, designed to make them less competitive with Manchester's and thus impeding the remarkable growth of the infant Bombay textile industry. Unfortunately for Curzon, all this bad news could now be broadcast far and fast: the circulation of the vernacular press had trebled to nearly 850,000 between 1885 and 1905. Moreover, there was no shortage of readers. This was the era when the super-abundant supply of English-speaking graduates from India's universities was decisively out-stripping demand.

But Curzon's real blunder was the partition of Bengal. Bengal, a huge province, had long been an administrative headache for the British. It was an unwieldy composite of multifarious linguistic frag-ments to which it was difficult to attract the best ICS recruits. There was a feeling that the province was poorly administered, and it was certainly becoming politically unmanageable. The splitting of the province into two was a characteristically gordian-knot chopping decision by Curzon, but one which tightened the noose on his Indian career. While the initial intention may have been administrative streamlining, there is no doubt that Curzon and his officials had also spotted an opportunity to confound the troublesome *babu* politicians of Calcutta. Curzon had already offended them by slashing the elected

Indian majority on the Calcutta Corporation and by breaching the autonomy of the Indian-run University council. The division of the province promised further to undermine these Calcutta-based Hindu troublemakers by splitting the province into predominantly Hindu and Muslim halves. As the home minister Risley observed, 'Bengal united is a power; Bengal divided will pull in several different directions.' With this in mind, early in 1904 Curzon hurried to Dacca (the capital of East Bengal) to tell the Muslim landowners that, 'the Mohammedans of Eastern Bengal [will have] a unity which they had not enjoyed since the days of the old Mussulmam Viceroys and Kings'.

From the announcement of the intended division to its enforcement in October 1905, Bengal heaved with protest, not all of it Hindu; over 2000 public meetings were held; press opposition was vehement, voicing a sense of wounded pride and outrage at declining influence. Infuriated by government intransigence even in the face of such concerted opposition, moderate Congress politicians were at a loss, and their only option was to join forces with the revivalists in a strategy of direct action. Tilak was the inspiration. He had proved himself a demiurge of direct action in his unsuccessful but well-organized no-tax campaign among famine-hit peasants in the Deccan in 1896, where he had also road-tested his new technique of mass boycotts of British-made goods – hitting the Raj where it hurt, in the pocket. Throughout Bengal, British cotton, textiles and salt were boycotted, while school-children refused British-made sweets as speech-day prizes. Soon the idea of boycott spread from consumption to any form of co-operation with the Raj: students truanted from government schools, civil servants abandoned their offices, lawyers and judges picketed the courts. Much of Bengal ground to a halt throughout 1906. From this essentially negative form of action, however, grew the more positive notion of 'self-help', and especially of economic nationalism or *swadeshi*. Indigenous businesses mushroomed: Indian banks opened, factories appeared making *swadeshi* chemicals, 'national' schools opened and the Shantiniketan University, offering a syllabus blending eastern and western humanities, was established by the poet Tagore. There were even experiments with Indian-run arbitration courts in the villages. Comparisons were made between this blaze of self-strengthening and similar movements in the rest of Asia; it did not go unnoticed that the previous year the Japanese had defeated the Russians in war – the first example of a modern victory by east over west (in Bengal it became briefly fashionable to name children Kuroki or Nogi after the conquering generals). The sweetest legacy of the times, however, was the symbolic triumph of the Mohun Bagan football club over its white rivals in the IFA Shield Final of 1911.

Most of the support for *swadeshi* was urban, professional and, to some extent, artisanal. Efforts were made to carry the movement to the villages through 'mass contact' at fairs and by the performance of *jatras* (popular morality plays). But often attempts to popularize *swadeshi* could smack of Hindu triumphalism: many of Bengal's peasants, craftsmen and workers were Muslim, and to them *swadeshi* could seem coercive. Muslim weavers were hard-hit by the boycott of British cloth, while Tagore recorded the ambiguities of the movement in the countryside in his novel *Ghare-Baire* (Home and the World), in which the supposedly patriotic *swadeshi* campaign is used merely as a ruse to cloak Hindu animosity towards Muslim traders.

Perhaps even more ominous was the radical turn taken by the *swadeshi samitis* or 'national volunteer groups'. Initially philanthropic bodies set up to train Bengali youth for various *swadeshi* projects, as the movement wound down between 1908 and 1909 many *samitis* morphed into underground terrorist cells. Journals like *New India* and *Bande Mataram* called for a more 'full blooded' struggle, not just for *swadeshi*, but for *swaraj* (self-rule). In Aurobindo Ghose, sparkling intellectual, educated at St Paul's school in London and then Cambridge and at one time the epitome of westernized urbanity, they had their prophet. His pamphlet 'New Lamps for Old' (1894), became the manifesto of the new extremists. Aurobindo rejected constitutional gradualism, favouring instead the example of the 'great and terrible republic' of the French. Inspired in part by Mazzini's Young Italy, British humiliation in South Africa and the epochal Japanese defeat of Russia, he chastised Congress for its pro-Britishness. He demanded that the moderate Indian 'burgess or middle-class' ally with the 'people' to champion revivalist Hinduism and *swaraj*.

By 1908 Aurobindo was organizing secret societies and planned an armed insurrection in India and a military mutiny, with Japanese assistance. Although he conceded that this might take up to thirty years to achieve, the first step could be taken immediately, by forming a network of underground cells of radical students in the cities run by men like Hemchandra Kanungo, who had been trained by Russians in Paris in the arts of non-judicial murder. Though clearly anti-British (indeed, several British officials fell to the assassin's bullet around this time), the precise goals of this revolutionary violence were somewhat vague. Much of it was informed by a rather mystical religious ethos, drawing inspiration, again, from the 'golden age' of the Vedas and the even more esoteric ideas of the Theosophists. In 1907, however, Aurobindo declared, ambitiously, that his ultimate goal was 'the Aryanization of the world'.

The era of *swadeshi* marked the crystallization of a 'new party' within Congress in self-conscious opposition to the methods and ideas of the old reformers and moderates. Men like Aurobindo and Bipin Pal in Bengal, Tilak in Maharashtra and Lajpat Rai in the Punjab, emerged as challengers for the leadership. Significantly, these men, though celebrities, were all essentially regional leaders; no national figure had yet emerged. Their challenge to the moderates failed, though in 1907 they did succeed in splitting Congress into two warring factions. The British, to some extent, were the engineers of this division; by hinting strongly that a round of significant power-sharing reforms was on the way, they steeled the will of the moderates to stand firm. Further assistance to the moderates was provided when Tilak was imprisoned for sedition. Aurobindo was forced into exile in French Pondicherry, where he lapsed into full-time mystical musing, while Lajpat Rai, after a spell of detention in Burma, embarked on a lengthy lecture tour in the United States.

By 1907 it seemed that the moderates had trumped their more radical challengers in achieving real political progress. But this was an illusion. The moderates had hardly advanced on their position of 1885; they were essentially dependent on the goodwill of the British and they were to be disappointed in their trust. The much-vaunted power-sharing reforms of 1909 turned out to be rather meagre. Moreover, the extremists had revealed a world of politics and proto-nationalist mobilization outside the polite realm of the Congress annual meeting. The aspirant farmers, traders and radicalized religious activists, novelists, wrestlers and campaigners for the protection of 'tradition' were not going to go away. Any successful nationalist movement would have to find a home for them.

Yet the nationalists found it very difficult to create this unity. In the manner of some fiendishly complex experiment of physical science, British power in India refashioned the molecular structure and internal dynamic of political life. Colonial cultural arrogance had provoked a powerful Hindu revival, and high-caste Hindu assertion had, in turn, provoked equal and opposite reactions from many other groups and regions. Proselytizing Arya Samajists in the Punjab, Brahmanical elitists in Maharashtra and the south, and the menacingly anti-Muslim timbre of *swadeshi* politics in Bengal had brought forth yet more atomic rearrangements among the various constituent parts of Indian society. Non-Brahman groups in the south and west, and Muslims in the north, reorganized themselves into new patterns of cultural distinctiveness in their rejection of the high-caste Hindu leadership proffered by Congress. None of this boded well for nationalism, especially when a shrewd colonial state was on hand ready to make political capital from the merest whiff of division.

However, it would be wrong to conclude that the goal of national unity was doomed from the moment of its birth. The fact that India eventually achieved independence as two states – India and Pakistan – was never inevitable. As we saw in the previous chapter, the Muslims of India were a very diverse group, riven by divisions of language, class, region and sect. Many of these Muslims were as potentially hostile to the British and as open to the Indian nationalist message as their Hindu counterparts. And in its very earliest days the prospects for Hindu-Muslim unity in Congress were rather promising. In Bombay the educated and partially westernized Muslim elite had prospered as merchants and bankers, and by the 1880s they too were becoming resentful of the Raj's economic priorities. Led by the wealthy and influential Muslim aristocrat the Aga Khan, these Muslims became keen adherents of Congress's brand of moderate nationalism. The Central Mohammedan Association of Calcutta and the Anjuman-i-Islam of Bombay were among Congress's earliest sponsors and in its first six years the number of Muslim delegates steadily grew to between a sixth and a seventh of all delegates, while the Bombay Muslim lawyer Badruddhin Tyabji became its third president. In Bengal, Syed Amir Ali's National Mohammedan Association advocated fellowship with non-Muslim Indians in promoting the advance of India as a whole. It even included Hindus on its central committee. They acknowledged that Muslims had distinctive interests as Muslims, but this did not prevent them urging Muslims to make common cause with Hindus in a broader spirit of nationalism.

More radical anti-Britishness surfaced with the appearance of pan-Islamic sentiment from the late 1870s and 1880s. Propagated during a brief sojourn in India between 1879 and 1882, pan-Islam was the brainchild of the globe-trotting intellectual Jamal al-Din al-Afghani. Support for Afghani's movement boomed as Muslims around the world looked on aghast while the French occupied Tunisia in 1881, Egypt fell to the British a year later, the Italians seized Eritrea in 1885 and, not content with Egypt, the British swooped on the Sudan in 1898. The British especially, it seemed, were determined to beat the 'gigantic drum' of Islam, which, as France's Marshal Lyautey observed, threatened to reverberate 'from one end [of the world] to the other'. Occidental aggression infuriated the younger generation among the *ashraf* (Muslim upper classes), who felt they were on the receiving end of a new crusade, an interpretation compounded by the torrent of denigratory scholarship now pouring from the pens of western orientalist scholars preoccupied with the supposedly ingrained anti-modernism of some varieties of Islam. The modish histories of Ranke and Burckhardt, stuffed with gloating accounts of the alleged decadence of Muslim culture, wounded deeply. But pan-Islamism was not exclusivist. Afghani passionately pleaded for Hindu-Muslim unity in his Indian lectures, and pan-Islam was to have a distinguished anti-imperial history, beginning with the riots of Muslim factory workers in Calcutta in 1897.

Educated and elite groups were not the only ones to harbour anti-British sentiments. Among the more traditionalist and lower-class Muslim organizations, anti-British feeling could run high. The famous Deobandi seminary (recently the sponsor of the latter-day pan-Islamism of Al Qaeda) and other *madrasas* observed the British with hostile eyes. These were, in some ways, the last vestiges of the *jihadi* fervour which had intermittently terrified the British earlier in the century. Crushed in 1858, such Muslim sentiment had turned inwards and became quietist, directing its considerable energies to consolidating a sense of Muslim *qaum* (community), determined to resist the west by refining its spiritual purity. Eschewing *jihad*, the seminary and its many branches wrestled instead with the theological problems presented by everyday life under alien rule, passing hundreds of *fatwas* (adjudications) on such matters as whether a man who accidentally touched his brother's wife's aunt's bare arm had technically committed adultery. Perhaps more significantly, they also trained thousands of *ulema* or theologians, usually men from poor backgrounds for whom the *madrasas* offered the only education available. Many would later become convinced Congress nationalists. Such nationalist feeling was doubtless a reflection of the harsh life experienced under the colonial heel by poorer Muslims. Insensitive official handling of the plague crisis of 1896–1903, with troops barging into Muslim homes to inspect their sanitary conditions and heedlessly violating purdah, left in its wake a level of anti-British anger not seen since the Rebellion. Meanwhile, the impressive show of fraternity as 10,000 anti-partition student protesters, many of them Muslim, marched through Calcutta in September 1905, suggested that not all opponents of Bengal's division were Hindu.

However, despite a promising courtship, a divorce between Hindus and Muslims was looming as early as the mid-1890s; at the 1894 Congress session a mere 23 of the 1183 delegates were Muslim. This was no accident: vigorous efforts were made to wrench the betrothed asunder. A leading architect of Muslim separatism in India was an aristocrat from the United Provinces, Syed Ahmed Khan. Born in 1817, his family boasted a long tradition of service in the Mughal court. His career had begun in the judicial service of the East India Company and by the time of the Rebellion he had become a sub-judge. He subsequently devoted himself to the cause of Anglo-Muslim understanding and played a leading role in the reconciliation of the two through his writings. His pamphlets – 'The Causes of the Indian Revolt' (1859), 'The Loyal Mohammedans of India' (1860) and 'The Refinement of Manners' (1870) – all strove to reconcile Muslims to their British overlords, arguing that British rule, far from being anti-Islamic, was a providential opportunity for Muslims to recover their former cultural, intellectual and, eventually, political glory. He was, effectively, the father of a modern, secular idea of Islam. The Muslims of India formed a separate nation within the subcontinent and their future lay in co-operating with the British, who would protect them from the Hindu majority.

For Syed Khan it was absolutely essential that Muslims retain their distinctiveness and usefulness to the British and not allow the crafty *babu* Hindus to outpace them in the acquisition of western education, something they seemed poised to do in Khan's home region of the United Provinces and Oudh. His newspaper, *Tadhib al-Akhlak* (Social Reform), disseminated these ideas and he collected monies (much of which came from the British) to found his Muhammadan Anglo-Oriental College at Aligarh, which would train a Muslim 'gentlemanly cadre' fit for government service and the higher professions. He insisted that there was no such thing as 'the general progress of India' as a single nation. The common interest of Indian Muslims lay in co-operating with the British and opposing Hindu power in India. Congress was a threat to these ideas, and his rival United India Patriotic Association made its debut only three years after Congress's own, in 1888. Disregarding taunts that it was neither united, nor patriotic, nor All-Indian, the Association skilfully exploited internal dissent in Bengal's Central Mohammedan Association and Bombay's Anjuman-i-Islam and secured the abstention of these organizations from Congress after 1890.

The activities of Hindu revivalists, with their distinctly anti-Muslim tone, lent credibility to Syed Ahmed Khan's views. Their histories now depicted Islam as the great destroyer of a Hindu-Aryan 'golden age', with much talk of the Mughal dynasty as an era of 'Muslim tyranny' and the 'medieval dark ages'. The Arya Samaj sought to 'cleanse' Hinduism of 'medieval' crudities (a code for Islamic influences), Tilak had striven to end Hindu participation in Mohurram, and Muslims were slaughtered in the north Indian cow-protection riots in 1893. Even more poisonous were the communal riots accompanying the *swadeshi* protests of 1907, after which many Muslims saw the partition of Bengal not as a British infamy, but as a deliverance from Hindu oppression.

Muslims began to respond to high-caste Hindu assertions with a cultural revival of their own. Poetic reveries about Islam's decline, the distant glory days of Aurengzeb and the great Muslim courts of Spain, and the pathetic plight of the last Mughal emperor were so regularly recited that even their authors began to regard them as clichés.

High-caste Hindu revivalist sentiment was also powerful in the south where considerable, though not insuperable, cultural differences already made the construction of an all-Indian national movement formidably difficult. The Madras presidency, along with the princely states of Hyderabad, Mysore, Travancore and Cochin, extended over nearly 170,000 square miles of highly diverse linguistic, cultural and economic terrain, which had never been fully integrated into the rest of India, even at the height of Mughal power. And British rule lay even more lightly south of Bombay than it did to the north; white officials were spread thin almost to vanishing point and local landlords, urban magnates and big-shot lawyers enjoyed an autonomy which often blurred into semi-independent power. Its forty million people spoke four Dravidian (native to the south) languages, unrelated to the Sanskritic language family of the north. It also possessed a radically different caste structure from north India, with Brahmans few and far between while most of the great landowners and substantial farmers of the region were often Shudras.

Nevertheless, despite these challenges, there were still opportunities for building a sense of national unity between south and north. During the *swadeshi* campaign the south showed sympathy with student and worker riots in Andhra (the region north of Madras). Support meetings were held and Bipin Pal, the Bengali Congress leader, embarked on a successful southern tour in 1907. Several *swadeshi* enterprises started up, most famously the Swadeshi Steam Navigation Company in Travancore. Many Brahmans were very proud of their southern heritage and pioneered the recovery of Tamil as an integral part of a more broadly based Indian cultural revival – the leading Tamil Brahman poet Subramanya Bharathi was a great champion of southern cultural revival within the context of an All-Indian unity. Others, like the Madras Congressman R. Kulasekharam, strove to present the nationalist movement as an exercise in organic oneness and unity, arguing that 'the central note of the evolution of religious unity in India has always been striving after unity. Buddha . . . taught the proud Aryan [the northerner] to love his dark brother [the southerner].'

As has been seen, the real obstacle to unity was, perhaps unwittingly, erected by the British. Since 1800 they had heavily promoted the traditionally literate Brahmans into positions of power and prestige in their southern administration. Though a mere 3 per cent of the population, Brahmans accounted for 70 per cent of students enrolled in Madras University between 1870 and 1918; by 1912 Brahmans held over 70 per cent of civil service jobs, 83 per cent of sub-judgeships and 55 per cent of deputy-collector posts. The middle castes – Vellalas, Reddis, Naidus and Nairs – had all been powerful clans in the pre-colonial period. Many were still wealthy landowners and aspired to western education; now they bridled under this novel subordination to Brahmans. In particular they resented the new-fangled census, which, compiled with the assistance of Brahmans, had classified them as Shudras (the lowest caste, just above dalits). This injury was compounded by the insult of Aryan race theory. This held that at some point during a misty and ancient epoch the south had been invaded by a master-race of Aryan Brahmans who had struggled to 'civilize' the coarse Dravidian peoples from whom all non-Brahmans were descended.

The Theosophical Society was heavily involved in propagating this myth, especially after its latest luminary, the sometime socialist, contraceptionist, atheist and Irish nationalist Annie Besant had holed up in Madras after Madame Blavatsky's scandalous departure from India in 1882. Although Besant had originally come to India to promote social reform, she soon fell prey to theosophy's seductive promise: to marry east and west, science and religion, male and female in a transcendent union of perfect oneness. Like other theosophists she was convinced that the mythical Aryans were the ancient race who had originally reconciled these antinomies, and would do so again if their descendants, high-caste Hindus, regained power. Besant became president of the Society in 1907, and made a great splash when her rather controversial attitude to non-Brahmans was unveiled. Her intention, it appeared, was to 'humanize them [because] here as in Britain they [the lower classes] are a menace to civilization and undermine the fine fabric of society'. Nor were articles from the Society's journal, the *Hindu Message*, calculated to endear it to the non-Brahman majority. One year it ran a long series entitled, 'Why the Brahman is the fit leader . . . in the sense that he alone is qualified to show the way to others'. Unfortunately for the fortunes of Congress in the south, its early membership tended to be almost exclusively Brahman and to overlap with that of the Theosophical Society.

These provocations coincided with a non-Brahman renaissance. Particularly important was the Tamil movement, based in the south eastern region of Madras presidency, and centred on the cult of Tamil-tay (goddess of the 'mother-tongue' Tamil). The fashioning of Tamil language into the symbol of a separate southern identity originated with the British bishop, missionary and sometime linguist, the Reverend Robert Caldwell, whose *Comparative Grammar of the Dravidian Language* of 1856 was the anvil upon which modern Tamil culture was hammered. The erudite bishop believed he could Christianize Tamil life by destroying the influence of corrupt priests and Brahmans, and a powerful weapon in this war was to stress the autonomy of southern Dravidian languages, especially Tamil, from the Sanskritic traditions of the north. Caldwell also hinted that underpinning this independent language was a unique and ancient civilization of the south that could rival that of the Aryans. Tamil intellectuals rejected conversion, but swiftly elaborated on the rest of his ideas. Soon 'histories' of a pre-Aryan Tamil utopia became wildly popular. There had been, they claimed, an ancient and heroic people of the south who had sailed the high seas, were tolerant and friendly, egalitarian, rational, philosophical, yet also fun-loving and creative. Some enthusiasts even suggested that Tamil civilization pre-dated the era of tectonic shifts, when Australia, Africa and Southern Asia had been a single continent – 'Kumarikkantam' and its mother culture, Tamil. Traces of this lost Tamil culture could, apparently, be detected as far a field as Palestine and Scandinavia. So convincing were these histories that soon even Raj authorities were insisting that the southern Dravidians possessed 'a culture of very great antiquity . . . speakers of Dravidian languages . . . [were] the ancient inhabitants of Mohenjodaro [an ancient and recently excavated city, now in Pakistan] and perhaps the givers of culture to India'.

This cultural assertion also had a religious dimension, curiously reminiscent of the puritan reformism of the Arya Samaj. Campaigns were launched to stamp out polytheism, which had supposedly been foisted on the non-Brahmans by Aryan-Brahman interlopers, the virtues of vegetarianism and teetotalism were extolled and 'irrational' customs, such as the worship of 'godlings' and animal sacrifice, censured. But unlike the northern revivalists, the southern Hindu reformers insisted that religious ceremonies should be performed by their own non-Brahman priests, and that Sanskrit should yield to Tamil as the 'divine' language of ritual and devotion. The sectarian Hinduism of the south, like that of the north, was being consciously upgraded and detached from its popular customs, but unlike its northern counterpart this version of 'classical' Hinduism was devoted to the veneration of non-Brahmans.

This duet of cultural and religious reawakening soon became a trio as political assertion joined the chorus. Predictably, the shrill rhetoric of the Brahman-dominated Madras branch of Congress, combined with the mystical musings of their Theosophical allies, kindled fears among non-Brahmans that nationalism was just a mask for aggressive, revivalist high-caste Hinduism, and that 'national feeling' was a ruse for grabbing more jobs and power from non-Brahmans. Efforts were made to promulgate Tamil pride to the educated through a prolific Tamil press, and to the illiterate through street songs and polemical plays, which portrayed a national 'India' as an evil mother, a blood-sucking demoness and a conniving strumpet. Political tension was ratcheted up during the controversy over the relative status of Tamil and Sanskrit at the University of Madras in 1905, during which both sides furiously lobbied the government. The non-Brahmans began to enjoy some success. The British, who had unwittingly elevated Brahman power in the south, now hoped to use the Dravidian movement to counterbalance the Brahman-dominated Congress. In 1912 the Madras Dravidian Association, with much British encouragement, was established to lobby for a greater share of official posts; by 1917 a non-Brahman party manifesto announced the movement's intention to compete with the 'automatic quill-drivers, indifferent school masters and pettifogging lawyers' of Congress. It was clear that non-Brahman elites were not going to accept a nationalist movement led by high-caste groups. The Maharaja of Panagal, a non-Brahman leader, put anti-national feeling bluntly:

While the British oligarchy touches us here and there and that too only superficially, the Brahman oligarchy pursues us at every turn and makes itself felt in the innermost recesses of our life.

Nor was the Brahmanical flavour of Congress politics to the taste of ambitious non-Brahmans elsewhere. Conflict between Brahman and non-Brahman soon became evident in Bombay presidency. Maharashtra, its largest region, had only a thin veneer of Brahmans; they had soon mastered the new language of power, English, and so dominated government employment and (along with the Persianate Parsis) modern professional employment in the major cities of Bombay and Poona. They were, however, anxious about the rise of educated and well-off non-Brahman challengers to their prestige, and they seized on nationalist politics and Congress as a means of protecting their status and recapturing influence. For these high-caste nationalists it was crucial to shape a nationalist movement able to meld the vast 'muddle in the middle' of prosperous peasant and trader groups into an alliance with Brahmans, not against them. But they had little success and only alienated non-Brahmans further.

Between 1870 and 1900 a curious, heated struggle simmered in Maharashtra over who should wear the (figurative) mantle of the region's great seventeenth-century warrior-king – Shivaji. Around this time Maharashtra was suddenly awash with histories and biographies of the great hero, who had resisted Mughal power and even given the East India Company a bloody nose. Several of these had been penned by aspiring politicians. Clearly Shivaji was an ideal symbol of some kind of Marathi patriotism and unity, but of what kind precisely? The moderate Congress leader, judge and historian Ranade, saw him as a pietistic soldier-cum-religious syncretist, a wise and humane man, whose legacy was neither exclusively Brahman, Ksatriya or indeed Hindu at all, but that of reformer and nation-builder. For the Congress extremist Tilak, however, Shivaji was an avenging angel of revivalist Hindu militancy whose politics were the prototype of Tilak's: culturally aggressive and Brahman-led. Tilak's *Kesari* exulted in his brutal treatment of Muslims and suggested that the great general's main purpose in life had been the protection of cows.

Neither Ranade nor Tilak succeeded in harnessing Shivaji to the nationalist juggernaut. Other more alluring 'Shivajis' appeared. For the low-caste activist Jyotirao Phule, Shivaji was the champion of the oppressed, the lowest castes and even dalits, and in his 1869 ballad, Shivaji the Shudra king returns as good king Bali to preside over a casteless paradise. The most successful Shivaji, however, was the one embodied by his closest living descendant, the Maharaja of Kohlapur. The Maharaja was of Ksatriya caste and an opponent of Brahman pretensions; he had effectively scuttled Tilak's plans for a Shivaji memorial by organizing a princely boycott (though he did stump up for a statue of Lord Harris, the well-known cricketer and much-disliked governor general of Bombay; with fitting irony, it was the British who eventually picked up the tab for Tilak's Shivaji memorial). Kohlapur's Shivaji was a non-Brahman Ksatriya hero who would lead the Maratha race to independence, free of Brahman dominance. Unfortunately for the Congress nationalists, this particular maharaja was both an adult and sane (several of his predecessors had been neither). He became a powerful and influential figure and had a plausible strategy for building a Marathi political identity around non-Brahmanism and British loyalism. In his own state government he assiduously promoted non-Brahmans over the heads of Brahmans and financed the education of Marathas. In 1902 he formally reserved 50 per cent of state jobs for non-Brahmans. They retaliated by insisting on elaborate purification rituals whenever they came before him, but despite these petty humiliations the Maharaja's Marathi identity policies were up and running by the turn of the century.

Meanwhile the Punjab, too, the parade ground of the Raj, was also beginning to splinter into a kaleidoscope of cultural and political identities – Sikh, Muslim, Hindu Brahman and Hindu non-Brahman. One aspect of Punjabi politics was very distinctive: the chasm-like gulf between urban and rural politics cutting across religious communities, which, by 1910, left the nationalist Congress with an almost exclusively urban profile. This urban-rural rift was skilfully engineered by British policy. The loyalty of the Punjab's peasants and farmers, whether Hindu, Sikh or Muslim, was absolutely crucial to the Raj;

they were the vertebrae of the Indian army, which was the backbone of British power. Since 1860 loyalty had been bought with the most generous developmental gifts available anywhere on the subcontinent, low taxes, land grants, superb irrigation, massive investment in land reclamation and, in 1901, the cherry on the cake, the Punjab Land Alienation Act. This act had, by imperial fiat, imported the novel notion of the 'agricultural tribe' (and its alter-ego, the 'non-agricultural tribe') into Punjabi life, and under the terms of the act land could be permanently owned only by those classified as belonging to 'agricultural tribes'. Everything now turned on how these entities were defined. It transpired that those groups and castes which provided most men for the army were 'agricultural'; those who did not (a group composed almost exclusively of Brahmans and trading castes) were not.

The British were increasingly wary of *banias* (small-time merchants), 'money-lenders' and other high-caste groups with a propensity to sympathize with British critics, and sought to exclude them from the now very valuable Punjab land, where many had ancestral holdings. One official put it very bluntly: 'Even if a *bania* has held land for thirty or forty years, he does not thereby cease to be a *bania*.' Soon a specifically ruralist cultural identity had developed to accompany what had begun as a purely legal persona, for while Raj officials mused on the virtues of the 'splendid yeoman peasants' and 'martial races' of the Punjab, the peasants themselves seemed equally keen to assume this manly bucolic mantle. Inevitably this identity crystallized into a political lobby, and in 1907 the Jats (a group of several million Hindu farmers whom the British now classified as one tribe) began to protest that they were an 'oppressed agricultural tribe' deserving of special treatment to help them catch up with urban, educated Brahmans. The *Jat Gazette* was launched in 1913 and contributed to this new sense of community by publishing colourful and highly imaginative 'histories' of Jat 'tribal' loyalty to the Raj, hinting that their true caste was Ksatriya, and not the not lowly Shudra status assigned to them by urban Brahmans.

For those not accorded the title of 'agricultural tribe' came the bitter realization that they were now legally second-class citizens. The Punjab Hindu Sabha complained: 'The high caste Hindus have been scrupulously kept out, even where they have held land and followed agriculture as a profession for several generations', and the Punjab branch of Congress, which was largely composed of Brahmans and *banias*, opposed the 1901 Land Alienation Act, a decision which made the nationalists spectacularly unpopular in the countryside and was never forgotten, even when belatedly reversed. Although there was a brief phantom of urban-rural accord during a Congress-led campaign in 1907, its cause was a set of particularly unwise government policies which infuriated farmers. As soon as these were dropped, the alliance collapsed. Signs of an emergent agriculturalist politics, detached from Indian nationalism, were now looming on the horizon. After the First World War this farmer interest found expression in its own Unionist party, which combined Hindu, Muslim and Sikh interests around one great issue – the defence of the Punjabi Magna Carta, the 1901 Land Alienation Act.

The immediate beneficiary of this seemingly endless chain reaction of political and cultural fission was the Raj. And while the British had not conjured these proliferating divisions and identities from thin air, they waved a magic wand that would entrench and institutionalize them. By the early 1880s the collaborative equations established after the Rebellion no longer added up. The prosperity of the two decades following the rebellion had nurtured a more aspirational peasantry moving beyond the control of 'natural leaders', while organized, urban and educated public opinion, much of it critical of the Raj and coming from erstwhile collaborators, were features of the political landscape that could not be ignored. The British may have longed to remove these unsightly eruptions, but the best they could do was go round them, digging fresh channels of influence and patronage with more amenable groups such as elite Muslims and the prosperous non-Brahmans in the regions. The predominantly Hindu and high-caste nationalists would be left, it was hoped, in hidebound political irrelevance.

So, by the eve of the First World War, the British had shrewdly manipulated the politics of cultural difference and elite competition to achieve a new political configuration and, in so doing, they had killed two birds with one very well-aimed stone. In 1909 a scheme of limited electoral politics was introduced at the provincial level. These ingenious reforms allowed the Raj to bask in the glow of progressivism, while effectively recalibrating the political scales to ensure that high-caste Congress nationalists would be greatly outweighed by non-Brahmans, loyal rustics and Muslims in the temples of power. In south India, the governor of Madras enthusiastically encouraged non-Brahman politics, prompting their requests for special quotas in education and official employment and assisting in the formation of the 'Justice' party in 1916. In Maharashtra, the Maharaja of Kohlapur and his patriotic movement was welcomed; such a strategy was, as one official commented, mutually beneficial, 'for we are subject to a common danger from the preponderance of Brahmans in the public services'. In the Punjab electoral reforms introduced throughout India in the 1890s were resisted, allowing the government to retain the right to nominate its rural allies on to courts and councils until such time as they had been organized into an effective electoral competitor with urban nationalists. And in 1909, in a policy unique to the Punjab, a ban was placed on urban politicians standing for election in rural constituencies. But for many Hindus and Congressmen the most egregious act of colonial gerrymandering was the creation of separate electorates for Muslims; Muslims would now be treated as an independent political constituency, with seats in the new assemblies allotted specifically to them. While the initiative for these came from Muslims themselves (albeit rather unrepresentative ones) with a deputation to the Viceroy in 1906, nationalists always maintained that this apparently unprompted request was, in fact, a colonial command performance.

Those at the very bottom of society generally escaped the direct attentions of both British patronage and Hindu self-strengthening movements. Nevertheless 'tribal' groups (forest and hill dwellers), the poorest Shudra peasants and dalits were inescapably caught up in colonial policy, and were often the victims of the aspirant castes clambering up the Indo-colonial social and economic hierarchy. Though generally illiterate and isolated, these so-called 'subalterns' (as historians now refer to them), were more than capable of responding with organizational, cultural and ideological innovations of their own. They too were a link in the great chain reaction set off by the control rod of colonialism. Their movements were spectacular, exotic and extreme, but they betrayed underlying patterns of resistance, a visceral egalitarianism, a rejection of the *Homo hierarchicus* of Hindu tradition and sometimes even the faintest inklings of class-consciousness and socialism.

Diverse though subaltern groups were, their experience of the Raj was depressingly similar – they were the losers. The particular version of economic 'modernity' intermittently imposed by the British destroyed their lives. Just as the British had enclosed their own common lands in the seventeenth century and cracked down hard on poaching and living off the land in English and Scottish forests, so also in India they determinedly privatized what had been public and made exclusive what had been common. By the 1860s the extensive hill territories and forests, with their millions of tribal dwellers and nomadic cultivators, had become just so many enterprise opportunity zones. Men from the plains – money-lenders, traders and labour contractors – poured in. Armed with British notions of private property and contract, they laid claim to the land and inveigled the hapless tribal peoples in highly disadvantageous contract-labour arrangements, often tantamount to a new slavery. In the plains themselves, court-enforceable notions of property rights etched sharp boundaries between the owner and the tenant that had not been visible before. In the cities the concept of untouchability also acquired a much sharper edge, partly because of the proliferation of 'unclean' tasks in the burgeoning cities – street-sweeping and night-soil clearing – but also because of the redefinition of Hinduism propagated by the Arya Samaj and other reformist sects. While these movements were the most critical of untouchability as an idea, they were often its most fierce enforcers in practice.

Subalterns did not take their new oppressions lying down. Violent rebellion among tribal people seems to have been endemic during the *Pax Britannica*. Moreover, these were not merely reprises of older types of resistance common during economic and cultural crises; potent new elements had been added to the brew of exploitation and misery, as notions of rights, freedom and equality mingled with the older ideologies of Christianity, Islam and sometimes Buddhism. The most dramatic of the Christian-inspired uprisings was the *ulgulan* (great tumult) of Birsa Munda, which erupted in the Chota-Nagpur forest districts of Bihar between 1899 and 1900. From the 1870s the age-old autonomy of the forest-dwelling Mundas was breached; interloper merchants and money-lenders rode rough-shod over traditional notions of joint property holdings, annexing territory and turning the Mundas into forced and indentured labourers. At the same time, the region was swarming with Lutheran and Anglican missionaries, people like the famous Reverend Lusty who promised to restore the Mundas' land if they became Christian, but failed to keep his word.

In 1898 a young Munda man – Birsa – announced that he was their real saviour, and urged them to abandon the Anglican Church and follow him, as he was a distant relative of Jesus Christ. He also promised the Mundas that if they killed all their white poultry and pigs (which were unclean), and sold all their possessions in order to buy smart clothes, they would be saved on the day of reckoning, which was 24 December 1899. On this date God would destroy their enemies and restore their lands. Throughout 1899 secret midnight meetings were held in the Munda forests, where Birsa urged his thousands of devotees to murder the usurping interlopers who had stolen their land. Effigies of enemies were ritually burnt, accompanied by energetic renditions of Christian hymns rewritten to encourage violent retribution against Munda foes. On Christmas Eve 1899 Birsa launched a mass revolt in the name of his new faith. The Mundas torched churches full of carol singers and waged war on the local police with bows and arrows. Over 5000 tribal people joined the rebellion and it was some weeks before the British re-established control of the area. Birsa was eventually captured and died in prison, but he left a long legacy: a cult of resistance and a potent folkloric tradition of radical egalitarianism.

Elsewhere subaltern rebels sought an Islamic millennium. Between 1870 and 1920 the Muslim Moplah peasants on the far south-west coast of peninsular India were aroused by mendicant Muslim clerics and Deobandi students to a state of virtually permanent rebellion against their oppressive Hindu landlords. Many dalit peasants had been recently converted to Islam by these Muslims, who promised a future of social equality and, like Birsa's movement, made direct links between violent retribution against oppressors and the recovery of a lost golden age of virtue and plenty. One cleric preached that murder in retribution for land seizure would be rewarded in paradise. All claimed to possess miraculous powers, and one *mufti* was thought to have the power to 'appear and disappear at will, to remain proof against bullets, to cause bullets to drop harmless the moment they issued from rifles', according to the *Times of Malabar*.

In the far south, on the other hand, radical egalitarianism acquired a Buddhist tincture. The plight of dalits in Travancore was particularly severe: they were thought to pollute on sight and were therefore 'unseeables'. The cosmically tactless Annie Besant made matters worse, insisting that untouchability was caused by failings in personal hygiene. The relatively affluent non-Brahman movement of the middle castes was either apathetic towards dalits, or anxious to distance itself, the better to press claims for Ksatriya status, and not surprisingly many southern dalits began to reject Hinduism entirely. In its place they developed an 'adi-Dravida' (original Dravidian) identity with its own foundation myth. According to the adi-Dravida version of history the true natives of southern India were the dalits. They had created a Buddhist utopia known as Indirar Desam, which had been destroyed by Aryan Brahman invaders who had promoted caste divisions, land-theft and untouchability:

They approached the illiterate chieftains and citizens of Indirar Desam and claimed falsely that they were enlightened men. They also sent their women to the kings, distracted them into debauchery and thus corrupted them ... Those who fell prey to the sophistry of the vesha [sect of] brahmins became Hindus. Those who rejected them ... came to be known ... as paraiahs.

Brahmans had Hinduized noble and rational Buddhist rituals into degraded and vulgar superstitions, polytheism and a variety of absurd behaviours clearly designed to oppress the adi-Dravidas and promote Aryan interests. Outraged by the hypocrisy of Hinduism, Southern dalits began to question caste rules, such as that which stated that mud pots sullied by the glance of a dalit had to be smashed, while similarly blighted silver pots need only be washed. They were unconvinced by the pseudo-scientific Brahmanical explanation that mud was a base material that secreted filth, while non-porous silverware could apparently repel the polluting glance. By the twentieth century this radical Buddhism had intermingled with other more contemporary philosophies and it was the adi-Dravida intellectual Ramakrishna Pillai who published the first biography of Marx in Malayalam.

Others subalterns retained Hinduism, but modified it in highly egalitarian ways. New ideologies emerged from an ingenious blend of the genuine folk traditions of Hindu-*Bhakti*, an egalitarian form of anti-caste Hinduism with roots in the fifteenth century. This philosophy was most evident in popular songs and in poetry, especially that of Kabir, an early *bhakti* poet.

> It's all one skin and bone
> one piss and shit
> one blood, one meat.
> From one drop, a universe.
> Who's Brahman? Who's Shudra?

Soon a genealogy was constructed, allegedly pre-dating Aryan India and Vedic Hinduism. The dalits were the 'real' Hindus. Their egalitarian version of the religion was the truer and more pure. It had been suppressed by Brahman interlopers, but kept alive through secret cults and a saintly tradition. Furthermore, they, the 'adi-Hindus', were the rightful rulers of India. In 1896 the British administrator William Crooke noted that there were a great many 'closed sects' or secret societies among rural *bhakti* sects. In the cities adherents called themselves *bhagats* (holy persons), who wore distinctive bead necklaces as sect marks, and built their own temples to *bhakti* saints, which became the foci of community building with devotional singing and rousing prayer meetings.

While some sought prestige and power by turning conventional hierarchies upside down, others demanded rapid promotion to the apex of the Hindu status pyramid. The *adivasi* (tribal) movements of south Gujarat asserted themselves by adopting the habits and demeanour of the regionally dominant high-caste Brahmans and *banias*. This bold bid for higher social standing took the unlikely form of a possession cult. Certain *adivasis* would be 'seized' by the spirit of the 'Devi' (the local goddess) and forced to implement her desires.

Curiously the Devi never seemed to want them to challenge high-caste groups, but did insist that the local (non-Hindu) Parsi landowners and Muslim traders be boycotted. She also insisted that the previously bibulous *adivasis* become teetotal. The mysterious Devi was, in fact, ordering the *adivasis* (via her 'mediums') to emulate high-caste habits: abandon drinking and brewing toddy, adopt strict vegetarianism, wash daily and use water instead of leaves for bottom-wiping. Coincidentally, such 'improvements' smoothed the way for the *adivasis*' post-war incorporation into the mainstream, high-caste led nationalist movement and, through it, the pursuit of their local power ambitions.

What is striking about all these groups is their powerful resistance, both ideological and organizational, to their own crushing subordination. These were shrewd and inventive people, who, though constrained by their isolation and lack of education, were conscious of the rapidly shifting political economy of later nineteenth-century India. Resourceful though they were, to make real progress they needed allies, but they had to decide who their real friends were. For many of these groups, perhaps surprisingly, it seemed to be the British. This was somewhat ironic since it was the British who had promoted high-caste Hinduism in the south and west and introduced and enforced the property and land laws that so disadvantaged many of them. Nevertheless, many found western concepts of rights, equality and freedom liberating. The Muslim peasants of Pabna in Bengal brought law suits against their oppressive landlords, insisting they were 'the *Ryots* [tenants] of Her Majesty the Queen and of her only'. At a more banal, but highly visible level, technological innovations associated with the Raj, such as the railways and later trams and buses, made a nonsense of caste distinctions, as did urban life more generally. Moreover, the arrival of the British could be seen as ending centuries of misrule not known since the humane governance of the pre-Aryan kingdoms. Missionary journals were crammed with letters from recently educated subalterns praising Christianity's respect for human equality and extolling the British as their liberators. So far the nationalists, with their disdain for tenancy reform, their ambivalence about caste and their apathy towards tribal people had not made convincing competitors in the contest for subaltern loyalties.

So by 1900 the great cultural chain reaction continued to transform the subcontinent. India was an extraordinarily politicized society, but also a kaleidoscopically fragmented one. The presence of a colonial state with its influential nostrums of race and hierarchy, its powerful predisposition to legitimize diversity and deny unity, and its dextrous ability to rapidly reshuffle the pack of collaborator loyalties seemed unbeatable. Any nationalist movement faced not only the obvious difficulties of forging a sense of 'unity in diversity', but also the infinitely greater task of doing so when the ruling state was determined to do the opposite. One area where division was wrenched from promising unity was the question of language, the story of which in many ways is a microcosm of the larger difficulties of Indian nationalism

In 1889 an extraordinary play was performed at a religious *mela* (fair) in the north Indian town of Meerut. *The Case of Hindi and Urdu* was a tense courtroom drama by one Babu Ratna Chandra, a barrister. In the play Hindi, the heroine – a Cinderella-like figure, despised and neglected, yet also beautiful and virtuous – brings a law suit against the defendant, a proud, wicked stepmother-type called Begum (widow) Urdu. During the trial Begum Wanton-Pleasure, Begum Urdu's sidekick, is called in her defence. She dismisses the claims of the maiden Hindi: 'she has stayed so long in the jungle . . . she is not fit to live in the city . . . She has become a savage.' But Begum Urdu turns out to be a woman of loose morals who attempts to sway the judge, Maharaja Righteous-Rules, with offers of sexual favours:

> This is my work: passion I'll teach
> Your household tasks we'll leave in the breach.
> We'll be lovers and rakes, living for pleasure,
> Consorting with prostitutes, squandering your treasure.

The play illustrates an arresting phenomenon of Indian cultural life in the later decades of the nineteenth century: the quest for 'pure' languages and the consequent dissolution of a venerable, popular and elegant language that had fostered some degree of communication within the linguistically diverse subcontinent for over a century. The play is a highly partisan account of one dimension of this curious episode. It dramatizes the battle between those who demanded the replacement of the official state language of the north-eastern provinces, Urdu (written in an Arab-Persian script), with another language called Hindi (written in the Sanskritic Devanagari script). Urdu, its opponents claimed, was an inherently immoral language: its script was difficult and often illegible, allowing plenty of leeway to fraudsters, and its vocabulary was ambiguous and 'depraved' – several words had double meanings and the second was usually obscene. All in all Urdu was a corrupting influence on pious Hindi and, by implication, on Hindu society in general. On the surface this seemed like a fairly clearcut morality play with an easily identifiable heroine and villainess. There was, however, a major complication. To the vast majority of Indians, 'Cinderella' Hindi and 'evil stepmother' Urdu were one and the same. Many knew them as a single language, Hindustani.

Though the fabled home of hundreds of tongues, there are essentially fifteen major subcontinental languages. Moreover India's many tongues trace their origins to one of two linguistic ancestors – Sanskrit (Bengali, Marathi, Punjabi, Gujarati, Hindi), or Dravidian (Tamil, Telugu, Malayalam, Kannada). There are strong family resemblances within each group, and even between the Sanskritic and Dravidian there is shared vocabulary, syntax and grammar. Language in India is more in the nature of a continuum than a set of absolutely distinct entities. Moreover many Indians spoke (and speak) roughly three versions of their mother-tongue – dialect, regional and 'correct'. Language in nineteenth-century India was fluid, malleable and protean, offering opportunities for practitioners of linguistic apartheid or miscegenation alike.

However, around 1900 many nationalist Indians decided that India needed a national language, or at least a link language that would serve as a lingua franca throughout the subcontinent. Clearly the big question was what should it be? In Kipling's *Kim* it is the Hindi-Urdu blend called Hindustani that clearly fitted the bill. Mahbib Ali, the Pathan horse dealer, uses it to speak to Kim, though his 'mother-tongue' is Pashto; the lama (Buddhist priest) knows Tibetan and Chinese, but speaks Hindustani; Huree Babu speaks everything – Bengali, Punjabi, *'Babu'* English ('offeecially, by jove') – and can read 'Court Persian', but he too habitually lapses into Hindustani. Kipling was not alone in his enthusiasm for Hindustani, and its merits were pressed by many Indians: it had the largest number of speakers (around 30 per cent of the population), was extensively spoken across the north, was quite widely understood in the south, and united Hindu and Muslim through a common tongue (if not script). But not everyone agreed.

In 1868 a campaign was launched to promote the use of the Devanagari script for Hindustani. In part this move had a calculated and pragmatic motivation: jobs for the (Hindu) boys. Some Hindus, particularly those associated with the Arya Samaj which launched the agitation, had not been taught the Arab-Persian script and were thus disqualified from official employment in the north-eastern provinces (where it was the official script). But strong emotions and a preoccupation with symbols of cultural power were also present. Revivalist Hindus regarded the official use of the Arab-Persian script as a slight to their culture and yet another example of the favouritism shown to Muslims. This sense of subordination and victimhood lent the Devanagari movement a surprisingly passionate intensity, and soon it seemed that merely displacing the Arab-Persian script was not enough. Hindustani had to be purged of all Muslim influence – vocabulary, grammar and syntax; thus cleansed, *shuddh* (pure) Hindi would emerge. And so, in an egregious example of putting the cart before the horse, a literary language was created to go with a script. Hindi was fashioned from several regional dialects – Awadhi, Khari Boli, Braj Bhasa among them – but purged of all Urdu influence. This linguistic cleansing not only destroyed Hindustani, but in its hyper-purist form rendered Hindi itself incomprehensible to the less well-educated and even, on occasion, to the very highly educated. India's first Prime Minister, Nehru, once complained that he found his own speeches, as reported by All-India Radio (a stickler for 'correct' Hindi), incomprehensible.

The promotion of Hindi dealt a death-blow to the idea of a link-language, confirming to many what they had always suspected: that this, like nationalism, was just a ruse for high-caste Hindu imperialism. It went down especially badly in the south, where, by the 1890s the semi religious cult of Tamiltay (goddess Tamil) was in full swing and the suggestion that a northern interloper language should become widely spoken, even if only as a second language, was regarded with horror. A campaign to 'purge' Tamil of all 'foreign' (i.e. Sanskritic) words was launched by the linguistic activist Maraimalai Adigal, who had dravidianized his embarrassingly Aryan name Swami Vedach-alam. He brought an apocalyptic fervour to the language wars. Those who opposed Tamil purification were denounced as murderers and degenerates; for him, 'defiling one's speech by mixing up with it extraneous elements simply indicates laxity of discipline, looseness of character and lack of serious purpose in life'. In 1916 the Tamiliyak-kam (Pure Tamil Society) set up shop to publish poetry and drama denuded of any remotely Sanskritic words. This proved difficult. Meanwhile the 'Tamil Scientific Terms Society' struggled to establish a modern scientific Tamil vocabulary. Though it eventually produced a glossary of 10,000 technical terms, it proved impossible to reduce the Sanskritic vocabulary to less than 10 per cent, or entirely to purge Tamil of Sanskrit-influenced syntax. So, just as pure Hindi had to be invented, so too the task of 'cleansing' Tamil to recover its 'authentic' form proved a quixotic task. Moreover the resulting 'pure' or correct languages were virtually unintelligible to the man on the Kanchipuram omnibus.

The trumpeting of Tamil linguistic superiority had inevitably triggered another stage in the chain reaction, this time among the Telugu speakers of the northern areas of the Madras presidency. Telugu was another Dravidian language, closely related to Tamil with many shared words and forms, and Madras itself was a city where Tamil and Telugu were spoken in equal parts. There had been something of a Telugu renaissance among poets and novelists since the 1870s. Yet by the eve of the First World War this had acquired a rather ominous political dimension as Telugu-speaking politicians began to demand their own 'linguistically' pure province, where the state language (and all the best jobs) would be Telugu. This was accompanied by moves to 'de-Tamilize' Telugu, to prove how very different it was to Tamil and therefore how it was wholly unreasonable that people speaking these two languages should be part of the same province.

The British, as usual, did well out of this linguistic fissuring. In 1903 the Raj launched the 'Linguistic Survey of India'. Reminiscent of the Census, this was not a wholly innocent project of detached scholarly enquiry, but partly a useful device for demonstrating how very divided India was. The survey eventually announced that there were over three hundred languages in India, the implication being that since language (according to the fashion of the time) underpinned the notion of a nation, India could not be a nation. However, British policy was frequently responsible for making language so contentious in the first place, using it to reward allies and punish enemies. In the north-eastern provinces where the Devanagari controversy erupted, the British had pursued the polarizing strategy of insisting on the use of Devanagari script in state-aided schools for Hindu boys, while retaining the Arab-Persian script in government.

In the India of 1860 language was a messy and syncretic melee of dialects, earthy vernaculars and, in the case of Hindustani, something approaching a lingua franca. The quest for linguistic purity, inspired in part by the British and in part by Hindu revivalism, sensitized Indians to language as an icon of status and identity. Meanwhile official manipulation of language as a technique of government gave difference and purity of tongue a hard political utility. By 1914 the fragile but palpable inklings of linguistic unity had dimmed.

For many it was the serene image of the Taj Mahal that symbolized India. But by 1914, after sixty years of Raj rule, India had become a Babel-Mahal – a palace of endlessly fragmenting languages, castes and regional identities. This was state-building of a type diametrically opposed to that practised by the nation-states of Europe. In Italy, France and Germany, powerfully integrative governments strove to standardize and homogenize language; the colonial state in India did the opposite. Nationalists could see that the resultant fracturing was a catastrophe and that prospects for unity were bleak. But the Great War offered unifiers unprecedented opportunities. One in particular, a certain South African-based lawyer and political alchemist M. K. Gandhi, saw unity in the fragments. But though Gandhi was a great experimenter, he discovered, like all scientists, that fusion was an infinitely greater challenge than fission.

3

Far Pavilions

At their most philosophical, the British saw empire as cricket. For some, cricket was the greatest gift imperialism could bestow, because it could transform 'natives' into gentlemen. In 1893 this 'wicket imperialism' acquired its most prominent theorist in the shape of Arthur Haslam, Oxford historian and wicket-keeper for the 'Oxford Eccentrics', the first British team to tour India. Cricket's rules and culture, he insisted, were the platonic embodiment of English virtue:

First the hunter, the missionary and the merchant, next the soldier and the politician and then the cricketer – that is the history of British colonization . . . the soldier may hector, the politician blunder, but cricket united . . . the ruler and the ruled. It also provides a moral training, an education in pluck and nerve, and self-restraint, far more valuable to the character of the native than the mere learning by heart of a play by Shakespeare or an essay by Macaulay.

For others, cricket could build not merely character but the nation itself, though there was profound disagreement about the nature of the 'nation' being constructed. For Lord Harris, the cricket-loving governor of Bombay from 1890 to 1893, it encouraged the multifarious castes, communities and religious of India to mingle while retaining their separate identities – an ideal displacement of potentially explosive political rivalries. Those of a more progressive temper than Harris saw it differently. For Sir Lancelot Graham, the first governor of Sindh, cricket was capable of dissolving such divisions to 'bind communities together and foster harmony on and off the field, and not only in cricket'. For a while, at least, it appeared that Graham's optimistic view might be vindicated.

Before the First World War cricket did indeed appear to be the cultural glue of an emerging national identity. By 1918 cricket had become a national obsession, played throughout the country, uniting rich and poor, high caste and low, Hindu and Muslim. The great tournaments were kaleidoscopic spectacles: the well-off inside the stadiums in tents and on divans, the less prosperous straining for a view of the pitch from the tops of trees, buses and telegraph poles. There were even signs of integration on the pitch with multi-caste teams and princes playing with paupers. Indeed the greatest stars of the pre-1914 game came from opposite ends of the social spectrum. The outstanding batsman was Kumar Shri Ramjitsinhji, Jamsaheb (prince) of Nawana-gar (1872–1933). Having taken up cricket at Rajkumar College, the princes' Eton, he proceeded to Trinity College, Cambridge, where he acquired the nickname Smith and a parrot called Popsey, and joined the University team in 1893. He went on to play for England against Australia in 1896, making three centuries in a style characterized by enraptured observers as 'an oriental poem of action'. The other great pre-war star was the fabulously gifted bowler Baloo, a dalit, who had honed his spinning as a practice bowler to British officers in the military encampment where his father worked as a camp orderly. Initially, he was not allowed to take tea with other team members but had his served outside the pavilion in a disposable cup. Triumphing over caste prejudice, however, he eventually captained the predominantly high-caste team that sensationally beat the Europeans in 1923.

However, Indian cricket soon came to embody not caste, class and religious unity, but division. This development is best encapsulated in the strange history of the greatest tournament of colonial India: the Bombay Pentangular. Bombay had been the birthplace of cricket for Indians. A proto-tournament had been initiated by Harris in 1893, with teams assembled along racial and community lines. Initially the Parsi team had haughtily declined to play the Hindus: only European opponents were equal to their dignity. But by 1907 the rift between Hindus and Parsis was healed and the first Bombay Triangular, between Hindus, Parsis and Europeans, was held. In 1912 a Muslim team joined, and thus the Quadrangular began. By the early 1930s the tournament was beginning to mirror national politics; the various teams roughly reflected the disposition of forces at the Round Table constitutional talks held at the time – Europeans, Hindus and Sikhs, Parsis and Muslims. In 1932 matches had to be cancelled owing to Congress's boycott of the constitutional talks. By the mid-1930s the question of how the 'minor' minorities should be incorporated into the game arose, just as their place in a reformed constitution was vexing talks in London. In cricketing terms the question was how the smaller communities of Indian Catholics, Protestants, Syrian Christians, Eurasians, Sinhalese, Buddhists, Luso-Portugese Indians and Jews might participate in the game. The solution came in 1937 with the formation of a fifth team, known as 'the Rest', and the first Bombay Pentangular was born.

The ethnicization of the game naturally led to conflict. The first Pentangular of 1937 proved something of a fiasco. The Hindus withdrew because they had not been allocated enough seats in the new stadium; the Parsis boycotted it in 1938, only to return in 1939, when the Pentangular commenced in earnest. By 1940, however, political tensions were again disrupting play: the Hindus decided they should withdraw in solidarity with Congress's resignation from government after the declaration of war. The tournament was not held in 1942 owing to the Japanese triumphs in south-east Asia, but was back in 1943, when the British had great hopes of winning with a team boosted by new infusions of talent from the swollen ranks of British servicemen (they were defeated in the first round). The last Pentangular was held in January 1946.

By the mid-1930s there were grave misgivings among many Indians about the communal turn team games had taken. Cricket crowds were deeply infected with communal feeling; in 1935 one journalist detected 'the unmistakeable tinge of communal partisanship which is the bane of these tournaments'. In 1939 the triumphant Hindus celebrated their Pentangular victory over the Muslims with the pointed chanting of the controversial nationalist hymn *Bande Mataram* and the ignition of thousands of firecrackers, the markers of triumph in war. When real war broke out, many concluded that it was time for the cricket to stop. The *Bombay Chronicle* insisted:

We must not play the game of the Britishers. They want us to remain divided ... so that they may point out our disunity to the world and keep us in subjection till eternity . . . as long as there is emphasis on community in the tournament the man who says let the best side win is either uttering a fiction or is a Mahatma.

The 'Mahatma' – Gandhi – himself agreed, arguing in 1941 that teams either integrate or pull up stumps altogether. The end of the war brought the future of the Pentangular into sudden sharp focus. The Hindu nationalist Veer Savarkar had exhorted 'the Rest' to 'revert to Hinduism', while the Muslim team was now generally referred to as 'Pakistan'. In a complete U-turn from its previous disposition, the Pentangular Board passed a resolution in December 1946, stating that it 'disapproved of communal cricket'. With the creation of Pakistan now virtually a certainty the Pentangular was an embarrassment. In 1947 the first 'zonal' Quadrangular, based on regional rather than religious or community-based teams, was held in Bombay; teams from North, West, East and South India met. The West, the victors, comprising a mixed team of Muslim, Christian, Parsi and Hindu, played an equally mixed team from the North.

The history of British India between the wars is strangely reminiscent of the history of cricket. In their last thirty years of power British politicians and officials were divided: some wanted to abandon the old *durbar*-Raj and recast the imperial relationship, ditching hierarchy and division for a new politics of development and nation-building. But for others the idea of India as a unified nation-state – a single team – was inconceivable. The appropriate model was an 'umpired' nation of competing 'teams'. A curious hybrid of Victorian orientalism and modern liberalism emerged from these conflicting approaches. The British promoted political, economic and social reforms which seemed, in some ways, to be liberal. But they were often ineffectual, and in practice, they entrenched the politics of division, rather than unity. Though Congress fought hard to counter these fissiparous tendencies, it was unable fully to transcend them, and, once umpire-less, the two most prominent Indian teams – the Hindus and the Muslims – found it impossible to play politics on the same pitch.

*

Curiously, given the reformist temper of the post-war Raj, the First World War itself brought the resurgence of a more self-confident and pugnacious imperialism. For some the Great War was an opportunity to attend to unfinished business in the Middle East, tying up loose ends left over by the final collapse of the Ottoman Empire, buttressing those last vulnerable flanks on the Raj's defences with new territory in the Middle East. And in the course of the war and subsequent peace, the imperial state had grabbed German South West Africa, annexed Egypt, and formalized its tutelage of Persia. Along with France, it had also become the residuary legatee of much of the dismembered Ottoman Empire, gaining the old vilayets of Palestine, Basra, Mosul and Baghdad, now clumsily shoe-horned into the new state of Iraq. In the imperial capital a resurgent Edwardian imperialist claque dominated the Lloyd George cabinet, thinned out with a scattering of progressive liberals. The former group included several men with great futures behind them, including imperial strongmen such as the former viceroy Lord Curzon, and Alfred Milner, the South African High Commissioner. Their vision was of an old-style *durbar* empire, short on 'native' involvement and long on white prestige. They were not disposed to be liberal in India. Others, however, were dubious about hard-line approaches, recognizing their potential to misfire. The Labour Party leader, Ramsay MacDonald, who had made a pre-war tour of the Raj, concluded that British conservative elements were making a mistake in treating Congress as an irreconcilable enemy and were allowing their long-standing dislike of the nationalists to harden into a prejudice that would ultimately damage Britain's interests. As his Labour colleague Keir Hardie wryly observed, Congress was in fact pretty loyalist: 'Part of it is extreme in its moderation, whilst the other part is moderate in its extremism.'

Within the Raj itself, progressives had, since before the war, been warning that failure to rally the moderates with generous reforms would push them into the arms of the extremists and terrorists. But they were in a minority. There was a party for more devolution of power from Delhi to the provinces among ICS officials, but their goal was to enhance their own administrative autonomy, save money and avoid the noisome daily grind of local politics, and certainly not to become bag-carriers to elected Indian ministers. The Viceroy himself,

Lord Chelmsford, though a proponent of modest devolution, was a notorious stickler for status, prestige and hierarchy, even by the exacting standards of Raj propriety. He was stiff, cold and formal even with very senior Indian politicians, and it was this frosty and parsimonious strand of reformism that set the tone.

Moreover, to the right of Chelmsford were more reactionary officials, who cavilled at the idea of sharing real power with Indians. In their opinion, India, despite its apparent loyalism, was in reality a cauldron of barely contained dissent and treachery. Nationalism was poised to strike when the Raj was at its weakest and the thin white line of order was at its thinnest. During the war the numbers of white troops posted in India had fallen to a post-1858 low, breaching the fetishistic ratio of three 'natives' to two 'whites'. Such apparent vulnerability fuelled phantasmagoric nightmares of a second rebellion. In support of their dire predictions, the conservatives pointed to incidents of Indian terrorist activity, both at home and overseas. Many had also been disconcerted by the pre-war blusterings of Bernhardi, the German nationalist polemicist, in his *Germany and the Next War*, who exhorted the Germans to promote 'Hindu-Muhammadan' unity in India, in preparation for '[shaking] the foundations of England's high position in the world'.

Cells of terrorist activity, some in league with enemies, had certainly thrived in the febrile pre-war and wartime atmosphere, but the phenomenon was always rather more sensational than substantial. In 1911 German agents had helped to found the Sikh Ghadr (Revolution) Party among disaffected Punjabi migrants in California, who planned to return to India and foment revolution, encouraged by the imminent defeat of England by 'the [German] Fatherland'. At the same time Paris hosted a coterie of elite Bengali malcontents clustered around the intriguing Madame Cama – a Parsi lady revolutionary, originally from Bombay. Meanwhile 'silk-letter' conspirators, who communicated by letters written on yellow silk carried by pilgrims to Mecca, plotted to overthrow the Raj with the aid of Arab 'Wahhabi' Muslims. However, throughout the war British intelligence kept well abreast of all this. The various to-ings and fro-ings of the Oxford-educated German-backed terrorist leader Har Dyal between London and Berlin, were well documented, and a cache of German arms heading for

Bombay via Bangkok was easily confiscated. The US-based conspirators were as leaky as a punctured sieve, teeming with double-agents and opportunists. The whole operation to organize a rebellion in the Punjab was blown after a gossipy exchange of information with a British-paid network of Czech informers in New York. Even the infamous silk letters were intercepted in the Punjab, and by early 1917 all fears of a German-backed terrorist insurrection in India had evaporated.

But Bolshevism soon replaced the German threat in the fevered imaginations of British officials. Perhaps the most convincing case for imminent revolution was among the Muslim tribesmen of the North West Frontier, who were thought to be in cahoots with Lenin and the Comintern. These previously loyal and doughty warriors seemed to have morphed, in the British imagination, into hostile conspirators at some point in 1915. In August of that year a 'Free Government of India' was declared to be operating out of Kabul, funded, it was rumoured, initially by the Kaiser and, after the October Revolution, by the Bolsheviks. There was said to be a plan to invade India through Afghanistan, fomenting revolution along the way. Obeidullah, a Sindi Sikh who had converted to Islam and had founded the 'Army of God' in 1916, was thought to be the principal Bolshevik agent. This was, however, a somewhat top-heavy force, boasting twelve field marshals and forty-eight generals, but only two captains, one lieutenant and no 'other ranks'. Neither was there any evidence that the Afghan Amir had any intention of hostaging his independence to this Islamo-Bolshevik army, however lavishly officered.

India's Great War conspirators were woefully short on arms, ideology and organizational elan. Arms supplies were cripplingly expensive and unreliably sourced (largely from Afghan fruit-dealers or foreign sailors), while the groups were endlessly fissuring into ever smaller warring factions: nationalists and Pan-Islamists squabbled, orthodox Sikhs rowed with the clean-shaven Hindus and so forth. In Bengal the revolutionaries split into two irreconcilable factions, the Yugantar group and the Dacca Anushilan Samiti. Bureaucratic hierarchies and centralized command-and-control structures were conspicuous by their absence, and charisma, personal ties and guru-disciple relationships only partly filled the vacuum. Furthermore, impulsive and sporadic acts of terror, rather than strategically planned campaigns of sabotage, were the order of the day. And finally, to this catalogue of revolutionary incompetence must be added an almost complete absence of popular support within India itself. Indeed, when the Ghadarites did stage an uprising in the Punjab in February 1915 it was swiftly foiled after betrayal by a mole, and the Punjabis themselves promptly rallied to the British, eagerly assisting in rounding up the terrorists.

Despite the somewhat farcical character of these movements, they provided ample grist for the rhetorical mills of Raj conservatives, and were offered as proof that Indian youth was riddled with sedition. Secret police were sent into Bengali high schools to flush out pubertal revolutionaries, among whom the seeds of sedition were sown in 'dark and ill-ventilated rooms and [by] the soul-destroying process of unceasing cram'. Meanwhile the *madrasas* of the western Punjab were scoured for Bolsheviks, Islamicists and other forms of dissident exotica, and in June 1917 the indomitable Annie Besant was arrested. A state of acute paranoid anxiety gripped much of the British administration, impeding clarity of thought. Rather than rallying the moderates, the Raj seemed to be set on alienating them. Conservatives had already scored a notable victory with the 1915 Defence of India Act, which brought a massive increase in security and surveillance. This act was closely modelled on the British Defence of the Realm Act passed specifically to deal with acts of Irish sedition. The act allowed for detention without trial, trial without jury, force-feeding of hunger strikers, indefinite detention and so forth, for the vague category of 'political crimes'. These ranged from 'extravagance of speech' to 'trafficking with the King's enemies'. The already hawk-like gaze of British surveillance became even more acute as the Bengal Special Branch acquired an extra five hundred men.

This machinery was tackling a threat that was not only small but diminishing. While in 1910 there had been over forty terrorist 'outrages' in Bengal, by 1917 the number had plummeted to ten. In 1919 a camp was established, at great expense, in Upper Burma to house revolutionary seditionists, but it had to be closed six months later owing to a lack of prisoners. Nevertheless, paranoia did not ease. The passage of the notorious Rowlatt Acts in 1918 extended the Defence of India Act and its extraordinary powers of detention indefinitely. The acts had been spurred by the alarming Rowlatt inquiry of late 1917, which continued to insist that India was enmeshed in intricate networks of seditious conspiracy. Meanwhile back in Britain, politicians issued blood-curdling alarms about the incendiary effect of reckless reform and the need to insert the iron fist of repression into the silk glove of concession. 'The more democratic the Government becomes the more fatal disorder is likely to be', Austen Chamberlain, Secretary of State for India until the spring of 1917, insisted, while Viceroy Chelmsford feared 'the sudden release from restraint and control of the forces of anarchy'.

At the same time as the leash of imperial control was tightened, efforts were being made by reformists to loosen it, with some form of power sharing. Progressive sentiment within the Cabinet was, however, rather weak; the most ardent advocate of generous reform was Chamberlain's successor as Secretary of State, Edwin Montagu. But Montagu was a rather isolated figure among an imperial executive which sought to concede the minimum required to ensure continued Indian co-operation. After much controversy Montagu issued the celebrated 'Declaration' of August 1917, which appeared, prima facie, to offer generous concessions to the Indian nationalists. It asserted clearly, and for the first time, that the goal of British power in India was the 'gradual realization of responsible government'.

However the 'realization of responsible government', regardless of how gradual, encountered bitter opposition from Indian officialdom. Moreover, Montagu had incautiously denounced the Government of India as 'too wooden, too iron, too inelastic, too antediluvian to be of any use for the modern purposes we have in mind'. These sentiments had not endeared him to the colonial administration; throughout the summer and autumn of 1918 the unfortunate Montagu toured the subcontinent supposedly to gather opinion and thrash out fine legislative detail, but in fact cajoling or pleading with the truculent mandarinate. Surprised at this official hostility, he concluded that his sympathy for Indian nationalism was a consequence of his being 'an oriental myself', and many others shared this opinion, though they expressed it in more starkly anti-Semitic terms. The whole experience destroyed his health, and after the final publication of the Government of India

Bill in late 1918 he retreated to a mental asylum for a lengthy 'cure'. It was not only Montagu's health that suffered as a result of these protracted negotiations, consultations and intra-imperial wrangles. The famous 1917 Declaration had already been diluted by dexterous redraftings, many supplied by the hand of Curzon, whose insistence on the slippery term 'responsible' rather than 'self' government rendered its meaning highly ambiguous. As for the Act itself, the devil of imperial power had always been in the constitutional detail, and the enigmatic import of its elegant and lofty phrases took a further twenty years to clarify.

Post-war reform was not confined to politics; some of the main initiatives came in the economic sphere where there had been a distinct change in attitude among many in government as a consequence of the war. At the turn of the century there had, under Curzon himself, been signs of a new interest in modernizing the Indian economy, but that tendency was now much more pronounced. Throughout the inter-war era India was the subject of a plethora of ambitious plans and projects for 'improvement'. Industrialization was espoused, schemes for urban beautification floated, economic planning contemplated, the nature of Indian banking, peasant spending and even Hindu sex lives were all enquired into. Though driven in part by wartime exigencies, these innovations were not entirely pragmatic. Behind it all was a shift in ideas, especially among a younger generation of Raj officialdom influenced by the progressive Fabian faith in the transformative power of an activist state prevalent in wartime Britain. Moreover, there was an understanding among some that if the colonial relationship was to endure it had to be put on a new footing, not just politically, but socially and economically. Progressive officials and politicians in Britain and India seemed to acknowledge that the old foundations of Indo-British trade – with Britain as exporter of industrial goods and India as exporter of primary commodities – had to change to reflect the changing realities of both economies. An industrializing India would be a better market for British machine tools and more advanced consumer goods, while it would also be less prone to the instability and poverty of a poor agrarian economy.

An early harbinger of the new interest in social and economic development was the ambitious, if ill-fated, Indian Industrial Commission of 1916–19, appointed to formulate policies to promote modern industry. It was headed by the visionary official Thomas Holland, who had pioneered state factories in Madras and had done sterling work at the Munitions Board during the war. Its principal recommendations were state provision of specialist advice, technical education, investment in infrastructure, the encouragement of industrial banks, state investment in the private sector and the creation of state-owned 'pioneer' factories. Equally revolutionary was the decision to violate the Raj's almost century-long commitment to free trade by setting up a Fiscal Commission to look into suitable cases for protection. Some proposed that this should take the form of 'imperial preference' – protection targeted to promote Indo-British trade and pull the two countries' economies closer together. But the most startling of all these economic initiatives were tentative steps towards economic planning. In 1932 the then finance minister in the Government of India, George Schuster, proposed the formulation of a 'five-year economic plan':

However much supporters of old-fashioned individualistic ideas may dislike government interference . . . [they are] merely burying their head in the sand . . . Practically every government in the world is now in actual practice interfering drastically in the flow of trade.

The government looked into the possibility of setting up a Council of Experts to advise it, along with an Economic Advisory Council made up of British and Indian industrialists, bankers, agriculturalists and commercial specialists.

But little came of these bold ideas. Finance (or rather lack of it), political expediency and administrative conservatism were chronic brakes on all new initiatives. Britain had borrowed £250 million from the Raj during the Great War, and military expenditure was pushed up from Rs. 233 million (26 per cent of the Raj's budget) in 1912–13 to Rs. 365 million (32 per cent) in 1918, absorbing two-thirds of all government spending throughout the inter-war period. This did not leave much money for anything else. More damaging still was the impact of the political reforms. The Industrial Commission had stressed the need for its recommendations to be implemented by an all-India central state department and, indeed, the Munitions Board briefly became the Board of Industries and Munitions. But within three years the ideas had fallen under the wheels of political expediency. London insisted that industry become one of the areas transferred to the control of Indian ministers in the new provincial assemblies, reasoning that, given their lack of power, whatever they did wouldn't matter much. In the end, the only elements of the Commission's proposals to survive were the creation of central cadres of specialist technical advisers, but local jealousies and financial stringency soon killed these off too. By 1923 nothing remained of the project. Holland was dismissed in 1921 and went to work for the princely state of Mysore, which subsequently underwent a remarkable industrial renaissance.

Tariff protection and planning suffered a similar fate. The Fiscal Commission was carefully packed to ensure that a rather limited and unimaginative view of protection emerged, not one that might promote a more radical synergy between the British and Indian economies. The government also cavilled at levels of tariff protection that might bite into customs revenue. The Tariff Board itself was merely an advisory and ad hoc body lacking the power to initiate inquiries and enforce recommendations. Planning was similarly emasculated. Annual state capital expenditure actually fell, from Rs. 27 million between 1920 and 1930 to Rs. 6 million between 1931 and 1939. A central office of statistics – essential to any planning body – was not established until the Second World War. Schuster's notion of a Keynesian-inspired scheme to use government borrowing to boost the inter-war economy through such projects as a state-funded Civil Aviation Authority and subsidizing the wages of cotton growers, were opposed by the Imperial Bank. His unsympathetic successor as finance minister, James Grigg, denounced such Keynesian ideas as either 'silly or vicious', because India was too backward:

The representative Indian is not to be found among the few tens of thousands of noisy politicians, journalists, stock exchange gamblers and clerks; he is the almost naked creature who squats among his crops by day and breeds like a rabbit at night.

Thus efforts to remould the economic relationship between Britain and India foundered; by the late 1930s Indian business was looking to the United States and Germany as possible partners in the future industrialization of India.

A similar conservatism blighted efforts to respond effectively to the inter-war crisis in Indian agriculture. Having grown fairly steadily from the 1860s, agricultural growth began to tail off at the turn of the twentieth century and prices of export crops fell steadily in the 1920s, collapsing to less than half their pre-war value between 1929 and 1931. Alongside the short-term crisis of the Depression were more long-term problems. Growing population pressure exacerbated the tendency for farms to fragment into uneconomically minute plots: the Agricultural Commission of 1928 recorded an instance of a 'farm' of only one third of an acre; elsewhere a coconut tree was recorded as an 'estate' whose ownership was disputed by several members of the same family. Relatively high revenue demands, poor infrastructure, unpredictable environmental dangers, drought, malaria and the high cost of rural credit all combined to further immiserate large swathes of the peasantry.

Government anxiety about the potential political and economic consequences of agricultural stagnation became acute in the wake of the catastrophic collapse in peasant incomes following the Great Depression of the late 1920s and early 1930s. It was clear to Delhi that this was fuelling recruitment to the nationalist cause. As with the industrial sector, imaginative and progressive policies were proffered by some British and Indian officials. The establishment of credit co-operatives to ease peasant dependence on money-lenders, investment in fertilizers and insecticide, and agricultural colleges to teach better farming techniques were all mooted. In an early intimation of the Green Revolution of the 1960s, research into the development of new high-productivity seed types was also considered. However, financial stringency and official fear of the political consequences of too radical an intervention in peasant lives combined to frustrate most of these proposals.

Moreover, persisting orientalist prejudices about the nature of the Indian peasant also blocked economic reform, colouring even the most esoteric debates, such as those on the rupee exchange rate in the late 1920s. A surreal dispute developed between advocates and opponents of devaluation of the rupee concerning its effects on the Indian peasant. Proponents of devaluation, while conceding it would raise the price of Manchester textile imports, making the cost of new clothes prohibitive, maintained that the move would still favour the peasant by making their crops cheaper on foreign markets, boosting exports and peasant incomes. Opponents countered that, on the contrary, the Indian peasant would prefer to be well-dressed and starving, for he would then, at least, be able decently to beg. Behind these curious deliberations lurked old ideas of peasant fecklessness and the need for 'uplift' as the key to agricultural improvement.

According to 'uplift' theory, peasant poverty was not caused by poor infrastructure, lack of money, environmental depredations or the unequal distribution of land; the real obstacle to prosperity was the Indian peasant himself. The leading proponent of this school of thought was Frank Lugard Brayne, a highly energetic and awesomely self-confident District Officer in the Punjab. He came to India with impeccable imperial credentials. The son of evangelicals and nephew of the African pro-consul Lord Lugard, he had won both the Kadir cup for pig-sticking and the Military Cross for bravery under fire. After service in the Great War he received his first 'independent charge', the district of Gurgaon 25 miles south-east of Delhi, a famine-ridden and disease-prone tract of land populated largely by an isolated and impoverished semi-tribal group, the Meos. Brayne reasoned that if he could 'uplift' the Meos he could 'uplift' anyone. And so began his 'Gurgaon Experiment' in rural reconstruction.

The message and the campaign mostly focused on the moral failings of the Meos. Brayne argued that because the Indian peasant was already inclined to idleness, canal irrigation, which made farming easy, was a very bad thing. The ancient Persian wheel method of water lifting, which entailed heavy physical labour, would be much more morally uplifting. Peasants were also wasteful, as demonstrated by their profligate use of manure as cooking fuel. Waste could be curbed, he insisted, by the use of his specially designed 'magic *bhoosa* box' – a sort of primitive Thermos flask made of two wooden boxes, which supposedly conserved cooking fuel. Thrift was a key virtue, and for Brayne the great enemy of thrift was the peasants' predilection for jewellery. He campaigned against offending gems and gewgaws; earrings were ripped from the earlobes and clanking anklets had to be removed in his presence. However, like many of the British, his greatest preoccupation was 'filth'. 'Uplift', he thundered, began with 'disciplined defecation'. Soon the unfortunate Meos were diverted from farming to digging state-of-the-art latrines.

Morally uplifting though all this effort may have been, it was less than effective. The Persian wheel method was costly, it used up valuable bullock power to lift the pots of water from the wells, and the water recovered was saline. Laboriously dug latrines soon became ideal breeding grounds for mosquitoes. Magic *bhoosa* boxes were not popular with the village women and, as their husbands pointed out, there was really little point conserving dung for manure as the light, sandy soils of Gurgaon could not absorb it. The peasants were right about 'thrift' too, for during the Depression it was the sale of offending gold gewgaws that, for many, provided a hedge against utter destitution.

Undaunted by peasant scepticism, Brayne bombarded them with propaganda. He himself gave hundreds of lectures illustrated with magic lantern slides, and even made a film: *Tale of Gurgaon, or Heaven Helps Those Who Help Themselves*. Village headmen were enjoined to behave like boy scouts, and Brayne approvingly reported a rather improbable encounter with one local, who met him with a scout salute and announced,

we are all Boy scouts nowadays, you know, we find it such splendid training . . . We have a good wash on Saturday, and on Sunday morning, after tidying up the village, we put on our best clothes or play our good old games for the rest of the day and in the evening we sometimes have a lecture or a magic lantern.

Most peasants, however, complained that the films were boring and what they wanted was entertainment. Brayne's propaganda was more successful among his colleagues. Despite its eccentricity, the whole Gurgaon enterprise was lent a certain credibility by its lucky timing. Launched in 1920, the region appeared to do well on the back of a series of favourable monsoons. Brayne had left the district in 1927 just before the Depression cut a swathe through peasant India. Buoyed by this apparent success, he was made Commissioner for Rural Reconstruction in 1933, and his handbooks became standard texts in many provincial agricultural departments.

The British reforms had little effect on the crisis, and agriculture remained in a parlous condition until the later 1930s. This combined with the striking surge in population growth after the First World War to drive mass migration into India's towns and cities. Between 1921 and 1931 the population of India's cities grew at double the rate of rural areas, whereas forty years earlier they had grown only half as fast. Established cities like Bombay and Calcutta were engulfed by new migrants, while newer ones, such as Kanpur in the United Provinces, grew exponentially. By 1931 it had a population density of 22,000 per square mile, and nearly half of these people were recent migrants. As striking as the pace of urban population growth was its extreme gender bias. In 1931 there were only 696 women to every 1000 men, and only 9 per cent of the workforce were women. The towns and cities of India were strikingly masculine environments.

Many were attracted by the jobs created by rapid industrialization. The inter-war era witnessed the sudden flourishing of Indian business houses. By the end of the 1930s it was new Indian business houses, not old British expatriate firms, that led the field in new industries such as motor vehicles, electricals and chemicals. The most dramatic example of this Indian business success was the house of Birla, which was second only to the older Parsi enterprise of Tatas in terms of the size and scope of its interests by the eve of the Second World War. The Birlas were Marwaris (a traditional Hindu commercial caste), who, like many Marwaris, had left their native Rajasthan in the mid-nineteenth century to do business in the booming colonial cities of Bombay and Calcutta. The Birla family firm had established itself in the opium trade, had then become agents, *banias*, to British firms, acting as their intelligence in the internal Indian markets which they knew so much better than the rather insular British. During the First World War the *banias* made enormous fortunes in currency and commodity speculation, and they ventured into jute and cotton manufacturing – areas traditionally dominated by Europeans and Parsis. They also began to buy up shares in the very British firms they had once served. By the end of the Second World War, many British companies discovered, to their intense dismay, that they were in fact owned by their own Marwari brokers.

Hundreds of less spectacular examples of Indian commercial enterprise could be given; the result was that in the inter-war era small factories and workshops manufacturing chemicals, dyes and textiles, offering work to poor migrants, sprang up in many towns and cities. Those who could not get factory work would be found in construction, municipal services, workshops, hawking and tonga driving.

The phenomenal growth of Indian cities in the inter-war era presented a complex and potentially destabilizing amalgam of economic, social and political problems, which demanded urgent intervention. But it also presented opportunities: a chance to mould these new urban Indians into a more cohesive society. A group of progressive urban planners was eager to do this, and particularly influential was Patrick Geddes. Yet again, various interests conspired to undermine this progressive impulse, however, and thwart Geddes' idealism. Geddes, the father of the British town planning movement, was in India between 1916 and 1919 to propagate his notion 'The Revivance of Cities'. India, like many other 'modernizing' countries, was plagued by what he termed 'Paleotechnic' or slum-ridden industrial cities; what was required was their transformation into 'Neotechnic' ones. Neotechnic cities would not only be beautiful but also morally improving: the creation of 'garden cities' which, through creative use of open space, would 'promote literacy, sanitation and good citizenship'. He had no time for colonial notions of crude westernization, but had fallen under the influence of the late nineteenth-century Hindu mystic Swami Vivekananda, and the temple towns of south India, which embodied, in his opinion, the essence of Indian spirituality.

What emerged from these influences was an organic view of how Indian cities should develop. Urban revivification had to be 'indigenized'. This was to be achieved by yoking modern notions of town-planning to traditional religious rituals. Through the tactful manipulation of religious festivals messages about urban renewal could be transmitted to the poor and thus help transform the lowly migrant into the new ideal national citizen. In 1917 the town of Indore became the site of a curious experiment. Diwali (the festival of lights welcoming Ram's triumph over the demonic Ravana) was restaged as a dramatic lesson in better sewage management. The intention was to illustrate the defeat of the god of dirt by the god of purity. In this revamped procession, Ram and Lakshmi were recast as the deities of cleanliness, mounted on a symbolically white elephant. Following them was Ravana, here decked out as the god of filth, accompanied by a gigantic model rat. More quotidian representations of filth succeeded him: a perambulating retinue of 'slum' floats exuding a 'general air of misery and dirt'. Bringing up the rear were the forces of goodness: the goddess of Indore City bearing a copy of the new city plan, sweepers wielding new brooms and garlanded bullock-driven refuse carts. Geddes had stipulated that as a reward the procession would be specially diverted through the cleanest locales of the town, and this competition had allegedly inspired the removal of over 6000 cartloads of rubbish.

The whole spectacle was described by Geddes as 'the symbol of the democracy of civic service', but it soon transpired that democracy, or at least democracy as it was practised in inter-war India, and civic service were ill-suited bed-fellows. Geddes did not stay in India to see his plans through; that task fell to more orthodox Raj officials, such as A. L. Saunders, Commissioner of Lucknow, who considered Geddes' schemes were likely to prove a 'source of friction' between the government and the poor, the most 'dangerous and easily excited class'. Moreover, town-planning, like industrial policy, took second place to political reformism. The 1919 provincial assembly reforms transferred urban affairs into the hands of elected municipal councils, but the electoral franchise was heavily biased towards the monied mercantile middle classes, who were disinclined to tax themselves more heavily in order to beautify their cities for the benefit of the poor. Thus the management of India's towns and cities lay not with utopian dreamers like Geddes, but with hard-headed officials and burghers more concerned with cost control. They considered ideas like Geddes' expensive and dangerous, and believed that his organicism, designed to coax and educate the poor into modern citizenship, would take far too long. What were needed were quick and cheap methods of dealing with India's filthy and congested conurbations.

Slum demolition and clearance, rather than elaborate and educative rituals, became the chief occupation of the new Civic Improvement

Trusts set up to implement urban planning. New powers gave these bodies rights of compulsory purchase and the *kuccha* (mud) hutments of the poor became the primary target as they occupied what came to be seen as valuable inner-city land. To the Committee for the Improvement of Kanpur this meant, essentially 'the removal of the superfluous population . . . they must be made to go', and in 1929 9000 of the poor – largely petty hawkers and traders – were 'dehoused', as slum clearance was euphemistically dubbed. Supposedly they would be 'rehoused' on new land bought outside the city, but it soon transpired that most of this new land had been cornered by property developers for rehousing more prosperous classes. By the 1930s Lucknow had apparently become 'a paradise for contractors and retired officials who have come to settle here', according to one report. The poor, by contrast, ended up in *kuccha* hutments and shanties on low-lying swampy areas lacking basic sanitation.

Urban improvement policies also tended to make the poor poorer by removing them from their places of work and heavily taxing them. Such policies rendered petty trading more and more difficult. In 1926 a community of Lucknow pulse-grinders was displaced from their market location, supposedly a site of 'immorality', and relocated faraway from its workshops, with no means of transport. In Kanpur a moving magistrates' court was introduced to tour the city and levy instant fines on offending carters, hawkers and labourers who had encroached on to the pavement; tonga and cart drivers were charged a wheel tax and butchers, milkmen and poulterers had to pay for special health licences. Much of this was designed to raise revenue and keep taxes on middle-class residents low.

The poor themselves often resisted their ghettoization and impoverishment through violent protest, alarming the middle classes even further. Having been benignly regarded as feckless rustics prone to gambling, prostitution and drink, the urban poor now assumed a more sinister aspect as an unruly, crime-ridden and violent mob. One Indian police official summed up widespread anxieties in 1929, reporting that: 'large bands of lawless folk have come into existence . . . always ready for mischief'. It now seemed to the authorities that this 'mob' was not to be easily tamed into Geddes' ideal citizens; firmer measures were required. The obvious solution was more rigorous policing, but police manpower was actually reduced in the inter-war period. The United Provinces' force declined from 88,000 in 1922 to 52,000 in 1923, and spending fell again in the Depression years. In straightened financial circumstances a tough policing policy did not mean more police – it meant armed police.

From the 1920s armed police were more and more frequently used in both real and anticipated disorders, from religious festivals to labour strikes. In 1927 an emergency reserve corps was created, armed with the latest weaponry and better paid than the regular police. In the mid-1930s a special force of 700 was authorized in United Provinces, complete with motor transport and telephone communications. Emergency forces were not, however, always on hand and ingenious impro-visation took place. One United Provinces town official, fearing an outbreak of disorder during a religious festival, spread the rumour (wholly untrue) that a regiment of mounted European volunteers was waiting just outside the perimeter. The authorities had, in fact, managed to enlist the services of only a solitary European. This plucky volunteer, decked out in uniform, paraded about the streets on horse-back brandishing a mini-armoury. By the early 1930s, armed police had become the backbone of civil administration, as the Raj and its allies considered that only the ferocious show of force could maintain authority.

Policing was often brutal. At religious processions the accom-panying police were ordered to fire at any sign of disorder. Curfews were routinely imposed during 'tense' periods, during which people visiting other neighbourhoods, or just fetching water, were liable to be arrested for loitering. The police were also associated with breaking up strikes and political pickets during nationalist rallies.

Yet despite police heavy-handedness during the 1920s, Hindu-Muslim and inter-caste violence was becoming endemic in many Indian cities. Riots of increasing violence and cruelty broke out in Amritsar and Agra, in Delhi in 1924, Indore and Lucknow in 1925, and Calcutta in 1926. In 1929 it was Bombay's turn, but the most massive and lethal riot of the era occurred in Kanpur in 1931. Observers at the time (and since) viewed this increasing violence as a natural, inherent feature of the Indian poor. British and Indian middle classes of the time assumed that what they were seeing was simply the reproduction in the cities of traditional rural culture. There was nothing to be done except apply tough policing. However, the causes of communal violence were rooted not in traditional mentalities, but in the conditions and politics of the modern city.

Much of the explanation lies in the extreme poverty and insecurity of the urban lower classes. Most were Shudras – lower caste pastoral groups – who formed the backbone of the migrant unskilled working class. But many were also dalits, who before the First World War had ended up in the cities as sweepers, scavengers or servants, occupations for which there was diminishing demand by the 1920s. Many towns also had colonies of Muslim artisans, weavers, dyers and embroiderers whose jobs were being destroyed by cheap imports and manufactures. Some became bricklayers, others worked in leather shops or as cigarette factory workers.

The labour market for the poor and unskilled was therefore increasingly overcrowded and intense rivalry for jobs meant that Hindus, Muslims and dalits saw themselves as competitors, not comrades, especially as employers, predominantly high-caste Hindus, tended to discriminate in favour of Shudra workers. Competition for housing, or just pavement space, was also fierce in an era of strenuous 'de-housing'. Soon urban workforces and neighbourhoods became divided along lines of caste and community, ferociously competing for jobs, space and security. The institutions that might have ameliorated these tensions did not do so. It proved difficult to organize stable trade unions that united the different caste and religious groups among such a fluid workforce, and community rivalries were often exploited by competing union organizers. In the Bombay textile strike of 1931, for instance, the communist union leaders tried to build solidarity among Hindu workers by spreading rumours that the Muslim Pathan workers, who had been brought in as strike-breakers, were kidnapping Hindu children. Likewise the police did not operate as impartial arbitrators in community disputes and the state offered no assistance with housing. In the absence of modern labour organization, arbitration or municipal housing, the poor formed their own protection networks.

One manifestation of this process was the emergence in poor communities of the 'Dada' ('elder brother'), in essence neighbourhood godfathers filling the vacuum left by the state, unions and the police.

Usually they had proved their mettle as great fighters in local wrestling competitions, and they could be involved in a number of neighbourhood activities – labour recruiters (jobbers), wrestling-club owners, organizers of religious festivals, managers of local housing committees or the chairmen of caste associations. They could also play the role of rent and debt-collectors, turn out the vote on election day and, on occasion, break strikes. They enjoyed a reputation for getting things done and gained much local prestige, often acting as arbitrators in local disputes.

The poor were not just interested in jobs and welfare. They also used their caste and community associations to gain respect, and they did so, in particular, by promoting various brands of aggressive religiosity. The Hindu middle classes had taken enthusiastically to temple-building, festival-sponsoring and extravagant displays of devotion as assertions of status and bids for prestige. Now poorer groups, too, adopted religion as a form of political expression. Religious organizations multiplied in poorer neighbourhoods, and the poor were more prominent in religious festivals and processions, transforming their previously rather staid and sober character by the additions of clowns, street theatre and acrobatics. The poor also promoted their own favoured festivals. One such was Holi, which drew on Shudra folk tales which heroized the lower castes. Holi was especially popular, involving the ebullient hurling of coloured powder at one's social superiors. It is intended to subvert, temporarily, the Hindu caste hierarchy, turning the world upside-down and putting the Shudras on top. By the 1930s Holi, now a seven-day event, had become the main festival of north Indian bazaars and remains one of the most popular festivals of India today.

This new religiosity was also connected with community defence, and thus promoted a sacralized martial culture. *Akharas* (wrestling clubs) and quasi-military defence and volunteer corps were established by Shudra groups, which taught drilling, marching, wrestling and *lathi* wielding, and often formed the basis of armed neighbourhood patrols. Again there was an element of emulation of the better-off in this. The image of Hinduism had become much more martial and aggressive under the influence of politicians such as Tilak in Bombay. Now the Shudras presented themselves as competitors of the higher castes, portraying themselves as a resurgent army of Hinduism, better defenders of the faith against Islam than the effete higher castes. When the British tried to ban a Ramlila festival in Allahabad after Muslims objected to loud music, members of Shudra *akharas* sought to outdo the protests of Hindu merchants by forming a *Khuni Dal* or Suicide Corps, pledged to sacrifice their lives to uphold the triumphal procession of Ram.

These popular Shudra organizations began to mesh with more elite organizations, like the high-caste Hindu reform movement, the Arya Samaj. This was a mutually beneficial relationship, for while high-caste Aryas sought to bolster Hindu solidarity in the towns by reaching out to lower castes, Shudras were keen to gain the respectability conferred by adopting pious Arya practices, and thus distinguish themselves from the more lowly dalits. During the 1920s Hindu festivals were increasingly adapted to make them more socially inclusive and attractive to the Shudra group. The Allahabad Ramlila procession of 1928 had a novel tableau, featuring a sweeper and a Brahman sitting together under the slogan 'The True United Organization of Hindus'. They encouraged new forms of worship among low-caste Hindus, especially the vigorous blowing of conches outside mosques, and performed *Nautanki* plays, designed to inflame Shudra passions with stories of Muslim fanatics, kidnappers of women and children and desecrators of shrines. *Aurangzebe*, ostensibly a dramatization of the life of the seventeenth-century Mughal emperor, was imbued with the message that Islam was 'born of violence and would always remain tied to religious warfare'. Unsurprisingly, the notion that Hindus were at war with Muslims soon gained widespread credence.

Muslims fought back. Soon they were forming their own *akharas*, often in defence against this highly assertive Hinduism. By 1930 every Muslim neighbourhood had its own volunteer force patrolling their area. They wore green badges and Turkish caps, carried red flags with white crescents, and would gather together for processions and drilling issuing words of command in Persian, chanting Allah-o-Akbar (God is Great) or Islam-zindabad (Victory to Islam).

Intense competition for work, space and respect, accompanied by religiously charged martiality, were an incendiary partnership. Secular conflicts swiftly became intermingled with religious passions. Previously unknown spiritual paraphernalia, shrines, statues and relics would mysteriously materialize at disputed sites. A market improvement scheme in Allahabad in the early 1920s that was seen by Muslim petty traders as a ploy to promote the interests of Hindu greengrocers escalated into violence when a Muslim graveyard was 'discovered'. People also became far more sensitized to supposed religious insults. Cow-killing and music before mosques, activities which had not occasioned much comment fifty years earlier, now became one of the most frequent causes of riots. In 1926, a 500-strong procession of singing Arya Samajists passed before a mosque in Calcutta and sparked off riots in which 128 were killed and 11,000 injured. When the government attempted to ban Hindu street music at Muslim prayer times, Hindus argued that playing music was a matter of *dharma*, or duty. But territory not theology was the real issue: music before mosques was an invasion of aural space.

The most savage riots of the period erupted in Kanpur in late March 1931. Lasting several days they engulfed nearly all the poor neighbourhoods. Between 300 and 400 were killed and 1200 injured; during the violence 23 mosques and 37 temples were gutted. The riots arose from Hindu frustration at Muslim apathy towards Congress's Civil Disobedience campaign then being conducted, but the immediate catalyst was the burning of a mosque. Throughout the riots the police were conspicuous by their absence, as was the local British magistrate who had fled in fear. He later faced furious criticism for not intervening when the mosque was burnt, action that many agreed would undoubtedly have reduced the subsequent violence. This incident typified the problems of wicket imperialism. The state limited its role to that of umpire, leaving the pitch clear for an assortment of caste, religious and community organizations to compete for influence and ascendancy, often with ferociously violent results.

It was against this backdrop of economic crisis and increasing caste and religious conflict that the Raj experimented with political reform. And it was on the field of politics, and especially the response to nationalism, that two very different British strategies met. Liberal progressives such as Montagu favoured a more integrative approach, compromise with the nationalists and power-sharing, not only in the regions but also at the centre – India as a single team. The conservative advocates of wicket imperialism pursued the politics of provincializ-ation, community identity and group division – India as many teams. Ultimately the wicket-imperialists won out, because it appeared, short-sightedly perhaps, but persuasively nevertheless, that it was only by encouraging the teams opposing the nationalists that the Raj itself could hang on to power. But the price of hanging on was, ultimately, India's unity as an independent nation-state.

For Montagu and other British progressives the constitutional experiments which began in 1919 were, in part at least, inspired by noble motives – to democratize, modernize and even to unify. But such idealists were in a minority in Delhi and London and the reforms themselves were born of the forced realization, effected initially by the Great War, that the *durbar* Raj was as inwardly empty as it was outwardly impressive. It lacked both the money and the administrative structures to impose radical reform and retain legitimacy. Its solution was half-hearted reform, disguised as devolution and designed to maintain control of those aspects of India essential to the British imperial state while out-housing the rest – the nation-building tasks – to provincial Indian politicians. The 1919 reforms created new provin-cial assemblies with elected majorities and limited cabinet power-sharing with Indian ministers. At the all-India level, a new elected assembly materialized, but it was purely consultative. And the system was only very partially democratic. Electorates of 5.5 million in the provinces and 1.5 million for the centre (out of a population of 350 million) were created. Even at the provincial level, moreover, full executive powers were not transferred to Indian ministers. Instead a rather elaborate hydra-headed power-sharing system known as 'dyarchy' was established, whereby officials ran the most important departments and Indian ministers dealt with the rest; joint meetings of the full cabinet of ministers were held purely at the (British) governor's discretion. This was reform as a training in the nets of government. The experiment was intended to run for ten years, and if Indians proved themselves sufficiently 'responsible', further increments of power would be bestowed.

The 1919 reforms did not go well. They created eleven elected provincial assemblies. Indians acquired so-called 'transferred' ministries – local government, education, health, commerce and industry and agriculture – while finance and law and order remained in the hands of bureaucrats. The precise powers of Indian ministers were rather unclear. While they supposedly ran the transferred portfolios, ICS departmental secretaries held the real reins of power. Inevitably it proved impossible to fully separate 'reserved' from 'transferred' ministries, making nonsense of co-ordinated policy-making. Some provinces, notably Madras, tried to ease relations between the two dyarchic halves of government by meeting together as a 'Happy Family', but the family was dysfunctional and soon collapsed into a Byzantine array of feuds. Reddi Naidu, an ex-minister, bitterly complained:

Intrigue seems the only way of success. Everybody seems to indulge in it. What for? To get power, to get more influence, to please His Excellency, to be known to have a great place in His Excellency's heart.

The two halves of government worked effectively only in blocking one another. The most important of the ministerial areas not transferred to Indians was finance. Finance ruled all else, but there wasn't much of it. The 1919 reforms had awarded land revenue, a stagnant pool at this time, to the provinces, but from this the central government in Delhi also demanded subventions to help pay off its war debt. The result was a chronic financial crisis. In Madras the development minister was privately known as the 'minister without portfolio', unable to develop anything.

Moreover, despite careful crafting of predominantly rural electorates to scupper the largely urban-based nationalists, Congress soon demonstrated its superior mastery of the new political game by bowling some devastatingly effective googlies at the edifice of reform. In 1920 it organized a widely observed boycott of the first elections, and subsequently the nationalists perfected even more devastating tactics: they used their electoral successes in 1923 and 1926 to block the formation of ministries, vote down finance bills thus forcing the governor to pass the budget by fiat, and generally halt political play. By 1927 it was clear that the dyarchic model was not working and three years ahead of schedule, under mounting Indian pressure and criticism, the British announced that they were pulling up stumps and returning to the pavilion to consider further improvements to the reform wicket.

In 1927, determined to pre-empt the potentially more progressive policies of an incoming Labour government, the Tory Secretary of State, Lord Birkenhead, appointed the seven-man Simon Commission to make recommendations for further reform. Headed by the Liberal politician John Simon, it included the young MP and future Labour Prime Minister Clement Attlee. Birkenhead had provocatively argued that Indians were incapable of agreeing a workable constitution, so Englishmen should do it for them. The commission was all-white, haughtily disdained prior consultation with Indians and was, unsurprisingly, regarded in India as an outrageous insult. The commission was boycotted by Indians when it visited in 1928, and was greeted across the subcontinent with thousands of protestors brandishing black flags and 'Go Back Simon' placards. It briefly solidified the otherwise fragmented particles of Indian political opinion into a stance of outright hostility.

By 1929 the Viceroy, Irwin, realized the forthcoming Simon report was effectively a dead letter and that a grand gesture was now required to rally Indians back to the cause of constitutionalism. Irwin had the insight and imagination to see that the issue was about race: in short, that India must be offered the same status as Britain's white dominions, with some kind of self-government at the central level, not just in the provinces. Having rallied the support of the new Labour government, on 31 October 1929 he declared that it was the opinion of His Majesty's government that 'it is implicit in the declaration of 1917 that the natural issue of India's constitutional progress . . . is the attainment of Dominion Status'. Dominionhood had been defined by Prime Minister Balfour in 1926 to mean a system of 'autonomous communities within the British Empire, equal in status, in no way subordinate one to another in any aspect of their domestic or external affairs, though united by common allegiance to the crown'. Birkenhead saw the point immediately and tartly expressed the views of more reactionary opinion: 'We are not dealing with the case of a daughter nation of our own creed and of our own blood.' Irwin however stuck to his guns, explaining, 'you could not, without losing

India from the Commonwealth, hold out a future for her less honourable than that to which constitutional development had brought Canada or Australia'.

Nevertheless, Irwin's intentions were slightly cloudy, at least to observers. Writing to the British Conservative leader, Stanley Baldwin, in 1929, he drew a distinction between what a British man might understand by self-government, and an Indian reading, i.e. a commitment to self-government in the distant future. But he told Gandhi that dominion status was meant in the full Balfour sense. Congress, along with other representatives of Indian opinion, was invited to a Round Table Conference in London to discuss the proposals. Congress, however, demanded that dominion status be announced immediately; the conference would simply be a forum for thrashing out the details. Negotiations broke down in December 1929, and in January 1930 Congress launched the Civil Disobedience campaign. Irwin now had to fall back on what he referred to as the 'stable elements of the community' – princes, landowners, businessmen, retired officials, prominent Hindus, Muslims, Sikhs, Parsis, Anglo-Indians and 'depressed classes' (Shudras and dalits) – to make a success of his revolutionary experiment in joint consultative constitutional talks.

On 4 October the *Viceroy of India* set sail from Bombay carrying most of the Indian delegates to the first session of the conference in London. There were 58 from British India and 16 from the princely states. The Indian Liberals were led by Sir Tej Bahadur Sapru, a Kashmiri Brahman lawyer and old friend of Motilal Nehru. He was staking his career and reputation on getting an agreement, having been denounced as a collaborator by Congress. The Muslim team included the Aga Khan and Muhammad Ali Jinnah, but its most powerful influence, Fazl-i-Husain, the leader of Punjabi Muslims, though a looming *éminence grise*, was not physically there. The Hindu right was championed by Dr Balkrishna Moonje, a Poona eye surgeon and president of Hindu Mahasabha. The 'minor' minorities were headed by the dalit rhetorician Dr Ambedkar. All went as nominees of the Viceroy, with no popular mandate. The rest of the delegates comprised eight British government and eight opposition members, including the Labour Prime Minister Ramsay MacDonald, who had written two books on Indian reform, Sam Hoare, a Conservative MP with an interest in India, and the former Viceroy Lord Reading for the Liberals.

Even before the *Viceroy of India* reached port, disagreement had broken out among the floating delegation and unshiftable positions were being marked out. The Muslims and the Indian Liberals believed the main difficulty would lie in reaching agreement on the representation of the non-Hindu minorities, and this had to be solved before there was any constitutional reform at the all-India level. But that was where accord ended. The Muslims insisted on maintaining their separate electorates. Members of the reformed assemblies stood either for the general seats and were elected by largely Hindu voters, or for the separate seats, voted for only by Muslim electors. In provinces where Muslims were a minority they elected a disproportionate (or weighted) number of assembly members, but this was not the case for Hindus where they were minorities. The Muslims wanted to maintain and even increase the proportion of seats elected by the separate electorates. This would effectively give them permanent majorities in the provinces of Bengal and Punjab, where they constituted a majority of the population. In addition, the Muslims sought full provincial status for Sindh and the North West Frontier, taking the tally of Muslim-majority provinces from two to four. The 'minor' minorities were inclined to support the Muslim position. Yet the Hindu right detected a sinister plot. Dr Moonje confided to his diary:

This is a time of great crisis for the Hindu Community; there is a conspiracy between the bureaucracy, the Anglo-Indians and the Muslims to put down the Hindus forever.

The British delegates were not in accord either, with Conservative and Liberal members highly dubious about India ever attaining dominion status.

Surprisingly, the first Round Table Conference went remarkably well. The breakthrough was the notion of an Indian federation, formulated by the Resident of Hyderabad, Lieutenant-Colonel Terence Keyes. The scheme would have meant the end of British India and the creation of a bicameral federal legislature, with representatives of the princely states and provinces in both houses. Prima facie this was the answer to everyone's prayers. It accorded with Irwin's notion of establishing some sort of organic unity of Hindu, Muslim and Princely India, a step on the road to forming a single all-Indian team; William Wedgwood Benn, a Labour member of the British delegation (and Secretary of State for India), saw it as a 'safe' legislature of experienced statesmen rather than 'lawyers and demagogues'; even the Conservative Sam Hoare approved the proposal, as it would strengthen 'the stabilizing influence of the Indian (princely) states', and thus 'rescue British India from the morass into which the doctrinaire Liberalism of Montagu had plunged it'. However these were early days, and though Muslims and the princes appeared to accede, there were ominous signs of dissent.

Meanwhile Congress's Civil Disobedience campaign had been boiling in India. However, by early 1931 Gandhi was willing to parley with the British if the terms were right. During February and March Irwin and Gandhi met like the commanders of two opposing armies to discuss terms. Winston Churchill was horrified by this, declaring, 'it is alarming and also nauseating to see Mr Gandhi, a seditious Middle Temple lawyer, now posing as a *fakir* of a type well known in the East, striding half naked up the steps of the Viceregal palace'. Luckily, Gandhi chose to see this as a compliment and the talks went well. Irwin, later to become the arch-appeaser of Nazi Germany, Lord Halifax, was a courteous, if calculating, High Anglican. He and Gandhi enjoyed a rapport which some attributed to their mutual religiosity, and the Gandhi-Irwin Pact was signed. This was essentially a truce rather than a peace deal, under which Gandhi agreed to suspend Civil Disobedience and attend the second of the Round Table talks later in the year.

In August 1931 Gandhi set sail for London. Though the sole official representative of Congress he was accompanied by a retinue of advisers and several gallons of ritually pure milk (it was forbidden to take a cow on board). He went in Micawberish mood, expecting little but 'hoping that something will turn up to make the conference a success'. He was warmly received even by politicians like the former Viceroy and Liberal hardliner Lord Reading, who had mocked the Mahatma in 1925 as a spent force – 'the last minstrel with his harp'. Gandhi, though only one of 112 delegates, insisted that he alone represented the whole of India – a contentious position to adopt at a conference where the biggest issue was the question of the representation of minorities. His approach to the talks was to employ a version of his *satyagraha* (soul-force) technique – shaming one's opponents into conciliation through love and self-sacrifice. This manifested itself in somewhat quixotic tactics. At one point he offered to issue the Muslims with a 'blank cheque', separate electorates, new provinces, reservations, if they desisted from supporting dalit demands for separate representation. This merely succeeded in alarming the Hindu right, strengthening Muslim delegates' suspicions, and hardening dalit determination to extract the very separate electorate Gandhi so deplored. He was more successful outside the committee room, making quite a hit with the British public, meeting Charlie Chaplin and even taking tea with the King. On this last occasion his scanty approach to wardrobe matters caused some disquiet. Was it appropriate to meet the monarch half-naked? The King, Gandhi quipped, would be wearing enough clothes for both of them. Yet Gandhi's inspired PR couldn't save the conference. With the talks at an impasse he returned to India, via Rome where he met Mussolini, to restart the Civil Disobedience campaign. But the British were ready for him this time and the movement was swiftly and brutally suppressed.

The deadlocking of the second of the Round Table Conference talks was not entirely the result of Gandhi's diplomatic insouciance. The federal idea itself was unravelling, and there was no agreement among the princes or the Muslims about the relative balance of power between centre and province in the putative federation. The princes split three ways, while Punjabi Muslims wanted a weak centre and strong provinces, and Jinnah, leading the Muslim League, wanted the opposite. Meanwhile, the onset of the Great Depression and the financial crisis of 1931, when Britain was forced off the Gold Standard, were hardening the hearts of the British. India could not be allowed the freedom to embarrass Britain economically or financially at such a sensitive time.

In the middle of 1931 the MacDonald Labour government fell and was replaced by a National coalition dominated by the Conservatives, though still led by MacDonald. MacDonald now proved far more open to the arguments of Conservatives like Sam Hoare, who insisted that 'One of the basic principles of Imperial policy is agreement with the Moslem world . . . To say that provincial autonomy would not be granted [for Muslim provinces] would put all the Moslems against us.' It seemed that the British were drifting towards a much emasculated version of the federal idea, in which reform focused not on Indian power at the centre, but on the greater provincialization of the Raj.

This approach gave far more security to Muslims in Muslim-majority provinces and was in many ways the logical outcome of the 1919 experiments in devolution coupled with separate electorates, which had given Muslims in Bengal and the Punjab (where they were in a majority) a taste of autonomous regional power. On 16 August 1932 MacDonald announced the 'Communal Award', under which entrenched Muslim electoral majorities were created in Bengal and Punjab – an abject defeat for Congress and a total victory for the provincial Muslims. The Award also created separate electorates for dalits, though these were subsequently negotiated away after Gandhi launched a fast-unto-death on the issue.

Discussion, with much less Indian involvement, continued through 1933 and 1934. Vigorous opposition to the federal idea in any form was spearheaded by Churchill, who mobilized constituency associations, Rudyard Kipling and even Michael O'Dwyer (infamous after the 1919 Amritsar massacre) against 'this monstrous federation built by pygmies'. As a result, in the committee stage of the bill many concessions were made to Conservative opinion.

In 1935, after eight years of discussion, the new Government of India Bill was finally published. It proposed to introduce a central bicameral chamber, in which the princes would nominate between 30 and 40 per cent of seats and the Muslims and other special electorates (such as Sikhs) also gained weighted representation. Under the bill Indian ministers at the centre would receive some portfolios, but not foreign affairs or defence, which the Viceroy would control. This was essentially 'dyarchy' at the centre with British interests defended by a battery of economic and financial 'safeguards'. The new central bank (which would free India from the formal financial control of London) was cordoned off from political influence, as were ICS salaries and the railways. Sam Hoare, now Secretary of State for India, approvingly noted that it permitted 'a semblance of responsible government and yet retains in our hands the realities and verities of British control'. The introduction of the central federal element of the reforms was dependent on the agreement of at least half of the princely states and never came into being. Effectively, therefore, Irwin's plan for greater Indian unity by establishing some power-sharing at the centre was abandoned in favour of old-style wicket imperialism – an India of many regional and religious teams, not a unified state. This defeat reflected, in part, a determination by the British to hang on to as much power as possible in India and to help old allies.

But underlying the realpolitik was also a powerful and persistent set of assumptions about India: the old Risleyean sociology of difference. Representative government in India, according to this philosophy, was an act of social engineering designed to integrate India in a very particular way – to restore a sense of order and rank by restraining the supposedly alien influence of westernized nationalists. The 'real' or authentic interests of India were its castes, communities and tribes; individuals' political affiliations counted for little. A genuinely representative system had to encompass these corporate identities and ensure balance and political equilibrium. These ideas had been largely shaped by the nineteenth-century Prussian model of conservative reform, which sought to bolster bureaucratic power at the centre while banishing democratic processes to the local level.

Unsurprisingly, this theory found many devotees among Raj officialdom. Separate electorates and provincialization would ensure that no single party or group would dominate, leaving officials in a dominant position. Although the system might resemble the parliamentary politics of Britain, in reality it allowed the Raj to maintain order and bolster its legitimacy by drawing groups more deeply into collaborative relationships, via regional elections. But the British, paradoxically, did not want politics to be based around religious groups. They believed that the communities on whom separate electorates were conferred were essentially local and tribal; they were religious only in the sense of indicating a common heritage and descent. Indeed, the rules of electoral competition limited the use of religious rhetoric and prohibited 'any attempts to induce a candidate or a voter to believe that he will be rendered an object of divine displeasure or spiritual censure'. However, the British soon discovered that they were power-less to prevent these community identities from becoming profoundly religious.

With their sanctification of the ideas of community and the exten-sion of separate electorates, the 1935 reforms initiated a new era of wicket imperialism. Indians would form teams; Muslims, non-Brahmans, Princes and Nationalists would take to the field umpired by the Raj. But rather than observing strict neutrality, the British employed all their powers of propaganda to hobble the nationalist team. Schoolmasters were employed to travel around the districts explaining to sceptical audiences that they faced a stark choice between the benign ministrations of a progressive Raj or the threat of nationalist anarchy. Congress, it was implied, was a threat to the stability of society; it was 'a state within a state', embodying 'the essence of totalitarianism', with *khadi* (home-made cloth) as its brown shirts and the *charkha* (the spinning-wheel icon of Congress) its swastika. Nehru, with his Soviet connections, posed a sinister 'red' threat. Under Nehru's command international debt obligations would be repudiated, foreign capital would flood out, interest rates would soar, property rights would collapse and the country would be ruined.

However, even with a biased umpire, the defeat of the enemy demands that the home team put up a decent performance. This was not the case. The 1935 Act envisaged a far greater role in all-India affairs for the princes. They would, it was thought, be 'a steadying element in a time of flux ... a bulwark of British prestige and influ-ence'. The rebranding of the maharajas as 'constitutional' monarchs supposedly began in 1921 with the creation of a new consultative Chamber of Princes. But the great south Indian states of Hyderabad, Mysore, Cochin and Travancore, and the only slightly less grand western principalities of Baroda, Jaipur, Jodhpur and Udaipur, regarded the chamber as beneath their dignity and had little to do with it, preferring direct relations with the Raj. The chamber was therefore dominated by medium-sized states, such as Patiala and Bikaner, which accounted for only 5 million of the 70 million inhabi-tants of princely India – the 'Rolls-Royce Rajas' as they were derisively known by their enemies. The 327 statelets with populations of less than 1 million had no representation at all.

From the beginning the Chamber of Princes was riven with dissension, and rather than cohering into a single aristocratic side it splintered into its several component parts. The princes, it appeared, were not content to be incorporated into a unified India as a prop for British power. The aim of most of them was quite the opposite – to slip the leash of British suzerainty and avoid, as the Maharaja of Bikaner put it, the fate of the 'loyalists of Ireland'. The federation idea was promoted by some princes at the Round Table Conference as another scheme to wrench their autonomy from the grasp of the Raj. However, they found it impossible to agree on what federation meant. The more far-sighted monarchs of the south saw clearly that the issue now was 'Swaraj [Independent] India vs. Rajas' India'; the Nizam of Hyderabad shrewdly recognized that it was worth trading the recovery of complete autonomy for a say in the evolution of an all-India federation. The 'Rolls-Royce Rajas', on the other hand, ultimately judged the creation of a strong federal centre too risky. The tiny statelets, seeking strength through numbers, threw yet another spanner into the federal works by floating the idea of an entirely separate princely confederation. The British dream of a revivified princely India saving the Raj thus perished. However, it generated the potentially Balkanizing notion that the princes were, in some sense, entitled to full independence.

The British also counted on another important home team, the 'non-Brahman' parties, which might be compared to 'the Rest' of the Bombay Pentangular. The most significant player in this team was the Justice party of Madras. Comprising city merchants, professionals, large estate owners and petty rajas, this diverse collection of interests was united only in its resentment of the power and influence of another group, the Mylaporeans. The Mylaporean faction was a set of western-educated and predominantly Brahman professionals who had gained great ascendancy in the public life of the province. Crucially they were associated with Congress and thus opposed the reforms of 1919. The Justicites, spotting an opportunity, declared themselves Raj loyalists.

They presented themselves as the leaders of Madras's non-Brahman community, which, broadly interpreted, meant 97 per cent of the population, and demanded special reservations to 'protect' them from the 3 per cent of Brahmans. This was something of a misrepresentation of social conflicts in Madras. Certainly the educated Mylaporean Brahmans were an influential group, but in much of the south it was the non-Brahman landowners who wielded power, while Brahmans were generally cooks and temple priests whose services could be had for a few broken coconuts, rather than monstrous oppressors. But the idea that Brahmans were a powerful and overrepresented minority suited the British, now desperate for loyal collaborators, and after the provincial elections of 1920 they directed the leader of the Justicites to form the first Indian ministry in Madras.

Even with a strong British steer the Justicites made a disappointing political team. The party's establishment consisted of a few tables at the Madras Cosmopolitan Club, and in 1928 it was forced to advertise in the press asking any local Justice party branches to get in touch. By the late 1920s it could list only 5000 members, 2000 of whom were in Madras city. In the 1920 elections, which Congress boycotted, many erstwhile Congressmen slid easily over to the Justicites. Unsurprisingly there was little party discipline; there was so much party-hopping that the perplexed governor, Goschen, despaired: 'the changes are so kaleidoscopic that it is impossible to follow the various intrigues and issues from day to day.'

But under dyarchy an elaborate party organization was unnecessary for winning elections. Only 1.25 million had the vote across 25 constituencies, turnouts were low, especially in rural areas (an average of 23 per cent) and 3–4000 votes were enough to win. These could be easily purchased. The most rational electoral strategy, therefore, was to court local big men – managers of temples, landlords and petty officials – who would then mobilize their clients to vote the right way. The Raja of Panagal, who led the Justice party until his death in 1928, learnt very quickly that the key to staying in power was through patronage, the life-blood of the system. So powerful and unchallengeable were ministers that one observer compared them to idols in a temple:

'Seeing people' is a fine art in this climate; and the man who wants to get on goes on a pilgrimage to those that have; and the man who has got on would be offended if ceremonial visits are not paid to him and the proper quantity of incense burnt . . .

Soon the distant relations of various ministers were elevated to district board presidencies, and temple committee membership was stuffed with loyal clients. But inevitably a patronage-based system produced losers as well as winners. The problem of disappointed clients was obvious in the myriad splits and fragmentations to which the Justice party fell victim. In 1923 a disgruntled raja formed a splinter group, the Tamil Districts Non-Brahman Conference; in 1925 two mutually hostile non-Brahman conferences were held simultaneously; and after the death of the Raja of Panagal in 1928, nine competing candidates emerged in a leadership struggle that lasted two years. In 1932 several district bosses jockeyed for ascendancy by shipping their supporters across the state on trains to do battle at the annual Justice Conference in Madras. Over 15,000 attended, but the conference opened and closed in less than two minutes as the various factions pelted one another with mud, smashed chairs and demolished the speaker's podium. Meanwhile any ideological coherence collapsed completely: some urged the party to abandon its communal origins and admit Brahmans, while others urged a moral crusade against them. The politics of steady conservatism and radical socialism coexisted uneasily, and Raj loyalism competed for support with proposals to ally with Congress. By 1934, in a final irony, one leader floated the idea of complete rapprochement with their erstwhile foe, the Mylaporean faction. In the midst of all this manoeuvring very little policy was actually implemented, and a 'cult of incompetence' reigned, as Congress put it.

Such problems afflicted many of the pro-Raj parties, such as the National Liberal Federation in Bengal, and the Agriculturalist Party in the United Provinces. The result of this dismal experiment in wicket imperialism was that in 1937 it was Congress, not the Raj's allies, that triumphed in elections to the new autonomous provincial assemblies established by the 1935 reforms. Congress won 54 per cent of the vote, 711 of 1585 seats, and majorities in 5 provinces. They also formed governments in two further provinces, putting them in power in seven of India's eleven regional parliaments.

The areas where Congress did not prevail were the Muslim-majority provinces. The 1935 Act had created statutory Muslim electoral preponderance in these regions, effectively creating Muslim-dominated islands in an ocean of Hindu majorities. This was essentially an Ulster-style solution to the minorities problem that had proved so intractable at the London conferences, and was, indeed, the logical conclusion of the politics of provincial devolution and separate electorates begun by the 1919 reforms. For in one, unintended, sense the provincializing tactic had been a great success: the decentralizing reforms had made Muslims in the Punjab and Bengal acutely aware of the advantages to be gained from splitting with the nationalists and co-operating with the British. But the reforms had also divided Muslims among themselves. While it was apparent that Congress was not the party of choice for South Asian Muslims, it was uncertain whether they could be moulded into a coherent political force at all.

The Ulster strategy left unsolved the not inconsiderable problem of the Muslim minorities in Hindu majority states. It also left unanswered the question of what an all-India Muslim political identity should be. There were many contenders for Muslim leadership, many versions of 'Islam' on offer, and many notions of what constituted a Muslim 'community'. These can perhaps be distilled into four broad groups: reformist clerics; traditional locally based religious leaders; secular regionalists; and secular 'modernist' nationalists.

The reformist clerics were the *ulema*: *muftis* (legal scholars), *imams* (prayer leaders) and *qazis* (judges) who, under the Mughals, had enjoyed state support and in return helped bolster the legitimacy of Mughal power. The collapse of Mughal power was something of a catastrophe for them, deprived now of any firm foundation for their authority. They would now have to establish a new rationale for their influence. From the late nineteenth century they began to recast themselves as custodians of the conscience of South Asian Islam rather than servants of the state. Assuming the role of teachers, they presented themselves as specialists in the 'correct' principles of Islam, which they promulgated through networks of schools or *madrasas*, of which Deoband was the most famous. This project, however, involved homogenizing South Asian Islam, which had previously been diverse. In a sense, an Islamic Reformation was being initiated which preached personal transformation through individual reading of the Quran and Hadith, rather than the practice of customary rituals. Religious solidarity and universal Muslim values were stressed over hierarchy and localism.

Though the promotion of equality and individualism implicit in this new Muslim 'fundamentalism' was, in many ways, at odds with the essentially hierarchical nature of the Raj, until the First World War the reformists had been relatively apolitical. But with the end of the Ottoman Empire and greater encroachment by the colonial state on areas close to their interests, such as education and family law, they became increasingly anti-British. They made their debut in politics as leaders of the Khilafat agitation, the movement founded to defend the Caliph following the dismemberment of the Ottoman Empire. And having got a taste of power they soon asserted their right to lead the Muslims of India. In 1919 the recently founded Jamiat-Ulama-e-Hind offered political leadership based on the universal values of shariah or religious law. An Amir-i-Hind, or leader to offer guidance to all India's Muslims, elected from the ranks of the *ulema* was mooted. This was a challenge not only to the British but to secular Muslim politicians, and to more locally based religious leaders.

These localists opposed the new individualist Islam of the reformers, advocating instead the revival of a particularistic and hierarchical version of Islam focused on the *Sufi* shrines and the *pir* landowners (descendants of saints) who dominated rural areas. Their theology was at odds with the egalitarianism of the reformers: for them saintly charisma, ritual and the authority of spiritual leaders were central. This kind of approach was well-adapted to rural society where local kin networks (*biradari*) and tribal leaders were the most important links between their communities and the Raj. The yoking of religious to political power underpinned the foundation of bodies such as Hizbullah (Party of God), organized as a spiritual army whose soldiers pledged themselves to follow their local *pir* leadership. *Pirs* themselves were generally pro-British, unlike the reformists, and were usually allies of the loyalist Punjabi Unionist party. One *pir*, Syed Muhammad Hussein, for example, was elected to the provincial council in 1920 as a Unionist.

The Unionist party was the leading exponent of the politics which advocated the devolution of power to Muslim-dominated regions.

Fazl-i-Husain, its founder, had successfully used the Round Table Conference to press for greater decentralization, thus enhancing Muslim power in certain areas. The Unionists dominated politics in the Punjab through skilfully uniting Hindu, Muslim and Sikh peasants, and its goal in politics was to preserve the autonomy of the Punjab and the power of its rural magnates.

Opposing both the reformist *ulema* and the localists were the modernizers, led by Muhammad Ali Jinnah. The modernizers were essentially the descendants of Syed Ahmed Khan and his Aligarh college movement, who saw Muslims as an ethnic, political community. For them belief was a matter of the 'private sphere'; they embraced western education and sought to modernize Muslim attitudes to women, education and law. By the First World War modernist Muslims believed their political interests were best served by an alliance with the Congress nationalists.

A number of groups therefore claimed to speak for India's Muslims, and the Muslims were clearly not the supposedly coherent community imagined by the Raj's bureaucratic mind. They were divided by sect and language. Class conflict was prevalent, with poorer Muslims, especially in the cities, resentful of the *ashraf* elite that sought to lead them. They were also divided doctrinally and debates about the rights of women, the place of the family and shariah law caused violent friction. Most importantly for their political future, they were divided into those living in Muslim majority provinces and those who were not. Attempts were made to mould the Muslims of south Asia into a more cohesive group. The most obvious basis for unity was the faith, but religious initiatives seemed merely to sharpen divisions. Control of festivals and rituals were areas of intense rivalry and competition as much among Muslims themselves as between them and the Hindus. The promotion of extreme piety, stressing Muslims' common love or devotion to certain sacred symbols, was a potential route to religious nationalism. But agitations around such symbols as the Khilafat often descended into sectarian and class disputes.

Another apparent tool for fostering unity were the new elections introduced by the Raj, especially as now the Muslims constituted a separate electorate in their own right. Elections, some hoped, would become events at which the values of community would transcend the reality of division. But others were not so sure. The irony of British devolution of power and separate electorates was that they actually politicized the cultural fragmentation of India's Muslims. In the Punjab separate electorates seemed to affirm unity, but in fact they became contests between competing networks of local interest: locality, language, *biradari* and so forth. Religious rhetoric was often used competitively rather than cohesively. In the 1937 election in Karnjal district, posters appeared equating a vote for the Shia candidate with a vote for a *kafir* (non-believer): 'Let Sunnis only vote for Sunni candidates' it proclaimed.

But if elections could promote disunity, they also made it clear to Muslims that the consequences of disunity were grave. The inter-war elections increasingly served to define groups' place in the nation, just as the *durbar* had done before. The Congress landslide in the 1937 elections, the greatest of the pre-independence era, vividly demonstrated that it was Hindus, not Muslims, who stood at the apex of the new order. The consequences of losing elections were potentially catastrophic: Muslims were excluded from coalitions, discriminated against in the job market and, many felt, their culture threatened. The 1937 elections were a sharp lesson in the danger of disunity and one not wasted on Muslim politicians. Jinnah, who had, since 1916, tried intermittently to establish a modus vivendi with the nationalists, now switched to a strategy of building common ground with his erstwhile foes, the regionalist Muslims of the Punjab. Regional politicians, in turn, now recognized that regional autonomy in Bengal and the Punjab was not going to protect them from domination by a co-ordinated Congress high command in the other provinces.

In the early 1930s another possible solution to the problem of Muslim disunity began to emerge: the idea of a Muslim nation. The idea began with the poet Iqbal, who argued that European-style democratic majority rule was not compatible with Islam. The Muslims of India were a distinct moral community which had to control its own political destiny, and religion could not simply be relegated to the private sphere. It followed from this that no non-Muslim body, however liberal or enlightened, could have political legitimacy over Muslims. There was, Iqbal insisted, a Muslim nation within India. This was not, he insisted, a territorial nation, but a spiritual one, but nevertheless Iqbal himself floated the idea that Muslims should form a large autonomous group in north-west India. This notion was elaborated upon by a group of Cambridge students in 1934 who formed the acronym PAKISTAN from Punjab, Kashmir and Sindh, alternatively known as the land of the 'pure' (*pak* meaning pure). However, it would take the conditions of war to crystallize Iqbal's vague notions into a hard demand for a Muslim nation state. Only then would the provincialization of politics promoted so assiduously by the British be transformed into a process of separation.

The British failed in their efforts to recast colonial politics to their own advantage. But in trying to enforce their very particular rules of the game, they had succeeded in radically altering the field of play in a way that would profoundly shape India's future. The logical, if unintended consequences of regionalist and community-based politics had, by the eve of the Second World War, fostered a separatist Muslim nationalism. Moreover, it was overwhelmingly obvious, however much the British might deny it, that politics in India was not a gentlemanly game played by several evenly matched teams. Instead one team, immensely bolder and more skilfully captained than all the rest, had emerged – the Indian National Congress.

4

Spinning the Nation

On 15 August 1947 the Union Jack of the Raj was lowered one last time and in its place was hoisted the Indian national ensign, a flag bearing the image of the humble spinning-wheel (*charkha*). For if the British saw India as a set of competing cricket teams to be marshalled into sportsmanly coexistence under the tutelage of an all-powerful umpire, the nationalists themselves favoured a more organic, hand-crafted metaphor and produced spinners of a very different kind. The notion of nation-building as a cottage industry ultimately found its way on to the national flag. Consciously eschewing the pompous and conventional insignia of power, India's leaders had chosen the quotidian spinning-wheel. The *charkha*, like all good symbols, was loaded with multiple meanings. It recalled Gandhi's great campaigns to spin the British out of India with *khadi* (home-made, coarse cotton cloth); it heralded the exclusion of foreign exploiters in favour of domestic economic power; and it was a spiritual, but non-denominational emblem of national creation. The simple wheel would spin the many threads of Indian identity into a single, hard-wearing tapestry of nationhood. But while British decline and miscalculation allowed the great spinner himself, Gandhi, to fabricate a nation, his project of weaving the various disparate skeins of India into a single cloth had, in fact, been only partly successful. The Indian nation was not a single bolt of roughly woven, but all-embracing coarse *khadi*; it was tissue of a more exclusive, fragile and potentially less durable variety. The *charkha* was a symbol of aspiration, not achievement.

In 1919 the British Empire was apparently at its zenith. But in the same year a sequence of catastrophic and interlinked uprisings cast a shadow of mortality over this impressive, if short-lived, imperium. On the streets of cities as diverse as Dublin, Cairo and Lahore, violent popular resistance erupted and was only halted by the concession of significant political and economic reform. In all cases the British used conciliating reforms to confound nationalism, juggling tentative devolution of power with the promotion of conservative, pro-imperial allies. In all cases, the consequence was the precise opposite of that desired: nationalism flourished.

Ironically, the outbreak of the Great War brought a surge of pro-British patriotism among many Indians. In August 1917 M. K. Gandhi visited London, where he praised the British government's foreign policy, urged Indians to 'think imperially' and did a brief stint as recruiting sergeant for one of the Indian regiments. Gandhi was not alone in thinking imperially. In December 1914 Congress offered the King-Emperor and the English people 'its profound devotion . . . its unswerving allegiance to the British connection, its firm resolve to stand by the Empire, at all hazards and at all costs'. Even hardened extremists like Tilak and Bipin Pal counselled co-operation with the government's war effort. Loyalty to the British was not only evident among nationalist elites. It could also be found among the urban population more generally. The government's 'loyalty postcard' propaganda campaign was an instant sell-out, as Indians flocked to purchase the cards showing pictures of the fluttering Union Jack accompanied by the stirring verse:

> Symbol of freedom, truth and right
> Proud 'neath thy folds our soldiers fight
> Each with his life thy cause defends
> And heaven to each its blessings sends.

Over 400,000 of these cards were printed in seven different languages, and another run featuring 36 different uplifting messages was immediately commissioned.

Loyalty of word was compounded by generosity of deed. Between August 1914 and November 1918 over 1,300,000 military personnel, including nearly 3500 Indian doctors and surgeons and 165 vets, were shipped abroad. Of these 1.3 million, 53,000 were killed, 64,000 wounded and nearly 4000 declared missing in action. Even the subcontinent's elephants, camels, goats and horses were expected to do their duty, and over 172,000 of them were shipped overseas, along with nearly 3,700,000 tons of fodder and supplies. In all, India contributed around £250 million worth of materials. Taxes rose by over 40 per cent. Businessmen and townsmen rallied to the cause, buying war loans to the value of £75 million, accepting government controls, financial shortages, transport bottlenecks and runaway inflation. The Indian princes and other wealthy individuals stumped up another £5 million in cash, all of this largely unforced generosity culminating in the 'gift' of £100 million in cash by the people of India as a contribution towards British war debts in 1918. By the end of the war India had contributed over £400 million to the British war effort.

Yet like many effusive demonstrations of affection, this enthusiasm for the Raj was highly conditional. For Indian politicians, moderate and extreme alike, conspicuous loyalty was meant to be a demonstration of political 'maturity', and as such a suitably grown-up reward was expected – namely self-government. The early years of the war witnessed a remarkable rush towards consensus among Indian politicians of every stripe as they awaited major constitutional advance. Sensing the promise of strength in unity, an unlikely alliance of extremists, moderates, Hindu nationalists and Muslim leaders came together to frame a demand for self-government.

In 1907 Congress had split into 'extreme' and 'moderate' camps. The moderates placed their faith in the good offices of the Raj, but were sorely disappointed by the barely detectable advances of the 1909 legislative council reforms. The extremists, meanwhile, were both defeated and depleted as their best men, including Tilak, were despatched to the Andaman Islands for lengthy custodial sojourns. But the apparent promise of post-war advance convinced the recently liberated Tilak and others that it was worth considering the reform option again, and in 1916 the prodigal son of radical nationalism was inducted back into the bosom of Congress through the good offices of the redoubtable Annie Besant. Tilak had not entirely given up his penchant for direct action, but his activities were now channelled into the newly established Home Rule Leagues. These organizations were consciously modelled on their Irish counterparts and recruited impressive numbers of new nationalist adherents from diverse backgrounds, but their modus operandi was a world away from the inflammatory activities of the self-sufficient *swadeshi* years. Even so, with nearly 60,000 members the Leagues were a significant advance on the erstwhile supplicant and 'moderate' politics of the pre-war era, characterized by polite petitioning rather than mass mobilization. Spreading the word with vernacular pamphlets, gaudy poster art, postcards, patriotic stamps, subtly modified religious songs and missionary-style rhetoric, they succeeded in rallying a constituency previously aloof from nationalist exhortations – petty tradesmen, lowly government clerks, farmers, students and people far beyond the great presidencies of Calcutta, Bombay and Madras.

This war-driven reunion of moderates and extremists was further bolstered by an extraordinary rapprochement between Congress and the Muslims. Since the death of the arch-Raj collaborator Syed Ahmed Khan, a younger generation of Muslim leaders had begun to question his separatist strategy. The new unity was crowned with the signing of the Lucknow Pact in 1916. The pact, designed to unite Hindus and Muslims behind a common demand for radical reform, was an impressive piece of political horse-trading, ably brokered by one Muhammad Ali Jinnah, a brilliant young Muslim lawyer from Bombay. Yet the pact was less radical than it first appeared. While employing the language of 'Home Rule', it stopped well short of demanding full independence. What it demanded was 'Home Rule' within the British Empire: that is, to enjoy the 'dominionhood' granted to Britain's 'white' colonies, such as Canada and Australia – a measure of domestic power in return for loyalty based on friendship, self-interest and mutual respect, in place of coercion, exploitation and sullen acquiescence.

The subsequent 1919 reforms were, then, profoundly dis-appointing. Many suspected the British of bad faith. The new provincial assemblies offered only dilute forms of power sharing and were partnered with the repressive and hated Rowlatt Acts. Moreover, the terminological ambiguity of the reforms immediately triggered suspicion among the nationalists, many of whom, being lawyers, understood only too well the evasive intent behind circumlocutionary language. Expectations, having risen very high during the war, were now crushed. And other features of British wartime exploits had begun eroding Indian respect for the Raj. Among the educated, the most notorious of these was the hopelessly botched military campaign in Mesopotamia (Iraq). In 1916 thousands of Indian troops had died for lack of adequate supplies owing to the incompetence of the Indian-based military administration. It was an open secret that the Viceroy, Lord Hardinge, would have been recalled in disgrace had he not already been homeward-bound. Returning soldiers joined the chorus of criticism. Thousands of Indian troops had been stationed in France throughout 1916, and many drew unfavourable comparisons between their treatment by the polite and solicitous French and the high-handedness of their British overlords. After the war was over, the US President Wilson's idealistic vision of war aims and the post-war order swiftly percolated into the subcontinent: if this was a war for national self-determination and against imperial despotism, why should India be excluded? Critical analysis of the British state abounded in the Indian press. In November 1918 *New India* heralded the fall of the three pre-war autocracies – Russian, German and Austrian – and demanded to know why the fourth, British India, should persist 'to the amazement of, and a menace to a world set free'. Racism was also becoming more broadly appreciated as a facet of British character somewhat incompatible with claims to superior moral status. Events at the Versailles Peace Conference of 1919 compounded these charges of racist hypocrisy. There was particular outrage at the denial of equal treatment to the Japanese over the parcelling out of the spoils of war, all of which seemed to be going to 'white' nations.

However, by far the most damaging consequence of Versailles was the acute alienation of India's Muslims, enraged at the dismember-ment of the now defunct Ottoman Empire. British indifference to the Balkan wars and Italian machinations against the Ottomans had already inflamed Muslim opinion before the war. In 1916 this radi-calism was reflected in the foundation of the Muslim lobby, the Jamiat-ulama-e-Hind, by clerics in alliance with a new generation of politicians, unimpressed at the Syed Ahmed Khan school of imperial conciliation. In 1917 the 'Khilafat' Committee was formed to protest against the treatment of the Ottoman Empire, and especially of the 'Khalif', the protector of the holy places of Mecca and Medina and thus effectively the figurehead of the Muslim world. These radical forces soon captured control of the Jamaiat's governing committee. Ill-feeling was further stoked when, in early 1918, the government released several non-Muslim Home-Rulers, including Mrs Besant, but declined to liberate the leaders of the radical Young Party of the Muslims – the Ali brothers. This fuelled suspicions that Muslims, in India and throughout the world, were being singled out for special victimization.

Discontent had, by this time, spread far beyond the elites, and in some regions popular confidence in the Raj had begun to buckle. Food prices, scarcity and heavy-handedness in army recruitment had particularly affected the peasants and townspeople of north India. In 1918 the economy had finally succumbed to wartime strains hitherto borne only with the aid of bumper harvests. Huge military demands, inflation and food shortages coincided with famine and epidemic: nearly six million died during the influenza of that year. The economy had been ill-managed, lurching from boom to bust; between 1917 and 1919 many Indian merchants had been ruined, while a few had become spectacularly wealthy through commodity speculation. And although food prices in the cities soared, little attempt was made, by the still doggedly laissez-faire government, either to curb such profiteering, or to control prices.

But discontent was not merely the politics of the empty belly. As early as 1917 officials reported the pervasiveness of 'vague notions that in some unknown way the British Raj is going wrong or is going under, and *swaraj* [Home Rule] is coming to put all things right'. In Bihar many believed that British power was collapsing. 'Germany *ki jai*' (victory to Germany) they chanted as they hailed the new 'kaiser-*baba*' (Emperor-father). Nor was fury at the repressive Rowlatt Acts just confined to the elites. Bizarre rumours swiftly sprang up about the acts: it was said that farmers would be forced to surrender half their bullocks to the government; all brides and grooms would be inspected by British doctors; parents would be taxed for each child born; and no more than four men at a time would be allowed to follow a funeral.

The first post-war crisis, when it came, struck in the very heart of Raj loyalism – its recruiting ground, the Punjab. Here the impress of war had been at its harshest: recruitment levels leapt from one in two hundred to one in forty, and with barely 7.5 per cent of India's population, the Punjab provided over 60 per cent of its soldiers. The province was run by the Anglo-Irish Lieutenant-Governor, Sir Michael O'Dwyer, a devotee of the iron-fist school of colonial government, who had bitterly opposed any reform or concessions to nationalist feeling. On the afternoon of 13 April 1919, just after 5 p.m., in the Sikh city of Amritsar, fifty riflemen of the 19th Gurkhas, 54th Sikhs and 59th Sikhs under the command of General Reginald Dyer, opened fire on an unarmed crowd of around 20,000 people gathered in the waste ground of the Jallianwala Bagh, a gulley about 200 yards long. It was wholly enclosed by the backs of houses and low walls and its three narrow entrances were too narrow to permit the armoured cars and mounted machine-guns that Dyer had hoped to deploy. At least 379 were killed and 1650 were wounded. Dyer had instructed his men not to fire over the heads, but into the thickest part of the crowd. Firing ceased only when the ammunition ran out. No provision was made for the wounded; 'it was not my job', Dyer later insisted.

The people on whom Dyer's troops fired were a diverse crowd. Some had just turned up for a festival, but others were part of the 'Rowlatt *satyagraha*', organized by a certain M. K. Gandhi, lately returned from South Africa, where he had spent twenty years discomfiting the imperial government. This demonstration was designed as an experiment in 'non-violent' direct action, intended to challenge the repressive Rowlatt Acts with 'truth or soul force' (*satyagraha*). The call to protest had brought a remarkable response, especially in the war-bruised provinces of Bombay and Punjab. But it was the arrest of Gandhi while en route to the Punjab on 9 April that had the greatest effect. The protest in Jallianwala Bagh on the 13th was only one of these.

Compounding the immediate crisis was the response of Governor O'Dwyer, who immediately imposed martial law. This permitted Dyer and others to exact what an official inquiry termed 'fancy' punishments on supposed rebels. These included a collective 'levy', imposed to recover 'incidental expenses', including the cost of sending European women and children to the hills; one protestor was even ordered to compose poems in praise of martial law to be read aloud in the market. But the most notorious example was the infamous 'crawling order', by which those wishing to pass through a major thoroughfare where an English lady had been 'insulted' could do so only on their stomachs. The power of rumour soon exaggerated these punishments into acts even more grievous than they already were. A *sadhu* (holy man), it was said, had been brutally whitewashed, while others had, allegedly, been ordered to draw pictures in the dust with their noses (the latter derived from the genuine 'punishment' of enforced ground-sweeping 'salaaming' in the presence of Europeans). None of this enhanced the British reputation for fair play and honest justice.

O'Dwyer later claimed that martial law had been justified because the Punjab was in the grip of a conspiracy and that full-scale rebellion had been narrowly averted. However, no evidence of any conspiracy or rebellion was found by any of the several subsequent commissions and committees of inquiry, even the most sympathetic. Indeed, O'Dwyer was stumped when asked how he could believe that Punjabis were in the pay of Bolshevik and Afghan revolutionaries, when only eighteen months before he had praised them for their 'common sense and sanity of judgement' and their affable understanding with the British, based on 'mutual comprehension, confidence and co-operation'. Among the British in India Dyer's actions were warmly received. C. F. Andrews (a friend of Gandhi's), wrote of a meeting with Lord Chelmsford shortly afterwards, during which the Viceroy was 'cold as ice with me and full of racial bitterness – referring again and again to the murders of English people at Amritsar, but resenting it when I spoke of the intolerable wrongs from which Indians suffered'.

While the event itself caused outrage in India, it was the response in Britain that set even moderate Indian nationalist opinion reeling. Back in England, where Dyer was sent for 'early retirement', having escaped a court martial, the House of Lords lauded his bravery and sagacity, and the *Morning Post*'s appeal for him raised £26,000. Retribution, when it came, fell not upon Dyer, but on such British critics as Ben Horniman, editor of the *Bombay Chronicle*, who was promptly deported for his scorching criticisms. The British political establishment moved to downplay Amritsar, claiming either that Dyer's judgement had been tragically impaired by arteriosclerosis, or that he was a one-off, bad-apple case of 'Prussian frightfulness'. But to many Indians he appeared more the embodiment of a governmental philosophy that was, *au fond*, despotic, and proof that the reforms heralded no new dawn. It seemed that martial law had been deployed not to avert an imminent threat to the state, but to set a terrifying example, to re-establish British morale and restore the prestige of the Raj. Dyer, in his evidence to the official commission of inquiry, tended to support this interpretation, stating that he was 'going to give them a lesson', that it was 'a merciful act . . . and they ought to be thankful to me for doing it'. He opined that, 'I thought it would be doing a jolly lot of good and that they would realize that they were not to be wicked.'

Amritsar was not in fact the wholly isolated event the British liked to believe. Elsewhere the Punjab disturbances had been met with lethal force: armoured trains and aeroplanes were sent from Lahore to the villages of western Punjab, where unarmed market crowds and schoolhouses were strafed with hundreds of rounds of ammunition and then carpet bombed – a strategy recently perfected in Iraq. Jury-less courts were used to try people retrospectively; many were sentenced to death without appeal, and public flogging was common.

These incidents, and especially Amritsar and its reception in Britain, had an inflammatory effect on Indian public opinion. Rabindranath Tagore, the poet and Nobel Laureate, who as late as 1917 had regarded British rule as 'providential', saw Amritsar as 'the monstrous progeny of a monstrous war'. Aghast at the massacre, he attempted to return his recently bestowed knighthood, though the government, perturbed at such 'insolence', continued, to his fury, to 'sir' him. By late 1918 virtually all moderate nationalist support had fallen away from the Raj. Motilal Nehru and C. R. Das, leading constitutionalists in United Provinces and Bengal respectively, now underwent a radical conversion, to become part of a novel coalition of Congress moderates, pragmatists and assorted hard-headed realists, led by the extraordinary and idiosyncratic utopian, M. K. Gandhi.

On returning to India in 1915 after an absence of over twenty years, Gandhi established an *ashram* – an ideal community. He had experimented with this kind of collective at the Phoenix Settlement and Tolstoy Farm in South Africa; both were modelled on his experiences in a Trappist monastery in Durban and, later, several months in a

South African jail. Installed in these model communities was an eclectic mix of Hindus of various castes, Muslims, Europeans, friends and relatives. They were alternately cajoled and bullied into conforming to Gandhi's notion of ideal citizenship: they built their own homes, they farmed, they scrubbed lavatories, they prayed and sang hymns – 'Lead Kindly Light' and 'When I Survey the Wondrous Cross' were particular favourites. Boys and girls were taught together, with an emphasis on practical skills, not 'book learning'. Everyone learnt to spin and sew, and in 1904, when Gandhi became a *brahmacharya* (celibate), other inmates, even married couples, were enjoined to abstain from fleshly pleasures. More controversial, perhaps, was his insistence on caste and religious intermingling: Brahmans were compelled to do physical labour, and interdining was compulsory, though not intermarriage. Gandhi established his ashrams at various locations around India, the Sabarmati Ashram in Gujarat, or 'Abode of Service', being the most famous. All survived on business donations, provoking the famous quip that it was costing a fortune to keep the Mahatma (or 'Great Soul', as Tagore had recently dubbed him), in poverty.

In practice these experiments proved a dismal failure, sowing discord not harmony and trying the temper of even the saintly Mahatma. Caste posed a particular problem. High castes balked at the requirement that they live as equals with dalits. It was rumoured that after socializing they would go off and secretly 'purify' themselves in the nearest river. One of the most stubborn of the ashramites was Gandhi's own wife, Kasturbai. Her chief offence, in Gandhi's opinion, had been her refusal to empty the chamber pot of a dalit Christian with sufficient 'cheerfulness', provoking a violent tussle. Most failed to live up to his expectations: the standard of living was too high, women insisted on wearing jewellery, and spinning and weaving were neglected in favour of constant squabbling, especially in the kitchens. Outre sexual experimentation took place, though not of the *brahmacharya* variety prescribed. Violent collapse was only avoided through the force of the Mahatma's iron will. He once wryly observed that being viceroy of India would have been less taxing than running one of his ashrams.

For Gandhi, building the nationalist movement, a feat of formidable political virtuosity, was much like managing an ashram – a marvel of integration accomplished against great odds. But the history of his ashrams hinted at a more general flaw in his conception of the nation, which he insisted was also a harmonious family community of like-minded truth-seekers. For, like the inmates of Gandhi's ashrams, many Indian nationalists heartily loathed one another, saw the movement as more akin to a prison than a utopia, and curtailed their ideological and factional disputes only in deference to the Mahatma's extraordinary charisma. But the price of success was a confusion of purpose that would later blight efforts at national transformation after independence.

Intellectual incoherence is, of course, a characteristic common to all nationalisms, but the Indian example was extreme. Gandhi had mixed a compound national vision that was either startlingly radical or deeply conservative, depending on the political proclivities of the beholder. However, despite his determination to eclipse enemies left and right, rival ideologies flourished on both flanks, invoking visions of the nation wholly at odds with Gandhi's ashramite utopia. At the extremes, militant radical right-wingers competed with Marxist socialists to mock the Mahatma's gentle idyll. At the centre, progressive liberals and moderate conservatives found his intemperate hostility to modern civilization, extravagant asceticism and anti-intellectualism alternately infuriating and embarrassing. Meanwhile, beyond the metropolitan intelligentsia and activist middle classes, the kaleidoscopic politics of the Indian people, poor and not so poor, often defied crude left/right categorization. In truth the Mahatma had many competitors for the right to cut the cloth of nationhood.

Mohandas Karamchand Gandhi was born in 1869 in Porbandar, a small-town backwater in Kathiawar on the south-west coast of Gujarat. Kathiawar was one of two hundred micro-statelets squeezed between the enormous British presidency of Bombay and the pseudo-independent principality of Baroda. Gandhi's homeland was untouched by either the material or spiritual paraphernalia of the Raj: no railways passed by and the intrepid band of Irish Presbyterians who had ventured there in the 1840s was soon seen off. Though formally of the Vaishya or merchant caste, his family had long been bureaucrats serving petty local princelings. Gandhi was steeped in the localist political culture of the old, pre-Raj, order. It was a tradition-soaked milieu, replete with notions of divine kingship and changeless paternalism, confident of its own values and suspicious of the west. Nevertheless his family was ambitious for the young Gandhi to make his way in the new order, and for this an English education was essential. At the Alfred High School in Rajkot he imbibed rich and undiluted draughts of high Victorian culture, memorizing 750 lines of *Paradise Lost*, and perusing the works of Jane Austen.

Thus armed with the cultural weaponry of modern civilization he felt free to flout the Hindu pieties of his mother, eating meat and lusting after women, like his much-wedded father. Nevertheless Gandhi was sufficiently deferential to tradition to marry Kasturbai Makanji, daughter of another Porbandar merchant, when they were both thirteen. He was a patriarchal spouse and, as he said, 'lost no time assuming the authority of the husband'. The unfortunate Kasturbai became his first project and was alternately coaxed and bullied towards virtue. 'I was a cruelly kind husband,' he wrote, 'I regarded myself as her teacher, and so harassed her out of my blind love for her . . . My ambition was to *make* her live a pure life . . . and identify her life and thought with mine.' He later admitted that it was her dogged obstruction to all efforts at her own 'improvement' that inspired his ideas on passive resistance.

Emulating fashionable elite behaviour of the time, he elected to train for the bar in London, where he arrived in 1888. While other Indian expatriates of the time were converting to revolutionary nationalism, Gandhi essayed ballroom dancing, the violin and elocution lessons, enunciating the more notable speeches of the younger Pitt in an effort to boost his rhetorical accomplishments. He also read with startlingly catholicity: Gibbon's *Decline and Fall of the Roman Empire*, Carlyle's *Heroes and Hero Worship*, pamphlets on vegetarianism, Tolstoy's *On Drunkeness or Why people become Intoxicated*, Stevenson's *Dr Jekyll and Mr Hyde* and, for the first time, the *Bhagavad Gita*, rendered into English by the theosophist Edwin Arnold as *The Song Celestial*. After passing his legal exams he returned to India, but his career did not flourish back in Bombay. Having failed to establish a successful legal practice there, he left for South Africa in 1893.

He was a success in South Africa, and became a respected and prosperous lawyer. But his 'faddism', as he termed it, was also quickly apparent: in Durban he became agent for the Christian Union, the London Vegetarians and the 'No Breakfast Society'. He also embarked on a journalistic career: *Indian Opinion*, the periodical he founded, carried articles on everything from public health to European history. He also developed a powerful distaste for modernity and a growing regard for traditional Indian culture. Much of this thought had 'occidental' rather than 'oriental' origins – he corresponded with Tolstoy (who cautioned him against excessive patriotism), and translated Ruskin's anti-industrial diatribe *Unto This Last* into Gujarati as *Sarvodaya* ('The Welfare of All'). The problem of opposing a violent and unjust state also began to preoccupy him for the first time. 'Civil Disobedience', Henry Thoreau's essay on the duty to disobey unjust laws, caught his attention, as did the biblical Sermon on the Mount, with its prophecy that the meek would inherit the earth. From these he began to theorize about the value of non-violent or passive resistance against injustice.

While in South Africa Gandhi remained an ultra-loyal subject of the Empire, composing a memorial to Queen Victoria on her Diamond Jubilee praising her 'glorious and beneficent reign'. He even organized a thousand-strong Indian ambulance corps to minister to British casualties during the Boer War, receiving the Raj's most prestigious gong, the Kaiser-i-Hind medal, for his trouble. Nevertheless his time in South Africa did provoke doubts about imperial beneficence. His sojourn coincided with a sharp upturn in racism, particularly towards immigrants from India. The 'white' press blustered luridly about the plague and epidemic that would ensue from this 'Asiatic invasion'. There were early calls for whites to be wholly segregated, to protect them not from Africans but from Indians, and Gandhi later recalled that 'I discovered [in South Africa] that as a man and an Indian I had no rights. More correctly, I discovered that I had no rights as a man, because I was an Indian.' Twenty years of campaigning against anti-Asian discrimination followed. The significance, impact and role of Gandhi in these struggles have been somewhat exaggerated: he remained notably aloof from Black Africans and only reluctantly embraced working-class Indians in his campaigns. Nevertheless, his persistence, resourcefulness and unpredictable methods, including early experiments with non-violent protest, made him a celebrated champion of the downtrodden and an irksome thorn in the side of the imperial lion. He was once greeted in Natal by a 'white' crowd chanting:

> Hang Old Gandhi
> from the sour apple tree.

When he finally left South Africa to return permanently to India in 1915 the then Governor General, Jan Smuts, hailed his departure with evident relief: 'The saint has left our shores, I sincerely hope forever.'

Gandhi's interest in Indian nationalist politics had been fired by the extraordinary events of the post-*swadeshi* era when Calcutta, Bombay and Lahore became crucibles of political conspiracy and terrorist intrigue. The politics of the era acquired a febrile Dostoevskian instability of which Gandhi thoroughly disapproved – he was always a Tolstoyan. During a journey from South Africa to London in 1909 he reflected on this extremist turn in Indian national life. His riposte was the pamphlet *Hind Swaraj* (Indian Home Rule), a thundering jeremiad against the frenetic and inhuman pace of modern life, written over ten frenzied days (he used his left hand when his right tired). The pamphlet takes the form of an imaginary Socratic dialogue (in reality a lengthy monologue) between Gandhi and a youthful Indian nationalist with extremist tendencies. Rebutting the imaginary activist's lust for modernity and westernization, he counsels simplicity, unity, non-violence and a return to the true 'traditions' of real India. Gandhi's distaste for modern civilization encompassed a curious, if broad, range of targets: doctors, lawyers, constitutions, railways, political parties, department stores, modern machinery and all the myriad manifestations of contemporary liberal society. Behind these supposed boons he detected a terrible malignancy: violence, hypocrisy and vice. Modern civilization was, he cautioned, incompatible with morality. Politics, greed and materialism had consumed humanity: 'Western civilization is the creation of Satan.' The only way back to a truly moral existence was to return to an older, simpler way of life revolving around the village, cottage industry, self-sufficiency and religious piety.

Ironically, much of this idealized arcadia was strikingly reminiscent of hoary Raj stereotypes. The simple peasant, the village republic, the antique benevolence of caste had all featured prominently in British colonial writing. To these romantic colonial concoctions Gandhi brought his own idiosyncratic version of the modish neo-medieval philosophies of *fin-de-siècle* Europe, derived from the stern sermons of Ruskin, Morris and Tolstoy. Rejecting the modern west as a false model of progress, he proposed that the blueprint of the perfect civilization could be found in India itself – in ancient India. The India of the Vedas, he suggested, had produced the ideal citizen, the humble villager ennobled by manual labour and simple piety, non-competitive and peace-loving. The village, with its harmonious caste-regulated organicism, was the natural unit of Indian society, and, what's more, the natural form of the Indian state and nation. What need was there for the modern, centralized nation-state – an ersatz copy of western civilization – when India had its own tradition of democracy and self-governing republics in the village *panchayat* (a council-cum-court of elders)? The economy of this ideal state would also be ancient and pastoral. Again the genealogy of anti-industrialism was distinctly European, with a lineage directly descended from Morris, Ruskin, Tolstoy and the administrative clerisy of the Raj. For the romantic dissidents of late nineteenth-century Europe, modern industry was the root of alienation and moral decay, while the British, somewhat self-servingly, had long denied India's suitability or capacity for mass industrialization. But non-industrialization was not, Gandhi argued, the result of any failing in Indian culture; it was its triumph. He insisted that the Vedic ancients had actually foreseen many modern machines and contraptions, but had disdained them as robbers of human dignity. The problem of India's gross poverty was not to be solved by cultivating the cornucopia of industrial progress, but by embracing self-sufficiency, free of the corrupting influence of luxury.

In a move that would hopelessly disorientate many on the Indian left, Gandhi also proclaimed himself a socialist, though typically, a somewhat unorthodox one. Socialism would come, he insisted, but only after a 'change of heart'; a spontaneous eruption of altruism, he predicted, would prompt the landed and the wealthy liberally to reapportion their largesse. These prophecies were accompanied by equally panglossian pronouncements on modern industrial capitalism.

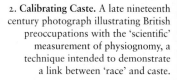

1. Categorising Indians. F. M. Coleman's *Typical Pictures of Indian Natives in Colours* presented hand-tinted photographs of the 'Gorgeous East', arranging Indians by caste, region, religion and occupation, complete with exotic and stereotypical descriptions; it proved immensely popular among British audiences, running to seven editions.

2. Calibrating Caste. A late nineteenth century photograph illustrating British preoccupations with the 'scientific' measurement of physiognomy, a technique intended to demonstrate a link between 'race' and caste.

3. Durbar Raj. The Royal pavilion of the 1911 Delhi Durbar, in which George V and Queen Mary presided over the inauguration of New Delhi as the new capital of India.

4. **Imperium Britannicum.** The roman-viaduct-style 'Gallery' bridge – one of 864 bridges on the Kalka–Simla Railway, begun in 1898. The construction of the line was masterminded, in part, by Bhalkoo, an Indian engineer known as the 'illiterate genius'.

5. **Rallying Round the Cow.** *Charasi Devata Auvali* (Cow with eighty-four deities), *c.* 1912. An example of the highly popular 'calendar art' associated with Hindu revivalism, in this case produced by cow protection movements. The cow is being menaced by the monstrous *Kali*, symbol of *Kaliyug* (the age of darkness). Above his head is the legend '*he manusyaho! Kaliyugi manasahari jovom ko dekho*' (mankind, look at the meat-eating souls of the *Kaliyug*). He is beseeched by the saffron-clad figure *dharmraj* (dutiful ruler), '*mat maro gay sarv ka jivan hai*' (don't kill the cow, everyone depends on it).

6. **Tropical Gothic.** The Bombay Municipal Corporation Building, known as 'BMC'. Begun in 1884, its architect was Frederick William Stephens, who specialized in the Gothic Revival style, here blended with 'oriental' features intended to demonstrate the raj's fusion of European and Moghul aristocratic forms.

7. **Eternal Empire.** The Residence of the Viceroy of India, now known as Rastrapati Bhavan. This was the centrepiece of Edward Lutyens' new capital for the raj at New Delhi, completed in 1929. For the design he created the 'Delhi Order', blending European classical forms with traditional Indian features – seen here in the great drum-mounted Bhuddist dome. The 'Delhi Order' columns below include sculptures of 'silent' bells that would never peel to herald the end of British rule.

8. **The Martial Alternative?** This highly symbolic painting of the late 1940s illustrates the cult of Subhas Chandra Bose, the Bengali nationalist whose founding of the Indian National Army challenged Gandhi's non-violent approach to national emancipation. An 'enslaved' mother India looks on as Bose, self-proclaimed leader of *Azad Hind* (Free India), stands over the grave of an Indian soldier who has fallen liberating a small portion of the homeland at Kohima in north-easter India in 1944.

9. **Famine.** Bengalis queuing at a soup kitchen in Calcutta in December 1943 in the midst of the Bengal Famine. The famine, now regarded as a man-made disaster, claimed 1.5 million lives.

10. **Partition.** Muslims crowd into and onto a train leaving Delhi for Pakistan in September 1947. In all, about 5 million Muslims migrated from India to Pakistan after Independence.

11. **Spinning the Nation.** A famous photographic portrait of Gandhi from the mid 1940s showing the Mahatma in his most iconic pose.

12. **Salt March, 1930.** Gandhi launches the Civil Disobedience Campaign. Gandhi, highly conscious of the power of iconography, managed his own image very carefully and ensured that international press photographers accompanied him every step of the way.

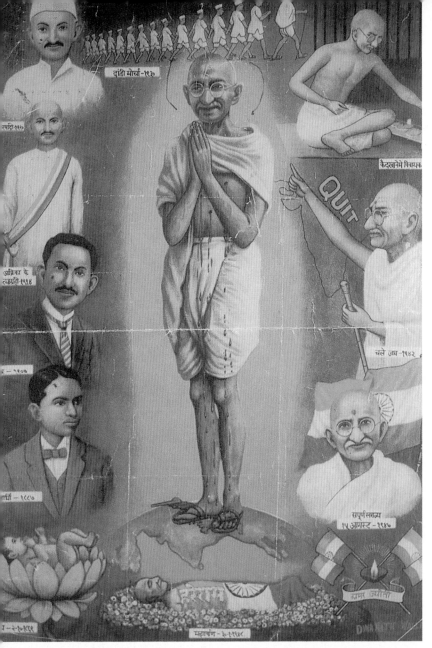

13. The Apotheosis of the Mahatma. This 1948 image of Gandhi, by the artist Dinanath, though consciously emulating Christ's Passion, is ambiguous. It had also become popular to depict the ten avatars of Vishnu in this stylized manner, suggesting a blending of Christian and Hindu iconography. The legend at the foot of the picture reads *He Ram* (Hail Ram), Gandhi's last words.

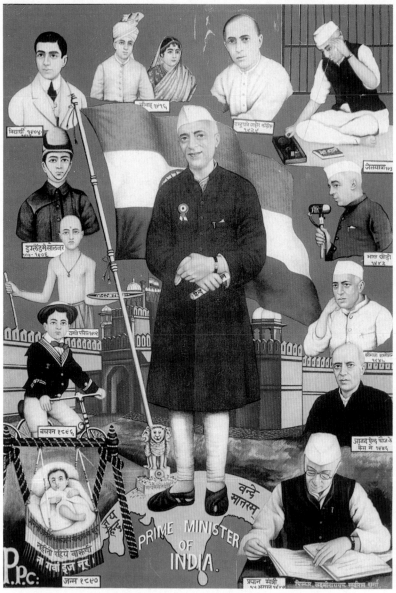

14. **From Public School to Public Servant.** This popular pictorial biography of Nehru shows his evolution from British-style public schoolboy to Congress icon through his changing headgear. As infant, schoolboy and juvenile he dons respectively a prep-school boater, a pith helmet and a ceremonial nuptial turban. However, for the political highlights of his career, political prisoner, president of Congress and, ultimately, prime minister, he sports the iconic Gandhi cap.

While basically a bad thing, factories had to be tolerated and, like the village, the factory owner and his workers were to be bound into a moral community based on mutual affection and reciprocity. Business magnates were to be seen as benign paternalists. More conventional socialists with their calls for nationalization and the 'dictatorship of the proletariat' were dismissed as the misguided dupes of modern western philosphies that merely disguised violence, coercion and greed.

Oddly, Gandhi was more sympathetic to the hypernationalism of modern Japan than he was to socialism, and like many Indians he had been awe-struck by the Japanese victory over Russia in the 1904–5 war, wondering:

What is the secret of this epic heroism? The answer is: unity, patriotic spirit, and the resolve to do or die. All Japanese are animated by the same spirit, they think of nothing but service to the nation . . . heroic indifference to life and death.

He concluded, however, that the military foundation of Japan's new strength was an unsuitable model for India. Indians were not suited, by reason of the *varna* system (the four-fold division of caste) which restricted arms-bearing to the warrior Ksatriyas, to physical battle:

India cannot rival Britain or Europe in force of arms. The British worship the war god and they can all of them become . . . bearers of arms [but] the hundreds of millions in India can never carry arms . . . [because] the *varnash-rama* is a necessary law of nature.

Having rejected the conventional routes to national power – liberalism, socialism and militarism – as unsuited to India's special genius, Gandhi formulated a mode of self-strengthening at which India could excel: the deployment of *satyagraha* ('soul-force'). *Satyagraha*, the ability to overpower your enemy with the moral truth of your position through infinite self-sacrifice, was, he claimed, a weapon of awesome power. It was more potent than physical strength and mere victory in war, because such conventional power ultimately bred pride, arrogance, decadence and decline (as the Boer War had in the British). It was, therefore, not simply the weapon of the weak (like passive resistance), but the weapon of the supremely potent. It would 'infuse manliness in cowards', and allow Indians to 'conquer our conquerors the English [and] make them bow before our tremendous soul-force'. But truth or soul-force could be effectively deployed only by those sufficiently perfected to attain 'truth'. A *satyagrahi* had to be a *brahmacharya*, supremely self-controlled in his personal habits, behaviour and desire. The task, therefore, was to fashion Indians into perfect souls and this would require a mass 'change of heart'. The rest of Gandhi's life was essentially devoted to achieving this collective heart-shift, but many of the experiments and techniques he devised struck others as eccentric, bizarre or incomprehensible. The Gandhian path to self-strengthening lay not in grand schemes for 'modern' education, industrialization and constitutional reform, but in the rigorous reform of the most quotidian and intimate aspects of Indian life. Reform and purification of the body, which Gandhi regarded as 'a mine of dirt . . . a bag of filth . . . [and] an incarnation of hell', was the route to moral power and self-rule (*swaraj*). It was through changing what people ate, how they dressed, their attitudes to sex and religion that he proposed to emancipate India from self-imposed colonization.

Gastro-politics were an all-consuming preoccupation. When his autobiography, *The Story of My Experiment With Truth*, was published in 1926, many were puzzled. Anticipating some sombre tract on great men and events, what they received was an excruciating exegesis of the Mahatma's alimentary anxieties and dietary didactics. Chapters sketched his search for the perfect nut, the pros and cons of goat's milk, the philosophy of fruit, the merits of one kind of egg, the toxicity of another. But this was not so very surprising, for as early as 1918 he had declared, 'It is impossible for unhealthy people to win *swaraj*.'

Preoccupation with the politics of food was not a new phenomenon among Indian nationalists, as the cow-protection movements of the late nineteenth century demonstrate. Many remained convinced that British power was in some way connected with what they ate, and even the youthful Gandhi, who was much embarrassed by his spindly physique, had been briefly carnivorous. However, Gandhi soon became convinced that it was the 'traditional' vegetarian diet, of the strictest kind, that would make Indians truly strong. According to certain Hindu theories each caste has its own special diet, of which the Brahman regimen, which not only prohibits flesh and alcohol but also excludes all spicy and even mildly pungent food (such as onions), was the most exacting. Dalits and the poor would improve themselves by giving up liquor, meat and other polluting substances. Over time Gandhi experimented and refined his diet, and ultimately would eat no more than five foods a day. Reasoning that all sensual pleasure generated selfishness and was an obstacle to truth and thus power, it is perhaps logical that Gandhi's ultimate weapon was the fast.

During his career as leader of the nationalist movement he embarked on no fewer than thirteen major fasts between 1918 and 1947, several of them, he threatened, unto death. While many criticized his fasting as a peculiarly effective form of moral coercion or 'white-mail', he insisted that the fast was simply the logical conclusion of his various experiments with food. He had found, to his immense irritation, that when he restricted his diet, instead of losing his appetite, he desired the few foods he allowed himself even more intensely. Restriction had in fact fed desire, not starved it. The obvious next step, he reasoned, was the complete fast, which would finally purge all vestiges of 'carnality' and release the spiritual energies needed to reach other people's hearts more effectively. So, on the occasion of his last great fast during the partition in 1947, he claimed, 'the reward will be the regaining of India's dwindling prestige and her fast-fading sovereignty over the heart . . . of the world'.

Though he occasionally suggested that the fasts were a quest for *akash* (emptiness), a Hindu concept related to spiritual power, in fact much of his thinking on health and diet was western. Gandhi was sceptical of Indian traditional medical Ayurvedic thought, which stressed the correct balance of heating, cooling, moist, dry and purifying food, and was far more attracted by some of the more outlandish pronouncements of western dietetic science. While in London he had read the works of Henry Salt, the vegetarian proselytizer, and Dr Kellogg, the experimental American nutritionist, both of whom asserted the 'scientifically' proven properties of a vegetarian diet as the most healthy. Indeed it seems that only when he had the imprimaturs of 'eminent and sober' voices from the west, was Gandhi willing finally to endorse vegetarianism as the correct national diet and health regimen. He outlined these theories in what became by far his best-selling publications – *The Key to Health* (1913) and *Self-Restraint vs. Self-Indulgence* (1927). These sermonized on the correct method of cleaning teeth, efficient mastication, keeping the nasal passages clear, abdominal mudpacks, the importance of the right bed-clothes and the perils of constipation. He also became a great advocate of yoga, now scientifically verified as efficacious by German theorists, as a 'non-violent' alternative to western-style military drilling for building up the stamina of *satyagrahis*, training them to 'withstand extremes of heat and cold, standing for long periods' and beatings. More controversial was his advocacy of the *sitz* or genital friction bath, a technique developed by the German naturopath Dr Kuhne as a cure-all for many diseases, though Gandhi was most interested in its role in curbing 'self-abuse'.

While in South Africa Gandhi had decided that sexuality was unnatural, a form of violence that had to be suppressed. Sex, like everything else, was subjected to his rigorous, if eccentric, experimental scrutiny. He concluded: 'it is surely wrong to take it for granted that because we have hitherto indulged the sexual appetite in married life, that the practice is either legitimate or healthy. Many old practices have been discontinued with good results.' He became a celibate at the age of 35. Many attributed his preoccupation with sex to guilt at the circumstances of his father's death – he had died while Gandhi 'lay' with his wife. However, his carnal concerns seem to have been as much politically as psychologically inspired, and he believed that bodily self-discipline was an indispensable preliminary to the exercise of political power. 'It is easier to conquer the whole world, than to subdue the enemies in our body', he once announced. Some of these views were derived from the god Krishna's advocacy to the warrior Arjuna in the *Bhagavad Gita* of celibacy as a recipe for success in war, promising health, longevity and tirelessness. Enforced impotence would, through some elaborate hydraulic channelling of 'energies', produce omnipotence. 'I saw that *brahmacharya* . . . is full of wonderful potency', he explained, and a nation of sober celibates would, he insisted, create a new moral order. Other connections between celibacy and nationalism were suggested by Paul Bureau's *L'Indiscipline des Moeurs* (1920), and its philosophy that 'the future is for the nations that are chaste'. From this Gandhi deduced that the defeat of colonialism required 'a halt to all reproduction for the time being', rather than bring 'weakling children into the slavery of colonial power'.

His views on masculinity were just as idiosyncratic. If Indian men were, as the British claimed, hopelessly effeminate, then effeminacy should be seen as a virtue. In 1926 he announced: 'My ideal is this: a man should remain man and yet should become woman', and on occasion he would present himself as an honorary woman. But only particular kinds of women were to be models. Virtue was essential, as was sobriety. Adornment was particularly frowned on, jewels harboured dirt and 'the cobra which has a precious stone on its hood still has poison in its fangs'. Underpinning his conception of the virtuous woman was a Gandhian proclivity for suffering as a moral and political weapon. Fashioned from Jain notions of *ahimsa* (non-violence) and inflected with the Christian belief in the potency of self-sacrifice, he seems to have developed an inclination towards self-harming as empowerment, and his views could sometimes veer perilously close to the proposition that women should suffer to atone for the vices of men. This vision of women was strikingly akin to that of the Hindu revivalist movement of the late nineteenth century, with its trope of the ideal Hindu woman: silent and submissive. As Gandhi explained, 'a real Hindu widow is a treasure. She is one of the gifts of Hinduism to humanity ... She has learnt to find happiness in suffering, has accepted suffering as sacred.' Women's true role was as 'the true helpmate of man in the mission of service ... like the slave of old', he once declared.

Gender differences, like distinctions of caste, were seen by Gandhi as natural. While he was an advocate of women's education and greater freedom, and believed that women were peculiarly well-adapted to non-violent forms of action and self-suffering, he didn't encourage their active participation in politics. He had not been enamoured of suffragette activity in pre-war Britain, which suggested an unappealing 'manly strength', and he forbad women's involvement in high-profile campaigns like the salt march. Women should come out of *purdah* only to teach men purity and non-violence; spinning was to be their forte.

And in Gandhi's utopia, there would be a lot of spinning to do. He had always been acutely sensitive to the political power of dress, and he insisted that his renewed Indian citizens were to wear a new, homespun wardrobe. Anybody who had known Gandhi as a youth would have been surprised at these ideas. He had been something of a dandy, and in London he had acquired the reputation of 'a nut, a masher, a blood' – a nineteenth-century fashion victim. He was once spotted strolling down Piccadilly in a top hat, morning coat and spats, swinging a silver-topped stick. It is possible that he was overcompensating for his vegetarian 'Indianness' (about which he betrayed much embarrassment) with sartorial hyperconformity. However, it was in South Africa that the moral and political significance of clothes really struck him. There he learnt that simply appearing in court in the 'wrong' headgear had the power to send the British into apoplexies of rage. From then on he wore only 'native' dress in court. He developed the publicist's eye for a striking image, and the crucial importance of dressing the part. The photographs of the loin-clothed Mahatama in London during the winter of 1931 were a worldwide press sensation, and he stuck stubbornly to his preference for political undress even when meeting the British monarch at court.

It was the capacity, within an Indian context, to combine utility with morality that made cloth and clothing such alluring symbols for the saintly pragmatist. His sartorial theories were clearly connected with his ideas about Indian economic development. Influenced by William Morris's writings in praise of cottage industries, Gandhi argued that the mass production of *khadi* (homespun) and *swadeshi* (homemade) cloth campaigns, along with the boycott of foreign cloth, would revive the national economy, provide employment for the poor, and unite rich and poor in the nobility of manual labour and uniformity of appearance. Gandhi also made *khadi* and *swadeshi* cloth the centre of mass political campaigns. In Jabalpur a parade of donkeys sporting English jackets, trousers and waistcoats was staged by the local Congress Committee. Elsewhere volunteers would dramatically strip themselves of their foreign clothing and hurl it on to a bonfire of the vanities, before plunging into the Ganges in an act of ritual purification. A thousand autos-da-fé of alien textiles illuminated the national landscape, accompanied by the sound of Gandhi's own clarion call: 'it is sinful to buy and use foreign cloth . . . On the knowledge of my sin bursting upon me, I must consign foreign garments to the flames and thus purify myself.'

Khadi was a brilliant political symbol, embodying the political, the practical and the transcendent. Gandhi exploited antique notions of the transformative power of cloth with virtuoso effect. Cloth has a peculiar resonance in Indian culture: colours, textures and weaves embodied particular qualities of power, goodness and purity. They could be auspicious or inauspicious, conferring or reducing status. *Khadi*'s very ambiguity lent it universal allure. Loosely woven, it was thought especially vulnerable to pollution – a poor man's cloth. But its whiteness evoked high-caste purity. Similarly, spinning and weaving were somewhat ambivalent activities. Both ennobling and humbling, they were, theoretically, able to unite high and low. On the one hand they were creative, and therefore godly tasks; but on the other, both were also potentially polluting, bringing the practitioner into contact with perilously unclean substances like dye.

Gandhi was very successful in associating the issue of cloth with the nationalist message. He argued that by wearing foreign cloth Indians had, in fact, become foreigners, and rumours reminiscent of Mutiny days were spread: foreign cloth, it was said, was made using hundreds of gallons of cow and pig blood. Wearing foreign cloth was likened to sin or disease, and clothes of a foreign cut denounced as a denial of *swadeshi* spirit. Indians, Gandhi said, were waging 'spiritual war' and 'the revival of hand spinning is least penance we must do for the sin of our forefathers in having succumbed to the satanic influences of the foreign manufacturer'. The message was clear: people would become stronger, more virtuous and more Indian by wearing *khadi*.

The whole phenomenon contributed to the appearance of a *khadi* army. Gandhi himself drew military parallels, likening spinning to the discipline of army drilling, regimented and instilling self-control. The famed Gandhi cap (deliberately white so that it would show up the dirt), became the near universal badge of nationalist allegiance after 1920. It was also a form of armour, believed, by some, to protect the wearer from bullets and even to repel the evil eye. In 1947 the English governor of Bengal was stampeded in his offices in Calcutta and several caps forced, one on top of the other, on to his head, and a Congress flag pressed into his hand, in a mock coronation. Brahman priests were censured for dressing temple gods in 'foreign cloth'; brides were urged to don *khadi* for their weddings; and Gandhi even tried to replace the traditional marigold garland with knitted *khadi* substitutes. With Gandhi's takeover of Congress, the simple white *kurta* pyjama replaced the suit and tie as the uniform of the Indian politician, and is still sported on ceremonial occasions by Congress ministers today. Nehru and other prominent convicts spun and wove their way through prison, while young volunteers painted the green, orange and saffron tricolour on to their *khadi kurtas* in ingenious defiance of the British ban on displays of the newly adopted Congress national flag.

Khadi could also endure where more flamboyant politics withered. After calling off the non-cooperation campaign in 1921, Gandhi devoted most of his energies to promoting *khadi*'s virtues: he spun in prison, on trains and on his sick bed. In 1925 he set up the All-India Spinners' and Weavers' Association, which collected funds and yarn, employed spinners and weavers and distributed the product. On one occasion he stated that social, economic and moral power was geometrically related to the spread of spinning-wheels in India. When each of India's fifty million families owned a spinning-wheel, the scale of national purification would be 'so high that we would regain that birthright of ours that we have lost'. Gandhi even insisted that spinning was a surer route to national independence than agitation: 'I say nothing will need to be done after you have universalized the spinning-wheel. You will have acquired a power and strength which everybody will automatically recognize.' In a certain sense this was true: the *khadi* associations in Bihar and Gujarat became the backbone for Congress organization, ready to revitalize the somewhat exhausted local committees during the Civil Disobedience campaign of the early 1930s.

But the Mahatma's dream of a class-free *khadi*-clad India never quite materialized. Ironically *khadi* itself was an expensive cloth relative to cheap Lancashire imports, putting it beyond the reach of the impoverished. All manner of significant differentiations soon appeared, which served to distinguish rather than homogenize: Hindu revivalists insisted on wearing saffron *khadi*, the well-heeled wore their *khadi* cut with conspicuous elegance, and soon a thriving cottage industry in silk *khadi* emerged. Concessions had to be made to Indian mill magnates whose machine-made output was nominated as 'honorary' *khadi*, in recognition of their indispensable financial services to nationalism. And on one matter Gandhi failed to prevail. The insistence that each and every senior Congress member should himself spin two hundred yards of pure *khadi* every month as a condition of office was quietly dropped when it became apparent that Congress's big-wigs were paying minions to do their spinning for them.

The last stitch in the tapestry of Gandhi's campaign for national renewal was religion. For Gandhi, religion was the essence of India, echoing the assumptions of many British scholars and officials that spirituality was India's national genius. Gandhi's own religiosity was profoundly eclectic. He had been impressed by aspects of Christianity, especially its preoccupation with self-sacrifice, but he was never tempted to convert. His ashrams were scenes for curious ecumenism, with hymn singing, rosary beads and eccentric liturgical practices. Crucial in shaping his ideas about religion and public life were his experiences in South Africa, where he had led successful campaigns of Hindus and Muslims against the pass laws. Back in India he eagerly seized on the Khilafat issue. What could be a more compelling basis on which to forge a political alliance than the defence of all India's various religious communities? In a reversal of conventional western secular politics, which strives (however unsuccessfully) to purge the religious from the political sphere, Gandhian secularism encouraged all religions to colonize the public sphere and revitalize the nation with their various faiths to create a composite nationalism. For Gandhi, the Vedas, the Bible, the Quran and the (Zoroastrian) Avesta were all ultimately derived from the same divine source. But this solution to India's 'religion problem' was dependent on the Mahatma's very particular interpretation of Hinduism. Hinduism, he argued, was unique among the world's great religions in its capacity to both tolerate and, indeed, absorb all others. This was a controversial interpretation.

Even if his ecumenism had succeeded in allaying Muslim fears, Gandhi's conception of caste was a fatal flaw in his religious vision of the united nation. Though viscerally opposed to untouchability,

Gandhi was favourably disposed to the *varnashrama*. He hoped to consolidate India's thousands of castes into the four foundational *varnas* (a suggestion strikingly similar to the project of the Raj's Census commissioners), and his solution to untouchability was to reabsorb its victims into the fourth and lowest rung of the caste ladder, the Shudras. Gandhi saw caste not as a rigid and unjust hierarchy, but simply as a rational and harmonious means of dividing labour: 'All [*varnas*] are good, lawful and absolutely equal in status. The calling of the Brahman – spiritual teacher – and scavenger are equal,' he claimed. If people inherited their occupations at birth, then individuality, selfishness and competitiveness would dissolve. To charges that caste exclusivity in matters of eating and marriage bred mutual suspicion and ill-will, he commented that if communal dining were a route to social harmony, 'there would be no wars in Europe'. However, this interpretation was utopian, unpopular and ultimately an obstacle, not a path, to national unity. For many Indians Gandhi's anti-modern national vision was reactionary, unappealing and incompatible with contemporary notions of national power and individual equality and freedom.

Gandhi himself was rather evasive about how these insights might be constructed into workable institutions. Sometimes he spoke vaguely of 'oceanic circles' – interconnecting sets of villages bound by invisible chains of love and reciprocity. On other occasions he likened his ideal India to 'Ram Rajya', the perfect kingdom of the mythical Hindu king Ram, drawn from the Hindu epic, the *Ramayana*. Gandhi's vision of an independent India may have been a little cloudy, but what was crystal clear was his nightmare India: a modern, centralized, industrialized and westernized nation-state – in other words, 'Englistan'.

Few Indians would have admitted to wanting Englistan, and the uncomfortable proximity of modernity to westernization was a vexed and treacherous issue for all third-world nationalists. The place of Indian religion, tradition and masculinity and a craving for self-respect in a world where occidental superiority was apparently inevitable, suffused all varieties of Indian political thought. But Gandhi's solution to these problems of cultural colonization and the annihilation of national identity was peculiarly hostile to modernity and found few adherents among India's intelligentsia, most of whom did indeed want some kind of modern state. There was, however, little agreement on which mix of industrialization, westernization, 'traditionalism', egalitarianism and individualism was most desirable. A number of possibilities emerged, from a fascist-style Hindu radical right to a communist-inspired left.

On Vijaya Dashami day 1925 (specially chosen as the anniversary of the defeat of the demon king Ravana by the ideal Hindu king Ram), five modern Indian warriors met in the city of Nagpur, Maharashtra. Modern because all were scientists: two doctors, an engineer and a zoologist; warriors because they were the founding fathers of the RSS or Rashtriya Swayamsevak Sangh (the national volunteer corps). Their inspiration was the erstwhile Irish nationalist, nun and Hindu convert, Margaret Noble (also known as Sister Nivedita), who had exhorted nationalists before the First World War to 'congregate and pray for fifteen minutes, every day, and Hindu society will become an invincible society'. Ram's saffron flag became its emblem. In 1927 the first training camp was opened. Boys of between 12 and 15 years of age were the target recruits. Wearing uniforms of khaki shorts, they followed a strict regime of physical jerks, weapons training with *lathis*, swords and daggers, prayer and political discussion (India's lamentable disunity was the favourite topic); every night, at exactly the same time, each volunteer sang *Bande Mataram* – the unofficial anthem of Indian nationalism, the later verses of which were found offensive by many Muslims – before going to bed. They also found time to play games and go on picnics, and in many ways this synchronized, semi-martial youth club resembled the British Boy Scout movement, except that its goal was Hindu world domination.

Building, to some extent, on the pre-war revivalism of the Arya Samaj, the RSS spread rapidly throughout north India, with 400 *shakhas* (branches) and 100,000 volunteers by 1940. Its membership was overwhelmingly urban, middle class and of either Brahman or Bania caste. University students, shopkeepers and clerks enjoyed this oasis of camaraderie in a desert of competitive and alienating insecurity. Conservative Congressmen like Vallabhbhai Patel and Madan Mohan Malaviya were early enthusiasts, welcoming its inculcation of reverence for elders, self-discipline and study in the young. In fact membership of the RSS and Congress overlapped to a considerable degree. The RSS's progenitor, Hedgewar, had been a disciple of the Maharashtrian Congress 'extremist' and Hindu cultural nationalist, Tilak, while disapproving of Gandhi, and especially his pro-Muslim sympathies. Hedgewar was a votary of the radical right nationalism of Vinayak Damodar (Veer) Savarkar, a sometime playwright, terrorist and author of the foundational text *Hindutva: Who is a Hindu?* published in 1923. Savarkar had been inspired by his proximity to Pan-Islamic Khilafatists while in prison in the early 1920s. Struck by their fervour for the Holy Places of Arabia, he concluded that it was impossible for Muslims (or Christians) ever to be true Indian patriots. By the late 1930s this approach to nationalism had acquired a more sinister spin, with the latest RSS leader, M. Golwalkar, citing Nazi Germany as a possible role model: 'Germany has shown how well nigh impossible it is for races and cultures, having differences going to the root, to be assimilated into one united whole, a good lesson for us in Hindustan to learn and profit by.'

Ironically Golwalkar and Savarkar, while denouncing Islam and Christianity, advocated a programme of action that was slavishly emulative. Savarkar praised these religions for their 'fierce unity of faith, social cohesion and valorous fervour'. Hindus, by contrast, were wedded to disintegrative notions of individual liberty, elaborate philosophizing and arcane traditions. What was needed was a sense of 'theocratic patriotism', an integrative temple and faith, and 'a state powerful enough to weld [Hindus] into an organic whole'. They had to embrace modernity, western science, European forms of the state and military organization. The greatest threat to this militant integrative nationalism, in their opinion, was Gandhi, with his wishy-washy dogmas of non-violence and love of the primitive. Denouncing the 'mealy-mouthed formulas of *ahimsa* [non-violence] and spiritual brotherhood', Savarkar's play *Sanyastha Khadga* (Renunciate Sword) suggested that Gandhian non-violence was the high road to Hindu subjugation and a heinous obstacle to national integration. According to Hedgewar, Gandhian non-cooperation encouraged disunity. Violence, he insisted, was an essential element in nation-building, and the destiny of the RSS was to counter Hindu fragmentation with 'disciplined organization' (*sangathan*) and to fashion a new muscular Hinduism.

However, while they chided Gandhi for his backward-looking promotion of the old four-*varna* caste system and claimed to want a reformed and integrated Hinduism without hereditary caste, in reality the leaders of the RSS were more determined to preserve a version of caste than the Mahatma was himself. They never intended that all castes should become equal. Even so they did try to 'convert' dalits and tribal peoples to caste Hinduism, encouraging them to identify themselves as Shudras, adopt the practices of 'clean caste' Hindus and to identify themselves in the official census as Hindus. These strategies had two purposes: to bolster Hindu numbers and increase their electoral power, and to disarm the political assertiveness of low-caste and dalit groups by stressing the necessity for 'Hindu' solidarity against supposed Muslim and Christian threats.

Underpinning the ideology of the RSS were older anxieties about high-caste Hindu status. RSS ideologues were acutely conscious of British disparagement of their masculinity, their exclusion from the military and the army's supposed dependence on low castes for martial duties. They also presented Muslims as a sexual threat. In one of his plays Savarkar has a rapacious Muslim brag of 'fulfilment of lust through faith and fulfilment of faith through lust . . . Enjoy the girls of the *kaffirs*, corrupt them, this mantra . . . is my Quran.' The notion of Hindu sexual and demographic victimization found its most hysterical expression in the writings of Swami Shraddhanand, a Punjabi Arya Samajist, in his *Hindu Sangathan – Saviour of a Dying Race* (1926), which sketched a lurid picture of exponentially multiplying Muslims soon out-numbering the more prudent and restrained Hindus in their own land.

This preoccupation with national machismo was in marked contrast to the Gandhian feminization of politics. The RSS saw itself as a manly corrective to such effeminacy: high-caste boys were certainly not to become more like women; they were to become muscular Hindus. Amidst these feverish xenophobic, caste and racial terrors, the one foreign group to escape RSS censure was that which ran the country – the British. The leaders admired British power and saw the Raj as a force for Indian revitalization. Unlike Gandhi, the RSS did not have a heroic history of anti-colonial struggle. Indeed, during the 1942 Quit India movement it co-operated with the British. Urged by Savarkar to 'stick to their posts and continue to perform their duties', his wartime slogan was not 'Quit India' but 'Hinduize Politics and Militarize Hinduism'.

Not all Hindu cultural nationalists espoused political violence. The Hindu Mahasabha, which shared the RSS's enthusiasm for building a Hindu nation, preferred to associate themselves with mainstream nationalism. For Mahasabha members there was a wing of Congress that they found most congenial to their culturally conservative and generally anti-socialist outlook. The chief proponent of this brand of Congress nationalism was Vallabhbhai Patel, Gujarati strongman and Gandhi's right-hand man. Born in 1875 Patel was a small-town lawyer (*vakil*) from the Patidar peasant group which dominated Gujarati rural and, increasingly, urban politics. This was a socially and economically ambitious group which had done relatively well under the British, but were frustrated by the economic stagnation of the post-First World War era and had begun to question the beneficence of British rule. Patel himself was steeped in the informal politics of *mofussil* (up-country) India, characterized by family, caste, community, professional and commercial organizations. This clever, bridge-playing *vakil* had first met that other clever small-town *vakil*, Gandhi, during one of his early campaigns in 1917. There was a strong mutual attraction based on genuine religious piety, a respect for order and a rich appreciation of the importance of institution-building and group co-ordination in politics. Patel was a genius not of rhetoric, but of organizational strategy. Shrewdly insightful, he had spotted the immense, untapped resource of the informal bases of authority in India, on whom the British relied but had never entirely co-opted.

Though previously a loyal adherent of non-cooperation, with the failure of Civil Disobedience in 1934 Patel concluded that Congress's future lay in constitutional politics. But this was not simply a matter of factional manipulation, log-rolling and pork-barrel deal-making. His networks of moderate nationalists had ideological goals and value systems of their own. Certainly they wanted India to be a great nation, economically powerful, free of western exploitation and cultural humiliation. But they did not want social revolution or violent disorder. The Indian nation was to be based on the preservation of a caste-hierarchical social order based on orthodox religious piety, the protection of property and control of the 'masses'. Patel embodied this more conventionally conservative nationalism. Its objectives were to rid India of British domination, while keeping in abeyance appeals to the more disruptive ideologies that often accompanied nationalism, be they selfish individualism or socialist collectivism, both of which threatened the traditional values of family, religious sentiment and proper social order. For Patel the best way to defeat these anarchic forces was not through argument and rhetoric – that could be left to Gandhi – but by institutional manoeuvres. While dominating the Congress politburo, the increasingly powerful All-India Congress Working Committee, Patel also scrupulously cultivated his links with the provincial-level leadership. It was this provincial level of leadership which tapped directly into India's most enduring social structures, networks that could be very effectively mobilized to keep at bay any challenge from the left. Presiding over these two great levers of the nationalist shadow state, Patel was able both to steer Congress's campaign against the Raj at the national level, while ensuring, through his provincial power, that the new nation would not be so very different from the old.

The main enemy of Patelite nationalism was the Indian left. But the left lacked Patel's genius for group co-ordination and was never able to transcend its internal differences. These divisions were broadly two-fold. The first concerned method; should socialism be achieved by force or by consensus? The second centred on the competing claims of nationalism and internationalism. Was India, as the orthodox Marxists claimed, simply part of a universal global movement whose socialism would look much like anyone else's? Or should the left be worried about foreign-influenced socialism – was this just another form of colonialism? Those in the latter camp insisted that India develop its own indigenous brand of socialism, one specifically tailored to India's unique culture. The failure to resolve these differences contributed to the left's conspicuous failure to impose its vision on the nationalist movement.

On the radical internationalist left was the Indian Communist Party founded by sometime Bengal revolutionary Narendra Nath Bhatta-charya, better known as M. N. Roy. Roy was an adherent of early twentieth-century Marxism, and his vision of India, radically at odds with Gandhi's, envisaged an urbanized, industrial and machine-based utopia, which quite eclipsed the modest developmental attainments of the Raj. Orthodox Marxist in vision, the Indian communists were initially unorthodox in strategy. While in Berlin in the early 1920s, they denounced Lenin's advocacy of a broad front with the national-ists, arguing that India's masses were already revolutionary and 'bour-geois' leadership should be spurned. However, despite their suspicion of Gandhi, 'the mascot of the bourgeoisie', by the late 1920s the Indian communists had adopted the orthodox Moscow line and supported the 'bourgeois' Congress. They continued to zigzag be-tween a pro- and anti-Congress stance, depending on the latest direc-tive from the Comintern, an approach which seriously weakened their credibility during the Second World War, when, following the Anglo-Soviet alliance, they took a pro-British and anti-nationalist line.

The slavishly pro-Moscow communists left room for another form of Marxism, more fully blended with nationalism. In 1928 the Hindustan Socialist Republican Army (HSRA), an out-growth of the older revolutionary tradition of the Punjab, was founded in Lahore. Led by a charismatic 22-year-old student, Bhagat Singh, it departed from its pre-war terrorist lineage by adopting Marxist militant atheism as its ideology. The HSRA favoured acts of 'exemplary' revolutionary violence. Between 1928 and 1929 Singh and his associates attempted to explode Viceroy Irwin's train, succeeded in blowing up a British policeman (though not the one they intended) and, most famously, threw a bomb into the Central Legislative Assembly in New Delhi. During its brief existence, it also attempted to gather a mass base in the countryside, a departure from orthodox Marxist thinking as strik-ing as Mao Zedong's Chinese peasant experiments. Calling for free republics of peasants and workers, the 'army' distributed revolution-ary leaflets at village fairs, established peasant 'front' organizations in the countryside, gave 'lantern' lectures on revolutionary martyrs and planned a massive recruitment offensive in the villages of the Punjab with emotive songs and poems in its journal, *Kirti*. ('The fat bellies which can be seen are swollen with flesh cut from our stomachs . . . We will cut off the nose of capitalism.') However, all this activity came to nought when the leaders of the movement, including Bhagat Singh himself, were arrested and executed in 1931.

Within Congress itself, elements on the left sympathized with Bhagat Singh's desire to indigenize socialism, but saw his atheism as incompatible with this urge. The most creative thinker on the Congress left was Sampurnanand. His thought blended Marxism and Hindu revivalism, Fabianism with Hindu reformism, to produce a Hindu socialism. Drawing deeply on his Banaras childhood, suffused with the ritual of the yearly 'mystery play' based on the life of Ram, the *Ramlila*, he believed that socialism in India had to reconcile democracy and social responsibility with spiritual values. This was best done by preserving the notions of *dharma* (duty), central to Hinduism, as these would act as a curb on selfish individualism. Moreover, Hinduism was the organic, spiritual cement of the Indian nation, able to transform mere society into a spiritual community. This was a deliberate conflation of western and Vedantic ideas. While democracy was desirable, every nation had to adapt it to its own 'genius and traditions'. His idea of combining Hinduism with public service to the nation were outlined in his book *Ganesha*, designed to coax ordinary Indians from their superstitious religiosity to a more socially aware form of spirituality. In common with many on the Hindu cultural right, Sampurnanand saw no problem with asserting Hinduism as the basis of national identity. It was, he insisted, a tolerant and essentially 'secular' faith, easily able to accommodate other beliefs. He was therefore happy to maintain links with Hindu communal organizations, convinced that a rejuvenated Hindu society would have radical social implications.

But others, while uncomfortable with the coercive and alien provenance of orthodox Marxism, were also unhappy with efforts to hitch socialism to Hindu revivalism. The most prominent of these nationalistic, but secular, socialists was Jawaharlal Nehru. Born in 1889, the son of the wealthy lawyer and Congress leader Motilal Nehru, he was educated in England and returned to India just after the First World War. In the mid to late 1920s he travelled extensively in Russia and Europe. Though much impressed by Bolshevik economic ideas, of which he approved as thoroughly modern and scientific, he was hostile to their repressive politics. Nevertheless Nehru was frustrated by what he regarded as Gandhi's excessive moderation and he became involved with the growing Indian labour movement. He even attempted to form his own youth party of mass action – the Independence for India League. This was a dismal failure, and Nehru concluded that only a magician like Gandhi could move India's peasant and pious masses. There was, he argued, no future for an independent left outside Congress or for class struggle. As he declared, 'The Congress is the country and the country is Congress.' Henceforth his objective was to imbue Congress with a social democratic programme of land reform, industrialization and social justice.

Nehru's views were popular among elements of the Indian intelligentsia. But perhaps more influential as a representative of the Indian-educated and westernized classes was Rabindranath Tagore. From a cosmopolitan family of wealthy merchants, artists and intellectuals, he was born in 1861, spent time in England as a youth and was much travelled. Awarded a Nobel prize in 1913 for his poem sequence *Gitanjali*, he briefly flirted with the identity of mystic eastern sage, and in the 1890s had even been attracted by the revivalist wing of nationalism. However, Tagore was a quintessential cultural hybrid, wholly immersed in modernity and the new, whatever its origin. In London he had delighted domestic audiences with his renditions of music hall classics such as 'Won't you call me Mollie, darling' and 'Come into the garden, Maud'.

His vision of a modern India was much closer to Nehru's than Gandhi's. Unlike Nehru, however, Tagore was ambivalent about nationalism itself, and came increasingly to see it as parochial at best, chauvinist at worst. The essence of India, he believed, was its openness to outside cultural influence, and its genius for assimilation. He deplored Gandhi's diatribes against modern, and by implication western, civilization, urging in the place of sullen isolation a fertile marriage. His model was Japan, which he had visited frequently and praised for its creative response to the west. Japan was 'where the East and the West found their meeting place and carried on their courtship for long enough to give assurance of a wedding'. He was interested in modern notions of internationalism, modern art, international institutions (such as the League of Nations) and progressive education (he founded the experimental arts university of Shantiniketan in Bengal immediately after the Great War).

Tagore also worried about the stultifying effect of Gandhi's notion of 'composite nationalism', a view of India composed of tolerant, but essentially separate and compartmentalized religions, which he linkened to 'worshipping with all ceremony a magnificent cage'. This approach, he argued, could produce only frosty co-existence or 'a federation of blocs', when what was needed was a more creative blending and deliberate mixing of religious cultures, to produce something unique to modern India. He called this his '*mahajati*' (nation as mega-caste) model of complete integration. Gandhi's fetishistic hostility to modernity and to the intellect also infuriated him, as it did many who shared his high-brow, Bengali *bhadralok* (western-educated and land-owning) cultural milieu. Again, he saw these postures as a denial of India's essence – an artistic, creative, intellectual and dynamic society. 'Mind,' he cautioned, 'is no less valuable than cotton thread.' And while he conceded that men had to be wary of enslavement by big machines, as Gandhi warned, there was the equal peril of 'being stunted by small machines also'. Again, he pointed to Japan as an example of the creative use of modern technology, praising its harnessing of 'the whirlwind of modern civilization'.

He was particularly hostile to Gandhi's attitude to caste, and in his *The Unapproved Story* of 1925, Tagore satirized the self-serving and condescending attitudes of high-caste young nationalists to their servants and low-caste groups. In the story the heroine, a young student, becomes a 'Goddess of Swadeshi', flitting from one pointless committee to another, finally ending up as chief busybody on the local orphanage board. Having conceived a jealous dislike of the servant girl who looks after her nationalist hero uncle, she conspires to have the girl and her sisters exported to the orphanage for 'improvement'. Poignantly, it later transpires that she herself is a low-caste orphan, who has enjoyed the loving nurture of an adoptive family that she now seeks to deny to others.

Tagore's views, unlike Nehru's and Gandhi's, were not institutionalized in a political party, but nevertheless they exerted a powerful influence. His call for a blending of western classicism with Indian feeling to express modern universal values shaped Indian fine art for the next fifty years. These ideas also found a receptive audience among early Indian filmmakers, among them the Bombay-based pioneer director Dhundiraj Govind Phalke. His films challenge caste and gender conventions to present an internationalized ideal nation, in contrast to Gandhi's pre-modern and insular arcadia. Film, he argued, was a powerful agent of egalitarian internationalism, not hierarchical nationalism, because it showed Indians how other societies were organized. It was also a medium for projecting democratic values into a hierarchical culture, because all, regardless of caste, class or gender, were equal before the big screen (Phalke was a great advocate of non-segregated cinema seating). He used cinema to dilute the high-caste influences that had taken over Indian theatre (*Henry V*, *Hamlet*, *Othello* and *Macbeth* were firm favourites), by reintroducing the influence of *tamasha* culture. *Tamasha*, or popular theatre, was generally bitingly satirical, irreverent, erotic and egalitarian. Moreover, cinema could dissolve religious and communal antagonisms because, in its very conception, it was syncretic. Early Indian cinema was heavily influenced by the so-called blended 'Islamicate' culture of north Indian urban life, and Phalke himself always referred to India as a 'Hindumusalman' enitity: 'All people, Hindumusalman, Chini, Japani are coming together in the cinema houses.'

Like Tagore, Phalke identified the four-*varna* caste system as a fault-line in Indian civilization, and for him film was an agent of change. His most famous intervention in the caste debate was also India's first example of its pre-eminent genre, the 'Hindu Mythological', through which he sought to shape an 'Indian humanism', a mix of western and eastern visions of the good. Much influenced by the French film of 1911, *Life of Christ*, Phalke had been inspired to make a celluloid biography of Krishna. He based his script on the traditional text *Raja Harishchandra*, the fabular tale of the good king of Ayodhya, another mythical ideal. However, he chose the text in order to make a deliberate point, and his version of *Raja Harishchandra* departed significantly from 'tradition' to press a more universal and modernist understanding of India. *Raja Harishchandra* is the story of a legendary Hindu Brahman king, who through a series of tests devised by his ritual inferior the Ksatriya sage Vishvamitra is driven from misery to misery, finally ending up a slave on a cremation ground. The real subject of the play is the nature of the caste order, in particular the humiliation of the Brahman by someone of lower status. The play had become very popular in Maharashtra in the late nineteenth century, where it was used by high-caste authors to drive home the evils of low-caste assertion. In these high-caste versions the wicked and uppity Vishvamitra gets a violent come-uppance and the 'correct' caste hierarchy is restored. In Phalke's version, lower-caste sage and high-caste king are harmoniously reconciled.

Phalke, like Tagore, believed that film had the capacity to reorder Indian mentalities, to bring 'ordinary' Indians into contact with other worlds. Cinema, he argued, was an ideal social space for effecting change, imitating the atmosphere of the village *mela* (festival) where the village forgot its narrowness. Film was to revitalize village culture, and a sense of modern individualism would be instilled into these 'traditional' people. As they were brought up close to gods and kings on screen, they would see them as human beings, shed their customary deference and begin to create a uniquely Indian modernity. Both Gandhi and the Raj also had great faith in the power of the new medium, which spread like prairie-fire through urban India and had, by the 1930s, even begun to acquire rural audiences.

The penetration of new ideas into even the most remote and impoverished corners of society was a phenomenon not just of culture, but of politics too. In recent years historians have been much concerned with the mental life of the so-called 'subaltern', or powerless ones, the very poor, tribal peoples and so forth. Some have surmised that such groups, hermetically sealed from the impress of colonial modernity, represent unspoiled or authentic India, which the force of nationalism used and then discarded. However, as previously seen, closer inspection suggests that it is both difficult to define the subaltern and to demonstrate that s/he was cut off from change and modernity. A great variety of popular mentalities, cultures and moral systems coexisted among the poor. Some were religious and millenarian, some paternalistic and hierarchical. But others were more modern, and manifested signs of class-consciousness and an appreciation of the values of the modern liberal state. Some found Gandhian nationalism appealing, others preferred greater radicalism. Yet none succeeded in breaking the bounds of locality or province to create nationwide networks or leaderships to compete with Congress.

The religiosity of the politics of some is undeniable, from adulation of Gandhi's *sadhu* (holy man) status, to the emergence of armies of mini-Gandhis who sprang to brief prominence as the leaders of dramatic rebellions. *Sadhus* became Congress's undercover propagandists: discreetly endorsing Congress while on politically financed 'religious' tours; adapting *kathas* (religious songs and poems) to nationalist ends; warning temple-goers they would be polluted by people wearing foreign cloth; making injunctions to boycott government taxes; and enunciating politicized versions of the epic *Ramayana*, identifying Ram's rule with Gandhi's.

Perhaps the most striking example of such religious millenarianism in popular politics was the Moplah Rebellion in coastal Malabar in 1920–21. Ostensibly part of Gandhi's non-cooperation movement, the Shia Muslim peasants of the region conducted an effective guerrilla war against the British. Local clerics promised peasants that with the coming of an Islamic state 'there will be no expensive litigation . . . No one shall have more than he actually needs', and the police would be abolished. The violation of the Tirurangadi mosque by British soldiers in boots during a search for arms provoked a full-blown uprising with attacks on police stations, post offices, rail and telegraph wires. The rebels took control of many districts for several months and proclaimed 'Khilafat republics'; in one case, a certain Variamkunnath Kunhammad Haji proclaimed himself Raja of the Hindus, Amir of the Muslims and Colonel of the Khilafat army from a buffalo-cart. Charismatic leaders emerged with the usual armoury of startling capacities: Umar Qazi could evaporate from prison, while Sayyid Alavi had the power to re-erect fallen trees. A certain suicidal element characterized the movement, with many electing to fight to the death. Forced conversion of Hindus was also a feature. And while the national Congress-Khilafat campaign was crucial in lending legitimacy to this uprising, it was also built on a long history of poor Muslim tenant grievances and periodic rebellions against Hindu landlords, and much of the conflict had incipient class motivations.

Elsewhere, low-caste and dalit politics sometimes took a strikingly modern form, espousing Enlightenment values and even atheism.

For these groups, Gandhi's idealization of the Hindu caste system as a paternalistic organic community was especially repugnant. They sought cultural separation from Hinduism, through atheism, conversion, or the pursuit of new Brahman-free religions. Some, such as Dr B. R. Ambedkar (a Colombia PhD), who led the Maharashtrian Mahar dalits, attempted to build hybrid caste-cum-class alliances between low-caste and dalit groups. In 1936 he founded the Independent Labour Party (ILP), an anti-Brahman and anti-capitalist party. His objective was to create a broad front of dalits, low castes and labouring poor across north India. In his powerful anti-Hindu diatribe, *The Annihilation of Caste*, Ambedkar likened Hinduism to 'a veritable chamber of horrors ... These very instruments which have mutilated, blasted and blighted the life of us are to be found intact and untarnished in the bosom of Gandhism.' He insisted that Hinduism must be radically reformed, with caste intermarriage and the replacement of the hereditary priesthood with state employees chosen by examination. Only then could the principles of 'liberty, equality and fraternity', the basis of true democracy, be established in India. This was the first manifestation of a strategy of yoking class to caste that would become a formidable political force fifty years later. In the 1930s it failed, as many low-caste groups in the north opted for the more socially respectable route of assimilation into the Gandhian Congress, rather than make common cause with dalits.

A more successful brand of low-caste political mobilization emerged in the south. With its wafer-thin layer of high castes, the south had always provided a more promising milieu for low-caste and dalit alliances. The onetime Congressman and low-caste journalist Ramaswami Naicker abandoned Congress in the mid-1920s over its refusal to endorse caste quotas in elections. In 1925 he founded the Self-Respect Association and its propaganda sheet, *Kudi Arasu*. Like Ambedkar, he identified Hinduism as the enemy of low-caste progress, but unlike Ambedkar, he thought it was fundamentally unreformable and became a militant atheist. His contemptuous attitude to the baleful influence of Hinduism on Indian public life is strikingly akin to the anti-Catholic diatribes of the Enlightenment *philosophes*. Indeed, Rousseau was one of his inspirations. Superstition and caste division,

Naicker argued, had to crumble before science, secularization and progress. Europe, he claimed, had been plagued by religious troubles even worse than India's, and had wisely got rid of God. 'Where have their gods and priests gone?' he enquired. 'They have all arrived here!' Atheism was the only answer.

Apart from anything else, as Naicker observed, the sheer cost of tending to 330 million gods was a terrible financial burden. The money, he insisted, could be much better spent: 'If only our idols would abstain from food for 25 years, we [would not] find even a single uneducated person in our country.' Naicker also shrewdly made common cause with a variety of non-Brahman sects, including dalits, Christians and Muslims, arguing that they all had a common need for special political privileges to protect them from the oppressive Brahmans.

Surveying the bewildering profusion of nationalist ideologies and teeming cadres of political heroes, all competing to challenge the Raj to its last great fight, it seems distinctly odd that the frail and eccentric Gandhi should have emerged as star rhetorician, strategist extraordinaire and commander-in-chief of the Indian freedom struggle. But he wielded his charisma with formidable skill and stuck single-mindedly to his goals: both to challenge British power, and to cement Indian social unity. His master strategy of non-violent non-cooperation was founded on the beguilingly simple premise that since the Raj depended on Indian co-operation, the withdrawal of that co-operation would automatically bring about its fall. While the Raj was never completely toppled, it did totter, and the Gandhian Congress was singularly adept at wounding its moral legitimacy and stealthily displacing its practical authority. These achievements owed much to Gandhi's success in building a remarkably broad, if not all-inclusive, national coalition. His anti-capitalist nostrums and concern for social justice attracted the left, while his religious piety and insistence on social order pulled in the conservative right. Despite this, however, his influence in Congress was not all conquering; by the late 1930s the movement he actually led bore scant resemblance to the one he had set out to create. It was not the all-embracing, idealistic force for transcendental freedom he had intended, but a spatch-cocked and motheaten agglomeration, in which idealism was in danger of being eclipsed by calculating self-interested pragmatism. For despite the leftism of some of its leaders, the body of the movement was decidedly conservative. Gandhian nationalism was a triumph, of sorts. It did succeed in undermining British power, while managing to avoid internecine strife. But it was a victory at the cost of narrowing the social base and idealistic ambition of nationalism.

In eight climactic months between April and December 1919, the Mahatma took the nationalist movement by storm. By the careful deployment of celebrity and charisma, the exploitation of his rivals' disarray and through a series of daring organizational coups, he successfully manoeuvred himself into the unelected post of lifetime leader of Congress. Returning from South Africa in 1915 he was already famous across the whole of a subcontinent in which celebrity had previously been localized. And despite taking a vow of political silence in 1915, he had, by 1917, elevated his moral authority even further. He had become involved with three prominent local political struggles in 1916 and 1917: a strike in Ahmedabad in Gujarat, the Champaram indigo growers' dispute in Bihar, and the land tax crisis in Kheda, also in Gujarat. Though not the instigator of any of these, he was called in by local leaders to lend some national glamour to the proceedings, and had shown himself a deft operator in both conventional and unconventional political battles. He parleyed with factory owners, bamboozled the British in the courts, choreographed mass protests and supplicated before numerous commissions of inquiry. The British were beginning to find him irksome and his reputation as a political fixer was spreading.

However, to explain his ultimate triumph it is necessary to mention another remarkable Gandhian asset: raw political cunning. Between April 1919 and December 1920 Gandhi effectively hijacked the Congress's high command at a series of key conferences, in the course of which he managed to impose a political programme radically at odds with its previous actions: the strategy of non-violent non-cooperation. This was not perceived to be an entirely friendly takeover; many older and more established Congressmen resented the interloper and distrusted his populism and taste for mobilization. They were, however, comprehensively outmanoeuvred. He proved himself a political operator of awesome skill, wrong-footing opponents, mobilizing hordes of new members from around the country and ushering small armies of *sadhus* in to clinch crucial votes. He was also a fundraiser and accountant of considerable gifts, who would sit on the floor and personally count donations, anna by anna. At the Nagpur Congress of 1920, he consolidated his hold by rewriting the party constitution and imposing radical regional reorganization. Henceforth Congress regions, rather than shadowing the territorial structure of the Raj's India, reflected real linguistic divisions. Telugu-speaking Andhra, in the south, was separated from Madras, and Gujarat from Maharashtrian Bombay. These linguistic concessions certainly made Gandhi popular, and brought new groups pouring into the movement, which now seemed much more 'theirs' and not an elite lobby. He deployed these tactics to great effect. By late December 1920 opposition had crumbled, crucial allegiances had had been switched and critical votes won. And at its famous Nagpur session Congress adopted a resolution to campaign with non-violent mass action for a vaguely defined notion of *swaraj*. The era of the saint had arrived.

The centrepiece of the non-cooperation programme was the boycott of all goods and institutions that made the Raj run. Indians were exhorted to disdain foreign goods, boycott the new elections, abjure the British-run courts, play truant from the state's schools and councils and reject the Raj's honours, titles and other demeaning baubles of servitude. Though the boycott of elections was strikingly successful, this 'middle-class' aspect of the movement had the least impact. Though middle-class students and children proved most obliging players, quitting school and college with alacrity, their more conservative and respectable parents were unconvinced of Gandhi's anti-establishment techniques and strongly disapproved of their children neglecting their education. Resignation of office, boycott of law courts and the refusal of titles were patchy and generally disappointing affairs – only 24 titles were returned.

The second stage of the movement was, by comparison, a runaway hit. This involved the mass burning of foreign cloth, *hartals* (sit-ins), *khadi* and *swadeshi*, and a controlled and peaceful assault on 'unjust' laws. Non-violence, or *ahimsa* was stressed and volunteers were enjoined not to return violence with violence, however provoked they might be by police or others. Also, no action likely to pit Indian against

Indian was permitted, strikes and rent boycotts were prohibited, and instructions specified no rudeness. Nevertheless, these protests were by no means sober or earnest events and made brilliant political theatre, with Gandhi an inspired dramaturge.

From a cast of millions, the starring roles went to the young, the poor and the Muslims. Muslim support was extraordinary, energized by the harsh treatment of the Ottoman Empire at the end of the First World War. The more radical of the Khilafatists were led by Gandhi's allies, the Ali brothers, who favoured mass agitation and were thus happy to make common cause with Gandhi's call for non-cooperation to attain *swaraj*. Westernized young graduates along with the more traditional *ulema* joined together to galvanize the Muslim villages and *mohulahs* (neighbourhoods) of India into action. This astonishingly unified Muslim action combined with an upsurge of protest among large portions of the urban and rural poor to generate an electrifying movement that rivalled the Rebellion in its fervour and, briefly at least, terrified the British.

From the impoverished sharecroppers of the United Provinces, who had laboured for decades under appalling conditions, to the ex-ploited tea-garden workers of Assam, from the tribal forest peoples of Kumaun to the immiserated Muslim tenants of the Malabar coast, 'Gandhi-raj' became a byword for revolt and renaissance. Nearly seven million workdays were lost through strikes in 1921, many associated with Congress, despite Gandhi's stern discouragement of labour militancy. Throughout 1921 Gandhi toured the entire subcontinent by train, mobbed wherever he stopped by heaving crowds of peasants and townspeople who had come to get *darshan* (a vision) of him. And he was not the only one riding the rails; tens of thousands of peasants trundled about the country ticket-less, convinced that 'Gandhi-raj' meant free travel. Throughout the land the Gandhi phenomenon acquired a distinctly magical air. Spiders, it was rumoured, were spinning his name in their webs; he was regularly spotted turning his *chakra* down village wells. In many places the movement became hitched to earlier cults, such as that of the pox goddess of Bardoli, now in full swing following the influenza epidemic of the post-war years. Unsurprisingly news spread rapidly that the Raj was collapsing, and by late 1921 the British were seriously rattled. In November the

Viceroy even suggested an amnesty for all political prisoners and called for a Round Table Conference of the British and Indians to review the reforms.

But most of these movements, far from being conjured up by the magus Gandhi, pre-dated the non-cooperation upsurge and already had their own leaders and programmes. In Gorakhpur, in rural east United Provinces, where Gandhi-raj was enthusiastically proclaimed, it proved impossible for Congress workers to impose anything resembling the Gandhian manifesto. Rumours flew that Gandhi had urged the people to loot markets and attack money-lenders, and the pious and puritanical nostrums of the Mahatma were spurned in favour of coarse and vengeful imprecations: ordure, it was said, would rain down of the houses of Gandhi deniers. Elsewhere tensions surfaced between the Gandhian and the Khilafat leadership, which maintained their separate organization. Radicalized *ulema*, infuriated by the jailing of the Ali brothers, launched *fatwas* against the Raj and it proved difficult to restrain their militarized drilling and menacing threats of Holy War. In November 1921 the rioting and strikes that marked the Prince of Wales's visit to Bombay provoked Gandhi to thunder, 'the spirit of *swaraj* stank in my nostrils'.

This barely contained violence revealed the great potential for class and community conflict, and for mass agitations to alienate the better off and split the nationalists. The non-cooperation movement had promised to integrate poor and wealthy, urban and rural, right and left against British oppression. But its effect was to raise the lid on a seething cauldron of conflict, not between the British and Indians, but between Indians and Indians. The problem now was to slam the lid back on. Gandhi's conviction that India enjoyed innate class and religious unity was clearly exposed as illusory. Henceforward breadth of mobilization would have to be sacrificed to the practicable unity of a narrow movement. On 5 February 1922 Gandhi called non-cooperation off, when a police station in the small railway village of Chauri Chaura in eastern United Provinces was burnt down by non-cooperators, killing the 22 Indian police inside. Heedless of all mitigation, Gandhi was implacable. Congress leaders demanded that the perpetrators own up and over 170 were sentenced to death.

For the next six years Congress led a curiously schizophrenic existence, its political personality uneasily divided between agitators and constitutionalists. Gandhi languished in Yeravda prison for two years, where he read the *Bhagavad Gita* and worked on his serialized autobiography. He had concluded that India was still not ready for soul-force and dedicated himself to *sarvodaya* (universal uplift), or 'constructive work' instead, emulated by provincial leaders like Patel in Gujarat and Rajendra Prasad in Bihar. Patel and Prasad were both convinced Gandhians, but they also shrewdly deployed constructive work to bolster their regional political satrapies. Elsewhere Congress membership plummeted and factionalism, reminiscent of the pre-Gandhian era, resurfaced. Party bosses were seemingly united only in the violence of the invective they periodically poured on one another.

Support for Congress was also increasingly undermined by the operation of the British-created provincial assemblies. Although the first elections had been boycotted by Congress supporters, for many the lure of electoral politics began to prove irresistible. Regional, community and caste-based politicians were now partially running provincial government and were assiduously cultivated by the Raj. The reformed assemblies had conferred palpable, albeit limited powers of bureaucratic patronage and influence over subjects like education which caste and community groups competed for in vicious zero-sum tournaments. Some politicians were also attracted to electoral politics out of principle: why shouldn't the nationalist struggle be carried into the electoral sphere, especially with the Mahatma in temporary retirement?

Some abandoned Congress completely to join rival parties, such as the anti-Brahman Justice party in the south. Within Congress too, electoral groupings emerged. In 1923 the Swarajist party was formed as an electoral 'wing'. The Swarajist strategy was to expose the sham of British reformism by winning elections but refusing office, using their numbers to obstruct administration by voting down budgets, and indulging in general obstreperousness. In this they had much success. Some Congressmen, however, found the glitter of office just as inviting. In the Central Provinces men elected on a pseudo-Congress ticket became cabinet ministers using their powers to promote the interests of their almost exclusively high-caste Hindu constituents.

Elsewhere, even Gandhian Congressmen launched themselves into city and municipal politics, where they avidly fought for the spoils of office.

Ultimately all of these erstwhile Congress members, whether opportunists, faction bosses, communal ideologues or nationalist idealists, were pre-eminently professional politicians, for whom premature obsolescence loomed if the 1919 reforms worked and the political allies of the British displaced them permanently. However, in 1927 deliverance came for the nationalists in the form of another great British blunder. Emboldened by the collapse of non-co-operation there had been a rallying of the right in Britain and India, and in 1927 the Conservative British government, determined to tie the hands of any new Labour administration on Indian policy, ordered an early review of the 1919 Indian Reform Act, performed solely by white politicians, in the form of the parliamentary Simon Commission. In one stroke the British had achieved the very thing that had eluded Gandhi since the end of non-cooperation – nationalist unity. Congress moderates, no-changers, pro-changers, office-takers and office-breakers were reconciled, albeit temporarily, in the heat of mutual rage. Boycotts and protests against the Simon Commission's stately progress across the subcontinent reawakened the excitement of direct action. It also coincided with an extremely alarming level of workers' strikes and communist and terrorist activity.

Many in Congress worried about a resurgence of radicalism and wanted negotiation, not agitation. Gandhi was called back into action to negotiate a balance between the radicals and moderates and prevent a split. In one of his classic moves, to please both sides he announced in December 1928 that the government would be given a year to concede *purna swaraj* (complete independence), in the absence of which civil disobedience would be launched. This was quite a radical advance on previous definitions of *swaraj* and was clearly aimed at appeasing the increasingly radicalized left, among them Jawaharlal Nehru. Between 1928 and 1929 the nationalists and the Raj gingerly circled one another, each looking to the other to make some concession that would allow the other to save face. Viceroy Irwin announced Round Table Consultations (described in the previous chapter) at the end of October 1929, but no agreement was reached on terms. On 26 January 1930 'Total Independence Day' was celebrated across major cities and declarations of independence were read to massive demonstrations. But Gandhi remained reluctant to launch another mass mobilization, still fearful of the violence of the previous one. He even attempted a last-minute compromise with the British, offering negotiation in return for various concessions ranging from revenue cuts for peasants to the devaluation of the Indian rupee and the immediate concession of dominion status – just some of his famous eleven points. But even this failed to unite British and nationalist negotiators and Congress now waited anxiously for the Mahatma's next move. In early April 1930 Gandhi announced that he was going to make salt.

This seemed such an anodyne gesture that initially sceptics like Nehru scoffed. But the Mahatma's critics were proved wrong and he soon had another hit on his hands. The salt tax was a relatively minor revenue, but one that caused much resentment among the poor as it was, in effect, a tax on life, made more galling by the fact that salt was so freely available in India. It was, as Gandhi soon demonstrated, a commodity lying on every beach just waiting to be picked up and used – except that it was illegal to do so. The Salt March was, like non-cooperation, intended as political theatre, both a spectacle and an education in disciplined confrontation. Gandhi and 28 followers set off on the 240-mile march from Ahmedabad to the coast of Dandi, accompanied by a posse of international photographers and pressmen, many from the USA, designed to create maximum embarrassment to the Raj. Gandhi's fragile *dhoti*-clad figure was filmed trudging solemnly across the Indian landscape, acquiring temporary followers wherever he went. Soon a great train of activists snaked across the countryside. The march took a month and quickly acquired a powerful religious aura – a 'holy struggle', as Gandhi called it. In his speeches he demanded a 'change of heart', not money, and he stressed the moral duty to disobey a corrupt state. Non-violent raids on government salt works were staged to force violent retribution from the police. Visions of stoical women withstanding *lathi* charges and police beatings generated precisely the moral effect desired.

All this proved very puzzling for the British, who had the Mahatma followed by relays of secret agents. Efforts were made at counter-propaganda, though these were not entirely effective. A Government of India Finance Department pamphlet, for instance, blandly rebuffed Gandhi's charges with the assertion that the salt tax was not 'satanic'. It was, the pamphlet continued, an ancient form of revenue, and it concluded with a historical disquisition and erudite references from the *Mahabharata* and Kautilya's *Arthashastra* (an ancient Sanskrit treatise on good government) in defence of the tax: 'Adulteration of salt shall be punished ... likewise persons, other than hermits, manufacturing salt without a licence.' But Gandhi's march was not to be halted by abstruse legalism, and meanwhile the campaign was seriously undermining the legitimacy of government. The Viceroy himself complained that 'the personal influence of Gandhi threatens to create a position of real embarrassment to the administration'. Formerly 'sane and reasonable' people were being 'seduced' by Gandhi, not because they expected any definite results from the campaign, but because they now believed that British laws were 'morally indefensible and economically intolerable'.

Despite the spectacular commotion of the accompanying Salt March, the Civil Disobedience campaign was in some ways a much more controlled phenomenon than non-cooperation had been a decade earlier. In part this was Gandhi's and the leadership's intention. They were determined to avoid the ebullient and potentially anarchic fervour of the first experiment, and to convince potential constituents that they were a responsible force. The result of this policy was that the nature of the movement changed. It was now made up of more prosperous and more Hindu groups than before. Among the most conspicuous abstainers were the Muslims. The only significant Muslim participation was on the north west frontier, where Abdul Ghaffar Khan, dubbed the frontier Gandhi, organized the extraordinary *Khudai Khidmatgars* (servants of God), known as the Red Shirts. It was a remarkable alliance of Pathan tribesmen whom Ghaffar Khan had persuaded forgo their customary blood-feuds and unite under the banner of Gandhian non-violence to protest against the British annexation of the area from the Afghan kingdom in 1926. The Red Shirts made an impressive show. The local governor had a nervous breakdown and had to be relieved. The British were sceptical that a non-violent movement could be sustained among such 'martial' races and were on standby for the never-to-materialize Holy War that they had feared since the Mutiny. However, the *Khudai Khidmatgars* were really campaigning for union with their Pathan kinsmen and in a sense this was, if anything, an example of Afghan rather than Indian nationalism.

Elsewhere, Muslims were unmoved. Since the collapse of the unity over the Khilafat issue relations between poorer Hindu and Muslim groups, especially in the towns, had been characterized by competitiveness, violence and mutual suspicion. Aspects of the Gandhian campaign – its use of Hindu symbolism, and its insistence on the boycott of foreign cloth, which especially hurt Muslim mercantile interests – antagonized Muslims. And their unwillingness to participate in grand demonstrations against the British was used as an excuse by local Hindu toughs to launch attacks on them, as happened in the town of Kanpur in 1931. Joining Muslims in their ambivalence to this new wave of nationalist mobilization were factory workers, the urban and rural poor and India's tribal peoples. Some had been disillusioned with the abrupt ending of the last agitation, others were disdained by Congress organizers for their supposed lack of 'discipline'. Increasingly, workers and poor peasants were organizing themselves in trades unions and *kisan sabhas* (peasant associations). In place of these groups, Congress was seeking supporters among other constituencies: wealthier peasants and businessmen.

Congress was helped in this by the Great Depression. Unlike non-cooperation, which had been staged in the midst of post-war inflation and high food prices, the Depression had sent food prices plummeting. As a result it was the relatively prosperous peasantry, and not the rural poor, who bore the brunt of the crisis. Prosperous peasants had been having a hard time since the end of the First World War, when lost markets were never fully recovered. However, matters took a distinct turn for the worse in 1927–28 when the average prices of Indian cash crops – cotton, wheat and jute – collapsed by over 50 per cent. By 1930 many of these previously comfortably off farmers were in deep trouble. Agriculture had always been dependent on money-lenders, and with the collapse in prices many farmers across India could neither repay old debts nor take out new ones to buy the next season's seeds, except at exorbitant rates of interest. They began

selling jewellery and gold (traditional forms of saving) to bail themselves out, but soon even that was not enough, and people faced the
prospect of actually forfeiting their lands to their creditors.

One source of relief could have come from the government in the
form of major revenue reductions or the cancellation of debt. Another
would have been a devaluation of the rupee, rendering Indian agricultural exports cheaper on the world market and boosting economic
recovery. Neither policy was forthcoming. A large part of the problem
lay in London, where the Treasury and the Bank of England were
adamant that the rupee could not be devalued without seriously damaging Britain's own international financial standing. At this time India
was still a large borrower from the City of London, and a rupee
devaluation was thought likely to accelerate a debt default. Here,
starkly, was the fundamental contradiction between the interests of
India's massive farming population and the imperial state.

As a result, prosperous peasants flooded into Congress: in the
enormous Madras presidency grain farmers joined, while in Bombay
presidency cotton farmers signed up. In Gujarat, Congress's spectacular 'no-revenue campaigns' increased its appeal. For months the
Patidar farmers of Kheda in Gujarat, led by Gandhi's loyal ally Patel,
withheld their taxes despite threats of land confiscation, and when
the British did confiscate their land the Patidars migrated en masse
to the neighbouring princely state of Baroda. Increasingly, the idea
percolated into public consciousness that a Congress raj might bring
a radically new economic dispensation in the countryside: more state-
led rural development, better credit facilities, and the promise of
permanent land reform to create secure owner-farmers from the ranks
of the Indian tenant classes who were now realizing their inherent
vulnerability under the Raj.

This rejection of the Raj by wealthier peasants was not just about
belly politics, and it signified more than short-term economic distress.
With the arrest of the frontline Congress leadership in early 1930 the
government had hoped that the movement would swiftly fizzle out.
But by now Congress had struck deep roots into the countryside, and
a whole cadre of second- and third-level leaders swiftly came forth
from the peasantry and small-town India to keep the protests alive.
Congress was, in effect, becoming a parallel government, collecting

fair revenues and administering the courts. Moreover Congress effectively ran many cities through bodies of volunteers and white-collar supporters and businessmen. According to Bombay's Governor Sykes:

Congress House [Congress's HQ in Bombay] openly directs the movement of the revolt . . . Gandhi caps fill the streets, volunteers in uniform are posted for picketing with the same regularity and orderliness as police constables. The numbers, the discipline, the organization . . . combined to produce a vivid public impression of the power and success of the congress movement.

In Amritsar, Delhi and Bombay, Congress succeeded in closing down the hugely valuable foreign cloth trade for the whole of 1930, while throughout rural India, village headmen and accountants, the front line of the state, resigned. British administration virtually collapsed in parts of Gujarat, where elected local government bodies co-operated with the campaign and Congress, not the Raj, collected taxes. The Bombay presidency was the hardest hit, buffeted by a social boycott of government officials, widespread official resignations, a refusal to pay land revenue and mass migrations. The *khadi* campaigns throughout India, the anti-alcohol movements in the south, the revitalization of *panchayat* village government and the conspicuous sacrifice on the part of the now imprisoned nationalist leadership had clearly impressed peasant India with an image of a different nation.

The Gandhian sensibility, in its broadest sense, was crucial to the success of the campaign among middling groups, as it was a bridge linking the urban elites who had long dominated the nationalist movement to small-town and *mofussil* (up-country) India. Throughout his ascendancy Gandhi gained his strongest support from these essentially conservative groups. His populist vision of village democracy in particular resonated with the better-off farmers. While they had learnt to appreciate the state as a source of patronage and resources, they were deeply suspicious of further intrusion. For merchants, traders, artisans and petty clerks, known for their piety and jealousy of more privileged and westernized elements, the coming of a modern nation-state was a dubious blessing which might ultimately lead to their disappearance as a distinctive social and cultural group. In Gandhi, both the rural and urban little men saw a national leader in their own image: a compelling political vision of an India imbued with their values, not those of the godless and materialist west. Gandhi's ambiguous endorsement of the caste system and the lure, therefore, of continuing dominance over the poor, proved irresistible to those eager for prestige within the conventional caste hierarchy.

However, in December 1931 Gandhi called a truce. After controversial discussions with Viceroy Irwin, and much horse-trading about the freeing of political prisoners, restitution of confiscated lands and so forth, Gandhi agreed to attend the second stage of the Round Table Conference talks in London. Many were critical of what they saw as a climb-down and suspected that those with commercial interests, to whom Gandhi was close, were exerting pressure for negotiations, eager to resume business as usual as India slowly emerged from the depths of the Great Depression. But the real reason for the retreat was that the movement was running out of steam. The Patidar experience had been bruising and the Mahatma did not relish the prospect of more land seizures, or of hordes of immiserated peasant protestors in refugee camps following no-revenue campaigns elsewhere. He may also have felt that in forcing the British Viceroy to parley with him as an equal he had, in some sense, achieved his objective. However, his gifts as a negotiator were rather less magical than those for mobilization. He returned from London empty handed and to a Raj well-prepared to crack down hard when Civil Disobedience was restarted in April 1932. Under the new Viceroy, Willingdon, the Raj had prepared tactics to knock out opponents with the draconian Indian Emergency Powers Act of 1932.

Under what amounted to a form of civil martial rule, the entire Congress organization was not merely decapitated, it lost several limbs too, as quite lowly leaders were rounded up and gaoled. By mid-1932 over 100,000 Congress volunteers, including, for the first time, many women, resided in the Raj's prisons. Imprisonment under the Raj was a rather mixed experience. For many it was brutal and demoralizing. For the Congress high command, it was, to a degree, an opportunity to regroup and strategize. Nehru spent most of the period 1930 to 1935 behind bars. While incarcerated he managed to read quantities of Shakespeare, Ruskin, Carlyle, Spengler's *Decline of the West*, Kropotkin's *The Great French Revolution*, Trotsky's *My Life*, Nietzsche and much else. He also wrote both a history of the entire world, *Glimpses of World History*, *Letters between a Father and Daughter*, a common-man's treatise on Indian current affairs, and an *Autobiography*. His prison years brought a sharp reappraisal of both his youthful socialism and his hero-worship of Gandhi. By the time he re-emerged in 1935 his views on India's social, economic, constitutional and international future seem to have crystallized into the form that would direct his subsequent career.

Gandhi spent much of his time in Poona's Yeravda gaol, or *mandir* (temple) as he called it, memorizing the *Bhagavad Gita*. He pursued his dietary experiments, refusing all luxuries sent by well-wishers and existing on a regime of goat's milk, fruit and bicarbonate of soda. He also maintained a rigorous daily timetable: working from 4 a.m. to 9 p.m., with two hours of ablutions and one hour praying. Preparing food and eating took three hours, an hour and a half was spent exercising, six hours spinning and stitching gaol-caps, two hours reading or in meetings. Despite this his gaol-time was not without its compensations. The prison steward did his shopping and six fellow convicts were assigned to assist him; he kept up a huge correspondence, and learnt Marathi. During this time he seems to have lost faith in political action. With his release he restarted Civil Disobedience, but restricted it to individual acts, mainly to be undertaken by himself. In 1933 he set up his 'Harijan' Association, devoted to the 'uplift' of dalits, and also spent much of the later 1930s on the *khadi*, ashram and language campaigns. He was also initially determined that the rest of Congress should follow his lead and abandon politicking for social work.

In April 1934 he officially ended Civil Disobedience, ordering all Congress organizations to be disbanded and insisting instead on a wholly non-political programme of individual protest and social uplift through the 'constructive programme'. The intention was that Congress would cease to exist as a political force and transform itself into an elite of apolitical social workers devoted to attaining the Mahatma's eccentric vision of a just society. But neither the left nor the right were going to let the great prize of Congress be dismantled so easily. It was unthinkable that Congress politicians would allow the organization and name, which had now become such a powerful political brand, simply to rust away. The British had pushed through the Round Table reforms; elections to the reconstituted central legislature were planned for 1935, and even more important regional elections in 1937. With Gandhi's apparent abdication, the question was whether Congress should take the constitutional path and transform itself from a movement into a party, and, if so, who should control and benefit from that transformation.

Congress was now sharply divided over these issues. The left had grown considerably, both in and out of Congress, fuelled by labour protests, youth radicalism and the apparent success of Soviet Russia. In the countryside hundreds of radical *kisan sabhas* were pressing for land reform, and in cities trade unionism was strong. By 1933, annoyed at Gandhi's back-tracking on mass action, the left had become formally organized into the Congress Socialist Party (CSP), which included both socialists and communists – following the recent U-turn in Soviet policy encouraging communists to collaborate with nationalist parties. The goal of this group was the continuation and escalation of mass agitation, the boycott of constitutional reform and the inclusion of the trade unions and *kisan sabhas* in Congress in order to strengthen the institutional representation of the radicals.

But the left, though large and not wholly disorganized, was not well marshalled within Congress itself. Despite the formation of the CSP it remained divided over strategy, goals and, in the end, it was hopelessly outmanoeuvred by Gandhi and the more conservative forces within Congress. The key radicals were Jawaharlal Nehru and Subhas Bose, though significantly neither of them joined the CSP. Nehru, though a brilliant and insightful leftist analyst, was constantly prevailed upon by Gandhi to retreat from his radical positions. In part this compliance arose from personal loyalty to the Mahatma, but it was also driven by a predisposition to put nationalist unity before all else. Gandhi's tactic was to bind Nehru with office: he twice made him accept the presidency of Congress in the mid-1930s, shrewdly calculating that, burdened with responsibility and denuded of power, the younger man would prove biddable. This was indeed the case, and on many issues of progressive policy and alliances with the peasant associations and unions, Nehru was defeated.

This was the culmination of a pattern that had begun in the late 1920s. In 1927 Nehru and Bose had succeeded in getting Congress to adopt *purna swaraj*, the goal of breaking all connection with the British Empire to form an Indian republic. But under pressure from Gandhi and the right, they were persuaded to compromise. In the early 1930s the battles shifted to the nature of Congress's social and economic policy and again Nehru tended to buckle before the Mahatma, who made full use of his charismatic power over the younger man. Commitments to land reform and radical social reforms were continually diluted.

A more formidable challenge to Gandhi's authority was to come from the young Bengali radical Bose. Bose hailed from a political tradition wholly at odds with the more culturally conservative and pious politics of the north Indian Hindi belt that Gandhi embodied. The scion of a Bengali *bhadralok* (gentry) family of high intellectual accomplishment, Bose had enjoyed a rather murky involvement with the terrorist revolutionaries of the Great War era. His political ambitions, however, were somewhat compromised by the collapse of Bengal's influence within the nationalist movement. Having been in the vanguard of nationalist politics in the Edwardian era, Bengal's Congress party had decayed into a backwater of infighting and back-stabbing in the later 1920s and 1930s.

Bose became a persistent and intermittently insightful critic of Gandhian strategy. He despised *ahimsa* (non-violence) as weakness, exhorted Congress to embrace worker and peasant radicalism, even if it meant violence, and bitterly denounced the Mahatma's eccentric negotiating style at the London Round Table Conference talks. Bose's own radicalism took something of a fascist turn in the 1930s when, after travelling in Europe, he became impressed by Mussolini. He seems to have envisaged a much more dictatorial role for Congress, which, he believed, should co-ordinate a corporatist strategy combining the state, business, labour and peasant interests in a heroic struggle to make India a Great Nation – Japan-style. This was in marked contrast to Nehru's more pluralistic brand of social democracy. Bose's popularity and the strength of leftist forces in Congress became manifest when he was elected Congress president with a large majority in 1938 and then re-elected a year later. However, at this point the Mahatma struck.

Bose's year as Congress president had convinced Gandhi that he was not to be tamed by office as Nehru had been. Moreover, the right of the movement, especially its business supporters on whom it depended for money, was thoroughly alarmed by the apparent strength of the radical elements. When Bose was re-elected Gandhi announced that he could not work with him on the Congress politburo (the All-India Congress Working Committee) and would quit politics completely. The defection of the Mahatma was simply inconceivable and Bose, realizing that his continuation in office would finally accomplish what many had spent the decade trying to avert – the splitting of the nationalists – reluctantly resigned.

By 1938 the radicals were being marginalized, but they did manage to get Congress to agree to develop a programme of economic planning, largely because this coincided with the interests of its big business backers. These men were happy for Nehru to assume the mantle of mascot of the left, confident of Gandhi's influence over him. The most prominent spokesman of these corporate interests was G. D. Birla, head of one of the largest Indian-owned industrial groups. As early as the 1936 Lucknow Congress session, where the right had feared the left might make gains, Birla had noted with satisfaction: 'Mahatmaji kept his promise ... He saw that no new commitments were made. Jawaharlalji's speech ... was thrown into the waste paper basket.' He also understood Nehru's willingness to give way to the right: '[he] seems to be a typical English democrat ... out for giving expression to his ideology, but he realizes that action is impossible and does not press for it'. Meanwhile Patel wryly observed, 'the difficulty with Jawaharlal, all said and done, is not insurmountable. He frets and fumes, he storms, he is often in a rage, but after all he is a great sport and so quickly regains his balance and sees that there is no unpleasantness left behind.'

The right of the party was a less conspicuous, but ultimately more powerful force. Boosted by the Depression, it was an eclectic mix of small and big business interests, urban professional groups and regional 'big men', along with small-town shopkeepers, merchants and clerks. Congress conservatism had also been immeasurably bolstered by the influx of India's dominant peasantry. Nearly half of all those joining Congress in the 1930s came from the prosperous rural classes, farming between 21 and 100 acres. These people were nationalists, but far from revolutionary in their aspirations. Small business interests had been alienated by the volatile financial policies of the British in the 1920s and 30s and the piecemeal development of the modern urban economy, which they both welcomed and feared. In particular, many felt highly competitive with Muslim mercantile rivals. But they were also culturally traditional, and they saw the Gandhian Congress as a vehicle for the perpetuation of their values in a modern Indian state and economy.

The right had also been strengthened by the growing interest of big business interests in nationalism, prominent among them was Birla, a close confidant of Gandhi's, though never formally a member of Congress. Birla came from the highly traditional and pious Marwari trader caste and the Birlas, like many of their caste, had made a fortune from share speculation immediately after the Great War. They had used the money to move from commerce into industry. First they competed with the traditionally British-controlled jute industry (Birla claimed he had been radicalized as a young man after being humiliated in a lift). Their antagonism to British business, which they believed was unfairly promoted by the racial policies of the Raj, had bred a fierce economic nationalism. This took the form of ambitions to create modern Indian industries in sectors as advanced and diverse as autos, chemicals and even aeronautics. The Birlas combined this economic patriotism with commercial shrewdness and had cleverly played the British and Congress off against one another in order to extort maximum concessions from both. However, by the mid-1930s Birla, along with India's growing body of big industrialists, had decided that British-style laissez-faire economics was insufficient for India's industrial needs and had been attracted by Congress's commitment to rapid development behind protective tariff boundaries and the removal of India, temporarily, from the global economy. They also wanted a more interventionist state – up to a point – and from this emerged their uneasy rapprochement with Nehru and other radicals.

Business interests, small and large, along with Congress's supporters among the dominant peasantry, had thrown up their own political leadership. Men like Patel in Gujarat, Rajendra Prasad in Bihar, Rajag-opalachari in Madras and Govind Pant in the United Provinces were typical. Many were first generation small-town lawyers who became ardent Gandhians, combining the Mahatma's charisma with their own intimate knowledge of India's rural and small-town networks to construct a dense matrix of power. They ran the All-India level of politics in uneasy compromise with the Nehruvian left, but wholly dominated provincial and local politics. The leaders of these local networks could be unscrupulous in gaining control of Congress in the districts, and were adept at manipulating membership lists. The Indian left was no match for them in this kind of politics, and it also lacked money. The right became particularly powerful when in 1937, after much wrangling, Congress decided to abandon Gandhian mass action once and for all in favour of constitutionalism. Nehru, who had vigorously opposed taking up ministerial posts in the new provincial assemblies, performed one of his notorious U-turns, and after a staggeringly successful campaign in 1937, largely financed by big business, Congress became the government in a majority of India's eleven provinces.

Nehru's misgivings about acceptance of office and its potentially corrupting effects on the great struggle for freedom turned out to be perspicacious. Though Congress fought the 1937 elections on a radical programme, once in power the agenda of the right came to predominate and Patel's strategy of replacing the Raj by stealth – whether the British quit India or not – came to fruition. Initially the new governments were greeted with a tidal wave of expectant adulation. As Reginald Coupland, a British historian who witnessed the process, wrote:

At Lucknow . . . they thronged the streets, gazed with a dubious sense of ownership at the public buildings, scrutinised the lobbies and lavatories of the Assembly house, and even penetrated the sacred precincts of the Secretariat to see what their ministers were doing.

But popular enthusiasm didn't last long. Much heralded, but costly, social reforms conflicted with the governments' enthusiasm for the prohibition of liquor. Excise taxes on drugs and alcohol were the mainstay of revenue in most states – in Bombay they amounted to 26 per cent of all government income. Losses were made up with property taxes, some of which fell rather heavily on Muslim religious foundations, causing much resentment.

There was also trouble over the issue of agrarian reform, which

Congress had promised but now seemed reluctant to deliver. On the first day of the Bihar Congress administration, thousands of peasants turned up at the assembly and threatened to turn out the ministry using civil disobedience if tenancy reform were not speedily passed. By late 1938 much of rural Bihar and the United Provinces were embroiled, ironically, in organized campaigns of peasant non-cooperation. These movements turned very radical and some in Congress feared that India was on the brink of revolution. The poorer peasantry now demanded the abolition of landlordism (and landlords), which they thought they had been guaranteed. Armed police were needed to protect the spring harvest, and ministers had to undertake personal tours of the United Provinces in 1939, begging the peasants to pay their rents and taxes. Eventually two rather mild tenancy reform bills were passed in the two states, which essentially benefited dominant peasant interests. More radical legislation in Madras and Orissa was aborted and policies to reduce land-revenue and implement land reform were not pursued.

The other source of embarrassment was labour. In their 27 months of office nearly all the Congress ministries had to deal with a series of major strikes, the most disruptive being in Bombay and Kanpur, both now centres of communist trade unionism. Congress took a hard line with strikers. Patel chastized them for waving red flags: 'Comrade Lenin was not born in this country, and we do not want Lenin here,' he declared. 'We want Mahatma Gandhi and Ram Rajya.' Congress's use of the Raj's powers of coercion also became controversial, with Gandhi himself coming out in favour of repression: 'Civil liberty is not criminal liberty,' he said. The repressive criminal procedure code was regularly used to counter 'breaches of the peace', and in May 1939 Congress organized a summit of Home Ministers in Simla to discuss internal security. Each minister (many fresh from gaol) was, somewhat incongruously, accompanied by his British Inspector General of Police. Coupland concluded, with some satisfaction, that the Congress ministries could be justifiably labelled 'Conservative'. Nehru was less complacent about the regional governments: 'provincial autonomy affords no scope for the self-government and growth which independence alone can give, and its capacity for good is rapidly being exhausted,' he thundered.

But while Nehru may have disapproved of Congress in office, its record was a testament to the success of the Patel strategy of undermining the British at the centre, while controlling radicalism in the provinces. And with the enthusiastic support of better-off groups Congress continued to replace the Raj by stealth. Its High Command, run by Gandhi, effectively made a mockery of British reforms, which had been intended to divert and then 'lock' nationalism into provincial politics. The All-India Congress Working Committee, rather than humbly fading away, acted as a shadow central state, presiding over and co-ordinating provincial ministerial policy from its headquarters in Delhi. Patel ran Bombay, Madras and Central Provinces, Abul Kalam Azad did the same in Bengal, United Provinces, Punjab and North West Frontier Province, while Prasad organized Bihar, Orissa and Assam.

Moreover, the Congress ministries went out of their way to marginalize those apparatuses of Raj power with which they had been supposed to co-operate. Congress politicians avoided socializing with British officials, lunched separately and refused to attend retirement parties. And new ministers were ordered not to fraternize with members of the Indian Civil Service, the Indian Police Service and other state bodies, despite the fact that many of these services had been largely 'indianized'. Lower down the hierarchy Congress institutions effectively displaced those of the state. Party committees and Congress's rural development schemes acquired a quasi-official mantle. Congress police stations were established, as was an embryonic Congress army. The United Provinces' government set up a military department intended to recruit 500,000 troops by 1940, including 1000 women. Officers' training camps opened in Bihar. Congress functionaries increasingly concerned themselves with the minutiae of political life, areas that were previously, and supposedly still were, the provenance of ICS officers. Congress High Command was intimately involved in all these affairs, as Coupland remarked: 'Nothing was too petty, too local, too palpably groundless not to justify, in the eyes of small local leaders, a reference direct to the centre over the head of district administration.' Finally, much patronage was dispensed and a new pageant of power was fashioned: 'Special trains, "profuse" garlanding, unhorsed carriages, beflagged cars, mass receptions, civic addresses and tumultuous processions' marked these experiments in Congress government.

One group, however, was ominously absent from this new parade of power – India's Muslims. During and immediately after the First World War the omens for Hindu-Muslim unity had been almost preternaturally auspicious. In 1916 Congress and Muslim League leaders had signed a power-sharing agreement, the Lucknow Pact, under the terms of which Congress happily conceded separate electorates to Muslims in return for a joint front against the British. In 1918 Gandhi embraced the cause of the beleaguered Caliph in the old Ottoman Empire, folding it into the first non-cooperation campaign and with it the support of a large proportion of India's diverse and far-flung Muslims. But with the collapse of the non-cooperation and Khilafat movements in the early 1920s, the paths of Congress and Muslim politics had sharply diverged. In part this reflected the success of British devolutionary reforms, which created alluring islands of autonomous power for Muslim politicians in the Punjab and Bengal where Muslims were the majority community. But the divergence was caused by more than just British machinations. As Congress grew it became, especially at the local level, a body with a distinctively Hindu tint. Gandhian rhetoric played a significant role in this, albeit unintentionally; his utopian projection of Ram's Raja and his preoccupation with unifying the four *varnas* of the caste system into a possibly threatening Hindu whole could not but alienate Muslim observers. Moreover, the Civil Disobedience campaign of the early 1930s, with its insistence on the boycott of foreign cloth, disproportionately damaged the business interests of imported cloth merchants, a traditionally Muslim trade. In Bengal the economic interests of Muslim peasant tenants were at odds with those of petty Hindu landlords – many of whom were Congress members, and even leaders. Finally, the tense and poverty-stricken urban milieu of inter-war India created vicious competition for space, jobs and local dominance; in this context supposedly non-violent Gandhian campaigns could all too easily turn into anti-Muslim mini-pogroms, and then be justified as 'nationalist'.

In 1928, Jinnah, the leader of the Muslim League, had attempted as he had in 1916 to forge unity between Congress and the League.

Though Jinnah had been willing to renounce separate Muslim electorates (now a minimum demand from Congress), Hindu nationalists wrecked the basis for a quid pro quo by refusing to permit the creation of more Muslim majority provinces in Sindh and on the North West Frontier. Again, the Muslim League co-operated with Congress during the 1937 provincial elections. After these elections, however, a number of Congress provincial cabinets reneged on a deal to share posts with League members, insisting that only the Congress was a truly 'national' organization, while the League was merely a 'communal' one. Following this, many Muslims felt they were unfairly treated by the Congress ministries, and discriminated against in the fields of official posts and education.

Underpinning these rhetorical, socio-economic and high political tensions was the unmistakable tendency for Congress, whatever its high command might say, to become associated with Hindu nationalism at the local level. By the late 1930s the membership of many town and district Congress committees overlapped with those of overtly Hindu nationalist bodies such as the RSS and the Hindu Mahasabha. This gave the Muslim League's allegation that Congress government was tantamount to 'Hindu Raj' a powerful resonance. Against this background attempts to build a mass Muslim support base by means of 'mass-contact' campaigns seemed doomed before they even began. They were perceived as aggressive moves by the predominant community to subsume the Muslims into a vast Hindu majority. One Muslim newspaper likened the campaigns to an advance by a spider tempting a fly into its web. Paradoxically, Gandhi's very success at weaving so many of India's hitherto fissiparous Hindu communities into a single cloth simply convinced many Muslims that British offers of a constitutionally protected separate identity was their only safeguard against total effacement as a distinct culture.

By 1939, then, Congress was the ruler-in-waiting. The nationalists had been remarkably successful in spinning a movement that could challenge the British, but the Gandhi era had posed a choice between radicalism and a more conservative, ideologically unambitious constitutionalism, which the Mahatma had hoped to duck. Unlike the Chinese nationalists – which had split into communist and more conservative nationalist factions – Gandhi had succeeded in keeping left and right together in one party. But the price of unity had been the alienation of the radical popular support that Congress had attracted during the first non-cooperation campaign. Gandhi's victory over the Congress left also, ultimately, led to the defeat of his own ideals. By the end of the 1930s it was clear that much of Congress politics was fast degenerating in an unedifying scramble for the spoils of office. Gandhi had not woven the tough, rough-textured and inclusive fabric he had originally designed. Rather, the Congress nation was silk not *khadi*. Threads from the prosperous peasantry, urban petty bourgeoisie, the progressive intelligentsia and big business had somehow been woven into a single cloth. But it was distinctly frayed at the edges. Skeins of regional, Muslim and low-caste politics hung loose and it would prove difficult, if not impossible, to weave these back into a united and independent Indian nation.

5

A House Divided

*. . . above the green tree tops, glitters the seat of government,
the seventh Delhi, four square upon an eminence – dome,
tower, dome, tower, dome, red, pink, cream and white washed
gold and flashing in the morning sun . . . Here is something
not just merely worthy, but whose like has never been. With
a shiver of impatience [the traveller] shakes off contemporary
standards, and makes ready to evoke those of Greece, of the
Renaissance, and the Moguls.*

Delhi has been rebuilt seven times since its foundation in 1450 BC,
surprisingly perhaps, as an old prophecy warns that anyone who
builds a new city in Delhi is sure to lose it. In 1911 the British began
work on a new imperial capital in Delhi, commissioned to testify, as
Viceroy Hardinge declaimed, to 'the idea and fact of eternal British
rule in India'. So grandiose a vision demanded a suitable monumental
style. But the precise character of this style led to ferocious disputes
between Hardinge and his architects. The Viceroy insisted on the need
to represent imperialism in an Anglo-Indian hybrid vocabulary: the
new capital had to be 'imbued with the spirit of the East such as will
appeal to Orientals as well as to Europeans', a 'plain classic style
with a touch of Orientalism', he suggested. But Edwin Lutyens, the
principal architect, was contemptuous of both Indian architecture and
Anglo-Indian hybridity. 'Would Wren, had he gone to Australia, have
burnt his knowledge and experience to produce a Marsupial-style
thought to reflect the character of her aborigines?' he thundered.
Hardinge won out. Nevertheless, Lutyens and his partner, Herbert

Baker, still presented their neo-classicism and geometric purity as emblematic of Britain's imposition of order on the chaotic subcontinent:

One rule confers order, progress and freedom within the law to develop national civilisations along the lines of their own traditions and sentiments: so in architecture there is infinite scope within the limits of order, true science, and progress for the widest self-expression in every field of art; but without the orderly control of great principles, there might result a chaos in the arts, as in governments, which History records our rule was ordained to supersede.

The new capital was laid out south-west of Shahjahanbad (Old Delhi), the seventeenth-century walled city of the Mughals. An enormous political, strategic and logistical undertaking, it took 20 years, 29,000 labourers, 700 million bricks and 100,000 cubic feet of marble to build the city. The overall conception was borrowed from Haussmann's Paris, Wren's unbuilt London and L'Enfant's plan for Washington DC, and was intended to surpass them all. But, as Hardinge had insisted, it also bowed to some Indian architectural influences. The merging of Indian and neo-classical styles was accomplished with varying degrees of success. Relatively trivial decorative embellishments, such as the sculptures of bells and elephants on the Secretariat buildings, was one approach. But Lutyens himself came close to achieving a genuine synthesis of neo-classical and Indic forms: Hindu *chattris* (small umbrella-shaped pavilions used to decorate Hindu buildings), were rigorously pared down to their platonic essentials, the red sandstone recalled the stone plinths of nearby Mughal tombs, while the great black dome of the Viceroy's palace (now Rashtrapati Bhavan) was a homage to the third-century BC Buddhist *stupa* at Sanchi. This was a genuine fusion of the three great religions of the subcontinent with European classicism – the perfect, if highly idealized, embodiment of the British vision of India.

The new capital was officially inaugurated in 1931. Robert Byron was awe-struck: 'how stupendous it is, and such a work of beauty, so unlike the English'. But the British tenancy of this fabulous monument to their own eternal rule was rather short-lived; within twenty years they had been evicted and replaced by Indian custodians. But these new owners were not, as anticipated by the architecture and, indeed, by the British themselves, a harmonious blend of all Indians, for India did not achieve independence as one united state, but as two.

On 3 September 1939 the Viceroy, Lord Linlithgow, announced that India was going to war for the defence of Poland. In Poland, he declared, the principles of international justice and morality were at war with 'the law of the jungle ... and nowhere do these great principles mean more than in India'. A few weeks later, all eight of the Congress provincial ministries, which had been in power since 1937, resigned in protest at this high-handed action. Surprisingly perhaps, many British officials were cheered by this news: this was now a war on two fronts – with the Axis powers and with the Indian nationalists. Here at last, it seemed to some, was an opportunity to recover the initiative, and after decades of strain, defiance, bickering and the 'melancholy, long, withdrawing roar' of British power, to restore the mastery of old Raj. Several senior officials, led by Linlithgow himself, believed that they now had a chance to adopt strong measures and 'knock Congress out', something they had conspicuously failed to achieve in the previous twenty years. In the Viceroy's opinion, 'we are dealing with this country in the happy conditions of 70 years ago, when it was our blessed business to clear up a mess into which India had got itself'. Such sentiments encouraged a reversion to old-style imperial government, assuming extraordinary powers of detention and arrest, restoring the old authority of governors, district officers and collectors in the ex-Congress provinces.

Meanwhile thousands of British troops poured in, forming the largest European armed contingent ever seen on Indian soil. To bolster this renewed white ascendancy even further, Linlithgow proposed the total abandonment of ICS recruitment for the duration of the war to avert 'over-indianization'. The ensuing vacancies, he added, would be filled by white army officers once the war was over. But the centrepiece of Linlithgow's project to efface Congress was the 'Revolutionary Movement Ordinance' promulgated in the summer of 1940. The idea of the ordinance had in fact been around since 1937. It included powers of wholesale arrest, seizure of bank accounts and premises and, in a new form of economic warfare, the denial of government contracts to supporters of such movements – i.e. Congress. It was intended that the ordinance would be accompanied by a bold manifesto of anti-nationalist assertion:

India can now best fulfil her destiny and take her due place among the nations of the world only after the total extinction of the political party which at this vital juncture had seen fit to betray them.

Officials in London cautioned greater circumspection. Cavilling at the term 'revolutionary' as likely to alarm allied opinion, especially in the USA, the 'Emergency Powers Ordinance' was settled on as a less inflammatory alternative, while Leo Amery, Secretary of State for India, also excised all reference to the 'total extinction of Congress'. Thus tempered, the ordinance acquired cabinet approval.

There was, however, a serious problem with the Emergency Powers Ordinance as a tactic for disposing of Congress. It depended on an 'emergency' occurring. In September 1940 there were promising signs of revolution afoot when Gandhi authorized a campaign of 'individual civil disobedience' against the government. Gandhi's chief disciple in the practice of *satyagraha*, Vinoba Bhave, gave a speech in a village denouncing all wars. His special qualification was, Gandhi explained, his unequalled dedication to hand-spinning, on which he had recently penned a textbook. But it proved difficult to construe Bhave's innocuous activities as either 'revolutionary' or an 'emergency'; the Raj was forced to wait another two years before launching a lethal strike against their nationalist nemesis.

Undeterred, the Raj pursued its strategy by other means. More biddable Indians, it was assumed, could be recruited to collaborate in the war effort with the incentive of post-war privileges. With Congress out of the game, the government could encourage smaller parties such as the Muslim League, the Hindu Mahasabha (now detached from Congress) and even the communists, which, Linlithgow mused, 'may be influenced in a better direction by the sunshine of official favour'. Indians had split into several factions on the issue of the war; the princes, the Hindu right and leaders of the provincial Muslim parties all fell into line with the British. The Hindu Mahasabha even considered setting up its own volunteer force, and the RSS leader, Veer Savarkar, called for 'the militarization of the Hindus', seeing an opportunity for a Hindu martial renaissance. The communists, though initially committed to an anti-capitalist struggle, did a swift U-turn when Germany invaded Russia and advocated maximum assistance to the British. With this motley array of allies the Viceroy's Executive Council was bolstered to give the appearance of Indian participation in the war effort. Muslim, Sikh and Dalit representatives acquired seats on the Imperial Defence Committee. Some were even sent to London to represent India in the War Cabinet, provoking a Churchillian quip that the proliferation of Indians would make it necessary to book the Albert Hall for cabinet meetings. This, however, was something of an exaggeration – in the end only two Indians were despatched.

Meanwhile a thriving local Nazi party was discovered operating in Calcutta, headed by the German consul. But heedless of the enemy in their midst, high society went on as ever. Boosted by fresh infusions of white manpower, life for expatriates became rather heady. Newly arrived British officers were constantly surprised at the conspicuous consumption, levity and luxury on offer. Whist-drives and bridge absorbed the day and cocktail parties filled the evenings. 'This was life with the lid off. Dinner jackets, drinks and demonstrations of dazzling dancing', observed one newly arrived and thoroughly bemused army officer. There were race meetings, golf and tennis tournaments, while in 1941 Gone with the Wind played to packed cinemas in Calcutta. Officers dined in luxury at the Bengal Club or at the Grand on Chowringhee, where seven-course menus, including 'quartier de mouton rotie à la Metternich', were to be enjoyed. A popular ditty, 'Sticking it out at the Cecil', satirized the surreal atmosphere:

> Fighting the Nazis from Delhi,
> Fighting the Japs from Kashmir,
> Exiled from England, we feel you should know,
> The way we are taking it here.

But life was not so sweet for all newcomers. Wartime, it seemed, was no time for lowering standards: old obsessions with class and race persisted unabated. European clubs maintained strict race bars, and 'temporary gentlemen', as recently promoted white officers of unknown pedigree were known, were made to feel distinctly unwelcome. Denied credit at the clubs, they were censured for their 'irregular' sexual liaisons with mixed-race women – one British woman complained that while it was all right for such officers to sleep with Eurasian women, it was outrageous to 'flaunt these "half-breeds" in public'.

However, the strange revival of the illiberal Raj was an illusion. Beneath the imperial bravado and snobbish insouciance all was not well. The colonial state, always short of money, was now close to broke. During the Second World War Rs. 3.5 billion were spent on defence. This was an imperial commitment even greater than that of the Great War, but with the crucial difference that this time it was the British, not Indians, footing the bill. Under terms conceded in the 1939 Imperial Defence Committee agreement, the use of Indian resources (including the army) for any purpose not directly related to India's own security had to be reimbursed after the war. In the meantime Indian war production had to be funded by credit. The Government of India paid private producers on behalf of His Majesty's Government in Britain by printing rupees. This was an unprecedented breach of the principles of sound finance that had governed Raj policy for sixty years and one that soon fuelled destabilizing inflation. It necessitated the levying of new taxes – always a dangerous move by the Raj – which rapidly alienated hitherto quiescent business opinion. Most of the cash went on the very belated modernization of the Indian army and its supplies.

Yet despite this expenditure, India was hopelessly unprepared for war. There was virtually no air defence in the crisis-stricken first half of 1942, with only eight serviceable Mohawk aircraft to defend Calcutta, and no suitable airfield for use by heavy aircraft. The army too was hopelessly unequal to its task. Starved of adequate funding since 1919, it was an unmodernized shambles, its shortcomings starkly exposed by a series of humiliating defeats at the hands of the Japanese in 1941–2. It lacked trained drivers, engineers and explosives specialists. Indeed it remained an oddly antiquated institution, composed for the most part of the old 'martial races' and largely officered by the British. But now not enough of the 'right type' of British men was available for commissions.

The army was not the only Raj institution showing signs of decay: the 'steel frame' of the ICS was also badly corroded. The service had been under pressure ever since the early 1920s, with new British recruits thin on the ground. Young British graduates preferred to stay in Britain, lured by new professional opportunities in the expanding economy at home, disenchanted with the project of empire, or discouraged by the erosion of the ICS's prestige by Indian reforms. By 1939 the number of Indians and British in the service had reached parity. And, because of Linlithgow's decision to freeze recruitment in 1940 to avert complete indianization, total numbers of British officers in the service declined from 587 to 429 during the war, leaving only 19 British men eligible for 65 posts in 1945. Total numbers in the service fell from 2101 to 939. This was an imperial manpower crisis writ large.

Moreover, among the younger generation of officials there was little appetite for old-style imperialism. There had been inklings of just such a *trahison des clercs* before the war. The British Chief Secretary to Madras had taken to wearing *khadi*, while the Revenue Secretary of Bombay had been spotted scuttling back and forth between first- and third-class rail carriages, jettisoning his dignity in his anxiety to appease the Gandhian sensibilities of the Bombay Finance Minister, Morarji Desai, with whom he was on tour. Many officials enrolled for active service, and among those remaining in post demoralization had clearly bitten deep. Some were unhappy with the Raj's tough repression of the 1942 Congress-led rebellion, the Quit India movement, and the refusal to release Gandhi even as he neared death during his fast of February–March 1943. At the height of the Quit India disturbances, British graffiti had responded to Congress's calls to 'Quit India' with 'We wish we could' on service buildings in Delhi.

Even more worrying than ICS morale were the allegiances of the predominantly Indian lower civil service, troops, war workers and the general population. Despite bravado about Congress's lack of support, the Raj was clearly worried about incipient disloyalty. Indians, now classified according to strategic worth into 'priority' and 'non-priority' groups, were presented with an elaborate sliding-scale of incentives and punishments devised to secure loyalty. The carrot of 'welfare', 'dearness allowances' (to compensate for inflation) and benefits-in-kind were offered to war industry workers. These inducements soon proved insufficient to prevent absenteeism and strikes, and the stick of punishment was more regularly wielded.

For Indians less directly involved in the war effort, propaganda was prescribed. Early propaganda aimed at the literate middle classes included a perplexing series of articles by Percival Spear, an academic at St Stephen's Anglican College in Delhi (and author, after the war, of the first Penguin *History of India*). Spear's 'Development of New Ideas through Danger and Suffering' developed the thesis that the fascist onslaught was in some way a good thing because India would be redeemed by suffering in the great fight against evil. More conventional approaches focused on Congress's pusillanimity. A cartoon in the English Calcutta paper *The Statesman* depicted Hitler, Tito, Mussolini and the Japanese Admiral Tojo chanting: 'I vote for the Congress resolution'. Company managers and clerks were encouraged to lead discussions among their employees on war aims through a series of government prepepared 'talking points', while ICS officers went on lecture tours to disseminate 'war news'.

Among troops 'Josh groups' (Japanese orientation sessions) were held to promote anti-Japanese feeling. These used government-supplied history courses, which dwelt on the evils of emperor-worship and the samurai ethos. Communist party cadres were employed to popularize pro-war ideas among factory labour, and in rural areas provincial and district war committees employed songsters and theatrical troupes to perform pro-war dramas. There were even free meals and itinerant cinema shows for the poor to celebrate allied victories in North Africa and Italy. Travelling exhibitions proved especially popular: a War Demonstration Train trundled around Bihar exhibiting models of the weapons of modern warfare – allied warships, tanks, planes, ammunition, shells, bombs and carbines. Meanwhile, in Calcutta, trucks bearing the remains of two Japanese bombers and the anti-aircraft guns that had shot them down proved a great attraction.

But the propaganda was more inventive than it was effective. Radio bulletins in the vernacular languages were thought to be an essential resource, but there were insufficient transmitting stations – only nine when at least one hundred were needed. War films proved hard to distribute: Bengal had only six motor cinema vans and eight bullock vans with projector sets, while Assam and Orissa had no itinerant cinemas, and trucks fitted out with 35 mm projectors were unable to negotiate the poor roads. Efforts at popular mobilization proved equally unsatisfactory. A volunteer corps of Civil Guards – a sort of Home Guard – was established, supposedly to allow Indians an outlet for their pro-war enthusiasms, but in Bihar it was still-born: at one meeting an audience of 1500, after attentively listening to a pro-British speech, dispersed with the shout of 'Gandhi *Ki Jai!*' (Victory to Gandhi!) In eastern India few enrolled, fearing they might end up at the front, while poorer peasants could see no point in patrolling villages to protect rich merchants and landowners.

In rural areas it appeared that the Raj was far too closely identified with rich landed loyalists, and government officials trying to implement the 'Grow More Food' campaign were attacked with impunity, their assailants protected by the silence of the local population. Unsurprisingly cases of defiance among local bureaucrats soon multiplied. Communist cadres also proved somewhat unreliable allies for the British, exploiting their access to labour as an opportunity to organize strikes. Businessmen became increasingly irate over the new wartime super-taxes, complaining that these levies were stifling 'legitimate national aspirations'. And there was also increasing non-cooperation among provincial government officers.

But perhaps the greatest blow to Raj authority was the slowly emerging news of catastrophe in Bengal – not invasion, but famine. During the spring of 1942, as the Japanese thundered through South East Asia, Bengal witnessed ominous signs of food scarcity as Burmese rice supplies dried up. In October a cyclone hit the east coast destroying the rice crop, the staple of the region, and by December the situation was clearly developing into a disaster, with all surplus rice consumed by the following spring. The crisis escalated through May and June of 1943 and peaked in the autumn. Thousands of villagers began flooding into Calcutta looking for food and spreading cholera. In mid-October the death rate in Calcutta, which was usually 1500 per month, had risen to over 2000.

The famine hit the poorest hardest, in particular low-caste groups dependent on wages for food, and impoverished peasants who were forced to sell their land and houses for a few pounds of rice. Women suffered most. In families men and boys were fed before women and girls. Many women were forced into prostitution, and girls were sold to the military by young boys acting as pimps. One relief worker reported: 'I saw nearly 500 destitutes of both sexes, almost naked and reduced to bare skeletons. Some of them were begging for food ... some lying by the wayside approaching death', while the journalist Wilfred Burchett described how 'each morning the trucks rolled around the suburbs of Calcutta like the plague carts of 17th century England'.

The context for the famine lay in the demographic and agricultural problems of Bengal, but its immediate cause was wartime government policy. From early in the war much of Bengal's and Bihar's rice was shipped to supply allied troops in the Middle East; the fall of Burma then produced a panicky 'scorched earth' policy in eastern India in which boats, carts and even elephants were destroyed, wrecking food supply networks. Finally grain from the Delta region was confiscated to supply troops and war-workers in Calcutta: the state was hauling grain into the city at the cost of feeding the rural poor. A famine created by official neglect desperately needed official intervention, but none was forthcoming. Dominated by a chaotic Muslim League coalition, the Bengal provincial authorities were weak and corrupt. Calcutta's government insisted for months that there was no real problem and cravenly declined to interfere with the profits being reaped by local politicians dealing in rice. There was no famine code in place, and for a year after the Japanese declaration of war, Bengal had no food department. Little real effort was made to curb inflation, and food prices rose steeply through 1942 and 1943.

But it was not entirely the fault of provincial politicians and officials. The war cabinet in London was warned in early 1942 of the impending crisis, but refused to stop the export of food from Bengal or to divert shipping to bring supplies to India. The government's scientific adviser took a bracingly Malthusian view of the situation: the cause of the famine, he asserted, lay in over-breeding among the weak Bengali race. The Calcutta paper *The Statesman* ran a shocking picture campaign: 'This sickening catastrophe is man-made,' it roared, 'and shows a shameful lack of planning, capacity and foresight by India's own civil Governments, Central and Provincial', while Nehru denounced the famine as the final tragic act in Britain's long history of 'indifference, incompetence and complacency'.

By the late summer of 1943 the famine was beginning to threaten the war effort. Army morale plunged and troops were ordered not to share their food with the starving. The military authorities warned that India would become an inadequate base for operations against Japan if the civilian economy collapsed and troops themselves might face food shortages. By the autumn Leo Amery, Secretary of State for India, managed to extract a commitment for a million tons of food to be sent, though this was only 25 per cent of what was required. The situation began to improve with the arrival of a new Viceroy, Wavell, in October 1943. Wheat deliveries were made from the Punjab, though the poor, used to rice, found wheat difficult to digest. Relief camps were established and the army was used to get food into the villages. Unlike his predecessor, Wavell visited Calcutta and toured famine relief centres. His impression of incompetence and complacency among local officials was confirmed when his special envoy was refused a meeting with one District Officer because he was detained at a tennis match. Ironically the Bengal and Bihar rice harvest of 1943 was one of the best ever, but there was nobody left to collect it. Between 3.5 and 3.8 million are thought to have died in the famine.

The catalyst for the famine had been the Japanese invasion of Burma in early 1942, and thus the crisis in Bengal was deeply entwined with the collapse of British power in the Far East between December 1941 and February 1942. This was not an event that the Raj had anticipated. In 1941 Victor Bailey, a former ICS officer, published a robust analysis of India's defence capabilities entitled *Is India Impregnable?* Decisively answering 'yes', he went on to explain that the real threat came from Russia via its old allies the Pathans, who would swarm down through Central Asia to loot the 'treasure house of the world'. But, defended by its martial races, plentiful food supplies and excellent railways, India would not fall. Nor was India vulnerable on her eastern flank. Singapore, he declared, 'cannot be attacked from the land; no army can march down the thousands of miles of tropical jungle which covers the Peninsula. It is a sheer impossibility.'

By the spring of 1942 the 'sheer impossibility' had been accomplished. In 55 days the Japanese had marched down through Malaya. Advancing at a rate of 20 kilometres per day, they fought 95 engagements and repaired 250 bridges destroyed by the retreating British force. On 15 February 1942 they took Singapore, where a British garrison of 85,000 surrendered to 30,000 Japanese. Two weeks later Rangoon was evacuated, and Mandalay surrendered in May after the bombing of the European club and golf course. Indian refugees began leaving in thousands. By autumn 1942, 600,000 plantation, mine and factory workers fled to India, while 80,000 died on the way.

Meanwhile bombs rained down on India's eastern borders, and there was now the real fear that the Japanese might invade eastern Bengal through Assam. Rumours of a Japanese fleet sailing to India from the Andaman Islands began to circulate, and much of the population of Madras decamped. In Vizagapatnam, on the southern coast, trenches were built in expectation of a Japanese naval assault, and when these were bombed the British, astonishingly, offered no retaliation.

Confidence in the Raj began to collapse as a consequence of these Japanese invasion stories. There was panic in Calcutta as the city filled with refugees from Burma claiming that the Japanese were only a few days' march away: they had come to free India; they possessed superhuman powers; they could use their parachutes like rockets to become airborne again. One Superintendent of Police in a district of Bengal reported that many ordinary people believed the Japanese to be Hindus and there was, therefore, no need to fear invasion. Meanwhile hoary rumours surfaced reminiscent of the 1857 Rebellion. In July a blind *sadhu* in Muzaffarpur (Bihar) predicted British rule would end 'in three months and thirteen days', though unhelpfully the British report did not say exactly when the prediction was made. In December a story that the government had ordered 10,000 wooden dummy planes from the firm of Chinoy and Co. gained currency. The dummy craft, it was said, were to be deployed on Indian aerodromes to deceive people into thinking that the British were well defended. Meanwhile leaflets appeared urging Indians to renounce the British yoke, and Subhas Bose, the leftist Congress leader, who had escaped to Germany from British custody, predicted the imminent destruction of the British Empire in his 'Free India' broadcasts from Berlin.

Suitably terrified, British firms had elaborate evacuation plans in place by late May 1942. The wife of an Indian Police Service officer wrote that British families began to 'think up wild plans . . . Could we stain the children's faces with walnut juice and let the *ayahs* take them to the villages?' Alarmed, but always with one eye on business, the Marwaris of Calcutta sold up and moved north; there was a run on the banks and mass absenteeism from factories in December.

The international context had now dramatically altered for the British. With the collapse of the European empires, the Americans became major power-brokers in the region, and they were, in part at least, fighting to liquidate empires. Churchill now came under enormous American pressure to move beyond gestures on the question of Indian independence. The first sign of this was the Cripps Mission in spring 1942. Stafford Cripps, a Labour minister in the war cabinet, arrived on 22 March with a brief to secure Congress's co-operation in the war effort. He offered Indians greatly increased representation in the Central Executive of the Government of India and de facto dominion status once the war was over. Even so, he failed to entice Congress back into government.

Officials blamed Congress for the failure of the mission. They believed that Congress had demanded too high a price for entering government – control of the Defence Ministry – which was unthinkable in wartime. Congress claimed that the problem was that the Cripps proposal, with its implied assumption that individual provinces might be allowed to secede from a post-war dominion, threatened the Balkanization of India. Subsequently suspicion has fallen on Churchill and Linlithgow for supposedly sabotaging the Cripps Mission from behind the scenes. Certainly Churchill was a shamelessly unapologetic imperialist. Infuriated at President Roosevelt's sympathy for the nationalists, he dismissed Congress as merely 'the intelligentsia of non-fighting Hindu elements, [who] can neither defend India nor raise a revolt'. Neither does Linlithgow seem to have been overly eager to promote accord, and is reported to have greeted Cripps' failure with the gloating 'Goodbye Mr Cripps'. But sabotage was not the root cause of failure. After two decades of stalled constitutional negotiations the problem was simply a complete lack of trust between the government and the nationalists.

The refusal of the Cripps offer raised the question of what Congress's next move would be. Despite their mass resignation from office on the declaration of war, the nationalists were divided on what position to adopt towards the war effort. Some were pacifists and opposed all war. Others saw Britain's war as India's opportunity. On the left, Subhas Bose's Forward Bloc advocated immediate mass action to lever the British out, citing Ireland as an example of freedom wrenched from a war-crippled colonial state. Nehru, however, worried about world opinion if Congress was seen to be offering support to fascists, refused to speak against the British directly, and many Congressmen, suspicious of Japan's motives given its record in China, felt it necessary to offer at least temporary support to the war effort.

Gandhi adopted a typically quixotic approach. Quoting the *Mahabharata*, he predicted that 'the end will be mutual exhaustion. The victor will share the same fate that awaited the ... mighty warrior Arjuna [who] was looted in broad daylight by a petty robber' – the message being that war, even for the victors, was invariably futile. But not wishing to embarrass the government too deeply, he initially declined to lead a mass campaign against the British. In the autumn of 1940 individual *satyagraha* was launched as a compromise between those wanting mass radical action and those who advocated caution. Despite the arrest of 23,000 *satyagrahas* by the spring of 1942, the government derided the movement as 'dull', concluding that Gandhi's influence was exhausted, while Jayaprakash Narayan, the Bihari socialist, denounced 'this farce of *satyagraha*' and advocated an alliance with underground revolutionaries.

Gandhi was stung by this contempt, and claimed that he was pondering a fresh attack on the Raj even before Pearl Harbor. 'Some form of conflict was inevitable to bring home the truth to the British mind,' he later wrote. After the fall of South East Asia, Gandhi's anti-British rhetoric hardened. The British, incapable of defending India effectively, had now forfeited the right even to moral support: 'The Nazi power has risen as a nemesis to punish Britain for her sins of exploitation and enslavement of the Asiatic and African races,' he thundered.

Gandhi seemed to believe that India would inevitably fall under Japanese control for a time while the 'two foreign mad bulls' fought it out. Since the imperial system had proved incapable of defending India it would be preferable for the British to leave altogether. Though not using the term itself, he seemed to be advocating something close to guerrilla warfare. India's city populations were to be evacuated to its 700,000 villages, which would then form self-help networks along the lines of communist rural communes in China. 'Leave India to god. If that is too much then leave her to anarchy', he exhorted the British. The war seemed to be an opportunity finally to implement the utopian anarchy of his 1909 credo *Hind Swaraj*.

Strikingly Gandhi seemed to be moving away from his advocacy of strict non-violence. Instead he spoke of non-violence as merely the apex of a hierarchy of action, followed by violence, with cowardice last. India, he suggested, was like a woman facing rape: ideally she would be protected by the 'flame of her dazzling purity', but in less ideal circumstances, 'God has given her teeth and nails . . .' On 8 August 1942 the All-India Congress Working Committee passed the 'Quit India' resolution, giving Gandhi complete authority to take whatever steps necessary to expel the British.

The Quit India movement became, by British admission, the greatest rebellion since 1857. The nationalist leadership was immediately arrested, but Gandhi had anticipated this, and in his speech of 8 August, which launched the movement, he declared that everyone who desired freedom would have be his own guide, even (he implied) if it meant violence, guided only by this mantra: 'Do or Die'. Although a secret Congress office continued to operate on Cathedral Street in Bombay, the real leadership of the movement swiftly passed to spontaneous, rudimentary underground organizations.

The Quit India campaign was a drama in three acts. It began with massive strikes, largely in urban areas, with a great deal of violence in Bombay, Calcutta and Delhi. From mid-August the action moved to the countryside, and though this had been more or less suppressed by September 1942, a third act, now largely an underground terrorist movement, opened and played on until early 1944. The rebellion was at its most intense in eastern United Provinces and Bihar. Smallholders were the movement's storm-troopers, but other groups, including tribal people, joined. There was an element of score settling over land disputes, but much of the anger was aimed at government wartime exactions and expropriations and suggested the utter collapse of respect for the *izzat* or 'honour' of the British. The movement assumed the character of a popular revolt. In Bihar, a parallel government in the name of Congress materialized, while in Banaras the Hindu University declared itself free Indian soil and the undergraduate military training corps became the army of Free India. In Ahmedabad and Bombay, European clothes became a particular target, with cases of 'rowdy urchins . . . molesting pedestrians clad in European dress' and burning their ties and hats.

A flood of underground leaflets and radio broadcasts offered guidance on action. In Nasik (Maharashtra), the police uncovered the 'ABC of Dislocation', a pamphlet elaborating plans for a nationwide guerrilla network headquartered in jungle areas. These bands were to inspire the masses and make the victory of any invader easier through a campaign of organized sabotage. The pamphlet was highly pragmatic in its approach, advising against blowing up big bridges without expert help, and suggesting that, if busy, an effective campaign of sabotage could still be conducted in one's spare time.

The Quit India rebels organized unprecedented attacks on the sinews and symbols of the state. 'The rails and roads that coil round the country like a black serpent and collect its blood in central reservoirs', as the Nasik pamphlet described them, suffered intense disruption: 332 railway stations, 945 post offices and 12,286 telegraph poles were destroyed in a worryingly systematic way. One District Officer reported that 'though the attackers were numerous they were not a mob but advanced in some sort of formation', assisted by two elephants. In Champaram (Bihar) peasants armed with spears, bows, arrows, pepper, syringes and nitric acid attacked police stations and burnt revenue records, while women armed with scythes, bamboo poles and sticks stepped into the front line once their husbands had been arrested. For several days the provincial government had little idea what was going on; the only link between the Bihar towns of Patna and Gaya was a daily shuttle by a Tiger Moth aeroplane borrowed from the Bihar Flying Club.

The British struck back hard. Responding to the pre-agreed code words 'Adolf' and 'Pantaloon', police began rounding-up Congress leaders only hours after the Quit India declaration was made. A special train carried prize prisoners, including Gandhi and Nehru, to confinement in Poona and Ahmednagar. Scuffles ensued at Poona station where a large crowd had gathered. Nehru briefly escaped, and the senior Congressman S. D. Deo kicked the Superintendent of Railway Police in the leg. So dire was the emergency that the British were even willing to contemplate the demise of the Mahatma who, in February 1943, undertook a fast in protest at the violence on both sides. Linlithgow dismissed this as a typical example of suicidal exhibitionism, but, as Gandhi neared death, he faltered and offered to release him, ignoring Churchill's apoplectic raging that this was not the time to 'crawl before a miserable little old man who has always been our enemy'. Gandhi, having effectively demonstrated that he loomed larger in the Viceroy's calculations than the British Prime Minister, refused to be released but began taking liquids.

The popular revolt was suppressed with great brutality. Gurkhas and British troops administered *lathi* charges, mass whippings, shootings and even aerial bombardments. Villages suspected of harbouring terrorists were torched, in an eerie echo of the Rebellion. A few Indian officers refused to shoot rioters, though this was hushed up, as was the nature of much of the repression, which was of dubious legality: the taking of hostages, the imposition of collective fines, the seizure and destruction of rebel property without due procedure, and the use of forced labour to repair sabotaged communications. In all 66,000 were convicted or detained and 2500 killed. But the movement had been suppressed.

The Raj had proved it still possessed plenty of raw power, but repression had come at a high price: 57 battalions of British troops in 60 locations had been required to quell the rebellion. Meanwhile all military training was halted, aerodrome construction stopped, khaki production fell by half and India almost ran out of cigarettes. And though the army and police had stayed loyal and Muslims had barely participated, the episode provoked defeatism among many British officials. They had received practically no co-operation from the general public in Bihar, and in Bombay it proved impossible to get evidence against saboteurs. It was no longer plausible to insist that Congress had no connection with 'the vast silent majority'. For Chief Justice Sir Maurice Gwyer, the ultimate consequence of the Quit India campaign was that 'Englishmen in India have ceased to believe in themselves or indeed in anything else'.

During the campaign many Indians had listened avidly to Subhas

Bose's broadcasts, now made from Kuala Lumpur where he was hoping to organize an invasion of India by his Indian National Army, which comprised Indian prisoners of war from the Malaya and Burma campaigns. Bose had enjoyed an eventful war. In the summer of 1940 he had been imprisoned by the British after staging a protest demanding the removal of the Holwell monument to the British victims of the so-called Black Hole of Calcutta atrocity of the late eighteenth century. In gaol he began to develop schemes to work with foreign powers for the military invasion of India. And in late December 1940, after consulting astrologers and palmists for a propitious day, he escaped confinement disguised as Mohammed Ziauddin, a travelling inspector for the Empire of India Life Assurance Co., and headed for Kabul by mule.

Once there he made contact with the Nazi regime through the office of the Siemens Company, and in April 1941, now posing as an Italian, Orlando Mazzotta, he arrived in Germany. In Berlin he entered talks with the Nazi government, which set him up with 'Free India' offices and radio equipment and two small training camps to prepare a crack force for the liberation of the subcontinent. But more ambitious plans to promote an early German invasion were greeted rather tepidly, and after an unsatisfactory meeting with Hitler in which accord was reached on the goal of expelling the British from India, but not on certain racist passages offensive to Indian feeling in *Mein Kampf*, Bose turned his thoughts to an alliance with the Japanese. Travelling by U-boat to Japan via Madagascar, in May 1943 he (or rather a mysterious Mr Matsuda) arrived in Tokyo.

Tokyo had long been a haven for a number of Indian revolutionaries, including the First World War extremist veteran Rash Behari Bose (no relation). He, along with intellectuals from the Indo-Japanese Black Dragon Society, had hatched grand schemes for linking up the whole of Asia in a 'Greater East Asian Order'. This notion was based on the premise that Japan, having learnt much from the ancient Asian civilizations of India and China, now had a duty to 'liberate' them from western imperialism. These ideas received a fillip when in 1940 the Japanese regime announced its commitment to creating a 'Co-Prosperity sphere', designed to pull the fraternal Asian nations together and, thus strengthened, they would throw off the shackles of western oppression. The boundaries and borders of this putative Co-Prosperity sphere were somewhat vague and it was unclear whether India was to be included. Nevertheless, the idea had taken hold among many Indians in Malaya and Burma that the Japanese were friends of the Indian motherland.

This was confirmed when, after over-running South-East Asia in 1941-2 the Japanese decided to corral the remains of the British Indian forces abandoned there into a free Indian force, the Indian National Army; many joined. Their motivation is uncertain. Some were coerced, while others, faced with the alternative of internment in a Japanese prisoner of war camp, understandably opted to join up. Whatever their rationale, by late 1942 45,000 Indian prisoners of war, nearly one third of the total, had joined. The force was led by a young and inexperienced Punjabi Sikh, Captain Mohan Singh. But by December 1942 Singh had fallen out badly with the Japanese over finance and training and the infant INA seemed already moribund. For many the problem was that Singh lacked the distinction and charisma necessary to inspire such a heroic enterprise. An Indian leader of real prestige was needed, and Subhas Bose was mooted for the role.

Bose, now the Indian samurai, determined to resurrect the INA and, with Japanese aid, liberate India by force of arms. To the main force of prisoners of war he added Indian plantation workers from Malaya, and traders and shopkeepers from Thailand. Breaking with traditional Indian army martial-race theory, the INA was an admirably multi-ethnic force: Punjabi and Pathan rubbed shoulders with Tamil and Malayali; there was a Muslim corps and even a women's detachment, named after the Rebellion heroine, the Rani of Jhansi. Muslim sensibilities were stroked with the adoption of the symbol of the springing tiger of Tipu, and the Urdu-Hindi compound, Hindustani, became the language of command. Cash was solicited from the wealthy Indian business diaspora of South East Asia (an Indian merchant from Rangoon was reported to have given his entire fortune). Nevertheless the operation was reliant on Japanese loans and always severely under-funded. Modelled on de Gaulle's Free French, a Bose-led provisional government of *Azad Hind* (Free India) was proclaimed in October 1943. In November the Japanese gave it the

Andaman and Nicobar Islands, renamed *Shaheed* (martyrs) and *Swaraj* (self-rule) Islands. As well as territory, Free India also acquired a governor, a trained cadre of civil and administrative staff, and its own currency. Bose's stirring 'Chalo Delhi' radio broadcasts whipped up INA fury with tales of 1857, the Amritsar massacre and the Bengal famine. With Japanese assistance, he insisted, *Azad Hind* would soon encompass the whole of British India.

British India, however, was beginning to show signs of reinvigoration. After the Japanese bombing of the American naval base at Pearl Harbor, the Americans finally entered the war and the South East Asian region. The South East Asia Command (SEAC) was created to co-ordinate all allied forces in the area, including those of the Indian army, and the Indian war effort was subjected to intense and highly critical American scrutiny. After a brief sojourn in Delhi, one American officer commented acidly that the Government of India

is not concerned about winning the war and is hopelessly inefficient, tangled in red tape, short-sighted, reactionary, uncooperative and strongly anti-American . . . a sort of composite of the [Austro-Hungarian] Dual Monarchy and the [French] Third Republic in their last days.

Unsurprisingly, if a little unfairly, the Indian army command was blamed for the humiliating defeats in Malaya and Burma, and India's Commander-in-Chief, Claude Auchinleck, was relieved of operational responsibility for defending the now vulnerable east Indian borders in Assam and Arakan. In his stead came Lord Louis Mountbatten, a British aristocrat, as Supreme Allied Commander of SEAC, in full control of all Indian forces and those operating out of India. Many thought this a somewhat surprising appointment; Mountbatten was regarded as lively, exciting and charming, but his judgement had been called into question on more than one occasion. One theory was that his lack of military distinction was precisely why he was appointed: someone more distinguished would have been more likely to tread on American toes. Yet, despite these unflattering assessments, Mountbatten proved a good choice. What he lacked in operational experience and judgement he made up for in charisma and 'people skills'. With his arrival in India the demoralized British began to rally, Indians became less resentful, and even the sceptical Americans were, partially, won over.

By 1944 the Indian war effort was finally getting into gear. Auchinleck, though relieved of operational command, was put in charge of production, army organization and recruitment, at which tasks he proved outstanding. He had always been an advocate of the indianization and modernization of the army, and now he was free to promote much needed change. The Indian army finally began to flourish under his ferocious attentions and the Indian navy and air force finally took shape. Army recruitment boomed, with 72,000 signing up between January and February alone, the princely states proving particularly rich recruiting grounds. More attention was paid to morale and welfare: the redoubtable Frank Brayne became inspector-general of amenities for the troops, charged with supplying better food and 'rest and recreation'. Nevertheless, old British misconceptions about potentially inflammatory dietary superstitions persisted, and cans of American corned beef were painstakingly rebranded bully mutton.

Most significantly, traditional martial-race theory was finally interred. Recruitment was now based on modern theories of psychological testing, and many of the new troops came from the supposedly effeminate peoples of the United Provinces, Bengal and Madras. On the eve of the war only a few hundred officers were Indian in a corps of thousands, and even they were confined to a single division where they would not have command of British troops. But by the end of the war 15,000 Indians from all regions, not just the 'martial' northeast, had received commissions and all the divisions of the Indian army were open to them. Indeed recruitment posters stressed modernity and opportunity: 'Pilot today. Airline executive tomorrow!' Technical training and specialization markedly improved: for the first time thousands of Indian troops became mechanics and drivers.

War production also finally started to boom. The Engineering Department budget alone now ballooned from Rs. 40 million to Rs. 1,000 million, vast acreages of land were requisitioned, and the 'aboriginal tribes' of Bengal, Bihar and Orissa found themselves pressed into aerodrome construction. The Tata Iron and Steel corporation established several new factories turning out motor engines, aircraft parts and munitions, while the princely states in the south began to produce sufficient rubber to fill the gap in supplies caused by the fall of Malaya. The massive East India Railway was put at the disposal of the military, its workshops now devoted to fashioning tanks and guns. Confidence seemed to be returning. In Calcutta bank deposits outweighed withdrawals for the first time since early 1942. Therefore the British were not so hopelessly unprepared as they had been two years previously when the Japanese launched another offensive in March 1944.

The Japanese advance on the Assamese territories of Imphal and Kohima was intended as a surprise preliminary to a fully fledged advance on India. It was enthusiastically supported by Bose, who, in anticipation of the invasion, had moved the INA headquarters from Singapore to Rangoon in early 1944. He had assured the Japanese high command that they would be met by a mass popular rebellion in Bengal, only kept in check, he claimed, by 'wild' West African troops imported to control the mutinous Indian sepoys.

However, the Japanese advance did not go well. The 95,000-strong Japanese forces were joined by 8000 INA men, but the combined army was ill-supplied and under-mechanized, and has been likened to a mass suicide squad. The advance depended on an animal force of 12,000 horses, 3000 oxen and 1000 elephants, of which only the elephants survived. This beast-borne army faced a British force over-whelmingly superior in tanks, heavy artillery and air power.

Moreover, far from joining an anti-British uprising, the local Naga and Chin peoples offered courageous support to the British armies. Dismissed by the Japanese as tribal primitives, they were allowed free access to Japanese camps as orderlies, and two such Naga camp attendants stole a crucial operational map which they gave to the British. But most important was the effectiveness of the 14th Army under General William Slim. This was a force of some of 80–100,000 men composed largely of British Indians, Burmese, Nepalese and Africans. Enraged by stories of Japanese atrocities against the wounded, they killed ruthlessly in retaliation, while mounting a brilliant campaign against the enemy. By September 1944 the Japanese were in full retreat.

Relations between the INA and the Japanese were appalling. The

Japanese regarded the INA troops as turncoats – inherently un-trustworthy and cowardly. Though trained for guerrilla warfare, the Japanese saw them, at best, as a propaganda unit intended to spread pro-Japanese stories among the conquered Indians, and, at worst, as merely a 'coolie' corps. The Imphal advance was delayed by wrangling over flags and whether the Japanese should salute INA officers. Supplies for the INA were also a problem: the Japanese themselves were ill-supplied, and the only food they offered the Indians was Japanese, which they hated. At one stage INA officers were driven to trading liquor with the Japanese in return for engine oil. Bose himself was regarded by the Japanese as incompetent and stubborn. This was not a wholly inexplicable view: Bose continued to insist that the march on Delhi was feasible in the midst of a catastrophic retreat, even as the Japanese demanded the return of their weapons. The retreating INA continued to fight in north and then south Burma, but without air cover or supplies they were in a hopeless position. Many deserted or surrendered. In late 1944 Bose abandoned his Rangoon head-quarters and withdrew his forces to Bangkok and then Malaya. By now Bose's great ally, General Tojo, had been deposed as supreme military commander in Japan. A desperate Bose began to send out feelers to the USSR, and it was on a flight to Russian-occupied Man-churia that his over-burdened plane (Bose had insisted on taking two heavy suitcases loaded with jewellery) blew up and killed him.

By the autumn of 1944 it was clear that, for the moment at least, British India had been saved. Things had improved so much that Noël Coward flew out to Delhi to entertain the troops and take cocktails with the Viceroy. But despite the military victory, Wavell was pessimistic about Britain's standing among the Indian population. In July 1945 he warned London that if a new mass rebellion were launched 'we could still probably suppress [it] . . . [but] should be driven to an almost entirely official [i.e. non-democratic] rule, for which the necessary numbers of efficient officials do not exist'. The psychological consequences of war contributed incalculably to the erosion of British authority. Indians had been shocked at Japanese military successes in South-East Asia. Prem Saghal commented: 'the fall of Singapore finally convinced me of the degeneration of the British people, and I thought that the last days of the British Empire had come'. But British prestige had plummeted further when news came out of the official abandonment of Indian troops and civilians in the wake of defeat. Refugees in Malaya and Burma had been abandoned by the British civil authorities, and rumours soon spread of racial discrimination on escape routes. Allegedly there had been a 'white' road and a 'black' road to Assam: Europeans followed well-supplied tracks with 'European' food and porters, while Indians were left to starve.

The behaviour of the enormous allied army in eastern India further eroded relations with Indian civilians. Cases of murder, rape, arson and robbery committed by British and American troops in Bengal and Assam were legion. Insult was added to injury when many of the culprits were tried by military rather than civil courts, where they tended to receive rather lenient sentences. Rumours of allied misbehaviour were soon rife, systematically spread by Congress propaganda. Pamphlets appeared blaming foreign troops for inflation, food shortages and the slaughter of 30,000 cattle daily (even pregnant cows) to feed their carnivorous appetites. Some suggested that American troops were there to take over India after the British left. Much of this literature manifested a striking preoccupation with attacks on Indian film stars. One official was driven to write to Gandhi:

I have now heard at least four different film stars named as the victim of this outrage and been told of all of them that they died of their injuries. So far as I know and have been able to find out, no film star has been in any way molested.

The British were not the only casualties in the war of opinion. The old Indian collaborator parties, which had stayed in power in some of the regions, were fatally tarnished. The Punjabi Unionists were now completely identified with the wartime economic shortages, inflation and intrusive regulation, and forced recruitment had a catastrophic impact on its relations with its Sikh and Muslim peasant constituencies. Even more damaging was the compulsory requisitioning of grain enforced on Punjab by the Central Food Department in Delhi, despite protests from the governor that such action could prove fatal to the Unionists. The implied British promise of dominionhood after the war made by Cripps in 1942 also weakened the party, as its core of wealthy landowners began to transfer their allegiance to the Muslim League as a better conduit to patronage and power in an independent India. By late 1945 a mass defection by Unionist assembly members to the League was under way.

Army loyalties were also severely strained. Strikes paralysed Kanpur, Karachi and Poona; violent protests broke out over delayed demobilization and rumours that Indian troops were to be deployed in Java and Vietnam. Sixty per cent of Indian commissioned officers were reported to be nationalists, angry at poor pay and racial discrimination in clubs, restaurants and trains, and traumatized by the effect of the famine on their families. Intercepted letters from Indian troops reported their resentment at their low pay compared to the British. One said, 'in the eyes of Mahatma Gandhi all are equal but you pay a British soldier Rs.75 and to the Indian soldier you pay only Rs. 18'.

One of the greatest causes of discontent was the treatment of INA prisoners. The government had insisted that INA rebels would be court-martialled once the war was over. The 11,000 prisoners interrogated in Calcutta, Jingaragacha and Nilganji were classified as 'whites', 'greys' or 'blacks' according to their degree of treachery. In Madras it was decided that trials would be too expensive and all prisoners were released with Rs.10 and a railway pass. But in Delhi it was decided to hold a show trial of three INA officers, one a Hindu, one a Sikh and one a Muslim. Nehru, who had been a bitter critic of Bose's INA exploits, dusted off his barrister's robes and appeared for the defence. Nevertheless all three were judged guilty of treason, cashiered and ordered to be transported. This caused riots in several cities, with order restored only after 33 had been killed and 200 injured when the police opened fire. The sentences were quashed and the three were paraded triumphantly through the country before rapturous crowds. One senior police officer in Lahore commented that the entire episode had been disastrous for police morale: 'From the police point of view I feared we could no longer expect to be able to call upon military forces of unquestioning integrity to support us.' The entire episode was described in Wavell's journal under the revealing title, 'On the Edge of a Volcano'.

Such forebodings proved well-founded. On 18 February 1946

Indian naval ratings on HMS *Talwar* mutinied in Bombay. They demanded action against their commanding officer, F. W. King, who had been accustomed to addressing them as 'black buggers', 'coolie bastards' and 'jungli Indians'. To a chorus of anti-British slogans, the British officers retreated, leaving the men to commandeer the signalling equipment and transmit the strike to other ships. On the nearby corvette *Hindustan*, sailors trained the main guns on the city, in the direction of the yacht club veranda where British officers were taking pre-prandial drinks. The mutiny spread to Fort Barracks and Castle Barracks onshore, where the white ensign was replaced by Congress and Muslim League flags. By 22 February, 20,000 naval ratings across the country – on land and at sea – were in a state of mutiny. They now demanded better food, better standards, parity of pay and conditions and a gratuity on release, as well as disciplinary action against racist officers.

Meanwhile communists had mobilized mass meetings, and by 19 February the whole naval dockyard was in uproar as 300,000 dockers and mill-workers went on strike. Congress, Muslim League and communist negotiators were brought in but talks broke down over clemency terms and the British decided that a show of force was necessary. At one point it seemed the first ever tank vs. ship battle was about to ensue. However, after bombardment by mortar, order was restored.

India had become frighteningly unstable. Cholera was rampant, rationing was severe, and only the black market thrived. The cost of living had risen 200–300 per cent in a few months, bringing middle-class distress and mass communist-led strikes among rail, postal and government workers. The classic post-war problems of unemployment and inflation were now compounded by a looming food shortage. A poor harvest in 1945 forced the government to cut rations drastically, to only 1200 calories per head. Officials feared another Quit India-style revolt. An unstable compound of agrarian unrest, labour strikes and a food crisis would be rendered highly incendiary by unrest in the army and a large reservoir of recently demobilized soldiers.

Despite its parlous financial state and the startling erosion of its authority, a surprising cross-section of British politicians harboured fond hopes that the Raj might yet be saved. After all, promises for constitutional advance during the war had spoken only of 'self-government', pointedly stopping short of the 'independence' word. Churchill had developed some bizarre plans. He suggested that the British attempt to outmanoeuvre the nationalists by wooing the poor with land confiscated from rich Congress supporters. If this proved impossible, he suggested reneging on the £1,335 million debt the British government had accrued to India for war costs, and instead present their own massive bill to India for services rendered, thus financially crippling any new Indian government. More surprisingly perhaps, even Labour Party leaders harboured notions of hanging on. Ernest Bevin, soon to be Foreign Secretary in the post-war Labour government, advocated a new reformist policy aimed at gaining the support of peasants and workers against Congress. Stafford Cripps, a friend of Nehru's, who had doubts about the socialist bona fides of Congress, pondered the possibility of promoting class politics in India. The Conservative Amery, in an equally unrealistic, though more resigned mood, mused:

Looking back one cannot help regretting that we did not keep Kashmir after the Sikh wars and use it for the large scale settlement of old British officers and soldiers and also for Anglo-Indians ... Possibly it was a real mistake of ours not to encourage the Indian princes to marry British wives for a succession of generations and so to breed a more virile type of native ruler.

But even hard-line imperialists were being forced to change their minds. The worrying erosion of British authority, the crisis-ridden British economy and, especially perhaps, American pressure to decolonize, simply could not be ignored. As Wavell himself confided to his diary, while Churchill, Bevin and Co. 'hate the idea of our leaving India but ... [they have] no alternative to suggest'.

Wavell himself had recognized the need to begin negotiating with Congress as early as September 1943 and had advocated setting-up a 'provisional political government' based on a Congress-Muslim League coalition. But Congress intransigence and what Wavell described as Churchill's 'Hitler-like attitude' towards Indian affairs, meant that nothing came of such initiatives. In 1944 there had been talks between Gandhi and Jinnah on an agreed separation of parts of the Muslim majority areas of north-west and north-east India from the rest after plebiscites, but the offer had been rejected by Jinnah, who denounced it as 'a shadow, a husk, a maimed, mutilated and moth-eaten Pakistan'. What was clear was that the position of the Muslims in an independent India was going to be the major issue in any subsequent transfer of power negotiations.

On 15 June 1945 the Congress High Command were released from gaol in order to attend an all-party conference convened by Wavell at Simla. This took place a month before the General Election in Britain, and the final end of the war in mid-August. Talks dealt with the setting up of a new Executive Council, which would be wholly Indian, bar the Viceroy himself and the Commander-in-Chief. It was proposed that 'caste Hindus' and Muslims should have equal representation. Inevitably Congress objected to being styled an exclusively 'caste Hindu' party, insisting on its right to nominate Muslims and dalits too – at this point the Congress president was the Muslim nationalist Maulana Azad (Abul Kalam Ahmed), who headed the Simla delegation. But the conference collapsed completely when Jinnah insisted on the right to nominate every single one of the Muslim members of the Executive, and effectively demanded that there should be some kind of Muslim veto, with all decisions opposed by Muslims requiring a two-thirds majority for acceptance. Wavell dissolved the conference, thus, in effect, conceding Jinnah's right to a Muslim veto on future constitutional negotiations. The complex and frustrating manoeuvres of the Simla session were satirized by the Viceroy in high Carrollian style:

> Twas Grillig; and the Congreelites,
> Did hearg and shobble in the swope,
> All jinsy were the Pakistaniites,
> And the spruft Sikhs outscrope.

Behind Jinnah's intransigence lay the fundamental question of the status of India's Muslim minority in a future independent state: were they a nation in their own right that was only represented by the Muslim League, as Jinnah claimed, or not? Since the Congress electoral landslide of 1937 Jinnah had set about reorganizing the hitherto tiny and aristocratic League into a mass party, thus closing the gap between popular and elite Muslim politics. The war acted as a great accelerator to this process. The Congress's refusal of all co-operation during the war had encouraged the government, anxious to promote its legitimacy in American eyes, to promote League participation in government. Jinnah, however, was not willing to be a bit-part player in a revitalized *durbar* Raj, and struck a hard bargain in return for co-operation. On 23 March 1940, in his address to the All-India Muslim League conference at Lahore, he declared: 'The Mussulmans are a nation by any definition, with the need for a homeland, territory and a state if we are to develop to the fullest our spiritual, cultural, economic, social and political life.' This was a bold and dramatic demand for Muslims to be recognized as a nation, Pakistan, in their own right, with the League as their 'sole spokesman', on a par with Congress.

After the Lahore declaration, the League was rapidly transformed. By 1943 it was in government in Assam, Sindh, Bengal and North West Frontier Province. It acquired a wardrobe of symbols appealing to the 'national' ideal – a flag, an anthem, Muslim League National Guards, a volunteer corps, a 'Pakistan' National Bank and Chamber of Commerce, even a Pakistan airline was mooted, all designed to present an image of a state in waiting. However, the precise nature of this putative 'Pakistan' remained unclear: was it a people, a faith, a piece of territory within India or a sovereign state? Initially it seems to have been envisaged by its progenitor, the poet Iqbal, as an autonomous territory within an Indian federation. Jinnah himself was rather vague about where or what Pakistan should be. The 1940 Lahore conference passed a resolution calling for 'geographically contiguous units ... demarcated into regions ... in which the Muslims are numerically in a majority ... grouped to constitute independent states'.

The very ambiguity of the idea of 'Pakistan', like Gandhi's notion of *swaraj* two decades earlier, made it highly potent. To the aspirant peasants of Punjab and Bengal it signified the end of Hindu landlordism and money-lending, while to businessmen and professionals it promised deliverance from Hindu competitors. To the poor and devout its appeal was emotive and religious, the promise of a post-British state that was not dominated by aggressive Hinduism. For politicians like Sikander Hyat Khan, the chief of the Punjabi Unionists, it worked as a magic electoral wand, 'a convenient slogan to sway the Muslim masses'. The nebulous symbol of 'Pakistan' thus succeeded where other symbols of Muslim identity had failed – it transcended the disunity of locality, sect, town, village and region. Deploying the language of unity long present in the rhetoric of Islamic reform and revival, Jinnah had hit upon a way of moulding a subjective 'imagined community' from the empty British bureaucratic category of Muslim separate electorates.

After the breakdown of talks at Simla and the election of a Labour government in Britain, events began to move more rapidly. In August 1945 the new Labour government announced that elections would be held in India, the first since 1935 at the centre and 1937 in the provinces. After the elections there would be constitutional talks with the newly elected Members of the Legislative Assembly (MLAs) and the princely states in order to establish a 'constitution-making body'.

Elections were held in the winter of 1945/46 on the basis of a still very limited franchise of only 10 per cent of the population in the provinces and less than 1 per cent at the centre. Congress swept the general (non-Muslim) seats, winning 57 of 102 seats in the Central Assembly. It also won every province except Punjab, Sindh and Bengal (all provinces with a majority Muslim population). Congress did, however, win the North West Frontier Province, despite its Muslim preponderance, a legacy of the long alliance with Abdul Ghaffar Khan (the 'Frontier Gandhi').

The Muslim League swept the other provinces. The League portrayed the contest as one of *haq aur batil* (truth or falsehood), not merely a battle with the Hindus. Voting for the League became a symbol of one's commitment to Islam. One electoral agent reported: 'wherever I went everyone kept saying, *bhai* (brother) if we did not vote for the League we would have become *kafir* (unbelievers)'. But Jinnah also tapped into the local, particular forms of political influence. In the Punjab and Sindh, careful account was taken of local identities based on tribe, *biradari* (kinship networks) and family in organizing the electoral lists. Supporters of Pakistan included prominent rural *pirs* (descendants of saints) who issued *fatwas* which threatened those who voted the 'wrong' way with exclusions from his *pir*'s *baraka* (charisma). In these districts the League achieved its best results. The recruitment of big landlords, ideally placed to marshal the Muslim tenant vote, was also crucial to the League in the Punjab. The unfortunate pro-British Unionists, whose wartime administration had already made them unpopular, were overly reliant on government machinery to mobilize their vote. The Unionists' electoral tactics consisted of a disastrous combination of coercion and the belated deployment of Islamic rhetoric, which merely served to alienate its erstwhile Sikh and Hindu voters. Jinnah and the League swept the board, taking every Muslim seat in the Central Assembly and 75 per cent of all Muslim votes cast in the provinces, and forming governments in Bengal and Sindh. However, they did not succeed in the Punjab, where the Unionists managed to construct a coalition with Congress and the Akalis (a Sikh party). Even so, despite the limited franchise, Jinnah and the League had massively enhanced their political leverage and with it the apparent legitimacy of the demand for Pakistan. But with Congress entrenched in eight of the eleven provinces and at the Centre, deadlock threatened the constitutional process.

The British government took the initiative and in March 1946 despatched a three-man Cabinet Mission, consisting of Cripps, Lord Pethick-Lawrence (the Secretary of State for India) and Horace Alexander (a long-time specialist in Indian affairs and a correspondent of Gandhi's), to negotiate the terms of a settlement. The mission argued that a sovereign Pakistan was unfeasible, but produced an ingenious compromise: a three-fold India federation. The existing provinces would be combined into three sets to elect members for the new constituent assembly: Section A would comprise Hindu-majority provinces, Section B would include Muslim-dominated provinces in the north west, and section C the north-eastern Muslim regions. Each grouping would then establish its own parliaments and cabinets, and the federal centre would have authority only over defence and foreign relations. Essentially, India would remain a unified state, but with a weak centre and strong regions. Congress would have its united India, but the League would get a de facto 'Pakistan' in the second-tier Muslim groupings.

In June 1946, agreement to this plan was triumphantly announced, and an interim government and Constituent Assembly was created to hammer out the details. But by November the agreement had collapsed. This was not wholly surprising as agreement had been based on wholly opposing interpretations of the plan. The League insisted that the groupings be compulsory and envisaged the Muslim B and C elements potentially seceding from united India after ten years. Congress insisted that the groupings were optional, and on 10 July, Nehru, now Congress president, used a press conference to suggest that the Muslim-dominated North West Frontier Province and Assam defect from the B and C groups respectively to join the Hindu A group, thus wrecking Jinnah's plans of establishing unified Muslim territories. Jinnah therefore retracted his acceptance of the plan, and a 'Direct Action Day' for the 'Muslim Nation' was announced by the League for 16 August. The question of Pakistan was now beyond negotiation: it was to be settled on the streets.

On Direct Action Day, riots lasting ten days broke out in Calcutta. Violence spread to Noakhali in rural Bengal and then to Bihar and finally the Punjab in March 1947 – an ominous prelude to the violence of partition; 45,000 troops were needed to restore order and over 4000 people were killed in Calcutta alone. The Sikhs were rumoured to be preparing for 'Holy War', and the Hindu nationalist right was arming itself in anticipation of civil strife. The political situation was now rapidly transformed: the Unionist-coalition government in Punjab fell victim to a League-led civil disobedience campaign in March 1947, and the Congress-dominated interim government, unable to cope with the violence, and paralysed by wrangling with its League members, effectively ceased to function.

In this context desperate measures began to be contemplated. Some Hindus and Sikhs began to demand the partition of India and the creation of a Muslim homeland. Indeed, on 10 March 1947 even Nehru privately confided to Wavell that 'the only real alternative was the partition of the Punjab and Bengal'. Wavell himself was concerned about the security of the British in India, and in January 1947 despatched his now notorious memo, in which he proposed a strategy of emergency withdrawal, dubbed 'Operation Ebb-Tide', in the event of order collapsing completely. This outlined in graphic terms a depressing scenario of mounting violence and anarchy as British control broke down in stages across India. He explained that the police were unreliable and there were fears for the loyalty of the army. He was particularly concerned that there were now fewer British troops in India than in Palestine. He predicted that the British had until the middle of 1948 to get out. After that they would, he said, be left with responsibility but no power. He proposed, therefore, that if no constitutional settlement had been reached by March 1947, a care-taker government of officials should be set up at the centre while the British withdrew, province by province, starting in the south with Madras, Bombay, Central Provinces and Orissa, and moving progress-ively north in a holding operation while Europeans were repatriated:

We propose to withdraw. Within our own method and in our own time, and with due regard to our interests and we will regard any attempt to interfere with our progress as an act of war.

Essentially Wavell's scheme amounted to an acceptance of Gandhi's 1942 demand that India be left to anarchy.

The Churchillian alternative to Wavell's Operation Ebb-Tide was an Ulster strategy writ large. The British would stay for another twenty years while staging a more prolonged retreat by signing separate constitutional arrangements with individual provinces and princely states. This approach threatened the complete fragmentation of the subcontinent, the logical culmination of a long-standing view that India was not a nation but merely a collection of races, sects and tribes.

Clement Attlee, the new Labour Prime Minister, was disinclined to accept either of these alternatives. He dismissed the Wavell scenario as defeatist, and Operation Ebb-Tide as 'an ignoble and sordid scuttle'. Meanwhile the Churchillian approach violated the principle of demo-cratic will that had informed Labour approaches to India since the 1930s. Attlee himself was something of an old India hand, having served on the Simon Commission in 1928. Since then he had formu-lated his own distinctive views on India. Nationalism, he concluded, was the only force capable of unifying India's welter of divisions and remedying its social and economic problems. In 1938 he, together with Cripps and Nehru, had agreed that the terms of the transfer of power would be based on a democratically elected constituent assembly. Though he, like Cripps, had reservations about Congress's commitment to democracy, Attlee believed that it alone could make or break any constitutional settlement and, if properly handled, could be a constructive force. The minorities could not be allowed to veto this process and a negotiator with full powers on the spot was now needed to break the impasse by means of private and informal talks. Attlee concluded that Wavell lacked the temperament for this strategy and had lost the confidence of Congress. In February 1947 the Viceroy was unceremoniously dismissed and replaced by the highly ceremonious Lord Louis Mountbatten, who had knowledge of India since his days as Commander of SEAC during the War.

Though Attlee had dismissed the messenger, he had absorbed one crucial element of Wavell's message: the need to impose a time limit on negotiations in order to force agreement. In a private directive to Mountbatten on 8 February (and to Parliament on 20 February), he stated that if the Indian constituent assembly had not produced an agreed plan for independence by June 1948, then power would be transferred to 'whomever is considered most appropriate' and in 'the best interests of the Indian People'. Early independence now carried the unmistakable threat of possible Balkanization or partition. Mountbatten rapidly decided that retaining a unified India, though desirable, was impractical in the timescale available. Soon after his arrival he announced his own proposal, tactlessly if accurately entitled 'Plan Balkan'. All provinces, and apparently now even the princely states, would have the right to choose whether or not to accede to the new Indian Union or become independent.

Aghast at this prospect, Congress suggested a clean break involving the creation of 'Pakistan' comprising a bifurcated state of two wings, one to the east, consisting of a partitioned Bengal, and one to the west made up of a portion of west Punjab, Sindh, Baluchistan and North West Frontier Province. This was precisely the 'moth-eaten' entity Jinnah had rejected in 1944. Its two wings would be separated by a thousand miles of Indian territory, with no land corridor linking them, as Jinnah had suggested. Mountbatten, eager to secure India's accession to the new British Commonwealth, accepted this proposal and a deal was struck. Congress would get most of India and a quick transfer of power, now accelerated to August 1947.

Plan Partition was announced on 3 June with the acceptance of Nehru, Jinnah and the Sikh leader Sardar Baldev Singh. The plan was put to the vote in the provinces affected: Bengal, Punjab, Sindh, North West Frontier Province and Baluchistan. In Punjab and Bengal the provincial assemblies were notionally divided into their Hindu and Muslim majority districts, and each half then voted separately on the disposition of their respective halves. All Muslim majority districts in both the Punjab and Bengal opted for Pakistan, but against partition. The non-Muslim halves of both states voted for India and for partition.

The partition of India has generated a great deal of controversy, and observers at the time and since have spent much time trying to assign blame to one or other of the three main parties involved. The British have been accused of attempting to weaken the successor states in order to ensure continuing British military and political influence. The Congress right has been seen as callously sacrificing a united India to a Hindu one, while Nehru has been depicted as an opportunist anxious to get his hands on power as soon as possible, regardless of the consequences. A megalomaniacal passion for power has also been offered as an explanation of Jinnah's actions. But, given the conditions of the period, the behaviour of the British, Congress and the Muslim League is readily comprehensible in terms of their interests, as they perceived them at the time.

The British, while recognizing that their authority was collapsing, disagreed, as they had always done, on how power should be transferred and to whom. But Clement Attlee had very decided views: the handover must be democratic. That meant cutting a deal with Congress. There was no ulterior motive or design to keep control. The British imposed no fine print, escape clauses, conditions, no military treaty or even an insistence on joining the Commonwealth (Mountbatten's personal hobby-horse).

Within Congress there had been tacit acceptance of the possibility of partition from as early as 1944, and a suggestion to hold referendums on the Pakistan question in north-west and north-east India. The right within the movement, especially Patel, greeted partition as a masterstroke, believing that the resulting 'moth-eaten' Pakistan stood little chance of long-term survival. In Bengal, especially, the Hindu right had become highly vociferous, and partition was welcomed with jubilation, as Hindus were now no longer doomed to minority status.

On the left, Nehru's commitment to rapid state-led economic development in an independent India predisposed him to favour a 'strong'
state over the idea of a 'weak' federation encompassing the Muslim
regions. Moreover both left and right were disturbed by the increasingly unstable conditions in India and wanted a swift transfer of power
in order to quell potentially socially radical movements.

Also pressing was the very real fear of Balkanization and civil war
as various princes, tribal groups and regions sought sovereign status.
Congress was thus eager to settle the question of independence rapidly.
Some of the larger princely states still had ambitions for sovereignty:
the largest, Hyderabad, was a landlocked state the size of France in
south central India with a population of eighteen million. Its ruler,
the Nizam, harboured ambitions for complete independence and,
equipped with a private army, had made plans for war. In early 1947
he unsuccessfully pressed the Portuguese to sell him Goa, a prized
seaport. Recognizing common interests with Jinnah, the two hatched
plans to fashion a 1200-mile land corridor linking Hyderabad to
eastern Pakistan via a newly established *adivasi* (tribal) homeland in
south Bihar and the northern districts of Central Provinces. Meanwhile in the far north-east the Sinic peoples of Assam, Nagaland and
the Mizos were agitating for nationhood. And to the west in the
Punjab, one faction of the Sikh Akalis lobbied for an independent
Sikh state carved from the south Sutlej region and Lahore. Even the
dalits had dreams of a sovereign 'Achutistan'. Given these ambitions,
Congress's leaders concluded that one partition was a reasonable price
to pay to avoid many.

Among the Muslims the switch to the Muslim League by the landed
elites in western Punjab and Sindh, along with the defection of patriarchal heads of *biradari* brotherhoods who had been loyal to the Unionists had, in part, been motivated by a desire to avoid the socialist leash
of an all-Indian state dominated by Congress. Jinnah's own views
remain something of an enigma. It has been suggested that the notion
of Pakistan as sovereign territory was always just a bargaining chip,
designed to elicit concessions from Congress in the form of weighted
Muslim representation and power-sharing deals. But this seems
implausible. It is difficult to see how Muslim self-determination could
have been accommodated in a united India, even one with the most

elaborately convoluted constitutional structure. Perhaps too little has been made of Jinnah's place in an intellectual tradition stretching back to Syed Ahmed Khan and the Aligarh school, which had always foreseen that majoritarian democracy in India was not compatible with the autonomy of a Muslim community; a view crystallized by Iqbal in the 1930s. As early as 1940 Jinnah had insisted: 'A democratic system of government' was not acceptable because Islam 'does not advocate a democracy which would allow the majority of non-Muslims to decide the fate of Muslims.' Ultimately, as Jinnah himself declared to Mountbatten, he didn't care how much territory Pakistan was given, as long as it 'was given completely'.

There was, therefore, a consensus on rapid partition, and the preparations for handover now had to be telescoped into 72 days. Mountbatten posted a large tear-off calendar on the wall of his office to give officials a sense of urgency, unofficially dubbed the 'count-down calendar'. Things to do ranged from the trivial – apportioning typewriters and other bureaucratic paraphernalia – to the momentous – the partition of peoples and territory. Among the latter, the demolition of the last flimsy edifices of the *durbar* Raj, the princely states, was a pressing concern. The princes had much to lose, including near despotic personal power and vast incomes derived from customs, taxes and mineral rights. In their final days a frantic rearguard action in their defence was staged by the chief of the Indian Political Service (which oversaw princely matters), Sir Conrad Corfield. Corfield, a convinced royalist, hoped to salvage the independence of at least two or three states. He had high hopes of an ally in Mountbatten, who was, after all, a cousin of King George. Mountbatten, though, regarded the princely states as absurd antediluvian entities which should have been reformed decades before.

Undaunted, Corfield decided to bypass the Viceroy and flew to London in early July to appeal for the preservation of the direct relationship between the British and each of the princes until the last possible moment. This would result in the newly independent India facing the infinitely tricky task of negotiating six hundred different deals, prince by prince. To make these negotiations even more irksome, officials in the princely states were ordered to start cancelling all previous agreements with British India over such issues as railway rights, customs duties and the stationing of troops. Corfield was also determined to deny Congress the satisfaction of reading about pyromaniac Maharajas, dalliances with dancing girls and evidence of other embarrassing princely peccadilloes: over four tons of confidential reports and communications were burnt or shipped back to London.

Mountbatten was furious at this back-room politicking, as was Nehru. In mid-July Congress established its own department to look into the integration of the princely states, headed by the first Interior Minister of independent India, the formidable Vallabhbhai, or Sardar, Patel. Patel and his able amanuensis, V. P. Menon, proceeded comprehensively to outmanoeuvre Corfield, with the enthusiastic assistance of Mountbatten. The Viceroy embarked on one of his notorious charm offensives. Appeals were made to princely vanities: those with no-gun salute status were elevated to nine-gun glory, and it was pointed out to others that if they stayed outside the Commonwealth they would be ineligible for future honours and decorations from the King. Most spectacularly, on 25 July the princes were gathered into an audience with the Viceroy in 108-degree Delhi heat, where they were alternately coaxed and cajoled into accession to either India or Pakistan. The question of acquiring sovereignty in their own right was, Mountbatten archly pointed out, merely a theoretical option.

Despite this pressure, a few states still entertained notions of independence. Each prince was theoretically free to opt for either India or Pakistan, but in reality location and the supposed wishes of the general population were the deciding factors. Given these conditions, the accession of the vast majority to India was a certainty. A few statelets, such as Bahawalpur in southern Punjab, lay within Pakistan, while the rest lay within India and had mainly Hindu populations. Those determined to defy absorption to the bitter end included Travancore, Bhopal, Jodhpur and Junagadh. But the offer of handsome permanent incomes, and some thinly veiled threats of popular mobilization and other 'pressures', brought these states swiftly to heel; they all joined India, though only after the Maharaja of Jodhpur had flourished a revolver at Menon in the Viceroy's private office. But difficulties persisted with Kashmir in the north and Hyderabad in the south, both of which had majorities with different religions to their rulers. Hyderabad also had a sizeable army. However, once Indian forces arrived at his borders in September 1948, the Nizam accepted the inevitable and acceded.

That still left the question of Kashmir. The state had been constructed as a mini-empire of various ethnicities and 'tribes' within an empire by Gulab Singh, the subtle scion of Rajput extraction. He had cannily remained aloof during the Anglo-Sikh war of 1846, and the British, in return for Rs. 7500 and the annual supply of 'one horse, twelve perfect shawl goats and three pairs of Kashmir shawls', agreed to 'make over, for ever, in independent possession, to Maharaja Gulab Singh and the heirs male of his body' the Kashmir Valley. By the First World War, Kashmir was a sprawling multi-ethnic entity, having acquired parts of Ladakh and Baltistan in addition to Jammu and the Kashmir Valley. Its population was mixed: 23 per cent were Hindu, Sikh and Buddhist, while the remaining 77 per cent were Muslim, of whom most were impoverished landless labourers working effectively as serfs for absentee Hindu landlords. The Maharaja was notoriously authoritarian and repressive and Kashmir remained very backward economically. A visiting British official reported to Delhi in the late 1920s that its capital, Srinagar, was a 'filthy, foetid place populated by illiterate people with no conception of rights'.

The state was contiguous with both India and Pakistan, though its border with Pakistan was longer; trade and transport links were also more integrated with those of west Punjab (which became part of Pakistan). However, the case for accession to Pakistan was complicated by the attitude of its main political movement, the National Conference. Formed in the early 1930s, it had become a mass movement during the 1940s. Much of its popularity derived from the charisma of its leader, Sheikh Abdullah, part of whose appeal rested on his ability to recite movingly from the Quran, while its support was rooted in its control of mosques. But its ascendancy was not based on promoting Hindu-Muslim rivalry, but on regional patriotism and the promise of social and economic progress. Its radicalism had made it a distant ally of Congress, and Abdullah himself was close to Nehru. In April 1946 the National Conference launched a Quit Kashmir agitation against the widely disliked Maharaja, which meant that by early 1947 most of Kashmir's effective political leadership were in prison and the Maharaja was, temporarily, back in full control.

On 15 August, Independence Day, the Maharaja signed a preliminary agreement to accede to Pakistan, which, though he was Hindu, had offered him more attractive powers and privileges than had India. However, in late August and early September relations with Pakistan began to deteriorate over minor tribal incursions into Kashmiri territory from over the border. On 21 October matters escalated when several thousand Pashtun tribesmen launched an offensive into Jammu and Kashmir from North West Frontier Province. Pakistan claimed it was a spontaneous rebellion in support of enslaved people. The incursion, however, seemed suspiciously well planned, with experienced leaders, a fleet of transport vehicles, modern arms and strikingly precise goals. With the rebels only 20 miles from Srinagar, the Maharaja urgently cabled New Delhi for assistance. Mountbatten advised Nehru to get an accession agreement signed before sending in troops or the action could be regarded as illegal. The accession was rapidly secured and accepted by Mountbatten, with the proviso that it be subject to popular ratification once law and order was restored.

The Indian army quickly recaptured much of the lost territory, assisted by the National Conference and by the general population, which had been alienated by the violence, rape and looting inflicted by the Pashtuns. Abdullah was appointed to head an interim administration and the National Conference emerged as the de facto government. But by late 1947, several regions of Kashmir, now infected by the partition violence affecting nearby Punjab, had descended into an orgy of ethnic cleansing: the entire Sikh and Hindu population of north-western Jammu were killed or expelled, as were Muslims in Hindu-dominated eastern Jammu. There now seemed little hope of a negotiated settlement. In the spring of 1948 the Pakistan army joined battle, and the first of three Indo-Pakistan wars over Kashmir ensued. The war ended in stalemate and in January 1949 a truce established a 'line of control', leaving India controlling the bulk of Jammu and Kashmir, while Pakistan held a long strip of territory running north to south, mostly in the border Jammu districts, part of Ladakh and the mountain zones of Gilgit and Baltistan, dubbed Azad Jammu and Kashmir. Thus began the Indo-Pakistan Kashmir dispute, a continuous running sore, and, potentially, the catalyst of a nuclear war in South Asia.

Nevertheless, the task of integrating princely India was compara-tively simple compared with the nightmarish complexity that beset efforts to partition the enormous provinces of Bengal and Punjab. Inevitably there was controversy about the 'shadow lines', the artificial map-made divisions imposed on Punjab and Bengal, shadowy because they were drawn with a rather thick lead pencil, leaving acres of territory and thousands of lives in the disputed penumbra of these markings. The British had initially attempted to devolve responsibility for the surgery elsewhere. The UN was considered, and even a com-mission composed of delegates from France, the US and Peru. These suggestions were rejected on grounds of time. Ultimately the role of chief surgeon fell to Sir Cyril Radcliffe, a Chancery barrister and latterly Director-General of the Ministry of Information, in which capacity he had met and impressed Mountbatten. He was considered qualified precisely because of his lack of experience of India. He famously decided that it would be best if he did not see the territories themselves, and made all his decisions on the basis of reports and written submissions, from a small room in the South Block of New Delhi's magnificent new administrative citadel. The whole procedure was completed in less than a month.

Demography was the governing principle of division and Radcliffe was charged with 'ascertaining contiguous majority areas of Muslims and non-Muslims', but he was also required to take into account 'other factors'. The vagueness and ambiguity in those terms of refer-ence would create serious problems, especially as it was not clear when 'other factors' should trump demographic criteria. At the evidence hearings held in Lahore and Calcutta, the Muslim League urged demography, while Congress and the Sikhs stressed 'other factors', such as economic stakes, property and historical and religious association.

Though its border was six times longer, the division of Bengal proved a simpler task than dividing Punjab, largely because there were only two population groups to consider – Hindus and Muslims. At the boundary hearings the Muslim League made somewhat extravagant claims, even suggesting that Calcutta, with a Muslim population of only 23 per cent, be divided between the two states or become a 'free city'. They argued, with some reason, that without the industrial hub of Calcutta east Bengal would become merely a grossly overcrowded poor agrarian state. Congress retaliated by demanding the whole of Calcutta along with its surrounding, largely Muslim-populated Burdwan region as a protective belt. In the end the final decision proved equally unfavourable to both sides. East Bengal received 54,000 square miles of territory, with a population of 40 million, 27 per cent of whom were Hindu. The west was allocated 28,000 square miles and 21 million people, including a 29 per cent Muslim minority. Calcutta went to India, with Pakistan compensated by the extensive swamp and wet forest of the Khulna district.

Apportioning the Punjab was, by comparison, a task of nightmarish complexity. Unlike Bengal there were not two, but three population groups whose claims had to be considered. The Sikhs, 20 per cent of the population and long the favourite sons of the Raj's armies, had acquired some of the best agricultural land in India, much of it in central Punjab. Any boundary would have to cut through the Sikh heartland close to the holy city of Amritsar and several sacred sites, including the birthplace of the most revered figure of Sikhdom, Guru Nanak. This was also the land of 'five rivers' with a highly complex system of dams, barrages and canals. Division would inevitably interrupt these irrigation works, damaging the Punjab's prosperous economy. These were 'other factors' of some significance.

As with Bengal, Radcliffe adopted demography as his guiding principle, but applied it somewhat inconsistently. With the exception of the Lahore and Gurdaspur districts, all Muslim-majority areas went to Pakistan. In all, west Punjab, allocated to Pakistan, received 63,000 square miles of land and a population of 16 million, of whom 4 million were non-Muslim. East Punjab was composed of the remaining 37,000 square miles of land, with a population of 12.5 million, of whom 35 per cent were Muslim. The most controversial decision concerned allocation of certain Muslim-majority sub-districts in the Gurdaspur region to India. Clearly 'other factors' had been at play here, though it was not clear which ones. Pakistanis have seen a conspiracy between Mountbatten and Nehru to pressure Radcliffe to change his initial allocations in order to guarantee India land access to Kashmir. Though it is now clear that Radcliffe did not operate, as was claimed, in monkish isolation, hermetically protected from official and political pressure, there is little evidence that Kashmir was the reason for his last-minute change of plan.

In part the problems over Gurdaspur seem to have been the result of difficulties over water and rail systems, but the real reason was the threat of violence from Sikhs. The Sikhs had made it very clear that they would not accept Muslim control of the areas east of the Ravi river, which would pose, in their view, a direct threat to Amritsar. On 9 August a train carrying Muslim officials and files from New Delhi to Karachi was mined, and although there were no fatalities the incident provoked a chain of revenge attacks. It was known that the Sikh militant leader, Tara Singh, had been planning an insurgency in league with the Sikh Maharaja of Patiala, and Mountbatten seems to have considered arresting him, but concluded it would simply escalate the violence. These concerns, rather than a Machiavellian scheme to secure Kashmir for India, help to explain Radcliffe's revision of his allocations. Radcliffe himself left India on the 17th, having destroyed all his notes. His famously Olympian approach to the proceedings was grimly satirized by W. H. Auden:

> Shut up in a lonely mansion, with police night and day
> Patrolling in the gardens to keep assassins away,
> He got down to work, to the task of settling the fate
> Of millions. The maps at his disposal were out of date
> And the Census Returns almost certainly incorrect,
> But there was no time to check them, no time to inspect
> Contested areas. The weather was frightfully hot,
> And a bout of dysentery kept him constantly on the trot,
> But in seven weeks it was done, the frontiers decided,
> A continent for better or worse divided.
> The next day he sailed for England, where he quickly forgot
> The case, as a good lawyer must. Return he would not,
> Afraid, as he told his Club, that he might get shot.

Partition, a harrowing event, has produced an outstanding literature. A superb example of this is Sadat Manto's partition tale, *Toba Tek Singh*, in which the Muslim writer grimly satirizes the bloody process. *Toba Tek Singh* concerns the exchange of 'lunatics' between India and Pakistan. The chief protagonist of the story is a Sikh 'lunatic',

Bishan Singh, known as Toba Tek Singh after his birthplace, the market town of Lyallpur district. The personal bonds between Hindus, Muslims and Sikhs that characterize Toba Tek Singh's town, not its national location in either India or Pakistan, are what define Singh's identity: 'A Sikh lunatic asked another Sikh: "Sardarji, why are we being sent to India? We don't even know the language they speak in that country."' But these human bonds are destroyed by the harsh division of territory. 'Where is Toba Tek Singh,' he asks, 'is it in India or Pakistan?' No one can give a clear answer:

Those who had tried to solve this mystery had become utterly confused when told that Sialkot, which used to be in India, was now in Pakistan. It was anybody's guess what was going to happen to Lahore, which was currently in Pakistan, but could slide into India at any moment. It was also possible that the entire subcontinent of India might become Pakistan. And who could say if both India and Pakistan might not entirely vanish from the map of the world one day.

Having been released from the asylum, a confused Toba Tek Singh refuses to cross into India where his home town is now located:

There he stood in no man's land on his swollen legs like a colossus. There behind barbed wire, on one side, lay India and behind more barbed wire, on the other side, lay Pakistan. In between, on a bit of earth which had no name, lay Toba Tek Singh.

The irony, of course, is that it is the 'lunatic' Toba Tek Singh who sees through the insanity of partition and its forced recasting of authentic personal and local identities into the artificial (or so Manto implies) idea of a 'nation'.

In the three and a half months after 15 August, 4.5 million Sikhs and Hindus and 5.5 million Muslims abandoned their home districts in Indian or Pakistani Punjab to live in the other half, traversing the bifurcated province either by train or on foot. It was one of the greatest mass migrations in history, and one accompanied by astonishingly brutal violence. Although there are no conclusive statistics it is estimated that there were 180,000 deaths and between 200,000 and 250,000 casualties. The Paharganj area of Old Delhi was, according to one despairing official, 'like a battlefield with blazing houses, hordes of refugees, dead cattle and horses and the rattle of automatic weapons'. The notorious rail track from Sialkot and Amritsar was, at one time, strewn with Sikh corpses. A train that had set out from Delhi with over a thousand Muslim refugees on board, arrived seven hours late with only eight survivors. Many were forced to convert before death, and men were branded and castrated. The toll on women was even worse: breasts were sliced off, genitals mutilated, and rapists carved their names on to their victims' bodies. One official reported seeing

3 women and 9 babies all dead in one well, a child of three or four with its face kicked in and then charred with fire, a woman beaten to death while in the act of producing a baby, girls of twelve or thirteen raped, and then killed by thrusting spears up them and ripping them apart.

It has proved difficult to account for this extreme violence. Some have attributed the catastrophe to British carelessness. Though Mountbatten dubbed partition one of 'the greatest administrative operations in history', many disagreed. In fairness to the British, they were now acting in concert with Indian politicians who wanted the handover to be as swift as possible and who also grossly under-estimated the turmoil that would ensue. Incredibly, few had given serious thought to the question of population transfers. Indeed many seemed to assume that such transfers would not be necessary. Officials in the Punjab were, however, not so complacent; they had warned of the violence and argued that a peaceful transition would take years. Similarly, opinion in the army was that a year, at the bare minimum, was necessary to ensure an orderly transfer.

Given the ludicrously tight timetable imposed on the handover it is hardly surprising that the whole process was ill-managed. The specially created Punjab boundary force of only 55,000 (drawn from both the Indian and Pakistan armies and commanded by a British officer) was hopelessly inadequate to its task of securing over 37,500 square miles of territory. The Pakistani authorities, as a matter of national pride, refused help from the Indian Evacuation Organization, but arrangements in India itself were hardly ideal, with Muslim refugees often being left to fend for themselves. Indeed, the British governor of east Punjab (in India) conceded that civil government effectively 'had ceased to exist' and local landlords and militias were in charge. The only option was to send in a neutral force of British or UN troops to quell violence, though it is far from clear that Indian and Pakistani politicians would have agreed to this. Mountbatten's chief adviser later lamented: 'Our mission was so very nearly a success: it is sad it has ended up such a grim and total failure.'

What the authorities seem not to have anticipated was that the violence, rather than being random or spontaneous, was well organized, much in the manner of a military campaign. In part this reflected the highly militarized nature of Punjabi society and the fact that there were many former soldiers in the region. At the beginning of the Second World War 48 per cent of the Indian army was recruited from this region, and during the war 71,500 Punjabis joined up, with another 90,000 from the surrounding princely states. By 1944, Punjabi villages were awash with weapons, and by early 1946 the province was flooded with demobilized Sikh, Muslim and Hindu soldiers.

But the ensuing violence was more than the reflex of battle-hardened veterans. It was also a response to the breakdown of civil society. It is striking that the violence which swept Punjab in March 1947, which many regard as the real beginnings of partition, came after the resignation of the inter-communal Unionist ministry. Inadequate though it was in many ways, the Unionist party had attempted to promote a regional identity and had offered a framework which fostered links between local communities, Hindu, Sikh and Muslim. However, the wartime Muslim League campaigns had anathematized these ideas in its drive to replace a Punjabi identity based on regional *biradari* ties with one founded exclusively on religious solidarity and the idea of a Muslim nation – Pakistan. The overarching regional identity common to all Punjab's communities for decades was thus systematically destroyed.

So, while the Punjab was a violent society and there had been clashes between its three communities before, partition violence was qualitatively different. In the past violence had been designed primarily to assert the dominance of one or other community in particular locales; it was now directed towards capturing territory for the 'nation' and expelling neighbours of other religions who were now defined as 'foreigners'. Moreover, territory in India had long been regarded as sacred and the sites, shrines and tombs of all communities were densely concentrated across the towns and countryside. The predominantly local and popular nature of much religious practice there meant that identities were deeply enmeshed in this 'hallowed' landscape. In this context any division of territory would inevitably become highly charged. Thus with the publication of the 3 June partition plan, Sikh posters were plastered all over Lahore announcing that Pakistan meant death to Sikhs. For Muslims, too, the demand for partition raised the fundamental issue of the relationship between the local community and the sacredness of place.

The violence therefore combined two highly explosive elements: national and religious passion. After the Attlee announcement in February 1947 of the end of the Raj within a year, all sides felt they had to mobilize their forces to secure territory swiftly, and private militias rapidly sprang up. The Calcutta riots of August 1946, a clear prelude to what would come later, were described by an official as 'a pogrom between two rival armies of the Calcutta underworld'. In the princely states of the Punjab, the RSS and the Hindu Mahasabha became very active immediately after the war. B. S. Moonje, the organizations' leader, exhorted the Hindu youth of Alwar city to arm and defend themselves. Both the states of Alwar and Bharatpur, on the fringes of Delhi, became centres for paramilitary training and, after completing rapid and intensive courses, the young 'troops' were sent to battle 'theatres' in Delhi and the Punjab. During the riots of March 1947 the Sikh leader was seen brandishing a sword in front of the Lahore Assembly Chamber proclaiming '*Raj Karega Khalsa*' (The Pure Shall Rule). From May 1947 the Sikhs had been collecting funds and arms to build their own militias which played a leading role in organizing attacks on Muslim border villages.

These private armies adopted the symbolism of religious warriors and their violence acquired a curiously ritualized quality. RSS troops would tie the sacred thread around their wrists before an attack. In Bharatpur armed squads were accompanied by *shuddhi* (conversion) specialists, who would shave their Muslim victims, make them eat pork, recite a Rigvedic hymn, and drink a mixture called *Panchgavya* (the five products of the cow). The widespread abduction and rape of women was also accompanied by religious ritual. Women were treated rather like territory, to be seized and occupied. They were regarded as easily convertible because, as one assailant reported, 'Women do not have any religion.'

These organized bands clearly felt they were acting justly and wielding almost state-like authority in a new territory which had to be 'cleansed' of alien elements to create a 'purified homeland'. As Manto recognized, partition involved the deliberate destruction of bonds based on locality and personal connections, and in their stead sought to establish an iron link between religious community and territory. In this it appears to have been, at least partially, successful. One refugee, on reaching Pakistan from Jullundur after seeing her entire family murdered, could still exclaim:

At last, somehow or other, after crossing the sea of fire and blood, we stopped on the lovely land of Pakistan. The slogans Long Live Pakistan, Long Live Islam, echoed from every corner . . . I had lost everything, forty people of our [extended] family were martyred, but the happiness I found when I saw the Pakistan flag flying at the Pakistan border, is still living in every cell in my body.

Whilst partition itself was about blood and violence (and even before independence there were ominous signs that this would be the case), in Delhi both Mountbatten and Nehru were determined that Independence would be a celebration, although they could not entirely agree on what, precisely, was being celebrated. For Mountbatten the events of 15 August were intended to demonstrate the successful fulfilment of British rule and India's continuing links with Britain through the Commonwealth. For Nehru, they were intended to symbolize the nationalist struggle to wrest freedom and democracy from empire and to demonstrate a clear break with the past. In the end the meanings of independence were to become the subject of even greater conflict.

Throughout July and early August Mountbatten was much pre-occupied with arrangements for the Independence Day rituals. In particular, he was having a lot of trouble with flags and astrologers. 'The astrologers have been rather tiresome since both the 13 and the 15 have been declared inauspicious days,' he wrote. 'One or two

superstitious members of the Cabinet wished to have all the ceremonies done at midnight, but as fortunately the older members . . .
go to bed at 9 o'clock, sleep won in the swearing-in battle.' More
vexatious still was the question of flags. Mountbatten was determined
to avoid any symbolism suggestive of British decline, and forbad any
ostentatious lowering of the Union Jack. The Union Jack over the
Lucknow Residency, which had flown constantly since the Rebellion,
was discreetly brought down just before sunset on the 14th and sent
home. Mountbatten was also desperately anxious that the new Indian
flag should acknowledge the continuity of the British connection.
Deeply interested in heraldry and insignia, he expended much energy
trying to persuade Nehru to incorporate the Union Jack into the new
Indian ensign, personally drafting a suitable design. Nehru refused,
arguing that many felt India was already pandering too much to
British sensibilities.

On the Indian side, by contrast, the point of the 14/15 August
celebrations was ritually to demarcate a new era in India's history.
Imaginative suggestions as to how this might be done included the
offering of one professor that a new calendar, with months named
after prominent national leaders, be promulgated, 'a novel and noble
idea to nationalize the very thing of our daily life'. Nehru himself was
determinedly hostile to anything that smacked of old-style *durbar*
symbolism, evincing lofty disdain for British 'court ceremonies, their
durbars and investitures, their parades, their dinners and evening
dress, their pompous utterances'. The focus of the day was to be
democracy and republicanism. The focus of the ceremonies could not,
therefore, be the viceregal lodge, as Mountbatten wished; Nehru, no
fan of Lutyens's architecture, dismissed it as the 'chief temple where
the High Priest [of imperialism] officiated'. Rather, it was decided that
the Council House (now the Indian parliament), had to be the location
for the official handover.

At 11 p.m. on 14 August the Council House rapidly filled with
starched *dhotis* and Gandhi caps. Ceremonies began with a rendition
of the controversial nationalist hymn *Bande Mataram*, an element of
the proceedings from which Muslim members were conspicuously
absent. Just before midnight Nehru gave his famous speech, and
then the philosopher Sarvepalli Radhakrishan spoke in an 'oratorical

time-bound relay race' crafted to end precisely at midnight, at which point a *khadi*-clad bugler sounded 'a haunting knell for empire and a summons to self-government' on a conch. On the morning of the 15th, attention shifted briefly to the viceregal house and Mountbatten, in full official dress, was sworn in as India's first Governor-General. Elsewhere proceedings were considerably less decorous: at Government House in Calcutta the day began with a flag ceremony for local worthies, but rowdy crowds soon took over, and the governor's wife, Lady Burrows, was surprised to find three Indians slumbering peacefully in her bedroom. The departing governor, his wife and aides-de-camp ultimately had to be smuggled out of the rear of the former governor's mansion.

Back in Delhi, the highlight of the evening was a parade in which Mountbatten processed down Lutyens's magnificent King's Way in a gold carriage and unfurled the new Indian flag at the War Memorial (now the India Gate), accompanied by a thirty-one gun salvo and a fly-past by fighter planes which dipped their wings in salute. Millions had turned out, Delhi had been specially tidied, and the city was decked out in saffron, white and green. Not even the legs of bullocks and horses escaped nationalist attention and were daubed in the new colours of the Indian national flag. On 16 August, Nehru appeared at the Red Fort, where a crowd of over a million turned out to see him raise the new flag over the seventeenth-century Mughal citadel. They then watched a display of fireworks – all made 'purely with *swadeshi* stuffs and with Hindustani skill'.

Clearly Independence was something to celebrate, as was the achievement of democracy. But however carefully planned, the celebrations themselves could not entirely efface the manifest divisions and controversies that underlay the meaning of Independence and the intended character of the new Indian state. Muslims celebrated, but with apprehension. Nationalist Muslims saw partition as a betrayal of the ideals of a secular India. Maulana Azad, the leading Muslim Congressman, sat through the ceremonies, 'his face', remarked one onlooker, 'a tragedy, sticking out from the sea of happy faces like a gaunt and ravaged rock'. Other Muslims objected to what they saw as Hindu triumphalism in the choice of the Mughal Red Fort as a venue for the celebrations. Potent symbolism was at play here: it was doubtless intended to underscore the continuity and legitimacy of the new Indian state from Mughal rather than British predecessors. However, it could also be seen differently. *Dawn*, the Muslim newspaper, reported it had caused agitation among Muslims:

we trust that there will be no petty-minded jubilation by the Hindus under the mistaken impression that by hoisting the flag of their state on the seat of power of the ancient Muslim kings they have somehow stretched a spiteful hand back into the historic past and dimmed the imperishable glory of Muslim rule.

On the other side, the Hindu right saw partition as a defeat, the vivisection of Mother India. They organized a major boycott of the ceremonies, dubbing 14 August a 'great day of shame, mourning and humiliation', and on Independence Day itself they convened their own alternative – the All-India Anti-Cow Slaughter Conference. Another dampener on the festivities was the presence in the city of over 100,000 refugees, including 25,000 Meo camping on the pavement following the burning of their villages in nearby Gurgaon by the prince of Bharatpur. Perhaps the illest omen, however, was the conspicuous absence from proceedings of the father of the nation himself. Gandhi, while he welcomed Independence, despaired at the manner of its coming and had declared that he wanted no part in the official ceremonies. Instead he had decided that his time was better spent trying to calm Hindu-Muslim violence and had gone to Calcutta, where he was commended by Mountbatten as a 'one-man boundary force' to prevent communal conflict. At the 'midnight hour' of 14 August, while India 'trysted with destiny', as Nehru put it in his remarkable speech in Delhi, the father of the nation was hundreds of miles away and sound asleep.

Soon after he took his one-man boundary force to Delhi, now the scene of appalling partition violence, and embarked on his last great fast on 13 January 1948. This had the effect of forcing pledges from police and government workers to work for peace. From then on the violence gradually subsided and Muslims began returning to Old Delhi. Then on 30 January, a few days after he ended his anti-riot fast, having begun the day with spinning and an abdominal mudpack, the Mahatma was shot three times by Nathuram Godse, a Hindu extremist, while on his way to a prayer meeting and died in the Birla gardens. By the afternoon of the same day Delhi was flooded with mourners. Thousands streamed down the Alburquerque Road towards Birla House, and even more gathered in the gardens. The Mahatma's body was carried on to the roof of Birla House and inclined until almost upright under the full glare of an army search-light. This was done twice to appease the now hysterical crowds. Clearly, in death as in life, a last vision or *darshan* of the Mahatma would be demanded.

Partition and its attendant violence had forced the army to take control of the city of Delhi, and so, in the most bitter of ironies, the last rites of India's peace-loving nationalist leader were entirely organized by a British general. The priest of non-violence and the father of the nation was borne to his funeral pyre on a 15-hundredweight British weapon carrier, drawn by 200 troops, followed by 4 armoured cars and 6000 soldiers, airmen, police and sailors. In a curious merging of British and national symbolism the cortège moved at a snail's pace down Lutyens's King's Way between the government offices and the statue of George V, but was accompanied by a crowd that dwarfed in magnitude and genuine awe any *durbar* ever assembled by the Raj. At the cremation site as a thousand conch shells roared, the assembled masses thundered: '*Mahatmaji amrho gae*' (Mahatmaji has become immortal).

A few days before 15 August Gandhi had expressed gloomy fore-bodings, drawing parallels between India's independence and the story of the troubled birth of the Universe in Hindu cosmology:

In the mythological churning of the ocean were discovered poison and nectar along with other valuable gifts . . . Lord Shiva had to swallow the poison to save the world. The mighty struggle for India's independence might well be compared with the churning of the ocean. It has yielded the nectar of independence and the poison of partition. There are many who have had to swallow the poison of partition. Let us hope the figurative Lord Shiva will emerge all the stronger for the deadly drink.

The assassination and funerary rites of the Mahatma held a meaning perhaps more potent than all the celebratory rituals of Independence

Day. They offered India's first and greatest martyr to its own struggles over national identity; they highlighted the indelible legacies of the British presence; and they established a fittingly paradoxical and sombre foundation myth for the new state.

6

The Last Viceroy

On 26 January India celebrates Republic Day with a great parade in New Delhi. It is staged on that great icon of the British Raj, Lutyens's awe-inspiring King's Way, now renamed Rajpath. Beginning relatively modestly with a few fly-pasts and flag-hoistings, successive celebrations became increasingly elaborate, and by 1960 had blossomed into full maturity, requiring a vast retinue of committees, planners and organizers and lasting over two-and-a-half hours.

Intended to dramatize a break with the past, the new state's rituals tended rather to throw the continuities with the old Raj into sharp relief. Announced by a thirty-one gun salute, the event began, *durbar*-like, with a formal march past by the Indian army. Decked out in Raj-style regalia, each regiment was heralded by a roll call of the various medals and honours it had earned from their departed imperial overlords. Following this came another echo of the Raj's image of India as a mosaic of nations, when a pageant of floats designed to dramatize the distinctive culture of India's various states, regions and 'tribes' trundled past. This part of the celebrations received the most planning and attention as each year every state submitted various proposals for their tableaux to an inter-ministerial committee in Delhi, which would decide what best captured the essence of the people supposedly being represented. No attempt was made to impose any kind of unity of theme on this cultural *mélange*; rather the opposite. Entries were judged for their originality and distinctiveness; the stated goal was that each float should be 'remarkably different' from any other. The inescapable logic was that each state and region was an unchanging cultural entity in its own right with its own highly distinctive identity without apparent connection to one another or, indeed, to the Indian state as a whole. So, in a typical year the Rajpath might quicken to the rhythms of Naga dancers, resound with chants of the 'tribal' 'Gonds' of Madhya Pradesh or enjoy elaborate re-enactments of Ladakhi marriage ceremonies, all scrupulously choreographed into a dazzling multi-hued kaleidoscope. Presiding over this curious mix of military march-pasts and cultural kitsch were the official elite of the new raj. From their own viewing platform built high above the centre of Rajpath – for all the world like the Viceroy and his flunkeys viewing one of their grand imperial *durbars* – the President, the Prime Minister, cabinet ministers and other dignatories gazed down upon the pageant.

Despite the apparent echoes of the Raj there was, however, a subtly different message encrypted into this novel republican ritual. For, while the imperial *durbars* sought to capture India's various castes, peoples and 'nations' in a crystalline hierarchy, the Republic Day *tamasha* or festival was a great plebiscitary pageant celebrating India as a vibrant, multi-cultural democracy, a theatrical display of India's various peoples co-existing of their own free will in a liberal state. The implicit message was that the state would foster unity in the manner of a progressive *deus ex machina*, up-lifting oppressed minorities and bestowing the benefits of modernity on a multifarious citizenry united in their diversity. Everyone was now welcome in the temple.

The Republic Day parades encapsulated the governing philosophy of India's first Prime Minister (though many would see him as its last viceroy), Jawaharlal Nehru. For Nehru, India was an experimental field for perfecting a modern, economically dynamic and socially progressive state. Central to this view was the determination to avoid the imposition of any kind of cultural unity. It did not merely tolerate, accept or even just celebrate India's cultural pluralism, but, rather as the British had, made a fetish of it. For what Nehru shared with his predecessors, the British viceroys, was the conviction that India was defined by its diversity. And, as he wrote to his chief ministers in 1952, folk traditions, peripheral cultures and neglected groups had to receive pride of place on Republic Day: 'the procession should be a moving pageant of India in its rich diversity'. The procession would dramatize the state's duties as guardian and promoter of minority groups and cultures, just as the new Indian constitution gave legal expression to this fragmented conception of the nation in its language policies, minority rights and federal structures.

It followed from this liberal commitment to pluralism that while, as Nehru insisted, massive social and economic change was needed, radical upheavals which suppressed minority and peripheral cultural identities had to be avoided at all costs. In India modernity would be beckoned by a consensual revolution. This was an attractive vision, and one developed in conscious antithesis to the violent disturbances attending modernization and state-building in Asia's other giant – China. However, while the Nehruvian version of liberal development enjoyed extraordinary success in entrenching democracy in the new state, his perpetuation of the Raj's orientalist vision of an India fragmented by groups, castes and tribes made the emergence of a sense of national cohesion and common purpose, both prerequisites of effective economic development, next to impossible. The cruel ironies of the Nehruvian liberal development project were dramatically displayed in later Republic Day parades, in which the rich cultural diversity of places like the Punjab, Assam, Kashmir and Nagaland were assiduously celebrated at the very same time that the central Indian state was engaged in violent struggles with secessionist insurgents in those very same regions.

Nehru was born into a wealthy and prominent north Indian family. His father, Motilal, was one of the most successful barristers in Allahabad. Motilal's antecedents had been Kashmiri Brahmans, and though they had left Kashmir some seven generations earlier and undergone certain set-backs in their fortunes since, when Jawaharlal (Red Jewel) arrived in 1889 the family was very wealthy, prestigious and prominent. Motilal had restored the family fortunes playing attorney to the aristocratic Muslim dynasties of the region and so the young Nehru hailed from a highly mixed and cosmopolitan milieu. The culture of Allahabad itself was Persianized, and Urdu was the Indian language Nehru himself spoke best. Though not remotely religious – a phenomenon he saw as essentially a 'women's affair' – he had picked up the basics of Hindu mythology from his mother and aunts. There had even been a brief dabbling with the esoteric pseudo-religion of Theosophy, promoted by his father's friendship with the redoubtable ally of Indian nationalism, Annie Besant. But in all essentials Nehru enjoyed a thoroughly anglicized Indian gentleman's upbringing. Motilal's affluence enabled the family to move from the 'native' quarters of Allahabad to the more prestigious and Europeanized Civil Lines, where the family lived for a few years at no. 9 Elgin Road. In 1900 they moved into the palatial Anand Bhavan (Abode of Bliss), where the young Jawaharlal could disport himself in two swimming pools and, owing to the impressive stables there, perfect his horsemanship. He also developed his backhand on the tennis courts.

An English governess was engaged for Nehru's earliest education, and from then until the age of fifteen he was educated at home by private tutors. At this point he proceeded to Harrow and thence to Cambridge. Perhaps the most influential of his early educators was a young tutor, Ferdinand Brooks, who had been engaged on the recommendation of Mrs Besant. Brooks, it later transpired, shared Mrs Besant's somewhat eccentric spiritual proclivities, which, when they appeared to be having undue influence on his young charge, led to his dismissal by the staunchly rationalistic Motilal. Nevertheless, Brooks left a strong impression and seems to have fostered one of Jawaharlal's main intellectual interests: science. From a childhood laboratory in Anand Bhavan to the decision to follow the Natural Science Tripos at Cambridge (a slightly outré choice for an Indian of his background), to his ambition to take India into the space age, science was a passion of Nehru's. He continued to read scientific books throughout his life. Indeed, towards the end, science seemed to have displaced literature and history as his principal reading matter.

However, Nehru himself was not a terribly distinguished scientist, taking a poor second-class degree at Cambridge, which rather put paid to his father's initial ambitions for him to join the Indian Civil Service. But despite this less than stellar examination performance, Nehru was a natural intellectual. At Harrow and at Cambridge he became phenomenally well-read in the English classics and in history, a pursuit that contributed to his own much admired literary style, brilliantly displayed in his later political and historical writing.

In a speech to the Cambridge Union thirty years after he had left, Nehru commented that 'coming to England is far easier for me, because a part of me, a fairly important part, has been made by England'. With his reserved temperament, fastidiousness, urbanity, dry sense of humour, partiality for bland food, and his tendency towards self-doubt and vacillation, all masking a certain vanity, he was, in many ways, a perfect English gentleman – 'a bit of a prig with nothing much to commend me,' he later observed. India remained to be discovered. After his return to Allahabad in 1912 Nehru spent the next seven years practising law in a rather desultory fashion, to his father's disappointment. Moreover, he and his father did not agree on politics. Motilal had belatedly joined Congress, in part as a career move once political lobbying became a necessary adjunct to his legal practice. His views erred, as one might expect, towards the moderate wing of the movement; Nehru's politics were more radical and emotional. He had been stirred by Sinn Fein after a short visit to Ireland as a student, and was briefly fascinated by the activities of the Suffragettes. He took a lively, if chair-bound interest in Indian nationalism during the 1905 *Swadeshi* movement, and had been elated by the Japanese defeat of Russia in the same year. Nehru's interest in Indian nationalism quickened during the Great War, while the internment of Mrs Besant had incensed him. And, like the rest of India, he was electrified by Gandhi's increasing dominance of the nationalist political scene after 1919.

Intoxicated by Gandhi during the first non-cooperation campaign of 1920–21, the most intensely lived year of his life he later claimed, Nehru not only read the *Bhagavad Gita* and briefly embraced vegetarianism, but he even took to driving around in a bullock-cart, much to his father's annoyance. However, though the relationship between guru and protégé was emotionally intense, it was also ideologically fraught. A close observer of Nehru once remarked that he was the sum of three rather conflicting influences: British liberalism, Russian Marxism and Gandhianism. Nehru himself insisted that Gandhi was the greatest of these influences, but this was a rather implausible claim, for he differed from Gandhi on perhaps the most important question of the age: modernity. While Gandhi romanticized the Indian past, both real and imagined, Nehru was in love with the future. Gandhi decried the Raj as the harbinger of modernity, while for Nehru it was the detested heart of the *ancien régime*. Nehru was a technophile, a religious agnostic, cosmopolitan in his tastes and an instinctive internationalist; the Mahatma was the opposite. And while both claimed to be socialists, each understood this to mean something entirely different to the other. For Gandhi, socialism was the slow paced idyll of arcadian village republics and the spinning-wheel; for Nehru it signified a dynamic utopia of the latest science, mechanized production and a globally minded modern citizenry.

Throughout most of his adult life Nehru claimed to be a socialist, but on the face of it, his intellectual trajectory was cyclical: from the moderate progressivism of the English Fabians, with their belief in the power of rationality and state intervention to promote social and economic betterment, through a serious flirtation with Bolshevik-inspired Marxism and finally back to the left-liberalism of his youth. However, behind the apparent vacillation between moderation and extremism there actually lay a core of consistent beliefs and action – a commitment to social justice, and a powerful conviction that rationality, in the form of modern science and economics, could deliver this social justice without resort to violence.

In the early years of mass nationalism, just after the First World War, Nehru encountered for the first time the poverty of village India. Fifteen years later, in his *Autobiography*, he recalled his shock:

A new picture of India seemed to rise before me, naked, starving, crushed, and utterly miserable. And their faith in us, casual visitors from the distant city, embarrassed me and filled me with a new responsibility that frightened me.

By the time he came to write this, he had moved beyond moralistic expressions of humanitarian concern to an absorbing interest in Marxist theory and its practice in the Soviet Union. His fascination coincided with the Great Depression, which appeared to many contemporaries to be the long-awaited fulfilment of Marx's prediction about the final crises of capitalism, as well as with the voguish interest in the Stalinist transformation of the Russian economy through planning; Nehru began to speak the language of international communism. However, closer inspection of his writings of the time reveals relatively little interest in class struggle or the other socially revolutionary aspects of communist politics. What seems to have appealed above all else was the reaffirmation in Marxist writings of Nehru's pre-existing belief in the transformative powers of modern science.

In *Glimpses of World History*, a nearly thousand-page collection of letters written in 1932–3 to Indira, his daughter, while he was in prison, many insights may be gleaned into his evolving approach to economics and development. The last few chapters deal almost exclusively with the symbiosis of science and economics achieved, supposedly, in the form of planning, and its efficacy in comparison with the failure of capitalism. Certainly he dwells at length on the achievements of the Soviet Union, but with rather more stress on the scientific marvel of rapid modernization, rather than the emotional appeal of egalitarianism:

This five-year plan has been drawn up after the most thought and investigation. The whole country had been surveyed by scientists and engineers . . . One thing is clear: that the five-year plan has completely changed the face of Russia. From a feudal country it has suddenly become an advanced industrial country . . . Everybody talks of 'planning' now. The Soviets have put magic into the word.

Nehru was never wholly bewitched by the Soviet magic though, and in the chapter 'President Roosevelt to the Rescue', it was the New Deal, Roosevelt's pragmatic, mixed-economy solution to the Depression, that attracted his admiration:

Roosevelt took swift and decisive action. He asked the American Congress for powers to deal with banks, industry, and agriculture . . . He became practically a dictator (though a democratic one).

This was the first explicit sign of his distaste for formal ideology, or 'dogma' as he termed it. Later Nehru would insist that India's problems could only be solved by:

Proceed[ing] scientifically and methodically without leaving things to chance or fate . . . the room for what we called ideological debate on matters like planning and development becomes less and less. The whole thing becomes a mathematical formula.

Clearly the real appeal of Marxism to Nehru lay not in radicalism, but in the appliance of science to economic disorders in the context of an essentially liberal government. And in a message to the Indian Science Congress of 1938 he went to some pains to defend his intellectual trajectory:

I realized that science was not only a pleasant diversion and an abstraction, but was the very texture of life, without which our modern world would vanish away. Politics led me to economics, and this led me inevitably to science and the scientific approach to all our problems and to life itself. It was science alone that could solve these problems of hunger and poverty, of insanitation and illiteracy, of superstition and deadening custom and tradition, of vast resources running to waste, of a rich country inhabited by starving people.

By the late 1930s Nehru seemed to have tired of his brief dalliance with Soviet socialism. In *The Discovery of India*, he denounced Soviet-style government as crude and violent. Revelations of the purges had by this time leaked into the global press, and Nehru, despite a period of alienation from Gandhi caused by the latter's apparent diversion of political energies into social rather than political action, was now firmly back under the Mahatma's wing. But perhaps more powerful than either of these was the strong influence in all his writing and actions of a fundamental commitment to liberal politics and economics. Revolutionary violence, and even mild coercion, was neither desirable nor viable, in his view, as a means to achieve social progress, because the forces of property and the right would not accept this short of defeat in civil war. The parallel with China was one always close to the surface of Nehru's mind. And though he tended to deny it, on occasion he made the comparison himself. It is striking that he never proposed the collectivization of agriculture along the lines followed in Russia and China, preferring instead what he saw as the consensual and pragmatic route to the same end – greater rural efficiency and fairness – through the voluntary co-operative.

The Nehruvian vision was, then, an ambitious left-liberal project designed to lead India from feudalism into modernity, bypassing the squalor, dislocation and violence that had accompanied this revolutionary change in the west. Like the Fabians, New Dealers and other progressives of the era, he was convinced of the boundless transformative potential of an enlightened, liberal state. Though the whole initiative smacked of the paternalism of do-gooding Raj officials, it was intended to be very different. This was to be an experiment in development with democracy. The masses were not to be passive, but were to be mobilized, following the example of Gandhi, to achieve their own liberation and 'uplift'. But, as Nehru had always been painfully aware, he lacked the Gandhian genius for translating new ideas into the vernacular of the ordinary Indian. There was little of the populist about Nehru; his style was rather that of an earnest and occasionally ill-tempered schoolmaster chastising his pupils. Early on in his political career Nehru had perfected the oratorical style of the lecturing teacher dealing with a class of likeable but recalcitrant children: 'I felt at home in the dust and discomfort . . . though their want of discipline often irritated me.' Once in power, he confided that one of the greatest challenges to modernizing India was the hidebound outlook of its peasants:

each one an individual problem, and three-hundred million problems in all . . . it's been a terrific job, pulling them out of their traditional ways . . . Mind you, they can be pulled out and they will be!

Thus the pedagogical style perfected by the more progressive Raj officials was now perpetuated in independent India. Symbolic of this continuity was the retention of the old 'steel frame' of empire, the Indian Civil Service, now seamlessly reincarnated as the Indian Administrative Service. Nehru, despite the strictures of his younger days, now became a keen defender of the old service, its style and method. Indeed, he took a personal interest in recruitment, determined that the importance of 'character', much stressed by the British, be retained. Forgetting, it seems, its principal role under the Raj as local tax collector and law-enforcer, the service appealed to Nehru's notions of a Platonic elite; not a steel frame, but a shimmering matrix of rational philosopher-bureaucrats, assisted by cohorts of technical and scientific specialists newly minted by the new, and highly elitist, Indian Institutes of Science, Technology and Management. The belief that technical training was the key to development was strikingly reminiscent of the ill-fated post-First World War British state's attempts to accelerate development precisely through the training of an elite technical cadre. As if to underline the continuities with the imperial past, the handbook of peasant uplift, made notorious by the evangeli-cal District Officer of Gurgaon, Frank Brayne, was reinstated as the official handbook for community development cadres during the second five-year plan.

However, in one respect Nehru was very different from the British. Unlike them he was uninterested in the religious life of 'the people', and strongly disagreed with British notions that religion constituted the existential alpha and omega of Indian existence. Late in life Nehru was forced to conclude that one of the most difficult tasks he had faced in his project of making the nation was introducing secular ideas into a profoundly religious society. But in his more optimistic moments he had seen excessive and politicized religiosity as an ailment, like economic backwardness or social injustice, that would succumb to the application of liberal and rational solutions. Here, Marxist historical analysis proved an appealing solvent of what Nehru regarded as an unhealthy combination of mass irrationality and the cynical manipu-lation by vested interests. In his *Autobiography* he described his struggle to understand the religious mentality and culture:

looking to the masses the most obvious symbols of 'Muslim culture' seem to be: a particular type of pyjamas, not too long and not too short, a particular way of shaving or clipping the moustache . . . and a *lota* (pot) with a special kind of spout, just as the corresponding Hindu customs are the wearing of a *dhoti*, the possession of a top-knot, and a *lota* of a different kind.

In a less flippant chapter on the same subject, Nehru admitted that there must be more to religion than this, citing the American Prag-matist philosopher John Dewey: 'religion is "Whatever introduces genuine perspective into the piecemeal and shifting episodes of exist-ence" . . . If this is religion then surely no one can have the slightest objection to it.'

It followed from this highly abstract understanding of religion that it was not something with which the new nation-state need be overly concerned. Essentially Nehru believed that the public and political manifestations of religious passion were whipped up by old 'feudal' classes (tacitly encouraged by the British), to subvert the development of a more rational class consciousness. With independence, these feudal residues would be swept away and with them the false consciousness that fuelled religious-political rivalry. As he argued:

> Having assured the protection of religion and culture, etc., the major problems that were bound to come up were economic ones which had nothing to do with a person's religion. Class conflicts there might well be, but not religious conflicts.

However, things were not so simple. A large contingent of the Congress rank-and-file saw Hinduism less as a discrete religion to be practised quietly in private, than as the basis of national identity. This was also, of course, the view of some Muslims and underpinned the demand for a separate Pakistan. In the *Discovery of India*, intended as an exploration of the nature of Indian identity written while in prison during the Second World War, Nehru was at some pains to detach the idea of Indianness from Hinduness, insisting that India had always been, and should continue to be, 'like some ancient palimpsest on which layer upon layer of thought and reverie had been inscribed'. In his 1948 speech inaugurating the debates on India's new constitution he proclaimed, 'India will be a land of many faiths, equally honoured and respected, but of one national outlook'. This was essentially a multi-culturalist approach to national identity, and raised the vexing question of how the state would both foster multi-culturalism, and simultaneously develop a single national outlook. Nehru's answer was secularism of the classical nineteenth-century liberal variety – one in which a strictly religiously neutral state would offer constitutional protection to all religions, now seen as a purely private matter. But the policy of state abdication from the religious sphere was precisely the strategy pursued by the British since the Rebellion. And, like the British before him, Nehru found that the task of relegating disruptive religious identities to the private sphere would tax these elegant liberal solutions.

While Nehru's love of modernity might suggest complete disdain for India's traditions, this was not the case. But with his elite, anglicized and secular background, more at home in Urdu than Hindi and in English than either, Nehru had, unsurprisingly, developed his own rather peculiar views about Indian culture. The glories of India were, for him, essentially ancient. In the *Discovery of India* Nehru seemed to reconsider the matter of the past's place in the future:

India must break with much of her past and not allow it to dominate the present . . . all that is dead and has served its purpose has to go. But that does not mean a break with or a forgetting of the vital and life-giving in that past. We can never forget the ideals that have moved our race, the dreams of the Indian people through the ages, the wisdom of the ancients, the buoyant energy and love of life . . . their spirit of curiosity and mental adventure, the daring of their thought, their splendid achievements in literature, art and culture . . . their love of truth, beauty and freedom, the basic values that they set up . . . their toleration of the ways of others, their capacity to absorb other peoples and their cultural accomplishments, to synthesize them and develop a varied and mixed culture . . . If India forgets them she will no longer remain India.

This passage is striking in its highly selective view of what constitutes India's core heritage and identity. Essentially it is two things: a classical culture of the ancients, which was precisely that aspect of India valued by the British; and a set of values – tolerance, intellectual curiosity, openness to outside influences and a capacity to synthesize all into a vibrant multi-cultural whole. These, while also attributed to the ancients, look very like the credo of a modern liberal internationalist. Clearly Nehru realized the necessity of grounding the seeds of a new India in some kind of traditional cultural soil, and the question of establishing a unifying cultural identity and set of national symbols was as important as the heroic social and economic policies of the Nehru years. In retrospect, a cultural and educational policy that would forge a sense of popular legitimacy for the new nation was probably equally if not more important than the ambitious plans for economic transformation and institutional change. But, as with those more concrete manifestations of the new nation, the Nehruvian cultural vision, though well-intentioned, often alienated the interests and emotions of those it was supposed to beguile.

Nehru's particular vision of the new state was not the only one in India, nor, indeed, the only one in Congress. Now that he is so inextricably associated with the economic, political and cultural contours of post-colonial India, it is surprising to consider how near to being still-born the entire Nehruvian enterprise was. Between 1947 and 1950 Nehru's vision had powerful challengers on right and left. The weaker of these two challenges was by far the most dramatic, and took the form of a violent guerrilla war in Telengana, an eastern province of the princely state of Hyderabad. The movement combined communist leadership with armed revolt by landless peasants, reminiscent of the Quit India movement. An uprising of real potency, it took the form of mass arson, looting and the murder of local landlords and officials, the object of which was to bring the whole area under the control of village 'soviets'. This turned out to be part of a master plan for a communist seizure of power arising from a network of co-ordinated peasant revolts centring on guerrilla units based in West Bengal, Madras and Bombay. The movement was swiftly beheaded, Hyderabad was annexed, and, in a show of authoritarianism harking back to the days of the Raj, the old British Public Safety Acts were invoked. The Communist Party of India (CPI) was banned and most of its leadership imprisoned. Confronted with total annihilation, the CPI switched tactics to pursue power through the ballot box, and the threat from the radical left seemed, for the moment at least, to have been dispatched.

The slayer of the left was, however, also Nehru's chief opponent on the right. Sardar Vallabhbhai Patel, who had been Gandhi's number three and was now home minister in the interim government, was essentially a machine politician who held the Congress party organization in a vice-like grip. His general prestige had soared in the late 1940s owing to his firm handling of the integration of the princely states, and he had also boosted his standing with the Hindu nationalists in Congress with his denunciation of the party's Muslims as traitors during the partition crisis. He had been censured by Gandhi for this and had agreed, at the Mahatma's beseeching, not to break with Nehru and cause a rift in the movement. And so, the interim governments of 1946–50, under which India's new constitution was hammered out, were effectively a duumvirate.

It seemed for a while that Patel would emerge as the first among equals in this relationship. For what he lacked in Nehruvian charisma and electoral chutzpah he more than made up for in behind-the-scenes political acumen. His was a very different vision of India to Nehru's: less liberal, less egalitarian and more 'Hindu'. This was an outlook, it would transpire, in greater accord with the rank and file of Congress's provincial members – the businessmen and farmers who had flooded the party in the late 1930s when its electoral star began to rise. During the interim governments Patel acquired the key portfolios of home minister, minister of information and finance minister, and from this powerful bastion he worked hard to marginalize Nehru's influence on domestic policy, while the foreign field was left free for Nehru's posturings, as Patel saw them. Nehru was effectively isolated within the party machine, and the Congress socialists, frustrated by the right's obvious command, assisted in this process by departing in 1949. Patel, not Nehru, was in the best position to shape the contours of the new state. Fate, however, intervened and the 75-year-old Patel died in late 1950. His death precipitated the constantly threatened breach between left and right in Congress, and on this occasion Nehru showed untypical political cunning. Pulling an old trick of the Mahatma's, he threatened to resign as leader of the party on the eve of the 1951 elections if the right's candidate for party president, Purshotamdas Tandon, a Hindu nationalist, were elected. Isolated though he was, Nehru was indisputably the party's greatest electoral asset, and thus outmanouevred for once, the right capitulated. Nehru became Congress president. Nevertheless, despite this seemingly unassailable position, he had not succeeded in decisively stamping his imprint on Congress; moreover the wily Patel had already had ample opportunity to contribute to the shaping of the new state, as soon became apparent. Within a few years of his ostensible victory Nehru faced a backlash from the right, and also from the left, which had not been wholly neutralized.

However, for the first five years of his premiership it seemed that the Nehruvian vision of India would become a reality. To the recently acquired post of Congress president he had added, since the triumphant election of 1951–52, the roles of prime minister, foreign minister and chairman of the planning commission. With this apparent monopoly of power how could he not succeed? In 1937, the *Modern Review* published an anonymous article which ominously warned of the dangers of the young Nehru and his lust for power. Behind the benign exterior, it warned, beat the heart of an autocrat, a Napoleonic figure, or a Caesar in the making. It seemed, for a while, that this Jeremiad had been acute, for to this collection of portfolios Nehru also added demonic energy. His day began at 6.30 a.m. with 30 minutes of yoga, a tough regime which included standing on his head (this activity became something of a cult among the nation's youth, and my father, a teenager in the Nehru years, was still given to doing head-stands in his sixties). After breakfast he would visit his pet pandas, before proceeding to his office in the Ministry of External Affairs in the South Block of the Lutyens government complex, or, if Parliament was sitting, to his office there. The rest of his day, when not closeted with statisticians and planners, he devoted to meeting peasant petitioners in the grounds of Teen Murti, his official residence. He would see up to 400 a day, and would reason patiently with them and attempt to explain the intricacies of modern agricultural techniques and industrial planning in layman's terms.

But despite the multi-headed authority he wielded, the multifarious official roles, the energy and the vision, Nehru lacked power. Far from being a Napoleonic dictator, Nehru seemed a curious hybrid of harassed schoolmaster, poet-legislator and lonely viceroy. It later transpired that the author of the mischievous piece in the *Modern Review* was J. N. Nehru himself. Paradoxically, a more dictatorial approach might have served his liberal vision better. For despite apparent success in institutional and economic reform, where his project was not flawed by compromise, it was thwarted by well-entrenched opponents.

The centerpiece of Nehru's reforms was economic planning. Though Nehru and his supporters indulged in leftist rhetoric and even talked of establishing a 'socialistic' pattern of society, in reality the plans were an eclectic blend of American New Dealism, projects incubated by British bureaucrats in the last days of the Raj, Soviet approaches and the latest thinking in development economics. The intention was not the systematic and radical transformation of power and property relations along Marxist-Leninist lines, but rather a scientifically inspired project to rectify the economic neglect of the Raj by creating the infrastructure of a modern economy, and laying the foundations for a modicum of social justice without coercion. Indeed, rather than a doctrinaire experiment in command economics, the essence of the approach was, as Nehru revealingly dubbed it, 'the method of trial and error'. Nehru and his economic advisers believed that a progressive liberal model of a mixed economy, combined with technical know-how and good will on the part of all social groups, could achieve in thirty years what had taken the Anglo-Saxon economies two hundred. If by a socialistic pattern was meant the manufacture of wildly optimistic growth plans, then the pledge was certainly honoured. But in truth planning in India was about science and self-sacrifice, not socialism. And even at its height the planned economy was always predominantly in private hands.

It was never likely to be otherwise, for the very structure of the new Indian constitution, with its assurance of the right to private property and its elaborate diffusion of powers between the centre and the regions, made it next to impossible for New Delhi to exert the kind of dictatorial economic power found in Stalin's Russia or Mao's China. The lack of tyrannical power was absolutely central to the Nehruvian vision, though it was certainly the source of much frustration to his chief economic lieutenant, the more interventionist architect of the plans, P. C. Mahalanobis.

Mahalanobis was, to all intents and purposes the father of Indian planning. With a flair for arresting phrase-making he had famously announced at the launch of the second plan, the most ambitious of the three for which Nehru was responsible, that planning must be a drama, not an anthology; by this he meant that it should progress through sudden, striking leaps forward, not by incremental and piecemeal change. This approach was unsurprising for Mahalanobis was, despite his statistician origins, a rather theatrical figure himself. From a religiously reformist background (his family were long-time members of the Bengali modernizing sect, the Brahmo Samaj), his father, a sports goods and gramophone record shop owner in Calcutta, was highly ambitious and the young Mahalanobis was encouraged to excel at school. After matriculating head of his class he proceeded to Cambridge and a first in physics, from whence he drifted though Samajist circles back in Calcutta, eventually coming into the orbit of the sage of Shantiniketan – the poet Rabindranath Tagore. After a brief and unlikely career as the Nobel laureate's sometime literary agent and theatrical impresario, Mahalanobis embarked on his first proper job, as professor of physics at Calcutta's prestigious Presidency College. In 1931 he established the Indian Statistical Institute (ISI) in Presidency College (Tagore attended the opening ceremony). He ran the institute as a virtual dictator and was a notoriously difficult boss, jealously blocking any attempt by his assistants to find employment elsewhere, and even interfering in their marital arrangements. During the Second World War the institute became a governmental quango, bringing it and Mahalanobis to Nehru's attention. By the early 1950s he had become Nehru's chief economic adviser and a member of the Planning Commission. This was despite the fact that his administration of the ISI, now with a branch in New Delhi, continued to raise eyebrows, for, ironically, Mahalanobis was not good with money. This had already been clear from his Cambridge days when he had been bailed out constantly by his doting (and increasingly impecunious) father. At the ISI he came under a cloud for diverting funds intended to pay staff salaries to building up the institute's physical establishment. This preference for capital investment at the expense of consumption was later echoed in his plan priorities, though with more deleterious consequences.

His rapport with Nehru was not surprising: the two shared both a certain leftism in their political inclinations, and a heady confidence in the power of science and mathematics to solve economic and social problems. As Mahalanobis confidently asserted:

the rate of economic growth in every country is determined both directly and indirectly by the rate of progress in science and technology, directly through the utilization of the result of research and development, and indirectly through institutional changes brought about by increasing influence of scientific outlook and tradition.

Yet Mahalanobis's ambitions would be extremely difficult to achieve without the assistance of a highly dirigiste and centralized state, and the new Indian constitution, much of it transplanted wholesale from the Raj, ensured that the central state actually wielded remarkably few effective economic powers. The plans would, therefore, be heavily dependent on the co-operation of important business and agricultural groups. Initially it seemed that such co-operation from business would be willingly forthcoming. After the First World War Indian businessmen had become increasingly critical of the laissez-faire economic policies of the Raj. There was much talk of the need for a public-private partnership for development, and indeed some of India's leading industrialists had ostensibly been advocates of planning since the late 1930s. In the famous 1944 Bombay Plan, hammered out between Congress and several of the greatest entrepreneurs, businessmen had welcomed the notion of greater state participation in the economy. This was, perhaps not as surprising as it appeared. Indian big business had grown dramatically in size and scope in the inter-war years, and in 1942, when it became clear that the British would decolonize at the end of the war, British business houses, which had previously dominated the Indian industrial economy, began to sell up, leaving the field entirely clear for their Indian competitors. In such circumstances the promise in the Bombay Plan of both greater tariff protection against foreign competition and massive state investment in infrastructure seemed to suggest that planning would be uncontroversial. Ominously, however, a private note exchanged by two businessmen who helped draft the Bombay Plan, hinted at ulterior motives:

The most obvious way in which extreme demands in the future may be obviated is for industrialists to take thought while there is yet time as to the best way of incorporating whatever is sound and feasible in the socialist movement . . . to examine how far socialist demands can be accommodated without capitalism surrendering its essential features.

Nevertheless, with the stunning electoral victory of 1951, delivered in no small part by the nation's farming classes, and the apparent support of its leading private businessmen, it must have seemed to Nehru and his advisers that they enjoyed the full support of the most important economic groups in society for a radical new approach to development.

However, almost as soon as it was launched the experiment in planning encountered serious problems. To begin with there were undoubtedly shortcomings in the very conception and execution of the plans themselves. The first plan, which covered the period

1949–54, had some marked successes, particularly in dam-building and power generation. It had not really been a plan at all, though, merely a loosely bundled collection of piecemeal measures – the anthology deprecated by Mahalanobis. Determined to stage his economic drama, the second plan, of which he was virtually sole author, was infinitely more ambitious. It was, indeed, too ambitious, and suffered from the defect known as voluntarism: the belief that through supreme effort serious constraints can be overcome in defiance of rational economic logic. His famous Plan Frame of 1955 bore all the characteristics of voluntarism. Mahalanobis proposed that the Indian economy be seen as two interlocking spheres: modern industries and cottage industries. This two-sector model (as he dubbed it), was the economic equivalent of an arranged marriage between Soviet planning and Gandhian village economics. The issue of this unusual alliance would, Mahalanobis believed, be India's long-awaited take-off into economic nirvana. The modern sector would be free to concentrate on the heavy and capital goods indispensable to modern development, while unemployment would decline as tens of thousands of cottage craftsmen made up the shortfall in consumer goods by their copious spinning and weaving. 'If,' he declared, 'hand industries could be activated, the era of unemployment would disappear in five years.'

Enthused by Mahalanobis's dazzling hybrid, many of the nation's politicians and economists caught planning fever. The commerce minister, T. T. Krishnamachari, previously a great foe of planning, declared himself a complete convert to the philosophy of the handloom. And while in 1954 planned investments had been relatively modest, by early 1955 output projections had become astonishingly inflated. The finance minister announced that an incredible 24 million new jobs would be created in ten years, the railways minister demanded a doubling of his investment budget allocation to raise passenger and freight loads, and it was confidently predicted that sufficient personnel could be trained to deliver another 21 million acres of irrigated land in five years and to nearly double electricity output. Meanwhile the Central Advisory Council for Industries criticized many of these targets for being too conservative. In the countryside, too, voluntarism held sway. The Community Development programme, designed to send workers into the villages to educate peasants in the latest agricultural techniques, was projected to extend from an initial coverage of 80 million peasants to 325 million – virtually the entire population of rural India – in just five years. This was to be accomplished by graduates from just five training centres.

A more serious problem still was lack of money, an obstacle also blithely ignored in the spirit of voluntaristic optimism. The rate of investment needed to fulfil all these new targets was estimated to be 11 per cent of national income, at a time when 7 per cent seemed the very maximum that could be mobilized. This financial shortfall, which amounted to Rs. 4 billion, perplexed, but did not deter the planners. The chief minister of one state proposed that the 'gap', as it came to be known, could be rectified by holding raffles; another suggested compulsory savings. Mahalanobis advocated an even more extraordinary solution. He suggested that since India was singularly abundant in one particular input – underemployed rural labour – the gap could be closed by persuading poor peasants to work for free. The ingenious suggestion was made to commute old feudal labour dues (against which Gandhi had led one of his most famous *satyagrahas*), into obligations to build roads, schools and irrigation channels. This policy proved unpopular and difficult to implement.

The obvious solution would have been to raise income taxes, especially those on farmers, who paid no income tax at all. But India, since Raj days, had had an astonishingly low tax take of only 7 per cent of national income, and state governors, under whose purview the power to raise agricultural income tax fell, demurred at the electoral perils involved in trying to increase this tiny total. No adequate answer was produced as to how the 'gap' would be closed, but the plan went ahead. In 1957 a poor monsoon precipitated an inflationary spiral, which coincided with a foreign exchange crisis, and Mahalanobis's dramatic second plan was only saved by the *deus ex machina* of foreign aid, largely from Germany and America.

Problems of conception and funding were compounded by serious shortcomings in execution. The planning project was continually handicapped by poor co-ordination and lack of control over what resources it did possess. The institutional headquarters and supposedly central command for the plan was the newly created Planning Commission, intended as the omnipotent hub of all economic decision-making. But it faced fierce opposition within the cabinet. The finance minister, John Matthai, made its creation a resignation issue, denouncing the proposals as tantamount to 'a super-cabinet running roughshod over elected ministers', and after his resignation Nehru reported several key ministers 'had no liking for the Planning Commission and failed to co-operate with it and facilitate its working'. The result was that economic policy-making lacked any central co-ordination or overview. Indeed, if anything, power over and information about the economy was even more diffused than it had been in colonial days, with jurisdiction over separate industries now scattered across an ever proliferating maze of ministries. The absence of an overarching co-ordinating body with teeth made the job of effectively implementing the plan impossible. Channels of information between various ministries silted up. The process of approving licences for new industries descended into chaos, as a consequence of which there was no real control over the spending of India's scarce foreign exchange reserves. The culmination of this un-coordinated spending was the foreign exchange crisis in 1957, after which the prestige of the Planning Commission, and of planning itself, was badly tarnished.

This resistance to attempts to co-ordinate policy was merely a symptom of something far more serious: a deep-seated ideological opposition to the very idea of planning at the highest levels of business and politics. During the Second World War Indian business had been willing to pay lip-service to the notion of greater state intervention when they felt themselves threatened by the radical politics of the Quit India movement. But they had not bargained for the degree of intervention planned by Nehru. Policy statements after the war revealed that a far larger proportion of the modern industrial sector would be reserved for the state, and that a complex network of licences would limit business's access to foreign exchange and imports; similarly the permit system, under which businessmen had to apply for official permission to open or expand their enterprises, was highly restrictive. Businessmen soon began to mobilize in opposition, buoyed by regained confidence and the willingness of many Congress politicians on the right, anxious to neutralize the wartime ascendancy of the left, to help them. Principal among these allies was Sardar Patel, who, in 1945, imposed a series of stringently restrictive laws governing union organization, thereby significantly boosting the bargaining power of corporations. Anti-planning pressure was also channelled into a concerted campaign of press and political lobbying. Patel received a steady stream of letters from G. D. Birla, longtime confidant of Gandhi and one of India's wealthiest businessmen, throughout the summer of 1946 in which he warned of dire consequences if businesses were overly restrained. In the same year a highly effective campaign of plan sabotage was launched. The centrepiece of this was an investment strike – businessmen simply refused to set up the new enterprises envisaged by the state. Nehru confessed privately that 'our monied people are on strike and trying to bring pressure on government'. The investment strike, coupled with systematic cabinet opposition, ruined plans to restructure the economic and finance ministries, and to create a powerful Planning Commission.

With the publication of Mahalanobis's second plan, which promised further encroachment by the state on sectors previously dominated by private industry, a new campaign of political and commercial opposition was launched. The Federation of Indian Chambers of Commerce and Industry published alarmist reports forecasting the collapse of business as a result of supposedly crippling taxes, a critical shortage of consumer goods if the state took over more areas of manufacturing and, ultimately, the collapse of the Indian economy in a hyper-inflationary crisis. In 1956 the government hit back with an inquiry into the growing monopoly power of the great business houses in the previous decade. The Hazari Inquiry revealed that a handful of great business conglomerates now dominated manufacturing through elaborate cross-meshing networks of subsidiary companies. However proposed legislation to break up these octopus-like entities was vigorously opposed, and Nehru, ever anxious to avoid a split in Congress, backed down. The anti-monopoly legislation was hopelessly diluted during its passage through Parliament; proposals to extend the state's industrial interests were also retracted and, instead, private business was offered tax holidays and other inducements to increase its investment.

In 1958, when the outline of the third plan was being mooted, the opposition, especially from the right, had become better organized and even had its own political party, Swatantra. Business opposition to planning now received an important new ally in the form of foreign expert reports by the World Bank and by the Ford Foundation, which heavily criticized the plans. In 1960 the private sector controlled 80 per cent of the modern manufacturing sector, and Mahalanobis noted, mordantly, that far from controlling the commanding heights of the economy, as its critics claimed, the Indian state was running hospitals for the sick industries that private business disdained.

Despite these limitations the first three plans of 1950–65 could claim some achievements. They ended the stagnation in agriculture that had marked the last fifty years of the Raj, and growth rates in industry accelerated as the industrial stagnation of the post-war era was overcome. By the mid-1950s private business was booming, iron and steel output grew, and food production targets had been over-fulfilled. The foundations for the later success of the Green Revolution in making India self-sufficient in food undoubtedly lay in the public investment in irrigation, power and fertilizers, rural credit and crop research launched during the plan era. Perhaps more importantly, the plans' concentration on power, irrigation, road building and heavy industry both improved the economy's infrastructural foundations and created a degree of diversification which had been greatly lacking under the British. Moreover, though the economy may have been overly protected, it was effectively insulated from the catastrophic shocks inflicted by the international economy that hit Africa and Latin America in the 1970s.

However, these achievements came at a very high cost, and they were relatively unimpressive compared with the achievements in growth and development seen in other planned economies, such as China in the early 1950s or South Korea in the 1960s. Moreover, the political distortions introduced into the planning process by lobbying and corruption ensured that many of the new industries were inefficient and uncompetitive. Ironically, the most striking effect of a project designed to promote efficiency, social justice and greater equality, was the entrenchment of pre-existing vested interests. Instead of the state being in control of business, the matter was rather the reverse. The big business houses, whose power the 1956 Companies Act was intended to curb, actually became more monopolistic. They dominated the licence application field, and used their control over their multifarious subsidiaries to bid for licences in profitable spheres, intending not so much to develop interests in these areas, as to exclude competitors. The result was that by the early 1960s a few very power-ful firms held the permits and licences needed for many new businesses, excluded new entrants and exploited their tariff-protected exclusive access to the home market to make excessive profits.

Agricultural reform and development was, if anything, an even bigger failure, and for similar reasons: as in business, vested interests were able to monopolize almost all the benefits of planned investment, with the consequence that by 1960 peasant life had become even more unequal. Radical land reform had been the policy of Congress since the 1930s. It was generally agreed that power in the countryside lay not with the real producers, but with networks of absentee landlords and other intermediaries who siphoned-off the hard-earned profits of the peasant cultivator. The poverty of most of India's peasantry caused by this and the proliferation of uneconomically small plots was, it was agreed, not only deeply unjust but also a major obstacle to economic growth, for as long as 70 per cent of the population remained abjectly poor there would be insufficient purchasing power in the economy to fuel a real economic boom. Despite these arguments, land reform was dodged or distorted. An initial wave of land reform in the early 1950s had dispossessed only the aristocracy and very large landowners – or *zamindars* – whose land now became the property of the state. The working of the legislation was manipulated to benefit larger farmers, and was, if anything, skewed against the interests of poorer groups, since permanent title to land went only to those who could afford to pay for it. Similarly, land ceiling legislation (designed to equalize the size of farms) announced in 1953 was not implemented until 1960, giving larger landowners seven years to arrange their holdings in such a way as to elude redistribution. During this seven-year breathing space large landlords evicted their poorer peasants and reclaimed their plots as so-called 'home farms', to which the ceiling legislation did not apply. Meanwhile those whose land was taken over by the state were given generous compensation, which allowed many to rebuild their wealth very swiftly. All this was made possible by the consti-tutional powers over all rural matters invested in the regional states. Regional governments were soon controlled by farmer Congressmen who had joined the party with the explicit intention of frustrating the land reforms.

In 1958, in a desperate attempt to circumvent some of these problems and help poorer peasants, Nehru attempted to promote the formation of co-operative farming, whereby smaller and middling-sized farmers were to pool their resources, act together to raise investment credit and thus, it was hoped, raise agricultural productivity and incomes. The proposals were met with a solid wall of opposition in the states, again bolstered by foreign expert reports which called for a policy of 'backing winners', that is, allowing poorer peasants to go out of business and concentrating public investment on richer and more efficient farmers. Politicians on the right both in and outside Congress castigated the proposals as coercive and communistic and Nehru was forced to back down, promising co-operatives would be purely voluntary. 'No Act is going to be passed in Parliament ... There is no question of coercion,' he declared:

I do believe in co-operation and I do firmly and absolutely believe in the rightness of joint cultivation. Let there be no doubt. I do not wish to hide my beliefs in this matter. I shall go from field to field and peasant to peasant begging them to agree to it, knowing that if they do not agree, I cannot put it into operation.

A similar coalition of big farmer and regional Congress opposition was effective in diverting state investment into the pockets of the better-off and frustrating broader infrastructural development, especially in education. Under the Raj, progress in basic education was snail-like; however since independence the percentage of children attending primary schools had risen not the 19 per cent predicted, but only 9 per cent. Secondary school performance was even worse, and not enough teachers were being trained. Meanwhile, as under the British, the university sector was blossoming, or, as some put it, had undergone a hasty and ill-thought out expansion. The higher education sector, unlike state basic education, catered almost exclusively to the wealthier sections of society.

In rural areas education was supposed to be advanced by the Community Development Programme. The programme's precedent had been provided in 1948 by Albert Mayer, an American architect, with his Pilot Development Project in Etawah. Assisted by the Uttar Pradesh (the renamed United Provinces) government, the pilot blended paternalistic with democratic impulses and involved sending a team of highly trained volunteers into 64 villages to educate poorer groups. It had been very successful, improving local agricultural techniques, establishing co-operatives, credit societies, rural industries, infrastructure, community works, housing and schools. However when it was extended to the rest of the Indian countryside the results were considerably less spectacular, because it was extended too rapidly using less skilled personnel. Once the presence of the development worker was phased out, the projects, once started, were soon neglected. Development workers also tended to concentrate on visible signs of success – road construction, well-sinking – at the expense of perhaps the more pressing, but less tangible task of instilling new ideas.

The centerpiece of the Community Development Programme was the dissemination of local democracy through the revival of village India's ancient councils, the *panchayats*, a project dear to Gandhi and now adopted by Nehru as a means of mobilizing popular democratic will behind economic and social reform. However, rather than evolving into engines of rural democracy, the *panchayats* swiftly emerged as new centres of rich peasant and dominant caste power, from which bastions these groups could monopolize the economic spoils of the development programmes. One worker reported:

The better-off classes get loans, are more easily able to adopt improved practices, and otherwise derive larger benefit from the development programmes. The non-owner classes have not got the status that possession of land alone can give them. Land reform still remains in the realm of thought and discussion ... The result of all this is that while some people are undoubtedly benefiting from the development programme ... these usually belong to those sections in the village that were somewhat better off than their fellow villagers.

Rather than providing a non-partisan forum for participatory village democracy, the *panchayats* were sectarian, factionalized and caste-ridden.

So, underlying the failure to promote economic development and social equality was not planning as such, but a fundamental flaw in the Nehruvian liberal notion of a gradualist and consensual form of planning in a society and economy that required drastic and radical institutional change. In South Korea, and in other cases of planned, mixed economic development, the problems with vested interests did not arise – business and landed groups had been discredited or destroyed by the Japanese occupation during the war. The state there was able to gain the upper-hand and use its power to shape and direct private economic development. But in India the contours of the weak colonial state soon reemerged behind the apparent innovations of the Nehruvian era. Crucially too, in Korea a decision was taken to promote export-led growth, while in India this did not happen. The departure of British firms with decolonization left the vast Indian domestic market an open field for Indian business, while the planners' commitment to heavy industrial development behind high tariff barriers made the incentives to concentrate on the home market and neglect exports even more compelling. By the time the government had realized its mistake in the late 1950s, the private sector was too well-entrenched and supported by political insiders to be prevailed upon to change course, condemning Indian industry to inward-looking inefficiency for another three decades. In the countryside investment was diverted to the already well-off at the cost of essential infrastructural and educational change. By 1964, when Nehru died, Mahalanobis's drama had turned into a tragedy. Big business had become even bigger, protected from foreign competition and cosseted by state subsidies, while the countryside was still dominated by the better-off peasants, now bolstered by new institutions for projecting their power over the villages and fertilized by generous dollops of state largesse.

Just as planning had inadvertently entrenched the power of the old elites, so too did Nehru's plans to create a more democratic and integrated society. The new Indian Constitution of 1950 was intended to bring the same practical rationalism to the problem of forging unity. The Constituent Assembly which worked to draft the new charter faced the unenviable task of transforming the toxic broth of separatism, regional and linguistic rivalries, murderous religiosity and rampant caste conflict into an elixir of unified nationhood. But in practice the implementation of much of this, as with planning, tended to perpetuate continuities with the British past. Indeed, much of the 1935 Government of India legislation was simply adopted unchanged, especially its provisions allowing the central government dictatorial rights in the regional states should an emergency arise. However, in contrast to the British, the intent of the Nehruvian legislators was to promote integration, not devolution and regionalism. This was in part motivated by the belief that effective economic development had to be co-ordinated from the centre, and in part by a liberal humanist commitment to universalist values of citizenship and rights.

Nevertheless Nehru was not an autocratic centralizer, and even had he been, it would have been very difficult to override the expectation of some regional political autonomy that the British experiments in limited devolved democracy had fostered. Princes had been bought off with large purses and protected prestige. Kashmir and the eastern 'tribal' states of Nagaland had been given 'special status', and the new nation was already beginning to acquire some of the ramshackle quality of the old Raj. The question then was how could unity be promoted while respecting the sensitivities of local identities. The answer lay, Nehru believed, in the question of a national language.

The language issue had long been on Congress's agenda and the Raj's gleeful recognition of proliferating language groups had been regarded as a mischievous ploy to thwart unity. That was certainly Nehru's view. In the *Discovery of India* he maintained this tough line:

The oft-repeated story of India having five hundred or more languages is a fiction of the philologists' and the census commissioners' minds, who note down every variation in dialect and every petty hill-tongue . . . according to the method adopted by the census commissioners, Europe had hundreds of languages and Germany was, I think, listed as having sixty.

Gandhi and others hoped that a single link-language would emerge across the whole of India. He advocated the northern Urdu-Hindi blend known as Hindustani, brushing away objections from the south; he was even undeterred when, on a visit to the south to celebrate the silver jubilee of the launch of the Hindustani cause, he discovered not a single Hindustani speaker. He was forced to resort to a religious sing-along with other platform speakers while his baffled audience looked on in silence. But Gandhi was not to be deterred, blithely proclaiming that, 'An average Bengali can learn Hindi in two months ... and a Dravidian in six months at the same rate.' Nehru, too, a fluent Urdu speaker, who disliked the over-Sanskritized starchiness of modern Hindi, also urged the claims of Hindustani, though he sometimes recommended Hindi (it was never entirely clear which he meant). Ultimately the choice settled upon Hindi, reflecting the successful efforts of political Hindu proselytizers to separate Hindi and Urdu into two distinct languages. When the new constitution was established, Hindi was designated the 'official' language of the Indian state, allowing a fifteen-year transitional period during which the use of English would still be permitted.

However, while advocating a single national language, Gandhi had simultaneously boosted the cause of linguistic pluralism when he restructured Congress's grassroot organizations according to linguistic units, rather than following the contours of the great multi-lingual provinces of British India. This, he insisted, would allow party work to proceed more efficiently. From then on, splitting the super-provinces of Bombay and Madras into smaller, single-language states became Congress policy, giving, albeit unwittingly, the green-light to regional linguistic patriotism. Linguistic plurality was not at that time seen as a threat to unity, and until Independence this had been Nehru's policy too. However, by the late 1940s, in the wake of partition, the redrawing of territorial boundaries had become an altogether more sensitive issue. In a 1947 speech to the Lok Sabha (the lower house of the Indian parliament), Nehru argued that though reorganizing India's regions to reflect linguistic entities was not being ruled out:

many other considerations have to be borne in mind. Apart from the linguistic and cultural aspects sometimes there is also no clear demarcation ... and areas overlap ... the country has had to face ... a very critical situation resulting from partition. A living entity had a part severed from it and this unnatural operation resulted in all manner of distempers.

By now, rather than seeing regional languages as benign phenomena, Nehru feared they could easily become a potentially Balkanizing force. The 1948 uprising in Telengana (the Telugu-speaking portion of the old princely state of Hyderabad), though led by the communists, had had a strong flavour of Telugu linguistic separatism about it. Nehru himself was cosmopolitan by temper and multi-lingual himself, and he came to lament the passing of the great multi-lingual states as a victory for small-minded parochialism. Compounding this was the not unwarranted suspicion that linguistic patriotism was actually a Trojan horse for an army of caste conflicts that Nehru did not wish to countenance. The Andhra agitation for a separate Telugu-speaking state, 'the Land of the Andhras', was certainly fuelled by caste and class resentments, as the Kammas and Reddis used the issue to challenge the wealth and power of Madras Brahmans. Caste rivalry also underpinned the demand for the unravelling of the multi-lingual province of Bombay. Kannada speakers, who sought to merge with the southern state of Karnataka, saw this as a means of gaining ascendancy over the Brahman farmer sub-castes, the Lingayats and the Vakkaligas, who had hitherto dominated these districts. The Dar Commission, appointed to look into the controversy over state boundaries, therefore recommended in 1948 that 'No new provinces should be formed for the present.'

Although the question of linguistic reorganization had thus been deftly relegated to the back-burner, it refused to go off the boil. Agitations continued among those demanding that the Madras province be divided into Tamil and Telugu regions, and that the province of Bombay be split three ways, into Marathi, Gujarati and Kannada-speaking portions. In 1952 the question could be ignored no longer. In Andhra a Congress loyalist and old Gandhian follower, Sri Potti Sriramulu, embarked on a Gandhian 'fast unto death' in order to attain a Land of the Andhras. While Sri Potti fasted, Nehru vacillated. Determined not to concede victory to 'casteist' and parochial coercion, he also had to consider the tricky political problem of Madras city. Part of Sri Potti's agenda included the assertion that Madras be jointly governed by Telugus, and should not be just the satrapy of Tamil speakers alone. But such adjustments were inconceivable while the venerable Congress chieftain of the south, the Tamil-speaking Rajagopalachari, was in power. In December, following Sri Potti's death, violent disturbances swept the Andhra region. Terrified of violence of all kinds, Nehru capitulated, and the day after Sri Potti's demise it was announced in the Lok Sabha that the Andhra people would get their state, though without Madras. It was now impossible to defer all demands for linguistic reorganization any longer, and in 1953 a commission was charged to investigate the flood of demands 'objectively and dispassionately'.

The commission published its findings in 1955 having read 152,250 submissions, only 2000 of which, it reported, were 'well-considered'. Nevertheless, the commission conceded demands to redraw state boundaries to coincide with language regardless of the logic of economic and infrastructural development. In south India this led to the creation of four new states: Malayalam-speaking Kerala, Kannada-speaking Karnataka, a Telugu-speaking state composed of Andhra and the Telengana portion of Hyderabad, and the Tamil-speaking heartland of Tamil Nadu. But in the north disputes were still not resolved. The commission eventually proposed dividing Bombay into its Marathi and Gujarati constituents, but that still left the problem of the status of Bombay city. Despite various proposals for dual control, rioting broke out in 1961 and forced the issue: Bombay city was given to the new state of Maharashtra. Meanwhile in the Punjab, already partitioned once in 1947, the Sikhs now demanded their own Punjabi-speaking Sikh state, raising the question of what should happen to the only recently completed new capital, Chandigarh. In 1966 Punjab was split into three: Himachal Pradesh, the hilly region to the north; Haryana, a largely Hindi-speaking state of rich Jat farmers; and the Punjab proper, though this was still not a Sikh state and the question of Sikh autonomy would re-emerge as a major problem in the future.

Nehru may have given way on regional linguistic reorganization, but he continued to hold the line on replacing English with Hindi as a link language. However, as the deadline for abolishing English began to approach, protests began. Critics argued that the reform would grant an unfair advantage in the intense competition for government jobs to the 35 per cent of the nation for whom Hindi was their first language. In 1959 Nehru began to retreat, promising that Hindi would not be imposed and that English would stay as an 'associate' language. By now the cause of Hindi as the pre-eminent national language had been taken up by Hindu nationalists, and Nehru's reassurances weren't enough. In 1960 incidents of serious rioting broke out in Madras in protest at the coming of Hindi. But for Nehru the turning point came in 1963, when Sarvepalli Radhakrishnan, the Indian President and a Telugu by birth, was barracked in the Lok Sabha when he attempted to give the Annual President's address in English rather than Hindi. In consequence the impending Official Language Bill made provision for English, as well as Hindi, to be used for official and political business after the original deadline of 1965. While Nehru argued that this was merely a pragmatic response to the growing international importance of English, and the need for Hindi to 'mature', in reality, as he later admitted, 'essentially the overriding reason for it is the necessity of not encouraging any disruptive tendencies in India'.

So, instead of the elegant integrated diamond of mono-lingual liberal nationhood, Nehru was forced to concede a pluralistic edifice of linguistic autonomies, regional differences and localism. Like the British before him he discovered that the price of unity was paid in the currency of central weakness. However, his fears that concessions to these fissiparous tendencies would bring about the rapid Balkanization of the nation were not realized; overarching the constitutional diffusion of powers between centre and states, and transcending the bickering over linguistic chauvinism and caste particularities, was the power of Congress. And for the two decades immediately after Independence it was this, rather than economic development or new ideas of common citizenship, that held India together. But though Congress was undoubtedly a powerful force, it was not without its weaknesses. Under the Mahatma, and especially under Sardar Patel, Congress had developed as an alliance of local and often shifting factions, united largely by antipathy to the Raj. Any apparent integration or ideological coherence was, in reality, a very thin veneer masking its essential identity as a coalition of regional and district party bosses. In its glorious nationalist heyday, with the British still around to rally against, the underlying tensions of this system had been contained. But with the departure of the British the spoils of economic development and political power now formed the chief object of factional contestation. Central power, instead of being used to drive through reform, was dissipated through endless bargaining, with the result that the delicate equilibrium between central and local party power began to shift in favour of the regional bosses.

This was, to all intents and purposes, the system of collaboration that had operated under the Raj. It was a situation tolerated by Nehru, partly because he had imbibed from Gandhi the belief that the unity of India was dependent on the unity of Congress, but also because he believed that in return for a high degree of regional autonomy local party leaders would co-operate in the implementation of centrally directed policy. Through Congress's dense network of bosses, deal-makers and middlemen, the ideals of reform would be osmotically transmitted to the general population. But Congress was not quite what it had been under Gandhi. With the era of freedom-struggle heroes fast fading the party's machinery was increasingly usurped by new men, and especially by the dominant peasant and business groups most likely to frustrate, not promote, Nehru's vision. Between 1945 and 1950 primary membership of the party grew from 5.5 million to 17 million, and by the early 1950s the regional and district Congress boards had been captured by conservative elements composed of large-landowning castes and urban businessmen. Soon the regional party apparatus fell foul of intense factional rivalries, often taking the form of bogus enrolment to bolster a particular faction's voting power. In every locality the party was in the hands of dominant-caste leaders, who proved highly effective in manipulating the diffuse loyalties of the peasants to win elections.

Regional politicians, far from co-operating with the Nehruvian centre to push through reforms, were competing with the centre for control of state resources and power. And very soon links between party and officialdom produced a catastrophic interpenetration of Congress and the local administration; this was not a marriage from which good government was likely to issue. Endless opportunities now beckoned to divert development funds to loyal clients, and from this it was a short step to outright fraud. Bureaucrats at all levels, all underpaid, developed lucrative sidelines selling influence (at fixed prices and with graded fees) with the open co-operation of local politicians.

Nehru tried to reform the party, but he had never relished organiz-ational politics. Moreover the problem was so systemic as to defy solution. Whole districts were sometimes involved in egregious fraud, and though the Congress High Command was supposedly in charge of the selection of candidates for the Lok Sabha and had imposed stringent requirements of virtue, it was impossible to enforce any of this on the ground. The spoils of office were now so alluring that tidal waves of new men gushed forth seeking the Congress ticket. They were willing to use the most unscrupulous means to secure it, making the task of policing party virtue next to impossible. The 1951 General Election brought 25,000 applications for 4000 central and state assembly seats. Accompanying these were over 100,000 complaints, allegations of corruption or other malpractice from jealous rivals. Congress officials despaired of ever getting to the truth of these allegations: 'The complaints made truly distressing reading, alleging about individuals concerned all possible crimes. Some of the charges were major and serious, many were flippant and frivolous.' It proved impossible to screen so many, so that ultimately, except where the regional committee was hopelessly divided, the Congress Election Committee had no leverage over candidate selection whatsoever. Increasingly the recommendations of state parties simply reflected appeals to traditional caste loyalties. Congress was degenerating into a patronage machine with a flair for managing plebiscites.

Despite this endemic corruption Congress did keep the country together, but there were ominous signs as early as the mid-1950s, at the height of the party's electoral successes, that it would soon be challenged by other political forces better able to attract committed activists and to mobilize genuine popular support. The best example of this was the rise of the DMK, a party built on foundations of ethnic populism in the south. The party grew out of the radical rationalist E. V. Ramaswami Naicker's DK (Dravidian Federation) movements. Ramaswami, known as Periyar, had been the low-caste scourge of Brahmanhood in the south since the 1920s. And though he still enjoyed telling his followers that if they encountered a Brahman and a snake on the road they should kill the Brahman first, these sentiments had not prevented him forming something of an alliance with Congress, now it was committed to caste reform. Despite Periyar's hero status in Tamil Nadu the DK split in 1951 when, at the age of 71, the old war-horse married a 28-year-old party worker and named her the heir to his presidency. This did not go down well, and rivals claimed he had violated his own strictures about the need for a progressive and rationally organized society. They proceeded to form the DMK (Dravidian Forward Federation).

The new party's leader, C. N. Annadurai, was a journalist and film scriptwriter of lowly caste origins, though like Periyar, this did not mean he was poor. His strategy was to move the DMK away from Periyar's exclusive stress on non-Brahmanism and, especially, from the espousal of radical atheism, to a more populist ideology, stressing the virtuousness of and honour due to the 'little man'. Even so, its specific policies for promoting equality remained delightfully vague, which was hardly surprising for it set out to mobilize the vast kaleido-scope of middle and lowish castes who made up the majority of the south's population. These were not necessarily the very poor, but modest farmers, small businessmen, lowly clerks, school teachers and students. They disliked the cultural pretensions of the Brahman elite and clamoured for respect. The DMK's organizing principle was the valorization of the Tamil language and Dravidian history. It made noises about secession from India, but in reality this was a bargaining chip: the DMK really wanted more autonomy, not independence.

Annadurai was highly accomplished in a skill Congress had lost since Gandhi's death – the ability to stir souls. He brilliantly linked the demoralization of the broad swathe of Tamil backward castes with the notion of an oppressive north bullying the virtuous and venerable culture of the Tamil south. The party developed an innov-ative repertoire of techniques for recruiting cadres and then training them in the arts of political rhetoric. Small shops became informal debating forums led by their owners, who, unbeknownst to their innocent clients, were skilled party workers trained to encourage their customers to linger and talk politics.

The DMK's greatest resource was the political deployment of film, and its foremost asset was the extraordinary actor-turned-chief minis-ter, M. G. Ramachandran (MGR). The popularity of this flamboyant thespian was extraordinary, as shown through a network of 22,000 fan clubs. When MGR suffered a paralysing stroke while touring America, dozens of his fans chopped off their own legs and digits in sympathy, and on his demise in 1982 33 fans committed suicide.

MGR starred in dozens of films, scripted by Annadurai and other party leaders, which focused on the plight and the unsung heroism of the little man. MGR would be shown protecting lower-caste women from the lewd attentions of predatory Brahmans, smiting hordes of the high and mighty single-handed (he was generally imbued with supernatural physical powers). Or he would be shown as the little man gaining prestige and honour through education, and then going on to acquire great wealth. This was a populist, not an egalitarian message. But it struck a powerful chord among the lower castes in the villages and lower middle classes in the towns, who increasingly felt that Congress, despite its leftist rhetoric, was a party of the haves.

The DMK's rhetoric about the venerability of Tamil culture was ridiculed by Nehru. But it retaliated brilliantly, launching a massively popular campaign against a Congress project designed to win low caste support by teaching children weaving. The campaign, which portrayed Congress's policy as a plot to condemn the little man's children to servitude, was wildly successful. In 1955 the DMK mounted a massive voter registration campaign, promising an autonomous Tamil Nadu and, significantly, job reservations for backward castes. Under the DMK, Annadurai announced, Tamil Nadu would be the land 'where everyone is a king'. The DMK flickered into the polls in 1957, won the municipal elections of 1959 and then, in a great shock to Congress, won 50 seats in the 1962 General Election. The writing may not have been on the wall, but the image of India's future was on the screen, and it was regionalist and populist.

While Nehru had tried to resist forces of linguistic and regional fragmentation, his well-intended reformism had the unfortunate effect of actually exacerbating those of caste and religion. By creating special electoral reservations and legal protections for low castes and Muslims respectively Nehru did not intend, as had the British, to divide and rule. He hoped, rather, that by accommodating different group identities temporarily, he would allow the underprivileged to use the processes of democratic and economic reform to catch up and, ultimately, dissolve these differences and produce a sense of a greater Indian identity. However, in practice, group and religious identities, rather than eventually withering away, became entrenched and rapidly, as they had under the Raj, developed a political life of their own.

The key mechanism for promoting an integrated identity was the new Indian Constitution, crafted between 1948 and 1950. The first task of the constitution was to define citizenship, and in so doing, the identity of the new nation. Although Congress had long opposed the proliferation of group rights and minority identities under the British and was determined to supplant them with one all-encompassing notion of universal citizenship, there were two hard cases for whom Nehru felt special exemptions should be made – Muslims and dalit groups. The trauma of partition had convinced him that the Muslims left in India needed special reassurance, in the form of complete freedom in the pursuit of their religion and customary practices, that they would not be bullied by the majority Hindus. Dalits were also thought, on account of their historical repression, to require special reserved seats in Parliament and preferential quotas to gain access to universities and government jobs. And so, despite having censured the British for their divisive deployment of such special measures, Congress maintained some of them.

The new constitution therefore embodied a profound and unresolved tension between the principles of legal universalism, treating all equally, and those of legal pluralism, treating different groups differently – an early experiment, in effect, with statutory multiculturalism. What followed from this well-intentioned foundational fudge was a catalogue of unhappy compromises as Nehru attempted to steer an impossible course between Hindu majoritarianism and minority veto power. The compromise took concrete form in the unhappy juxtaposition of the Fundamental Rights section of the constitution, which entrenched a gala of minority interests and privileges, with aspirations to universalism embodied in the section on Directive Principles. The content of these two sections was often blatantly contradictory. So, while religious minorities were permitted, under the Fundamental Rights, to establish their own private faith schools, the Directive Principles declared the state's intention to establish a free and universal education system. Likewise, while the Directive Principles undertook to 'secure a uniform civil code throughout the territory of India', covering marriage, divorce, family property rights, inheritance and so forth, the Fundamental Rights guaranteed minorities freedom in the pursuit of their 'cultural practices'.

The definition of a religious minority, or of a backward caste, was left open to interpretation, allowing for a proliferation of such entities. Moreover, the constitution also permitted, though did not force, individual regional states to enact educational and job reservations for other 'backward' groups, as they judged fit. These were well-intentioned provisions, and were, in the case of caste reservations, meant to last for only ten years, until the processes of education and economic development had removed the structural disadvantages afflicting these castes. However, contrary to intentions, caste reservations proliferated, as did the numbers of groups claiming special minority status. Policies intended to foster unity in diversity only exacerbated conflict, and in a manner that had the potential to become politically toxic. This was because the decision to treat minority groups differently could, perversely perhaps, but nevertheless, persuasively, be presented as examples of discrimination against the Hindu majority. India was a society where many who were not 'minorities' also suffered economic and other deprivations, or at least the frustration of their aspirations. Their response would most likely be either to demand such status themselves, or to fume against the 'pampering' of special interests. In short, legal pluralism, or multiculturalism, both encouraged groups to demand minority or 'backward' status and exacerbated high-caste Hindu chauvinism.

The latter tendency was strikingly in evidence during the protracted and ill-tempered debates over the creation of a uniform Hindu code. This was intended to systematize and modernize the variety of Hindu local practices affecting marriage, divorce and property law. But, in an effort to reassure Muslims, traumatized by partition, that their religion and identity would be protected in independent India, no similar attempt was made to regularize and update Muslim family law. Creating a uniform Hindu code was first attempted in 1950 under Nehru's first law minister, Dr B. R. Ambedkar, leader of the dalits and committed, as he put it, to reforming Hinduism. Barracked and blocked by a wave of Hindu protest in Parliament, the controversy drove him to resign. Nehru retaliated by breaking the reform up into parts, covering marriage, divorce and inheritance, and brought them back to the Lok Sabha as four bills in 1952. Nevertheless it still took four years and much wrangling to pass what in the end were rather moth-eaten pieces of legislation, which had perhaps rather more symbolic than substantive effect.

Opponents relied on two sets of arguments. First, that Hindus should not be required to give up polygamy and the resulting high birth rate, as to do so would be 'race suicide' in the face of the aggressively reproducing Muslims. The second argument, that Nehru was acting hypocritically, was the more powerful. Several critics pointed out the inequity of insisting that Hindus should reform their customary law in accordance with what was 'modern' and 'rational', while Muslims should be left free to carry on their traditional practices. This, of course, was uncomfortably true, and a similar argument was adduced in support of a constitutional amendment making cow slaughter illegal. Nehru took a tough stance on this, as the cow issue had long been a *casus belli* in politically inspired communal violence, and was determined not to allow the amendment. The issue threatened to become explosive, and even to force Nehru's resignation, when a 'compromise' was hit upon. It would become illegal to slaughter cows, but only in the interests of rational and scientific husbandry.

Ultimately, rather than treating Hindus and Muslims as completely equal before the law, and insisting upon the absolute neutrality of the state towards religious identities, secularism in India was a contorted compromise. Hindus and Muslims were treated very differently for the purposes of personal law, and the state found itself playing exactly the same role the Raj had assumed – that of acknowledging rather than being blind to religious difference, and acting as a referee. The real losers from this unfortunate accommodation were India's women, both Muslim and Hindu. Muslim women and Hindu women were, unless their husbands chose to be bound by secular law, still covered by discriminatory customary practice. In particular, Muslim women had no right to maintenance after divorce, while Hindu women did not enjoy equal rights with men over the inheritance of property. This was in striking contrast to the property rights of religious idols and deities, which, under the constitution, acquired a legal identity of their own. As long as they had become deities according to an approved procedure, the *pranapratistha*, or 'life-implacing' ceremony, they became juristic persons with inalienable proprietory rights over any gifts donated.

In Nehru's time, the potentially explosive consequences of treating Hindus and Muslims as different legal persons were not yet apparent, largely because the Hindu right, which championed these issues, had gone somewhat into abeyance since the assassination of Gandhi. In contrast, the caste issue threatened to become an elemental force shaping the future of the Indian state and society. The writing was on the wall when a legal case was brought to the Supreme Court in 1963 – that of Balaji vs. State of Mysore – which raised the question of what precise percentage of places in universities and governmental agencies should be reserved for backward castes. The court was asked to reconcile the constitution's guarantees of 'equality of opportunity in matters of public employment' with its provision that 'Nothing in this article shall prevent the State from making any provision for the reservation of appointments or posts in favour of any backward class of citizens.' It decided to limit possible reservations to 49 per cent. Anything beyond that would be 'a fraud on the constitution'. So, the court had measured the relative weight of absolute equality of citizenship and privileges for 'backward' groups at 51 per cent and 49 per cent respectively. With nearly half of all government jobs now potentially reserved by quota, it was inevitable that lower caste groups would demand the status of 'backwardness' and that higher castes would feel increasing resentment. The process began in the south in the 1960s, but by the 1980s it had also become the principal dynamic of north Indian politics too.

In the face of this legal and political atomization the Nehruvian project of unification had only one weapon left in its armoury – culture. Nehru's government took cultural matters tremendously seriously, commissioning hundreds of new buildings and even new cities from the world's leading architects, establishing a plethora of museums and art galleries, creating state academies for the encouragement of classical dance, theatre and literature, and even developing a policy on radio music. However, the single most important cultural arena in modern India filled it with anxiety: Nehruvian India was deeply hostile to Bollywood. Nehru's was essentially an elitist project designed to elevate high cultural values, whether 'classical', international or modern, and deprecated the supposed vulgarity of contemporary popular culture. It sought to bridge the two by creating state-approved folk and regional cultures that could be incorporated into a new 'classical' tradition. But this official version of popular culture failed to take root, and left the disdained aspects of a genuinely vibrant popular culture to be co-opted by regional and sectional politicians.

The classicizing approach was particularly evident in music, as is shown in the policies planned by All-India Radio. All-India Radio passed into Indian hands in 1946, and came under the purview of the new minister for information, Sardar Vallabhbhai Patel. Although Patel was a Hindu of conservative tastes, his musical objectives accorded with Nehru's. His strategy was to increase the dominance of a few stations, shutting down those of the princely states, and leaving only a handful of broadcasters in regional languages. Ultimately it was thought that this would raise standards by countering the lamentable influence of vulgar, commercial film music, and create a more integrated culture. Patel immediately set about imposing a 'classical' canon on the station's music output. Musicians from the 'courtesan' tradition – i.e. those trained in Islamic music schools or *gharanas* – and anyone whose 'private life was a public scandal' was banned, in favour of graduates from 'classical' music schools. Auditions for artists were enforced, following the model used by the Public Services Commission to recruit civil servants. They were graded A, B or C on performance, and had to pass a test in 'theory', involving knowledge of scholarly texts on classical forms. By the late 1950s the 10,000 musicians regularly employed were, it was proudly reported, largely from 'educated and respectable families'.

However, this high-minded policy was singularly ineffective, and popularity of the despised popular songs from the films continued to grow. This was a direct threat to the edifying and classicizing policy of the state. The language used in film songs was, in fact, merely a more Urduized form of Hindi, not the rarefied, formal and Sanskritic kind favoured by All-India Radio. Moreover, their lyrics were generally erotic, and (worse) the songs were tainted by infusions of western orchestration, melody and rhythm, which Patel's successor regarded as emblematic of a lower stage of human evolution. Drastic measures were imposed. In 1954 all film music disappeared from state radio after a dispute with the industry, though its corrupting rhythms could still be enjoyed by those with sets tuned to Radio Goa or Radio Ceylon. But an outright ban was not really in the spirit of the new democratic India, and an alternative was followed: the invention of a new genre of edifying 'light' classical music to compete with the Bollywood hit machine head on. A young musician named Ravi Shankar was employed to develop this style, and what emerged was a set of light ragas, 'romantic, bright, lilting pieces with exciting rhythms and lively melodies', to be played by the National Radio orchestra, the Vadya Vrinda. Meanwhile, in the regions, light music units were created and classical musicians, together with state-approved poets, were charged with composing two new songs a week. Yet this too proved ineffective, and in 1957 a survey of ten households commissioned to discover the success of the new light music plan revealed that nine of the sets were permanently tuned to the film-music specialist, Radio Ceylon, while the tenth was broken.

Commercial film had the potential to be a vehicle of national identity and cohesion, but was only rarely so used. It had become a hugely popular medium in the 1930s, and there was now an opportunity to influence film as the studio system responsible for the escapist mythologicals and musicals of that era had largely been wiped out by the war. However, Congress officials' most recent foray into the world of popular entertainment – they had attended a gala in 1939 to celebrate twenty-five years of Indian cinema – had not been a happy experience. The delegation of earnest politicians was appalled to discover a cinematic landscape populated by leather-booted temptresses beating the living daylights out of sleazy gangsters, to the ecstatic joy of the assembled onlookers. Nehru himself was no fan of film, and this disdain was underlined when film was excluded from the new system of national academies created to promote classical theatre, dance and literature. In fact, rather than seeing film as a resource, the industry was shackled with a punitive entertainment tax and besieged by an obsessive regime of censorship and prohibitions, each film minutely scrutinized for the faintest glimmer of vulgarity. Even the Raj's notorious ban on film kissing was preserved.

Some effort was made to shape cinema to national purposes. Directors whose output was thought to promote a progressive message were rewarded with tax exemptions, and in 1952 an international film festival was launched, to bring over the best examples of film-making in the rest of the world. The main goal of the Indian Film Finance Corporation, belatedly created in 1961, was to encourage the 'realist' style in preference to the over-heated melodramas favoured by the studios. The result was films of great artistic merit, such as Satyajit Ray's dreamy elegy to the lost innocence of the countryside, *Pather Panchali* (*Song of the Little Road*, 1955); although this ambiguous film, in which the railway features as an alluring symbol of modernity, arguably embodied an implicitly Nehruvian message.

The state also attempted to influence film-making more directly. It forced cinemas to screen edifying 'shorts' and documentaries before the main feature, which generally took the form of newsreels informing the audience of ever more impressive economic and infrastructural achievements: dams built, tonnages of steel output, the virtues of family planning. Shorts demonstrating the benignly transformative influence of machines on peasant life, or documentaries celebrating India's classical cultural heritage were also common. Another favourite topic of this edificatory genre were celluloid representations of folk dances, tribal customs and other examples of India's diverse and far-flung cultures. These generally took the form of a specially mounted performance for either Nehru or his representative, often his daughter Indira, in which the honoured guest would view these anthropologized pageants from an elevated distance.

Some films, however, were more successful in promulgating elite messages through popular culture. A few directors working in commercial film did produce films which blended 'progressive' messages with the popular musical and melodramatic style. Bimal Roy, an accomplished leftist film-maker, produced a number of films which were popular in the cities. His *Udayer Pathe* (*Awakening*, 1944), in Bengali but remade in Hindi as *Humrahi* (*Fellow Travellers*, 1945), dramatized the struggle to bring economic prosperity and social justice to the countryside. *Humrahi* had a classic poor-boy-meets-rich-girl plot, in which the girl, increasingly alienated from her rich industrialist family, begins to wear simple clothes and read improving books. It was unashamedly populist and clichéd, and, using common speech patterns rather than elevated, classicized Hindi, it was also a powerful moral parable about social change achieved through an inter-class alliance. This was the Nehruvian project in celluloid form. Films like this, Roy's later *Do Bigha Zamin* (*Two Acres of Land*, 1953), and the urban block-buster *Mother India*, could have been successfully marketed in rural areas to link the state's modernizing policies to individual peasant ambitions, but they were not. Instead the state backed the high-brow neo-realist style which produced films that, rather like the Republic Day Parade, presented 'village India' as a sphere for middle-class uplift, rather than speaking directly to the objects of uplift themselves.

Perhaps an even more powerful means of transmitting the new vision of India to the masses lay in reshaping their environment, and architecture was the centrepiece of the new state's cultural ambitions. In the first few decades of its existence the Nehruvian state built many temples to the flame of modernity. Significantly, the architects of most of these new icons were not Indian. Though one school of thought maintained that the new nation should be designed by home-grown talent, another concluded that the experience and skill was lacking. The architectural style of the Raj's Public Works Department, dominated by sanitary engineers, cast a long shadow over India's architectural profession. It was decided, therefore, to engage foreign architects for the most prestigious projects, the preferred choice being Americans – deemed to embody the spirit of the age more persuasively than their British or European counterparts. Louis Kahn was engaged to create the famous Indian Institute of Management in Ahmedabad, a sort of Athenian academy dedicated to training a new generation of enlightened technocrats who would go out among the people to create the brave new world. Another such academy of modernity and high culture, also designed by an American, Joseph Stein, was the highly prestigious Indian International Centre. This was a pet project of Nehru, who with his long-standing interest in international affairs, saw it as a beacon of Indian intellectual and cultural influence on the global stage. Stein created an elegant, but not noticeably Indian, complex of buildings and gardens abutting the beautiful Lodhi Gardens in the heart of Lutyens's Garden City extension of New Delhi. The Centre still operates as a conference hall, library and study retreat for Indian and foreign scholars and diplomats. The whole complex wears something of the air of a deluxe monastery for refined intellectual pursuits. But, like many of the edifices established at this time, it remains a serene island of high culture and lofty ideals adrift in the burgeoning and bustling capital.

By far the most famous example of the Nehruvian vision in concrete was the new capital of Punjab, the planned city of Chandigarh. The loss of Lahore, the old capital of Punjab, to Pakistan at partition had created an unprecedented opportunity to plan a whole new metropolis, an opportunity relished by Nehru as a chance to create a monument to his moment in history that would rival Akbar's ruined Fatehpur Sikri, or the Raj's magnificent, if unloved, New Delhi. The planning and building of Chandigarh became something of an object lesson in the flawed aspirations of the new elite, and the problems they would encounter in garnering popular legitimacy for their vision. From the start there were battles over where exactly the city should be placed. Ambala in the princely state of Patiala was ideal geographically, but obtaining the site would have entailed tricky negotiations with the ex-prince. The land at Chandigarh itself immediately became contested territory. Angry and soon to be dispossessed farmers, egged on by socialist opponents of the government, organized a Gandhian protest against the necessary land purchases. No sooner had this crisis been resolved than another threatened. The first choice of architect, the American Albert Mayer, dropped out after the death of his assistant and it transpired that the government could not afford to engage another American owing to an acute dollar shortage. Reluctantly, therefore, the choice fell upon a European. The chosen one, rather ironically, was the Swiss-born Le Corbusier, a prophet of high-modernism who also harboured a soft spot for old-style colonialism, regarding it as a *force morale*. For Nehru at least, perhaps unsurprisingly, given his own unacknowledged fondness for civilizing missions, the Swiss *force morale* turned out to be a happy choice.

Le Corbusier believed that modern cities, unlike their predecessors, should not offer opportunities for 'anarchic individualism', but should be centrally controlled, hierarchically organized, and administered from above by highly qualified specialists. Like Nehru he was enraptured by machines and mathematics and believed, also like Nehru, that India, through the ingenuity of brilliant technicians, could transcend the ills and disorderliness of the first industrial revolution, to arrive harmoniously in the second – the age of the automobile, sectors, zoning and the plan. The original plans, drawn up by Mayer and his assistant, he deemed overly reliant on 'Indian idioms'. He determined to have no truck with bustling bazaars, zig-zag streets, village communities and the other paraphernalia of existing Indian cities. Chandigarh would be 'a city of rectangles and pure volumes, the symbols of perfection', adding, 'what is the significance of Indian style in the world today if you accept machines, trousers and democracy?' Geometry, Le Corbusier declared, was the sculpture of the intellect:

a battle of space, fought within the mind. Arithmetic, geometrics: it would all be there when the whole was finished. For the moment, oxen, cows and goats, driven by peasants, cross the sun-scorched fields.

The cows, goats and peasants would soon be removed.

The new city, unlike the messy labyrinths usually associated with Indian urban life, was constructed around what Le Corbusier termed sectors and zones. The residential sector, now dubbed a 'container of family life', was bounded on all sides by roads intended for fast-moving traffic – Le Corbusier assumed a population of two-car families on the American model. Housing would be segregated hierarchically, though, in a nod to social engineering, along class, not caste lines. There were three more sectors or zones, for education, industry and the city centre, complete with a 'leisure valley' and exhibition space, envisaged as a 'Centre of Itinerant Exhibition' devoted to the 'synthesis of the Major Arts', and folk-dancing displays. But the climax of the plan was the fifth zone, the Capitol, a complex of government, legal and administrative buildings set slightly apart from and elevated above the other zones. It was made even more monumental by the creation of man-made hills to frame it, and through the artificial lowering of the surrounding approach roads and pavements. Inspired by a pair of cooling towers he had spotted in Ahmedabad, Le Corbusier's Capitol, like Lutyens's New Delhi, was a city on a hill from which the government could look down on the people.

The cold perfection of the finished Capitol was a source of comment at the time, criticized for its homogeneity and lack of colour, alien to the noise, excitement and vibrancy of the authentic Indian city. The poet Aditya Prakash wrote of it:

> Are the spaces human or inhuman?
> Waiting to realize their full potential
> Awaiting a landscape
> Awaiting crowds of people
> Awaiting traffic

In fact the crowds of people arrived all too soon, rendering the perfectly planned city clogged and congested. Although intended for a maximum population of 500,000, by the early 1990s it had over 750,000 denizens. Today one quarter of the population live in unauthorized huts on streets choked with traffic, lacking adequate power and water supplies. Despite Le Corbusier's desire for a 'regulated' city, the living metropolis is wholly chaotic. People have opened shops on the ground floors of their apartments, small manufacturers have annexed open spaces and shacks occupy every spare inch of land, beginning where the airport runway ends. Even the spatial perfection of the city's grand centerpiece, the Capitol, has been breached by special parking spaces for judges and top officials. Moreover, the stern geometric perfection of Chandigarh's parliament has not bred a democratic style. The acropolis on which the parliament is mounted lends it an elitist air, evoking a sense of awe, not inclusion, in onlookers. The assembly chamber, designed to promote civilized debate among its politicians, seems rather to promote angry confrontations. All assembly members are equipped with separate microphones, making fluent debate near impossible. Indeed Punjabi politics has been notable for its violence and controversy. At Chandigarh two cultures were created – the icy elegance of the perfectly planned and monumental Capitol, and the disorderly vibrancy of the people – with no harmonious meeting between the two.

By the early 1960s the Nehruvian project was unravelling. The third plan was in crisis, agricultural reform had stalled, and grain output actually declined in 1962–3. The rate of industrial growth was stuck at 8 per cent p.a., not the forecast 14 per cent, impeded by shortages of coal, electricity and transport, while inflation was running at 9 per cent. This was a dangerous situation for a party in power, and on the eve of the third General Election of 1962 Congress was confronting a crisis of rising expectations at the very moment that its own reputation was at its lowest, dogged by corruption scandals at every level. The Santhanam Committee, appointed to investigate corruption in public life in 1962, had produced alarming revelations. Between 1958 and 1962, over Rs. 23,800,000 worth of business licences had been obtained fraudulently and then re-sold on the open market for up to five times their face value; this was thought to be only 25 per cent of the real figure. A conservative estimate of bribery in the construction sector under the second five-year plan was put at a Rs. 1,400 million loss to the exchequer. Overall it was thought that corruption was costing the country Rs. 1,200 million annually, not allowing for 'leakages' from the railway and defence budgets.

Several senior Congress state politicians were implicated. The former chief minister of Punjab, Pratap Singh Kairon, was found guilty of running an organized racket in gold and currency smuggling – his sons had all become millionaires. Mrs Easwaramma Mitra, wife of the chief minister of Orissa, had built up a business worth Rs. 160,000 in two years after an initial investment of only Rs. 2,000, while Biju Patnaik, another leading Congress figure in Orissa, had acquired Rs. 100 million in just ten years of industrial activity. Haridas Mundra, 'a flamboyant personality and a financial adventurer whose only ambition is to build up an industrial empire by dubious means', was also, it transpired, an exceedingly generous donor to Uttar Pradesh Congress coffers. The Santhanam Committee had received a large number of complaints about top politicians at the centre too, including charges, later upheld, against Nehru's close friend and foreign affairs minister Krishna Menon and his personal secretary, M. O. Matthai.

The culture of corruption had gone beyond gossip in the press and government circles and had begun to penetrate society more deeply. In 1961 the great novelist R. K. Narayan published *Mr Sampath*, a grimly comic depiction of a city milieu. The eponymous anti-hero is shown to be wholly immersed in fraudulent city life, a liar and an opportunist without family ties, someone who turns every occasion to his own advantage and someone else's loss. He is surrounded by a large cast of big-talking politicians, grasping merchants, phoney philanthropists and hard-bitten journalists. The reader is forced into a grudging sympathy for Mr Sampath, able to live on his wits in a rough and corrupting environment. Bimal Roy's film *Parakh* (*Test*, 1960) dealt with similar themes, but more judgementally, offering a scathing satirical attack on venal politicians allied with vested interests manipulating the life of a small village for their own gain. The entire cast of stereotypical village characters, with the exception of the teacher and postmaster, embody greed, meanness, dishonesty, pomposity and pretentiousness.

In 1960, in a desperate effort to recapture the spirit of renunciation and sacrifice of the Gandhi era, Congress High Command put into effect the famous Kamaraj plan. Named after its instigator, the powerful Congress chief minister of Tamil Nadu, the plan required a select number of top Congressmen, including chief ministers and cabinet ministers, to resign their posts and return to the villages to do Gandhian 'constructive work' among Congress's sadly dilapidated cadres. The bona fides of the scheme were, however, called into question when it was revealed that of the six chief ministers chosen for the renunciatory ordeal, two were serious contenders for the leadership after Nehru's (now anticipated) demise. One of these was the old Gandhian war-horse, Morarji Desai, number two in Congress seniority, austere, incorruptible, right-wing and cordially loathed by many other top figures in the party. The Kamraj plan, rather than a scheme to revivify the party, came to be seen by many as merely a stop-Morarji campaign.

The collapse of esteem for Congress was already noticeable in the elections of 1962. Despite winning a comfortable majority in the highly unfair first-past-the-post voting system, it was clear that Congress's support was starting to drift away. It only just hung on to power in several states, and 49 Congress ministers lost their seats. These elections also showed for the first time how well organized Congress's opponents were becoming, with their more disciplined and committed party workers able to attract disaffected voters using appeals to caste or ethnic identity and populist messages. The DMK doubled its vote in Tamil Nadu, and in the Punjab the Akali Sikhs deserted their alliance with Congress and took to the hustings demanding their own state. At the All-India level the Hindu nationalist Jan Sangh party, founded 1951, began to make electoral break-throughs, greatly assisted by its mother-organization, the paramilitary RSS. The RSS provided a ready-made and popular local network, and exposed the dangers of Congress's neglect of its grassroots membership. It had been banned in the wake of Gandhi's assassination, but once the ban was lifted in 1950 it had returned to its very successful inter-war strategy of building up Hindu nationalism as a social and cultural network devoted to the physical and cultural training of high caste Hindus and to the forced conversion or 'nationalization', as it put it, of all non-Hindus. By 1960 the RSS had about one million members, mainly small businessmen, petty civil servants, police officers and local notables. It combined a mildly egalitarian populist rhetoric with bitter attacks on land reform and on Congress as a party of godless closet communists. This strategy was rewarded when, after the 1962 elections, it became the chief opposition party in Uttar Pradesh, Punjab and Madhya Pradesh.

The combination of electoral, moral and economic crises both climaxed in, and was crystallized by, the disastrous border war with China in October 1962. Despite the talk of Chini-Hindi *Bhai-Bhai* (brother-brother), and cultural exchange visits with the Chinese, an unresolved dispute simmered between the two countries concerning their overlapping borders in the Himalayas. Nehru had tended to dismiss these as a minor side-effect of incompatible maps, concerning a scantily populated patch of the Himalayas, Aksai Chin, over which the imperial British had long been in dispute with China. This land was not without some importance, however, as it abutted the disputed Indian state of Kashmir and was also close to the unstable north-eastern state of Nagaland. But the crisis began to escalate because of events in Tibet. The Chinese claimed Tibet, a claim disputed by the Dalai Lama, who, backed by the Americans, led an exodus of Tibetans from the region into India in 1959. The Chinese, aggrieved at the recognition thus tacitly afforded to Tibetan separatism, and by India's acquiescence to American pressure, began to press for settlement of the Aksai Chin issue. Skirmishes began on the border.

At this point what was a minor foreign policy issue began to assume domestic political dimensions. The right, now efficiently organized in the Jan Sangh party, had long sought a stick with which to beat Nehru, and the allegation that he was insufficiently anti-communist and anti-Chinese was a good one. The right came out in strong support of the Dalai Lama, and the press began to make noises about Nehru's weakness. In the same year as the Tibetan crisis, Nehru lost his important Nagpur amendment to introduce co-operative farming, defeated by a peculiar coalition of rightists, claiming it was a heinous import from communist China, and the Indian communists, who were pro-Soviet and anxious to distance themselves from any taint of Chinese sympathies.

By now the Chinese were raising the negotiating stakes by claiming additional pieces of land and the Indian right was clamouring for Nehru to abandon non-alignment and join an anti-Chinese defence pact. When the Chinese prime minister, Zhou Enlai, visited India for talks, nationalist fervour began to grow: Nehru was castigated in the press for not being tough enough; Hindus spoke of their 'mystical affinity' with the Himalayas; and N. G. Ranga, leader of the business-dominated Swatantra party, declared that because of Nehru's perfidy the 'Chinese are soiling our motherland with their cancerous fingers'. Thus pressed, Nehru embarked on a very Indian 'forward policy', and troops were sent to assert the 'moral rightness' of India's claim in a form of armed *satyagraha*. In September 1962 they began to cross into what was undisputed Chinese territory. Nationalist hysteria erupted in India when the Chinese retaliated with devastating force. On 20 November Nehru was forced to request US assistance, and the Chinese withdrew the same night, having made their point. The government was now openly allowing CIA-trained Tibetan insurgents to drill on Indian soil, while the CIA itself was given free access to Indian territory in its campaign against China. Nehru's non-aligned foreign policy was in disarray, his domestic policy in tatters, and Congress in decline. Within eighteen months he was dead.

'My profession', Nehru once said, 'is to foster the unity of India . . . The glory of India has been the way in which it has managed to keep two things going at the same time: that is, its infinite variety and at the same time its unity in that variety.' Nehru's goal was to make a virtue of India's variety by creating the world's first self-consciously multi-cultural modern nation-state, and to do so without employing the tools of tyranny and coercion. Nehru is now often seen as a tragic figure, a great man with a great vision weakened by a fatal flaw – his own reluctance to fight vested interests. Certainly Nehru did not particularly relish battles. But neither did he avoid them. He should, perhaps, be more properly compared to Arjuna, the great warrior of the Pandava clan in the *Mahabharata*. Confronting a terrible war with his own cousins in order to regain the Pandava kingdom, Arjuna is tormented by the prospect of violence and struggle that will inevitably ensue. 'Why must I fight? Cannot you see the horrible destruction that will follow?' he asks his charioteer, the god Krishna:

> Saying this in the time of war,
> Arjuna slumped into his chariot
> And laid down his bow and arrows,
> His mind tormented by grief.

But steeled by Krishna Arjuna does fight, and the kingdom of Bharat is restored to the Pandavas. Nehru too disliked violence and confrontation, but he was a fighter. His flaw lay not in his lack of courage, but in his choice of weapons. The main weapon in his armoury was left liberal progressivism borrowed from the British; his army, the Congress party. Neither was sufficient to the task. No society has been able to achieve greater economic dynamism and social equality by entrenching the very interests who are most threatened by such change, but that is precisely what Nehru's model accomplished. The project was not without its benefits, laying the foundations of democracy and avoiding the systematic state violence associated with modernization in China and Russia. But the price was very high: India remained an exceptionally inegalitarian society, lacking in cohesion and a sense of common citizenship. Moreover, he bequeathed to his successors unresolved problems of political integration and thwarted expectations that would come to threaten the very integrity of the new nation.

7

Flames

In 1975 the most successful Indian film of all time – *Sholay* (*Flames* or *Embers*) – was released. Despite its vast expense it was, initially, a flop. A grizzly revenge drama, heavily influenced by Sergio Leone's *The Good, the Bad, and the Ugly*, and through that by the Japanese classic *Seven Samurai*, *Sholay* was a chappati western. It tells the story of Baldev Singh, a powerful village boss or *thakur*, and sometime police officer, who, over the course of a decade pursues a vicious bandit chief, Gabbar Singh, who, not satisfied with terrorizing the local village, has massacred the landlord's entire family and lopped off the arms of the unfortunate *thakur* for good measure. Realizing that the official forces of the state are literally armless in the face of this anarchic violence, the landlord enlists the assistance of two petty criminals whose intelligence and resourcefulness he had encountered while a policeman. After a series of hair-raising encounters with the villain, including a famous episode where the heroine is forced to dance on broken glass to save the life of her lover, the anti-heroes eventually bring nemesis upon the terrifying bandit.

Though declared a failure within two weeks of release, the film became a word-of-mouth super-hit – the first Indian film to gross more than Rs. 10 million. Indeed it eventually went on to make an unheard of £25 million at the box office and in 1999 BBC India declared it the film of the millennium. Very rapidly it established itself as a cult. Fans would go and see it dozens of times. And not only were its songs released on record, but also substantial clips from its dialogue, with the result that soon viewing the film had become something akin to a karaoke experience as the audience chanted along with the actors; the scene in which the terrified hero regresses into the pidgin Hindi spoken by many poorer Indians was especially popular. Most strikingly, it created India's first unassailably world-class super-star in Amitabh Bachchan, who became a household name across Russia and the Middle East. Bachchan played the more moody and romantic of the two anti-heroes – Jaidev – and launched a wholly new kind of Indian film hero – the angry outsider. In subsequent films he would reprise the role which, in its essentials, consisted of a brooding young man, usually from the wrong side of the tracks, who is forced to enact revenge upon a bewildering variety of bandits, crooks and scheming stepbrothers, who seem, during the 1970s, to have taken over celluloid India.

At the time many theorized about the popularity of the film. Some saw it as radical, with its narrative of a poor man standing alone against dark forces of injustice and anarchy. But that did not seem to be what the film-makers intended, for Jaidev and his partner did not lead a band of poor villagers against the depredations of the old order, but were enlisted by the chief representative of that old order (Baldev Singh is not only a big landlord, but a retired policeman to boot), to restore his authority over the countryside. And to drive home the point that old hierarchies cannot be breached, the low-caste character of Jaidev has to die rather than be allowed to consummate his love for the *thakur*'s widowed daughter-in-law. Bachchan himself, though physi-cally a far cry from the chiselled perfection supposedly associated with high-caste leading men, was in reality the starry son of impeccably elite parents – a Cambridge-educated poet and society-hostess mother. Controversy over the film's message continued to rage when the Indian film censors insisted on a new ending. In the original Gabbar Singh is annihilated under the spike-shod feet of Baldev Singh. But in the censors' conclusion the police, representatives of state authority, arrive in the nick of time and cart Gabbar off to face due process.

The ambiguities of the film's message were further compounded by the absence of any clear motive or identity for the bandit Gabbar Singh. Gabbar seemed to be merely an embodiment of senseless cruelty and evil. Was he, perhaps, supposed to be a Jat, representative of the newly enriched farmer class which was proving so politically problematic in this era? Or was he rather a symbol of the rapacious violence and thuggery that now seemed to infect Indian public life?

Whatever he was, it was notable that all the major actors in the film wanted to play him. And the most popular line in the film – soon a catch-phrase across the subcontinent – was '*Ab tera kya hoga Kaliya*' (And what will happen to you, you Darkie?), muttered at one of the heroes during a sadistic game of Russian roulette. While less menacingly, but tellingly, Gabbar's Choice, a rapidly popular brand of biscuits, was launched in his honour.

The film seemed to encapsulate the degree to which the issue of proper authority had become contested in the post-Nehru era. The temple of power may have finally opened to all, but the worshippers were by no means agreed on who should preside over its rituals and who should benefit from its sacrifices. India itself, like the village location of *Sholay*, was a battleground between warring groups as old hierarchies crumbled. *Thakurs*, bandits, heroized hoodlums and a host of external influences competed to fill the ensuing vacuum. Here was an India far from the insular and autarkic regime of journalistic imagination, but instead awash with foreign influences. While Bollywood offered its own answer to Clint Eastwood and the spaghetti western, others looked to Mao's China, Brezhnev's Russia, and even, in the case of Indira's son Sanjay, to Ferdinand Marcos of the Philippines. What *Sholay* depicted was an India beset by ferocious group conflict, with a faltering state; an India unsure of what or who constituted legitimate authority. Twenty years of democracy had dramatically dented respect for traditional power-holders and the gentlemanly and civilized ethos of the Nehru years dissolved into an ugly and more visceral politics as the old elites sought to defend their threatened dominance. Both the films and the politics of the era gave ambivalent but tangible support to the idea that the delivery of justice was not necessarily the monopoly of the state, and might *in extremis* fall to other actors. This was a form of justice the nation's chief power-holder, Indira Gandhi, would come to know at first hand, while the Nehruvian vision and legacy that she had fought to preserve was consumed by flames.

In 1967 India held its fourth General Election, the first election since the death of Nehru, and Congress was led by his daughter, Indira Gandhi. On the eve of the poll the question was posed: 'Will [Mrs

Gandhi], as her father so very often did before her, so charm the crowds, reaching out to them over the heads of party bosses and faction leaders, that the party admits that she is indispensable to it?' She did not. Congress's vote dipped alarmingly, its support in the cities, among the young and poor having plunged. It barely hung on to power at the centre, and lost it in many of the regions. Beyond that, the outcome was somewhat hard to decipher, for while radical Marxists triumphed in Kerala and a melange of factionalized communists took over West Bengal, in Madhya Pradesh, Gujarat and Rajasthan princes enjoyed startling success in turning their aristocratic charisma to democratic purposes.

In retrospect, what is really significant about the 1967 elections were the first flickering signs of agrarian populism – the rise of regional and sometimes caste-based parties representing a broad spectrum of peasant and farmer interests. Though it is impossible to offer a categorical definition of this group, as it varied from region to region, for the sake of simplicity they are best seen as middle-to-backward castes and those who comprised the principal farming groups – Jats, Kurmis, Ahirs (Yadavs), and Gujars. There has been much controversy over their proper name, and they have been dubbed variously commercial peasants, bullock-capitalists (to indicate the continuing use by many of animal power) and even 'kulaks' (the Russian term meaning 'fist', which the communists used to describe the rich commercial peasants of the 1920s). But they were essentially rich farmers drawn from the lower tiers of the Indian caste hierarchy, who had been the principal beneficiaries of the land reforms of the 1950s and in the mid-1960s of the so-called 'Green Revolution', when the government switched to a more market-based strategy of agricultural development. It soon became apparent that their economic dynamism was rapidly being translated into political self-assertion. Tiring of their political subservience to their 'betters' they rejected the role of passive recipients of high-caste developmental policy and were determined to storm the temple of Indian politics in their own right.

On 23 December 1978 Chaudhary Charan Singh, a well-known politician from Uttar Pradesh, held a birthday party. But this was no modest event, for Charan Singh had invited over a million guests, and armies of peasants and farmers from across the region descended on

Delhi to celebrate his 76 years on earth. This was an example of a very literal form of party politics: within a year Charan Singh's impressive display of peasant power had made him the first peasant Prime Minister of India. Though his premiership may have lasted a mere three weeks, it nevertheless marked the decisive arrival of the rich farmer into the political temple. Charan Singh, a Jat, had been born into a modest peasant family in western Uttar Pradesh. An intelligent youth, he had graduated with an MA in economics and began what would be a lengthy political career in Congress. An adherent of Gandhi, he had participated in the great Salt March and spent many years in prison as a political detainee before independence. Afterwards he had been rewarded with several ministerial posts in the Uttar Pradesh state government. But Charan Singh was no ordinary political operator. Spurning the factional jockeying of his higher-caste peers he had devoted himself to cultivating the broader constituency of the state's 'kulak' classes.

Charan Singh was, then, the unofficial ideologue of the new farmers, reprising, in some ways, Gandhian notions of the essentially rural character of the 'real India' and directly challenging the technocratic, westernized vision of India advocated by Nehru. This neo-Gandhian utopia was encapsulated in the notion of '*Bharat*', the Hindi name for India, suggesting an alternative, populist India, rooted in the rural soil, not in the seedy cities, urban sprawl and industrialized 'India' of the plan. In Charan Singh's bucolic vision, 'true' virtue inhered in the peasants, in villages and in small-scale agriculture, while the cities harboured alien technologies, hard-nosed wheeler-dealers and every sort of immorality. The very essence of democracy, he implied (like Gandhi), resided in the family smallholding, while large-scale farms were its utter antithesis: hellish institutions where the few give orders to the many, threatening to turn the countryside into 'a huge barracks or gigantic agricultural factory'. Most importantly, an India founded on small-scale farming would be safe from class conflict. This was the very essence of the agrarian populist vision, for there were, he asserted (rather implausibly), no real conflicts between those who worked the land, only between the yeoman peasant and urban and rural parasites such as traders and money-lenders, bureaucrats and big business.

Charan Singh propounded a theory of development to accompany these philosophical and sociological musings, and one radically opposed to that of Nehru and the planners. His *Joint Farming X-Rayed* of 1959 was a trenchant attack on Nehruvian plans to push these middling farmers into joint co-operatives. A consistent theme in both his policies and theorizing was the importance of the medium-sized farmer to India's development, which, he argued, given India's vast rural population, should be labour, not capital intensive. In *Joint-Farming X-Rayed*, he claimed that the most efficient size for an Indian farm was between 2.5 and 27.5 acres. The best way to develop Indian agriculture was not, he thundered, through Nehruvian structural change and the imposition of joint-farming, but by giving small family farmers more 'water, manure, seeds and pesticides'. While not exactly a technophobe, Charan Singh had very decided ideas about what did and did not constitute appropriate technology. Believing, like Gandhi, that excessive enthusiasm for machines was the high-road to un-employment in the countryside, he deprecated the grand dam-building and mechanized irrigation schemes of the five-year plans, advocating sinking more labour-intensive tube wells and using Persian wheels to raise water. He despised tractors, preferring the services of the trusty bullock. Chemical fertilizers, the holy grail of the American-inspired Green Revolution, also provoked his ire. These were a poor substitute for good old-fashioned manure, which did not, unlike the detested chemicals, 'give rise to plant maladies'.

These were potent ideas that did indeed resonate with many of India's middling peasants. The constituency to whom Singh's ideas were addressed were the very groups who were now participating in India's so-called Green Revolution. The failure of Nehruvian co-operative schemes to raise agricultural productivity had caused a crisis in food production, which, compounded by the poor harvests of the mid 1960s, threatened India with both famine and inflation. The inauguration of the Green Revolution in 1965 heralded the abandon-ment of Nehru's ambitions to couple agricultural development with social justice. It was, essentially, a wager on the strong – the middle caste peasants especially – and the scheme of co-operative farming, intended to boost poorer peasants, was dropped in favour of an all-out dash for growth fuelled by the latest technology. High-yielding seed varieties, fertilizers, irrigation and so-forth, it was hoped, would make

India self-sufficient in food. But while the middling farmers welcomed the opportunity for enrichment, they did not necessarily go along whole-heartedly with the scientific and 'western' approach to agronomy associated with it. Many had their own ideas about how the land should be cultivated. Charan Singh's eulogies to labour-intensive and more 'traditional' methods struck a chord with those who still saw the land in 'humoral' terms, where the heating effects of manure had to be balanced by the cooling properties of water, an equilibrium potentially imperilled by the indiscriminate application of synthetic chemical fertilizers, or by the harsh churning of heavy tractors. It would be wrong to dismiss all of their ideas as 'backward' – indeed they incorporated much of the 'foreign' knowledge into their own understanding of farm science – and Singh's ideas and rhetoric showed a respect for their expertise and experience that was often disdained by experts and officialdom. And his attacks on bureaucracy and defence of middling peasant interests against attempts to increase land revenue or levy agricultural income tax played powerfully among groups both increasingly economically powerful and politically ambitious.

Middle peasants were not the only group beginning to show signs of serious discontent with the Nehruvian order. The expectations of lower castes, dalits and tribal groups had also been at once raised and then dashed. Under the Nehruvian dispensation they had been promised land redistribution, which, because of the very weakness of the central state and the co-option of local bureaucracy by more dominant groups, had not materialized. Moreover, the very rise of the farmer castes could often make life worse for them. Evicted from the small tenancies they had cultivated, many became landless and increasingly dependent on newly prosperous middle-peasant agriculturalists for employment. Moreover, the eclipse of high-caste dominance by middling groups had also brought about the erosion of paternalistic traditions which had made the lives of the rural poor at least tolerable; the newly prosperous tended to expect the same 'feudal' deference of their inferiors, without observing the associated obligations to them.

The consequence was that in much of the countryside the poor were experiencing something akin to serfdom. They were expected to labour for very low wages and were increasingly forced into forms of long-term debt bondage merely to feed themselves. More galling still were the 'seigneurial' aspects of this neo-feudal arrangement: the sexual harassment and rape of their women by their superiors being among the more egregious of various forms of humiliation inflicted. These practices tended to go unchecked, for as well as supplanting many of the higher-caste *zamindars* in the ritual hierarchy of the village, the middle castes were also increasingly capturing the local state – buying their way into the bureaucracy and the police. So, abandoned by the government, the very poor groups began to take justice into their own hands, and as the 1969 report of the Home Ministry ominously concluded, the failure of land reform and the rise of wealthy middle peasants was threatening to turn the Green Revolution into a red one.

The most spectacular example of this was the Naxalite Rebellion – a communist-led strategy of guerrilla warfare in the countryside and lightning strikes and assassinations in the cities. While it originated in the borderlands of the West Bengal region of Darjeeling and those of Assam, the movement soon spread far beyond, and entrenched pockets of armed peasant guerrillas emerged in Bihar and Andhra. Since the late 1950s, communists had been organizing among the very poorest rural labourers, many of whom were *dalits* (untouchables) and tribal groups, *kisan sabhas*, or peasant trade unions. These had initially adopted lobbying and other kinds of legal action to gain control of land they believed should be theirs. However, in the mid-1960s some of these movements began seizing land, and a conflict broke out within the ranks of the West Bengal communists, then in government, over whether the police should be permitted to intervene to suppress these seizures. As a result a group of communist local leaders broke away and formed the Maoist-inspired CPI (M-L), to work for armed revolution and the seizure of the state.

The initial Naxal uprising, led by Jangal Santal, an educated man of tribal origins, and Kanu Sanyal, a Brahman from the Naxalbari district, who spoke the tribal dialects, soon became Maoist in style and intention. Having failed to protect the tribal Santals from encroachments by money-lenders and others through legal measures, Sanyal and Santal organized an armed rebellion in May 1967, declared the area a 'liberated zone', and ordered police and officials to keep out. Local committees were formed to run the schools and courts. On 5 July the Chinese Communist official paper, *The People's Daily*, declared, SPRING THUNDER BREAKS OVER INDIA. The article went on to sketch a strategy of armed revolution, which envisaged mobilized militias of armed peasants circling India's cities and seizing power. A similar movement developed in the Srikakulam district of Andhra, among the Girijan, a mountain-dwelling tribal people. The Girijan had lost control of their forests to plainsmen, money-lenders and labour contractors who had bought up land on the Girijan reserves and now employed the Girijans, at extremely low wages, in conditions that resembled serfdom. Organized by Maoists, the Girijans seized land and crops, occupying 2000 acres. The landlords retaliated with their own private militias to battle with the Girijans, who were weak, armed largely only with axes, bows and arrows. By early 1968 the state had ceased to function in the region.

The theorist of Naxalism was Charu Mazumdar, from a rich peasant background and a communist since the 1940s, who developed the notion of the 'annihilation campaign'. The Indian state, he argued represented the interests of feudal princes, big landlords and bureaucratic capitalists, all sheltering under the umbrella of Congress. The electoral politics of the revisionist Marxists had, he insisted, failed and there was no alternative to an armed struggle. This, it was surmised, would be readily achievable in Indian as the state had no real popular support and once the spark of revolution was ignited, the whole country would soon be aflame. Peasants would lead the revolution, establishing one base after another. As he argued, 'they will eventually develop such areas from isolated points into a vast expanse . . . an expansion in a series of waves'. The first stage in the guerrilla war would be to create 'Red Terror', by embarking on especially brutal forms of killing to create an atmosphere of fear and panic.

Mazumdar had very particular ideas about the nature of this terror. In February 1970 he published an article, subsequently dubbed the 'murder manual': guerrilla units were to be formed in a wholly conspiratorial manner, on a one-to-one basis. He suggested that a poor peasant considered likely material should be approached and asked: 'Don't you think it is a good thing to finish off such and such a *jotedar* (landlord)?' If their answer was affirmative they would be secretly recruited into the local Naxalite cell. Mazumdar insisted that Naxalites should eschew guns and firearms in favour of knives, choppers, swords, rods and spears, because this would entail close physical contact with the enemy and would intensify the 'revolutionary hatred' required. 'He who has not dipped his hand in the blood of class enemies can hardly be called a communist', he declaimed. Naxalite attacks were thus peculiarly sadistic, and slogans were painted on the walls of victims' houses in their own blood. 'Blood for Blood . . . You murdered P.K., so we annihilate you all', thundered one. The Communist paper *Liberation* quoted another participant: 'I hit the agent on the head and killed him with one stroke, but it did not seem enough, so the peasants cut him into three pieces'; and another: 'After this [the killing] we then severed his head and hung it in front of his house and wrote in his blood slogans like "Long Live Chairman Mao".' Meanwhile, in Andhra 'class enemies' were routinely decapitated and their heads stuck on nearby gate posts.

Though Mazumdar had demanded that the uprisings be led by peasants themselves, the movement had attracted a following among college students, particularly those of the highly elite Presidency College of Calcutta – 'the flower of Bengal' as romantics imagined them. However, once in the countryside many of them felt revulsion at the realities of the annihilation campaign and were labelled 'doubtists' by the more doctrinally rigorous. Nevertheless, over time the movement became a curious alliance of largely tribal groups (steeped in the ethics of communitarianism) and elite ideologically charged students. In the more settled villages the extreme violence tended to alienate the poor peasantry it was intended to liberate. Because Mazumdar insisted on only 'word of mouth' propaganda, the Naxalites failed to justify their violence effectively, and the lurid killings of 'class enemies' often appeared to the peasants to be wanton murders of co-villagers by strangers. Bereft of broader peasant support, the Naxalites became increasingly reliant on socially marginal groups. They were often then dismissed in the Indian press as 'lumpen elements', and in subsequent official inquires as 'pseudo-political criminals', 'vagabonds' and 'bandits'.

These lumpen elements became even more conspicuous once the

campaign moved out of the villages of West Bengal and into the capital, Calcutta, in the spring of 1970. Once urbanized, the annihilation strategy was renamed the 'Cultural Revolution' in conscious imitation of its Chinese prototype. It took the form of attacks on schools and colleges, described as 'factories for class enemies', and iconoclastic violence against statues of the heroes of the Freedom Movement. Statues of Gandhi were especially popular targets, ironically given that only fifty years earlier he too had launched an all-out attack on British educational institutions in the same city. This aspect of the movement became immensely popular with schoolchildren, many seizing the opportunity to intimidate disliked masters and heads for wholly non-political motives. Nevertheless, enthusiastic observers predicted great things from this: 'Didn't the cultural revolution start in Peking University? Didn't Mao Tse-tung rely on young students, who are not hidebound but are full of energy and daring, to fire the first salvoes of the revolution?'

More convincing revolutionary salvoes were launched in August 1970 with the beginning of the 'Annihilation Campaign' proper. For a year Calcutta descended into an orgy of violence: Naxalite murder squads roamed the streets annihilating 'class enemies' with Mazumdar's approved weapons – knives, iron rods, spears and pipeguns. The latter was an especially inefficient form of homemade firearm that required a string to be pulled to release the bullet, making accuracy problematic. In August 1971 the Naxalites were themselves decapitated, though not by the state authorities – the ruling Congress state government having resigned in despair. A posse of armed persons (possibly recruited by the state) penetrated the Naxalite stronghold of Cossipore-Baranagore on 12–13 August and massacred between 70 and 100 Naxalites; the bodies could be spotted floating down the Ganges for some days afterwards. Naxalism in the city had been controlled. But at its peak law and order in Calcutta had all but broken down, with unpunished killings running, at one stage, at the rate of 60 per day, policemen, businessmen and politicians being the favoured targets. Indeed in a sense the project of Red Terror had been partially accomplished, for a career in professional politics had become so dangerous that hardly anyone in their right minds would contemplate it.

Though the Naxalite movement in both city and countryside was largely extinguished by the early 1970s, it had been at a heavy cost in terms of respect for established authority and the rule of law. Elected Governments in West Bengal had twice been suspended to make way for presidential power, and politics had been criminalized to a degree previously unheard of. In Calcutta the Congress party, which had an undistinguished record in dealing with the Naxalites (at one point it encouraged their attacks on other communists), was systematically recruiting *goondas* (thugs) and petty criminals known as *mastans*. This process appears to have begun when a group of *mastans* running a boxing club in south Calcutta fell out over the division of spoils garnered from a protection racket they were running over local cinemas. One group sought police help in the dispute, while the other enlisted the support of local Congress politicians to protect them from the police. Soon the *mastans* themselves were running the district Congress committee. This is surely not what Nehru had in mind when he contemplated Congress as the heart and soul of the new nation.

Where politics was not collapsing into urban gangsterism, it was degenerating into low-level civil war, as high-caste groups struck back at these challenges to their dominance. In the Naxalite-plagued villages of Bihar and West Bengal the police ceased to function, displaced by paramilitary 'syndicates', or private militias of rich and then later of middling peasants, known as *senas* (armies), committed to waging just war on real or imagined 'Naxal insurgents'. The phenomenon first appeared in the late 1960s, but by the mid-1970s *senas* had proliferated and reflected caste divisions pretty accurately: the Brahmarshi Sena was a high-caste outfit, the Bhumi Sena relied on youths of the Kurmi low-to-middle castes, while the Lorik Sena recruited from the middle caste Ahirs or Yadavs. Though these peculiar military-cum-devotional entities claimed they were defending the community, their real purpose was the intimidation of poorer groups. The consequence of this was that in north and central Bihar agricultural wage rates were now determined not by negotiation, nor by market forces, but by the relative balance of power between the armed might of the haves and have-nots.

The rise of the middle peasants, the grievances of the poor and the resort of the higher-castes to violence in the defence of their interests seriously undermined the ability of the system established by Nehru to contain the burgeoning political fall-out from democracy. The power and dominance of Congress had hitherto held in check the potentially violent conflicts between social and economic groups, but with the election results of 1967 it became clear that this always shaky edifice was crumbling. Congress's power at the centre had been seriously dented, and in eight of the regional states entirely swept away. Into the vacuum left in its wake poured chaos, as contending groups struggled for pre-eminence. A rag-tag group of rightist parties contended with various fractions of communism, and embryonic parties of the middle peasantry emerged as politicians previously loyal to Congress began to split away. But no clear alternative emerged from the wreckage to run the state. Instead an era of defection and counter-defection was ushered in, during which politicians elected under the banner of one party would, lured by a variety of blandishments and inducements (usually the promise of office or money), defect to another. Between 1967 and 1970 these manoeuvrings attained bizarre levels with nearly 2000 defections in the states, where the total number of legislative seats was only 3500. Weak coalition ministries toppled one after another like so many skittles. The result was that central rule, under the President's ordinance, had to be imposed in five states between 1967 and 1969.

In Uttar Pradesh Charan Singh led the attack on the Congress system when he and seventeen associates left the UP Congress government to form the Bharatiya Kranti Dal (BKD or People's Revolutionary Movement), ushering in thirteen changes of government in five years. In Bihar, too, parliamentary politics descended into chaos: three hundred days was the maximum lifespan of these whirligig regimes, and the shortest lasted a mere four. Moreover, this regional instability affected the power of the centre to impose any order, coherent policy or economic reform. In Uttar Pradesh much-needed legislation to tax the newly prosperous peasant farmers was consistently blocked, and in Bihar no progress was made on long-standing commitments to further land reform. It seemed that far from the centre dominating the regions, it was the states, and the newly emergent rich farmers, who threatened to engulf the centre.

But in February 1971 Congress made a stunning comeback. In the

General Election of that year Indira Gandhi won 350 of the 515 Lok Sabha seats, and restored the party to power at the centre, and in subsequent regional elections in eleven states. The principal right-wing opposition was decimated, winning a combined total of only 30 seats. Most striking was Congress's massive support among the poor, scheduled castes and minority groups – constituents who had begun to desert it only four years before. This was Mrs Gandhi's answer to Charan Singh's populism, a regime in which the ranks of politicians and vested interests that supposedly stood between the goodly government of New Delhi and the virtuous masses – obstructing reform, corruptly creaming off the wealth of the nation and, at their worst, promulgating violence and disorder – would be swept away. It appeared that Nehru's daughter had revivified the party as an alliance of high and low, not so much against the middle (though the middle peasants were a problematic constituency for her), but against the middlemen or political bosses that stood between her and the 'people' – the *Sholay* strategy writ large. However, the early success of this populist experiment later soured into dismal failure as the apparently re-empowered state proved too weak an instrument to by-pass entrenched vested interests, whether new or old, and far from cleansing the Augean stables of corruption and violence soiled them even more.

Indira Nehru was India's third Prime Minister, the daughter of its first and mother of its sixth. She was born in late 1917 just as the high tide of Gandhian nationalism was about to break over India. It is ironic that one to whom the soubriquet Mother India was so readily attached was, in reality, Daughter India – not simply Nehru's only child, but sole scion of a great dynastic political family, born into the political fray and never to escape it. Expectations of her were high, and the very earliest – that she be a boy – she could never fulfil (though, tellingly, she adopted the alter-ego and nickname of Indu-boy as a young adolescent). Despite this initial disappointment, she grew up freighted with 'destiny'. The first lines of *Glimpses of World History*, written by Nehru for his daughter, portentously noted that she had been born on the very same day as the Russian Revolution, and the nationalist poet Sarojini Naidu hailed her birth as the coming of 'the new soul of India'. Her earliest memories were of the Gandhian bonfires of foreign goods during the non-cooperation campaign, flames to which her own favourite clothes and dolls were consigned. At the age of four she was dandled on the knee of her grandfather Motilal during his first trial for civil disobedience as a knowingly manipulated symbol of the new India. A celebrity from an early age, she was recognized wherever she went, and a photograph of a thirteen-year-old Indira in Gandhi cap and *khadi* uniform flanked by her parents became a Congress icon. Closely acquainted with the Mahatma from infancy, it was she who squeezed the orange juice with which he broke his famous Poona fast-unto-death. But despite these highlights, her childhood was largely blighted by the nationalist cause. Her parents were frequently absent, either campaigning or in jail, the family finances were neglected (and ultimately ruined), and she herself finally experienced the rite of passage of all Congress luminaries, spending a gruelling nine months incarcerated during the Quit India rebellion of 1942. 'Politics is the centre of everything', she told the *New York Times* in the year she first became Prime Minister; and for her this had quite literally always been true.

Unsurprisingly, she developed a somewhat ambivalent attitude to her compelling destiny, on occasion attempting to escape it altogether, but also impelled by the logic of dynastic duty. At the age of eleven, in 1928, she had watched Motilal, ensconced in a stately carriage, drawn king-like through the streets to be inaugurated as Congress president; the following year it was her own father she saw atop a white charger parading through the streets of Lahore followed by outriders and an escort of elephants, also on his way to be inaugurated as Congress president – the first of many instances of Nehruvian dynastic succession in Congress's history. On becoming Prime Minister in 1966, she told Rajiv, her elder son, that the words of the poet Robert Frost had run incessantly through her mind: 'How hard it is to keep from being King, when it's in you and in the situation.' On the night when she was expelled from the party (some forty years after she had watched her father 'crowned' president of Congress), she tearfully reminisced about her family's long involvement with Congress, how she had been born into it at Anand Bhavan (Motilal Nehru's Allahabad palace), and how membership was her birthright:

Nobody can throw me out of Congress. It is not a legal question, nor one of passing a resolution . . . It is a question of the fibre of one's very heart and being.

Her mother, Kamala, was a very young woman from a high-caste but less westernized background than her father. Kamala was despised by some of the other women in Nehru's family for her lack of sophistication, though she soon learnt English, took an active role in Congress politics and, indeed, became something of a feminist. She was ill for most of Indira's life, and died of tuberculosis when her daughter was only seventeen. The neglect and condescension that Kamala suffered at the hands of her father's family rankled, fostering a bitterness that fed Indira's depressive, introverted personality and sense of being undervalued. Nehru himself was a fond, absent and extremely demanding father. Indira was the recipient of his many gaol-penned letters (written for publication), in which she was enjoined to study closely the careers of Joan of Arc, Garibaldi and Socrates, among others. And, although it seems likely that she too suffered from tuberculosis until her forties, he also chastised her for enjoying indifferent health. He had the highest hopes of her, as he confessed, though his idiosyncratic views on education meant that hers was erratic and disrupted. She attended a variety of diverse schools and colleges, from a primer for sons and daughters of political prisoners, a convent school in Allahabad, an interlude at a Swiss finishing school, a stint at Tagore's university of arts at Shantiniketan, and eventually ended up rather incongruously at an English girls' boarding school, Badminton, to be crammed for Oxford entrance. She briefly attended Oxford to read Modern History, but left after a year. Nevertheless she was not without accomplishments, speaking fluent French and Italian, and with an interest in art and design, which led her on later occasions to claim that ideally she would have liked a career as an interior designer. She certainly had an artistic bent and was extremely well-read, though Nehru's own works, with the exception of the *Discovery of India*, which she proof-read, did not figure among her favourites (indeed she complained that his *Glimpses of World History*, dedicated to her, was too bulky and unwieldy). Nevertheless she had, by her late teens, imbibed her father's internationalism and centre-left leanings. She was not, however, her father's stooge. In the late 1930s she became a strong anti-fascist and rowed with Nehru when he insisted that they visit the right-wing appeaser Lord Lothian. But the precise nature of her ideological proclivities is hard to discern, and as an active politician her decision-making seemed guided principally by pragmatic calculation rather than conviction. She always professed to be on the left, and as a young woman in London in the late 1930s she came into the orbit of the group of radical and communist Indian students for whom the brilliant, if unstable, Krishna Menon was the focal point. One of these was Feroze Gandhi, who had been an acolyte of her mother Kamala's many years earlier, and whom Indira was later to marry. Others included P. N. Haksar, then studying with Malinowski at the London School of Economics, but later to become one of her chief political advisers. Another was Mohan Kumaraman-galam, an Etonian communist, and later an influential member of her cabinet. An intriguing display of her leftism was noted at the Oxford Majlis (an Indian debating society), during a debate on the proposition that Congress's politics were insufficiently revolutionary. Though Indira did not speak, her hand was seen to rise in favour of the motion at the end. Moreover, despite extreme reticence about public speaking, she was so appalled by the treatment of blacks in Durban where she stopped off on her return to India in 1941, that she made an impromptu speech comparing white colonialism and the colour bar to the Nazi persecution of the Jews.

Her husband, Feroze Gandhi, was an exuberant extrovert of Parsi background and the marriage was controversial. Indeed, like every-thing in her life, it soon became a public issue and heated debates ensued in the national press about Feroze's suitability. Nehru was opposed and even the Mahatma himself became involved (he approved, but suggested that the marriage should be celibate). But Indira showed iron resolve and the marriage was made and produced two sons. Feroze became an MP in 1952 and joined Indira in the prime-ministerial residence in New Delhi, where she had been living as political consort and domestic amanuensis to Nehru since the late 1940s. Relations between the two were not good. Feroze was a womanizer, who, moreover, adopted an oppositional stance to his illustrious father-in-law and was prominent in exposing the high-level corruption scandals that dogged Nehru's last ministries. He and Nehru did not get on; one lunch guest at Teen Murti reported that Feroze sat in complete silence over lunch except to contradict each and every opinion proffered by Nehru, ranging from the quality of the food to the trajectory of international politics.

Mrs Gandhi appears to have been at her happiest as Nehru's help-meet, organizing official dinners, bringing up her sons (she took a great interest in theories of child-rearing) and managing the family zoo. Inevitably, however, her proximity to power drew her into the political realm. Nehru himself seems to have decided by this stage that Indira was not the right material for a high-level political life, and she herself toyed with the idea of leaving India altogether and moving to England where her sons were being educated in the early 1960s. But others had very different ideas. Many, like Nehru, under-estimated her ability and will-power; indeed she had to endure endless insults, condescension and disparagement both before and after she entered politics. Tired perhaps of the various dismissive or insulting labels, ranging from dumb doll to evil genius, she once quipped that since no one could agree on her identity a seminar should be held to establish whether she was 'Hitler, Stalin, Mussolini or George III'. But clearly to many it was her own name that made her a priceless political asset. From the mid-1950s she was encouraged by people on both the left and right of Congress to dip a toe into active politics. She began in earnest in 1958 when she consented, with genuine reluctance, to stand for the Congress presidency. Indeed, she seems to have been goaded into agreement by reports in the press that she wasn't up to it. She won the election easily and at the subsequent celebrations concluded her inaugural address with a quote from a popular Hindi film song:

> We are the women of India
> Don't imagine us as flower maidens
> We are the sparks in the fire.

By nature well-organized, she made a success of the Congress presi-dency and other party jobs. And after her father's death she became a cabinet minister in his successor, Shastri's, short-lived government. But in 1966, following Shastri's sudden death, she was pressed by the party hierarchy to become Prime Minister herself, and now she accepted without much demurral. The group of regional party bosses, known by the sinister tag of the Syndicate, that ran Congress, saw in her a useful stopgap leader and a valuable hustings prop for the forthcoming 1967 General Elections. Her role was to be a pliant cipher, holding the fort while the big men fought out the leadership battle proper. But it was very soon apparent that Indira did not see herself as a cipher, pliant or otherwise.

The situation she inherited in 1966 was unenviable. The economy was suffering from food shortages, industrial stagnation and inflation, with near-famine conditions in parts of India. The latest five-year plan had stalled and there were signs of growing disillusionment with Congress in the country. To deal with the short-term food and financial crises Mrs Gandhi adopted a pragmatic, some said rightist, strategy. She paid a much-heralded visit to the USA, and while she insisted this was merely routine diplomatic protocol and she would not be taking a 'begging bowl' with her, that is precisely what she did. President Johnson and his advisers, knowing that India was desperate for aid, struck a very tough deal: in return for three million tons of food aid and $9 million in cash, they insisted on a swingeing cut (57 per cent) in the value of the rupee, more investment opportunities in India's protected market and the creation of high-level Indo-American educational projects intended to pull India more closely into the orbit of the west. Though Congress economic advisers had already recommended devaluation, when it came at the behest of the USA it was regarded by party leaders as deeply humiliating, as was the concession of greater American influence over Indian education. Both measures were depicted by left and right as examples of blatant neo-colonialism and Mrs Gandhi was censured for her weakness. This sense of humiliation was not alleviated by the manner in which the Americans dispensed their assistance, employing a drip-feed 'ship-to-mouth' policy of releasing the grain in tiny amounts on a month-by-month basis in order to squeeze the maximum amount of political leverage from the deal. This was the period during which Johnson was escalating the war in Vietnam, and it seems that Mrs Gandhi had also agreed to curb Indian criticism of American foreign policy.

From this point Indira's position as Prime Minister became very precarious. Her supporters on the right now abandoned her, and Congress's less than stellar performance in the 1967 elections did nothing to improve her standing with them. Indeed, immediately after the elections she suffered a leadership challenge from her father's old enemy on the right of the party, Morarji Desai. Desai was a senior cabinet minister and the chief political boss of Gujarat. He was also a highly orthodox Hindu devotee of Gandhi, who had taken a vow of celibacy at 27 and rejected all forms of western medicine in favour of drinking a glass of his own urine every morning. Until now his relations with the rest of the Syndicate had been very poor, and indeed both Shastri's and Mrs Gandhi's premierships had been choreographed with the more or less explicit aim of blocking his ascendancy. However, the devaluation crisis and other signs of prime-ministerial recalcitrance to the Syndicate's bidding had, for the first time, united him and the other party bosses in their determination to get rid of her. Though she survived this latest leadership challenge, she was forced to make Desai deputy prime minister – a dilution of authority that Nehru had never endured. Desai did not hesitate to make his contempt for her obvious, referring to her publicly as a mere *chokri* (slip of a girl), and excluding her from top-level discussions on the economy, saying 'Indirabehn [sister Indira], you don't understand this matter. Let me deal with it.'

Between the elections of 1967 and the Congress split of 1969 there were proliferating signs that Mrs Gandhi was rethinking her political strategy and abandoning the pragmatic, rightwards drift she had followed since 1966. Given that her key enemies were on the right, that she had been humiliated by the Americans and that the 1967 election results had delivered handsome rewards to India's various communist parties, there was logic in her apparent strategy of moving to the left herself. Freeing herself from reliance on the Syndicate, she sought new allies in the Congress Forum for Socialist Action, a ginger group of ex-communists and communist sympathizers to which Feroze Gandhi had belonged. This group hoped to re-energize Congress as a grass roots party dedicated to socialist transformation, and saw in Mrs Gandhi, whom some of them had known in London in the 1930s, a powerful ally. This set the scene for a reprise of old skirmishes dating back to the 1930s and 1940s, when the battle had been joined for control of Congress between the left and the right. On previous occasions the right had prevailed, aided in part by the mediating efforts of Gandhi, the organizational muscle of Sardar Patel and the pliancy of Nehru. But this time they faced a more formidable opponent, not in Mrs Gandhi, but in P. N. Haksar.

In May 1967 Mrs Gandhi appointed Haksar, her old friend from student days and a communist sympathizer, as her principal private secretary in the prime-ministerial secretariat, and together they comprised a team of supremely astute political tacticians who effectively plotted the overthrow of the Congress old guard. Their motives appear to have blended genuine ideological impulse with a gut determination to stay in power. Haksar had written the famous Ten-Point Programme which became official Congress policy after the 1967 elections, the most striking elements of which were plans to nationalize India's top banks and to abolish the large state incomes paid to India's former princes. These two measures were intended to generate much needed capital for investment in infrastructure and other developmental schemes now languishing for lack of money, and to appease the country's farmers and small businessmen with cheap loans. Though the Syndicate endorsed these radical propositions, they did so, as they had under Nehru, confident that any real radicalism would perish in endless factional bargaining and bureaucratic foot-dragging. But they had miscalculated. Determined to out manoeuvre her rightist opponents, Mrs Gandhi readily seized on Haksar's scheme to sack Desai from the Finance Ministry, take over the post herself and proceed with the nationalization of the banks by ordinance. This was duly accomplished in July 1969. Desai and the Syndicate were stunned; the Indian poor were delighted. The measure was presented as a transfer of wealth from monopolists to the masses. The latter, promised a jamboree of easy credit, danced jubilantly on the streets.

Bank nationalization was, however, part of a longer tactical game. For some months the right had been moving once again to oust Mrs Gandhi. This time the plan consisted of imposing on her a new Indian President, Sanjiva Reddy, with whom it was known she could not work, over her preferred candidate V. V. Giri. Had they succeeded she would have had little choice but to resign. But the hunters soon became the hunted. Mrs Gandhi responded by insisting that the choice of new President should be a vote of conscience, thus freeing Congress Lok Sabha members from the obligation to vote for the official Congress candidate. It was also made clear, covertly, that she did not support the official candidate. This was essentially a gamble on the careerism of Congress MPs, who, having witnessed the massive surge of popularity for the Prime Minister in the wake of the bank nationalization, did not wish to lose her as party leader and chief electoral mascot. This risky wager paid ample rewards and the official Congress candidate was defeated in favour of V. V. Giri. Such perfidy was too much for the Syndicate, and in December 1969 Mrs Gandhi was charged with disloyalty and expelled from the party. Anticipating this move, she and Haksar immediately 'requisitioned' a meeting of Congress MPs still loyal to her, and declared this group to be the authentic Congress (R) (Requisitioned). The Syndicate's wing of the party retained most of the organizational muscle of the old Congress and was hence dubbed Congress (O) (Organization). And so, after 75 years of fractious unity, the Indian National Congress had finally split.

Though Mrs Gandhi was able to remain in power with the support of her rump of Congress MPs, informally supported by communists, she decided to bring the next General Election forward one year and India went to the polls in March 1971. Electoral pundits confidently predicted that, denuded of the grassroots organizational machinery of the old united Congress, Congress (R) would be lucky to win more than one third of parliamentary seats. They were, therefore, confounded by her extraordinary sweep of nearly two-thirds of the Lok Sabha. But her victory was not about organization but personal charisma. Newly recruited party workers and volunteers pledged themselves not to the party but to her personally. The young proved particularly susceptible to heroine worship and the previously moribund Congress Youth Movement sprang into life to rally the urban vote for her. In the countryside the vacuum of organization was filled with Mrs Gandhi's own person. Old Congress heroes like Nehru and Gandhi received scant mention, and instead she herself was carefully projected as a symbol of change. Her face beamed not only from posters but from Mao-style badges, stamped in their hundreds of thousands and pinned to the breasts of peasant supporters. Meanwhile

Mrs Gandhi herself undertook exhausting whistle-stop tours of marginal rural constituencies, covering 30,000 miles by plane and helicopter, and another 3000 by road and rail. She spent 41 days on the campaign trail and addressed 409 gatherings, reaching, it was estimated, 20 million people.

The intention, amply fulfilled, was to insist that she personally, not the party, embodied a renewed commitment to delivering social justice. The previous slow progress of reform, she explained, had been caused by obstructive party bosses and she appealed for a decisive electoral mandate to strengthen her hands against the forces of reaction. Her speeches were simple, homely and effective. Already in the 1967 elections there had been signs that Indira was developing a style of political rhetoric that skilfully wove her dynastic legacy of sacrifice with her womanly persona into the image of mother of the nation:

My family is not confined to a few individuals. It consists of crores of people. Your burdens are comparatively light, because your families are limited and viable. But my burden is manifold because crores of my family members are poverty-stricken and I have to look after them. Since they belong to different castes and creeds, they sometimes fight among themselves, and I have to intervene, especially to look after the weaker members of my family, so that the stronger ones do not take advantage of them.

In the 1971 campaign she extemporized on this theme of maternal valour. Referring to herself as merely a 'weak and frail' woman, she painted a picture of herself battling the multi-headed demon of boss-ism and rich vested interests for popular justice. Congress (O) was portrayed as a claque of factional 'big-men' who, caring nothing for little people, had contracted marriages of convenience with princes and other forces of reaction, with whom they shared only one common goal – 'Indira Hatao' (remove Indira). To this she developed a brilliant response which both personalized the struggle and collapsed complex economic issues into a simple formula:

> Kuch log kehtai hai, Indira hatao,
> Mai kehti hu, garibi hatao.
> (Some people say, get rid of Indira,
> I say, get rid of poverty.)

The scale of the Congress (R) victory was greeted as little short of a miracle, or certainly the product of some kind of magic. Astounded opponents suggested the polls must have been rigged through the use of invisible ink and chemically treated ballot papers shipped in from the Soviet Union. But the election victory was undeniably Mrs Gandhi's personal triumph, and to this she added later in the same year the prestige of becoming a successful wartime leader, as the Indian armed forces decisively defeated those of West Pakistan (now Pakistan) during the war over East Pakistan (Bangladesh). The conflict began when Indian forces intervened to halt a campaign of repression by West Pakistan against a secessionist movement in East Pakistan which had forced millions of refugees to cross into Indian West Bengal. In December 1971 West Pakistan launched a surprise air attack, but the Indian army, which had already formulated a plan for the efficient takeover of East Pakistan, rebuffed the attack and swiftly achieved an all-out victory. In one fell swoop the new state of Bangladesh was created and Pakistan's pretensions to equal status with India in the region destroyed. The triumphant war was seen as yet another example of Mrs Gandhi's almost mystical powers (though Haksar was behind the strategy). Her divinity was now actively asserted. Some offered prayers to her image, while others contented themselves with comparisons to Mother India, the omnipotent mother goddess, Durga the Goddess of war, and Shakti, the very incarnation of female energy.

Goddess or not, Mrs Gandhi's vivisection of Congress and subsequent landslide electoral victory were events of undeniable import in the history of Indian politics. The very scale of her support, now unmediated by party middlemen, vote-banks and the old-school paraphernalia of the 'Congress System', was proof that increasingly large sections of the Indian electorate could, and would, vote independently. This, in turn, could only be a reflection of a profound challenge to the culture of hierarchy and deference that had hitherto bound Indian society. Whatever the shortcomings of the Nehruvian decades, they had undoubtedly brought emancipation of sorts to the Indian masses. Under his daughter the era of machine politics and the mechanics of the vote bank had given way to that of the charismatic populist. But this was a dangerous role to play and could easily metamorphose into that of authoritarian demi-god of the plebiscite.

Having severed the Gordian knot of Congress factionalism that had bound her father and frustrated radical reform, Indira was able to concentrate in her own person not only overwhelming charismatic authority, but also the effective instruments of state power. By the early 1970s under Haksar's tutelege, the powers of the Prime Minister's office had undoubtedly flourished. It now controlled the Indian intelligence services and revenue information, routinely circumvented cabinet and departmental decisions and was supported by a 'committed bureaucracy', in which recruits were scrutinized for their political convictions in order to reduce official obstreperousness. Indira now controlled the choice of party candidates across India, and was able to reduce the previously entrenched and truculent chief ministers of the regions into docile poodles entirely dependent on her favour. Attempts, less successful, were also made to curb the powers of over-mighty judges, who were empowered under the constitution to block populist policies affecting property rights. All of this was done in the name of 'democracy', now interpreted not as a delicate equilibrium of checks and balances, but as brute people power, embodied in the prime-ministerial mandate. In place of the old Congress system now stood Mrs Gandhi's pyramid. But for what purpose would this impressive concentration of puissance and prestige now be employed?

To her enemies on the right the answer seemed clear enough. According to Mrs Gandhi the Congress split was about ideology, and in the course of the struggle she wrote an open letter to all members of Congress:

What we witness today is not a mere clash of personalities and certainly not a fight for power. It is a conflict between two outlooks and attitudes in regard to the objectives of the Congress ... It is a conflict between those who are for socialism and change ... and those who are for the status quo ... The Congress stands for democracy, secularism and socialism ... But within Congress has been a group which did not have total faith in these objectives ... I know that this group constantly tried to check and frustrate my father's attempts to bring about far-reaching economic and social changes.

It seemed then that she was committed to a socialist model – indeed she had the constitution amended to proclaim India a democratic, secular and *socialist* republic. And her stunning victory had been accomplished with much assistance from the Marxist left, not only in the ideas of her various communist-sympathizing advisers, but also in electoral deals with the communists themselves. Her opponents insisted Haksar was a Soviet stooge and that Mrs Gandhi was planning to sell India to the Russians, but her victory was so categorical that she could now easily dispense with the support of the communists – advisory or otherwise. Moreover, her own speeches suggested that something rather less than full-blown socialism was her intention. Just before the election she subtly appealed to an association of businessmen that if they funded her and not her opponents their interests would be better served:

In other countries whole classes have been wiped out ... We are trying to have a kind of change that will prevent it, which will be peaceful, which will give a place to all in our community without thinking of wiping them out.

She told the Indian journalist Kuldip Nayar, 'If I don't do anything to take the wind out of the sails of the Communists, the entire country will go Red.' And, in the wake of bank nationalization she assured the assembled crowd at the Independence Day celebrations:

I want to assure the rich and the capitalists that the step is not directed against them. It is only in the interests of the people, and a measure that is in the interests of the masses is in their interest also.

The 1971 election manifesto promised modestly to reduce 'glaring disparities in income and opportunities', but also to 'give scope to the private sector to play its proper role in the economy'. The propertied middle class was promised stability and economic growth which only a strong Congress central government could deliver. Meanwhile the poor were largely offered hope. This was not socialism but a symbolic populism, confined to politically costless gestures like bank nationalization and the abolition of princely privilege, but barely touching the essential interests of commercial and landed groups.

Moreover, even when the commitment to radicalism was more deep-seated experience soon revealed that personal charisma, despite being coupled with greater state power, was not enough. Mrs Gandhi's pyramid was built on quicksand. Having bypassed party bosses, departmental officials, state functionaries, awkward judges and the like, she could still get nothing done. Her only real commitment to radical structural reform seems to have been the fulfilment of promises of greater equality in the countryside. But this soon foundered. Without an effective party organization it proved just as difficult to impose policies at the grassroots level as it had under Nehru. Indeed it was more difficult. In some ways she had become the victim of her own success: her astounding electoral victory had made Congress an attractive vehicle again, and so many of the old vested interests, and some new ones, recolonized it. But the decay of the old institutional structure meant the end of membership dues which had helped finance elections, and in their place came the commercialization of politics. The corruption and trafficking in office already apparent in the Nehru years became endemic as gangsters, shady characters and other varieties of political entrepreneurs entered the electoral field with plump purses and the expectation of a good return on their investment.

A more profound obstacle to Mrs Gandhi's populist policies in the countryside was the continuing rise of the commercialized peasantry, who felt that they had been neglected in the Nehru years. Now increasingly well organized into interest groups, they resisted all attempts to tax them, to charge them for their state-subsidized electricity or to collect interest on their state-financed loans. Efforts to redistribute land foundered again on the rocks of entrenched farmer opposition. Ram Dass, a landless dalit in bondage to the local landlord in a remote district of Uttar Pradesh, had greeted Mrs Gandhi as a Messiah of the poor, but recalled: 'Nothing much happened to me from Mrs Gandhi's promises of *Garibi Hatao*. My family was left as poor as we always were. There used to be orders from government: *Hatao, Hatao, Hatao*. But who will remove poverty? The orders came from government but they just stayed on paper.' Though the government launched yet another campaign to impose land-holding ceilings of 10 to 20 acres for the best irrigated land, those with privately owned irrigation were allocated far higher ceilings of another 27 acres of irrigated and up to 54 acres of 'dry' land or orchards – a major victory for the rich farm lobby. As Ram Dass commented of the Indira years:

There were some small improvements . . . Almost none of the scheduled castes had any land. This did change because of Indira Gandhi's *Garibi Hatao*. But today, it is only the *thakurs* and some of the middle castes who have enough land to feed their families from . . . All the landless people in the village have got titles to land, but some were never able to take possession . . . The *thakurs* threatened that they would cut us into pieces if we tried . . . they filed legal cases against our taking over the plots, and we poor people were ensnared in these cases for years . . . Some of them don't even know today where the land is that they have been allotted.

In the end the ambitious hopes of achieving a peaceful revolution in the countryside shrank to well-meaning but ineffective welfare schemes. While some of these projects had positive results, many were essentially doles which placed an even greater burden on already overstretched state finances. This was the first lesson of populism – it entailed ruinous outlay with very little return. And when in 1972 the harvest failed, and in 1973 international oil prices rocketed, the second lesson was swiftly driven home: power that arrives in a populist wave can be just as easily washed away in a tsunami of populist opposition.

By 1974 India was in the grip of a full-blown economic crisis. Industrial output had been stagnating since the late 1960s with conse-quent shortages of consumer goods; food was rationed, and oil price rises had pushed inflation to 30 per cent. Attempts to requisition cheap grain from the nation's farmers had failed, but had caused great anger; the state had been forced to impose cuts on public spending and public sector incomes were falling way behind prices. People now joked that the slogan '*Garibi hatao*' (get rid of poverty), had, in fact, meant 'get rid of the poor'. Meanwhile, public life after the Indira wave slid steadily into a swamp of petty and grand corruption, graft, black-marketeering and general criminalization, in the midst of which popular resentment simmered.

On 1 January 1974 students at the Morvi Engineering College in the state of Gujarat rioted over their spiralling hostel charges; running amok, they destroyed Rs. 300,000 worth of laboratory equipment. Four days later they were joined by striking students at the L. D. Engineering College in Ahmedabad, who rampaged through their lecture halls and residences wrecking everything in their wake. The State Reserve Police intervened, and with exceptional brutality the

rioting students were quelled. But not for long. Demonstrations provoked by the police action resulted in the creation of the Nav Nirman
Yuvak Samiti (Youth Reconstruction Committee), which comprised
not merely youths but university professors, teachers, lawyers, doctors, housewives and all manner of the outraged middle classes. For
two months the Nav Nirman movement staged state-wide protests,
processions, silent marches, relay fasts, bus-hijackings, *thali* (tin plate)
bashing, effigy burnings, mock courts and macabre pantomime –
funerals of Indira Gandhi and the Gujarat Congress chief minister,
Chimanbhai Patel.

Patel was a corpulent sometime college principal who had risen to
power through the serpentine and murky networks that now passed
for Congress organization in the wake of the great 1969 split. His
power was based on an alliance with the leaders of the state's farmer
castes, a deal sealed at the luxurious Panchavati farm near Ahmedabad
(a location much mocked in opposition slogans). He had then
embarked on an orgy of shady wheeler-dealing: his election had been
bankrolled by a claque of peanut oil magnates, after which food oil
prices soared. He was also involved in complex negotiations with the
Delhi government to divert scarce grain to Uttar Pradesh, in return
for which he would get the cash to begin work on the controversial
Narmada Dam project. The upshot of all this was astronomic food
prices and fury about the manipulation of the state's resources to
please New Delhi. The Nav Nirman movement was determined to
have his scalp, and, now that politics had poured anarchically on
to the streets, they got it. In March 1975 he resigned and President's
Rule was imposed from New Delhi.

However, this merely fed the popular appetite for political blood.
Fury was now focused on the entire Gujarat State Assembly, whose
resignation was demanded, as was that of Indira Gandhi herself,
routinely denounced as a witch. By now demonstrations had spread to
the villages. Members of the provincial Legislative Assembly (MLAs)
were confronted by angry constituents, their families menaced, their
homes surrounded by baying crowds in a new form of political action,
the *gherao* (encirclement). Several Congress politicians were debagged
and paraded through the streets on donkeys. Unsurprisingly, within
a fortnight 95 MLAs had resigned. Unappeased, the students moved

on to New Delhi and there enlisted the opportunistic support of Indira's old *bête noire*, Morarji Desai, who on 11 March embarked on a Gandhi-style fast to force fresh elections in Gujarat. Desai was now 79, and not wanting his demise on her conscience, Mrs Gandhi submitted. On the 15th the Gujarat Assembly was dissolved and new elections were scheduled for June. It seemed that mobilization could bring astounding rewards, though at the cost of 103 lives and 832 arrests.

Further evidence that popular pressures were threatening the government had come in May 1974 when the whole of India was gripped by a massive rail workers' strike. Nearly one and a half million rail workers, almost 10 per cent of the entire public sector, were demanding an eight-hour working day, and a 75 per cent increase in wages. The leader of the union, George Fernandes, had made menacing speeches:

Realize the strength which you possess. Seven days' strike of the Indian Railways – every [power] station in the country would close down. A ten-day strike – every steel mill in India would close down ... A fifteen-day strike in the Indian Railways – the country will starve.

Though the strike was swiftly and brutally extinguished it did succeed in causing acute food shortages and near-famine conditions in some parts of India. Moreover, it was notable as the first example of a strike aimed not at a regional, but at the national government in New Delhi.

This new phase of populism now assumed an even more threatening form in a state on the other side of India, one as indigent as Gujarat was affluent – Bihar. Taking up the baton almost the moment the Gujaratis laid it down, Bihar erupted on 18 March. Students began agitating in Patna for the dissolution of the state assembly, and within a week 27 people were killed in a botched police effort to restore order. Like Gujarat, the students of Bihar quickly found a figurehead for their movement, in the unlikely form of Jayaprakash Narayan. Narayan, along with Desai, was virtually the last living vestige of the heroic age of nationalism, but he had considerably more charisma than the urine-sipping Gujarati. A close friend of Nehru, sometime socialist and now a born-again Gandhian, he had impeccable political credentials as the voice of morality in a world of soiled and sordid politics. For the previous 25 years Narayan had abjured active politics in favour of Gandhian social work among the poor peasants of Bihar. He had been brooding for a while on the state of the State and had developed a superficially appealing, if rather vague notion of *Sampurna Kranti* (Total Revolution). This seemed to entail not merely the removal of the Bihar government, but an all-out assault on the causes of backwardness in Bihar, and, beyond that, in the whole of India. Narayan's political elixir was a blend of Gandhian arcadianism and Indian-style socialism. What was needed, he insisted, was *lok-niti* (people politics), not *raj-niti* (ruler politics), which would wipe out corruption and restore civil liberties. He demanded the creation of a 'communitarian society', based on village councils or *panchayats*, from which, apparently, 'partyless democracy' would mysteriously emerge. He created *Chhatra* (student) and *Jana* (people's) *Sangharsh Samitis* (Struggle Committees), which would somehow simultaneously bring about the fall of the New Delhi regime and the 'uplift' of India's village poor. Despite a proliferation of seminars and study groups devoted to the exegetical minutiae of these lofty musings, it remained unclear how exactly, once the corrupt governments of Bihar and New Delhi had been ejected, this utopia would be created. Moreover, Jayaprakash, now 72 and afflicted with a variety of heart, kidney and prostate ailments, seemed less than ideally placed to lead any kind of revolution, total or otherwise.

The JP Movement (JPM) was, in fact, yet another populist cure-all to go with Charan Singh's *Bharat*, and Mrs Gandhi's *Garibi Hatao* movement. Nevertheless his endorsement of the student protests in Patna had an electrifying effect. Its populist appeal was readily apparent and soon drew in a constituency way beyond that of aggrieved adolescents. *Sampurna Kranti* crystallized a generalized sense of injustice at the failings and corruption of the existing system. And certainly Bihar was an almost perfect case study in the collapse of good government and public probity. Narayan's movement to depose corrupt government appeared, albeit briefly, to unite all shades of opposition, from Hindu religious right to Maoist revolutionary left. But there were also signs that Narayan's challenge was running out of steam and that the appetite for popular protests was waning. But it then received a boost from an unexpected quarter.

Some months before, a little known side-kick of Charan Singh, the journalist Raj Narain, who had been Mrs Gandhi's opponent in the election battle for her own Uttar Pradesh constituency of Rae Bareilly, had brought a case to the courts charging the Prime Minister with misuse of state resources during her campaign. The charges related to the presence of a civil servant as a party-political aide, the commandeering of an Indian Airforce plane and the deployment of state employees to erect podiums and public-address systems for election rallies. And in mid-June 1975 the court finally announced its judgment: Mrs Gandhi had indeed been guilty of election offences, a ruling which, if upheld, would bar her from office for six years. Moreover, the day before the judgment the results of the Gujarat elections were announced – a landslide victory for Congress's opponents, a newly formed coalition of forces known as the Janata Front. Overnight the Prime Minister had become a lame duck.

For a fortnight it was unclear what would happen. Attempting to fight populist fire with populist fire, pro-Indira rallies were orchestrated. Fleets of Delhi buses were diverted from their habitual routes, delivering their bewildered occupants to 'spontaneous' demonstrations of support outside 1 Safdarjang Road (the prime-ministerial residence). Specially chartered trains trundled into New Delhi from as far afield as Varanasi and Lucknow bearing crowds of Indira fans. Supplied with hot drinks and snacks (and, some muttered darkly, money), they would chant 'Indira *Zindabad*' (long-live Indira) on the prime-ministerial lawn for hours. But the opposition was not to be outdone. Once the court ruling was announced a *Lok Sangharsh Samiti* (Committee for the People's Struggle) was formed headed by Morarji Desai, which demanded Mrs Gandhi's resignation and began organizing a *gherao* of her residence. Jayaprakash announced a massive Gandhian *satyagraha* (civil-disobedience campaign) to force her resignation. And a mass rally was planned at Delhi's gargantuan Ramlila grounds at which, it was said, he would call on the police and army not to obey 'wrong orders'. At midnight on 25 June the Indian President declared a state of National Emergency. All opposition leaders, critical politicians, certain judges and a few recalcitrant journalists, along with various princes and their mothers, were arrested. Meanwhile the nation's presses ground to a halt as supplies of electricity were cut to their print shops. Democracy had been indefinitely suspended.

The various agitations of the previous eighteen months had essentially been manifestations of the same phenomenon, populism. But populism – the mobilization of groups behind simplistic anti-elite slogans, unrealistic expectations, the vilification of political opponents, and the promulgation of the notion that if one controlled the state all would be well – was a political strategy championed most effectively by Mrs Gandhi herself. It was a high-stakes game in a society as fluid and divided as India's and she was now paying the price.

Mrs Gandhi, ignoring advice from Haksar and others that the protests were transitory and did not require the pressing of the 'panic button', decided that disaster would ensue if the opposition were not suppressed. She cited in justification the vagueness and indiscipline of the JPM, and, more particularly, its association with the Jan Sangh and the RSS. These latter entities were components of the Hindu nationalist right which aimed to revise the Indian constitution's commitment to secularism. They were well organized, the RSS in particular operating as a kind of paramilitary scout-movement with drilled ranks of young student volunteers. In the absence of its own organizational structures, the JPM had become quite reliant on the RSS, allowing Mrs Gandhi to denounce the whole movement and the court case against her as evidence of a potential 'proto-fascist' putsch. 'Forces seeking to strangle democracy [are] similar to those which backed the rise of Nazism in Germany,' she raged. 'If the Jan Sangh comes to power, it will not need an emergency. It will chop off heads.'

Moreover, she claimed, these 'forces' were not working alone, but had become willing tools wielded by a 'foreign hand', namely the CIA, which was, she insisted, plotting her overthrow, if not her assassination. Though lurid, this scenario was not entirely implausible. Mrs Gandhi had enjoyed poor relations with the USA ever since her humiliating aid-seeking visit of 1966. Her swing to the left domestically, accompanied by renewed warmth towards the Soviet Union, had not improved matters. More specifically, her support for the East Pakistan secessionist movement and the creation of Bangladesh had antagonized the US, then a close ally of Pakistan's. And, within less than a year of becoming president in Bangladesh in early 1975 her ally Sheikh Mujibur Rahman, had been assassinated. Added to this circumstantial evidence were Indian and Soviet intelligence reports that seemed to support suspicions of a planned coup, and also the chilling example of Salvador Allende, the socialist President of Chile who had been killed in 1973 and replaced by General Pinochet, an acknowledged friend of the USA. Fidel Castro, who was close to Indira, insisted that the Americans had similar plans for her. The similarity between the pot-and-pan demonstrations by Chilean housewives against Allende and the *thali*-bashing matrons of Gujarat struck the Prime Minister as no coincidence. And Narayan's call to the army and police to disobey 'wrong orders' was depicted as incitement to mutiny.

Changing international attitudes to development seem also to have influenced Mrs Gandhi's reasoning. In the late 1960s and early 1970s the economic success of the East Asian Tigers – Singapore, South Korea and Taiwan – was much remarked upon and thought to be the consequence of their undemocratic polities. Many in the international financial community, including the World Bank and the IMF, had begun theorizing a possible correlation between political authoritarianism and economic development. Indeed, within a year of the suspension of democracy both heaped praise upon the economic performance of the Emergency regime. Mrs Gandhi seems to have viewed the Emergency as a chance to pursue the economic goals she had failed to achieve democratically. Her experience since 1971 suggested that the vested interests entrenched in, and the new forces released by, democracy had wrestled one another to stalemate, and the consequence was chronic and deepening economic crisis. In an interview immediately after the Emergency was imposed she bemoaned the selfish, anti-social behaviour and politically destabilizing indiscipline of her countrymen. Comparing them to a flaccid new-born baby, she asserted that they needed to be 'slapped and shaken' into life, and that the country needed 'shock treatment'. During the Emergency itself, chief ministers and party workers were summoned to workshops and lectured on the wasteful garrulousness of legislative politics, and the importance of action. Informing these perceptions were her very particular personal history, psychology and, perhaps, isolation. Her sense of responsibility, if not destiny, as scion of the Nehru clan seems to have engendered a genuine conviction that only she personally could save democracy and India from the forces threatening it. Interviewed after the Emergency was over, she asked rhetorically: 'Had Gandhiji seen a threat to India, how would he have reacted?'

Though the Emergency entailed a suspension of civil liberties, the repression of opponents and press censorship, it was in many ways merely an intensification of the centralized and personalized form of government Indira had initiated in 1971, with its reliance on top-down fiat, rule by bureaucrats and sloganizing. Posters pasted on buses and the walls of government offices, and nailed to trees and lamp-posts across India, proclaimed: 'The Leader's Right, The Future's Bright', 'She Stands Between Chaos and Order', 'Discipline is the Watchword of the Hour', 'The Only Magic is to Remove Poverty', 'Talk Less, Work More', and the worrying 'Marching to a Better Tomorrow'. More tangible policies were embodied in the much heralded '20 point programme'. But the magical 20 points amounted to little more than the populist package she had presented before: promises of land reform, the abolition of bonded labour, an end to rural debt, higher agricultural wages, lower prices and a war on tax evasion.

But in its first few months at least, the Emergency seemed to be working. Peace reigned across the nation's troubled campuses; students abandoned their *bandhs* (sit-ins) and *gheraos* and returned meekly to their libraries and examination halls. The number of man-days lost in strikes tumbled from over 40 million in 1974 to 13 million in 1976. Prices fell, the rupee stabilized, the blackmarket shrank as 2000 smugglers were gaoled, along with grain hoarders and tax evaders, and the income from taxes increased by 27 per cent. Businesses were the chief beneficiaries: they were promised no further nationalization, an easing of controls and licensing procedures and support against workers. Virtually all strikes were banned and statutory bonuses (a form of deferred income) slashed. Industrial productivity rose, as did food output, though this was largely due to fewer strikes and more rain. Orderliness broke out: stray cows disappeared from the streets of Delhi, as did also, and more disturbingly, the beggars; clerks attended their offices, and queues replaced the angry throngs at bus stops. Even the trains ran on time, or at least not egregiously late.

Even in the countryside the Emergency seemed, initially, to be making a difference. Programmes aimed at improving access to credit among Muslims and dalits had some effect, and around one million acres of land was requisitioned from the better-off for redistribution, against the 62,000 acres made available in the previous four years. Houses for the poor were built, though not always in places where the poor wished to live. Otherwise, at first, the Emergency meant merely a new set of slogans – though sloganizing itself raised difficulties in a multi-lingual nation, and produced some very puzzling messages as officials struggled to translate idiomatic Hindi and English into regional tongues. In Marathi, 'Emergency Means Discipline', became '*anibani mhajne shist*', 'Commotion Means Discipline', while 'The Only Magic is Hard Work', morphed into the confusing claim that '*ekatz jadu*' (trickery) is the only thing that works. Like *Garibhi Hatao*, which had coincided with monsoon failure and near-famine conditions in Maharashtra, this new set of imperatives soon met with resigned scepticism.

Initially, the Emergency barely registered on village horizons. The peasants of the Satara district of Maharashtra had heard of JP and his movement, but appeared unconcerned about his fate, and the Emergency hardly figured in public or private discussion for months, and when it did it was often welcomed. One old villager told an American researcher that of the two forms of government, *lokshahi* (democracy) and *hukumshahi* (authoritarianism), the latter was best suited to Indians who were too irresponsible and undisciplined to govern themselves. Reminiscing wistfully about the days of *Vhiktoria rani* (Queen Victoria) and *Jyorj pancham* (George V), he declared that, '*Lokshahi mhanje gundashahi, lokshahi mhanje gunhegarshahi*' (democracy has brought the rule of thugs and crooks).

More remarkably, perhaps, in its first months, there was very little opposition in urban areas either; indeed quite the reverse. While the press was tightly censored, many journalists and editors seemed to fall willingly into line, or as one moralist put it, '[they] crawled when they were only asked to bend'. Levels of sycophancy reached stratospheric heights, some officially engineered, but not all. India's leading artist, M. F. Hussein, depicted the Prime Minister as victorious Durga, tiger-mounted and smiting her foes. *The Times of India* was dubbed by wits the 'Times of Indira'. Adulatory books were published with such titles as *Freedom is not Free* (1975), and *Thank You Mrs Gandhi* (1977); and a set of laudatory essays, *A Decade of Achievement* (1976), announced that the prime-ministerial decade had brought more boons than the previous thousand years of Indian history. Indeed, among many of the urban middle classes the Emergency was rather popular; some hailed it as a much needed 'breathing space', while others suggested a bonfire of the constitution and the promulgation of a presidential system.

Part of the reason for this quiescence lay in the official insistence that the Emergency was only a temporary measure to face down anarchy. It was, moreover, carefully buttressed with tortuous claims to constitutional legality. There were certainly abuses: Morarji Desai and Narayan were gaoled for several months, Desai, vindictively, in solitary confinement. There were also cases of torture and killings in gaol, though these almost exclusively concerned supposed Naxalites. But there were no Gestapo or storm troopers; very few prominent journalists were detained and those that were were generally released soon after. The opposition leadership rapidly sought forgiveness. Narayan sent the Prime Minister contrite messages through high-level intermediaries, and asked for release in order to resume his Gandhian social work. The leader of the RSS also wrote an abject letter of apology, with assurances of good behaviour if freed. The right-wing journalist and Emergency opponent Arun Shourie lamented: 'We collapsed without a struggle in the face of the mildest possible dictatorship.'

However this calm did not last and from early 1976 circumstances rapidly deteriorated. At the eye of the oncoming storm was the Prime Minister's younger son, Sanjay. There will probably never be consensus among the armies of writers who have attempted to fathom the depths of this particular Oedipal drama, but all agree on one thing: Sanjay was a very bad influence on his mother. Born in 1946, he erupted on to the Indian public stage in 1970 after winning a government licence to manufacture an Indian automobile, the Maruti, his qualifications being an incomplete apprenticeship with Rolls-Royce in England. Nevertheless he beat several more experienced enterprises in the bid to make the first all-India manufactured car. This proved an abysmal failure; it never went into production and the prototype displayed at a Delhi trade fair was discovered to have no engine. Maruti then metamorphosed into Maruti Technical Services, a dubious, if ambitious enterprise dabbling, *inter alia*, in banking, bus chassis manufacture, chemicals, company and criminal law, import licensing and as agent for various multinationals. Sanjay became very wealthy.

Though bereft of any administrative or political experience, he developed, with his mother's assistance, a popular power base in the Youth Congress, a body which, like Mao and the Naxalites, fetishized the supposedly regenerative powers of the young (though its upper age limit was 40). Though it claimed a mass membership of 5 million, it is chiefly remembered as an umbrella under which various 'thugs, criminals, bad characters and anti-social elements' sheltered. By late 1975 its chief activity seemed to be running a protection racket among the unfortunate traders and shopkeepers of Delhi, its members levying instant and astronomical fines on those found not displaying price tags clearly – an offence under the Emergency. Soon a personality cult developed around the 'rising son' inspired by the press. The *Illustrated Weekly* put him on the cover of its Independence Day edition, with the tag-line, 'the hope of the future'; inside, the balding and bespectacled Sanjay was described as 'an incredibly handsome man'. An article in the September 1976 edition of *India Today* reassured the nation that, 'significantly and happily, Sanjay Gandhi has today leapt out of the wings ... and raced to the centre of the Indian political theatre', adding, apparently without irony, 'He won this prize in the space of 12 months, or even less ... He is ensconced today in a position of political leadership that comes naturally to him.'

But beyond the Youth Congress and a breathlessly adoring press Sanjay had more tangible access to the levers of power. He had close links to a number of cabinet ministers, especially in the Home and Health departments, and also to the chief minister of Haryana state, Bansi Lal, the principal benefactor of Maruti. Moreover, living as he did with the Prime Minister in 1 Safdarjang Road, he was very close to the pulse of power, and soon developed what many saw as an *imperium in imperio* known as the 'PMH', the Prime Minister's House, in opposition to the 'PMO', the Prime Minister's Office. It was from here that Sanjay had personally compiled the lists of those to be arrested on 25 June, and it had been Sanjay's idea to cut electricity to the press that same night. It was also from the PMH that he intruded into the affairs of various departments, shunting ministers and officials around willy-nilly, and even attempting to meddle in the nation's security services.

Sanjay, his mother fondly observed, 'is a doer, not a thinker'. This was not quite true, for Sanjay did have thoughts, and developed a rudimentary political philosophy that blended the authoritarian populism of Ferdinand Marcos, whose *Democratic Revolution in the Philippines*, was one of the few books he owned, with intense anti-communism. In a notorious press interview Sanjay described the Soviet-aligned Communist Party of India as inept and dishonest ('I don't think you'll find richer or more corrupt people anywhere,' he declared), while proclaiming his whole-hearted support for free-market capitalism. This proved acutely embarrassing to his mother, for the Soviet Union was one of her few supporters abroad, and the CPI the only one at home. Sanjay subsequently 'clarified' his remarks, but he did not retract them. He also informed a West German journalist that he rather liked dictatorship, 'though not of the Hitler type'. But his philosophy is probably best encapsulated in a quip of his own coinage: 'the best ideology for the people of India is Mydeology'.

'Mydeology' was embodied in Sanjay's own five-point programme, which soon eclipsed that of his mother. The programme ranged from the stupendously ambitious – 'Eradicate Casteism' – to the bathetic – 'Plant More Trees' – and in between encompassed the admirable but challenging objectives of ending the dowry system, higher literacy ('Each One: Teach One') and urban beautification. Initially it seemed that the point closest to Sanjay's heart was urban beautification, which took the form of bulldozing the houses of the poor and clearing the land for property-developer cronies, planting trees and ridding the streets of stray dogs. Areas of Agra and Varanasi were subjected to such 'beautification', which seemed, as often as not, to mean the demolition, either by intent or accident, of streets of seventeenth- and eighteenth-century houses and their replacement with concrete blocks owned by Sanjay's chums. But it was Delhi, and especially Old Delhi, or Shahjahanbad, which attracted his particular attention. Here he was able to make his writ run rather effectively through his influence over the head of the Delhi Development Authority (DDA), Jagmohan, who also doubled as chief executive of Sanjay's crack urban beautification committee, the Sanjay Action Brigade. Between July 1975 and the end of 1976 over 120,000 *jhuggis* (slums) were bulldozed, and their 700,000 inhabitants carted off to undeveloped and disease-ridden 'resettlement' colonies on the other side of the Januma river, where they were given plots of 25 square feet of land and left to their own devices.

Though strongly resisted by its victims, this process received little coverage in India's censored press until the tragic events surrounding one particular pet project of Sanjay's and the DDA. This was the clearance of the labyrinthine warren of largely Muslim-occupied streets in Old Delhi, which, according to Sanjay, sullied the vista from the Turkman Gate to the seventeenth-century Jama Masjid mosque. On 19 April 1976 crowds of local men, women and children tried to block the bulldozers that had been sent in to flatten their homes and businesses. Anticipating resistance, the DDA had come equipped with twenty companies of the Delhi armed police. In the ensuing battle between 6 and 20 protestors were killed, but rumours that the death toll was over 1,000 spread rapidly across north India, leading to charges that this was another Amritsar massacre. Jagmohan later insisted, not unreasonably, that the protests were not exclusively about the slum-clearance – the whole issue of urban development had become intertwined with another of Sanjay's schemes, family planning. This was a sensitive subject among Indians, and especially among Muslims, and possibly the brash Sanjay was not best placed to promote its benefits among the pious Muslim poor of Old Delhi. Undeterred, he had recruited a small army of Delhi socialites to press the cause. One of them, Rukhsana Sultan, a glamorous Muslim lady, had set up her own family planning clinic in the environs of the Turkman Gate and had succeeded, before the eyes of astonished journalists, in persuading two imams to be vasectomized.

'Come have yourself vasectomized, make your family systemized', proclaimed government posters launching its family planning campaign in early April 1976. Certainly the burgeoning size of India's population was a very serious problem and one worthy of state intervention. The death rate had fallen from 47 per thousand in 1921 to only 17 per thousand in the early 1970s, while the birth rate threat-

15. **Independence Day.** *Dilli ke Lal Kile Par Bharat Dhwaja Sthaapana* (The National Flag being hoisted on the Red Fort in Delhi), artist unknown, after 1947. A popular depiction of part of the 14–15 August 1947 Independence Day Ceremonies, showing Nehru and other nationalist leaders, watched over by the heavenly warrior triumvirate of Shivaji, Bose and Pratap, as they are saluted by the Indian Air Force.

16. **Indian Modern.** The Assembly Building, Chandigarh, new capital of the recently partitioned Punjab. Designed by Le Corbusier and intended by Nehru to symbolize India's break with both the British and Indian past and embracing of 'modernity', encapsulated by the high modernist 'International' style.

17. National Infantry.
This depiction of a highly
sentimentalized nationalism
at the height of Indo-Chinese
border tensions in the
Himalayas made the name
of Yogendra Rastogi, the
self-taught 'calendar' artist
who painted it. His work
captured the preoccupations
of the era, often showing the
nation imagined as a small
child against a background
of protective troops or
productive tractors.

18. **A Fecund Future.** The style of this mid 1950s calendar poster, *Agricultural Beauty*,
is redolent of Bollywood '*filmi*' gloss. Note especially the young woman's tight sari. The
poster elides state concerns over boosting agricultural production with filmic stereotypes of
eroticism, both slyly evoked by the prominently placed sacks of fertilizer.

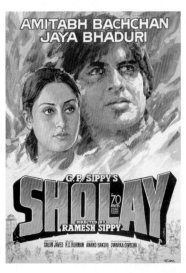

19. **Flames.** One of many film posters of *Sholay*, this one intended for a British audience.

20. **Mother Love.** In this portrait it is Sanjay, Indira Gandhi's younger son, and not the prime minister herself, who is foregrounded. The artist, Yogendra Rastogi, has captured the widely held perception in the mid 1970s that it was Sanjay, not Indira, who was running the country.

21. **The Indian "Royal" Family.** A typical shot of the Gandhis, from left to right: Sanjay, Rajiv, Indira, Rahul (son of Rajiv and Sonia), Manekar (wife of Sanjay), Sonia (wife of Rajiv and now President of Congress) and Priyanka (daughter of Rajiv and Sonia).

22. **High and Low.** Suburb of Mumbai (Bombay), 2004. In contemporary Mumbai, luxury high-rise apartments nestle among shanty towns in the suburb of Bandra.

23 and 24. Angry Ram. BJP politician L. K. Advani poses with bow and arrow in emulation of Ram (*left*). In this VHP poster of the early 1990s (*right*), Ram has acquired an impressive musculature and a vengeful demeanour not previously associated with him. He is bestriding the proposed new Ram temple that the Hindu right would like to build at Ayodhya on the site of the Babri Masjid. The legend below reads: *Shri Ramjanmabhumi Ayodhya mem prastarit Shri Ram Mandir* (proposed Sri Ram Birthplace Temple at Ayodhya).

25. Demolishing the Mosque. Hindu nationalist activists celebrate atop the sixteenth-century Babri Masjid on 6 December 1992. Later that day they demolished the mosque using pickaxes, hammers and swords.

26. **Amplified Hinduism.** Devotees pull a chariot of Lord Jagannath (an avatar of Vishnu) at the Jagannath *Rath Yatra* (pilgrimage) festival in November 2006 in Puri.

27. **Vishnu's Temple Challenged.** A bust of the low-caste leader E. V. Ramaswami Naiker, 'Periyar', contemplates the Srirangam Vishnu temple in Tiruchi, Tamil Nadu. The statue, erected by the DMK ruling party, was a rebuke to the high-caste Hinduism embraced by its rival party, the AIDMK. Unveiled in December 2006, it was soon 'beheaded'.

28. **Against the West.** Protestors burn effigies of Indian Prime Minister Manmohan Singh and US President George W. Bush after the sealing of a landmark nuclear cooperation pact in March 2006.

29. **Your Own Indian Super Hero.** An example of street graphics – a very popular form in India – here, perhaps, satirizing India's post-liberalization ambitions to superpowerdom. The image was used to advertise the Indian national television network, Doordarshan, in Rajasthan in the late 1990s.

30. **Chaharva in a Chopper.** Laloo Prasad Yadav and his wife Rabri Devi celebrate his re-election as national president of the Rashtriya Janata Dal (RJD) party in August 2005.

31. **Icon of the Oppressed.** A display of photographs of untouchable leader B. R. Ambedkar as part of an Untouchable political march in Mumbai in January 2004. Ambedkar's image is consciously placed among those of the Buddha, evoking his rejection of Hinduism and conversion to Buddhism.

32. **Hanuman Triumphant.** A statue of the monkey god towers over the recently built New Delhi Metro at Karol Bagh. At 108 feet he is not quite the tallest Hanuman in India, but 108 is Hanuman lucky number – he is said to eat 108 *laddoos* (sweets) and to chant Lord Ram's name 108 times every day.

ened soon to hit 35 per thousand. But the government's heavy-handed action during the Emergency probably set back the patient work done by medical and educational authorities for at least a decade. Alarmist Malthusian pamphlets appeared. One breathlessly announced: 'Every nineteenth second a child is born in West Bengal, every minute, three new born babies, every hour, one hundred and eighty new born babies!' And while the project launched in April had set relatively modest targets, under Sanjay's tutelage this rational plan soon turned into an all-out military style campaign. In Uttar Pradesh, targets for sterilization were unilaterally raised from 400,000 to 1.5 million in one year. Moreover the system of incentives – tins of ghee, clocks and radios offered to volunteers for sterilization – was replaced by mandatory quotas imposed on government workers, now dubbed 'motivators'. Thus clerks, policemen, schoolteachers, and later factory owners seeking licences, had to produce a certain number of 'cases' of people they had 'motivated' to get vasectomies in order to be paid.

For slum-dwellers entitlement to a resettlement plot after eviction became tied to the production of a *nasbandi* (vasectomy) certificate. The canny could, moreover, gain rights over another's plot by producing the *nasbandi*. Tightening the screw still further were rules that the hated *nasbandi* certificates were to become a form of identity card that had to be produced to entitle its bearer to all manner of state goods and services. The director for the Centre of Social Medicine at Jawaharlal Nehru University, who undertook field work in Uttar Pradesh villages later that year, discovered that:

The issue of licences for guns, shops, sugar-cane crushers and vehicles, issue of government loans, registration of land; issue of ration cards; exemption of payment from school fees or land revenue, supply of irrigation canal water; submissions of application for any job; any form of registration; obtaining of bail and facilitation of court cases; all these were linked up with the procurement of cases for sterilization.

Inevitably a market developed for *nasbandi* cards, and a macabre trade reminiscent of the trafficking of non-existent serfs in Gogol's *Dead Souls* developed. As with any market, traders emerged, called *dalals*, to bring buyers and sellers together, and soon certificates could be had for as little as Rs. 100 (these were usually forgeries) and as much as Rs. 1000, though the going rate was Rs. 400. This was an astronomical sum, representing two months' wages for a lower civil servant or schoolteacher.

Soon vasectomy clinics sprang up in the poorer areas of towns, and though volunteers were supposed to be of reproductive age and already to have three children, young boys, old men, vagrants and anyone in any way dependent on the state found themselves pressed by 'motivators' into having vasectomies. In September 1976 mobile *nasbandi* vans, and armies of 'motivators' seeking to fill their quotas, began descending on the countryside. In Satara, police rounded up eligible men, took them to rural health centres and more or less coercively sterilized them.

By now *nasbandi* was encountering serious resistance. The riot at the Turkman Gate had, in part, been roused by the local imams against the hated Rukhsana Sultan's vasectomy clinic. In the countryside of north and west India men ran off and hid from encroaching convoys of *nasbandi* trucks and police jeeps in the surrounding hills and jungles. In Muzaffarnagar in western Uttar Pradesh forty people were killed by police when a crowd assembled to stop them from seizing men for *nasbandi*, and in Haryana State over 100,000 villagers assembled, enraged by the death of a young man after a botched *nasbandi* operation. *Nasbandi* became a dreaded word, giving rise to the kinds of lurid atrocity rumours last heard during the 1857 Rebellion. It was said that *nasbandi* caused de-manning, loss of virility, low libido and impotence. In rural areas, where the principal experience of sterilization was the emasculation of bulls, *nasbandi* meant castration. It was no surprise, therefore, when in Uttar Pradesh, teams of Tantric priests began to pray for Sanjay's and his mother's annihilation.

By late 1976 the Emergency was beginning to alienate those who had previously been either its supporters, or, at least, indifferent bystanders. For the rural poor it had brought no magical deliverance: bonded labourers were not freed; women field workers were not paid the same as men – they were just sacked. The debts owed to money-lenders were not pardoned, as the government had ordered, and the poor made no protest knowing that this was their only source of credit. Rule by order, fiat and ordinance dissolved into merely quixotic gestures. Small-time officials turned up for work, but did very little, often going on long 'tours' of the district to avoid the avalanche of paperwork that now assailed them. The Emergency had only succeeded in transforming villages relatively untouched by the hand of the state into petty satrapies of unchecked arbitrary power. Every district seemed to have its little-Sanjay, and the police, now buttressed by the loathsome Maintenance of Internal Security Act, could bully and extort at leisure; peasants took to hiding their wrist-watches and other status symbols for fear of police confiscation. But it was *nasbandi* that provoked sharp politicization among the previously quiescent peasantry. Men who had fought in the Quit India campaign insisted they had not struggled for independence in order to submit to *saktine* (coercive) sterilization. Some even adopted the rhetoric of the JP Movement and talked of *kranti* (revolution).

Arbitrary state power was also alienating more affluent sections of society in the cities. One problem was press censorship, because without reliable news, credence was attached to the most bizarre rumours: Morarji Desai and Jayaprakash Narayan were being force-fed, the government had a massive network of spies and could detect the slightest dissent, 1 Safdarjang Road had descended into violent court intrigue and Sanjay Gandhi had been seen slapping his mother. But more tangibly the Emergency was not, as had at first appeared, delivering law and order but petty and unchecked official tyranny; local government officials themselves resented being made the scapegoats of the unpopular slum-clearance and sterilization campaigns. Meanwhile urban business interests, though initially the beneficiaries of the emergency crackdown, came to dislike the restrictions on trade, and found that campaigns to stop corruption simply made bribery more expensive, for, as officials reminded them, the risks were higher. Moreover, the cronyism and racketeering associated with Sanjay was deeply unpopular; not all businesses, it now seemed, would prosper under the new regime, but only those close to the Gandhi family.

In mid-January 1977 the prayers of the Tantric priests and all other opponents of the regime were answered. The Emergency was abandoned, and six weeks later an election was held which swept Mrs Gandhi and her satraps from power. It was the biggest turnout so far in Indian electoral history. Across the country, though especially in the north, poor peasants donned their best *dhotis*, saris and bangles, queued patiently at the tens of thousands of poll booths across the country, and cheered exuberantly on news that they had massively voted 'Mother India' and her cohorts out of power. Janata, the newly formed opposition party, had campaigned on the single issue of ending the Emergency and restoring democracy, and the Indian Bar association, galvanized by the egregious attacks on the judicial system, provided its rudimentary organizational framework. Janata, along with its allies, the Akali Dal, a Punjabi regional party, and the Communists, won 328 of the 542 seats in the Indian parliament. Mrs Gandhi's Congress won only 158, and in Uttar Pradesh, its traditional heartland, Congress did not win a single seat. The party did better in the south, a phenomenon explained by the relatively light experience of the Emergency there, which had been buffered by more independently minded chief ministers. This shocking landslide delivered power to the first non-Congress national party. Mrs Gandhi, along with her western-style bathroom suites, was unceremoniously ejected from 1 Safdarjang Road. Morarji Desai, her arch-enemy, auto-urine therapist and hater of all things western, was installed as Prime Minister, along with several Indian-style lavatories.

All sorts of theories abounded as to why Mrs Gandhi had made this appalling miscalculation. Some said she feared that Sanjay was now controlled by the CIA and planned a coup, others that she had followed the advice of ascetics and astrologers who had assured her that the portents and stars were favourably aligned. Others argued that she feared to go down in history as a dictator, or wanted to curry favour with the new and more liberal President of the USA, Jimmy Carter. But the most likely explanation is that Mrs Gandhi thought she was going to win. Dismissing tales of *nasbandi* excesses as malicious tittle-tattle, she believed she could now consolidate Sanjay's succession by giving so many party 'tickets' (Congress nominations to contest electoral seats) to Sanjay's lieutenants that he would be transformed overnight into the biggest faction boss in the organization.

How had Mrs Gandhi arrived in a place so deeply at odds with reality? It is clear that she lacked sound advice. She had dispensed with the services of the trusty P. N. Haksar when he had dared to draw attention to some of Sanjay's more unsavoury exploits. And while she still had excellent advisers such as Manmohan Singh, in charge of economic policy, the Prime Minister was increasingly surrounded by a coterie of sycophants, swamis and charlatans. Among the swamis was the glamorous guru Krisnamurthy, who kept an ashram in south India to which ladies of a certain age seemed magnetically drawn, among whom the Prime Minister figured prominently. Chief among the charlatans was her yoga teacher, who appeared to play a Rasputin-like role in the court of 1 Safdarjang Road. The six-foot Brahmacharyi, discontented with his role as yoga instructor-in-chief to the Delhi elite, acquired a pilot's licence and flew around India supposedly raising funds for his ashrams; he was, inevitably, dubbed the flying swami. He later went on to host his own TV show before a sudden fall from grace, if not from the skies – a fate which befell Sanjay in 1980 while piloting his Cessna over New Delhi.

However, Mrs Gandhi was not alone in her miscalculations. Indeed, most of the Indian elite were astounded by both the turnout and the results of the 1977 election. In part this was a consequence of press censorship, which had stifled the volume of opposition. But it also reflected deep cynicism among the elite about their countrymen's commitment to and understanding of democracy. For while the Emergency may not have 'shocked' India back to life economically, it had certainly done so politically; it had made many Indians aware that however corrupt and debased their elected politicians, they did at the very least offer some protection from arbitrary state power. Moreover, the election had, apparently, resolved the party political chaos of the last decade into a disciplined two-party system at the national level. For, to the great surprise of Mrs Gandhi and all informed observers, the diverse forces of the opposition, regional, right, left, peasant and urban, seemed to have sunk their differences into the newly formed Janata government. Paradoxically, India's half-baked experiment in dictatorship had the effect of entrenching democracy.

Unfortunately the Janata dispensation, which lasted a little over two years, did not fulfil its initial promise of ushering in a new era of a stable two-party system. This was never likely, as the fundamental conflict in Indian society, which was now seemingly drawn between urban businesses (symbolized by the western term 'India') and rural farming interests (aligned under the banner of '*Bharat*'), far from being resolved by the Janata party had merely been crystallized and embodied within it. Moreover the rumbling division between adherents of strong central government and advocates of a looser federal system was also reproduced in the very constituents of the supposedly united opposition. The Total Revolutionaries may have come to power but their impact was merely to renovate, not revolutionize, the old system.

Janata comprised the old Jan Sangh party, which advanced a Hinduized vision of the nation and drew predominantly upon urban small business interests, the Bharatiya Lok Dal (BLD), the latest manifestation of Charan Singh's north Indian rich farmer party, and various elements of the left, among whom figured yet another fraction of Congress which had split away from Mrs Gandhi's segment. This portion, calling itself Congress (D) for democracy, was led by Jagjivan Ram, the septuagenarian leader of India's dalits. The new Prime Minister, Morarji Desai, now over eighty, was also an old Congress war-horse though, unlike Jagjivan, one of decidedly high-caste and right-wing economic proclivities. Hovering over this opportunistic assemblage was the saintly figure of Narayan, now in his last days, but still able to lend his immense moral standing to the rickety enterprise and, for a while at least, able to prevail upon its fractious constituents to cohere. But the constituent parts of Janata never really trusted one another, made no effort to integrate their grassroots support bases or to co-ordinate their organizations into a cohesive and effective political entity.

It was surprising then that the government was able to develop an agreed set of economic and social policies, which might be dubbed neo-Gandhian. These first entailed greater decentralization: the return to state-centre norms violated under Mrs Gandhi, and an attempt to resuscitate Nehru's local *panchayats*, or village councils, as beacons of local, participatory democracy. Economically, the government committed itself to the Gandhian (and arguably pro-rich farmer) policies of rebalancing public investment away from the cities and towards the countryside, favouring 'independent cultivators' and 'cottage industries'. Its most Gandhian feature, however, was undoubtedly its espousal of 'intermediate technology'. This accorded with the Mahatma's nostrums that production in India should be man- and animal-based as far as possible, should be appropriate to Indian resources and should reflect Indian society. The pursuit of intermediate technology became the most eye-catching aspect of the new regime. These efforts were mercilessly satirized by V. S. Naipaul who visited India in 1977 and found it gripped by the cult of the bullock cart. In south India research institutes had been established in which bullocks were 'wired-up like cosmonauts', the better to assess the loads and stresses they endured while hauling their trusty carts. What Naipaul found particularly odd was that large sums were being spent to 'improve' the productive potential of the 3000-year-old form of technology, when the substitution of a simple tractor would have been much cheaper. As Naipaul pungently observed:

Intermediate technology should mean a leap ahead, a leap beyond accepted solutions, new ways of perceiving coincident needs and resources. In India it has circled back to something like the old sentimentality about poverty and the old ways, and has stalled with the bullock cart: a fascinating intellectual adventure for the people concerned, but sterile, divorced from reality and usefulness.

This was not about cost-saving; it was ideological – a blunt refutation of the westernizing modernization of the Nehru years.

Intermediate technology was about all Janata could agree on. The various factions that comprised Janata soon began to pursue their own rather different projects. The Jan Sangh element, represented by Atal Behari Vajpayee, pursued Hindu cultural goals, banning Muslims from slaughtering cows and establishing rest homes for these superannuated bovines instead. It had carved up the regions of north India in a power-sharing deal with Charan Singh's BLD, which both sides attempted systematically to subvert. But the Janata government will chiefly be remembered for the undignified shennanigans of its three gerontocrat principals, Desai, Singh and Jagjivan Ram, as they wrangled for power. Ostensibly the issue at stake was the punishment of Mrs Gandhi and Sanjay for their misdeeds. Desai was inclined to clemency, but Singh wanted blood. In June 1978, this conflict culminated in Singh accusing the rest of the cabinet of collective impotence because of their failure to bring 'the lady' to justice. Desai promptly sacked him for violating the norms of collective cabinet decision-making, and after a tearful farewell, Singh rallied his menacing mass assemblage of peasant power at his famous birthday party. He was soon hastily reinstated to the cabinet, from where he continued to conspire against his octogenarian Prime Minister.

While all this was going on in New Delhi, Mrs Gandhi had engineered her own remarkable comeback. Within a month of her defeat she was to be found brandishing her populist campaigning credentials during a UP by-election which drew attention to violent attacks on Dalits. By November 1978 she was back in the New Delhi Parliament after winning a by-election in a very poor district of Karnataka in a constituency specially chosen for its pro-Indira elements: it was 45 per cent untouchable and nearly half the population lived below the official poverty line. She won the seat by a margin of 70,000 votes. This was a portent of things to come. Back in New Delhi rows regarding her punishment for 'Emergency crimes' rumbled on; though arrested in late 1978, she was released only a week later. In the meantime the battles between Singh, Desai and Jagjivan Ram were threatening the Janata with collapse. In the summer of 1979 this unedifying spectacle culminated in Desai's resignation after losing a parliamentary vote of confidence on 11 July. This followed an orgy of lurid accusation and counter-accusation concerning Desai's son's supposed involvement in corruption, and a scandal in which pornographic snaps of Jagjivan Ram's son and an unnamed young lady appeared in the national press. Astonishingly, Charan Singh, Indira's avenging fury-in-chief, then became Prime Minister with the support of her rump of supporters, now known as Congress (I) (Indira). With Charan Singh's premiership, the Indian farmer, it was said, had finally stormed the New Delhi fortress. But his ascendancy was brief: within fifteen days Charan Singh too was subjected to a vote of no-confidence. Congress (I) now perfidiously abandoned him, and he was left with the modest prize as head of a caretaker administration until new elections were held in January 1980.

The Janata era had ended. It had not brought about stable two-party government at the centre, but merely reproduced there the coalitional chaos that had dogged regional government for the previous decade. Charan Singh had not succeeded in imposing his vision of a populist *Bharat* on the nation, but neither had Desai and his allies on the

Hindu right gained legitimacy for an alternative vision. Moreover, as an observer of the time noted, Janata had displayed at its most naked *matsyanyaya* (an ancient Indian principle that in public life the big fishes consume the smaller ones), and it was no surprise therefore that the electorate should emulate them by re-electing the biggest fish of all – Mrs Gandhi. In the 1980 elections Mrs Gandhi and Congress (I) swept back to power on another unprecedented populist wave. Unlike her 1971 victory, this was not built on an alliance of high and low against bosses, but of rich and poor against the middle, and more specifically, the middle-caste farmer. Her electoral slogan, 'Not for caste, not for region, but for Indira put your vote on the hand' (Congress (I) had adopted the electoral symbol of the open palm), positioned Congress as the party of unity, social justice and secularism. She received massive support from the very richest and the very poorest, Muslims and dalits.

But the rise of the rich peasantry was now an unstoppable force. Though briefly subdued by the Emergency, under Janata and Charan Singh it had come into its own, but not as the populist force envisaged by Singh. The Green Revolution, though controversial, had undoubtedly brought unprecedented prosperity to India's wealthier farmers and had made the country finally self-sufficient in food. Moreover, though many had worried that its uneven impact might bring a 'red' revolution in its wake, after a decade its effects had trickled down to create a diverse but potentially cohesive farming lobby out for its own interests. These included higher grain prices in the cities, and control over fertilizer prices, electricity costs, seed subsidies and the multitude of goods and services required by the new technology of the Green Revolution. The richer farmers had, to an extent, succeeded in co-opting some of the poorer peasantry who seemed to have abandoned the hope of radical change held out in the Naxalite era, symbolized by the collapse of the communists into regional parties with little influence beyond their electoral strongholds of West Bengal and Kerala. But even where they could not rely upon the co-operation of poorer groups, rich farmers had other means. Under the Janata dispensation they had used their political dominance in the districts to impose a more menacing form of power. A sinister sign of this was the astonishing proliferation of guns. By the mid-1980s there were

20,000 licensed firearms in the Uttar Pradesh district of Moradabad alone (in the 1950s it had been less than 2000). For every licensed gun, there were said to be another three unlicensed, which meant there were more guns in the district of Moradabad than in the whole of Great Britain. The localities of Bihar and Punjab were undoubtedly harbouring even more. In Bihar, it was said, grooms now regularly demanded a pre-nuptial Sten gun from their prospective in-laws.

These were probably not the simple democracy-loving, bucolic communities envisaged by Charan Singh in the late 1950s. But by the 1980s new farmers' movements were a phenomenon across India – eschewing broad-spectrum party politics, they had very specific economic goals. They employed the techniques of mass rallies, *gheraos* (encirclements), road blocking and the destruction of the odd bridge to get their way. They sought to shift the whole balance of economic power in India away from big business and the towns, to the commercial farmer and, increasingly, that meant directly challenging the power of New Delhi and seeking to focus much more economic and political power in the regions. There were some defensible reasons for this. Increasingly entangled in the pettiest aspects of district politics through its intervention in party and factional disputes, New Delhi had reduced local administration to farcical levels of incompetence. Politicians routinely demanded the transfer of top-level local officials and police so that they could reward allies, a practice that soon destroyed years of accumulated expertise and experience. In Uttar Pradesh one former inspector-general of police wrote of how at the beginning of his career an officer was expected to spend three months becoming acquainted with his district, and prepare guidebooks to pass down to successors containing essential information. Now, he said, no one bothered with such things, and during a spate of rioting in the district a posse of armed police had had to stop and ask passers-by for directions.

Moreover Delhi, with its control of the planning mechanism, of financial allocations between the states, and of the apparatus of price setting, commodity trading and irrigation, had immense influence over regional economies in what was supposed to be a federal system. And what really made regional groups chafe was the overt manipulation of their economic resources to suit the purposes of Congress's power battles. With her return in 1980 it quickly became apparent that Mrs Gandhi was determined, by hook or by crook (usually crook), to keep control of the states. Since 1971 this had been done in an increasingly cavalier and cynical fashion: sacking chief ministers, dismissing elected but unfriendly governments, bribing the opposition's supporters to defect. In June 1983 a conference of the four southern states, along with parties opposed to Congress in Punjab and Kashmir, demanded a radical modification of the constitution to deprive New Delhi of the power to dismiss elected state governments, to give states more power over their own finances, and to loosen the net of central planning. The crude actions of Congress (I) to crush these demands had the effect of turning regionalism into separatism in some states.

The most bizarre example of this occurred in the southern state of Andhra. Though the Congress vote had held up well in 1977, by 1983 it was challenged by a new party, which only ten months after its inception had trounced Congress at the state assembly polls, winning 202 of the 294 seats. It espoused a mishmash of regional culturalist causes, and was led by the flamboyant film superstar, Nandamuri Taraka Rama Rao (NTR). NTR was a populist who united various disgruntled rich peasant and urban professional groups who resented the depredations imposed on them by the north, or more accurately by the government in New Delhi. Habitually swathed in bright yellow robes he called himself a *Raja Yogi* (kingly monk), though his enemies dubbed him the 'Saffron Caesar'. His narcissism knew no bounds and all major policy announcements invariably coincided with his birthday. Vowing to restore the *aatma gauravam* (self-respect) of the Telugu-speaking majority of Andhra, he introduced a package of populist measures egregious even by the standards of the time. Land revenue was abolished, bus journeys made free (as were all school meals), widows received pensions, the poor got cheap rice and university fees were abolished, while civil servants' retirement age was cut by three years, to 55.

Determined not to let a regional election defeat get in the way of power, Mrs Gandhi began a systematic campaign to unseat NTR. After a triple heart-bypass operation in Texas, NTR returned to Hyderabad to discover that despite his massive majority he had been dismissed by the state governor. His finance minister, Bhaskara Rao, was, it seemed, going to form a new government composed of Congressmen and defectors from his own party, whose allegiance had been purchased, at some expense, by Mrs Gandhi. However, to consolidate his new premiership, the putative chief minister had to 'prove' that he had a majority. There then followed weeks of ludicrous manoeuvrings as NTR hid his rump of 168 MLAs in his old film studio to shelter them from the opposition's blandishments. He then carted them en bloc to New Delhi to prove to the President of India himself that he, not Bhaskara Rao, held the majority of seats. Despite these measures two of his flock still defected to Congress, while the train taking the rest to New Delhi (he had been mysteriously unable to charter a plane), took nearly three days to reach the capital, rather than the more usual one. It had, again mysteriously, spent much of its time stranded in sidings.

Though these happenings received no coverage on Indian TV, the people of Andhra followed the events on the BBC and rose in popular uproar. Mass rallies reminiscent of Jayaprakash Narayan's were held to oppose the 'murder of democracy', 15 August was named 'Save Democracy Day', protests and strikes were held across the state, and bombs were thrown in the assembly. In an effort to appease both sides a speaker of the house was appointed, who could speak neither English, nor the state language, Telugu. However, by the end of September NTR had been restored to power, after a month of chaos and fifty deaths. Though no one believed her, Mrs Gandhi denied all involvement in the affair, but *The Times of India* declared that 'no other issue since the Emergency has stirred the Indian people as the wholly illegal and unjustifiable dismissal of the NTR ministry has done'.

Regional revival took a far more dangerous form in the northern state of the Punjab, where Congress's Machiavellian scheming to wrest control of the state from its elected opponents had far more disastrous consequences: consequences that seemed at the time to threaten the very integrity of India itself. Following partition in 1947 a radical element within the Sikh community organized in the Akali Dal (a regional party of Sikhs) demanded that the Punjab be made a Sikh 'homeland'. After agitations and negotiations, Nehru agreed to divide Punjab in two, creating the new Hindi-speaking state of Haryana, while making the rump Punjab into a Punjabi-speaking region. Though the Sikhs now constituted 60 per cent of the new Punjab's population, Nehru had been very careful to rebuff calls to create an exclusively Sikh state. Nevertheless, the division of the Punjab had robbed the more radical Sikhs of their fire, and the Akali Dal became a moderate party with no further ambitions to revise the Indian constitution. The Sikhs, however, were not a united group, but riven by caste differences, and increasingly since the Green Revolution by those of class, as Jat Sikh farmers living on the best irrigated lands became more prosperous. Many poorer Sikhs therefore tended to vote for Congress, with the result that the Akali Dal could only form governments in partnership, rather bizarrely, with the Hindu rightist party, the Jan Sangh. After 1967 the Punjab therefore experienced the musical-chair politics of most north Indian states, as the Akali Dal and Jan Sangh formed unstable, faction-ridden coalitions, and Congress vied to unseat them.

Matters however took a more sinister turn in the late 1970s, when Sanjay Gandhi plotted with leading Sikh Congressmen to destroy the Akali-Jan Sangh coalitions permanently. The Punjab was important to the centre, not because it had many MPs in the Lok Sabha, but because politics there had ripple effects over the rest of Hindu north India. While continuing the tried and tested methods of faction-splitting and encouraging defections, Sanjay and his allies turned to new tactics: the promotion of communal ill-feeling between Sikhs and Hindus (to undermine the Akali Dal's understanding with the Jan Sangh) and a divide and rule approach to the Sikhs themselves. The latter was accomplished through Congress's promotion of an obscure wandering preacher, *sant* (holy man) Bhindranwale. Bhindranwale was a Sikh fundamentalist who denounced the Akali Dal's alliance with the Hindu Jan Sangh, warned of the threat to Sikh culture from wealthy and westernizing Sikhs, exhorted young Sikh men to wage holy violence against heretics, and, most electrifyingly, revived the old demand of the 1950s for an independent Sikh homeland – Khalistan.

Preaching soon became practice, and in the late 1970s Bhindranwale began organizing attacks on the supposedly heretical Sikh sect of

Nirankaris. His passionate mix of radical and nationalistic rhetoric won him an eager audience among poorer groups, while his credo – 'to be armed is the birthright of every Sikh ... a Sikh without a weapon is naked' – was taken quite literally by many young men. By the early 1980s he had slipped the Congress leash and was assembling an army of young terrorists, some trained by Sikh officers in the Indian army who were alienated by the determination of the New Delhi government to recruit more heavily from among Hindus and end the Raj-established predominance of Sikhs in India's military forces. These young guerrillas sheltered in *gurdwaràs* (Sikh temples), where they amassed impressive arsenals. Attacks now escalated and victims included prominent members of the Jan Sangh, Congress politicians and Sikhs considered by Bhindranwale to be his opponents. Spectacularly, in early 1982, Bhindranwale installed himself and his men in the Holy of Holies for Sikhs, the Golden Temple at Amritsar, from where he directed his campaign of terror with impunity. Though surrounded by several companies of police and army, the *sant* still maintained a well-stocked armoury – suggesting that the police and soldiers on duty (many of whom were Sikh) were making few attempts to stop him.

These actions not only catapulted Bhindranwale centrestage as the defender of Sikh purity, but caused intense embarrassment to the moderate Akali Dal, whose members were now routinely depicted by the bellicose *sant* as the weak and selfish running dogs of the Jan Sangh and their Hindu business supporters. Observing the growing popularity of the obscure preacher, the Akali Dal leadership, headed by another *sant*, Longowal, decided they had no option but to try and recapture Sikh support by espousing more radical ideas themselves. In 1981 Longowal resuscitated a long-forgotten demand dating from 1973, the Anandpur Resolution, which appealed for more state protection for Sikh identity, the recitation of *Gurbani* (holy texts) on government media and instruction in Sikhism in schools. He also demanded control of the disputed canal waters which fed the irrigation systems of both the Punjab and Haryana, arguing that Delhi was intent on diverting precious water out of Sikh Punjab and into Hindu Haryana for naked electoral gain. Though not secessionist, the Anandpur Resolution was an attempt to compete with Bhindranwale and references were made to a Sikh homeland, albeit vaguely. But unlike Bhindranwale, the Akali Dal hoped for a negotiated solution with New Delhi, eschewed violence and pursued a strategy of non-violent direct action, including the threat of roadblocks to stop Punjabi grain (Punjab was the bread-basket of India), from leaving the state.

Now seriously frightened, Delhi engaged in negotiations throughout 1983 with the Akali Dal leadership. But Congress proved unable or unwilling to prevail on Haryana over the canal water dispute and the talks eventually failed. With Sikh support now haemorrhaging from the Akali Dal, and humiliated by the failure of these negotiations, the moderates adopted the radicalism of Bhindranwale. Longowal formed his own crack corps and took up residence in another section of the benighted Golden Temple. Meanwhile unchecked attacks on innocent Hindus continued to escalate and Hindu rightist groups such as the RSS set up militias to retaliate. By the middle of 1984, having dithered for two years, Mrs Gandhi now demanded a swift resolution, and on 2 June the Indian army stormed the Golden Temple. Starved of accurate intelligence beforehand, the army's Operation Blue Star (as it was called), proved a fiasco. Instead of the swift surgical excision planned, it became a blood-soaked three-day siege, killing nearly 600 people. Rumours were soon rife that over 1000 had been slain and that the Harmandir shrine, most sacred to Sikhs, had been destroyed. Though Bhindranwale and his men had indeed used the shrine for gun emplacements, it had not in fact been destroyed; even so, many other holy sites and artefacts in the Golden Temple had been. The entire operation was viewed by Sikhs as an act of sacrilege and in the aftermath mutinies broke out among Sikh troops in eight different rebellions across India. In Bihar 1000 Sikh soldiers killed their Hindu commander, commandeered trucks and rode to New Delhi proclaiming 'Death to Mrs Gandhi', though the vast majority of the 120,000 Sikhs in the Indian armed forces remained loyal. But the Punjab itself was now effectively under military rule, and the Sikh population deeply alienated. The idea of Khalistan, which had until then existed largely in the imaginations of diasporic Sikhs as far afield as Birmingham and Toronto, now had a substantial following in the Punjab itself.

*

On 31 October Mrs Gandhi took a walk in her garden at 1 Safdarjang Road. She had dismissed warnings about the possible unreliability of the two Sikh soldiers who formed her habitual bodyguard. As she walked towards them they opened fire with several rounds and killed her. Another 3000 people were killed in the ensuing anti-Sikh riots in Delhi. Though her son Rajiv was immediately made Prime Minister and Congress won the subsequent election with an even more massive wave of support than had greeted Mrs Gandhi's return in 1980, this was an illusory triumph. The era of Congress's dominance was over. The populist strategy of marshalling high and low against a variety of 'enemies', be they party bosses, rich farmers or the CIA, had failed to bring stability to Indian politics or dynamism to the Indian economy. The nation's brief detour into authoritarianism had also achieved little, except, paradoxically, to entrench democracy. Jayaprakash Narayan and Charan Singh had proffered their own bespoke neo-Gandhian populisms, but neither had produced a solution to the overwhelming conflicts both unleashed and generated by democracy. To some it seemed as though the nation itself was falling apart.

In the same year as Operation Blue Star, the assassination of Mrs Gandhi and the slaughter of thousands of innocents on the streets of New Delhi, an event banal by comparison but ultimately of equal import took place. The sleepy Indian State TV Corporation, Doordarshan, began screening a new series, *Hum Log* (We the People). This prosaic tale of north Indian Hindu family life proved immensely popular, as did the adverts for Maggi's Two Minute Noodles which accompanied it (noodle sales rocketed from 1600 tons to 95,000). Though *Hum Log* was intended to reinforce the Nehruvian message of religious tolerance and national unity, it was plot-lines concerning the lives of pious modern Hindus that engaged the audience, and the Nehruvian nostrums were soon dropped. The broadcasters quickly saw the audience-luring potential of dramas with traditional themes. And what could be more traditional than the great Hindu epics? In 1987 Doordarshan broadcast its first *dharmic* (spiritual) serial, an adaptation of the *Ramayana*, which ran for several hundred episodes. The following year came the even more protracted *Mahabharata*. On every Sunday that the *dharmic* soaps were shown, India stood still. The rich watched in their lounges; the poor, urban and rural, congregated around TVs in shops and cafés, having come, they said, to receive *darshan* (a holy vision). For those looking for alternatives to the failed populism and authoritarianism of the previous decade the message was clear: religion, among Hindus at least, could unite.

8

Levelling the Temple

On 25 September 1990 a pilgrimage began from the ancient temple city of Somnath in Gujarat. The pilgrim caravan was an untidy assemblage of trucks, scooters, buses and lorries festooned with marigolds and bedecked with huge images of Ram – the mythical king of the *Ramayana* – images of fearsome lions and the Hindu mantra *Om*. Others bore the more mundane emblem of the recently formed Bharatiya Janata Party (BJP), a fetching lotus flower. Accompanying these unlikely 'chariots' was a motley collection of pilgrims; these included young people in yellow bandanas waving lotus-emblazoned orange banners, hordes of cheering old ladies proclaiming themselves 'The Lord Ram Birth Festival Assembly', and dozens of youths dressed-up as heroes from the *Ramayana* and the *Mahabharata*. In their wake marched a bizarre escort of young men in simian costumes, in emulation of Ram's famous monkey army, and brandishing swords and *trishuls* (tridents). But the centrepiece of the spectacle was a rather humdrum vehicle – a DCM-Toyota truck – bearing a far less exotic occupant – a portly BJP politician of advanced years, L. K. Advani. The grille of this truck-cum-chariot bore the legend 'From Somnath to Ayodhya', and some of the banners exhorted this unlikely avatar of Ram to build a great temple.

Ayodhya was held, by some, to be the birthplace of Ram, and thus a supremely holy place as Ram was a manifestation of the god Vishnu. But Ayodhya was also home to the Babri *masjid* (mosque), named after the fifteenth-century conqueror of north India, Babur. This mosque, some said, had been built on the very site of Ram's birth, in an act of deliberate humiliation that now required expiation. The *Rath Yatra* (chariot pilgrimage) and its thirty-five-day trek from Somnath through eight states, innumerable towns and villages, across the 10,000 kilometres to Ayodhya was intended to demonstrate the yearning of the nation's Hindus for the righting of this wrong. And the object of the pilgrimage was to elicit the consent of the Indian government to the demolition of the Babri *masjid* and the construction of a *Ram Janmahbhoomi* (temple of Ram's birthplace) in its place. The *Rath Yatra* transmitted a calculatedly mixed message. Advani, though occasionally snapped posing with a *sudarshana chakra* (Vishnu's indestructible discus), insisted he was merely a moderate, and indeed mild-mannered, politician. And his artfully adapted Toyota-chariot bore not godly insignia but the more quotidian instruction to 'Vote BJP'. But its attendants, the saffron-clad *sadhus*, monkey-militia and excitable Hindu women-folk projected a less placid image. And as the *yatra* trundled through hundreds of villages – 600 in Gujarat alone – people rushed to touch the Toyota's tyres in a gesture of religious obeisance, women danced the *ras*, supposedly invoking the god Krishna's dalliance with milkmaids, and dozens of devotees offered Advani vials of their own blood, swearing to convert '*Rama bhakti*' (devotion to Ram) into '*rashtra shakti*' (national power).

Though dismissed by some as tasteless 'Toyota Hinduism', the *Rath Yatra* attracted a surprisingly positive press from many of India's elite English-language dailies. Many simply adapted the breathless press releases issuing from the offices of the BJP itself, exclaiming at the ever-growing crowds massing to cheer the pilgrims. On closer inspection it turned out that these crowds consisted of essentially the same people who were being bused from place to place, the locals preferring to remain bemusedly aloof. But there were also many critics who labelled the *yatra* incendiary and accused Advani of an opportunistic stunt designed to hitch religious passions to the wagon (or chariot) of chauvinist politics. However, it was not until it reached Bihar, famously the most lawless and corrupt state in the entire subcontinent, that the *yatra* was halted, its unlikely chief charioteer deposed and bundled off unceremoniously for a short and involuntary sojourn in the Bihar state guesthouse. The author of this surprise detention was the recently elected chief minister of Bihar, Laloo Yadav. Laloo was a low-caste man, the Yadavs having traditionally been cow-herders, and Laloo's elevation to power had been among the more symbolically arresting events of recent years, just as his imprisonment of the Brahman Advani was a brutally literal one. Laloo, though he affected a bumpkin persona, was a shrewd politician, and quickly made the most of this richly comic event, soon parading about Bihar in his own customized chariot, a double-decker camper van converted to resemble a tank by the excision of a roof panel, from which Laloo's grinning visage bobbed ebulliently.

Both Advani and Laloo were in a sense warriors battling over temples, both literally and figuratively. While Advani may have claimed he was only fighting the 'pseudo-secularism' of Nehru, its favouritism towards Muslims and its callous lack of concern for Hindu sentiment, others saw his campaign as a holy war for Hindu unity against the supposed depredations, however long past, of the Muslims. Laloo, opportunistically perhaps, but nevertheless effectively, had gallantly defended the temple of Indian secular democracy. Moreover, he was a conspicuous example of the belated colonization of the Indian state by the lowliest but most numerous tiers of Indian society. Signs and portents of this latest and most dramatic advance on the temple of power had been around for many years, not least in the south. But the movement had crystallized around a recently revived government report, from the Mandal Commission of 1980, which had recommended that a sizeable percentage of prestigious state jobs now be reserved for people from the lower castes. This was a striking return to the assumptions of the Raj, which had also constructed caste as the alpha and omega of political and cultural life. But unlike the Raj, which had attempted to arrange India's castes into a great pyramidical hierarchy, the intention of Mandal was to level them. Advani's *Rath Yatra*, by contrast, was the latest in a series of concerted moves to subsume the uppity lower castes into a high-caste-led campaign to unite the Hindu 'nation' against its 'real' enemies – the Muslims; the building of the Ram *mandir* (temple) would be the crowning glory of the triumph of *Hindutva* (Hinduness). However, the 'Mandal-Mandir' confrontation, as it soon became known, was to have repercussions that neither of its principal protagonists could ever have imagined. For the alarming prospect of religious war permitted a determined battalion of politicians to advance on entirely different fronts – the liberalization of the nation's economy, and the battle to revivify India's global status.

The unprecedented majority won by the Congress party in the wake of Mrs Gandhi's assassination seemed at first to presage a renaissance of the Nehruvian glory-days. Led by his grandson, Rajiv, elevated monarch-like to the leadership within hours of his mother's death, Congress seemed revitalized. Rajiv, sedulously depicted as the Mr Clean of Indian politics was, it was said, poised to sweep the Augean stables of Congress politics clean of corruption, revitalize the party organization and regenerate the stagnant economy. Icon of a new generation, he was a tech-savvy Indian Airline pilot and devotee of computer gadgetry of all kinds; a role model for the aspirant middle classes, with his Gucci watch and loafers, a man, furthermore, commentators enthused, who understood the importance of colour TV. Marginalizing the old-timers associated with his mother, he preferred the company of a younger generation of advisers, many of whom were old school-friends from his days at the prestigious Indian Doon School. But he was also careful to nurture the party's traditional image as protector of the downtrodden, and in a neat PR stunt designed to project both his image as Mr Clean and friend to the poor (such as the sweepers) he was sometimes photographed wielding a broom.

His first months of office seemed promising. Accords were signed with the various regional groups in Punjab, Assam and Kashmir, whom his mother's crassly centralizing policies had antagonized. He also intervened in the ethnic conflict that had broken out in Sri Lanka between the Sinhalese and Tamil groups – diplomacy that would later cost him his life. While these initiatives did not solve all the problems of instability in these areas, they did, at least, signal an apparent return to the federalism of his grandfather's day. Plans were announced to rebuild Congress as a genuine mass party, to rid it of factionalism and corruption and to induct new blood and new groups into its fold. More striking still were the government's economic initiatives, which took the form of a mild loosening of controls on Indian businessmen and a concerted push to boost middle-class spending power. A few weeks after assuming office the youthful premier announced, 'Only a few decades ago made-in-Japan was synonymous with shoddy goods. Today . . . Japanese technology, finish and servicing have become a by-word for the best that is available . . . I am sure that we in India can do the same – and in a much shorter period.' The government's first budget, presented by the new finance minister, V. P. Singh, reduced licensing controls on many industries, loosened restrictions on investment, tore up a catalogue of controls on imported techno-logy, and lowered many tariffs and cut corporate taxes, with the intention of encouraging India's entrepreneurs to boost investment and expand at will into new spheres. Meanwhile personal tax rates were also slashed in an effort to create a more affluent domestic market for these new businesses. The Prime Minister was hailed as 'Rajiv-Reagan' for these new capitalist and market-friendly initiatives. And by the late 1980s the policies seemed to be working: the Indian economy was growing at around 8 per cent per annum, a pace not witnessed since the heyday of the Nehru years.

However, by mid-term it seemed that all this was not so much a new broom as old hat. Peace did not break out in the troubled regions, nor was Congress revitalized; indeed after disastrous results in state elections any purchase Rajiv may have had over the party evaporated and the old guard regrouped. Moreover, the new vigour in the econ-omy owed less to liberalization than to a revival of old-style state borrowing and public-sector investment. Emboldened by the now easy availability of credit on the international money markets and by healthy remittances from the burgeoning Indian diaspora in Europe, North America and the Gulf, the government had borrowed vast sums and ploughed them into infrastructure, and also into a bonanza of subsidies to the rich farming classes. Alarmingly, between 1982 and 1990 India's external debt had spiralled from $7.94 billion, or 11.4 per cent of GNP, to $70.12 billion – nearly 28 per cent of GNP. Moreover, the most striking effect of the liberalization was not the transfiguration of India's lumbering elephant of an economy into a roaring Asian tiger, but the transformation of its hitherto rather puritanical upper-middle-classes into insatiable consumers. Relaxed controls on foreign technology imports had not fostered a Japanese-style globe-conquering export drive but merely prompted India's slug-gish industrialists to import the technology needed to manufacture consumer durables cheaply and then sell them on to Indian consumers. For the 'middle class' – an unwieldy category embracing internationally educated and dazzlingly wealthy professional and business elites at its pinnacle to petty shopkeepers and modest farmers at its base – the possession of a certain 'suite' of goods (air-conditioning, a colour TV, a fridge and a washing machine) became the defining emblem of status.

Another unintended, but significant, consequence of the mild economic liberalization was the creation of yet more opportunities for graft. American businessmen were reporting that in return for contracts they were regularly required to deposit 5 per cent of the contract's value in offshore 'welfare' funds, and an IMF report of 1986 estimated there were 1.08 billion dollars deposited in private Indian accounts in Switzerland. The most spectacular of the various business scandals concerned the alleged payment of nearly $5 million in bribes or 'kick-backs' to senior politicians and defence personnel by the Swedish arms company Bofors. In return for a $1.3 billion contract to buy 400 howitzers, Bofors, it was claimed, had placed around $5 million in Swiss accounts held in the name of various Indian politicians and defence officials. Though nothing was ever proved against Rajiv Gandhi himself, his incorruptible image was hopelessly besmirched. The view developed that Rajiv must have something to hide, for otherwise why had he not, in the course of the tortuous investigations of the Swedish and Indian governments, insisted that Bofors divulge the identities of the persons in whose name the notorious bank accounts were held. Soon rumours sprang up that the disputed and costly howitzers didn't even work. This was all grist to the mill of Congress's political opponents, one of whom, the farmer-populist Devi Lal, sometime chief minister of Haryana, blustered: 'We don't want foreign wives, foreign money or foreign banks', in a slur designed to censure Rajiv not only for supposed shady dealings, but also for having chosen an Italian wife, Sonia. Rajiv himself was forced to resort to the old tactics of his mother, claiming the scandal had been trumped-up by a 'foreign hand' eager to destabilize India.

The principal beneficiary of this debacle was Rajiv's erstwhile finance minister, V. P. Singh. During the scandal Singh emerged as the new avatar of probity, whose personal incorruptibility, as *The Times* of London put it, 'made him stand out in a field crowded with racketeers'. Singh, scion of a small princely state, had arrived in politics by way of an early career in the Gandhian *Sarvodaya* (welfare) movement. He had made himself unpopular in political circles with his pursuit of big-business tax-evaders, involving police raids on the homes of well-known businessmen (a humiliation previously reserved only for film stars). He was swiftly transferred to defence. But in 1987, following his instigation of an anti-corruption campaign that some political colleagues regarded as unduly rigorous, he was expelled from the party. In the summer of 1988 he resigned his parliamentary seat and successfully fought a very high-profile by-election against Amitabh Bachchan, star of *Sholay* and dozens of other blockbusters, friend of Rajiv and latterly a Congress MP who, now also embroiled in the unsavoury Bofors affair, had decided to resign and fight again for his seat. During the election Singh's supporters chanted, 'Rajiv – return the nation's money. Rajiv – return to your senses.' The publicity generating impact of this victory was somewhat blunted by Bachchan's last-minute withdrawal of his candidacy. Nevertheless the momentum generated by the by-election had positioned Singh as a potential leader of the opposition. Singh, though he had been chief architect of the 1985 economic liberalization, now refashioned himself as a born-again socialist. And, invoking the impeccable credentials of such illustrious political forebears as Jayaprakash Narayan, set about crafting a left-of-centre coalition to oppose Congress in the impending 1989 General Election. An important component of this tricky brokering was a pitch for the support of the newly assertive groups known as the 'other backward castes or classes' (OBCs).

As has been seen, the linkage of caste identities with electoral politics dated back to the late nineteenth century, when the Raj had begun to use the caste categories of the census to create political interests for whom special privileges, in the form of positive discrimination in government recruitment, education and even government, were designed to cement their loyalties to the British. With the coming of independence some of these privileges – or 'compensatory measures' – were kept in order, it was claimed, to speed the integration of India's most oppressed groups. A set of supposedly time-limited quotas and reservations in government office, parliament and universities was made for dalit castes and tribal peoples, now known as the 'scheduleds' after the government schedule on which the beneficiaries of these measures were listed. But the constitution had also made it possible, though not mandatory, for individual states to make reservations for so-called 'other backward classes' or OBCs, an enormously broad collection of underprivileged persons previously dubbed the 'Depressed Classes' by the Raj.

The OBCs were a rather nebulous entity – not as oppressed as the 'scheduleds', but still hampered by low ritual status in the Hindu hierarchy, compounded by poverty and lack of education. Building on already entrenched British traditions, these new constitutional provisions for OBC quotas and reservations were adopted with some alacrity in the south and, to a lesser degree, in western India. Parties such as Tamil Nadu's DMK successfully amalgamated the fissiparous OBCs into over-arching quasi-ethnic identities defined, in essence, by their difference from the Brahmanical north, and rallied by the promise of quotas in universities and state jobs. By the early 1980s there were moves to reserve over 50 per cent of such posts for OBCs in Tamil Nadu. In western India, too, lower-caste groups had also been roughly forged into more cohesive blocs by movements such as Jyotirao Phule's late-nineteenth-century Satyashodhak Samaj. And while not as cohesive as the Dravidian-based DMK, this loose conglomeration of the Maharashtrian lower castes, notably Mahars and Kunbis, had forced the high-caste dominated Congress to assimilate them as something akin to equals. The result was that in much of the south and west these OBC groups had effectively colonized government jobs and higher education, either sharing power with high castes or, in the south, pushing them to the margins or forcing them to the north or, in many cases, abroad.

In north India, however, the British had not promoted the interests of low-caste groups so insistently; the legacies of positive discrimination had been much diluted and the lower castes had not forged the broader horizontal alliances found in the south and west. In part this was because in the north the British had relied on Muslim groups to counterbalance assertive high-caste Hindus, but also because lower castes were not, as they were elsewhere, such an overwhelmingly large proportion of the population. Moreover, the cultural context of the north differed markedly from that of southern and western India. This was the heartland of Brahmanical Hinduism with its more rigid notions of hierarchy and ritual purity. Here ambitions for social mobility among lower-caste groups tended not to take the form of rejecting Brahmanical Hinduism *tout court* in favour of non-caste-based ethnic identities; instead individual 'backward' castes had attempted to climb the ladder of status by emulating the higher castes – a process known as 'sanskritizing' themselves. As we saw in Chapter 2, the various *jatis* within the Shudra castes began to fabricate elaborate genealogies for themselves intended to 'prove' their high-status descent. The most numerous lower castes in Bihar and eastern Uttar Pradesh had all engaged in 'sanskritizing' strategies. The Yadavs (Ahirs), a cow-herding caste that could be found throughout the Ganges plain, acquired for themselves an 'Aryan' past, and in 1959 the *Divine Heritage of the Yadavs* confidently asserted that they were descended from the cow-herd god Krishna, that they were really high-caste Ksatriyas and asserted that they had been 'ancient Aryans, who . . . possessed the highest virtues which attracted God to be incarnated amongst them'. While this bid for self-esteem had the effect of knitting the hitherto fractious Yadavs into a more cohesive caste identity, it did not impress higher castes, among whom the Yadavs continued to be regarded by antagonists as 'dull, miserly, loud-mouthed people lacking in grace and culture'.

The Yadavs were not the only 'backward' caste in the region, though they were the most numerous. Other groups included the Kurmis and the Koeris. These too were cultivating castes, like the Yadavs, though usually less prosperous. They too had embarked on sanskritizing strategies, adopting a 'pure lifestyle' of vegetarianism and teetotalism, complete with elaborate caste histories tracing their ancestry to Ksatriya warriors. But efforts to unite with the Yadavs foundered on internal status jockeying – the Yadavs insisting on their superior descent. The Koeris, by contrast, had once been labelled a 'criminal caste' by the Raj's sociologists and their reputation had never quite recovered from this arbitrary appellation. Rather than make common cause with the Kurmis and Koeris, the Yadavs manifested their superiority complex by, for example, demanding the formation of a separate Yadav regiment in the Indian Army after the 1962 Indo-China war, claiming they were not a caste at all, but, employing Raj nomenclature, a 'martial race', like the Rajputs and Sikhs.

Nevertheless efforts had been made in the 1960s to unite the fractious OBCs into a unified political constituency around the issue of quotas and special representation. One such effort was led by the Samyukta Socialist Party of Ram Manohar Lohia. Though Lohia was as eager as any socialist to see caste wither away, he had been converted to the opinion of the great dalit leader Ambedkar, that precious little withering would occur until the lowest castes held the reins of political power in their own hands:

Many socialists honestly but wrongly think that it is sufficient to strive for economic equality and caste inequality will vanish of itself. They fail to comprehend economic inequality and caste inequality as twin demons, which both have to be killed.

And, as he astutely pointed out to those liberal Congressites who argued that equality of opportunity, not special quotas, was all that was required: 'When everybody has an equal opportunity, castes with the five thousand years old tradition of education would be on top. Only the exceptionally gifted from the lower castes would be able to break through this tradition . . . To make this battle a somewhat equal encounter, unequal opportunities would have to be extended to those who have so far been oppressed.' Lohia, though he became a mentor to a new generation of low-caste young men such as Mulayam Singh Yadav, future chief minister of Uttar Pradesh, made little headway. It was, rather, the agrarian populism of Charan Singh, which sought to dissolve caste divisions into a homogenous 'peasant' identity led by rich farmers that became the best-organized alternative to Congress. However, by the late 1970s Charan Singh's rich farmer constituency, many of whom, though prosperous, were OBCs themselves, sought to translate the economic power bestowed on them by the Green Revolution into social prestige. Anxious that their sons should have access to the best higher education and prestigious government jobs, they were not averse to the revival of the question of caste reservations. One of the few lasting achievements of Morarji Desai's short-lived

Janata government was the appointment, in 1978, of the second Government of India Backward Classes Commission – the Mandal Commission.

The first Backward Classes Commission had been appointed nearly thirty-years before in 1953, and had, somewhat unpromisingly, been headed by a Brahman, Kakasaheb Kalelkar. This commission, in the event, made little impression and had, indeed, stumbled over the very definition of the 'Backward Classes'. Operating during the high tide of Nehruvian 'socialism', this body had baulked at using caste as the primary definition of social and cultural status because this smacked too redolently of Raj stereotypes. Instead the commission had blurred the distinction between class and caste, with caste recognized as only one of a number of markers of oppressed status. Though one member of the Kalelkar Commission issued a minute of dissent, demanding that the backward classes should 'snatch away the power' of the upper castes through the creation of reserved parliamentary seats, the majority of the commission struck a less incendiary posture with recommendations of 70 per cent quotas in technical education only, and a 40 per cent quota in the lower tiers of government administration. But even these mild prescriptions were swiftly dismissed. Govind Pant, the Brahman Congress chief minister of Uttar Pradesh argued, somewhat disingenuously, that, 'With the establishment of our society on a socialist pattern . . . social and other distinctions will disappear as we advance towards that goal.' He also aired an argument that soon became popular among upper-caste groups: 'If we go in for reservations on a communal and caste basis, we swamp the bright and able people and remain second-rate or third-rate. Let us help the backward people by all means but never at the cost of efficiency.'

The second Backward Classes Commission, unlike the first, was headed by an OBC, B. P. Mandal, a Yadav – indeed there were no upper-caste members. But like the first commission, the most taxing task facing this inquiry was to define who precisely the OBCs were, and then to recommend such reservations as would promote their 'social emancipation'. Mandal had been a sometime member of Lohia's Samyukta Socialist Party, and then of the Janata Party and thus, unlike his predecessor, had no qualms about elevating caste as the pre-eminent measure of under-privilege. Caste, the commission insisted, was at the very root of India's structural inequality, adding: 'To treat unequals equally is to perpetuate inequality.' And, echoing some of the assumptions of the Raj, Mandal argued that in India persons could not, with fairness, be judged merely according to notions of individual merit; the 'Other Backward Castes' should be regarded as a 'class of citizens . . . socially and educationally backward', and deserving of special reservations as a collective, regardless of individual wealth or merit. The commission assembled a table of castes, oddly reminiscent of those found in the census data of the British era, and indeed drawing on those very Raj-authored artefacts for some of its information, for the last occasion on which India's castes had been catalogued so comprehensively was in the 1931 census. Using this and a variety of other vigorously disputed guides, the Mandal Commission identified 3743 distinct castes (the first commission had found only a paltry 2000) and then went on to calculate that 52 per cent of India's population were OBCs. It recommended that 27 per cent of posts in government bureaucracy and the public sector be reserved for them, along with 27 per cent of places in all scientific and professional institutions run by the central and state governments.

The Congress government of Indira Gandhi shelved the report, castigating its dubious methodology and arguing that discrimination should be on economic grounds only. However, at the very same time it and its Rajiv-led successor adopted a style of politics likely to make caste identity not less but more salient. For Congress, like the Raj before it, had embarked on the perilous path of appealing to supporters not as individuals with personal ideological proclivities, but as groups to be induced into ramshackle coalitions by the promise of special collective boons. The only real difference between this approach and the Raj's was while the British identified their clients/collaborators as 'minorities', in the era of mass democracy such beneficiaries were bluntly dubbed 'vote-banks'. In Gujarat, for example, this strategy had taken the form of the infamous 'KHAM' strategy, whereby Congress had cobbled together a majority for itself composed of the Ksatriya, Harijans, Ahirs (Yadavs) and Muslims. No effort was made to create a unifying ideology among these groups, for that would have imperilled alternative equations of group power in other states. Unsurprisingly, the constituents of these gimcrack assemblages began to see elections principally as the means to stake collective claims to state employment and largesse.

For Congress's opponents, among them the dissident ex-finance minister V. P Singh and his hastily formed party, the Janata Dal (People's Party), the imperative need was to create a vote-bank of their own. Given that Congress depended on its Brahman-cum-scheduled-caste 'coalition of extremes', the obvious strategy for Singh and his cohorts was to mobilize the OBCs en masse by disinterring the hastily buried Mandal Commission report and promising 60 per cent of his party's seats in the coming election to 'the weaker sections of society'. And, on 15 August 1990, Independence Day, as Prime Minister of the fragile National Front coalition government, Singh announced his intention to give 'a share to the poor in running the government', promising them a 40 per cent share in parliamentary and state assemblies.

In this year of justice, in memory of Dr Bhimrao Ambedkar [whose birth centenary would fall in 1991] the government has recently taken the decision to give reservation to the backward classes in jobs in government and the public sector . . . We want to give an effective [sic] here in the power structure and running of the country to the depressed, the down-trodden and backward people.

The effect was immediate – electrifying and alarming in equal measure. Anti-Mandal forums were hastily convened among students in top universities, and student agitations turned violent, culminating in a number of high profile self-immolations. At the same time Advani launched his motley crew of pilgrims on their baleful *Rath Yatra*. OBC leaders struck back, organizing mass demonstrations of angry crowds chanting, '*Brahman saala desh chhado*' ('Rascally Brahmans, get out of the country'). Caste, the defining social identity of India under the Raj, had been re-enthroned. The Mandal Commission, like the British censuses before it, had had the effect of reifying what had hitherto been abstractions. For it was only when the Mandal Commission set about counting, defining and measuring the concept of OBC-ness that the thing itself came into existence and the hitherto disparate and warring fractions of the north Indian lower castes began to see themselves, albeit briefly, as a unified interest group.

Seen in isolation, reservations of 27 per cent of official and public-sector posts did not amount to much, representing relatively few jobs in relation to the overall size of the working population. But they had immense symbolic significance. Bureaucratic office was highly valued: in 1989, for example, over 2.5 million people had applied for 204,000 central administrative posts. Mandal would have the effect of reserving 55,000 of these prized positions for OBCs only. Moreover, command of the best government posts was seen as virtually the birthright of the higher castes, which, while only a bare 15 per cent of the all-India population, held 90 per cent of top administrative posts in 1980. The OBCs, by contrast, held a mere 5 per cent of these jobs, despite constituting, according to the commission, 52 per cent of the Indian people. In the state governments the situation was similar: in Uttar Pradesh, 94 per cent of principal secretaries and secretaries to the governments, 85 per cent of the headships of departments, and 93 per cent of section officers were upper caste. And even locally nearly 79 per cent of district magistrates were upper caste.

But the greatest impact of the Mandal Commission was not on administration, but on politics. The gradual replacement of high-caste Members of Parliament and state-level Legislative Assembly members by low-caste counterparts in the late 1980s and 1990s has been described by some as India's second democratic upsurge (the first being the rise of the farmers in the 1960s), and as a silent (or at least relatively subdued) revolution. In the 1989 General Election the proportion of high-caste MPs fell below 40 per cent for the first time. The political impact of Mandal is not, however, so very surprising, for in many ways the mobilization around reservations was primarily intended not to capture administrative posts but to rally OBC voters to politicians who promised to promote OBC interests. The Mandal issue had crystallized the hitherto fractious OBCs into a cohesive whole capable of turning their massive voting strength into real power. The effects were not evenly distributed and OBCs did better in some states than others. However, in the two most populous northern states, Uttar Pradesh and Bihar, the OBCs displaced Congress and the high castes as the dominant power-brokers, a development signalled by the ascendancy of two politicians of Yadav background. From 1989 to 1991 and again in 1993–95 Mulayam Singh Yadav became chief minister of Uttar Pradesh, while in 1990 and again in 1995 Laloo Yadav occupied the *gaddi* (throne) of the chief minister in Bihar, and remained there, overseeing state affairs. Even when imprisoned on suspicion of a state-procurement fraud in 2000, he governed through his proxy, his (allegedly illiterate) wife, Rabri Devi.

The coming of the Laloo-raj was viewed with unmitigated horror by the upper castes and unabashed delight by his low-caste supporters. One of seven children born into a poor farmer's family in 1948, the gregarious Laloo did well enough at school to enter Patna's Bihar National College, though he neglected academe to become president of the Student Union. In 1974 he came to the attention of political leaders in the state with his involvement in the anti-Indira JP Movement, and was imprisoned during the Emergency. His arrival as chief minister ushered in a whole new style of politics, and one calculated to provoke the high-caste elites who had previously dominated Bihar.

Roguish, but charismatic and reckless, he is an accomplished and irreverent wit. On becoming chief minister he refused, initially, to move to the chief minister's mansion in Patna, preferring to stay in his brother-in-law's bungalow, a labourers' hut attached to Bihar Veterinary College. To this modest residence, senior, generally high-caste government officials were summoned to meetings held in public under a hastily erected marquee. Though educated, Laloo chose to address his audiences, both elite and popular, in either local Bhojpuri dialect or English heavily inflected with Bhojpuri. He also perfected a plebeian political style – leaping from his ministerial car, megaphone in hand, to marshal the traffic on Bihar's chaotic roads, or hugging elderly supporters and granting them immediate state pensions. A brilliant stump politician (he is reputed to have visited every village in Bihar), he would often descend on unsuspecting villagers and sweep them off for a few circuits in his chief ministerial helicopter, where they were exhorted to munch on his plentiful supply of Cadbury's Melody chocolate kept in a bucket in the cockpit: 'Eat, eat, have fun in Laloo Raj.' He was soon dubbed the 'Charvaha in a chopper' –

Charvahas being another low-caste group in Bihar. His campaigning message was the crude, but effective, '*Bhurabal Hatao*' ('wipe out the high castes'): 'Bhurabal' was an acronym of his own coinage, which amalgamated the various upper castes – the Bhumihars, Rajputs, Brahmans and Lalas (Kayasths) – into one compound bogey. To his enchanted supporters he thundered: 'These people have oppressed and suffocated you for thousands of years . . . they are about to be cast into the dustbin . . . there has been a revolution in Bihar.'

Laloo did not run Bihar very well, and spent a sizeable portion of his term of office in prison. But his appeal was not founded on claims to competence and probity, but on the assertion of plebeian ascendancy. As he told his biographer:

Look at my rosy cheeks, this is the colour of rebellion against the upper castes. Haven't I changed things for myself and my people? I am eating the best chocolates in the land, I am wearing crisp white muslin, I can do what I want. I have given [the people] a sense of self-respect.

Both Laloo and Mulayam Singh Yadav made dramatic changes in the personnel of government and administration. Upper-caste bureaucrats found themselves spirited into non-essential posts. In Bihar a scheduled-caste officer replaced a Brahman as Chief Secretary in 1993, and an OBC took over as Director General of Police. Within three years of Laloo's ascent, 70 upper-caste bureaucrats had requested new postings in another state; 12 of 13 divisional commissioners were transferred and 250 of 324 returning officers were moved to make way for lower-caste occupants. Both states implemented the Mandal reservations in recruitment, but in addition Mulayam Singh Yadav had introduced quotas in the local Uttar Pradesh *panchayats* in 1994. He even, controversially, extended reservations of 27 per cent to the region of Uttarakhand, where only 2 per cent of the population was actually OBC, while Laloo imposed 50 per cent reservations for OBCs on the governing senate of Bihar University. Clearly these initiatives were not merely intended to redress historic community imbalances, but were carefully staged PR coups designed to rally a vote-bank around the very symbol of reservations. This became clear when a new administration attempted to remove the egregious Uttarakhand reservations and Mulayam Singh Yadav, now in opposition, launched an *aarakshan bachao* (save reservations) campaign, directed not so much at the handful of direct beneficiaries in Uttarakhand itself, but to rally a broad OBC constituency in the whole of Uttar Pradesh behind the notion that their interests were being attacked.

It was not, however, the symbolic nature of reservations' politics that would cause problems for Laloo and Singh, but its very concrete operation. Mulayam Singh Yadav's Samajwadi Party, formed in 1992, espoused ostensibly broad and inclusive socialist goals, but its governing councils, candidates and supporters soon turned out to be overwhelmingly Yadav. Moreover, in a manner highly reminiscent of the collaborator parties of the Raj era, both Laloo and Mulayam used their power to dispense patronage to their closest supporters only. Of 900 new teachers appointed in Uttar Pradesh in 1993, 720 were Yadavs, while 1223 of the state's police cadets were also of Yadav origin. And in 1996, when the Bihar University Service Commission recruited 1400 lecturers, nearly all of them were Yadavs. In Laloo's cabinet a mere two of the seventy-six ministers were Kurmis. Yadavs also occupied the headships of the various public-sector commissions and boards of control, including the Public Services Commission, the Secondary Education Service Commission, the Bihar Electricity Board and the Bihar Industrial Development Corporation. Such favouritism soon had the effect of fracturing the recently won unity of the OBCs themselves and their alliance with the scheduled castes. By 1999 many dalits and smaller OBC groups such as the Lodhis and Kurmis were either voting for the high-caste BJP, or the dalit-led Bahujan Samaj Party (BSP).

In an extraordinary volte-face, which illustrated both the centrality of caste to north Indian politics and the bizarre alliances leaders of caste parties were prepared to make in order to get power, the dalit BSP brokered an arrangement with the high-caste BJP in order to remove Mulayam Singh Yadav, and they succeeded in replacing him with the BSP's leader, Mayawati. The BSP had been nurtured by a Punjabi dalit Kanshi Ram, who, one of the elite among the scheduled castes, had benefited from the original reservations policy of the 1950 constitution. After university he began work as a government chemist in Maharashtra, where, unlike in the Punjab, untouchability was highly stigmatized. Radicalized by the oppressive treatment of the dalit Mahars, and also by personal humiliation in his own career, Ram founded the Backward and Minority Communities Employees Federation (BAMCEF) in 1973. In essence this was a pressure group for the educated elite of dalits, and it soon boasted among its 200,000 members 500 PhDs and 15,000 university-trained scientists. By the early 1980s Ram began to change his strategy away from elite lobbying to popular political mobilization, having concluded, like Ambedkar and Lohia before him, that without power no amount of lobbying would improve the conditions of the scheduled classes. In a pamphlet, *The Chamcha Age*, he denounced other dalit politicians as stooges and in 1984 he formed the BSP, intended not only for dalits but all *bahujans* (common people), in order to, as he put it, '*jat todo, samaj jodo*' ('break caste, unite the common people'), and thereby to seize power from the upper-caste 15 per cent who controlled Indian life. The BSP's most famous (some thought infamous) slogan was the rhythmic and rather menacing chant: '*Tilak, tarahu, aur talvar isko maro joote char*' – a metonymic ditty inviting the Chamars, traditionally cobblers, to thrash the other castes, symbolized by the *tilak*, the mark of Brahmanhood, the *tarahu*, the weighing scales of the merchant castes, and the *talvar*, the sword of the warrior castes, with their shoes.

In the 1984 elections the BSP won one million votes, while in 1989 it polled over six million – largely from rural dalits. In 1993 the party formed an alliance with Mulayam Singh Yadav's Samajwadi Party to take power in Uttar Pradesh. Relations between the two parties soon deteriorated. During these years there were increasing numbers of violent attacks on dalit labourers, many by OBC farmers, in the Uttar Pradesh countryside; the 1067 cases reported in 1989 had spiralled to 14,000 in 1995. In Kanshi Ram's opinion Mulayam Singh had not done enough to suppress this violence. The BSP also objected to the continuing Yadavization of public life and, most of all, to Mulayam's cynical manipulation of caste quotas and reservations to capture the village *panchayat* councils. In the 1995 *panchayat* elections the Samajwadi Party took thirty of the fifty districts, while only two districts were won by the BSP. Dominance in these increasingly important rural institutions promised Mulayam a near unassailable power-base in the countryside, and thus brought about the remarkable rapprochement between the predominantly high-caste BJP and the largely dalit BSP. On 2 June 1995 the BSP withdrew its support from the Mulayam government, and, with BJP support, its leader, Mayawati, became chief minister the very next day.

Mayawati, a woman from a Chamar family, was born in the Ghazibad district of the province in 1956. Like Kanshi Ram she had been one of the beneficiaries of the Nehruvian scheme of affirmative action designed to help dalits. After acquiring a slew of degrees she began working as a schoolteacher, but then decided to prepare for the Indian Administrative Service exams, a decision, along with her impressive oratorical powers, that brought her to the attention of Kanshi Ram. She swiftly ascended the BSP hierarchy to become second only to Ram himself in the party organization. In her two brief terms of office in Uttar Pradesh she deployed a largely symbolic, but nevertheless highly effective brand of politics designed to consolidate her own scheduled-caste support, and also to forge an alliance with the poorer, non-Yadav, elements among the state's OBCs. Her speciality was the politics of public space, particularly the iconic occupation and renaming thereof. Agra University, for example, was transmogrified into Dr Bhimrao Ambedkar University, the Agra stadium became the Eklavya stadium (to commemorate the dalit bowman of the *Mahabharata*), and in the state capital Lucknow, an Ambedkar Udhyan (park) appeared. The many towns of the state soon hosted statues of the great dalit leader, Ambedkar; even more provocatively, the figure of E.V. Ramaswami Naicker, or Periyar ('wise one'), the leader of the south Indian low castes and razor-tongued scourge of Brahmanhood, began to appear in a variety of locations frequented by Brahmans. These gestures had their intended effect, both in raising low-caste esteem and provoking high-caste vandalism. Less symbolic was Mayawati's decision to increase the funding of programmes targeted at dalit villages where, she insisted, 'all roads, hand pumps, houses etc are to be built in their neighbourhoods'. Grants were given to dalit children to enable them to attend school and a rehabilitation programme initiated for Bhangi (ordure collectors) children.

Dalits and OBC groups may not have succeeded in forging themselves into a single cohesive or unified political constituency, but in the

1990s they did develop sufficient independent political organization to begin translating their voting strength into executive power. Some have likened this phenomenon to a silent revolution, and, like all revolutions, silent or otherwise, this one produced a reaction. High-caste groups, both incensed and threatened by this apparently unstoppable assault on their power and privileges, sought to suppress and divert it into alternative, less directly threatening channels. The most conspicuous example of this was the striking electoral success of the BJP. Formed in 1980 from the ashes of the old Jan Sangh, it was able to harness upper-caste resentments to its Hindu nationalist programme far more successfully than its predecessor. But in doing so it, along with its partners in the VHP (the *Vishva Hindu Parishad* or World Hindu Council) and the RSS, launched a broadside against one of the great foundational myths of the Indian Republic – secularism. And, paradoxically, the violence and turmoil aroused by Hinduization permitted another silent revolution to unfold – economic liberalization.

The Janata Dal government was plagued by internal rivalry, and in November 1990 V. P. Singh was deposed by Chandra Shekhar who held the premiership very briefly with the support of Congress. Fresh General Elections were called in May 1991, and during the campaign Rajiv Gandhi was assassinated by a suicide bomber attached to the Tamil Tigers, a group opposing his policy in Sri Lanka. Rajiv had not really fulfilled the promise of his massive majority. His economic reforms had become enmeshed in scandal, and by the late 1980s it seemed that India was heading for a major debt and foreign exchange crisis. Moreover, there seemed to be little appetite for further reform, with vociferous opponents spanning the social and political spectrum – from the wealthy farmers, business interests and Hindu nationalists on the right, a rainbow of low-caste groupings and communists on the left and much of the rest of India in between. It is surprising, therefore, that when the long-impending foreign exchange crisis finally broke in the summer of 1991, the new Congress Prime Minister, Narasimha Rao, leading a weak minority government, was able to embark on an infinitely more far-reaching set of economic reforms than Rajiv with his massive majority had ever attempted. What is even more arresting is that there had been no fundamental realignment of political opinion – those who had opposed reform in the mid-1980s were still opposing it in the early 1990s.

Narasimha Rao, India's twelfth Prime Minister, was its first from the south. Born in Andhra Pradesh in 1921, Rao had enjoyed a long and distinguished career in Congress politics, rising from Gandhian freedom fighter to chief minister of Andhra Pradesh in the early 1970s. He then became a minister holding various portfolios in both the Indira and Rajiv Gandhi cabinets. He was, therefore, an archetypal political insider. He also, however, had a pronounced literary bent, writing political commentary and satire in the 1980s under the apt pseudonym, 'The Insider'. In 1998, after leaving office, he caused a momentary stir in Indian elite circles with the publication of his semi-autobiographical novel, *The Insider*. Though it was the faintly lubricious sex scenes and scathing castigation of colleagues that caught the attention of reviewers at the time – Rao described the members of Congress's parliamentary party as a 'strange crowd – simple, complex, heterogeneous, spineless, variously motivated, united, divided, and on the whole undefinable' – the central story is a more poignant tale. This concerns the career of a neophyte politician, Anand, and his dismal trajectory from the idealism of the Nehru years, during which he imbibes the rhetoric of revolutionary social transformation, to his dispiriting political demise during the cynical Indira era. Anand is presented as a paragon of the Indian intelligentsia: 'Anand was a committed devotee of logical thinking. He had overwhelming compassion for the afflicted. He suffered from total absence of personal ambition. He possessed a storehouse of knowledge accumulated over a long period of study and reflection.' But despite these remarkable virtues, Anand's story is the classic tale of lost illusions. Thwarted in his goal to eject India's reactionary 'landlord lobby' from their entrenched privileges with his brilliantly conceived land reforms, he is reduced, instead, to presiding impotently over the chaotic scandal-ridden fictional state of Afrozabad.

Rao's own career proved rather more productive, though not perhaps in the manner that his fictional alter ego, who had dreamt of embarking on the semi-mystical 'path to revolutionary social transformation', might have envisaged. For while Anand had concluded that the Naxalites had 'served notice that social tensions can lead to unmitigated disaster; there has to be change', it was World Bank and IMF warnings of unmitigated financial disaster to which Rao responded. And with further irony, it was Rao, much given to such laconic aperçus as 'inaction is a form of action', who lit the bonfire under much of the planning framework and regulatory mechanisms of the post-independence Indian economic system. As a consequence of the heavy borrowing and relaxation of import controls in the mid-1980s, India's fiscal deficit – the excess of spending over revenue – had risen from 6.4 per cent of GDP in 1980–81 to 9 per cent in 1990–91, inflation was running at over 10 per cent, its balance of payments position had seriously deteriorated, government debt was growing alarmingly and India's foreign exchange reserves were so low that by the summer of 1991 it had barely enough foreign currency to cover two weeks' worth of imports. At the same time India's credit rating was downgraded by international agencies alarmed at the economic trajectory and by the political instability attending the Mandal-Mandir imbroglio – a move that made it very difficult for the state to raise funds from foreign lenders. And in a manoeuvre strikingly reminiscent of its colonial years, the nation's gold reserves had been put in hock to the Bank of England in return for short-term advances of foreign currency.

The summer of 1991 saw India in the midst of what economists call a liquidity crisis – it did not have enough cash to fund its foreign trade and debt obligations. The government insisted it had little alternative but to negotiate a 'stabilization' package with the IMF, under the terms of which India secured stand-by loans to cover its trading and borrowing obligations. In return for these it agreed to a 20 per cent devaluation of its currency, and to a series of cuts in state spending (largely on defence and subsidies) intended to reduce the fiscal deficit to the manageable proportions of the early 1980s. What was remarkable, however, was the ensuing assault on the entire ethos and apparatus of 'permit raj'. Not content with merely stabilizing the economy, Rao and his finance minister, the career official and professional economist Manmohan Singh, embarked on a set of policies intended to restructure the economy's fundamental basis.

Between 1991 and 1996 this radical reorientation brought dramatic change in some areas (though very little in others), and established a course from which its successor ministries have barely diverged.

The most striking feature of the policy revolution was the switch from an emphasis on government intervention and public spending to an all-out campaign to attract private business, both Indian and foreign. Before 1991 the private sector in India, though large, was shackled by a vast array of licensing, permit requirements and exclusions designed to give the government control over what could be produced, where and by what technological processes. Setting up a new business often required as many as eighty distinct 'permissions'. By 1998 most of this paraphernalia had been swept away and all but nine industries were now wholly open to private enterprise. The power sector was now open to private operators, as was much of the airline industry; indeed the only major state-held monopolies were in railways and insurance. More striking still, in a nation with a keen memory of imperialism, foreign business interests were assiduously wooed. Before 1991 foreign firms were even more bound by regulations than the home-grown variety: foreigners were allowed only a 40 per cent share in any Indian firm, were prohibited from borrowing in India, from taking over other Indian-owned firms, and required government permission to appoint foreign technicians and managers. But in 1993 it was announced that foreign businessmen would be welcomed like prodigal sons, subject to exactly the same treatment as the sons-of-the-soil. They would be permitted a 51 per cent controlling share in 48 industries, rising to 70 per cent in a further 9 and, astonishingly, 100 per cent ownership rights in the power sector. Foreign investors were allowed, for the first time, to buy and sell Indian stocks, and Indian companies could now offer their shares on foreign stock exchanges. This new approach soon had its intended effect and foreign direct investment leapt from a mere $80–100 million per annum before 1991 to $3 billion by 1997–98, while portfolio investment (foreign holdings of Indian stocks and shares) soared to $14 billion.

Not content with beckoning foreigners inwards, the government was also determined that Indian business should move outwards, and set about promoting the nation's dormant export trade. Again, in a hangover from colonial days, international trade had often been equated with exploitation; moreover, the decades spent huddling behind stratospheric tariff and quota barriers had produced among India's own industrialists the not unjustified fear that they could not compete with foreign entrepreneurs. Such trepidation was again brushed aside and tariff walls crumbled from an average rate of 87 per cent in 1990 to 20 per cent in 1997, while quotas were abolished on all but consumer goods and agricultural products. Dismissing accusations that any influx of foreign capital and commodities was tantamount to a neo-colonial putsch, Manmohan Singh declaimed that 'Indians must not remain permanent captives of a fear of the East India Company, as if nothing has changed in 300 years.'

Less dramatic but still significant alterations were made to India's banking and financial sectors. Most sweeping was the freeing of India's capital markets. Share issues had been strictly controlled by government boards, but now India's stock exchanges were allowed to emulate the practices of liberal economies, regulating their own operations under the Securities and Exchange Board of India (SEBI). Banks were not quite so liberally treated. Under Mrs Gandhi India's banks had been nationalized and their freedom of action severely restricted. They were required to hold large reserves with the Indian central bank (the Reserve Bank of India, or RBI), and much of their lending took the form of low-yield government debt. In essence their role was to support the government's social and political goals, not to make profitable investments. After the reforms, though many banks still operated under strict regulation, new private banks, including those owned by foreigners, were permitted and state banks were encouraged to direct more of their funds towards commercial lending. Statutory deposits with the RBI fell from 25 per cent to 10 per cent and compulsory holdings of government debt were reduced from 38 per cent of deposits to 25 per cent. Subsequent changes gave banks some discretion in setting their own interest rates and allowed them to offer especially attractive terms to Non-Resident Indians (NRIs) – the burgeoning community of affluent Indians now living abroad in North America, Europe and the Gulf – hoping, thereby, to turn the trickle of foreign exchange into a flood. They were, however, still required to allocate 40 per cent of their lending to so-called 'priority sectors' – essentially small businesses and farmers.

Finally, efforts were made to cut India's spiralling public debt and to reorient the tax system away from an over-reliance on indirect revenues towards the direct taxation of personal and corporate incomes. Government debt was reduced, though not to the degree projected. In an economy where politically sensitive food and fertilizer subsidies absorbed almost the entire sum raised by personal tax, this would have been a Herculean task. However, there was some success in tax reform, with the percentage share of direct taxes rising from only 19 per cent to 30 per cent of the total in 1997; this was achieved by cutting marginal rates and simplifying the tax rules in the hope of discouraging India's endemic degree of tax evasion. Even so, no attempt was made to levy a tax on agricultural incomes.

Despite the international brouhaha over liberalization, the issue was hardly a new one and the decision to embark on reform did not signify a miraculous conversion from socialism to the unfettered market, as was sometimes suggested by its most enthusiastic proponents. India's economy had never been socialist in any meaningful sense and the reforms were very far from marking the triumph of untrammelled capitalism. Debates and controversies between advocates of plans and markets were as old as the post-independent state itself – indeed older, as several of India's most prominent early nationalists had been economists. Moreover, such economic arguments were bound to be endemic in a society where 'the dismal science' had attained such prestige. It has been observed that the success of a nation's economy seems to be inversely related to the brilliance of its economists, and in the output of one commodity at least – brilliant economists – India has been a world leader. From the late nineteenth century the subcontinent began to produce a professional corps of economists in numerous schools and institutes, many with nationalist roots and devoted, in part at least, to dissecting the economic failings of the Raj. And after independence India has continued its production of renowned economists and influential institutions. Most prominent, of course, was P. C. Mahalanobis and the Indian Statistical Institute, though many maintained that it was really the Calcutta-Delhi axis, referring to the professors of Presidency College, Calcutta and the Delhi School of Economics, that had the greatest hand in shaping India's planorama.

By the 1970s the repute of India's economariat was so great that they had become an export industry in their own right, the most prominent being Amartya Sen, who, after teaching at the Delhi School of Economics, moved on to chairs at the LSE, Oxford and Harvard and was feted as a Nobel laureate for his work on poverty. Manmohan Singh, the architect of India's reforms who became Prime Minister in 2004, had also been both an academic and an IMF and government economist. Singh, modestly, refers to himself as not a distinguished, but an extinguished economist. Others, such as Jagdish Bhagwati and T. N. Srinivasan, have also held high-profile chairs at US universities while maintaining close links with both the Indian government and international institutions such as the World Bank. Indeed it might be argued, if there is an axis of academic influence operating in India today, one of its poles now points sharply towards the Indian diaspora.

While Nehruvian-style dirigisme had commanded broad, if not uncritical, assent among professional and government economists throughout the 1950s and much of the 1960s, by the early 1970s dissenting voices became more prominent, and by the late 1970s there was agreement only that the economy's performance was distinctly below par – particularly by comparison with other Asian late-developers such as South Korea and, latterly, China. Many bemoaned the apparently unshiftable 'Hindu' rate of growth – around 3–4 per cent per annum from 1950 to 1980. While there were pockets of success largely associated with the Green Revolution, industry was stagnant, inefficient and possessed virtually no export markets save those of the Soviet Union and its various satellites. Poverty was still endemic, a high percentage of the population remained illiterate and poorly trained confined to, ill-paid rural employment. Taxes as a percentage of GNP were dangerously low and declining, and the black-market accounted for between 20 and 30 per cent of all economic activity. Moreover, the economy was highly vulnerable to monsoon failure and to periodic balance of payments crises.

Two broad diagnoses emerged, one preoccupied with economics, the other with politics. Among neo-liberal economists such as Bhagwati, the chief ailment was the inefficiency inherent in a state-planned economy. India's planners, among whom Bhagwati had once been numbered, had committed a catalogue of errors, the principal mistake being excessive emphasis on protectionism and the promotion of 'infant-industries' in the misguided hope of making India independent of the world economy. As a consequence there had been excessive concentration on heavy industry and not enough on consumer goods and, compounding these calamities, a general neglect of agriculture. India had become a hostile jungle of licences and permits that sapped the 'animal energies' of India's entrepreneurs, but which provided a veritable paradise for grasping and corrupt officials. On the left, economists such as the professoriat of the Centre for Economic Studies and Planning at Jawaharlal Nehru University insisted that there had been nothing inherently wrong with planning; indeed the pursuit of import-substituting industrialization had been the strategy of choice for many late-developers from Germany to South Korea. The failure in India lay not with economic ideas but with political execution. To be effective planning required a fundamental redistribution of productive assets such as land and education to the masses – as had happened in Japan and South Korea – and a massive public investment in infrastructure. Both of these worthy goals had foundered on the rocks of vested interest. As a result the population remained too abjectly poor to constitute a viable mass market and India was stuck in a low consumption trap. Those of a less combative bent maintained that there was some truth on both sides of this argument, and that their respective prescriptions were not necessarily wholly incompatible.

These debates had penetrated official circles where already there was concern that chronic lack of funds for public-sector investment might require some tinkering with the operation and assumptions of planning – and even limited liberalization. The balance of payments crisis and devaluation of 1966 had been followed by a 'plan holiday', after which, though planning officially resumed in the 1970s, plans had ceased to play the determining role they had previously enjoyed. Market forces, though undoubtedly constrained, were already much more important in shaping outcomes and growth patterns. Increasingly, official commissions and inquiries concluded that economic administration was cumbersome and ineffective and suggested piecemeal measures of reform of some or other aspect of the economy. By the 1980s this quiet shift in official attitudes found favour with Mrs Gandhi, who, assured of her pre-eminence among the poor, was now seeking not only a constituency among businessmen and the urban professional classes, but also to negotiate a sizeable disbursement from the IMF. The not insignificant deregulatory measures pursued under her administration were, however, carefully glossed as essentially 'technical' matters – lifting a ceiling here, lowering a restriction there.

Pro-market policies gathered pace under her son Rajiv, but were declared by 'computerji' (as he was known) and his coterie of ambitious young technocrats and entrepreneurs to be harbingers of a major ideological change. The overt acknowledgement that the economy was being 'liberalized' allowed critics to polarize the debate as a rich versus poor issue in a way that his mother had studiously sought to avoid. Soon the Rajiv liberalization was drowning in a flood of opposition, which managed to unite leftist intellectuals with fearful businessmen, and rich farmers with poor peasants. While some employed the pseudo-Gandhian rhetoric of protecting national pride from foreign exploiters, others insisted that the poor were being sacrificed on the altar of capitalist greed. The result was that while in 1986 Rajiv had announced his willingness to confront 'vested interests in almost every field . . . including our own party, including industry, in business, in administration, the whole lot, the farmers', by 1988 his chief economic adviser glumly concluded, 'there seems little room for further concessions.'

By 1991, therefore, there was already a sizeable reform constituency among academic and official economists. At first glance, however, the policies initiated that year seemed even less likely to thrive than Rajiv's. While the Rajiv government had a massive majority of 415 out of 545 seats, the Rao ministry had no majority at all. It benefited, however, from a radically altered international context. The communist model of development, on which Indian planning was loosely based, was held to have been discredited not only by the fall of the Berlin Wall in 1989, but also by the economic success of China's economic liberalization. More immediately pressing than these theoretical considerations, the demise of the Soviet state had also robbed India of an important trading partner from whom it had received strategically important industrial and defence goods. Moreover the 1991 Gulf War threatened not only the end of cheap oil, but also of essential foreign exchange remittances from Indian workers in Kuwait and Iraq. The downgrading of India's international credit status in the wake of the collapse of the V. P. Singh government in late 1990 completed a disastrous series of shocks that effectively, it seemed, ended an era of cheap international credit and with it the high-risk debt-fuelled growth strategy of the 1980s. It was this short-term liquidity crisis, rather than some catastrophic breakdown in the fundamentals of the Indian economy – the manufacturing, agricultural and service sectors, though not exactly booming and dynamic, were hardly moribund – that required immediate action. For officials and their advisers who had imbibed the nostrums of fashionable 1980s neo-liberal ideas, and for those who simply sought to escape the cumbersome and interest-clogged paraphernalia of permit raj, the liquidity crisis was a heaven-sent pretext upon with which to hang far more radical change.

However, it was the radically altered domestic context, rather than international or financial imperatives, that created the political opportunity to initiate and consolidate that change. Paradoxically, it was liberalization's relative lack of political importance that most assisted its cause. Since the mid-1980s the remarkable ascendancy of the Hindu nationalist right from a meagre two seats in the 1984 parliament to the position of second largest party in 1991 had dramatically reconfigured Indian political life. The BJP was seen not only as a major threat to India's secular traditions among elite groups, but also as a menace to stability among the Indian masses. During the latter stages of the 1990 *yatra*, the VHP had also launched a series of *Ram Jyothi Yatras* (processions bearing the light of Ram). In towns in Uttar Pradesh slogans shouted by these flame carriers had provoked Muslims into throwing stones and petrol bombs, while in Rajasthan the Ram procession coincided with birthday celebrations of the Prophet Mohammed – with predictable results. After Advani's arrest violence became countrywide when a *Bharat Bandh* (national protest movement) announced by the BJP triggered riots in many commercial districts where Muslims had refused to close their businesses – in all around 260 people died. And so while in the past Congress had usually been the principal opponent in the eyes of the burgeoning array of caste, regional and left parties, their chief enemy now was the BJP. While these groups heartily detested many of the reforms, they detested the BJP even more. Moreover, the very weakness of Congress made it a more attractive coalition partner than it had ever been in the past. So, while almost all the MPs on the BJP right voted against the pro-market liberalization, the broadly centre-left representatives of the Janata Dal voted for them. By the early 1990s questions of economic policy, however ideologically charged, had been eclipsed by caste and communal conflict. The crisis occasioned by the Mandal-Mandir controversies had created a political space through which dramatic economic change could be smuggled.

The subsequent success of the reform process also owes rather more to India's idiosyncratic political dynamics, not to mention the craftiness of its politicians, than to any broad-based popular support for its content; indeed a survey in 2000 revealed that most Indians knew nothing about the reforms. Nevertheless, India confounded many theorists of liberalization by introducing a catalogue of potentially unpopular policies as a democratic state, and, furthermore, a state that defied almost all the norms of transparency and good governance that such *savants* propound. Indeed many of the aspects of Indian democracy so bemoaned by critics – its tolerance of graft, expedience and corruption – have become assets for liberalizers rather than liabilities. The new order emerged seamlessly from the old, and provided ample opportunities to engage in time-honoured forms of official corruption, while even, on occasion, revealing new ones. Similarly, the principle-free, faction-ridden style of India's politicians with their pragmatic traditions of deal-brokering, rule-bending and interest-accommodation, enabled the new regime to root itself far more deeply than a more open and principled approach would have permitted. It became, indeed, part of the rhetorical repertoire of the reformers to insist that very little had changed.

This is not to suggest that there was no conflict over liberalization – there were heated ideological exchanges. Hailed by the international press and domestic boosters, Manmohan Singh and Rao were feted for finally liberating India's tiger spirit from the cage of Nehruvian socialism, while opponents were subjected to scathing abuse. Bhagwati suggested that Amartya Sen was the author of almost all the nation's economic ills: 'these economists are like the politicians who espouse the cause of the poor but are themselves the unwitting cause of the perpetuation of that poverty', he thundered. On occasion proponents adopted a positively evangelical tone. One senior finance official suggested that the reformers were men of extraordinary valour, willing to risk life and limb in the battle for economic emancipation. Writing of a meeting with the communist chief minister of West Bengal, Jyoti Basu, he claimed: 'We were greeted with black flags, and just escaped being attacked with sticks by CPI(M) activists.'

Parliamentary opponents employed equally inflammatory rhetoric, accusing the government of prostrating the nation before the forces of resurgent imperialism; 'the economy of the country has been subjected at the feet of the World Bank and the IMF', said one. Others denounced the reforms as anti-poor, anti-farmer, anti-development and devoted solely to promulgating unlimited consumerism and mass unemployment. The chief malefactor himself, Manmohan Singh, despite his famous quote from Hugo – 'No power on earth can stop an idea whose time has come' – generally deflected these attacks with the abstract and passionless language of a supreme technocrat:

Macroeconomic stabilization and fiscal adjustment alone cannot suffice, they must be supported by essential reforms in economic policy . . . a transition from a regime of quantitative restriction to a price-based mechanism . . . Overspecialization and excessive bureaucratization have proved to be counter productive.

The reforms were not about giving free rein to the profit motive but merely 'getting government out of activities where governments are not very efficient at doing things'. When announcing the potentially incendiary step of freeing India's capital markets Singh coolly observed: 'The practice of government control of government issues has lost its relevance in the changed world of today', and private business should be free to raise money as it wished, 'provided the issues are in conformity with published guidelines . . .'

The strategy of presenting change as continuity with, perhaps, some mild technical tinkering, was key to entrenching the reforms and neutralizing opposition. Reform was spun as a rather minor and low-key affair, and indeed, was barely mentioned by Congress during the elections of 1996 and 1998. Instead party leaders reiterated their commitment to traditional goals: development, social welfare and self-reliance. 'No multinational will build a primary school in India, no foreign investor will set up a health centre. These are jobs for the government. Let the multinationals handle the top sector, we will manage the grass roots,' insisted the Prime Minister. Rao also spoke in misty terms of Gandhian ideals of village self-sufficiency, hinting that Gandhi had, in some unspecified way, always intended the triumph of free market capitalism. Manmohan Singh, too, claimed that opening the Indian economy to foreign multinationals was merely another route to self-reliance and was, therefore, simply the culmination of Nehruvian ideals. 'When Panditji [Nehru] wrote the opening chapter of the Third Plan,' he explained, 'he never talked about self-reliance in the autarchic sense, that we will never use foreign brands.' Chastising his critics, he exclaimed it was 'utter hypocrisy to say that all these years we were self-reliant and suddenly Dr Manmohan Singh and Mr Narasimha Rao have surrendered the country's sovereignty'. Some have suggested that the habit of presenting change as merely the continuation of tradition is a feature inherent to Indian culture, others saw it as merely cunning obfuscation. Whatever its origins, it created a pervasive sense of 'business-as-usual' which disarmed critics and allowed for a much deeper embedding of reform than was immediately apparent.

Such stealthy techniques were employed to erode India's extensive anti-poverty programmes and labour laws, while avoiding embarrassing headlines and parliamentary confrontations. Though both Singh and Rao continually proclaimed their stalwart resistance to demands from the World Bank to cut food aid for the poor, in reality the scheme was slowly withering on the vine, prices in government food shops floated up to near market levels and all but the destitute simply ceased to visit them. In 1990 20.8 million tonnes of food was sold at ration prices; in 1994 the figure had fallen to 14 million tonnes. Similarly, though the government shied away from openly tackling restrictive labour laws – factory workers essentially have jobs for life – it simply looked the other way as businessmen locked factory gates against their workers, failed to pay their bills and invited de facto closure, only to reopen under a new guise and with a more compliant workforce.

In the states, too, stealth proved an effective way of entrenching reform. In 1995 the newly elected right-wing Shiv Sena-BJP government in Maharashtra made a great show of implementing its election promise to protect the state from the predations of international capitalism by cancelling the contract its predecessor had signed with Enron – the soon to be disgraced US power conglomerate. While this spectacle unfolded on the front pages, the supposedly anti-liberalization ministry quietly pursued further reforms and, behind the scenes, renegotiated the self-same deal. Another feature of Indian politics that unexpectedly assisted the quiet embedding of reform was the federal system. With the government's categorical announcement of the abandonment of all pretence that the central state would be the main financer of state infrastructure and economic development, liberalizers forced state governments to become the authors of their own economic destinies. Moreover, the central government could now shuffle the more unpalatable consequences of reform, such as the relative decline in food aid and loss of jobs in defunct enterprises, on to the states. Meanwhile other potential enemies of reform, such as the hitherto powerful trade unions, now found themselves fighting liberalization on not one central but several regional fronts.

But the reforms did not have to rely solely on central government stealth, for one unexpected consequence of liberalization was the almost miraculous conversion of many local politicians to the reform cause. Though one might have expected regional governments to oppose liberalization and the resulting loss of central subventions, the greater freedom of manoeuvre it offered soon turned them into votaries of the new dispensation. Local politicians soon discovered that they could cloak contentious political favours in the garb of necessary 'reform'. The decision of the Maharashtra state government to slash the sales tax on diamonds from 20 per cent to 2 per cent was not only promoting liberalization, but also, some suggested, the interests of the diamond merchants – major donors to party funds. Meanwhile the scramble among businessman for the best commercial land offered several openings for entrepreneurial local politicians, from speeding up approvals of compulsory purchase orders, to the hiring out of loyal 'toughs' (with whom many had long connections) to evict recalcitrant owners. In Bangalore the state government acquired land greatly in excess of what was actually required for the building of the new airport and then sold off the surplus to private developers. And though many imagined that the ruthless pruning of permit-raj's thicket of licences and clearances would make bribery obsolescent it had, in fact, simply devolved it on to the states. It had also, moreover, provided the politicians with an invading army of new 'clients' in the form of foreign firms anxious for assistance in navigating these new commercial waters. Enron, for example, claimed that it had spent $20 million 'educating' the politicians of Maharashtra on how to go about seeking private investments in power projects.

The desire to accumulate the prestige, patronage and other boons that came with private investment soon created a powerful incentive for states to compete with one another. This brought a flurry of beggar-thy-neighbour activity as states rushed to offer tax incentives and all manner of alluring packages to prospective investors. Chief ministers began scouring the subcontinent for business, and the communist boss of West Bengal was so appalled by the appearance of the predatory chief minister of Maharashtra, Sharad Pawar, prowling the streets of Calcutta touting for business that he became determined, communist or not, to join the fray. Soon adverts beckoning American plutocrats to try their luck in the Marxist province appeared in the US press: 'No Red Flags. No Red Tape. Just A Red Carpet', they promised. This, of course, rather undermined the credibility of leftist ideological opponents of reform, and the West Bengal communist MP who castigated the central government for selling the nation's birthright to the WTO was greeted with gales of parliamentary hilarity. The intense inter-state competition to become more business-friendly was often pursued by stealthy means. In Karnataka the chief minister, Deve Gowda, disguised the erosion of affirmative action schemes for backward castes by announcing in 1994 that half the jobs in all new private-sector projects would go exclusively to those resident in the state for at least fifteen years. He thus deftly sublimated contentious and damaging caste conflict into a more manageable 'sons-of-the-soil' movement, while quietly reassuring foreign investors that there were sufficient loopholes in the legislation to ensure the smooth running of their operations. In Rajasthan the chief minister, Bhairon Singh Shekhawat, disguised liberalization as a form of state patriotism. Welcoming the return of the Marwaris, a group who figured prominently among leading businessmen, and who had, in the late medieval era, originated in that state, he insisted that this sudden influx of hungry entrepreneurs was essential in order to 'rebuild the people's pride'. The regional appetite for liberalization was fully revealed in the United Front government that immediately succeeded Rao's in 1996. Composed of an array of regional parties, many of supposedly left-wing proclivities, this ministry assiduously courted foreign business and in its first three months in office had approved $5.5 billion of new foreign investment.

The rise of the regions produced a new Indian phenomenon – the celebrity chief minister. During the Indira years state chief ministers had been rather grey and anonymous placemen whose principal role was to know their place. But in the reform era they too were liberated. Throughout the 1990s and 2000s chief ministers became nationally, and even internationally renowned, regularly shuttling between Dallas and Davos, meeting and greeting CEOs, European heads of state and US presidents, all in the cause of attracting private investment. The most conspicuous among them was Chandrababu Naidu, who became chief minister of the southern state of Andhra Pradesh in 1995. Though Naidu's rise had not been unconnected with the fact that he was the son-in-law of the previous Andhra chief minister, the film superstar and populist boss N. T. Rama Rao, he soon developed his very own personality cult. Naidu was hailed in the Indian press as the 'Generation-Next C-M', in *Time* as 'South Asian of the Year', and as 'IT Indian of the Millennium' by *India Today*. His chroniclers, in *From Cattle Carts to Cyber Marts*, breathlessly depicted his CEO-style approach to governing Andhra Pradesh:

Every morning Naidu boots up his IBM Thinkpad to check the water levels in the state reservoirs, power generation statistics . . . and the number of files cleared by state bureaucrats. Bottlenecks are identified, and Naidu uses his cell-phone to call the erring official with his signature line: 'This is Chandrababu Naidu speaking.'

An early exponent of e-governance and the IT revolution, the flamboyant Naidu eschewed the low-key and stealthy methods of Rao and Singh to propound a clear conception of what liberalization meant. In his Vision 2020 document he announced:

we are trying to telescope into one generation what it took decades, and possibly centuries, for other societies . . . to achieve. But the new technologies of today . . . give us opportunities that earlier societies did not have. Besides, learning from the experience of others, it is possible for us to leapfrog several stages of development.

He went on to sketch a prosperous future for Andhra Pradesh, which, fuelled by foreign investment, would be transformed within twenty years into a global technological 'hub', with the best infrastructure and a workforce of highly skilled, but competitively waged, cyber-technicians. Twenty million new jobs would be created every year, and the state's hitherto very backward agricultural economy would be restructured into a service-sector powerhouse. The centrepiece of this vision was a new city, Cyberabad, to be built on the outskirts of the capital Hyderabad. Cyberabad would be an 'intelligent' city of modern houses, unfailing power supplies, modern roads, shopping malls and, in deference to his famous father-in-law, cinemas. Close by the recently established Indian Institute of Information Technology and a new business school jointly run with the American Kellogg and Wharton schools of management, Cyberabad would become the education capital of India. But this was all in the future. In the meantime he contented himself with bringing e-governance to Hyderabad: citizens could pay their utility bills on line, register land deeds and order driving licences. Using a large World Bank loan and funds from the BJP-led central government, for whom the support of Naidu's Telugu Desam Party was essential, Hyderabad's infrastructure was modernized so that it could become the destination location for the world's backroom outsourcing centres. Foreign investors were lured by the new Software Technology Park, a super streamlined system of clearances for export-led companies and exemption from corporate tax. The idea was that this high-tech hub of well-paid knowledge workers would have a multiplier effect on the rest of the state. It was calculated that for every IT engineer or software programmer paid close to an international salary, five additional lesser paid ancillary jobs would be created, spreading affluence across the state.

Naidu's 'Vision' was the most conspicuous example of a form of neo-liberal voluntarism which became popular in the later 1990s among those gripped by liberalization fever, the mirror-image of the planners' paradise envisioned in the 1950s. Both sides believed that India could by-pass the slow and disruptive processes of modern development, but while the planners had fetishized the fusing of dirigisme and science, the liberalizers feted the marriage of the market to information technology. And while planners dreamt of an egalitarian socialistic pattern of society founded on agrarian co-operatives and heavy industry, liberalizers envisaged a post-industrial cyber-utopia built on services and the knowledge economy. Fuelling these fantasies was the undeniable success of India's IT industry in the 1990s and 2000s. Between 1991 and 1999 IT contributed 59 per cent of India's growth, and in the next four years 70 per cent. Exports of software and services grew 50 per cent annually to reach $6 billion in 2000, and $9.5 billion in 2003. Many new IT companies and call centres and other businesses specializing in the 'back-office' operations of western firms were founded, especially in Bangalore, Mumbai (Bombay), Chennai (Madras) and Hyderabad. By the late 1990s over 200 information technology academies were processing half a million new graduates every year. International commentators gasped as India began its out-sourced colonization of the west's white-collar job markets.

There were, however, dissenters who doubted the sustainability of IT growth and the plausibility of moving immediately to a post-industrial economy. Bottlenecks caused by poor infrastructure and dubious training appeared, and even the most feverish boosters of the IT revolution revised their growth projections down from 50 per cent to 30 per cent per annum, while in 2002–03 the sector achieved the impressive, but nevertheless disappointing figure of 26 per cent. Meanwhile there was trouble in Naidu's cyber-paradise. Massive fiscal deficits and near bankruptcy put paid to further infrastructural investment and the state had to be bailed out by the World Bank. Naidu's e-governance did not impress the poor rural groups who constituted the majority of the state's population, and efforts to raise electricity, irrigation and transport prices provoked riots. Andhra Pradesh was, in fact, one of the weaker regional economies, with 70 per cent of its population dependent on agriculture, an unusually high number of whom had incomes below the official poverty line, while the state's health and education spending was below the Indian average. In 2001 the state that had projected itself as the global hub of the new knowledge economy was forced to start rationing power supplies. The following year hundreds of poor Andhra farmers committed suicide in despair at their increasing poverty.

Andhra Pradesh is an extreme case, but it illustrates in microcosm some of the potential constraints on the success of liberalization throughout India. The need to ration power was, in part, related to inadequate investment in basic infrastructure. Between 1990/91 and 1997/98 state spending on roads, ports, schools and power transmission fell from 1.4 per cent of GDP to only 0.7 per cent, while the quality of India's transport, roads, power, telecoms and ports placed it in the bottom 10 per cent of the world's poorest economies. Neoliberal proponents of reform insisted that the private sector would supply infrastructural investment and that any shortfall should be funded by the proceeds of privatisation. But experience suggested that foreign businessmen tended to place their cash where it could be turned to profit and not necessarily where it was needed. In 1998 even the great proponent of liberalization, the World Bank, conceded that there was a strong case for state investment. However, after half a decade of reform the state still lacked the resources to make such investments. Nearly 50 per cent of annual revenues were spent on interest charges on central and state government accumulated debt.

In some spheres, however, the policy changes of Narasimha Rao's five-year administration were highly successful. The emergency stabilization package quickly eased the liquidity crisis and by early 1998 India had sufficient foreign exchange to cover seven months' worth of imports – a significant proportion of it derived from holdings by NRIs. Moreover the economy began to grow quite rapidly, reaching a relative high, by Indian standards, of 7.2 per cent per annum in 1994/5. Manufacturing did especially well, reaching growth rates of 10 per cent per annum. Deregulation had promoted restructuring and modernization in many Indian firms, especially those involved in chemicals, engineering, electronics, pharmaceuticals and finance, and much of this had been accomplished by going into partnership with foreign companies drawn largely from the USA, Germany, Japan, the UK and South Korea.

In 1996, however, growth rates began to falter and by 2000/01 sank to a mere 5 per cent; the old 'Hindu' rate of growth seemed to be reasserting itself, and with it old controversies. Neo-liberal economists and international agencies attributed the slow-down to the failure to implement the much mooted second stage of reforms, namely, the full-scale sell-off of all state enterprises and the abolition of all remaining controls on investment, restrictions on labour and subsidies. Or, as Jagdish Bhagwati put it: 'if we are truly to reproduce the East Asian miracle (rather than a pale and anaemic copy thereof) ... the public sector ... cries out to be privatized now ... and the ability to extract greater efficiency from the labour force [is necessary]'. The left's view was rather different. The recession was to be expected, for liberalization had simply exacerbated the very inequalities that had blocked progress before. Despite the reforms the poor remained poor – some said even poorer – and their lack of purchasing power was both an injustice, and an insurmountable obstacle to sustainable growth and development. This critique did not fall on deaf ears, and the chief architect of the reforms, Manmohan Singh, himself conceded, 'The impoverished rural poor do not any longer need to walk twenty miles to see how rich people live in cities. They are able to see this on TV, which magnifies disparities further by the use of glamorous advertisements. Frustrated people without jobs or prospects are likely to turn to violence.' The principal exponents of the politics of violence were not, however, the poor, but the Hindu nationalist right, who had their own theories about liberalization and its depredations.

In 1995 flies were discovered in the kitchen of a Kentucky Fried Chicken outlet in Delhi and the Delhi government, at that that time run by the political wing of the Hindu right, the BJP, closed it down. Though ostensibly a hazard to health and hygiene, the Kentucky Fried Chicken kitchen was also, many nationalists insisted, a symbol of all that was wrong with global capitalism. It was dirty, polluting and foreign, a threat to Hindu cultural values and to the livelihoods of the nation's small businessmen – an important BJP constituency. Though top BJP politicians maintained a studiedly ambiguous attitude to liberalization, the rhetoric of many of their supporters could not have been less so. 'We are reduced to beggars,' some declaimed, 'India will not allow itself to be raped.' In the 1996 elections the BJP became the largest party in the Indian parliament.

In the same year, the BJP formed the government of India. Though this government lasted for only a fortnight, as the minority party was unable to secure enough coalition supporters, it marked an extraordinary moment for a party which only twelve years earlier had been able to command just two seats in the Delhi parliament. And though it had to wait another two years, it then succeeded in becoming the leading party of government for the following five years. The BJP's vision embodied yet another project to unify India, but unlike Gandhi's notion of a composite culture, or Nehru's modern idea of secular citizenship, the BJP vision focused on *Hindutva* – Hinduness. In particular it sought to construct a 'modern' nation built upon what it claimed were Hindu 'traditions'. According to this view, Hinduism was less a religion than an all-encompassing way of life to which all Indians must subscribe, whether they were Hindu or not. The core ideology of *Hindutva* had been propounded in the 1920s by Veer Savarkar. A Hindu, he insisted, is a person who regarded '*Bharatvarsha* [the land of Bharat – India], from the Indus to the seas, as his *pitribhumi* [fatherland] and as his *punyabhumi* [holy land] that is the cradle of his religion'. This could include Hindus, Jains and Sikhs, but not Muslims and Christians, whose holy land lay outside *Bharatvarsha*. This was a cultural vision of the nation, in which national identity was defined more by what it excluded than what it embraced. Its success, however, owed less to enduring Hindu traditions and loyalties than to the particular circumstances of the late 1980s. The Mandal controversy, coupled with the embrace of a more open and market-driven economy after years of control and near autarchy, offered the Hindu right the opportunity to break out of its ghetto of hard-core, culturally conservative, small-town supporters to create, for a while at least, a broader constituency.

The rapid ascendancy of this form of politics took many by surprise, for though a specifically Hindu nationalism had been around for seventy years it had made little direct impression on the contours of political life, and its prospects in the early 1980s seemed most unpromising. Its advocates had, indeed, tended to concentrate less on conventional means of acquiring power from above through the state, than on the slower, but more utopian project of Hinduizing the nation from below. Concentrating on this goal through its numerous social and cultural organizations, its forays into the political field had not been conspicuously successful. Its origins lay in the *Rashtriya Sway-amsevak Sangh* (RSS, Association of National Volunteers), a high-caste Hindu volunteer corps founded in 1925 supposedly to protect Hindus from the depredations of their enemies – Muslims and Christians, and, though this was less explicitly stated, the threat posed by assertive lower castes. The RSS offered young high-caste men a regime of physical and mental training intended to develop an appreciation of national 'culture', while also blunting inter-caste conflict by positing the notion of a unified Hindu community threatened by external 'others'.

Ideologically the RSS was xenophobic, hierarchical, bellicose and reactionary. From Savarkar's veneration of all things native to India followed a visceral suspicion of the foreign; any idea, technology or institution that had not originated in *Bharatvarsha* was deemed threatening. Preoccupied with British stereotypes of high-caste Hindus' physical effeminacy Savarkar entreated young men to pursue physical training and informal 'militarization'. To these preoccu-pations a more systematically racist account of what it meant to be Indian was adumbrated by M. S. Golwalkar, the supreme chief of the RSS throughout the 1940s and 1950s. Golwalkar had been much influenced by Nazi thinking on the race question. In his 1939 tract, *We, Our Nationhood Defined*, he professed admiration for German race spirit and its 'struggle for national regeneration'. 'German national pride', he exclaimed, 'has now become the topic of the day. To keep up the purity of the nation and its culture, Germany has shocked the world by her purging of the Semitic races – the Jews . . . a good lesson for us in Hindustan to learn and profit by.' India had to be built upon the five unities of race, language, religion, culture and geography; those not native-born, or not of its religions, fell 'beyond the pale of national life . . . they deserve no privileges, far less any preferential treatment – not even citizen rights'. Golwalkar had also produced a rambling critique of the depredations of modernity, particularly its disruption of hierarchies, including those based on caste – though he was more vague about this. 'We live in strange times . . . nobility is at a sad discount . . . we are rolling down . . . into the bottomless abyss of degeneration', he declared. Unity and strength among Hindus was the only remedy; Hindus must not be rivals with one another, but must merge into a harmonious, organic and corporate whole – and the vehicle for this was a unitary state. Golwalkar opposed federalism and the reorganization of the states along linguistic lines, demanding instead 'One Country, One State, One Legislature and One Executive'.

Nehruvian India did not offer an environment friendly to these absolutist prognostications and a somewhat softer version of *Hindutva* was crafted in the 1950s and 1960s by Deendayal Upadhyaya, who had founded the political wing of the RSS, the Jan Sangh, in 1951. From a version of Golwalkar's corporatism, combined with a generous admixture of pseudo-Gandhian philosophy, he concocted the creed of 'integral humanism'. This was encapsulated by the idea of '*Bharatiya*', a neologism which blended 'Hindu' and 'Indian' to produce something that might be roughly translated as 'Hindian', and which deftly side-stepped the secular prohibitions on the use of overtly religious language in politics. *Bharatiya* was supposed to connote a gentler and more inclusive sense of Hinduness, modelled on ideas dating from reformers in the late nineteenth century (and adopted in part by Gandhi himself), of Hinduism as a uniquely tolerant and all-encompassing culture and religion (and by implication, superior to all others). But derived, as it was, from the Hindu reformist concept of *adhikarbheda* – the sense that Indians constitute a graded pyramid in which each group had its own separate place and traditions reconciled into a harmonious Hindu solidarity – *Bharatiya* also embodied the idea of hierarchy within community. Indeed Upadhyaya employed a metaphor for the relationship between groups and the nation, 'one of limb to body', strikingly reminiscent of the *Purusha* creation myth which justified the hierarchical four-caste order. He was, however, a little more generous than Golwalkar towards Indian Muslims, and was prepared to concede them citizenship as long as they were not 'pro-Pak'.

On economic affairs, though less stringent in his strictures about foreign technology and modern development than his predecessors, Upadhyaya harked back to Gandhian notions of *swadeshi* (self-sufficiency), cottage industries, and a paternalist relationship between employers and their workers. Factories were seen as 'occupational families', not spheres of class war or communism. 'Labourize industry, industrialize the nation, nationalize labour', he urged. In a formulation reminiscent of many 'third-way' ideologies, Upadhyaya insisted that while capitalism and socialism produced progress only by means of conflict, the path of harmony and adherence to *dharma* (duty) – a term deeply imbued with connotations of caste – was more efficacious. Hostile to the consumerist hedonism of western life and its despoliation of the environment, Upadhyaya implied that Hindu attitudes to nature, and its veneration of the cow in particular, was also a doctrine of ecological harmony.

Despite these revisions and softenings, the constituency for Hindu nationalist ideas had remained rather narrow. It was confined to the Hindi belt of Uttar Pradesh, Madhya Pradesh and the Punjab, and within it to traditionally pious small-town businessmen, resentful lower professionals and other downwardly mobile high-caste people, to aspirant wealthy farmers who had not been swept up by Charan Singh's agrarian populism and a kaleidoscopic crew of 'god-men' and *sadhus* annoyed at their loss of status in the secular India. Joining them were disgruntled elements among the Indian diaspora, who felt aggrieved at India's supposedly low status in the world and were, moreover, anxious to distance themselves from other minority immigrant communities by stressing their venerable cultural provenance. For these groups the curious medley of racism, pseudo-Gandhian cultural conservatism and 'third-way' economic nostrums that constituted *Hindutva* ideology proved appealing.

By the 1970s the RSS claimed to have over a million members organized into a disciplined corps. At its apex stood the supreme leader, or *Sarasanghachalak*, presiding over a network of *pracharaks* or propagandists, who were intended to be a celibate group of saffron-clad ascetics and who would combine the functions of political organizers with the charisma of karma yogis. From the trunk of the RSS a curious multi-branched entity of various associations, volunteer organizations and quasi-religious outfits soon grew; the most important were the *Rashtriya Sevika Samiti* for wives and daughters, the *Akhil Bharatiya Vidyarthi Parishad* for students, and the *Bharatiya Mazdoor Sangh* for workers. In the 1980s two new shoots, sprouting somewhat different constituencies, were cultivated – the *Bajrang Dal*, set up to induct lower-caste boys as a rough and ready reserve force, and the *Matri Mandal* for old ladies. The object of this broad family, the *Sangh Parivar*, was *sangathan* (organization), for it was lack of organization that had, it was held, made Hindus weak.

In 1964 the family's activities began to reach more directly into the religious world. In that year the *Vishva Hindu Parishad* (VHP), or the World Hindu Council was founded. This was designed to bridge the divide between the RSS and the Hindu clerisy and was envisaged as a kind of Hindu Consistory, its foundation a direct retaliation to the announcement by the Pope that the Catholic International Eucharistic Congress would be held in Bombay that year. Before this the RSS had been ambivalent about moving so obviously into religious territory, regarding itself as a cultural, not a theological movement, but now, as S. S. Apte, an RSS activist and founder of the VHP insisted, Hindus had to be protected from 'the insidiously spreading clutches of alien ideologies' – Christianity, Islam and communism – who all 'consider Hindu society as a very fine food on which to feast and fatten themselves'. The VHP, then, was intended to rally the various disparate elements of institutionalized Hinduism into some kind of ecclesiastical corporation, one moreover with subsidiaries not just within India but like the Catholic Church itself across the globe, especially in east Africa and north America, where the Hindu diaspora was substantial. The VHP crafted a 'Hinduism' for the modern age, simplified and accessible, providing the various sects of the *Pitribhumi-Punyabhumi* (Fatherland-Holy-land), including Jains and Sikhs, with one umbrella under which the displaced diaspora could shelter from the onslaught of foreign mores. Soon a cadre of space-age gurus and jet-set god-men were shuttling between India and California to offer spiritual-cum-political succour to the affluent Hindu middle classes.

In the field of politics, however, the Nehruvian and early Indira years had brought an uncongenial climate. In 1951 an act was passed forbidding the use of religious symbols or invocation of the 'threat of divine displeasure' in elections, and a similarly hard line against any breach of 'secularism' was maintained until the early 1980s. In 1951 the RSS leadership had decided to form a political party – the Jan Sangh – which, because it was supposedly quite distinct from the RSS, would avoid the strictures banning the use of religion in politics. But the Jan Sangh was always reliant on the RSS for its organization Moreover its manifestos were essentially dilute versions of the RSS message, designed to make it more attractive to potential coalition partners. This coalitional approach culminated in its merging itself within the Janata Party during the Emergency and taking two ministerial posts in the 1977–79 Janata government. But this partnership with a motley array of forces, including those on the socialist and atheist left, was a 'dilution' too far and alienated the more ideologically pristine members of the RSS. Indeed by the early 1980s many RSS members were supporting Congress, which was now also dabbling in the waters of Hindu cultural politics.

A revived Jan Sangh, now called the Bharatiya Janata Party, arose from the wreckage of the Janata government, with an agenda that emphasized competence, not culture. Its leader, the one-time RSS regional organizer Atal Behari Vajpayee, stressed reform, 'clean-government', and 'openness', even inviting Muslims to join. Its 1984 election manifesto stressed the party's commitment to a 'composite' Indian culture, and sought, by thus distancing itself from hard-core *Hindutva* ideology, to displace the waning Congress as the only truly national party. But, without its engine of RSS activists, it performed disastrously in the polls, winning only two seats, while Vajpayee himself lost his deposit. The movement seemed to have reached an impasse, confined to a hard-core of supporters who found its xenophobic and backward-looking ideology attractive.

However, from the beginning of the 1980s a combination of international and domestic circumstances combined to make the *Hindutva* message seem less arcane and irrelevant. The Iranian revolution of 1979 had raised the profile of Islam, and in the Indian context, where expatriate Indian Muslims were enriching themselves in the Arab oil-economies and then returning to India with supposedly objectionable fundamentalist ideas, Islam could once more be portrayed as a threat, as it had been in the years after the Khilafat campaign when the RSS was founded. Muslims could again be depicted plausibly as foreigners, loyal to other nations, a fifth column (an increasingly prosperous one, to boot) using their petro-dollars to spread their influence among India's poor. And just as the RSS blamed Christian conversion of tribal peoples for the various separatist movements in the north-eastern parts of the country, they now feared Muslim conversion might do the same elsewhere: in 1981, an dalit sub-caste in the village of Meenakshipuram in Tamil Nadu had converted en bloc to Islam, induced, it was thought, by Islamic proselytizers with oil money.

This more favourable atmosphere was aided by the decision of Congress to jettison the tough secularist stance of the Nehru era. Beset by successful Muslim and Sikh political rivals in Kashmir, Assam and the Punjab in the 1980s, Mrs Gandhi seemed to conflate the safeguarding of national integrity with the mobilization of Hindu sentiments. And Rajiv Gandhi declined to bring to justice the perpetrators of one of the worst examples of communal violence in the history of independent India – the mass slaughter of Sikhs in Delhi that ensued after the assassination of his mother by her Sikh bodyguards in 1984. It was also Rajiv who agreed to the reopening of the Babri mosque/Ram temple, a disputed site since the 1940s that his grandfather had closed to all communities. To 'balance' this concession he had bowed to the demands of conservative Muslims that they continue to be allowed to ignore state jurisdiction on matters of divorce and maintenance and follow instead the precepts of Islamic family law. Compounding this sin, in the eyes of many Hindus, was Rajiv's decision to ban Salman Rushdie's controversial novel *The Satanic Verses*, again, as it seemed to Hindu nationalists, 'pandering' to the minority.

The RSS and VHP responded to this new climate by adopting a strategy intended to push their influence more deeply into India's towns and villages by appealing to a broader social constituency and, for the first time, making a concerted effort to penetrate the south. This involved closer co-ordination of the VHP and religious leaders in a *jan jagaran* (people's awakening), which sought to extend

Hindutva to dalits and to the south. *Munnani* 'fronts' in Kerala and Tamil Nadu were opened and mission centres, ashrams, schools, clinics and *Vanvasi Kalyan Ashrams* (Tribal Development centres), were founded. But the most striking aspect of this new move was the adoption of a novel politics of ritual. A series of nationwide *yatras*, designed to tap middle-class enthusiasm for pilgrimages, was launched. The first of these was the *Ekatmata Yajna* (sacrifice for unity) of late 1983, a massive tri-partite spectacle consisting, it was claimed, of 60 million people, and intended by its geographical-cum-religious sweep to underline the essentially Hindu nature of the nation. The *yatra* took three routes, all beginning and ending at sacred sites, and all completed simultaneously. One began in Hardwar in the north, heading for Kanyakumari in the south; the second, inaugurated by the King of Nepal, set out from Kathmandhu and headed for Rameshwaram in Tamil Nadu; the last was initiated in Gangasagar and ended in Somnath. The three crossed simultaneously in the centre of India, not at some great sacred confluence but at Nagpur, home of the RSS. In all the religious centres they passed, the processions were greeted and blessed by local abbots, *sadhus* and priests. Leading figures travelled in 'chariots' – converted trucks – evoking the militant imagery of Arjuna's war chariot, and carried water from the sacred Ganges. Behind them followed smaller trucks selling bottled Ganges water. The *yatra* garnered blanket publicity and with it new clusters of VHP branches mushroomed throughout the country.

The popular success of these mobilizations suggested that there might now exist a 'soft' constituency for *Hindutva* consisting of those angered at Congress's alleged favours to Muslims, those threatened by the revival of the Mandal Report and its threats to old caste hierarchies and, a little later, those uncertain as to their fortunes under a new liberalized economy. Supporters could be found, for example, among the burgeoning urban lower-middle class in cities like Bombay, where recently built high rise blocks housed such families in their thousands. Threatened by the slums or *zopadpattis* that surrounded their middle-class enclaves, many harboured highly exaggerated notions of how many Muslims lived around them. There was also a pervasive sense that Muslims were being favoured by the Congress-run city council: a particular grievance was the proliferating use of amplifiers by mosques for the call to prayer, creating the impression, they said, of Hindus being 'dominated'. Competitiveness over space also informed another common complaint – that Muslims, unrestrained by the Common Civil Code applying to Hindus, were free to take 'four or five wives' and have families of 'ten or twelve children'. The refusal of the government to permit the demolition of the mosque at Ayodhya was viewed, in this context, as a brute denial of Hindu sentiment.

Compounding this was a growing sense of insecurity about the rise of lower-caste groups, who, it was claimed, were festooned with undeserved privileges by the Congress-led Maharashtra state government. Among these disgruntled communities older ideas of high-caste superiority persisted. One Brahman clerk reported, 'People know you are a Brahman, and still, to be frank, an honest man would consider a Brahman to be a person to be followed for his intelligence, his good habits and all that.' But such families were losing status and the children of civil servants were often, it was claimed, reduced to labouring and driving rickshaws. As one declared: 'Promotions are given to people who cannot read or write . . . I lost three chances because of such a policy . . . The government is not paying attention to the middle classes. They are just trying to get votes from labourers and other uncivilized and uncultured people.' So the RSS struck a chord when its journal, *The Organizer*, stated that 'the havoc the politics of reservation is playing with the social fabric is unimaginable. It provides a premium for mediocrity, encourages brain drain and sharpens caste divide', concluding that respectable people needed to 'build up the moral and spiritual forces to counter the fall out from the Shudra revolution'. It appeared, therefore, that the climate was ripe for a confluence of the aggressive activism of the RSS-VHP and the smoother politics of the BJP, appealing simultaneously to the *Hindutva* hard-core and a penumbra of increasingly disgruntled middle-class voters. The key moment in bringing these constituencies together, and a breakthrough in its electoral support, was the decision of the BJP leadership to participate in the 1990 *Rath Yatra*, thus embracing, though covertly, the strategy of invoking religion to achieve power.

Ayodhya is an old north Indian pilgrimage town of many mosques and temples where, supposedly, in 1528 a general of Babur's, the founder of the Mughal dynasty, demolished an ancient temple marking the birthplace of Ram, and used its pillars to build the Babri mosque. Beneath this colourful local legend, however, lay a far more complex story. In 1856 the first British District Commissioner of Faizabad wrote of a Sunni Muslim agitation about a mosque that supposedly existed in Hanumangarhi, a Hindu temple complex also in Ayodhya. This agitation had provoked a retaliatory attack by Hindu monks on the Babri mosque, until then not an object of much veneration or dispute. Moreover, the District Commissioner observed, at that time it seemed that both Muslims and Hindus used the mosque-temple for worship. The British, however, intervened in their typically categorical manner to clarify who could worship where. A railing was erected around the mosque to keep Hindus out, and a platform built outside the railings where Hindu *puja* (worship) was permitted. The railing seemed to solve matters until the mid-1930s when the mosque was damaged during a cow-slaughter dispute, and the local Hindus were taxed to pay for its repair. Resentment simmered, fuelled by the riots of partition, and by the late 1940s it had acquired police protection. The protection was not sufficient, however, to prevent the 'miraculous' appearance of an image of Ram in December 1949. Though closed to the public on Nehru's orders in 1950, one day every December a group of Hindu worthies was permitted inside to perform *puja* before the image. But no effort was made by local Hindu leaders to act on the notion that the mosque rested on the birthplace of Ram, reflecting, perhaps, their realization that such sanctification of a new temple might create a threatening commercial rival to their own.

In the early 1980s the dispute in Ayodhya acquired a rather mundane dimension involving competitive tourism. In the 1980s the government, now keen to promote tourism within India by catering to middle-class interest in both pilgrimages and holidays, set about developing the Ayodhya waterfront, abutting the sacred Sarayu river, into a tourist attraction by constructing an expensive pier or platform – 'Ram's Footstep'. It was hoped that thus equipped Ayodhya might emulate the more prosperous holy city of Hardwar. In this context the possession of Ram's birthplace acquired immense commercial potential. In 1984, the VHP initiated a *'Tala kholo!'* ('Open the lock!') campaign, and thus revived the dusty dispute over the old mosque. But though protests and processions were begun – a few monks in cars – they were subsumed by the aftermath of the anti-Sikh riots following the assassination of Mrs Gandhi. Nevertheless pressure continued, and in 1986 a local judge ruled that the site should be reopened, triggering more communal violence and, in 1987, the biggest Muslim protest in New Delhi since Independence.

In this same year another manifestation of mass market Hinduism unwittingly gave the obscure controversy further prominence. In January 1987 the state television broadcaster, Doordarshan, began a 78-episode serialization of the *Ramayana*. It soon became the most popular TV programme ever, with 100 million people watching the most exciting episodes on sets often put up in public. Though it blended the various local tellings with the more famous textual versions, the effect of the serialization was to homogenize the tale, and, by stressing Ram's war-like proclivities, it lent a new militancy to Ram worship. It also greatly increased public knowledge of Ayodhya, effectively merging the mythic with the real city in people's minds. The entire series was later released on video, billed as 'The Greatest Indian Epic. Treasured for over 10,000 Years. Enshrining Ideals That Are Ageless. Teaching Lessons That Are Timeless'. Its actors became revered throughout the land and some ventured into politics – happily the gods were even-handed: while Ram campaigned for Congress, Sita stood for the BJP.

By late 1987 the matter had acquired such prominence that even Rajiv Gandhi claimed to support the VHP's case. The Ram *mandir*, L. K. Advani, senior BJP leader and sometime charioteer, insisted, was 'not just a legal issue, nor is it merely a question of history. It is essentially a question of the nation's identity. Whom must this nation identify with, Ram or Babur [the Mughal emperor]?', and by 1989 the whole matter had been transformed into a symbol of the 'threatened' Hindu majority. One RSS leader wrote in *The Organizer*:

Hindus over the centuries have been subjected to aggression, tyranny and indignities. Thousands of temples have been destroyed ... Muslims beat Hindus time and again, not because Hindus lacked bravery or sacrifice, but just for one reason – Disunity ... After centuries of humiliation the Hindu's soul had arisen phoenix like from the ashes. Hindus want to possess what is theirs.

Moreover, because the BJP wanted to win the forthcoming general and state elections, the *mandir* campaign was also a covert election campaign. Timed for maximum electoral impact, in September 1989 another political ritual-cum-spectacle was launched: *ramshila* – worship of the holy bricks of Lord Ram. Vasant Rao, a VHP activist in Maharashtra recalled:

Pre-manufactured bricks were given to us by the VHP in Aurangabad. Then we took the bricks in jeeps to the villages ... There the *sarpanch* [village headman], the police *patil* [commander], or some elderly respected person was asked to perform *puja*: to apply tumeric paste, put flowers, and burn incense sticks. Then the bricks were carried around in the village, a small meeting was held with a speech or two, then we took the bricks back to Aurangabad, and from there by rail to Ayodhya ... I think we covered some one hundred and seventy villages that way.

Bricks came from all over the world, all eventually ending up in a pit on undisputed land just outside the mosque, awaiting employment in the construction of a Ram temple. The campaign stirred communal tensions in villages and towns, especially in Bihar where allegedly between 1000 and 1800 Muslims were killed in the city of Bhagulpur. Meanwhile VHP and *Bajrang Dal* (VHP youth wing) leaders were simultaneously promoted as BJP candidates in the coming election, *sadhus* operating as their canvassers.

The results were gratifying for the BJP. It became the third largest party in India, its humiliating 2 seats of 1984 now multiplied to 89. Some of its support came from old core constituencies, but others were won where communal tension had intensified and caste resentments were strong. The next stage in the campaign was Advani's decision, after V. P. Singh announced plans to implement the Mandal Report, to launch the *Rath Yatra* against the 'raja's caste war' (a jibe at Singh's princely origins) and the 'pampering of Muslims'. In linking these issues Advani broadened the BJP's appeal while deftly deflecting accusations of communalism by claiming he was campaigning not against secularism as such, but against the pro-Muslim pseudo-secularism of Congress and the nation-weakening policies of caste reservations. Fortuitously, the new campaign was able to focus these two resentments on to the single person of the new chief minister of Uttar Pradesh, Mulayam Singh Yadav. For Mulayam, an OBC himself, had won his pre-eminence by mobilizing the state's Muslim vote, and after his deployment of Border Security Forces to keep the *kar sevaks* (RSS 'temple-builders') from attacking the Babri mosque on 30 October 1990, creating fifteen *Hindutva* 'martyrs', he was dubbed 'mullah Singh'.

The new campaign was notable for its no-holds-barred *Hindutva* rhetoric and deployment of religious symbolism. Mountains of small icons were distributed, stickers depicting the putative Ram *Mandir* and postcards of a sickly sweet 'Baby Ram' proliferated (some noted his striking resemblance to the Glaxo Baby seen on advertising hoardings). During the campaign all Hindus were told to fly the saffron flag of *Hindutva*, and many obeyed. Another striking innovation was the appearance of a number of remarkable female orators – in apparent contravention of *Hindutva* strictures concerning the correct modest and motherly behaviour properly befitting Hindu women. Among them was Sadhvi Ritambra. Ritambra was a renunciate, a female monk, who, some said, now channelled her feminine passion into the Hindu cause. Ritambra could declaim for hours at a time with barely a pause, her high-pitched voice at times rising to screams, at others descending to pitiful moans as she evoked lurid images of the horrors inflicted on innocent Hindus by rapacious Muslims. Using rhyme and rhythm to build to crescendos of hatred, her harangues recalled folk traditions of endless improvisation on a single line – in her case usually an invocation to extreme violence – punctuated by incidental riffs on mythological and domestic matters. Her constant theme was the unquenchable bloodthirstiness of all Muslims, their desire to dismember India and tales of the grotesque Muslim-inflicted disfigurement of Hindu women in the Kashmir Valley. Many thought that her vivid evocations of vulnerable and defiled Hindu womanhood were intended to incite dreams of violent revenge in the young, low-status and frustrated men who comprised the greater part of her audience.

In the elections of early 1991 the BJP vote increased again, making it the largest opposition party. It won state elections in Uttar Pradesh, Madhya Pradesh and Himachal Pradesh; it also, for the first time, acquired some support in eastern and southern India. It was set fair to become the party of choice among India's 'respectable' and rapidly growing middle classes, disgusted by the corruption-enveloped Congress. The BJP itself was generously funded by hefty business donations at home and from overseas, and was remarkably popular among ex-military types, as well as serving officers and policemen. They were attracted it seemed by promises of more defence spending, nuclear armament and an aggressive stance towards the Muslim insurgency in Kashmir, as well as more generalized promises to project national greatness and honour on the global stage.

Following the elections, and undeterred by the revelation of a local religious functionary, Abbot Ram Chandra Das Paramhams, that it had been he who, in December 1949, had placed the 'miraculous' image of Ram in the Babri mosque, the VHP accelerated the pace of agitation over the Ram *mandir*. It set its own deadline of December 1992 for the demolition of the Babri mosque, and Advani announced in November that he would repeat the last lap of his *Rath Yatra*, allowing him to approach Ayodhya from the highly symbolic city of Varanasi. Another RSS and BJP leader, Murli Manohar Joshi, decided to make his advance on the unfortunate mosque from the equally holy site of Mathura. On this occasion both *yatras* made a great show of the bones and ashes of the martyrs of 30 October, carried on trucks in sacred pots.

On 6 December Joshi and Advani arrived in Ayodhya, with fifty VHP leaders. At 11 a.m. RSS volunteers easily broke the thin police cordon and by 5 p.m., using picks, shovels and their bare hands, they had demolished the mosque. The Congress Prime Minister, Narasimha Rao, had vacillated – the BJP chief minister of Uttar Pradesh had sworn to protect the mosque and so the pre-emptive imposition of President's Rule would have seemed a provocative token of mistrust. However, once the demolition was underway, stopping it would have meant sending in troops, probably by air, to disarm the RSS mobs, creating both another collection of 'martyrs' and, Rao feared, leaving the impression that Congress was anti-Hindu. Rao concluded, therefore, that the demolition of the mosque was the lesser evil.

President's Rule was imposed on Uttar Pradesh and on the other BJP-controlled states the next day and the VHP, RSS and the *Bajrang Dal*, along with two Islamic groups, the Jamaat-e-Islami and the Islamic Sevak Sangh were banned – though in the case of the *Hindutva* organizations, only for two years. Several BJP leaders, including Advani were arrested and charged with inciting communal violence, though their cases then languished for several years in the courts. The now ruined site of the mosque was taken over by central government, as were 68 acres of surrounding land, and the whole issue of ownership and archaeological provenance handed over to the courts. None of this, however, prevented the ensuing orgy of violence. Massive communal riots followed in Ahmedabad, Surat and Calcutta. After its previous *yatras* the RSS had often brought riots in its wake; indeed many believed that it had perfected the art of riot-creation. One method involved sending cars to play amplified recordings of riots in Muslim areas, alarming and bewildering the inhabitants and often leaving, as they sped off, a real riot behind them. In many areas cells of volunteers noted incidents that might incite violence, keeping their local communities in a state of tense paranoia, and, when the moment was judged ripe, 'conversion' specialists would be sent in to transform the tension into outright violence. The worst communal riots occurred in Bombay in early 1993 and involved the bloody intersection of various flammable elements, including not only the communal machinations of local politicians, but the ambitions of property developers and their shady Mafiosi connections, all exacerbated by the blatantly anti-Muslim behaviour of the police. More than a thousand people were killed, with repercussions as far afield as Pakistan and Bangladesh, and even precipitating attacks on Hindu temples in Great Britain.

The destruction of the Babri mosque, however, left the BJP in something of a quandary. Now lacking a clear focus for mobilization and afraid that its association with violence might harm its image with the 'respectable' middle classes, it turned instead to socio-economic issues and, especially, the effect of liberalization. This, however, was itself a tricky area, as too harsh a condemnation of the reforms might also alienate its more affluent potential constituents, as well as its big-business donors. So while neo-Gandhian rhetoric about *swadeshi* reappeared and pugilistic postures were struck towards the World Bank, the IMF and Kentucky Fried Chicken by some RSS groups, the BJP's own stance was rather more ambiguous. What was needed, it claimed, was a 'calibrated' approach to liberalization, an

'Indian model . . . in consonance with our cultural mores and ethos'. The party also turned its attention to recruiting support among the now unignorable OBCs, who had been alienated by its apparent hostility to reservations. Many OBC politicians were now promoted in the party apparatus and it fielded high-profile OBC candidates of its own in constituencies where the electoral arithmetic demanded it. With apparent disregard for its own strictures about the organic wholeness of the Hindus, the BJP also indulged in remarkably populist appeals, offering a galaxy of specially tailored boons and incentives to every conceivable category of voters. These included special employment schemes for youth, integrated welfare projects for women dalits and, most surprisingly for a party committed to national 'One State, One Language', priority employment schemes to regional language speakers.

With the more shrill *Hindutva* agenda now somewhat muted, and with declining support for the once-again scandal-ridden Congress, the BJP did well in the 1996 elections when the party emerged with the largest portion of seats, though still far short of an absolute majority. These elections had also confirmed a more long-term and profound change in Indian politics: the emergence of powerful regional parties at the centre. So while the BJP's manifesto may have pithily proclaimed: 'One Culture, One Religion, One Nation', the reality was very different: to achieve power the party would have to collaborate with other cultures, religions and, most importantly, regions. It won 25.5 per cent of the vote and 179 seats, compared with Congress's 141 seats, and took government for 13 days, but was unable to forge a lasting coalition with other regional parties, who went on to create their own United Front government between 1996 and 1998.

The new electoral arithmetic made it impossible to form a government alone. The BJP, therefore, had no alternative but to improve its relations with regional parties. Over the next two years it built its coalitions, cutting pre-election seat-sharing deals with the AIDMK in Tamil Nadu, and with local parties and various offshoots of Congress in Bihar, Punjab, Maharashtra and West Bengal. Gone from the manifesto were promises to introduce a uniform civil code, to abolish the special constitutional status of Kashmir, to introduce a US-style presidential system and to build a 'magnificent' Ram temple at Ayodhya. After the elections in 1998, the BJP was able to form a longer-lived government as leader of a thirteen-party coalition (four of the thirteen parties had only one member). Short-lived though it was – the coalition collapsed in April 1999 – it managed to impress the more nationalistically inclined by exploding five underground nuclear devices, marking India's emergence as a nuclear power. Moreover a BJP caretaker government was in control when the near-war crisis arose when Pakistani-backed Kashmiri insurgents crossed the Line of Control in the autumn of 1999. The ensuing general election of late 1999 again demonstrated not the triumph of *Hindutva*, but the fragmentation of the electorate along regional and caste lines. The regional parties trebled their share of seats from 56 to 158 seats; the BJP vote fell slightly, while that of Congress rose, but it was the BJP that proved more adept at alliance-building. After much brokering, a coalition between the BJP and twenty-three alliance partners (accounting for nearly 40 per cent of seats) emerged to govern – the National Democratic Alliance (NDA). But this was not a government well placed to impose a unified agenda. The BJP leadership had now to cater for its chauvinist activists intent on Hinduizing the nation and *swadeshi*fiying the economy, a soft-core of 'respectable' high-caste supporters who did not relish the prospect of government by violent obscurantists, and an array of regional allies with their own highly particularistic agendas. Success would require a virtuoso display of political acrobatics.

Once in power some effort was made to please this diverse crowd. For the *Hindutva* die-hards there were a series of cultural 'interventions'. Renaming became something of a sport: Bombay had become Mumbai in 1995, and soon Port Blair Airport was Veer Savarkar Airport, and Savarkar's portrait now hung in Parliament opposite that of the man many believed he had conspired to assassinate – Mahatma Gandhi. The most attention-grabbing exercises in cultural politics were propagated by the new Minister for Human Resources, and long-time RSS activist, Murli Manohar Joshi. He became internationally notorious for the 'astro-fiasco', the decision to fund 'Vedic astrology' courses at Indian universities. In his defence Joshi cited not only the importance of not kow-towing to 'western' science, but also the tremendous job opportunities for professionally trained astrologers, not least among the wealthy dollar-earning disapora. Wits suggested that India's prestigious elite bureaucratic corps, the IAS, be renamed the Indian Astrological Service. Other like-minded interventions included the dropping of communism from social science courses to leave only liberalism, Gandhism and fascism; the suggestion that university maths professors should learn Sanskrit; and that universities establish *Purohitya* courses to professionally examine Brahman priests, for whose services there was also, apparently, an insatiable demand in America. More seriously, Joshi was determined to establish a long-term *Hindutva* legacy among the nation's schoolchildren by commissioning a complete re-write of all history textbooks.

Hindu nationalists had long been pre-occupied by history, and more particularly by the supposed distortions of Indian history propounded by academic-cum-communist professors. These included the allegedly false notion that the Aryans were originally outsiders and that, therefore, Vedic culture might be seen as a foreign import. When another university academic showed conclusively that the Aryans had been beef-eaters it was the final straw. Amateur and web-based *Hindutva* historians and archaeologists fought a long battle challenging these now academically orthodox hypotheses and, using the various *puranas* (ancient texts), epics and other mytho-poetic sources had constructed their own chronologies, geographies and time-lines, which 'proved' that the case was entirely the opposite: the Aryans had been indigenous to India and had, in fact, invaded other societies and cultures, spreading the Vedic civilization. This and other historical 'distortions' were to be decisively cleared up under Joshi's management. Educational institutions such as the University Grants Commission, the Secondary School Board, the Indian Institute of Advanced Study and the Councils of Social Sciences and Historical Research were filled with BJP and RSS sympathizers. After a protracted and high profile struggle, the newly commissioned history textbooks were finally published in 2003. Critics trawled them for howlers and were not disappointed. In the text dealing with the nationalist movement, the butcher of Amritsar, General Dyer, was confused with the less bloodthirsty Lieutenant-Governor, Michael O'Dwyer; Subhas

Chandra Bose acquired an entirely unrelated brother, the terrorist Rash Behari Bose; and the freedom-fighting Chapekar brothers were hanged on the orders of two British officials whom only a few pages earlier they had assassinated. Nevertheless, children in VHP-run schools continued to learn that Jesus had visited Vedic gurus in the Himalayas and that the human race originated in Tibet. They could also expect to have their 'spiritual quotient' tested.

For those more interested in tangible signs of power the BJP instituted a high-profile foreign policy. The testing of nuclear devices in March 1998 transformed India's national security position. The government rejected US-led pressure to sign the Comprehensive Test Ban Treaty and in 1999 revealed its plans for a strategic defence system involving land-based missiles, planes and submarines. This antagonized international opinion, and, at first, looked like a miscalculation, bringing damaging US economic sanctions. But after 11 September 2001 US and Indian security goals began to converge. In December 2001 the US lifted sanctions, and a year later at a meeting of the Indo-US security co-operation group in New Delhi, the US announced the elevation of India to 'friendly country' status on a par with Japan and Singapore; India was now allowed to purchase weapons worth up to $40 million without Congressional approval. At last, it seemed to some, Savarkar's dream of militarizing the Hindu nation had been fulfilled.

These cultural and nuclear initiatives pleased hardliners, who had always been critical of India's non-aligned internationalism and were not averse to closer relations with America. But the discipline of government, especially a government resting on such a diversity of interests and ideologies, brought dissension. Part of the BJP's pursuit of electability after the demolition of the Babri mosque had entailed efforts to recruit scheduled caste and OBC support, and, to a degree, this continued in government. To be effective in the post-Mandal era, the party had to embrace the logic of reservations. Moderate elements had suggested that they should accelerate their recruitment of OBC candidates and party workers and, more dramatically, dilute their hostility to reservations based purely on caste – a strategy dubbed 'social engineering'. This approach came into conflict with the elitist ethos of the party and its associates in the RSS, who denied the saliency of caste divisions and insisted on organic 'oneness'. It also went against the grain of its other 'soft' support base, 'respectable' high-caste Hindus who felt threatened by the Mandalization of public life. For hardliners, the correct way to deal with caste conflict was through sanskritizing the scheduled and lower castes, a rather patronizing approach that involved 'uplifting' them to the same 'cultural' level as their 'betters', while inculcating sentiments of deference and respect. In Uttar Pradesh the contradictions within the party became manifest. While the BJP recruited OBC leaders such as Kalyan Singh to appeal to certain fractions of the OBC vote, in cities like Agra this alienated their high-caste supporters who preferred the RSS sanskritzing strategy designed to drive a wedge between dalit and more assertive OBC groups.

Another contradiction lay in the BJP's coalitional strategy with regional parties. This in itself was a violation of *Hindutva*'s professed hostility to federalism. Nevertheless, apart from the obvious necessity of making alliances in order to gain power, the party also hoped, in the longer term, to insinuate itself among their supporters and eventually displace them. But rather than riding on their coat tails, the BJP became besmirched by the highly irregular politics of many of these parties. The opening act of regional coalition politics was high farce. The first Vajpayee-led coalition of 1998 was entirely dependent on the whims of one of India's more colourful and volatile politicians, Jayalalitha. Jayalalitha had hitherto been chief minister of Tamil Nadu and leader of the AIDMK, a mantle she had inherited from her sometime film co-star and, some said, lover, M. G. Ramachandran. Jayalalitha, a Brahman, was not averse to the BJP's wooing since promotion of her high-caste status offered a cloak of respectability to throw over her rather dubious political origins. She was also, however, involved in a vicious tit-for-tat struggle with her rival, Karunanidhi, leader of the DMK and the new chief minister, who had instigated criminal proceedings against Jayalalitha for corruption when in office. Jayalalitha was selling her eighteen MPs to the BJP coalition for a very high price. She wanted the new government to impose President's Rule on Tamil Nadu, both to punish Karunanidhi and so that she could escape criminal prosecution, and just for good measure she demanded the right to nominate the Indian finance minister. Sordid negotiations dragged on for nearly a year until Jayalalitha withdrew her support, threw in her lot with Congress and precipitated another general election. After the elections her nemesis, Karunanidhi, joined the BJP coalition himself. Jayalalitha's mortification continued when a six-day search of her home revealed 29 kg of jewellery, 91 wristwatches and 10,500 saris – though a subsequent court case cleared her of all charges of graft.

However, the greatest source of ire for *Hindutva* hardliners was Vajpayee's vacillations, as they saw them, on the Kashmir issue, and his tolerance, to their eyes, of incidents of supposed Pakistani-sponsored terrorism in India. The autonomy granted to Kashmir under Article 370 of the Constitution had long been one of the *bêtes noires* of the right and deletion of the offending article had become a mantra among many. Letters signed in blood had been sent to the Indian President pleading for a stronger line. In 1992 Murli Manohar Joshi's *Ekta Yatra* (procession for unity) had traipsed from Kanyakumari in the south intending to fly the national flag at the very spot in Srinagar where it had so often been burnt by militant Kashmiri nationalists. Joshi's march was stopped at the border of Jammu and a much smaller contingent was helicoptered to the Kashmiri capital; the national flag was hastily unfurled, but not hoisted – the flagpole was broken. Though the revocation of Article 370 had disappeared from the BJP manifesto, the issue hadn't and it was revived by the escalation of the Pakistani-backed insurgency in the region. But Vajpayee adopted a moderate line and, in the right's eyes, kow-towed to American interests and diplomacy. In July 2001 the American-brokered Agra summit between India and Pakistan on the issue not only produced no advance, but saw an escalation of terrorist attacks in Kashmir, when, in October, a Pakistani suicide bomber killed twenty people at a railway station in Jammu. Criticism of Vajpayee reached fever pitch when suicide bombers attacked the Indian parliament on 13 December, an event soon likened to the earlier destruction of the World Trade Center in New York. As a result the Indian army was mobilized along the western borders.

Nevertheless, Vajpayee stuck to diplomacy and with apparent success when in January 2002, President Musharraf of Pakistan, under pressure from the US, outlawed five extremist sects, withdrew support

427

from terrorist groups in both Pakistan and Pakistan-controlled Kashmir and agreed to stop incursions. But infiltration continued throughout March and April and on 14 May Pakistani terrorists stormed the Indian army barracks at Kaluchak killing 32. Though Vajpayee told the army to prepare for war, the crisis was again resolved by US intervention; Pakistan agreed to control the jihadists and India consented to free elections in Kashmir. This was not likely to please the VHP hard-core and, coupled with the party's recent loss of the Uttar Pradesh state elections, marked a nadir for Vajpayee's strategy of stealthy moderation. Rajesh Ramachandran, a member of the National Democratic Alliance, observed, 'for the Sangh, Vajpayee's utility is almost over. He is no longer a vote catcher and in the scheme of *Hindutva* politics, he is a liability.'

The revival of the Ayodhya issue was a clear sign that the extremists in the party and its broader Hindu 'family' were conspiring to subvert Vajpayee's moderate path and return to religious mobilization and cultivation of communal violence. In early 2003 the VHP announced a rally of Ram *bhakts* (devotees) to start building the Ram *mandir* on the now closed site of the demolished mosque. The day after this rally fifty-eight returning Gujarati Ram *bhakts* were immolated in the carriage of their train just outside the Gujarati town of Godhra. Accounts varied as to the causes of this conflagration, the BJP maintaining that it had been planned with the connivance of Pakistan, but others noted that the *Hindutva* volunteers had been abusing Muslim passengers and vendors along the route. Hearing of these insults a crowd of 2000 poor and angry Muslims had gathered just outside Godhra, and when the train stopped they had surrounded the *bhakts*' carriage, allegedly dousing it with 60 litres of fuel before setting it alight.

Though Vajpayee had tried to calm the situation by permitting a single pillar of the Ram temple to be transported to the Ayodhya site, the RSS's riot system had already been primed. The supposedly peaceful protest held in Ahmedabad on 28 February marked the launch a massive onslaught of anti-Muslim violence, which spread across the towns and villages of north and central Gujarat. Official figures set the number murdered at 1000, unofficial figures at 2000.

In a subsequent independent report into the riots, the authors described what appeared to be an organized pattern of violence:

Attackers in their thousands in trucks, clad in saffron scarves and khaki shorts ... shouting slogans of incitement to kill, they were armed with swords, *trishuls* [tridents], sophisticated explosives and gas cylinders. Guided by computer printouts listing the addresses of Muslim families and their properties, information obtained from the Ahmedabad municipal corporation among other sources, they embarked on a murderous rampage. In many cases the police led the charge, aiming and firing at Muslims who got in the mobs' way.

The report by the Concerned Citizens' Tribunal of January 2003, based on 1500 eyewitness accounts gathered in 16 districts, claimed that swords, iron rods and *trishuls* had been used to sever limbs and even to quarter victims, women and girls were stripped and paraded through the streets before being raped and burnt. This report also claimed to have identified VHP and BJP leaders and even Legislative Assembly members among the attacking crowds. Some of the young *Bajrang Dal* men interviewed by the Tribunal reported that they had been attending weekly training camps since September 2001, where they were told of a 'coming war', exhorted to focus hatred on Muslims and assured that there would be no punishment. The 'war' seemed not only aimed at life and limb, but also at livelihoods – businesses were targeted and thousands of trucks, taxis and auto-rickshaws destroyed. Confidential information was offered to the Tribunal implicating the state's BJP chief minister, Narendra Modi, and his cabinet in the formulation and broader dissemination of a fully worked-out plan of attack. The report concluded that this had been a pre-planned pogrom aimed at terrorizing and economically crippling Muslims, for which the Godhra fire had been a pretext. The National Human Rights Commission also reported that no effort had been made for three days to quell the violence and that officials who had tried to do their duties had been transferred. Police reports were either poorly recorded or distorted, entering those accused as 'unknown'. 'The government's response' the report continued, was 'often abysmal, or even non-existent, pointing to gross negligence, or worse still, as was widely believed, to a complicity that was tacit if not explicit', indicting the Gujarat government for its 'comprehensive failure'.

Vajpayee made one brief visit to Gujarat to inspect the scenes of slaughter, after which many believed he would dismiss Modi. However, within a week, he too had adopted the Pakistan-conspiracy line, some thought under pressure from Advani and others. In a speech in Goa he explained the riots were simply in retaliation for the supposed massacre at Godhra, adding that the threat to India was not from anti-secularists, but from religious terrorism. Militant Islam, he maintained, was 'sowing thorns' for elected government the world over: 'these days, militancy in the name of Islam leaves no room for tolerance. It has raised the slogan of jihad.'

Though the English-language press condemned the riots as a cynical election manoeuvre, and efforts were made to depose the BJP-led government with a vote of no-confidence over its refusal to dismiss Modi, the NDA-BJP combine survived. The hardliners drove home their advantage by insisting on bringing the Gujarat state elections forward to capitalize on the after-effects of the pogrom. The Italian origins of Congress's leader Sonia Gandhi, widow of Rajiv, became a significant election issue – though she was not contesting any seat there. As part of his election campaign Modi launched a *Gaurav Yatra* to reassert pride in the Mahatma's home state, pride to which Congressmen, he said, had become blind because they wore 'Italian spectacles on their eyes'. The BJP won with nearly 50 per cent of the vote and a two-thirds majority; most of their gains had come from the most riot-struck areas, offering proof, or so it seemed, of the electoral gains to be had from the propagation of religious hatred.

But perhaps the most significant issue on which the Vajpayee moderates clashed with the RSS hardliners was economic reform. There had been an apparent consensus against liberalization after 1993 but the moderates had not wanted to alienate entirely those urban middle-class groups who were benefiting from reforms. This led to some friction, as hardliners wanted a more full-blooded assault on Congress's economic policy, and one expressed in both anti-consumerist and xenophobic terms. Jay Dubashi voiced the darker fears of the Hindu right: 'To a person who has not left India, the feeling is now that the Americans are coming, and they think they can partition the country again, they can break up the country again.' In 1991 the RSS issued a pamphlet listing 326 consumer goods made by multi-nationals next to a list of Indian substitutes, declaring, 'Every morning we begin the job of cleansing our bodies with help of products manufactured by these filthy companies.' In 1994 they launched the *Swadeshi Jagran Manch* (Self-Reliance Awareness Front), which opposed India's application for WTO membership launched by Rao, calling it 'a new centre of imperialism' out to destroy in league with the IMF, the World Bank, multinationals and the USA. A BJP government, it insisted, should abandon globalization and protect traditional industries.

Once in government it seemed, initially, that the hardliners would have their way and reforms would slow to a glacial pace. Vajpayee's first choice of finance minister, Jaswant Singh, a cavalry officer of pro-liberalization views and no RSS connections, was blocked. Moreover, Advani, as home minister, and Joshi at human resources seemed set on influencing economic policy. Joshi had pronounced himself a devoted *swadeshi*te: 'The *swadeshi* I have been propounding is an economy for, by and with the Indian people . . . We need to make . . . India economically and politically strong so that our voice is heard in the international arena.' Businessmen were now surprised to find themselves expected to make their case to the home minister and his circle of RSS advisers, often Hindi-speaking 'RSS *pracharaks*, living in small Spartan rooms, without television, and with no knowledge of what changes were taking place in the world'. The government's first budget imposed across-the-board import duty surcharges to offer some protection and satisfy ideologues. But the negative reaction abroad gave Vajpayee, more ambivalent about reversing liberalization, an opportunity to strike out alone, his resolve stiffened by officials in the Prime Minister's Office who suggested he consider his long-term reputation. Soon he had established and personally chaired two high-profile pro-reform advisory councils, one of eminent economists, the other of business CEOs.

Thus, while the National Executive and National Council of the BJP under RSS influence passed resolutions criticizing globalization for its one-sidedness, Vajpayee committed the government to speeding up internal liberalization and aborted planned SJM campaigns against various multinationals including Coca Cola. Heedless of hard-line strictures against foreign investment, on his visit to the USA in 2000 he called for $10 billion of foreign investment annually. Liberalization, though 'calibrated' and hedged with qualifications, had been resumed. The government announced that it would conform to WTO demands to abolish all quantitative restrictions on all imports by 2002, and it opened more sectors of the economy to full foreign ownership, including mass rapid transport systems, hotels, tourism and drugs. It also approved foreign ownership, of varying degrees, for a range of other sectors such as civil aviation, real estate, banking and telecoms. Foreign investment was even permitted in the highly sensitive insurance and print industries, though, in deference to *swadeshi* opinion, foreign holdings could not exceed 26 per cent. In one area the BJP government pursued liberalization with even more vigour than its Congress initiators. In 1999 Vajpayee created a Ministry of Disinvestment headed by his pro-privatization ally, Arun Shourie and answerable to a cabinet committee chaired by himself and designed to accelerate approvals. The entire public sector, with the exception of defence, atomic energy and the railways, was now subject to sales of government shares and even complete privatization. By July 2001 twenty-seven state-owned enterprises, including VSNL, the state's international telecommunications monopoly, were either at an advanced stage of the process or had already been privatized, raising $2.3 billion.

Matters did not proceed entirely smoothly. K. S. Sudarshan, leader of the RSS, condemned those who 'ape the west' and do 'the bidding of the IMF and WTO' as 'sons of Marx and Macaulay'. Privatization provoked most hostility, and RSS activists launched a 'Warning Day' when the privatization of insurance was mooted. Privatization of oil companies also proved highly controversial; Joshi and others argued it risked the state's energy security and the criticism was assisted by the maelstrom of business scandals that began to engulf the government. The partner of George Fernandes, the defence minister, was caught taking bribes in a press sting, while Ram Naik, the petroleum minister, supposedly gave petrol-pump licences to BJP supporters. Soon the press began to report that the corruption of Mrs Gandhi's

Congress, 'pale[d] in comparison' to that of the BJP-NDA government, and the IAS was now referred to not as the 'steel', but the 'steal' frame of India.

Despite these conflicts and scandals the 2004 General Election was brought forward and largely run not on the question of religion, but of economic success. Though this seemed justified by India's much improved growth figures, it proved ultimately a grave miscalculation, for the benefits of growth had not been so widely distributed as to have created a broad mass of support. It also left the leadership open to the charge that it was pandering to international opinion at the expense of its true *Hindutva* principles.

Nevertheless an advertising agency was retained and built the BJP message around the triumphalist slogan, 'India Shining'. This insouciant campaign, apparently forgetting that nearly 70 per cent of Indians were still dependent on agriculture, dwelt obsessively on images of booming big cities and exultant upper-middle-class consumers. Vajpayee, who had almost resigned in late 2002, was now revived as a key vote-catcher. A personality cult developed around the lugubrious poet, recasting him as another father of the nation, sagacious, moderate and avuncular, a visionary in the footsteps of Nehru. 'Shri Atalji', ran the ad-copy, is 'inspiring countless Indians with his poetry, his thoughts, his *tapsya* [renunciation] and towering personality'. An 'Atal wave' was predicted. Advani predictably set off on a *yatra*, this time the *Bharat Uday Yatra* (India Rising Pilgrimage) by bus, proclaiming an 'Agenda for Development, Good Governance and Peace'. And, in a radical volte-face from his earlier incarnation as Gandhian scourge of technology, he borrowed heavily from Chandrababu Naidu's lap-top vision of India's future. India, he announced, would be developed by 2020, would experience a 'quantum improvement in the quality of life', would acquire world-class infrastructure, and would become a 'global manufacturing hub'. Congress meanwhile campaigned ruthlessly on the BJP-NDA failures. The government had not provided jobs for youth, had neglected the poor, damaged agriculture and worsened security by spreading religious hatred. Referring frequently to Nehru, campaigners claimed they would 'rekindle the flame of all-inclusive, composite, pluralistic nationalism'. This was no ordinary election, but a 'clash of sharply competing values and diametrically opposite ideologies'. Even V. P. Singh emerged from a lengthy retirement to campaign for Congress, declaring, 'Gujarat was the last straw, its [the BJP's] real fascist character has been revealed now'.

The polling itself was characterized by widespread violence and unrest. Twenty-seven of eighty seats in Uttar Pradesh were labelled as 'highly sensitive'. Meanwhile in Bihar, where 15,000 of its 49,700 booths were regarded as vulnerable to 'booth-capturing', the police were authorized to shoot if they encountered any serious unrest. High-caste private armies clashed with Maoists in some places, and in Andhra Pradesh Chandrababu Naidu was the victim of an assassination attempt by the People's War Group. The results, when they came in, stunned observers and participants alike. The BJP lost 44 seats with its vote falling back to its 1991 level of 21 per cent. Its allied parties in the NDA did even worse, losing 68 seats, their vote share dropping from 17 per cent in 1999 to 13.8 per cent. Congress, while gaining seats, lost votes, its poll share falling by 1.6 per cent. The most striking winners were the parties of the left. The Indian electorate had apparently rejected both the economic liberalization of Congress and the diluted version proffered by the BJP. Whether they had wholly rejected the *Hindutva* project was unclear, as the BJP had not made the issue central to its campaign.

In August 2003 however, *Hindutva* suffered a slightly clearer defeat at the hands of official archaeologists investigating the disputed Ayodhya site. Earlier investigations by a project calling itself 'Archaeology of the Ramayana Sites', which had excavated the site in the 1970s, had found a fifth-century BC urban settlement in its environs, but it could not say conclusively whether this was Ram's Ayodhya. Later another dig, led by the archaeologist Hans Bakker, produced another theory. Ayodhya, Bakker suggested, may once have been Saketa, a city mentioned in Jain and Buddhist texts, raising the intriguing possibility that the subterranean temple, if there was one, could be Buddhist. In August 2003 the Supreme Court revealed that there was indeed a 'massive edifice' below the now demolished mosque. The artefacts uncovered, however, suggested that it was probably not a Hindu temple.

Epilogue, or Divine Developments

On 18 September 2006 students at the prestigious Ahmedabad Indian Institute of Management were presented with a curious case study. The subject of the presentation was the remarkable metamorphosis of an industry many had dubbed a lumbering white elephant into a model of managerial efficiency and commercial élan, a transformation, moreover, masterminded by a CEO of world-class business acuity. What made the presentation curious was that the company in question was not some private-sector high-tech software giant but the Indian Railways – the largest state-owned business in the world. More remarkable still was the identity of the corporate wizard who had engineered this management miracle, for it was none other than Laloo Prasad Yadav, sometime chief minister of Bihar, scourge of Brahmanhood and political showman extraordinaire. In 2004 Laloo, armed with a valuable cache of parliamentary seats and thus considerable leverage over the Congress-led coalition now running India, became Minister for Railways. And despite much hand-wringing in expert committees and management consultancies and predictions of imminent financial demise, in 2005/6 the Indian Railways turned in a profit of Rs.150 billion, with further substantial increases confidently promised for the following year. Laloo's astonishing achievement attracted the attention of management academics not only in India but as far afield as Harvard and Paris, while the CEO of the US corporate giant General Electric sought advice on 'strategy' from the 'Chaharva in a chopper'.

Laloo's much-studied success combined raw commercial cunning – cutting fares but increasing freight loadings – with eye-catching populism – replacing plastic cups with *kulhads* (earthenware beakers), insisting that only *khadi* cloth be used for upholstery, laying on *Garib Raths* (poor-people's 'expresses'), and offering free travel for the unemployed as they scour the country for jobs. Laloo himself claims no affection for the principles inculcated in management schools, preferring instead the homely adages of his mother: 'never handle a buffalo by its tail, but always catch it by its horns,' he has sagely observed. Meanwhile his realization that the railways could be turned to profit by the simple expedient of moving higher volumes of freight without adding to capacity, he attributes to the rustic recognition that, 'Wagon is the bread-earning horse of the railways. Load it adequately. Make it run and don't stable it.' Laloo's impact on the railways does not, however, even begin to capture his commercial significance, for Laloo has also become a brand. Laluji ('loved and revered Laloo') dolls are the toy of choice for many Bihari infants, Laloo chocolate bars depicting Laloo as politician on one side and Laloo as magician on the other have become a confectionary coup. A range of Laloo cosmetics has been launched; one product, *Lalu Chale Sasural* (Laloo Visits His In-Laws), comprising face powder, lipstick and a necklace, has proved peculiarly popular with pre-teen consumers.

Besides demonstrating yet another example of the bizarre vagaries of Indian public life, Laloo's apotheosis from rambunctious ruffian to management guru might also suggest something rather more significant. In the late 1990s and early 2000s Laloo was not a celebrated cultural icon but a gaolbird, having been indicted for embezzling from the Bihar public purse $267 million meant for cattle fodder (although, characteristically, the recently launched Laloo Cattle Fodder brand has been a runaway commercial success). His chief-ministerial reign in Bihar, dubbed 'jungle raj' by his detractors, was most notable for its egregious favouritism towards one caste – the Yadavs – and an insouciant disregard for broader considerations of public welfare and official probity. Yet as railways minister his record, if not perhaps as exemplary as management manuals proclaim, does suggest a new concern for efficient service, financial stability and good management. Could Laloo's personal transformation, then, be the harbinger of India's long-awaited transition from the politics of bossism, factionalism and caste competition to an ethos of common welfare and respect for the state as the embodiment of public service? Though this may indeed be the case, it is also clear that such a transformation will not come overnight. A few months after the Laloo management presentation in Ahmedabad, Laloo's in-laws were caught travelling first class, but conspicuously ticketless, on the Hajipur Express in Bihar. The elderly couple protested that there was 'no need' for them to buy tickets, and they had been assured that this was the case by the Hajipur station master himself. Though trivial in itself, the incident does suggest that ingrained habits of patronage and the notion of the state as a private exploitable resource, rather than a public good, will be hard to break.

In this book I have tried to show how India has developed its own peculiar form of modernity, the most striking feature of which is its highly variegated, fragmented and diverse citizenry. Identities of caste, religion, community and region often overpower broader-based loyalties to the nation state and also account, in part, for the very weakness of that state. Lacking deeply entrenched popular legitimacy, the Indian government has found mustering and deploying the resources and general will for development almost insuperably difficult. Paradoxically, while this lack of common purpose and identity has helped to perpetuate poverty and create only the most skeletal infrastructure, it has also fostered a robust democratic temper: India's kaleidoscope of contending castes and communities have seized on elections as a relatively peaceful means of brokering their competing claims. The question now is whether this paradox can be resolved into the harmonious co-existence of democracy and diversity with economic growth and equality. And, in particular, can the state sustain stability, legitimacy and economic dynamism as it emerges as a new superpower?

In the last decade there have been flickering indications that India is building on its difficult legacy to succeed in the global economic competition, improving living standards and strengthening political stability. Since 2004 the Indian economy has, in parts at least, done remarkably well, moving from the old 4 or 5 per cent per annum 'Hindu rate of growth' common in many of the preceding decades, to a much healthier 8 or 9 per cent. India's seizure of export markets in software engineering and business outsourcing (back-office administration) has astonished the world, and even manufacturing growth has of late moved into double figures. The country has attracted foreign investment in volumes not seen even during the high point of empire, with international corporate giants competing to construct massive power projects, refit airports and build city metros. But it is also clear that though the Hindu rate of growth may have been banished, in its place has come the Hindu rate of liberalization. India has disdained the Big Bang, 'red in tooth and claw' style of capitalism adopted in other liberalizing economies. Indeed, as liberal economies go it is remarkably regulated. New businesses are still bound by complex labour laws and thickets of bureaucracy cover everything from building permits to power connections. But though international commentators bemoan this apparent addiction to state control, it is in fact a consequence of the very features for which India is so commonly praised – its democracy and pluralism. In India politics trumps economics; the highly participatory democratic system offers all groups the chance to check and balance the ascendancy of one interest only, and so the pursuit of radical economic liberalization is effectively a political impossibility.

For this reason, among others, democracy, the great icon of Indian nationhood, has its detractors. The best formulation of this critique is that India has too much of the 'wrong' kind of democracy. Its multifarious groups act to check one another in a manner at once selfish and chaotic, but also ultimately self-defeating. Groups, whether they be castes, farmers, businessmen, regionalists or cultural-religious enthusiasts operate with no sense of common purpose or welfare, and politics is a set of unseemly skirmishes for resources in which the greater 'battle' for development will always be lost.

However, since the 2004 elections there have been inklings of more of the 'right' kind of democracy. The elections suggested Indian parties might be abandoning their old strategies of 'bribing' an unlikely collection of groups to vote for them, without any concern for broad strategy or principle. Instead they seemed to be forging more integrated coalitions, which might unite their supporters behind a coherent programme. This has held out the promise of a political process in which rival strategies of development – leftist and liberalizing – are debated and compromises arrived at. The elections themselves, though they produced no overall winner, did indicate broad left–right divisions among voters. The chief beneficiaries were regional parties of a leftist disposition, which have formed a Congress-led United Progressive Coalition, offering a moderately social-democratic future; opposing them stood the champions of more full-blooded nationalism and liberalization led, at that time, by the BJP.

Another example of the 'right' kind of democracy is suggested by the Laloo story. For the last twenty years high-caste groups have resisted the democratic logic of numbers and tried to prevent the entry of India's majority lower castes into the temples of political power, high office and prestigious education. In their defence they have invoked reasons of efficiency and 'merit', citing the lawlessness of Bihar or the dalit chief minister Mayawati and her statue-erecting antics as evidence. In a society where hierarchies have been extreme and powerfully discriminatory, it is inevitable that early manifestations of equality will often be rancorous and apparently trivial – such as the statue wars in Uttar Pradesh, where petty symbolic victories can count for far more than effective government. However, in south India, where there has been special discrimination to favour specific castes for much longer, governmental efficiency, state spending on education and welfare and something more akin to a sense of the common weal are far more conspicuous than they are in the north. These public 'goods' have been produced not by a lofty clique of high-caste mandarins, but by low-caste politicians themselves. And Laloo has, in a small and doubtless flawed way, demonstrated that the lower castes are not fundamentally incompetent or unmeritorious, but capable of leadership that attracts global attention.

Global attention is a 'good' that Indian elites prize, whether they be indigenous or diasporic. In the last few years India has acquired a clout on the world stage that the Nehruvian era of pious and preachy non-alignment had failed to deliver. In part this is a reflection of shifting geo-strategic realities. The US, discomfited by the rise of China, and less favourably disposed to Pakistan since the eruption of global Islamist terrorism, has pursued a closer understanding with India. Symbolic of this has been American recognition of India's status as a nuclear power, brought by the agreement in 2005 to support India's civil nuclear programme. India's recent economic successes have also been acknowledged internationally. It is now a net donor in the IMF, not a borrower, and has mounted, alongside Brazil and

South Africa, a powerful intellectual critique of the trading inequities embodied in the World Trade Organization – one that has effectively paralysed the manoeuvrings of that institution. It also has the support of many major powers, including China, for its ambition to acquire a permanent seat on the United Nations Security Council – the crown jewel of superpowerdom. Its corporations, moreover, are engaged in a frenzy of acquisitions of prestigious western businesses, for reasons that sometimes appear to owe more to the imperatives of national pride than commercial logic. The global benefits of unity have not been lost on India's elites and this, coupled with much improved centre–state relations since the mid-1980s, has quelled the incipient separatism simmering in some regions. It is even possible, though not immediately likely, that the bloody imbroglio of Kashmir may be solved as New Delhi pursues a more pacific strategy, supported by the US with whom it now has a common cause in suppressing Islamist terrorism.

India's leaders, however, have little cause for complacency, for intimations of triumph are easily matched by gloomier portents. India's current economic buoyancy relies on cheapish energy (it is heavily dependent on imported oil and gas) and the fickle whims of international bond and share traders; it could be badly buffeted by a sharp rise in energy prices, or by a 'cooling' of international 'hot money' towards the Indian market. But the greatest impediments to sustained growth lie in infrastructural shortcomings and political opposition to economic liberalization, for the popular legitimacy of this project is highly conditional.

India has been hamstrung by poor infrastructure since the days of the Raj, for it was under the Raj that the state acquired its stubborn inability to tax adequately. As a consequence, it has never commanded the revenues necessary to establish extensive and good-quality roads, ports, irrigation or power supplies. Social capital has been as much neglected as the physical variety. Though India's boosters make much of its proficiency in English – now the international business language and a powerful weapon in the battle for export markets in software design and call centres – good English is still the preserve of a tiny elite. Many Indians recognize the supreme value of mastering the global tongue, but can afford only the unregulated tuition proffered by private academies, colleges and 'English shops'. Many thousands of these institutions have mushroomed across Indian cities and towns to spread the boon of English among a broader constituency. But while their enterprise is undoubted, the product they purvey – a bizarre and sometimes barely intelligible version of the language – is more dubious. Sadly, fluency in this mangled hybrid-tongue will not help India in its long-term competition with China, the Philippines and much of South East Asia as those states embark on the task of teaching their citizens 'standard' English. And so the language of the colonizers, a sometimes embarrassing but lately priceless heirloom from the Raj, could rapidly become a wasting asset. This is a symptom of a more general problem: the poor quality of mass education in contemporary India, which has also inherited the Raj's flair for elite rather than popular instruction. India has a number of world-class schools and universities, which have catered, on the whole, only to the most privileged. Yet public education has been egregiously under-funded, with school buildings collapsing and teachers vanishingly rare. Though recent budgets have redirected funds to education, it still accounts for barely 3 per cent of GDP, not the 6 per cent often promised. Indians, meanwhile, have some of the lowest literacy rates in the developing world.

India also has strikingly rudimentary infrastructural and communications networks. While Bangalore, the cyber-capital of south India, may be constructing a state-of-the-art metro with foreign investment, the city was engulfed by flooding in the autumn of 2005 because of an unusually heavy monsoon – its water-draining systems having been steadily eroded since Independence as property developers were permitted to fill in 340 of the city's 400 lakes and waterways. Delhi, too, has nearly completed a metro with Japanese assistance, but in the summer of 2005 its road traffic was continuously gridlocked by citizens furious at their already intermittent and now virtually non-existent water and electricity supplies. India consumes only 30 per cent of the electricity used in most developed economies, its generation and supply are subject to regular cuts, its port facilities are miniscule compared with China's and, despite the vagaries of its monsoon climate, it has only 3 per cent of the water-storage capacity of the USA. Only 3 per cent of its roads are classified as 'highways' and only 1 per cent are dual carriageways. It is estimated that the country needs at least $350 billion of physical infrastructure investment. The government hopes to raise much of this from abroad, and though foreign investment is at a historic high it is still only $11 billion per annum.

In early 2006 the government announced a new initiative that it hoped might help close the infrastructural gap, the creation of 117 Special Economic Zones (SEZs). But the vexed fortunes and rapid demise of this policy vividly illustrates what is potentially the greatest obstacle to sustained liberalization – its lack of political legitimacy. The SEZs, modelled on Chinese forerunners, were intended to provide domestic and foreign businesses with enclaves in which they could operate relatively free from regulation while enjoying a bonanza of subsidies and tax breaks. In return, participating corporations would undertake infrastructural investment of (it was hoped) $20 billion in three years. The SEZ idea soon became a victim of its own success. Rather than the 117 zones intended, applications were made for over 500. To provide the territory necessary the government proposed to invoke an old colonial law that gave states rights of compulsory land purchase. These enclaves seemed to many unpleasantly reminiscent of the bad old days of the Raj, when wealthy foreign businesses clustered in a few cities, making large profits, which they then exported back to Britain. Meanwhile the freedom these businesses would enjoy from the regulatory and tax obligations shouldered by 'ordinary' Indian citizens also carried a distinct whiff of imperial extra-territoriality.

Soon the SEZ proposal had rallied a remarkably diverse coalition of opponents, ranging from the mighty finance ministry to the most humble peasant and virtually every class and ideological proclivity between. For the finance minister, the SEZs, a project emanating from the commerce ministry, meant the loss to the Exchequer of billions in tax revenues. To the romantic neo-Gandhian middle classes, the SEZs were a crass commercial encroachment on 'village India', and yet another harbinger of the ecological despoliation of the countryside – already continuing apace elsewhere as thousands of acres of forests were felled and even rivers partially privatized. Communists denounced the SEZs as the 'biggest land grab movement in the history of modern India', while Hindu nationalists have railed against the mortgaging of the nation's future to predatory foreigners. In West Bengal a mass protest was held over plans to hand over a 1000-acre site to Tata Motors, one politician mounting an appropriately Gandhian hunger strike. By the spring of 2007 a government committee, chastened by these commotions, recommended that SEZs would be capped at 1 per cent of the land in any one state, and the initiative seemed potentially moribund. The attitude of poor farmers and peasants was more ambivalent. While the SEZ scheme may not be as bad for them as well-heeled neo-Gandhians claim, offering such indigent peasants reasonable cash deals to sell up, it has, like the BJP's disastrous 'India Shining' election campaign, pushed liberalization out of the shadows of stealthy manoeuvring and into the forefront of political debate, and sharpened peasant suspicion of it.

Agriculture has been the black hole in India's economic universe. While other sectors have recorded annual growth rates in double figures, the performance of agriculture, though there are belated signs of dynamism, has been stagnating. Having been the engine of the economy in the 1970s and 1980s, the recipient of much public investment, it has grown at only 3 to 4 per cent since the mid 1990s. This is a deadly drag on Indian development, as over 60 per cent of the population are dependent on agricultural incomes. In the most aggressively liberalizing regions, such as Andhra Pradesh, Karnataka and Maharashtra, poor rural locales have been labelled 'suicide belts', areas where impoverished and indebted farmers have killed themselves in their thousands.

So, the exposure of liberalization to public gaze risks revealing its potentially disabling deficit of popular legitimacy, for there is something of a mismatch between the 'groupist' sentiments of Indian politics and the individualist ethos on which free-market liberalization is founded. The most significant political movement of the last few decades has been the rise of caste parties demanding positive discrimination, an approach that, in the short term at least, explicitly sacrifices open and individualistic competition on the altar of group equality. And beyond the wealthiest 10–20 per cent of the population who have enjoyed the affluence brought by liberalization, its benefits appear highly debatable. The other 80 per cent are the 'ordinary' people: peasants, artisans, shopkeepers, bazaar merchants, clerks, middlemen and teachers – the very groups to whom the original Gandhian brand of anti-modern and anti-market economics proved irresistibly attractive. As the SEZ fiasco demonstrated, 'ordinary' people, along with Hindu rightist communitarians, socialists, middle-class ecologists and OBC group-rights parties, can be mustered into a powerful force. To them, liberalization appears as nothing more than a selfish and rapacious scramble for the dispossession of the little man and the ruination of the environment.

More extreme opposition is to be found among the indigenous, or 'tribal' peoples, and very poor peasants living in India's 'unquiet forests' and mountain regions. In these areas the Maoist Naxalite movement has made a stunning comeback since its demise in the 1970s. In 2004 a number of peasant and 'tribal' Marxist groups, including 'People's War' and the 'Maoist Communist Centre', merged to form the Communist Party of India (Maoist), committed to waging violent struggle against government and private-sector encroachments on common land in the pursuit of mining and forestry rights. There are pockets of Naxalism in the remote regions of many states, though it is most threatening in Bihar, Andhra Pradesh and Orissa, through which a 'Red Corridor' has been sliced. Emboldened by Maoist successes in Nepal, the Naxalites have increased the audacity and sophistication of their attacks. In 2004 they succeeded in raiding a government armoury, and in 2007 killed forty policemen in Chhattisgarh. The movement has been ruthlessly suppressed by mass police and army operations, but even so, India's Prime Minister, Manmohan Singh, has stated that the Naxalites pose the greatest threat to Indian security since Independence.

The process of adjustment to a more liberalized economy, with its attendant mass migrations, farmer bankruptcies and rural unrest, places a heavy burden of management on India's politicians. The elections of 2004 marked the decisive end to the era of national party dominance. Neither Congress nor the BJP did well, losing out to a rainbow of regional and caste parties. And though Congress is now in government, it has been constrained by the necessity of coalition with an array of broadly left-of-centre regional groups and has curbed the excesses of liberalization. It is also by no means clear that it will be able to produce the leadership necessary to transcend the fractious and populist politics that have bedevilled efforts at sustained development. Regionalism itself, often seen as a 'good thing' by modish proponents of good governance, is clearly problematic if the state aspires to sustained economic growth. Responsibility for infrastructural development is untidily divided by India's constitution between central and regional governments, and a World Bank report of 2007 ominously stated that the financial and administrative acumen required to navigate complex infrastructural projects to successful completion were lacking at the regional level. It is conspicuous that it is only those sectors under central control – oil, gas and telecommunications – that have made significant process. Here too, the drift of Indian politics towards greater regional autonomy conflicts with the imperatives of economic development.

The 2004 elections created an opportunity for Congress, despite its poor electoral showing, to revive itself as the arch-co-ordinator of Indian political life. It has emerged as the leader of a centre-left coalition favouring moderately paced economic reform tempered with greater social welfare. However, its success in this co-ordinating role depends on it accepting that the politics of coalition is not a temporary disturbance on the calm seas of Congress hegemony, but a permanent feature of the political landscape. And there is a serious obstacle to this necessary adjustment – the party's addiction to a quasi-monarchical style of leadership. While Congress has ostensibly shed its dynastophilia and the economist-technocrat Manmohan Singh is Prime Minister, in reality the Nehru-Gandhi dynasty continues in the rather unlikely form of Sonia, the Italian-born widow of Rajiv Gandhi, who presides over the coalition. Many Congress politicians, despite the evidence of recent polls, seem convinced that they can dispense with the services of low-caste and regional collaborators and rely, instead, on the hereditary principle. By grooming Nehru's great-grandson, Rahul Gandhi, and great-granddaughter, Priyanka Vadra, for leadership, they hope to deploy the charisma of descent to recapture the massive majorities of the 1970s and 1980s.

There are signs too that the party is returning to the populist strategies of the Indira era, determined to outmanoeuvre regional collaborators by cobbling together a miscellany of 'vote-banks', lured by the promise of group boons and positive discrimination. This approach promises to perpetuate, not diminish, the hold of caste and religious identities on the popular imagination through the extension of job 'reservations' to new groups. Muslims in particular have attracted much recent attention. The government-commissioned Sachar Report of 2006 identified them as a group even more stricken by poverty and discrimination than dalits. Poverty and anger at denigration and discrimination has clearly fuelled recruitment to Islamist terrorist cells in various regions, some under Pakistani influence. One such cell, the banned Students Islamic Movement of India, is suspected of a series of train bombings in the summer of 2006, which killed 206 people in Mumbai. Though the government has responded with extreme repression there have also been calls, strengthened by the Sachar Report, to include Muslims among those groups receiving special discrimination. There are also proposals to expand positive discrimination into hitherto 'open' spheres, such as the elite Indian Institutes of Science, Management and Technology, and even into the private sector. While there may well be short-term electoral gains to be made from this, and even long-term improvements in social equality, it is a perilous game as it threatens to revive the querulous constituency of the chauvinist Hindu right. The BJP has been in some disarray since its debacle in the 2004 polls, but the revival of 'Mandal' reservation politics, the clumsy politicking of Congress against its regional and OBC allies, and simmering anxieties concerning Islamist violence in India are all grist to its paranoid mill, and recent regional election results suggest that it is by no means a spent force.

It is possible, though unlikely, that India will develop a west-European style of politics in which voters and parties form broadly coherent left and right blocs. More likely, however, is the continuation of government by an ever shifting kaleidoscope of unstable coalitions which seek to harness a vast array of diverse caste, regional and community groupings heedless of ideological incompatibilities. The rather hesitant pace of economic liberalization that follows from this causes frustration to some who demand that India free up its labour markets, slash social expenditure and open itself fully to the global economy. But there are some advantages to India's haphazard and wayward trajectory. Unlike China, India is an open, pluralistic and highly diverse society, and from these virtues flow great creativity – a commodity that even the mighty Chinese now fear may be lacking in their own more streamlined developmental drama.

In 1907 the Raj was beset by political, economic and social crises. Agricultural growth was stagnating, strategies to boost industrial production, pursued most energetically by the previous Viceroy, Lord Curzon, had enjoyed little success. Monsoon fluctuations had recently caused famine in much of western India, and little money could be found for railway, road or irrigation building. At the same time there were increasing demands from various regional, caste and religious communities for special treatment. The Muslim League, citing the 'backwardness' of the Muslim community, were demanding reservations and were soon to receive their own separate electorates. In the south also, non-Brahman groups clamoured for, and were given, quotas in state universities and government jobs. In Bengal a massive popular agitation had recently developed to oppose the division of the state in two, invoking Bengali patriotism in justification. Meanwhile portions of the countryside were scarred by peasant and 'tribal' rebels violently resisting the annexation of their forests and common lands. Terrorism was also a problem: recently there had been a flurry of bombings, shootings and other atrocities in which senior Raj officials had perished. On the North West Frontier the instability of Afghanistan continued to pose problems for the Raj and apparent agreements over borders and 'lines of control' were, in fact, far from settled. The government itself was constantly challenged and undermined by Indian nationalist politicians, who criticized everything from its recruitment policies in the Indian Civil Service to its free-market economics.

To a casual observer this gloomy catalogue of ills and controversies of a century ago might seem remarkably similar to those that still afflict India today. But India has changed. It has freed itself from the hierarchical cosmology decreed by the Raj; it is a democracy, not an autocracy; and there is an overarching sense of 'Indianness', albeit a fragile one. This is a change so profound that even the gods have bowed before it. In recent years India has witnessed a strange religious phenomenon. The landscape, both urban and rural, has become increasingly populated by enormous *murtis* (icons) of the so-called

monkey god, Hanuman, known as Maruti in the west and also sometimes as Anjaneya. This flurry of competitive monkey-building began
in the mid-1970s when an 18-foot statue of the lovable anthropo-
morph appeared perched on a hill near Bangalore; in 1982 the moun-
tainous northern state of Himachal Pradesh hosted a 30-foot icon
seated atop a Himalayan hillock; eight years later this sedentary deity
was surpassed by a 45-foot granite Hanuman which had manifested
itself in Vasant Gaon – a suburb of New Delhi. In a matter of months
this too had been overshadowed, by a 70-foot concrete *murti* in Andhra
Pradesh. The Andhra giant was, however, surpassed by the 98-foot
representation of the tutelary godling built in New Delhi in 1998, and
all these vertiginous erections have since been dwarfed by the 108-foot
colossus which now looms over the New Delhi Metro line at Karol
Bagh. Elsewhere, from Allahabad in the north to Nanganallur in
Chennai, Hanumans of varying dimensions, though never less than
25 feet tall, bestride highways and villages across India. There is even
an 85-foot NRI Hanuman in Trinidad and Tobago. These monkey
colossi have been financed by the broadest caste and class spectrum
of Indians, from millionaire US-based entrepreneurs to poor villagers,
from powerful government officials, to pious renunciate *sadhus*.
Clearly Hanuman, long regarded as a mere godling, now threatens to
displace Vishnu, and his avatar Ram, as India's presiding deity.

Vishnu – 'the Preserver' – is a stern and patriarchal figure, most
famous for having measured out a carefully graded cosmos in three
giant strides. He is, therefore, the god of rank and order par excellence.
Hanuman, by contrast, is a less conservative, more protean figure. The
Son of the Wind, progeny of Shiva and a beautiful monkey-woman, he
is neither wholly man, nor monkey, nor god, but something in
between. Among the most famous of Hanuman legends is the story
of his vaulting leap as an infant towards the sun, which in his impudent
hubris he tried to swallow. Struck by a thunderbolt hurled by an angry
god, his jaw was dislocated and he thus acquired his distinctive simian
visage. But Hanuman, a quick-witted youth, learned from this childish
misdemeanour not to essay projects of galactic ambition, and settled
down to life as a fleet-footed, shape-shifting 'fixer'. Indeed he is most
famous as Ram's devoted and deferential servant-cum-general in the
epic *Ramayana*. Hanuman has traditionally been regarded as a subal-

tern deity, venerated largely by the lowly, but worship of Hanuman has also been associated with eras of change and social fluidity when his ingenuity, flexibility and resourcefulness have been particularly prized. He is the intermediary-sublime, the communicator, the negotiator and, in the *Ramayana*, the builder of bridges. Hanuman's India is not a place of fixed orders and gradations, but of fluidity, practicality, compromise, change and connection.

Vishnu's temples are rather less popular than they once were, though still the recipient of pious libations and entreaties, and his godly forte – the measurement and preservation of rank – seems less in demand of late; this deity, as Indians say, has fallen 'asleep'. Hanuman, by contrast, with his skills as 'helper', 'facilitator', 'protector' and 'guide' is indispensable. To rich and poor alike, Hanuman's adaptable, even entrepreneurial style embodies the new ideal. And Hanuman is no longer merely a servant. In an era now more comfortable with social mobility, Hanuman has been promoted and has displaced his erstwhile master. His temples proliferate and provoke real passion. Hanuman is 'awake' and his pervasive influence seems a highly promising cosmological development. The creative and consolatory capacities entwined in this most ingenious but also most compassionate of gods, and captured in his devotional hymns, seem well-suited to India as it enters the twenty-first century:

> Victory to Hanuman, ocean of wisdom and virtue,
> Hail monkey lord, illuminator of the three worlds . . .

> Supremely wise, virtuous and clever,
> You are ever intent on Rama's tasks . . .

> Every arduous task in this world
> Becomes easy by your grace . . .

> Sheltered by you, one gains all delight,
> Protected by you, one fears no one . . .

> Your splendour fills four ages,
> Your fame shines throughout the world . . .

> Pay no heed to any other deity,
> Serving Hanuman, one obtains all delight . . .

Glossary

Adhikar-bheda: seventeenth- and eighteenth-century Brahmanical doctrine designed to uphold harmony in society by the maintenance of conservative rules applying to each caste, sect and community.

Adi: prefix suggesting aboriginality.

Adivasi: collective term for some of India's 'tribal' peoples.

Ahimsa: literally the 'avoidance of violence'; used by Gandhi to mean non-violence.

AIDMK: All India Dravida Munnetra Kazhagam, a Tamil political party formed from a split in the DMK.

Akhara: wrestling gymnasium.

Akhil Bharatiya Vidyarthi Parishad: all-India Students Council and part of the *Sangh Parivar*.

Arya Samaj: literally 'Noble Society', an important Hindu reform movement founded in 1875.

Aryans: supposedly ancient precursors of high-caste Hindus.

Ashraf: plural of *sharif*, meaning eminent Muslim.

Ashram: a spiritual community, usually led by a religious leader or mystic.

Babu: orginally a term of respect in north and east India meaning 'sir' or 'Mr', but used disparagingly by the British to refer to low-status clerks.

Bajrang Dal: refers originally to Ram's monkey army in the *Ramayana*, but latterly the name of the RSS's militant youth wing.

Bandh: literally 'closed' – another term for a strike.

Bania: a collective anglicized term for a member of one of the merchant castes.

Bhadralok: literally 'respectable people'; used to refer to the well-educated Hindus of Bengal.

Bhakti: literally 'devotion' or 'the path of devotion'; a form of popular Hinduism.

Bharatiya Mazdoor Sangh: Indian Workers' Union, a branch of the *Sangh Parivar*.

Biradari: a brotherhood or kinship group common in the Punjab and western India, akin to a clan.

BJP: Bharatiya Janata Party (India People's Party).

BLD: Bharatiya Lok Dal, farmers' party formed by Charan Singh.

Brahman: the 'priestly' caste, and considered to be the highest class or *varna* in the Indian caste order.

Brahmo Samaj: literally 'Society of the Worshippers of the One True God'; a Hindu reform movement founded by Raja Rammohun Roy in 1828.

Brahmacharya: one who practises a life of complete celibacy in pursuit of spiritual enlightenment.

BSP: Bahujan Samaj Party.

Busti: slum area or shantytown.

Charkha: spinning-wheel.

CPI (M): Communist Party of India (Marxist).

CPI (M-L): Communist Party of India (Marxist-Leninist).

Crore: 10 million.

Dalit: term meaning 'oppressed' which has replaced the colonial term 'untouchable' i.e. those beyond the pale of the caste system.

Darshan: literally 'sight or vision', commonly used to refer to visions of the divine.

District Officer: principal local official under the Raj.

DMK: Dravida Munnetra Kazhagam, regional party of Tamil Nadu founded in 1949.

Dravidian: originally referring to the family of languages in south India, now sometimes used to mean the people of south India.

Durbar: literally a court or audience chamber, but used by the British to refer to formal assemblies of notables called by the government.

Fatwa: literally a 'legal pronouncement' on some aspect of Islam.

Gaurav Yatra: journey or pilgrimage of pride.

Gaushala: cow refuges founded by cow protection societies.

Ghee: clarified butter, often used for ritual purposes in Hinduism.

Gharana: a sort of music academy devoted to a particular musical style and often based around kinship networks.

Gherao: literally 'encirclement'; a form of popular protest.

Gurbani: sikh holy texts.

Hartal: a strike or sit-in.

Hindu Mahasabha: literally 'Great Hindu Assembly', a Hindu nationalist organization founded in 1915 to counter the Muslim League and the secular Indian National Congress.

Hindustani: also known as Hindi-Urdu; a term used to describe several closely related idioms and dialects found in north India – a vernacularized blend of Hindi and Urdu.

Hindutva: literally 'Hinduness'.

Hizbullah: literally 'the party of God'; a radical Muslim movement.

Janata Dal: a centre-left political party founded by V.P. Singh in 1988.

Janata Party: literally 'the People's Party', formed in 1977 to oppose the Emergency.

IAS: Indian Administrative Service, the most elite level of the Indian civil bureaucracy, formed from the Raj's ICS.

ICS: Indian Civil Service, the most prestigious branch of the Raj's official bureaucracy.

Imam: in the context of Shi'a Islam, one qualified to interpret theological concepts.

INC: Indian National Congress.

Jati: a sub-caste within the four major *varnas* of the caste system; often reflects regional, linguistic or occupational associations.

Jihad: literally 'struggle in the way of God'; now often used to mean 'holy war'.

Khadi: hand-spun cloth.

Kisan sabha: peasant association.

Ksatriya: 'warrior', the second tier in the four-fold caste system.

Kurta: a long, loose shirt.

Lathi: stick or truncheon.

Lok Sabha: the lower house of the Indian Parliament.

Madrassa: arabic word for school; often used to mean Sunni Islamic religious school.

Maharajah: 'Great King'.

Mahatma: 'Great Soul'.

Maidan: area of large open space.

Marathi: language of Maharashtra

Mastan: often used to mean a thug.

Math: Hindu monastery

Matri Mandal: Association of Mothers, part of the *Sangh Parivar*.

Mela: Festival.

MLA: member of (a regional) Legislative Assembly.

Mofussil: literally 'up-county'; refers to provincial or small-town India.

Mufti: Islamic scholar

NRI: Non-Resident Indian.

OBC: Other Backward Caste or Class.

Panchayat: elected village-level councils.

Paraiyar: a dalit caste group in south India.

Parsi: ethnic group found in India, descendants of Persian Zoroastrians.

Pir: Muslim saint or mystic, sometimes commanding devotion of Hindus as well as Muslims.

Presidency: term for the principal administrative regions of British India (Bengal, Madras and Bombay).

Pujari: term for a Hindu priest.

Qazi: a judge in Islamic Shariah law.

Rath Yatra: Chariot Pilgrimage

Resident: British official adviser in a princely state.

RSS: *Rashtriya Swayamsevak Sangh* (National Volunteer Union); a Hindu nationalist organization founded in 1925.

Sadhu: Hindu male ascetic or monk.

Sadhvi: Hindu female ascetic or monk.

Sahib: term of respectful address under the British Raj.

Sanskrit: classical language of India.

Sangh Parivar: literally 'family of associations'; overarching organization of many bodies associated with Hindu Nationalism.

Sanyasi or *Sanyasin*: 'renouncer'; the ultimate stage of life in Hinduism, traditionally undertaken by older people in pursuit of spiritual enlightenment.

Satyagraha: literally 'to hold firmly to truth'; coined by Gandhi to mean 'soul-force'.

Shia: the minority Muslim sect in India.

Shudra: the fourth and lowest category in the Hindu caste system, Shudras are traditionally not 'twice-born', are not permitted to study Hindu sacred texts (the Vedas) and are theoretically confined to menial labour. In fact the Shudra *varna* is an enormously wide category encompassing wealthy landowners at one end, dalits at the other, and most of the so-called Other Backward Castes (OBCs) in between.

Swadeshi: self-sufficiency; associated with economic nationalism and movements to boycott foreign goods.

Swaraj: self-rule, home-rule or independence.

Sunni: the majority Muslim sect in India.

Taluqdar: a tax-collector, local law-officer and provider of soldiers under Mughal rule; but often meant a landowner under the British.

Tamasha: traditionally a folk-play, now often used to mean a public commotion or excitement.

Tamil: member of the Dravidian family of languages, widely spoken in Tamil Nadu.

Tapsya: spiritual exercises involving rigorous self-abnegation.

TDP: Telugu Desam Party, regional party in the southern state of Andhra Pradesh.

Telugu: member of the Dravidian family of languages widely spoken in Andhra Pradesh.

Thakur: 'lord'; feudal and colonial title in north India.

Ulema: Islamic scholars-cum-clergy; those well-versed in Islamic studies and jusrisprudence.

Urdu: language closely related to Hindi; now largely associated with Muslims and widely spoken in Pakistan, but before Independence also a major language of India.

Vaishya: third of the four *varnas* of the caste system, especially associated with mercantile occupations.

Vakil: lawyer

Vanvasi Kalyan Ashram: literally 'Forest-Dwellers' Welfare Community'; an arm of the RSS/*Sangh Parivar* devoted to 'tribal' 'uplift'.

Varna: literally 'colour'; refers to the four-fold orders of the Hindu caste system: Brahman, Kstatriya,Vaishya, Shudra.

Varnashramadharma: a social order governed by the notion that people should follow the *dharma* (duty) of their particular caste (*varna*) and the four prescribed stages of life.

Vishva Hindu Parishad (VHP): World Hindu Council, offshoot of the RSS founded in 1964.

Wahhabi: a highly puritanical branch of Islam that in the eighteenth century became associated with aggressive reform and proselytizing.

WTO: World Trade Organisation.

Zamindar: Mughal tax-collectors, who often acquired land rights and great prestige under the British.

Sources and Bibliography

INTRODUCTION

There is an account of the Guruvayur Temple entry movement in O. Mendelsohn and M. Vicziany, *Untouchables: Subordination, Poverty and the State in Modern India* (Cambridge, 1998), pp. 100–7. For a magisterial survey of the trajectory of European state building in the nineteenth century see M. Mann, *The Origins of Social Power*, vol. 2 (Cambridge, 1993), chs. 3, 4, 11–14. For the view that India, with its diverse identities, might become the model for other 'post-modern' democracies see Sunil Khilnani, *The Idea of India* (London, 1997). For a recent liberal account of the British imperial impact on India see N. Ferguson, *Empire: How Britain Made the Modern World* (London, 2003). There are many Marxist-influenced analyses of Indian history; among the most subtle and stimulating is S. Corbridge and J. Harriss, *Reinventing India* (Cambridge, 2000). There is no single 'subaltern' text offering an overarching view of India's historical evolution; indeed such a project would contradict the avowed approach of this school, which disputes the legitimacy of 'grand narratives'. However, a representative example of the approach may be found in P. Chatterjee, *The Nation and Its Fragments: Colonial and Postcolonial Histories* (Princeton, 1993). For a powerful critique of the philosophical and methodological assumptions underlying 'subaltern' approaches see R. O'Hanlon, 'Recovering the Subject: Subaltern Studies and Histories of Resistance in Colonial South Asia', *Modern Asian Studies*, 22 (1988), reprinted along with other critiques in V. Chaturvedi (ed.), *Mapping Subaltern Studies and the Postcolonial* (London, 2000). For a balanced analysis of the evolution of the Indian caste system in the modern period and especially of the impact of the British, see S. Bayly, *Caste, Society and Politics in India from the Eighteenth Century to the Modern Age* (Cambridge, 1999). For a very clear account of the 'Janus-faced' ideological character of the Raj, which simultaneously employed a rhetoric of 'modernization' while also claiming to govern India according to its own 'traditions', see T. Metcalf, *Ideologies of the Raj* (Cambridge, 1995).

1. TROPICAL GOTHIC

A description and analysis of the symbolism of the Great Assemblage may be found in B. S. Cohn, 'Representing Authority in Victorian India', in E. Hobsbawm and T. O. Ranger (eds.), *The Invention of Tradition* (Cambridge, 1983). For British ideas about governing India before the Great Rebellion see J. Majeed, *Ungoverned Imaginings: James Mill's The History of British India and Orientalism* (Oxford, 1992); R. Guha, *A Rule of Property for Bengal* (Paris, 1963); B. Stein, *Thomas Munro: The Origins of the Colonial State and his Vision of Empire* (Delhi, 1986); E. T. Stokes, *The English Utilitarians and India* (Oxford, 1959); T. Metcalf, *Ideologies of the Raj* (Cambridge, 1995), esp. chs. 1–3.

Recent historiography of the 1857 Mutiny-Rebellion has drawn attention to its broad social base and complex ideological motivations, but for an older contemporary account see M. R. Gubbins, *An Account of the Mutinies in Oudh, and of the Siege of the Lucknow Residency* (2nd) edition, London, 1858). For a survey of the debates on the 'mutiny' or 'revolt' question see A. T. Embree (ed.), *1857 In India. Mutiny or War of Independence?* (Boston, 1963). See also S. B. Chaudhuri, *Civil Disturbances during British Rule in India, 1765–1857* (Calcutta, 1955) and his *Civil Rebellion in the Indian Mutinies* (Calcutta, 1957); F. W. Buckler, 'The Political Theory of the Indian Mutiny', in M. N. Pearson (ed.), *Legitimacy and Symbols: The South Asian Writing of F. W. Buckler* (Ann Arbor, 1985). For more recent analyses see C. A. Bayly, *Origins of National Identity in South Asia* (Delhi, 1998); T. Metcalf, *The Aftermath of the Revolt, 1857–1870* (Princeton, 1964); E. T. Stokes, *The Peasant Armed: The Indian Revolt of 1857* (Oxford, 1986), and also Stokes's *The Peasant and the Raj. Studies in Agrarian History and Peasant Rebellion in Colonial India* (Cambridge, 1978); R. Mukherjee, *Awadh in Revolt. A Study of Popular Resistance* (New Delhi, 1984); T. Roy, *The Politics of a Popular Uprising – Bundelkhand in 1857* (Delhi, 1994); G. Bhadra, 'Four Rebels of 1867', in R. Guha, *Subaltern Studies*, vol. 4 (New Delhi, 1985); E. I. Brodkin, 'The Struggle for Succession: Rebels and Loyalists in the Indian Mutiny of 1857', *Modern Asian Studies*, 6 (1972).

For analyses of changing British architectural styles in India see T. Metcalf, *An Imperial Vision: Indian Architecture and Britain's Raj* (Berkeley, 1989); M. Dosal, *Imperial Designs and Indian Realities: The Planning of Bombay*

City, 1845–1875 (Delhi, 1991). For interesting discussions of the 'traditionalising' impact of British policy on nineteenth century India see C. A. Bayly, *Indian Society and the Making of the British Empire* (Cambridge, 1988); R. Inden, *Imagining India* (Oxford, 1990); C. A. Brekenridge and P. van der Veer (eds.), *Orientalism and the Postcolonial Predicament: Perspectives on South Asia* (Philadelphia, 1993).

For the reconstruction of British power and 'natural leaders' see T. Metcalf, *Land, Landlords and the British Raj: Northern India in the Nineteenth Century* (Delhi, 1979), and also his *Ideologies* chs. 3–4; P. D. Reeves, *Landlords and Government in Uttar Pradesh. A Study of their Relations until Zamindari Abolition* (Bombay, 1991); S. F. D. Ansari, *Sufi Saints and State Power. The Pirs of Sind, 1943–1947* (Cambridge, 1991); R. Frykenburg (ed.), *Land Control and Social Structure in Indian History* (London, 1969); C. A. Bayly, *Local Roots of Indian Politics: Allahabad 1880–1920* (Cambridge, 1975). For the evolution of British state apparatus see B. Spangenburg, *British Bureaucracy in India: Status, Policy and the ICS in the late 19th Century* (Delhi, 1974); D. Arnold, *Police Power and Colonial Rule: Madras 1859–1947* (Delhi, 1986).

For an insight into British romanticization of India's aristocracy in the nineteenth century see James Tod, *Annals and Antiquities of Rajasthan* (Madras, 1832, 1880), and for a modern critique see N. Peabody, 'Tod's Rajas'than and the Boundaries of Imperial Rule in Nineteenth Century India', *Modern Asian Studies*, 30, 1 (1996). For other modern accounts of princely India see R. Jeffrey (ed.), *People, Princes and Paramount Power: Society and Politics in the Indian Princely States* (Delhi, 1978); B. Ramusack, *The Indian Princes and their States* (Cambridge, 2004); N. Dirks, *The Hollow Crown: Ethnohistory of an Indian Kingdom* (Cambridge, 1987). For British attitudes to elite education see D. Kopf, *British Orientalism and the Indian Renaissance, 1773–1835* (Berkeley, 1969); G. Vishwanathan, *Masks of Conquest: Literary Study and British Rule in India* (New York, 1989).

On the creation of 'village India' and the traditionalising imprint of British agricultural policy see H. S. Maine, *Village Communities in the East and West* (London, 1871); A. C. Lyall, *Asiatic Studies, Religious and Social* (London, 1884). For more modern studies see Inden, *Imagining India*; Louis Dumont, 'The "Village Community" From Munro to Maine', *Contributions to Indian Sociology*, 9 (1966); C. Dewey, 'Images of the Village Community: a Study in Anglo-Indian Ideology', *Modern Asian Studies*, 6 (1972). For a survey of changing British approaches to land and agriculture see B. Stein (ed.), *The Making of Agrarian Policy in British India* (Delhi, 1992). For assessments of British agricultural policy see C. Dewey and A. G. Hopkins (eds.), *The Imperial Impact: Studies in the Economic History of Africa and India* (London, 1978); D. Ludden, *Peasant History in South Asia* (Princeton, 1985); R. Kumar, 'The Rise of Rich Peasants in West India', in D. A. Low, *Soundings in South Asian History* (Berkeley, 1968); T. G. Kessinger, *Vilyatpur 1848–1968. Social and Economic Change in a North Indian Village* (Berkeley, 1974); N. Charlesworth, *Peasants and Imperial Rule. Agriculture and Agrarian Society in the Bombay Presidency, 1850–1935* (Cambridge, 1985). On the immiseration of agricultural labour see J. Breman, *Patronage and Exploitation: Changing Agrarian Relations in South Gujarat* (Berkeley, 1974); G. Prakash, *Bonded Histories: Genealogies of Labour Servitude in Colonial India* (Delhi, 1990). On the 'traditionalising' effect of British legal policy on the agricultural economy see D. A. Washbrook, 'Law, State and Society in Colonial India', in C. Baker, G. Johnson and A. Seal (eds.), *Power, Profit and Politics: Imperialism, Nationalism and Change in Twentieth-Century India* (Cambridge, 1981), his 'Economic Depression and the Making of "Traditional Society" in Colonial India 1820–1855', *Transactions of the Royal Historical Society* (1993), and his 'Progress and Problems: South Asian Economic and Social History 1729–1860', *Modern Asian Studies*, 22 (1988). A. Yang, *The Limited Raj: Agrarian Relations in Colonial India, Saran District, 1795–1820* (Delhi, 1989), also argues that the impress of British rule was very light.

For assessments of British economic policy in the post-rebellion era see M. D. Morris, *The Indian Economy in the Nineteenth Century: A Symposium* (Delhi, 1969); N. Charlesworth, *British Rule and the Indian Economy, 1800–1914* (London, 1982); and B. R. Tomlinson, 'India and the British Empire, 1880–1935', *Indian Economic and Social History Review*, 12, 4 (1975). Useful material on aspects of the economy, especially agriculture and irrigation, is to be found in D. Kumar and M. Desai (eds.), *The Cambridge Economic History of India, Volume 2, c. 1757–1970* (Cambridge, 1983). For canal building and irrigation see I. Stone, *Canal Irrigation in British India. Perspectives on Technological Change in a Peasant Economy* (Cambridge, 1984). For a view more critical of British irrigation policy see E. Whitcombe, *Agrarian Conditions in Northern India. Volume I. The United Provinces under British Rule, 1860–1900* (Los Angeles and London, 1972). For the railways see I. M. Kerr (ed.), *Railways in Modern India* (Delhi, 2001) and his *Building the Railways of the Raj 1850–1900* (Delhi, 1995). For the development of modern pilgrimage see I. M. Kerr, 'Popular Religious Practice: the Effects of the Railways on Pilgrimage in 19th and 20th Century South Asia', in Kerr (ed.), *Railways*, and R. Ahuja, ' "The Bridge-Builders": Some Notes on Railways, Pilgrimage and the British "Civilizing Mission" in

Colonial India', in H. Fischer-Tine and M. Mann (eds.), *Colonialism As Civilizing Mission: Cultural Ideology in British India* (London, 2004).

The account of the Mohurram in Bombay comes from J. Masselos, 'Power in Bombay' in his *The City in Action: Bombay Struggles for Power* (Delhi, 2007). Studies suggesting powerful syncretistic traditions in Hindu and Muslim ritual include S. Freitag, *Collective Action and Community: Public Arenas and the Emergence of Communalism in North India* (Berkeley, 1989); G. Pandey, *The Construction of Communalism in Colonial North India* (Delhi, 1990); Ansari, *Sufi Saints*; S. Bayly, *Saints, Goddesses and Kings in South India* (Cambridge, 1989). However, most of these writers would also argue that even before the British the manipulation of caste had become an aspect of South Asian statecraft. See for example C. A. Bayly, 'The Pre-History of "Communalism": Religious Conflict in India 1700–1860', *Modern Asian Studies*, 19 (1985), and S. Subrahmanyam, 'Before the Leviathan: Sectarian Violence and the State in Pre-Colonial India', in K. Basu and S. Subrahmanyam (eds.), *Unravelling the Nation: Sectarian Violence and India's Sectarian Identity*, (New Delhi, 1996). For British perceptions of Indian culture and religion see P. J. Marshall, *The British Discovery of Hinduism in the Eighteenth Century* (Cambridge, 1970); L. Mani, 'Contentious Traditions: the Debate on Sati in Colonial India', in K. Sangari and S. Vaid (eds.), *Recasting Women: Essays in Colonial History* (New Delhi, 1989). On the various forms of Christian missionary activity see J. Cox, *Imperial Fault Lines: Christianity and Colonial Power in India 1818–1940* (Oxford, 2002) and J. M. Brown and R. G. Frykenburg (eds.), *Christians, Cultural Interactions and India's Religious Traditions* (Cambridge, 2002). For a contemporary account of British official attitudes to Islam see W. E. Hunter, *The Indian Mussalmans* (London, 1871, reprinted Lahore, 1964). For more recent studies see P. Hardy, *The Muslims of British India* (Cambridge, 1972). For the 're-writing' of Hindu–Muslim history, and other unreliable histories of the colonial era see Pandey, *The Construction of Communalism*.

For a penetrating overview of the impact of British ideas and policies on Indian society and culture see B. Cohn, *Colonialism and its Forms of Knowledge*, (Princeton, 1996). The effect of British policy on shaping caste identities remains highly controversial: for the view that the British effectively 'created' the modern caste system see N. Dirks, *Castes of Mind: Colonialism and the Making of Modern India* (Princeton, 2001). For an approach that stresses the importance of pre-existing indigenous attitudes to caste see S. Bayly, *Caste, Society and Politics in India from the Eighteenth Century to the Modern Age* (Cambridge, 1999); B. Cohn, 'Notes on the History of the Study of Indian Society and Culture' in M. Singer and B. S. Cohn (eds.), *Structure and Change in Indian Society* (Chicago, 1968). For the role of elite 'informers' in the shaping of caste ideas see E. F. Irschick, *Dialogue and History: Constructing South India, 1795–1895* (Berkeley and London, 1994). For the development of the Nadar caste identity and history see R. L. Hardgrave, *The Nadars of Tamilnadu* (Berkeley, 1969), from whom the accounts of caste assertion movements and history writing are drawn. For the evolution of ideas of 'race' in the later nineteenth century see P. Robb (ed.), *The Concept of Race in South Asia* (Delhi, 1995); J. Leopold, 'British Applications of the Aryan Theory of Race to India 1850–1970', *English Historical Review*, 89 (1974). The ideas behind and role of the census and British academic anthropology on shaping Indian caste may be followed in H. H. Risley, *The People of India* (Calcutta, 1915); F. Conlon, K. W. Jones and N. G. Barrier (eds.), *The Census in British India* (Delhi, 1981); C. Pinney, 'Classification and Fantasy in the Photographic Construction of Caste and Tribe', *Visual Anthropology*, 3 (1990). For studies of the impact of British policy on various aspects of Indian identity see R. Fox, *Lions of the Punjab: Culture in the Making* (Berkeley, 1985) on Sikhism; D. Gilmartin, *Empire and Islam: Punjab and the Making of Pakistan* (Berkeley, 1988) on the 'agricultural "tribe"'; and D. Omissi, *The Sepoy and the Raj: the Indian Army 1860–1940* (Basingstoke, 1994) on the so-called 'martial races'.

For the social life and mores of the British in India see: F. Hutchins, *The Illusion of Permanence: British Imperialism in India* (Princeton, 1967); K. Ballhatchet, *Race, Sex and Class under the Raj: Imperial Attitudes and Policies and their Critics, 1793–1905* (London, 1980); V. Oldenberg, *The Making of Colonial Lucknow* (Princeton, 1984); E. Buettner, *Empire Families: Britons and Late Imperial India* (Oxford, 2004); T. Metcalf, *An Imperial Vision: Indian Architecture and Britain's Raj* (London, 1989); D. Kennedy, *The Magic Mountain* (Berkeley, 1995).

Quotation Sources

'They have struck tin shields and battleaxes . . . atrocious taste', Val Prinsep, *Imperial India. An Artist's Journal* (London, 1879), p. 20. 'Stepped into the shoes of the Great Mogul', George Curzon, 1902, cited in Metcalf, *Ideologies*, p. 197. 'They do not value these rights . . . cherished system of the country', Lord Canning, November 1857, cited in Metcalf, *Aftermath*, p. 148. 'Great repository of verifiable phenomena . . . ancient judicial thought', Henry Maine, cited in Inden. 'Barring oriental scenery . . . and the peasant is at their mercy', Alfred Lyall, 1875, cited in Metcalf, *Ideologies*, p. 72. 'A system which recognizes . . . level of a demi-pauperized peasant proprietary', James Outram, May 1868, cited in Metcalf, *Aftermath*, p. 171. '. . . now lent their hearty support . . . in re-establishing order', Lord Canning, April 1858, cited in Metcalf, *Aftermath*, p. 139. 'It is of immense benefit to the people . . . settled in a paternalist fashion, rather than in an alien court', Charles Wood, August 1860, cited in Metcalf, *Aftermath*, p. 156. 'Much very much of the unpopularity . . . offend the dignity of his superior', Robert Montgomery, December 1858, cited in Metcalf, *Aftermath*, p. 156. 'Were I to tell you', H. Bartle Frere, 'Speech on the Opening of the Bhore Ghaut Incline of the General Indian Peninsular Railway', 21 April 1863 in Kerr (ed.), *Railways*. Citations from R. Kipling, 'The Bridge-Builders', reprinted in *Kipling's India* (New Delhi, 1994). 'Goods travel . . . evil has wings', from A. Parel, *Gandhi's Hind Swaraj and Other Writings* (Cambridge, 1997), pp. 47–8. '. . . built upon enormous and tormenting . . . grotesque and frivolous ceremonies', from James Mill, *The History of India* (London, 1818), cited in Metcalf, *Ideologies*, p. 30. '. . . in a vast swamp . . . disorderly superstitions', from G. W. F. Hegel, *The Philosophy of History*, trans. J, Sibree (New York, 1956), pp. 141–61. '. . . something in their religion makes warriors of them . . . fanatic spirit', John Lawrence, cited in Metcalf, *Ideologies*, p. 140. '. . . a network of conspiracy . . . merges into the sea', W. W. Hunter, *The Indian Mussalmans* (London, 1871). '. . . men of inert convictions . . . very little about the matter', Hunter, *Mussalmans*, cited in Hardy, *Muslims*, p. 88. '. . . anarchy is the peculiar peril . . . solidarity can penetrate', H. H. Risley, *The People of India* (London, 1908), p. 293. 'It is well to begin by clearing . . . mutually repellent groups', J. D. Baines, *The Indian Census* (Calcutta, 1891), cited in Dirks, *Castes*, p. 211. 'It is a subject upon . . . differ hopelessly', W. R. Cornish, 1871, cited in Dirks, *Castes*, p. 205. 'It is British officers . . . old standard', G. F. MacMunn, *The Armies of India* (London 1911), p. 137. Quotations from *A Short account of Tamil Xatras* cited in Hardgrave, *The Nadars*, p. 89. '. . . no doubt they have . . . unfounded pretensions', from E. Thurston, *Castes and Tribes of Southern India* (Madras, 1909). '. . . were brought more and more . . . for the season', Theodore Hope, September 1886, cited in Kennedy, *Magic Mountain*, p. 198. '. . . the voice of silence . . . Great Unseen hand behind', K. C. Bhanjal, *Darjeeling at a Glance* (Darjeeling, 1942), cited in Kennedy, *Magic Mountain*, p. 213.

2. BABEL-MAHAL

Accounts of early temple entry movements can be found in O. Mendelsohn and M. Vicziany, *Untouchables: Subordination, Poverty and the State in Modern India* (Cambridge, 1998), pp. 100–7, and R. L. Hardgrave, *The Nadars of Tamilnadu* (Berkeley, 1969). For the broader political importance of south Indian temples see A. Appadurai and C. Breckenridge, 'The South Indian Temple: Authority, Honour and Redistribution', *Contributions to Indian Sociology*, 10 (1976); C. Baker, 'Temples in South India', in C. Baker and D. Washbrook, *South India: Political Institutions and Political Change 1880–1940* (Delhi, 1975). For changing Indian attitudes to the British and cultural revivalism see T. Raychaudhuri, *Europe Reconsidered. Perceptions of the West in Nineteenth Century Bengal* (Delhi, 1988); B. Parekh, *Colonialism, Tradition and Reform. An Analysis of Gandhi's Political Discourse* (New Delhi and London, 1989), ch. 1. On the Brahmo Samaj see D. Kopf, *British Orientalism and the Indian Renaissance 1773–1835* (Berkeley, 1969); K. W. Jones, *Socio-Religious Reform Movements in British India* (Cambridge, 1989). On the famines of the late nineteenth century see M. B. McAlpine, *Subject to Famine: Food Crises and Economic Change in Western India, 1860–1920* (Princeton, 1983) and D. Arnold, *Famine* (Oxford, 1988). For early nationalist critiques of British economic policy see Dadabhoi Naoroji, *Poverty and Un-British Rule in India* (London, 1901); R. C. Dutt, *Economic History of India* (2 vols. London, 1901 and 1903); B. Chandra, *The Rise and Growth of Economic Nationalism in India. Economic Policies of the Indian National Leadership, 1881–1915* (New Delhi, 1966).

For British approaches to town-planning and segregation see K. Ballhatchet and J. Harrison (eds.), *The City in South Asia* (London, 1980); A. D. King, *Colonial Urban Development* (London, 1976). For the evolution of proto-nationalist politics see S. R. Mehrotra, *The Emergence of the Indian National Congress* (Delhi, 1971) and B. T. McCully, *English Education and the Origins of Indian Nationalism* (New York, 1940). For disputes over racial discrimination in ICS recruitment and in criminal cases see H. Singh, *Problems and Policies of the British in India 1885–1898* (Bombay, 1963); K. Ballhatchet, *Race, Sex and Class under the Raj: Imperial Attitudes and Policies and their Critics, 1793–1905* (London, 1980). For the Ilbert Bill crisis see E. Hirschman, *White Mutiny: The Ilbert Bill Crisis in India and the Genesis of the Indian National Congress* (Delhi, 1980). For an excellent study of the interaction of British and Indian political culture and ideas see D. Haynes, *Rhetoric and Ritual in Colonial India: The Shaping of a Public Culture in*

Surat City, 1852–1928 (Oxford, 1991). For the emergence of the Indian National Congress see J. McLane, *Indian Nationalism and the Early Congress* (Princeton, 1977); A. Seal, *The Emergence of Indian Nationalism. Competition and Collaboration in the Later Nineteenth Century* (Cambridge, 1968). For regional particularities see J. Gallagher, G. Johnson and A. Seal (eds.), *Locality, Province and Nation. Essays on Indian Politics 1870–1940* (Cambridge, 1973); R. K. Ray, *Urban Roots of Indian Nationalism. Pressure Groups and Conflict of Interest in Calcutta City Politics, 1875–1939* (New Delhi, 1979); G. Johnson, *Provincial Politics and Indian Nationalism. Bombay and the Indian National Congress 1880–1915* (Cambridge, 1973); J. H. Broomfield, *Elite Conflict in a Plural Society in Twentieth Century Bengal* (Berkeley, 1968); L. A. Gordon, *Bengal: The Nationalist Movement 1876–1940* (New York and London, 1974); D. Washbrook, *The Emergence of Provincial Politics. The Madras Presidency 1970–1920* (Cambridge, 1976).

For Hindu reform and revivalism and the Ramakrishna movement in Bengal see K. W. Jones, *Socio-Religious Reform Movements in British India* (Cambridge, 1989); W. Radice (ed.), *Swami Vivekananda and the Modernisation of Hinduism* (New Delhi, 1999); A. Sen, *Hindu Revivalism in Bengal, 1872–1905: Some Essays on Interpretation* (Delhi, 1993). The account of Bankim's *Kamalakanta* are drawn from S. Kaviraj, *The Unhappy Consciousness: Bankimchandra Chattopadhyay and the Formation of Nationalist Discourse in India* (Delhi, 1995); P. Chatterjee, *Nationalist Thought and the Colonial World. A Derivative Discourse* (London, 1986), ch. 1. See also Bankim's *Anandamath* (trans. Basanta Koomar Roy, 1882, reprinted New Delhi, 1992). For the development of wrestling and the *akhara* movement see J. Alter, *The Wrestler's Body: Identity and Ideology in North India* (Berkeley, 1992). For the evolution of notions of 'Vedic Aryansim' see R. Thapar, 'Imagined Religious Communities? Ancient History and the Modern Search for a Hindu Identity', *Modern Asian Studies*, 23 (1989). For Indian appropriations of ideas of race see the essays in P. Robb (ed.), *The Concept of Race in South Asia* (Delhi, 1995).

On the politics of gender and nationalism see J. Rosselli, 'The Self-image of Effeteness: Physical Education and Nationalism in Nineteenth Century Bengal', *Past and Present*, 86 (1980); M. Sinha, *Colonial Masculinity: The 'Manly Englishman' and the 'Effeminate Bengali' in the Late Nineteenth Century* (Manchester, 1995), which includes an essay on the 'Age of Consent' controversy from which much of this material is drawn; K. Sangari and S. Vaid (eds.), *Recasting Women: Essays in Colonial History* (New Delhi, 1989); P. Chatterjee, *The Nation and Its Fragments: Colonial and Postcol-*

onial Histories (Princeton, 1993); R. O'Hanlon, *A Comparison Between Men and Women. Tarabai Shinde and the Critique of Gender Relations in Colonial India* (Madras, 1994). For the history of the Cow Protection Movement, and the *Gau Mater* song, see McLane, *Indian Nationalism*; G. Pandey, 'Rallying Round the Cow: Sectarian Strife in the Bhojpur Region, c. 1881–1917', in R. Guha (ed.), *Subaltern Studies*, vol. 2 (Delhi, 1983). The best biography of Dayanand is J. T. F. Jordan, *Dayanand Sarasvati: His Life and Ideas* (Delhi, 1978). For the Arya Samaj see K. W. Jones, *Arya Dharm. Hindu Consciousness in 19th-Century Punjab* (Berkeley, 1976). For Tilak and the creation of the *Ganpati* and *Shivaji* festivals see R. Cashman, *The Myth of 'Lokamanya': Tilak and Mass Politics in Maharashtra* (Berkeley and London, 1975). For Curzon and the partition of Bengal see D. Dilks, *Curzon in India, vol. 2: Frustration* (London, 1970). On the Swadeshi Movement see S. Sarkar, *Swadeshi Movement in Bengal 1903–1908* (New Delhi, 1973). For Tagore's views see R. Tagore, *Nationalism* (London, 1917). For secret societies and 'extremist' politics see H. Chakrabarti, *Political Protest in Bengal: Boycott and Terrorism 1905–18* (Calcutta, 1992); Aurobindo Ghosh, *New Lamps for Old* (Pondicherry, 1894, reprinted 1974). For Congress moderates and the politics of reformism see S. Wolpert, *Tilak and Gokhale* (Berkeley, 1962); B. R. Nanda, *Gokhale, the Indian Moderates and the British Raj* (Delhi, 1977).

For accounts of Muslim society and ideas in the late nineteenth and early twentieth centuries see S. Mohammad (ed.), *Writings and Speeches of Sir Sayid Ahmad Khan* (Bombay, 1972); A. Jalal, *Self and Sovereignty: Individual and Community in South Asian Islam since 1850* (London, 2000); B. Metcalf, *Islamic Revival in British India: Deoband, 1860–1900* (Princeton, 1982); D. Lelyveld, *Aligarh's First Generation* (Princeton, 1977); A. Ahmad, *Islamic Modernism in India and Pakistan 1857–1964* (London, 1967); F. C. R. Robinson, *Separatism among Indian Muslims. The Politics of the United Provinces' Muslims 1860–1923* (Cambridge, 1974); F. Shaikh, *Community and Consensus in Islam. Muslim Representation in Colonial India, 1860–1947* (Cambridge, 1989); R. Ahmad, *The Bengal Muslims 1871–1906: A Quest for Identity* (Delhi, 1981). For Al-Afghani and Pan-Islamism see M. Hasan (ed.), *Communal and Pan-Islamic Trends in Colonial India* (New Delhi, 1985); N. Keddi, *Sayyid Jamal al Din al Afghani* (Calcutta, 1973). For the impact of British ideas on notions of Islamic law see S. A. Klugle, 'Framed, Blamed and Renamed: The Recasting of Islamic Jurisprudence in Colonial South Asia', *Modern Asian Studies*, 32 (2001); M. Anderson, 'Islamic Law and the Colonial Encounter', in D. Arnold and P. Robb (eds.), *Institutions and Ideologies* (London, 1993).

For the development of non-Brahman politics in south India see Annie

Besant, *The Future of Indian Politics* (Adyar, 1922); E. F. Irschick, *Politics and Social Conflict in South India. The Non-Brahman Movement and Tamil Separatism, 1916–29* (Berkeley and Los Angeles, 1969); C. J. Baker, *South India 1920–1940* (Cambridge, 1975). For the evolution of a Tamil identity see S. Ramaswamy, *Passions of the Tongue: Language Devotion in Tamil India, 1851–1970* (Berkeley, 1997); K. Nambi Arooran, *Tamil Renaissance and Dravidian Nationalism 1905–1944* (Madurai, 1980). On caste associations see D. Washbrook, 'The Development of Caste Associations in South India, 1880 to 1925', in Baker and Washbrook, *South India*. For the regional and caste politics of the Bombay Presidency see Johnson, *Provincial Politics*; Cashman, *Myth of 'Lokamanya'*; R. O'Hanlon, *Caste Conflict and Ideology. Mahatma Jotirao Phule and Low Caste Protest in Nineteenth-Century Western India* (Cambridge, 1985); G. Omvedt, *Cultural Revolt in a Colonial Society. The Non-Brahman Movement in Western India, 1873–1930* (Bombay, 1976). For a now classic analysis of 'subaltern' rural rebellions see R. Guha, *Elementary Aspects of Peasant Insurgency in Colonial India* (Delhi, 1983); S. Fuchs, *Rebellious Prophets: A Study of Messianic Movements in Indian Religions* (Bombay, 1965); K. S. Singh, *Dust Storm and Hanging Mist: A Study of Birsa Munda and his Movement in Chota Nagpur* (Calcutta, 1966). On the Moplahs see C. Wood, 'Peasant Revolt: An Interpretation of Moplah Violence in the 19th and 20th Centuries', in C. Dewey and A. G. Hopkins (eds.), *The Imperial Impact: Studies in the Economic History of Africa and India* (London, 1978). For the *adivasi* movements see D. Hardiman, *The Coming of the Devi: Adivasi Assertion in Western India* (Delhi, 1987). For *bhakti* reformism see J. Lele (ed.), *Tradition and Modernity in Bhakti Movements* (Leiden, 1981); N. Gooptu, *Politics of the Urban Poor in Early Twentieth-Century India* (Cambridge, 2001); for other examples of Dalit mobilization see M. Juergensmeyer, *Religion and Social Vision: The Movement against Untouchability in 20th-Century Punjab* (Berkeley, 1982). For the assertion of the 'pariahs' in south India see V. Geetha and S. V. Rajadurai, *Towards a Non-Brahmin Millennium. From Iyothee Thass to Periyar* (Calcutta, 1998).

For the politics of language see R. King, *One Language Two Scripts: The Hindi Movement in Nineteenth Century North India* (New Delhi, 1994) from which the account of the Hindi-Urdu play comes, (pp. 135–9). On the construction of a canonical 'Hindi' see V. Dalmia, *The Nationalisation of Hindu Tradition: Bharatendu Harischandra and Nineteenth-century Banares* (Delhi, 1997). For other treatments of the Urdu-Hindi controversy see Robinson, *Separatism* and P. Brass, *Language, Religion and Politics in North India* (Cambridge, 1979).

Quotation Sources

'. . . inert torpid . . . to subordination', W. C. Bonnerjee, cited in R. K. Majumdar, *Indian Speeches and Documents on British Rule, 1821–1918* (London, 1937). 'I have come to hate . . . in the world', Bonnerjee, cited in Majumdar, *Indian Speeches*. 'A Church Universal . . . fullness of time', from Keshub Chandra Sen, *Nava Samhita* [The New Dispensation] (Calcutta, 1869). 'I thank God . . . govern themselves', B. N. Dhar, cited in Majumdar, *Indian Speeches*. '. . . the peculiar character . . . Oriental methods', Surendranath Bannerjea, cited in Majumdar, *Indian Speeches*. 'Babus are invincible . . . regenerate their country', from *Bankim Racanvali (BR)*, ii, 11–12, cited in Kaviraj, *Unhappy Consciousness*, p. 44. 'True, these creatures . . . I'm not good to them!' from *BR*, ii, 112, cited in Kaviraj, *Unhappy Consciousness*, p. 70. 'Behold . . . five cubits tall!' M. K. Gandhi, *Autobiography: The Story of My Experiments with Truth*, trans. M. Desai (1927, London 1982), p. 35. '[Her] foremost vice . . . ropes to their necks', *Prachina Evam Naviha* [Old Women and the New], *BR*, ii, p. 251, cited in Kaviraj, *Unhappy Consciousness*, p. 251. '. . . females in groups . . . their lust', from *Bagabasi*, cited in Sinha, *Colonial Masculinity*, p. 168. '. . . no one who has seen a Punjabi . . . physique of the race', Denizel Ibbotson, 1908, cited in Sinha, *Colonial Masculinity*, p. 157. 'Gau Mater's Song', cited in McLane, *Indian Nationalism*, p. 276. '. . . they are prepared to use . . . unhealthy influence', from *The Regenerator of the Aryavata*, cited in Jones, *Arya Dharm*, p. 47. 'At the time of answering the call of nature . . . wash again', cited in Jones, *Arya Dharm*, p. 54. 'Oh! Why have you abandoned Hinduism today . . . do not forget her!' cited in Cashman, *Myth of 'Lokamanya'*, p. 78. 'They approached the illiterate chieftain . . . came to be known as pariahs', from I. Thass, *Indirar Desa Charitham* (1932), cited in Geetha and Rajadurai, *Towards a Non-Brahmin Millennium*, ch. 3. 'It's all one . . . who's Shudra?' from Prem Chand, *A Translation of Kabir's Complete Bijak into English* (Calcutta, 1911). 'This is my work . . . squandering your treasure', cited in King, *One Language*, p. 137.

3. FAR PAVILIONS

The accounts of the communalization of Indian cricket are drawn from Lord Harris, *A Few Short Runs* (London, 1921); R. Guha, *A Corner of a Foreign Field: The Indian History of a British Sport* (London, 1999); A. Nandy, *The*

Tao of Cricket. On Games of Destiny and the Destiny of Games (Delhi, 2000); A. Appadurai, 'Playing with Modernity: The Decolonization of Indian Cricket', in his *Modernity at Large: Cultural Dimensions of Globalization* (Minneapolis, 2000); R. Cashman, *Patrons, Players and the Crowd: The Phenomenon of Indian Cricket* (Bombay, 1980).

For India during the First World War see D. C. Ellinwood and S. D. Pradhan (eds.), *India and World War I* (New Delhi, 1978) and essays in D. A. Low (ed.), *Soundings in Modern South Asian History* (London, 1968); J. M. Brown, *Gandhi's Rise to Power: Indian Politics 1915–1922* (Cambridge, 1972); M. H. Siddiqi, *Agrarian Unrest in North India: United Provinces 1918–22* (New Delhi, 1978); C. Baker, *The Politics of South India, 1920–27* (Cambridge, 1976). For contemporary accounts and memoirs see M. K. Gandhi, *Autobiography: The Story of My Experiments with Truth*, trans. M. Desai (1927, London, 1982) and J. Nehru, *An Autobiography with Musings on Recent Events in India* (first published 1936, reprinted London, 1989).

On the various terrorist movements and 'scares' of the era see: A. C. Bose, *Indian Revolutionaries Abroad, 1905–22* (Patna, 1971); E. C. Brown, *Har Dayal: Hindu Revolutionary and Rationalist* (Delhi, 1975); R. Hees *Nationalism, Terrorism, Communalism: Essays in Modern Indian History* (New Delhi, 1998); S. S. Josh, *Hindustan Ghadr Party: A Short History* (New Delhi, 1977); H. Chakrabarti, *Political Protest in Bengal: Boycott and Terrorism 1905–18* (Calcutta, 1992). For British perceptions of the 'extremist' threat see *The Sedition Committee* (Rowlatt): *Report into Revolutionary Violence* (Government of India, Delhi 1916); N. G. Barrier, *Banned. Controversial Literature and Political Control in British India 1907–47* (Minneapolis, 1974). For innovation in British modes of control see D. Omissi, *Air Power and Colonial Control: the Royal Air Force 1919–39* (Manchester, 1990). For the Amritsar or Jallianwala Bagh Massacre see the official *Hunter Commission Report* (Government of India, New Delhi, 1920); D. Sayer, 'British Reactions to the Amritsar Massacre 1919–20', *Past and Present*, 31 (1991).

For British constitutional policy see *Report on the Indian Constitutional Reforms* (Cmd. 9109, London, 1918); P. Robb, *The Government of India and Reform Policies towards Politics and the Constitution 1916–21* (London, 1976); S. R. Mehrotra, 'The Politics Behind the Montagu Declaration of 1917', in C. H. Philips (ed.), *Politics and Society in India* (London, 1973); E. S. Montagu, *An Indian Diary* (London, 1930).

For the economic impact of the First World War on the Raj see B. R. Tomlinson, *The Political Economy of the Raj, 1914–47: the Economics of Decolonization* (London, 1979). For British economic policy during and after the First World War see *Report of the Indian Industrial Commission, 1916–1918* (Delhi, 1919); *Report of the Committee on Indian Currency and Finance* (Delhi, 1920); *Report of the Royal Commission on Indian Currency and Exchange and Finance* (Delhi, 1926); *Report and Evidence of the Indian Tariff Board* (Delhi, 1927); *Royal Commission on Indian Agriculture* (Delhi, 1928); *Report of the Indian Central Banking Enquiry Committee* (Delhi, 1931); Maria Misra, *Business, Race and Politics in India, c. 1860–1960* (Oxford, 1999); C. Dewey, 'End of the Imperialism of Free Trade: Eclipse of the Lancashire Lobby and the Concession of Fiscal Autonomy to India', in Dewey and A. G. Hopkins (eds.), *The Imperial Impact: Studies in the Economic History of Africa and India* (London, 1978), and his 'The Government of India's "New Industrial Policy" 1900–1925: Formulation and Failure', in C. Dewey and K. N. Chaudhuri (eds.), *Economy and Society* (New Delhi, 1978); B. Chatterji, *Trade, Tariffs and Empire: Lancashire and British Politics in India 1919–39* (Delhi, 1992). For the effects of the Great Depression and ensuing agricultural crisis see *Royal Commission on Indian Agriculture*; C. J. Baker, *An Indian Rural Economy 1880–1955. The Tamilnad Countryside* (Oxford, 1984); S. Bose, *Agrarian Bengal. Economy, Social Structure and Politics, 1919–1947* (Cambridge, 1986); D. Rothermund, *India and the Great Depression, 1929–39* (Delhi, 1992). The extraordinary story of Frank Brayne and the Guragaon experiment is drawn from C. A. Dewey, *Anglo-Indian Attitudes: The Mind of the Indian Civil Service* (London, 1993), ch. 4.

On the emerging strength of Indian business and entrepreneurship between the wars see C. A. Bayly, *Rulers, Townsmen and Bazaars. North Indian Society in the Age of British Expansion 1770–1870* (Cambridge, 1983); C. Markovits, *Indian Business and Nationalist Politics, 1931–39: The Indigenous Business Class and the Rise of the Congress Party* (Cambridge, 1985); R. K. Ray, *Industrialization in India. Growth and Conflict in the Indian Corporate Sector, 1914–47* (Delhi, 1979); A. K. Bagchi, *Private Investment in India 1900–1939* (Cambridge, 1972). The story of Geddes' city beautification festival is drawn from N. Gooptu, *Politics of the Urban Poor in Early Twentieth-Century India* (Cambridge, 2001), pp. 77–82. I have also used this excellent monograph for sections on urbanization, along with R. Chandavarkar, *The Origins of Industrial Capital in India* (Cambridge, 1994); D. Chakrabarty, *Rethinking Working Class History. Bengal 1890–1940* (Princeton, 1989) and S. Basu, *Does Class Matter?* (Delhi, 2004). For a study of the changing nature of Hindu–Muslim violence between the wars see *East India (Cawnpore Riots): Report of the Committee of Enquiry and Resolution of the Government of the United Provinces* (Cmd. 3891, Delhi, 1931); *Report of the Bombay Riots Committee* (Bombay, 1929);

S. Das, *Communal Riots in Bengal 1905–1947* (Delhi, 1991) and P. K. Datta, *Carving Blocs: Communal Ideology in Early 20th Century Bengal* (Delhi, 1999).

For the operation of dyarchy see *Report of the Reforms Enquiry* (Delhi, 1924); R. J. Moore, *Crisis of Indian Unity 1917–1940* (Oxford, 1974), and his 'The Making of India's Paper Federation, 1927–35', in C. H. Philips and M. D. Wainwright (eds.), *The Partition of India. Policies and Perspectives 1935–47* (London, 1970), pp. 54–78; S. Gopal, *The Viceroyalty of Lord Irwin 1926–31* (Oxford, 1957); C. Bridge, *Holding India to the Empire. The British Conservative Party and the 1935 Constitution* (New Delhi, 1986). For Congress policy in the 1920s see B. R. Tomlinson, *The Indian National Congress and the Raj* (Basingstoke, 1979). For developments in the princely states see R. Jeffrey (ed.), *People, Princes and Paramount Power: Society and Politics in the Indian Princely States* (Delhi, 1978); J. Manor, *Political Change in an Indian State: Mysore 1917–55* (Delhi, 1977); S. R. Ashton, *British Policy towards the Indian States 1905–1938* (London and Dublin, 1982). For a literary memoir of life in a southern Indian state see E. M. Forster, *The Hill of Devi* (London 1953, reprinted 1984). For the development of the Unionist party in the Punjab see D. Gilmartin, *Empire and Islam: Punjab and the Making of Pakistan* (Berkeley, 1988). For Muslim politics between the wars see M. Hasan, *Nationalism and Communal Politics in India 1916–32* (Delhi, 1979); G. Minault, *The Khilafat Movement: Religious Symbolism and Political Mobilization in India* (New York, 1982); D. Page, *Prelude to Partition: All-India Muslim Politics, 1921–32* (Delhi, 1981); A. Jalal and A. Seal, 'Alternative to Partition: Muslim Politics between the Wars', in C. Baker, G. Johnson and A. Seal (eds.), *Power, Profit and Politics: Imperialism, Nationalism and Change in Twentieth-Century India* (Cambridge, 1981); A. Jalal, *The Sole Spokesman. Jinnah, the Muslim League and the Demand for Pakistan* (Cambridge, 1985); F. Shaikh, *Community and Consensus in Islam. Muslim Representation in Colonial India, 1860–1947* (Cambridge, 1989). For the paradoxical impact of separate electorates on Muslim political identities see D. Gilmartin, '"Divine Displeasure" and Muslim Electorates: The Shaping of Community in 20th Century Punjab', in D. A. Low (ed.), *The Political Inheritance of Pakistan* (London, 1991). On the ideological formation of the idea of Pakistan see C. M. Naim (ed.), *Iqbal, Jinnah and Pakistan: The Vision and the Reality* (Syracuse, N.Y., 1979).

Quotation Sources

'First the hunter . . . essay by Macaulay', A. Haslam, cited in Guha, *Foreign Field*. 'We must not play . . . is a Mahatma', N. M. Madruddin, March 1937 in *The Bombay Chronicle*, cited in Guha, *Foreign Field*, ch. 10. 'However much supporters . . . flow of trade', from George Schuster, 'Indian Economic Life: Past Trends and Future Prospects', *Journal of the Royal Society of Arts*, 83 (1935). 'The representative Indian . . .', Grigg, cited in Tomlinson, *Political Economy*, p. 91. '. . . we are all . . . a magic lantern', cited in Dewey, *Anglo-Indian Attitudes*, p. 93.'Intrigue seems the . . . His Excellency's heart', Reddi Naidu, May 1923, cited in C. J. Baker, *South India 1920–1940* (Cambridge, 1975), p. 50. 'This is a time . . . put down the Hindus forever', B. S. Moonje to M. R. Jayakar, 8 January 1930, cited in Moore, *Crisis*, p. 105. ' "Seeing people" . . . quantity of incense burnt', C. R. Reddy, *Dyarchy and After*, cited in Baker, *South India*, p. 41.

4. SPINNING THE NATION

For the symbolic meaning of *khadi* cloth see E. Tarlo, *Clothing Matters* (Chicago, 1994); S. Bean, 'Gandhi, *Khadi* and the Fabric of Indian Independence', in A. Weiner and J. Schneider (eds.), *Cloth and Human Experience* (London, 1989); C. A. Bayly, 'The Origins of Swadeshi (Home Industry): Cloth and Indian Society, 1700–1930', in A. Appadurai (ed.), *The Social Life of Things* (New York, 1988). For an account of the global crisis of empire in 1919 see J. D. Gallagher, 'The Decline, Revival and Fall of the British Empire', in A. Seal (ed.), *The Ford Lectures and Other Essays* (London, 1982). For the Home Rule Leagues see H. Owen, 'Towards Nationwide Agitation and Organisation: The Home Rule Leagues, 1915–18', in D. A. Low (ed.), *Soundings in Modern South Asian History* (London, 1968). For the Amritsar or Jallianwala Bagh Massacre see the official *Hunter Commission Report* (Government of India, New Delhi, 1920) and for a different interpretation, *Congress Punjab Inquiry Committee Report* (Delhi, 1920); see also D. Sayer, 'British Reactions to the Amritsar Massacre 1919–20', *Past and Present*, 31 (1991).

For Gandhi's life see J. M. Brown, *Gandhi, Prisoner of Hope* (New Haven, Conn. 1989). For Gandhi's ideas see M. K. Gandhi, *Autobiography: The Story of My Experiments with Truth*, trans. M. Desai (1927, London, 1982); A. Parel (ed.), *Hind Swaraj and other Writings* (Cambridge, 1997); B. Parekh,

Colonialism, Tradition and Reform (New Delhi, 1989) and his *Gandhi's Political Philosophy. A Critical Analysis* (London and Basingstoke, 1989). For a brilliant discussion of Gandhi's adaptation of Indian tradition to modern politics see L. I. and S. H. Rudolph, *The Modernity of Tradition. Political Development in India* (Chicago, 1967); for an intriguing analysis of Gandhi's ideas as the inversion of colonial 'orientalist' stereotypes see R. Fox, *Gandhian Utopia: Experiment with Culture* (Boston, 1989). For an alternative view that Gandhi transcends western influence to craft a truly indigenous nationalism see P. Chatterjee, *Nationalist Thought and the Colonial World. A Derivative Discourse* (London, 1986), ch. 2. See also A. Nandy, *The Intimate Enemy: Loss and Recovery of the Self Under Colonialism* (Delhi, 1983). For a fascinating account of Gandhi's use of contemporary western notions of health, hygiene and sanitation, including his adventures with the 'sitz' bath see J. Alter, *Gandhi's Body: Sex, Diet and the Politics of Nationalism* (Philadelphia, 2000). For Gandhi's views of gender and the role of women see P. Joshi, *Gandhi on Women* (Ahmedabad, 1988).

For the origins of the RSS and the Hindu nationalist right see V. D. Savarkar, *Hindutva: Who is a Hindu?* (1923, New Delhi, 1999); M. S. Golwalkar: *We, or Our Nationhood Defined* (1939, Nagpur, 1947); D. Keer, *Veer Savarkar* (2nd edition, Bombay, 1966); C. Jaffrelot, *The Hindu Nationalist Movement and Nationalist Politics, 1925 to the 1990s: Strategies of Identity Building, Implantation and Mobilization* (London, 1996); R. Gordon, 'The Hindu *Mahasabha* and the Indian National Congress, 1915–1926', *Modern Asian Studies*, 9 (1975). L. McKean, *Divine Enterprise: Gurus and the Hindu Nationalist Movement* (Chicago, 1996), ch. 3. For a broad study of populist leftwing movements see K. N. Panikar, *Left and Nationalist Movements in India* (Delhi, 1980). For Sampurnanand see his *Memories and Reflections* (London, 1962), and W. Gould, *Hindu Nationalism and the Language of Politics in Late Colonial India* (Cambridge, 2004). For Baghat Singh see his *Why I am an Atheist* (reprinted Delhi, 1974). For the Self-Respect movement, E.V. Ramaswami Naicker, *Essays on Religion and Society* (Madras, n.d); A. Diehl, *Periyar: E.V. Ramaswami Naicker* (Madras, 1978). For communism in the inter-war years see P. Ghosh, *The Meerut Conspiracy Case and the Left Wing in India* (Santa Barbara, 1974). For M. N. Roy see S. Roy, *India's First Communist* (Calcutta, 1988), and for communism in the south E. M. S. Namboodiripad, *How I Became A Communist* (Trivandrum, 1976), V. M. Fic, *Kerala: Yenan of India* (Delhi, 1984) and D. Menon, *Caste, Nationalism and Communism in South India* (Cambridge, 1994).

For Dalit politics see B. R. Ambedkar, *The Annihilation of Caste* (Bombay, 1936, reprinted New Delhi, 1990), and his equally pungent and incisive

What the Congress and Gandhi Have Done to the Dalits (Bombay, 1945). For a source-based account of Gandhi's anti-Untouchability campaign see Baren Ray (ed.), *Gandhi's Campaign Against Untouchability 1933–34: An Account From the Raj's Secret Official Records* (New Delhi, 1996). See also E. Zelliot, 'Gandhi and Ambedkar: A Study in Leadership', in J. Mahar (ed.), *The Dalits in Contemporary India* (Tucson, Ariz., 1972); F. Omvedt, *Dalits and Democratic Revolution: Dr Ambedkar and the Dalit Movement in Colonial India* (New Delhi, 1994) and C. Jaffrelot, *Dr Ambedkar and Untouchability: Analysing and Fighting Caste* (London, 2000). For Nehru see J. Nehru, *An Autobiography with Musings on Recent Events in India* (first published 1936, reprinted London, 1989); B. Zachariah, *Nehru: A Political Biography* (London, 2004). For Tagore see K. Dutta and A. Robinson, *Rabindranath Tagore: the Myriad-Minded Man* (London, 1997); R. Tagore, *Selected Short Stories*, trans. W. Radice (London, 1991); R. Tagore, *The Home and the World*, trans. S. Tagore (London, 1985). For his disagreements with Gandhi see R. Tagore, 'The Call of Truth', *The Modern Review*, 30 (1921).

For government intelligence views of the non-cooperation movement see P. C. Bamford, *Histories of the Non-cooperation and Khilafat Movements* (Delhi, 1925, reprinted Delhi, 1974). For scholarly interpretations of Gandhi's impact on the Indian national movement see J. M. Brown, *Gandhi's Rise to Power* (Cambridge, 1974), and her *Gandhi and Civil Disobedience: The Mahatma in Indian Politics 1928–34* (Cambridge, 1977); G. Krishna, 'The Development of the Indian National Congress as a Mass Organization, 1918–1923', *Journal of Asian Studies*, 3 (1966); S. Sarkar, 'The Logic of Gandhian Nationalism: Civil Disobedience and the Gandhi–Irwin Pact (1930–31)', *Indian Historical Review*, 3 (1976). For accounts of Gandhi's first *satyagraha* campaign in India see R. Kumar (ed.), *Essays on Indian Politics: The Rowlatt Satyagraha of 1919* (Oxford, 1971). For his involvement in the Khilafat Movement see G. Minault, *The Khilafat Movement: Religious Symbolism and Political Mobilization in India* (New York, 1982) and B. R. Nanda, *Gandhi: Pan-Islamism, Imperialism and Nationalism in India* (Delhi, 1989). For a highly original account of popular perceptions of Gandhi see S. Amin, 'Gandhi as Mahatma: Gorakhpur District, Eastern UP, 1921–22', in R. Guha, *Subaltern Studies III: Writings on South Asian History and Society* (Delhi, 1984), and his *Event, Metaphor, Memory: Chauri Chaura, 1922–1992* (Delhi, 1995). For the influential argument that the Indian National Congress appropriated and de-radicalised popular politics see Guha's *Subaltern Studies* series, volumes 1 to 5; for sympathetic but critical analysis of this approach see S. Sarkar, *'Popular' Movements and*

'Middle Class' Leadership in Late Colonial India: Perspectives and Problems of a 'History from Below' (Calcutta, 1983). For an illuminating study of the symbolism of Swadeshi see L. Trivedi, 'Visually Mapping the "Nation": Swadeshi Politics in Nationalist India, 1920–30', Journal of Asian Studies, 62 (2003).

On the regional differences in Congress mobilization during the non-cooperation and Civil Disobedience campaigns see D. A. Low (ed.), Congress and the Raj: Facets of the Indian Struggle 1917–47 (London, 1977); C. Baker, G. Johnson and A. Seal (eds.), Power, Profit and Politics: Essays in Imperialism, Nationalism and Change in 20th Century India (Cambridge, 1981); G. Pandey, The Ascendancy of Congress in Uttar Pradesh 1926–34. A Study in Imperfect Mobilization (Delhi, 1978); D. Hardiman, Peasant Nationalists of Gujarat: Kheda District 1917–1934 (Delhi, 1981); M. Siddiqi, Agrarian Unrest in North India: United Provinces 1918–22 (New Delhi, 1978); C. Baker, The Politics of South India, 1920–27 (Cambridge, 1976), and his 'Non-cooperation in South India', in Baker and D. Washbrook, South India: Political Institutions and Political Change 1880–1940 (Delhi, 1975); S. J. M. Epstein, The Earthy Soil. Bombay Peasants and Indian Nationalism 1919–47 (Delhi, 1988); D. E. U. Baker, Changing Political Leadership in an Indian Province. The Central Provinces and Berar 1919–39 (Delhi, 1979); D. Arnold, Congress in Tamilnad. Nationalist Politics in South India 1919–37 (London and Dublin, 1977).

For an analysis of the competing groups within Congress in the 1930s see B. R. Tomlinson, The Indian National Congress and the Raj (Basingstoke, 1976); see also the collection of essays edited by R. Sisson and S. Wolpert, Congress and Indian Nationalism. The Pre-Independence Phase (Berkeley and Los Angeles, 1988). For the propaganda battle between the British and Congress see M. Israel, Communication and Power: Propaganda and the Press in the Indian Nationalist Struggle 1920–47 (Cambridge, 1994). On ideological divisions within Congress see R. Som, Differences within Consensus: The Left and the Right in Congress, 1929–39 (New Delhi, 1995); Nehru, An Autobiography; S. C. Bose, The Indian Struggle 1920–42 (New York, 1964); G. D. Birla, In the Shadow of the Mahatma – A Personal Memoir (Calcutta, 1953); C. Markovits, Indian Business and Nationalist Politics, 1931–39: The Indigenous Business Class and the Rise of the Congress Party (Cambridge, 1985); Zachariah, Nehru; L. Gordon, Brothers Against the Raj: a Biography of Indian Nationalists Sarat and Subhas Chandra Bose (New York, 1990). Research into the 1937–39 Congress provincial ministries is still at an early stage, but among useful monographs is V. Damodaran, Broken Promises. Popular Protest, Indian Nationalism and the Congress

Party in Bihar, 1935–46 (Delhi, 1992), and a contemporary, partial but very colourful account of the Congress ministries may be found in R. Coupland, *Indian Politics 1936–42: Report on Constitutional Problems in India, Part II* (Oxford, 1943).

On the vexed relationship between Congress and India's Muslims see M. Hasan, '"Congress Muslims" and Indian Nationalism, Dilemma and Decline, 1928–34', *South Asia*, 1–2 (1985), and his 'The Muslim Mass Contacts Campaign. An Attempt at Political Mobilization', *Economic and Political Weekly*, 21 December 1986. A stimulating study of a Muslim region that did adopt Gandhian tactics is M. Bannerjee's *The Pathan Unarmed* (London, 2000).

Quotation Sources

'Hang Old Gandhi' is cited in Gandhi's *Autobiography*, part IV. 'I was a cruelly . . .', Gandhi, *Autobiography*, part I. 'What is the secret . . . life and death', *Collected Works of M. K. Gandhi (CWMKG)*, vol. 3. 'India cannot rival . . . necessary law of nature', *CWMKG*, vol. 13. 'Germany has shown . . . learn and profit by', M. Golwalkar, 1939, cited in Jaffrelot, *Hindu Nationalist Movement*, p. 55. '. . . a veritable chamber . . . bosom of Gandhism', from B. R. Ambedkar, *The Annihilation of Caste*, ch. 1. 'If only our idols . . . in our country' E.V. Ramaswami Naicker, 'Hinduism and Social Reforms' in his *Essays on Religion and Society*, p. 58. 'At Lucknow . . . ministers were doing', Coupland, *Indian Politics*, p. 113. 'Mahatmaji kept . . .', G. D. Birla, cited in M. M. Kudaisya, *Life and Times of G. D. Birla* (New Delhi, 2003), p. 169. 'Comrade Lenin . . .', V. Patel, in P. Chopra (ed.), *Collected Works of Vallabhbhai Patel*, Vol. VII (New Delhi, 1984).

5. A HOUSE DIVIDED

For the building of New Delhi see Robert Byron, *New Delhi: First Impression* (New Delhi, 1997); R. G. Irving, *Indian Summer: Lutyens, Baker and Imperial Delhi* (New Haven, Conn., 1982).

For India during the Second World War see J. H. Voigt, *India in the Second World War* (New Delhi, 1987); C. Bayly and T. Harper, *Forgotten Armies. Volume I: The Fall of British Asia 1941–4* (London, 2004); C. Bayly and T. Harper, *Forgotten Armies, Volume II: The End of Britain's Asian Empire* (London, 2007); D. A. Low (ed.), *The Political Inheritance of Pakistan*

(London, 1991); and, despite its title, S. Bhattacharya, *Propaganda and Information in Eastern India 1939–45: A Necessary Weapon of War* (Richmond, Va., 2001) also contains much useful material on the more general conduct of war by the British. For Linlithgow and British official attitudes to Congress on the announcement of war see R. J. Moore, 'British Policy and the Indian Problem, 1936–40', in C. H. Philips and M. D. Wainwright (eds.), *The Partition of India: Policies and Perspectives* (London, 1970); G. Rizvi, *Lord Linlithgow* (Oxford, 1980). For more on Victor Bayly's *Is India Impregnable?* (London, 1941), see Bayly and Harper, *Forgotten Armies. Vol. I*, p. 77. See also their comments on the continuation of British social life in India during the war, pp. 80–1. Though written later, Paul Scott's fictional *Raj Quartet* (London, 1975) is based on his memoirs as an officer in India. For wartime propaganda see M. Israel, *Communication and Power: Propaganda and the Press in the Indian Nationalist Struggle 1920–47* (Cambridge, 1994), and Bhattacharya, *Propaganda and Information*. For the inter-war crisis in the Indian Civil Service see D. C. Potter, *India's Political Administrators 1919–83* (Oxford, 1986), and his 'Manpower Shortage and the End of Colonialism. The Case of the Indian Civil Service', *Modern Asian Studies*, 7 (1973); A. Ewing, 'The Indian Civil Service 1919–24: Service Discontent and the Response in London and in Delhi', *Modern Asian Studies*, 18 (1984); S. Epstein, 'British Officers in Decline: The Erosion of British Authority in the Bombay Countryside, 1919–47', *Modern Asian Studies*, 16 (1982). An excellent set of accounts by ICS officers themselves of their lives after the 1919 reforms can be found in R. Hunt and J. Harrison, *The District Officer in India 1930–47* (Oxford, 1986).

For the fall of Singapore, see B. Farrell and S. Hunter (eds.), *Sixty Years on: the Fall of Singapore Revisited* (Singapore, 2002). For the Bengal Famine of 1943 see S. Bose, 'Starvation amidst Plenty: the Making of a Famine in Bengal, Hunan and Tonkin, 1942–45', *Modern Asian Studies*, 24 (1990); P. Greenough, *Prosperity and Misery in Modern Bengal. The Famine of 1943–44* (New York and Oxford, 1982); A. Sen, *Poverty and Famines: An Essay in Entitlement and Deprivation* (Oxford, 1981). For the Quit India Movement see G. Sahai, *42 Rebellion* (Delhi, 1947); A. Prasad, *Indian Revolt of 1942* (Delhi, 1958); F. G. Hutchins, *India's Revolution. Gandhi and the Quit India Movement* (Cambridge, Mass., 1973); P. N. Chopra (ed.), *The Quit India Movement: British Secret Reports* (Faridabad, 1976); M. Harcourt, 'Kisan Populism and Revolution in Rural India: the 1942 Disturbances in Bihar and Eastern UP', in D. A. Low (ed.), *Congress and the Raj: Facets of the Indian Struggle 1917–47* (London, 1977); G. Pandey (ed.), *The Indian Nation in 1942* (Calcutta, 1988).

For Bose and the Indian National Army see L. Gordon, *Brothers Against the Raj: a Biography of Indian Nationalists Sarat and Subhas Chandra Bose* (New York, 1990); P. W. Fay, *The Forgotten Army: India's Armed Struggle for Independence, 1942–45* (Ann Arbor, 1994); S. A. Das and K. B. Subbaiah, *Chalo Delhi! An Historical Account of the Indian Independence Movement in East Asia* (Kuala Lumpur, 1946); K. K. Ghosh, *The Indian National Army: Second Front of the Indian National Movement* (Meerut, 1969).

For the conduct of the war by the British after 1943 see B. Prasad (ed.), *Official History of the Indian Armed Forces in the Second World War* (Calcutta, 1956); J. Connell, *Auchinleck: a Biography of Field Marshal Sir Claude Auchinleck* (London, 1959); Tan Tai Yong, *The Garrison State: The Military, Government and Society in Colonial Punjab, 1849–1947* (New Delhi, 2005), ch. 7; A. Grajdansev, 'India's Wartime Economic Difficulties', *Pacific Affairs*, 16 (1983).

For the debate on the Cripps mission see R. J. Moore, *Churchill, Cripps and India, 1939–45* (Oxford, 1979), and H. V. Brasted and C. Bridge, 'The Transfer of Power in South Asia: An Historiographical Review', *South Asia*, 17 (1994). For a different view of the Cripps-Churchill initiative see P. Clarke, *The Cripps Version: the Life of Sir Stafford Cripps 1889–1952* (London, 2002).

The best published documentary source for the transfer of power era is N. Mansergh, E. W. R. Lumby and P. Moon (eds.), *Constitutional Relations Between Britain and India: The Transfer of Power 1942–47*, 12 vols. (London, 1970–83). For the various 'plans' of demission developed between 1944 and 1946 see P. Moon (ed.), *Wavell. The Viceroy's Journal* (London, 1973); R. J. Moore, *Escape from Empire. The Attlee Government and the Indian Problem* (Oxford, 1983); A. Campbell-Johnson, *Mission with Mountbatten* (London, 1951); L. Mosley, *The Last Days of the British Raj* (London, 1962). For the impact of Attlee see H. V. Brasted and C. Bridge, 'Labour and Transfer of Power in India: A Case for Reappraisal?' *Indo-British Review*, 14 (1988). An incisive analysis of the British economic calculations at this time may be found in B. R. Tomlinson, *The Political Economy of the Raj, 1914–47: the Economics of Decolonization* (London, 1979).

For the politics of Congress in the last two years of the Raj see S. Sarkar, 'Popular Movements and National Leadership 1945–47', in his *Critique of Colonial India* (Delhi, 1985). For the interesting view that Congress wanted a swift transfer to avert a feared revolution see A. K. Gupta, *Myth and Reality: The Struggle for Freedom in India 1945–47* (New Delhi, 1987). The scholarly controversy concerning Jinnah's motivations and intentions is now voluminous. For the revisionist view see A. Jalal, *The Sole Spokesman. Jinnah, the Muslim League and the Demand for Pakistan* (Cambridge, 1985) and A. Roy, 'The High Politics of India's Partition: The Revisionist Perspective', *Modern Asian Studies*, 24 (1990). For the older view that Pakistan was always Jinnah's 'bottom line' see A. I. Singh, *The Origins of the Partition of India 1936–47* (Oxford, 1987); Moore, *Escape from Empire*; and F. Shaikh, 'The Making of Pakistan', *Modern Asian Studies*, 20 (1986). For the acceleration of separatist politics in the Punjab see D. Gilmartin, *Empire and Islam: Punjab and the Making of Pakistan* (Berkeley, 1988), and for the development of separatist politics in Bengal see J. Chatterji, *Bengal Divided: Hindu Communalism and Partition, 1932–47* (Cambridge, 1994). For integration of the princely states see I. Copland, *Unwanted Allies. The Princes of India in the Endgame of Empire* (Cambridge, 1997); C. Corfield, *The Princely India I Knew. From Reading to Mountbatten* (Madras, 1975); V. P. Menon, *Story of Integration of Indian States* (Bombay, 1956). For the background to the Kashmir conflict see S. Bose, *Kashmir: Roots of Conflict, Paths to Peace* (Cambridge, Mass., 2003); R. J. Moore, *Making the New Commonwealth* (Oxford, 1987); C. Dasgupta, *War and Diplomacy in Kashmir, 1947–48*, (Delhi, 2002). A highly detailed account of the events surrounding the crisis can be found in A. Lamb, *Incomplete Partition: The Genesis of the Kashmir Dispute 1947–48* (Hertingfordbury, 1997).

Old but still useful essays on partition may be found in C. H. Philips and M. D. Wainwright (eds.), *The Partition of India. Policies and Perspectives 1935–47* (London, 1970). Interesting accounts by contemporaries include A. K. Azad, *India Wins Freedom* (London, 1988); H. V. Hodson, *The Great Divide. Britain-India-Pakistan* (London, 1969); C. Khaliquzzaman, *Pathway to Pakistan* (Lahore, 1961); G. D. Khosla, *Stern Reckoning: a Survey of the Events Leading up to and Following the Partition of India* (1947, reprinted Delhi, 1989). For an excellent account of the drawing of the Radcliffe boundary in Bengal see J. Chatterji, 'The Making of a Borderline: The Radcliffe Award for Bengal', in I. Talbot and G. Singh (eds.), *Region and Partition: Bengal, Punjab and the Partition of the Subcontinent* (New Delhi, 1999). For scholarly analyses see D. Gilmartin, 'Partition, Pakistan and South Asian History: in Search of a Narrative', *Journal of Asian Studies*, 57 (1998); M. Hasan (ed.), *India's Partition: Process, Strategy and Mobilization* (3rd edition, New Delhi, 1994); D. A. Low and H. Brasted (eds.), *Freedom, Trauma, Continuities: Northern India and Independence* (New Delhi, 1998); I. Talbot, *Provincial Politics and the Pakistan Movement. The Growth of the Muslim League in North-West and North-East India 1937–47* (Karachi, 1988); S. Settar and I. B. Gupta (eds.), *Pangs of Partition: Volume I, The Parting of the Ways* (Delhi, 2002). For the popular experience of partition see I. Talbot,

Freedoms' Cry: The Popular Dimension in the Pakistan Movement and Partition Experience in North-West India (Delhi, 1996). Manto's *Toba Tek Singh* is available in Sadat Hasan Manto, *Black Milk: A Collection of Short Stories*, trans. H. Jalal (Lahore, 1997). For analyses of the accompanying violence see M. Hasan (ed.), *Inventing Boundaries: Gender, Politics and the Partition of India* (Delhi, 2000); S. Settar and I. B. Gupta (eds.), *Pangs of Partition: Volume II, The Human Dimension* (Delhi, 2002); G. Pandey, *Remembering Partition* (Cambridge, 2001); S. Kaul (ed.), *The Partitions of Memory: The Afterlife of the Division of India*, (Bloomington, 2001). Work dealing especially with the experience of women includes U. Butalia, *The Other Side of Silence: Voices From the Partition of India* (London, 2000), and R. Menon and K. Bhasin, *Borders and Boundaries: Women in India's Partition* (New Delhi, 1998).

For the celebrations of Independence see J. Masselos, ' "The Magic Touch of Being Free", Rituals of Independence on August 15th', in his *The City in Action: Bombay Struggles for Power* (Delhi, 2007); Campbell-Johnson, *Mission with Mountbatten*; Tai Yong Tan and G. Kudaisya, *The Aftermath of Partition* (London, 2000), ch. 2. For Gandhi's final days and assassination see M. Pyarelal, *Mahatma: The Last Phase*, 2 vols. (Ahmedabad, 1956–58); N. K. Bose, *My Days with Gandhi* (Calcutta, 1953).

Quotation Sources

'. . . above the green tree tops . . . of the Renaissance, and the Moguls', Byron, *New Delhi*, ch. 1. 'Would Wren, . . . of her aborigines?' Lutyens; 'One rule confers order . . . ordained to supersede', Herbert Baker, both cited in Irving, *Indian Summer*. 'The Nazi power has arisen . . . Asiatic and African races', Gandhi 1941, *CWMKG*, vol. 76. '. . . the fall of Singapore finally . . . Empire had come', Prem Saghal, from *INA Heroes: The Autobiographies of Prem. K. Saghal and Colonel Gurbax Singh Dhillon of the Azad Hind Fauj* (Lahore, 1946), cited in Bayly and Harper, *Forgotten Armies: Vol. I*, p. 146. '. . . stain the children's faces', cited in Bhattacharya, *Propaganda*, p. 42. 'I have now heard . . . in any way molested', cited in Bhattacharya, *Propaganda*, p. 26. 'Looking back . . . type of native ruler', Leo Amery, cited in Mosley, *Last Days*. 'Twas Grillig . . .', Wavell, *Viceroy's Journal*. 'Shut up in a lonely mansion . . .', W. H. Auden, *Collected Works* (London, 1976), p. 604.'Three women . . . ripping them apart', F. W. Baynes, 1946, cited in Pandey, *Remembering Partition*, p. 71. 'At last . . .', T. F. Manazar, cited in Talbot, *Cry Freedom*, p. 200. 'The astrologers . . .', Mountbatten, cited in Tan and Kudaisya,

Aftermath, p. 32. 'We trust that . . .', *Dawn*, cited in Tan and Kudaisya, *Aftermath*, p. 60. In the mythological churnings . . . the deadly drink', Gandhi, 10 August 1947 in *Harijan*, cited in Tan and Kudaisya, *Aftermath*, p. 77.

6. THE LAST VICEROY

For this account of India's Republic Day celebrations I have drawn from S. Roy, 'Seeing a State: National Commemorations and the Public Sphere in India and Turkey', *Comparative Studies in Society and History*, 98 (2006), and S. Freitag, 'Visions of the Nation: Theorizing the Nexus: Creation, Consumption and Participation in the Public Sphere', in R. Dwyer and C. Pinney (eds.), *Pleasure and the Nation: The History, Politics, and Consumption of Public Culture in India* (New Delhi, 2002).

There are many biographies of Nehru including the compendious, if a little uncritical, official biography by S. Gopal, *Jawaharlal Nehru: a Biography* 3 vols. (London, 1975–84). See also J. M. Brown, *Nehru: A Political Life* (New Haven, Conn., 2003), which has used new private sources and is excellent on personal detail and family relationships. A biography based on personal acquaintance is M. Brecher's old but still stimulating, *Nehru: A Political Biography* (Oxford, 1959). More recent and strong on political context and ideas is B. Zachariah, *Nehru* (London, 2004). The best source for Nehru's ideas is still his own voluminous writings, including *An Autobiography with Musings on Recent Events in India* (first published 1936, reprinted London, 1989), *Glimpses of World History* (Allahabad, 1934–35, 14th impression, New Delhi, 1999), and *The Discovery of India* (Calcutta, 1946, revised edition New Delhi, 1999); see also G. Parthasarathi (ed.), *Letters to Chief Ministers, 1947–1964*, 5 vols. (Delhi, 1985–89), and S. Gopal (ed.), *Selected Works of Jawaharlal Nehru* (Delhi, 1952). For Nehru's ideas in the latter part of his career see R. K. Karanjia, *The Mind of Mr Nehru: An Interview* (London, 1969). For critical analyses of Nehru's thought see P. Chatterjee, *Nationalist Thought and the Colonial World. A Derivative Discourse* (London, 1986), ch. 3; M. Israel (ed.), *Nehru and the Twentieth Century* (Toronto, 1991); B. Parekh, 'Jawaharlal Nehru and the Crisis of Modernisation', in U. Baxi and B. Parkeh (eds.), *Crisis and Change in Contemporary India* (London, 1995). For the development of Nehru's ideas on development see P. Chaudhuri, 'The Origins of India's Development Strategy', in C. Simmons (ed.), *The Indian National Congress and the Political Economy of India, 1885–1985* (Aldershot, 1988). For his approach to religion and secularism see S. Khilnani, 'Nehru's Faith', in A. D. Needham and R. Sunder Rajan (eds.), *The Crisis of Secularism in India* (Durham, N.C., 2007). For a critical view of the essentially elitist nature of the Nehruvian project see S. Kaviraj, 'A Critique of the Passive Revolution', in P. Chatterjee (ed.), *State and Politics in India* (Delhi, 1997), and his 'On State, Society and Discourse in India', in J. Manor (ed.), *Rethinking Third World Politics* (Harlow, 1991). For a more sympathetic view see S, Khilnani, *The Idea of India* (London, 1997).

On Sardar Patel and the rightist dominance of Congress in the late 1940s and early 1950s see W. Gould, *Hindu Nationalism and the Language of Politics in Late Colonial India* (Cambridge, 2004); R. D. Shankardass, *Vallabhbhai Patel: Power and Organisation in Indian Politics* (Delhi, 1988); Francine Frankel, *India's Political Economy 1947–2004: The Gradual Revolution* (New Delhi, 2005), ch. 3; S. Das, 'The Indian National Congress and the Dynamics of Nation-Building: Aspects of Continuity and Change', in T. Sathyamurthy (ed.), *State and Nation in the Context of Social Change*, vol. 1 (Delhi, 1994). On communism and the Telengana uprisings see G. D. Overstreet and M. Windmiller, *Communism in India* (Berkeley and Los Angeles, 1959); P. Sundarayya, *Telengana People's Struggle and its Lessons* (Calcutta, 1972); Ravi Narayan Reddi, *Heroic Telengana: Reminiscences and Experiences* (New Delhi, 1973). On Nehru as Prime Minister see J. Manor (ed.), *Nehru to the Nineties: the Changing Office of Prime Minister in India* (London, 1994).

On the pre-history of planning see G. D. Birla, *Path to Prosperity: A Plea for Planning* (Allahabad, 1950); D. Washbrook, 'The Rhetoric of Democracy and Development in Late-Colonial India', in S. Bose and A. Jalal (eds.), *Nationalism, Democracy and Development: State and Politics in India* (Delhi, 1997); B. Zachariah, *Developing India: An Intellectual and Social History c. 1930–1950* (New Delhi, 2005). On the 'cult' of planning see R. Inden, 'Embodying God: from Imperial Progresses to National Progress in India', *Economy and Society*, 24 (1995). See also P. Chatterjee, 'Development Planning and the Indian State' in Chatterjee (ed.), *State and Poltiics*. For Mahalanobis see P. C. Mahalanobis, *Talks on Planning* (Bombay, 1961); B. Zachariah, 'The Development of Professor Mahalanobis', *Economy and Society*, 26 (1997); A. Rudra, *Prasanta Chandra Mahalanobis: a Biography* (Calcutta, 1996). For an excellent set of essays analysing the ideas and ideologies behind Indian economic policy see T. Byres (ed.), *The Indian Economy: Major Debates Since Independence* (Oxford, 1998). For detailed analysis of the processes and outcomes of planning see A. H. Hanson, *The Process of Planning: A Study of India's Five-Year Plans, 1950–64* (Oxford, 1966); T. Byres (ed.), *The State and Development Planning in India* (Delhi,

1994); P. Streeten and M. Lipton (eds.), *The Crisis of Indian Planning* (London, 1968). For a critical contemporary account see D. R. Gadgil, *Planning and Economic Policy in India* (Poona, 1961). For an evaluation of planning from a leftist perspective see Frankel, *India's Political Economy*, chs. 3–8. A lucid insider's assessment is provided by S. Chakravarty, *Development Planning: The Indian Experience* (Oxford, 1987). For the rural experience of planning and the relative failure of land reform see *Implementation of Land Reforms: A Review by the Land Reforms Implementation Committee of the National Development Council* (New Delhi, 1966); H. Maddick, *Panchayati Raj. A Study of Rural Local Government in India* (London, 1970); T. Metcalf, 'Landlords without Land: The U.P. Zamindars Today', *Pacific Affairs*, 40 (1967); W. C. Neale, *Economic Change in Rural India: Land Tenure and Reform in Uttar Pradesh, 1800–1955* (New Haven, Conn., 1962); D. Thorner, *Agricultural Cooperatives in India: A Field Report* (London, 1964); R. Herring, *Land to the Tiller: The Political Economy of Agrarian Reform in South Asia* (New Haven, Conn., 1983). For arguments about the impact of planning on the balance of class power see P. Bardhan, *The Political Economy of Development in India* (1984, revised edition 1998) [?]. For a stimulating comparative approach to the history of planning in India see V. Chibber, *Locked in Place: State-Building and Late Industrialization* (Princeton, 2003).

For a prescient but overly alarmist view of regionalist, caste and language politics see S. Harrison, *India: The Most Dangerous Decades* (Princeton, 1960). On language see R. D. King, *Nehru and the Language Politics of India* (Delhi, 1997). For an original comparison of India's and Pakistan's approaches to problems of regional integration see A. Jalal, *Democracy and Authoritarianism in South Asia: A Comparative Historical Perspective* (Cambridge, 1995).

On Congress organization see M. Weiner, *Party-Building in a New Nation: The Indian National Congress* (Chicago, 1967); S. A. Kochanek, *The Congress Party of India. The Dynamics of One-Party Democracy* (Princeton, 1968); P. Brass, *Factional Politics in an Indian State: The Congress Party in Uttar Pradesh* (Berkeley and Los Angeles, 1965). For the increasing power of dominant castes in Congress see G. Hawthorne, 'Caste and Politics in India since 1947', in D. MacGilvray (ed.), *Caste Ideology and Interaction* (Cambridge, 1982). For detailed regional analyses of shifting patterns of caste dominance in politics see the essays in F. Frankel and M. Rao (eds.), *Dominance and State Power in Modern India: Decline of a Social Order*, 2 vols. (Delhi, 1989 and 1990). For an analysis of the emergence and operation of the Congress 'boss' system see R. Kothari, *Politics in India* (Delhi, 1970) and A. Kohli, *Democracy and Discontent: India's Growing Crisis of Governability* (Cambridge, 1990). On the relationship between party and bureaucracy see D. C. Potter, *India's Political Administrators 1919–83* (Oxford, 1986); R. Taub, *Bureaucrats Under Stress: Administrators and Administration in an Indian State* (Berkeley and Los Angeles, 1969). For the view that despite its many shortcomings Congress acted as an integrating force in this era, see J. Manor, 'Parties and the Party System', in A. Kohli (ed.), *India's Democracy: An Analysis of Changing State-Society Relations* (Princeton, 1988).

For the DMK see N. Subramanian, *Ethnicity and Populist Mobilization: Political Parties, Citizens and Democracy in South India* (New Delhi, 1999); S. Ramaswamy, *Passions of the Tongue: Language Devotion in Tamil India, 1851–1970* (Berkeley, 1997); P. Price, 'Revolution and Rank in Tamil Nationalism', *Journal of Asian Studies*, 55 (1996). For MGR and an analysis of the political symbolism of his films see M. S. S. Pandian, *The Image Trap: M. G. Ramachandran in Film and Politics* (New Delhi, 1992); S. Dickey, *The Cinema of the Urban Poor in South India* (Cambridge, 1993).

On the formation and working of the Indian Constitution see G. Austin, *Working a Democratic Constitution, The Indian Experience* (Delhi, 1999); on the Hindu Code controversy see R. Som, 'Jawaharlal Nehru and the Hindu Code Bill: A Victory of Symbol over Substance?' *Modern Asian Studies*, 28 (1994); U. Baxi, 'Siting Secularism in the Uniform Civil Code: A "Riddle Wrapped Inside and Enigma"?' in Needham and Sunder Rajan, *The Crisis of Secularism*. On caste reservations see M. Galanter, *Competing Equalities: Law and the Backward Classes in India* (Delhi, 1991). For a critical view of the constitutional approach to 'secularism' see T. N. Madan, *Modern Myths, Locked Minds: Secularism and Fundamentalism in India* (New Delhi, 1987), ch. 8; G. J. Larson (ed.), *Religion and Personal Law in Secular India: A Call to Judgement* (Bloomington, 2001).

For a discussion of the gap between elite and popular political culture see S. Kaviraj, 'The Culture of Representative Democracy', in P. Chatterjee (ed.), *Wages of Freedom: Fifty Years of the Indian State* (New Delhi, 1998). For radio see D. Lelyveld, 'Upon the Sub-Dominant: Administering Music on All-India Radio', in C.A. Breckenridge (ed.), *Consuming Modernity: Public Culture in a South Asian World* (Delhi, 1996). For film see R. Vasudevan, 'Dislocations: The Cinematic Imagining of a New Society in 1950s India', *The Oxford Literary Review*, 16, 1–2 (1994); R. Dwyer and D. Patel, *Cinema India: The Visual Culture of Hindi Film* (New Delhi, 2002); D. Cooper, *The Cinema of Satyajit Ray: Between Tradition and Modernity* (Cambridge, 2000); C. Brosius and M. Butcher, *Image Journeys: Audio-Visual Media and*

Cultural Change in India (New Delhi, 1997); R. Vasudevan (ed.), *Making Meaning in Indian Cinema* (New Delhi, 2000); M. M. Prasad, *Ideology of Hindi Film* (New Delhi, 1998); A. Nandy (ed.), *The Secret Politics of Our Desires: Innocence and Culpability in Indian Popular Cinema* (New Delhi, 1998). For post-Independence architecture see J. Lang et al., *Architecture and Independence: The Search for Identity in India 1880–1980* (New Delhi, 1998); R. Kalla, *Chandigarh: The Making of an Indian City* (New Delhi, 1999). Kalla's *Bhubaneshwar: From Temple Town to Capital City* (New Delhi, 1994) gives an account of the ideological alternatives to Nehruvian high modernism.

For the unravelling of Nehruvian political and economic ideals in the later Nehru years see Frankel, *India's Political Economy*, ch. 6; for details of corruption scandals see J. B. Monteiro, *Corruption* (Bombay, 1966) and S. Kohli (ed.), *Corruption: The Growing Evil in India* (New Delhi, 1975). For the battles over the succession see M. Brecher, *Nehru's Mantle* (Westport, Conn., 1966) and K. Nayar, *India: The Critical Years* (Delhi, 1971). For a contemporary attack on Nehru from the right see M. Masani, *Congress Misrule and the Swatantra Alternative* (Delhi, 1996). On the Jana Sangh see C. Baxter, *The Jana Sangh* (Philadelphia, 1969). On foreign relations and the war with China see N. Maxwell, *India's China War* (London, 1970). For an attempt to analyse Nehru's attitude to China see J. S. Mehta's article in Israel (ed.), *Nehru and the Twentieth Century.*

Quotation Sources

'A new picture . . . that frightened me', Nehru, *Autobiography*, p. 57. 'This five-year plan . . . magic into the word', Nehru, *Glimpses*, p. 857. 'Roosevelt took . . . (though a democratic one)', Nehru, *Glimpses*, p. 928. 'Proceed[ing] scientifically . . . mathematical formula', Nehru 1960, cited in Karanjia, *Mind of Mr Nehru*, p. 49. 'I realized that . . . starving people', Nehru, cited in Zachariah, *Developing*, p. 238. '. . . each one . . . and they will be!' Nehru, cited in Karanjia, *Mind of Mr Nehru*, p. 46. '. . . looking to . . . different kind', Nehru, *Autobiography*, p. 471. 'Religion is . . .', *Autobiography*, p. 380. 'Having assured . . .', *All Parties Conference Report* (Delhi, 1928). 'India must break . . .', *Discovery*, p. 509. '. . . the rate of . . . outlook and tradition', Mahalanobis, cited in Rudra, *Mahalanobis*, p. 226. 'The most effective . . . its essential features', John Mathai to P. Thakurdas, December 1942, cited in Chibber, *Locked In Place*, p. 96. 'I do believe in co-operation . . . it into operation', Nehru, February 1959, *Lok Sabha Debates*, cited in

Frankel, *India's Political Economy*, p. 167. 'Our monied people . . .', Chibber, *Locked Minds*, p. 143. 'The better off . . .', cited in Hansen, *Process*. 'The oft-repeated story . . . listed as having sixty' and ' . . .many other . . . all manner of distempers', Nehru, cited in King, *Nehru and the Language of Politics*, pp. 97–140. 'The complaints . . . flippant and frivolous', cited in Frankel, *India's Political Economy*, p. 92. 'A battle of space . . .', Corbusier, cited in Kalia, *Chandigarh*, p. 113. 'Are the spaces human . . . Awaiting traffic', Aditya Prakash, cited in J. Lang et al., *Architecture and Independence*. 'My profession . . .', Nehru 1956, cited in King, *Language Politics*, p. 132. 'Why must I fight . . . tormented by grief', see *The Bhagavad Gita*, trans. W. J. Johnson (Oxford, 1994).

7. FLAMES

For *Sholay* see A. Chopra, *Sholay: The Making of a Classic* (Delhi, 2000); W. Dissanayake, *Sholay, a Cultural Reading* (Delhi, 1992); R. Dwyer and D. Patel, *Cinema India: The Visual Culture of Hindi Film* (New Delhi, 2002); M. M. Prasad, *Ideology of Hindi Film* (New Delhi, 1998); A. Nandy (ed.), *The Secret Politics of Our Desires: Innocence and Culpability in Indian Popular Cinema* (New Delhi, 1998).

For the electoral decline on Congress in 1967 see Francine Frankel, *India's Political Economy 1947–2004: The Gradual Revolution* (New Delhi, 2005), ch. 9; R. Kothari, *Politics in India* (London, 1970), and for the ensuing coalitions in some states see P. Brass, 'Coalition Politics in North India', *American Political Science Review*, 62 (1968). For the rise of agrarian populism see Charan Singh, *Joint Farming X-rayed: The Problem and its Solution* (Bombay, 1959); T. Byres, 'Charan Singh – An Assessment', *Journal of Peasant Studies*, 15 (1988); A. Gupta, *Post-Colonial Developments: Agriculture in the Making of Modern India* (Durham, N.C., 1998); A. Varshney, *Democracy, Development and the Countryside. Urban-Rural Struggles in India* (Cambridge, 1995). For analyses of the impact of the Green Revolution on Indian politics see T. Byres, 'The New Technology, Class Formation, and Class Action in the Indian Countryside', *Journal of Peasant Studies*, 8 (1981); C. H. Rao, *Technological Change and the Distribution of Gains in Indian Agriculture* (Delhi, 1975); P. Bardhan, *The Political Economy of Development in India* (1984, Delhi, 1999); L. I. and S. H. Rudolph, *In Pursuit of Lakshmi: The Political Economy of the Indian State* (Chicago, 1987).

On Naxalism see S. Ghosh, *The Naxalite Movement: A Maoist Experiment* (Calcutta, 1974); R. Ray, *The Naxalites and their Ideology* (New Delhi,

1988, 2nd edition 2002); M. Franda, *Radical Politics in West Bengal* (Cambridge, Mass., 1971); Mohan Ram, *Maoism in India* (New York, 1971). For the rise of private armies see S. Bayly, *Caste, Society and Politics in India from the Eighteenth Century to the Modern Age* (Cambridge, 1999), pp. 355–9.

For Indira in her own words, or those of her speechwriters, see I. Gandhi, *Democracy and Discipline: Speeches of Shrimati Indira Gandhi* (New Delhi, 1975) and *Selected Speeches and Writings, Vol. 3, September 1972–March 1977* (New Delhi, 1984). For a more intimate sense of her personality see D. Norman (ed.), *Indira Gandhi: Letters to a Friend 1950–1984* (London, 1985). There are several biographies, but in the absence of access to full official and personal sources these necessarily remain limited and a little speculative. For recent studies see K. Frank, *Indira: The Life of Indira Nehru Gandhi* (London, 2001); P. Jayakar, *Indira Gandhi: A Biography* (New Delhi, 1992); I. Malhotra, *Indira Gandhi: A Personal and Political Biography* (London, 1989); Z. Masani, *Indira Gandhi: A Biography* (London, 1975).

For an excellent analysis of the chaotic politics of the late 1960s and early 1970s see A. Kohli, *Democracy and Discontent: India's Growing Crisis of Governability* (Cambridge, 1990). For an exhaustive account of the Byzantine politics of defection in this era see S. C. Kashyap, *The Politics of Power, Defections and State Politics in India* (Delhi, 1974). For the Congress split see Frankel, *India's Political Economy*, ch.10; K. Nayar, *India: The Critical Years* (Delhi, 1971); T. N. Kunhi Krishnan, *Chavan and the Troubled Decade* (Bombay, 1971). For the shift in attitudes to caste dominance that underlay the 1971 election result see M. Robinson, *Local Politics: Law of the Fishes – Development Through Political Change in Medak District, Andhra Pradesh* (Delhi, 1988). For analyses of Indira Gandhi's policies and style in office see the essays in H. C. Hart (ed.), *Indira Gandhi's India* (Boulder, Colo., 1976). For accounts of the 'deinstitutionalization' of public life in these years see S. Kochanek, 'Mrs Gandhi's Pyramid: the New Congress', in Hart (ed.), *Indira Gandhi's India*; P. N. Haksar, *Premonitions* (Bombay, 1979) and Mohit Sen, *A Traveller on the Road: The Journey of an Indian Communist* (Delhi, 2003), esp. ch. 13 offer personal insights into Indira Gandhi's mind and motivation at this time.

For the JP Movement see Jayaprakash Narayan, *Towards Total Revolution*, 4 vols. (Bombay, 1978). For a flavour of the rhetoric of the era see R. K. Karanjia, *Indira–JP Confrontation: The Great Debate* (New Delhi, 1975). For a more analytical account see B. Chandra, *In the Name of Democracy: JP Movement and the Emergency* (Delhi, 2003); R. G. Fox, 'Gandhian Socialism, Hindu Identity and the JP Movement: Cultural Domination in the World System', *Journal of Commonwealth and Comparative Politics*, 25

(1987); J. R. Wood, 'Extra-Parliamentary Opposition in India: An Analysis of Populist Agitation in Gujarat and Bihar', *Pacific Affairs*, 48 (1975).

For lively contemporary accounts of the Emergency years see Dilip Hiro, *Inside India Today* (New York, 1977) and Kuldip Nayar, *The Judgement: Inside Story of the Emergency in India* (New Delhi, 1977); see also D. Selbourne, *An Eye to India: The Unmasking of a Tyranny* (London, 1977); Arun Shourie, *Symptoms of Fascism* (New Delhi, 1978). For judicious analyses of the Emergency see Chandra, *In the Name of Democracy*; Frankel, *India's Political Economy*, chs. 13 and 15; P. B. Mayer, 'Congress (I), Emergency (I): Interpreting Indira Gandhi's India', in R. Jeffrey et al. (eds.), *India: Rebellion to Republic: Selected Writings, 1857–1990* (New Delhi, 1990); B. Puri, 'Afterthoughts on the Emergency Debate', *Economic and Political Weekly*, 12 August 2000. For insider accounts see P. N. Dhar, *Indira Gandhi, the 'Emergency' and Indian Democracy* (New Delhi, 2000); Haksar, *Premonitions*; Sen, *A Traveller*; and B. L. Nehru, *Nice Guys Finish Second* (New Delhi, 1997). For details of the Emergency in Satara district I have relied on L. I. Schlesinger, 'The Emergency in an Indian Village', *Asian Survey*, 17 (1977). For the sterilization campaign in Delhi see E. Tarlo, *Unsettling Memories: Narrative of the Emergency in Delhi* (London, 2003). Some interesting evidence on the Emergency is available in Gangadharan et al., *The Inquisition: Revelations Before the Shah Commission* (New Delhi, 1978).

For analyses of the New Farmer Movements see Varshney, *Democracy, Development and the Countryside*; T. Brass (ed.), *New Farmers Movements in India*, (London, 1995); M. V. Nadkarni, *Farmers Movements in India* (Delhi, 1987). For the growing inequality in rural wealth and incomes see J. Breman, *Of Peasants, Migrants and Paupers: Rural Labour Circulation and Capitalist Production in West India* (Delhi, 1985) and Z. Hasan, 'Aspects of the Farmers' Movements in Uttar Pradesh in the Context of Uneven Capitalist Development in Indian Agriculture', in T. Sathyamurthy (ed.), *Industry and Agriculture in India since Independence* (Delhi, 1995).

For the Janata era see P. Chatterjee's insightful contemporary articles, reprinted in his *A Possible World: Essays in Political Criticism* (Delhi, 1997); Frankel, *India's Political Economy*, pp. 570–9; J. Wood (ed.), *State and Politics in Contemporary India: Crisis or Continuity?* (Boulder, Colo., 1984) and Rudolph and Rudolph, *In Pursuit of Lakshmi*. The description of experiments in intermediate technology comes from V. S. Naipaul, *India: A Wounded Civilization* (New Delhi, 1977), pp. 116–25.

For a socio-economic analysis of the regionalist crises of the 1970s and early 1980s see A. Vanaik, *The Painful Transition: Bourgeois Democracy in India* (London, 1990). For approaches that stress institutional problems see Jalal, *State of Martial Rule* (Cambridge, 1990); P. Brass, 'Pluralism, Regionalism and Decentralizing Tendencies in Contemporary Indian politics', in A. Wilson and D. Dalton (eds.), *The States of South Asia: Problems of National Integration* (London, 1982); P. Brass, *The Politics of India since Independence* (2nd edition, Cambridge, 1994). For the views of a frustrated insider see Nehru, *Nice Guys*. For the Punjab crisis see G. Singh, 'Understanding the Punjab Problem', *Asia Survey* (1992); S. S. Gill, 'Genesis of the Punjab Problem', *Economic and Political Weekly*, 7 April 1984; S. S. Gill, 'Agrarian Capitalism and Political Processes in Punjab', in Sathyamurthy (ed.), *Industry and Agriculture*; H. K. Puri, 'The Akali Agitation: An Analysis of the Socio-Economic Bases of Protest', *Economic and Political Weekly*, 22 January 1983; H. Telford, 'The Political Economy of the Punjab: Creating Space for Sikh Militancy', *Asia Survey* (1992). For the cultural dimension see J. Pettigrew, 'Take Not Arms Against Thy Sovereign: The Punjab Crisis and the Storming of the Golden Temple', *South Asia Research* (1984) and C. Mahmood, *Fighting for Faith and Nation: Dialogues with Sikh Militants* (Philadelphia, 1996). For a good narrative account of 'Operation Blue Star' see M. Tully and S. Jacob, *Amritsar: Mrs Gandhi's Last Battle* (London, 1985). The story of the rise of the *Dharmic* TV serials comes from A. Rajgopal, *Politics After Television: Hindu Nationalism and the Reshaping of the Public in India* (Cambridge, 2001), pp. 79–81.

Quotation Sources

'Will Mrs Gandhi . . .', *Statesman*, cited in Frank, *Indira*, p. 353. 'Nobody can throw . . . heart and being', Indira Gandhi, 1969, cited in Frank, *Indira*. 'My family . . . advantage of them', Indira Gandhi, 1967, cited in Frank, *Indira*, p. 303. 'What we witness . . . economic and social changes', Indira Gandhi, cited in Frankel, *Political Economy*, p. 427. 'In other countries . . . wiping them out' and 'I want to assure the rich . . . in their interests also', Indira Gandhi, cited in Nayar, *The Judgement*. 'There were some . . . have been allotted', Ram Das, cited in S. C. Dube, *In the Land of Poverty: Memoirs of an Indian Family* (London, 1998), p.104. 'Realize the strength . . . country will starve', George Fernandes, 1974, cited Dhar, *Emergency*, p. 241. 'If the Jan Sangh . . .', cited in Jaffrelot, *Hindu Nationalism*, p. 273. 'The issue of licences . . . cases for sterilization', Dr D. Banerji, October 1977, cited in Chandra, *In the Name of Democracy*, p. 204. 'Had Gandhiji . . .', cited in Frankel, *Political Economy*, p. 653. 'Intermediate technology . . . and usefulness', Naipaul, *India: A Wounded Civilization*, p.121.

8. LEVELLING THE TEMPLE

The description of Advani's *Rath Yatra* is drawn from C. Jaffrelot, *The Hindu Nationalist Movement and Nationalist Politics, 1925 to the 1990s: Strategies of Identity Building, Implantation and Mobilization* (London, 1996), pp. 416–20; T. B. Hansen, *The Saffron Wave: Democracy and Hindu Nationalism in Modern India* (Princeton, 1999), pp. 164–5; and R. H. Davis, 'The Iconography of Rama's Chariot', in D. Ludden (ed.), *Contesting the Nation: Religion, Community and the Politics of Democracy in India* (Philadelphia, 1996).

The degree of euphoria surrounding Rajiv's ascendancy can be gauged in I. Narain's, 'India in 1985: Triumph of Democracy', *Asian Survey*, 26 (1986). For more sober assessments of the Rajiv years see P. Chatterjee, *A Possible World: Essays in Political Criticism* (Delhi, 1997); Francine Frankel, *India's Political Economy 1947–2004: The Gradual Revolution* (New Delhi, 2005), pp. 677–87; S. Corbridge and J. Harriss, *Reinventing India* (Cambridge, 2000), ch. 5; James Manor, 'Parties and the Party System', in A. Kohli (ed.), *India's Democracy: An Analysis of Changing State-Society Relations* (Princeton, 1988); Hansen, *Saffron Wave*, ch. 4; V. Mehta, *Rajiv Gandhi and Rama's Kingdom* (New Haven, Conn., 1994); P. Chatterjee, *A Possible India: Essays in Political Criticism* (Delhi, 1997). For the rise of India's 'consuming' middle classes see S. Dubey, 'The Middle Classes', in P. Oldenburg and L. A. Gordon (eds.), *India Briefing* (Boulder, 1992). For V. P. Singh see S. Mustapha, *The Lonely Prophet. V.P. Singh, a Political Biography* (New Delhi, 1995).

For the history of caste reservation in India see C. Jaffrelot, *India's Silent Revolution: The Rise of the Lower Castes in North India* (London, 2003); S. Bayly, *Caste, Society and Politics in India from the Eighteenth Century to the Modern Age* (Cambridge, 1999), ch. 7; *Report of the Backwards Classes Commission* (K. Kalelkhar, Chairman), (1955, reprinted Delhi, 1983); *Report of the Backward Classes Commission* (B. P. Mandal, Chairman), 2 vols. (Delhi, 1981). On the OBC upsurge see Z. Hasan, *Oppositional Movements in Post-Congress Politics in Uttar Pradesh* (Delhi, 1998); M. Weiner in A. Kohli (ed.), *The Success of India's Democracy* (Cambridge, 2001); S. Mitra, 'Caste Democracy and the Politics of Community Formation in India', in M. Searle-Chatterjee and U. Sharma (eds.), *Contextualising Caste: Post-Dumontian Approaches* (Oxford, 1994); L. I. and S. H. Rudolph, *In Pursuit of Lakshmi: The Political Economy of the Indian State* (Chicago, 1987), chs. 4–6, 12–13; T. Sathyamurthy (ed.), *Social Change and Political Discourse in*

India, Vol. III: Region, Religion, Caste, Gender and Culture in Contemporary India (Delhi, 1996), esp. essay by Suresh. On the high caste backlash see S. Mitra, 'The Perils of Promoting Equality: the Latent Significance of Anti-Reservations Movement in India', *Journal of Commonwealth and Comparative Politics*, 25 (1987). For background on Bihar see P. K. Chaudhary and Shrikant, *Bihar mein Samajik Parivartan ke Kuch Aayaam* (New Delhi, 2001). On caste identities see B. P. Yadav, *Ahir Jati Ke Niyamavali* (Benares, *Vikram Samvat* 1984, *c.* 1927). For OBC leadership see A. Kumar, *Laloo Prasad Yadav. Aaj ke netal/Alochnatmak Adhyaynamala* (New Delhi, 1994); S. Thakur, *The Making of Laloo Yadav: The Unmaking of Bihar* (New Delhi, 2000); R. Singh and A. Yadav, *Mulayam Singh. A Political Biography* (New Delhi, 1998).

On Dalits see Kanshi Ram, *The Chamcha Age – An Era of Stooges* (New Delhi, 1982); B. R. Joshi's overview article in D. Allen (ed.), *Religion and Political Conflict in South Asia* (Westport, 1992), and her edited collection *Dalit! Voices of the Dalit Liberation Movement* (Delhi, 1986); G. Omvedt, *Reinventing Revolution: New Social Movements and the Socialist Tradition in India* (Delhi, 1993); Bayly, *Caste, Society and Politics*, chs. 7–9; M. Galanter, *Competing Equalities: Law and the Backward Classes in India* (Delhi, 1991), ch. 16; M. Jurgensmeyer, *Religion as Social Vision* (New York, 2005); O. Mendelsohn and M. Vicziany, *Dalits: Subordination, Poverty and the State in Modern India* (Cambridge, 1998); P. Kumar, 'Dalits and the BSP in Uttar Pradesh: Issues and Challenges', *Economic and Political Weekly*, 3 April 3 1999; G. Shah (ed.), *Dalit Identity and Politics* (Delhi, 2001). The account of the Hindu nationalist attacks on Kentucky Fried Chicken come from T. Hansen, 'The Ethics of Hindutva and the Spirit of Capitalism', in C. Jaffrelot (ed.), *The Sangh Parivar: A Reader* (New Delhi, 2005), p. 383.

For the intellectual and academic debates between proponents and opponents of liberalization see T. Byres (ed.), *The Indian Economy: Major Debates Since Independence* (Oxford, 1998). For the neo-liberal view see J. Bhagwati, *India in Transition: Freeing the Economy* (Oxford, 1993) and for a trenchant critique see Corbridge and Harriss, *Reinventing India*, ch. 7, who also analyse the nature of the economic crisis of the early 1990s, as does Frankel, *India's Political Economy*, pp. 585–95. On the origins of economic liberalization in the Rajiv era see A. Kohli, *Democracy and Discontent: India's Growing Crisis of Governability* (Cambridge, 1990), ch. 11. For the view that liberalization was made possible by the distraction of Mandal-*Mandir* politics see A. Varshney, 'Mass Politics or Elite Politics? India's Economic Reforms in Comparative Perspective', in J. D. Sachs, A. Varshney, N. Bajpai (eds.), *India in the Era of Economic Reforms* (Delhi, 1999). See also B. R. Nayar, 'The Politics of Economic Restructuring in India', *Journal of Commonwealth and Comparative Politics* (1992), and his *Globalisation and Nationalism: The Changing Balance in India's Economic Policy, 1950–2000* (New Delhi, 2001). For the theory of liberalization by stealth see R. Jenkins, *Democratic Politics and Economic Reform in India* (Cambridge, 1999). For a positive view see Sachs et al. (eds.), *India in the Era of Economic Reform*. For liberal voluntarism see G. Das, *India Unbound* (New Delhi, 2000). For Chandrababu Naidu's Vision 2020 document see *http://www.aponline.gov.in/quick%20links/vision2020/.html*, modelled on A. P .J. Abdul Kalam, *India 2020: A Vision for the New Millennium* (New Delhi, 1998); L. I. and S. H. Rudolph, 'The Iconization of Chandrababu: Sharing Sovereignty in India's Federal Market Economy', *Economic and Political Weekly*, 5 May 2001; A. Wyatt, 'Re-narrating Indian Development: Economic Nationalism in the 1950s and the 1990s', Paper presented to the Institute of Commonwealth Studies and Birkbeck School of Politics and Sociology Seminar, 13 November 2004.

For the history of the Ayodhya dispute see P. van der Veer, *Religious Nationalism: Hindus and Muslims in India* (Berkeley, 1994). On the TV *Ramayana* and the rise of Hindu nationalist politics see A. Rajgopal, *Politics After Television: Hindu Nationalism and the Reshaping of the Public in India* (Cambridge, 2001). On the changing image of Ram see A. Kapur, 'Deity to Crusader: The Changing Iconography of Ram', in G. Pandey (ed.), *Hindus and Others: The Question of Identity in India Today* (New Delhi, 1993). For the impact of TV on cultural and political change more generally see L. Babb and S. Wadley (eds.), *Media and the Transformation of Religion* (Philadelphia, 1995); C. A. Breckenridge (ed.), *Consuming Modernity: Public Culture in a South Asian World* (Minneapolis, 1995); L. Rudolph, 'The Media and Cultural Politics', in H. A. Gould and S. Ganguly (eds.), *India Votes: Alliance Politics and Minority Governments in the Ninth and Tenth General Elections* (Delhi, 1993). On riots and the generation of political violence, see S. J. Tambiah, *Levelling Crowds: Ethnonationalist Conflicts and Collective Violence in South Asia* (Berkeley, 1996); S. I. Wilkinson, *Votes and Violence: Electoral Competition and Ethnic Riots in India* (Cambridge, 2004).

On the rise of the BJP see J. McGuire and P. Reeves (eds.), *South Asia* Special Issue: After Ayodhya, 17 (1994); T. Basu et al., *Khaki Shorts and Saffron Flags: A Critique of the Hindu Right* (New Delhi, 1993); Jaffrelot, *The Hindu Nationalist Movement* and the collection of essays edited by him *The Sangh Parivar*. See also D. Ludden (ed.), *Contesting the Nation: Religion, Community and the Politics of Democracy in India* (Philadelphia, 1996);

A. Vanaik, *The Furies of Indian Communalism: Religion, Modernity and Secularization* (London, 1997). For BJP ideology see Y. K. Malik and V. B. Singh, *Hindu Nationalists in India: The Rise of the Bharatiya Janata Party* (Boulder, Colo., 1994), ch. 4. On the BJP's connections with the Indian diaspora see I. Therwath, '"Far and Wide": The Sangh Parivar's Global Network', in Jaffrelot (ed.), *The Sangh Parivar*. For accounts of the BJP's extraordinary women rhetoricians see P. Bacchetta, 'Hindu Nationalist Women as Ideologues: The "Sangh", the "Samiti" and their Differential Concepts of the Indian Nation', in Jaffrelot (ed.), *The Sangh Parivar*. For an analysis of Hindu nationalist politics in Bombay/Mumbai and how that city came to change its name see T. B. Hansen, *Wages of Violence: Naming and Identity in Post-Colonial Bombay* (Princeton, 2001). For the biased and sensationalized reporting of the VHP campaigns see *Swatantra Bharat*, 30 October 1990 and 27 November 1990, and *Aaj*, 27 November 1990.

For the BJP in government see J. McGuire and I. Copland (eds.), *Hindu Nationalism and Governance* (New Delhi, 2007). On BJP cultural politics see T. Jayaram, 'Vedic Astrology and all that', *Frontline*, 12–25 May 2001; S. Watkins, 'Saffron Gastonomy', *New Left Review*, 17 (2002); M. Hasan, 'The BJP's Intellectual Agenda: Textbooks and Imagined History', in McGuire and Copland (eds.), *Hindu Nationalism*; P. Chatterjee, 'History and the Nationalization of Hinduism', in V. Dalmia and H. von Stietencron (eds.), *Representing Hinduism: The Construction of Religious Traditions and National Identity* (New Delhi, 1995); T. Sarkar, 'Educating the Children of the Hindu Rashtra: Notes on RSS Schools', in Jaffrelot (ed.), *The Sangh Parivar*. On the nuclear bomb tests see A. Roy, 'Domestic Politics and National Security', in *Economic and Political Weekly*, 7 July 1998; S. Sarkar, 'The BJP Bomb and Aspects of Nationalism', *Economic and Political Weekly*, 14 July 1998. On the broader background to India's rise to nuclear power see I. Abraham, *The Making of the Indian Atom Bomb: Science, Secrecy and the Post-Colonial State* (London, 1997); A. Vanaik and P. Bidwai, *New Nukes: India, Pakistan and Global Nuclear Disarmament* (New York, 1999). For the Kashmir imbroglio see B. Puri, *Kashmir: Towards Insurgency* (London, 1993); R. G. Thomas (ed.), *Perspectives on Kashmir: The Roots of Conflict in South Asia* (Boulder, Colo., 1992); S. Widmalm, 'The Rise and Fall of Democracy in Jammu and Kashmir, 1957–89', in A. Basu and A. Kohli (eds.), *Community Conflicts and the State in India* (New Delhi, 1998).

On the BJP's economic policy, see L. K. Advani, 'Globalisation on the Solid Foundation of Swadeshi', Lecture delivered to the 71st annual session of the Federation of Indian Chambers of Commerce and Industry, 25 October, 1998; Nayar, *Globalisation and Nationalism*, ch. 7; Hansen, 'The ethics of

Hindutva', in Jaffrelot (ed.), *The Sangh Parivar*. For the BJP's economic performance in government see Frankel, *India's Political Economy*, pp. 723–39; P. Mayer, 'The Hindu Rate of Reform: Privatization under the BJP – still waiting for that *Bada Kadam*', in McGuire and Copland (eds.), *Hindu Nationalism*. J. Mooij (ed.), *The Politics of Economic Reforms in India* (New Delhi, 2005). For the Godhra incident and its aftermath see Frankel, *India's Political Economy*, pp. 739–70; P. Brass, 'The Gujarat Pogrom of 2002', *Items and Issues*, Social Science Research Council, 4 (2002–03); M. L. Sondhi and A. Mukarji (eds.), *The Black Book of Gujarat* (New Delhi, 2002); National Human Rights Commission, *Proceedings*, 31 May 2002 at *http:// nhrc.nic.in/gujfinalorder.htm*. A summary of the findings of the Concerned Citizens' Tribunal can be found at *http://www.pucl.org/Topics/Religion-communalism/2003/gujarat-tribunal-report.htm*.

Quotation Sources

'Only a few . . . much shorter period', cited in Varshney, 'Mass Politics'. 'We don't want foreign . . .', cited in Mehta, *Rajiv*, p. 137. 'Many socialists . . . have to be killed', R. Lohia, 1953, from 'Class Organisations: Instruments to Abolish Caste' in *The Caste System*, p. 20. 'When everybody. . .so far been oppressed', Lohia, 1958, from 'Towards the Destruction of Castes and Classes', in Lohia *The Caste System* (Hyderabad, 1964), p. 96. 'ancient Aryans . . .', cited in Jaffrelot, *Silent Revolution*, p. 195. 'dull, miserly, loudmouthed . . .', cited in Jaffrelot, *Silent Revolution*, p. 188. 'With the establishment . . . never at the cost of efficiency', G. B. Pant, 1961, cited in Jaffrelot, *Silent Revolution*, p. 228. 'These people . . . revolution in Bihar', Laloo, cited in Thakur, *Making of Laloo*, p. 85. 'Look at my . . . of self-respect', Laloo, quoted in Thakur, *Making of Laloo*, p. 91. 'Tilak, Tarahu . . . Joote char', is from Kanshi Ram, *Bahujan Samaj ke lye asha ki kiran* (New Delhi, 1992), and cited in Jaffrelot, *Silent Revolution*, p. 397. 'Every morning Naidu . . . Chandrababu Naidu speaking' and '. . . we are trying to . . . stages of development' are from A. Singhal and E. M. Rogers, *India's Communication Revolution: From Bullock Carts to Cyber Marts* (New Delhi, 2001). 'German national pride . . . profit by', and 'We live in strange times . . . abyss of degeneration' M. S. Golwalkar, *We, or Our Nationhood Defined* (Nagpur, 1947), pp. 1, 6. 'People know . . . and all that', 'Promotions are . . . uncultured people', 'The havoc . . . caste divide', 'Hindus over . . . what is theirs', and 'Premanufactured bricks . . . villages that way', are from interviews with Maharashtrian and Mumbai residents in the early 1990s and articles in *The Organiser*, cited in Hansen, *Saffron Wave*, ch. 5. 'Attackers in their ... in the mob's way', Sondhi and Mukarji, *Black Book of Gujarat*, p. 219. 'The swadeshi ... international area', M. M. Joshi, August 1998, cited in Frankel, *India's Political Economy*, p. 730.

EPILOGUE

For an analysis of the 2004 election results see Yogendra Yadav, 'Radical Shift in the Social Basis of Political Power', *The Hindu*, 20 May 2004. For an overview of recent political and economic developments I have drawn on Oxford Analytica and Oxford Economics, *India: A Five Year Outlook* (private publication, Oxford, September 2006). For early academic assessments of the prospects for liberalization see M. E. John, P. V. Kumar Jha and S. S. Jodhka (eds.), *Contested Transformations: Changing Economic Identities in Contemporary India* (New Delhi, 2006); T. Dyson, R. Cassen and L. Visaria (eds.), *Twenty-First Century India, Population, Economy, Human Development and the Environment* (Oxford, 2004). For analyses of the impact of liberalization and globalization on various strata of Indian society see B. Harris-White and S. Janakarajan, *Rural India Facing the 21st Century: Essays on Long Term Village Change and Recent Development Policy* (London, 2005); J. Breman, *Footloose Labour: Working in India's Informal Economy* (Cambridge, 1996); J. Assayag and C. J. Fuller (eds.), *Globalizing India: Perspectives from Below* (London, 2005); L. Fernandes, *India's New Middle Class: Democratic Politics in an Era of Reform* (Minneapolis, 2006). For the Nehru-Gandhi dynasty see S. S. Gill, *The Dynasty: A Political Biography of the Premier Ruling Family of Modern India* (New Delhi, 1996) and I. Malhotra, *Dynasties of India and Beyond* (New Delhi, 2003). For assessments of India's post-BJP politics see M. Vicziany (ed.), *South Asia*, 28 (2005) Special Issue: India At the Dawn of the Twenty-First Century: The Tough Question; K. Chandra, *Why Ethnic Parties Succeed: Patronage and Ethnic Head Counts in India* (Cambridge, 2004); M. Hasan (ed.), *Will Secular India Survive?* (New Delhi, 2004). For India's great power prospects see B. R. Nayar and T. V. Paul, *India in the World Order: Searching for Major-Power Status* (Cambridge, 2003). The rise of Hanuman is brilliantly told in P. Lutgendorf, *Hanuman's Tale: The Message of a Divine Monkey* (New York, 2007), and the saga of competitive Hanuman *murthi* building comes from this source, pp. 3–9. The devotional couplets to Hanuman are extracted from *Hanuman Calisa* (Forty Verses to Hanuman), attributed to Tulsidas.

Index

PENGUIN POLITICS

THE SHADOW OF THE SUN
RYSZARD KAPUŚCIŃSKI

'Written with love and longing, as sharp and life-enhancing as the sun that rises on an African morning' *Sunday Times*

'For more than forty years, Ryszard Kapuściński has been the definitive voice on all things African ... Almost every page in this book comes alive with his quick brilliance ... He brings the world to us as nobody else' Ian Jack, *Observer*

'One of the finest books I have ever read about Africa ... Kapuściński has been visiting Africa as a journalist since 1957 ... he has avoided "official routes, important personages and high-level politics" ... it is here, in the margins, that Kapuściński has achieved something no other commentator I know of has done' Justin Cartwright, *Daily Mail*

'He has V. S. Naipaul's gift for characterization and Isaac Babel's openness to life-threatening experience ... *The Shadow of the Sun* is an indispensable book for anyone interested in great humanitarian writing about an indefinable continent' Russell Celyn Jones, *The Times*

PENGUIN HISTORY

THE NEW PENGUIN HISTORY OF THE WORLD
J. M. ROBERTS

A book of breathtaking range by the pre-eminent giant-scale historian of our age. One of the most extraordinary history bestsellers on the Penguin list, John Roberts's book has now been completely updated to the end of the last century and revised throughout to make sure it keeps its amazing appeal to a new generation of readers. The entire text has been overhauled to take account of the great range of discoveries that have changed our views on early civilizations and to bring it fully up-to-date. The book has also been completely redesigned and reset. The result is a book that is both an essential work of reference for anyone with the slightest historical interest and a great reading experience.

'A stupendous achievement – the unrivalled World History for our day. It extends over all ages and all continents. It covers the forgotten experiences of ordinary people as well as chronicling the acts of those in power. It is unbelievably accurate in its facts and almost incontestable in its judgements'
A. J. P. Taylor, *Observer*

'A work of outstanding breadth of scholarship and penetrating judgements. There is nothing better of its kind' Jonathan Sumption, *Sunday Telegraph*

'This is a book I would like to put into the hands of anyone interested in the past' Alan Bullock

'Anyone who wants an outline grasp of history, the core of all subjects, can grasp it here' *Economist*

PENGUIN HISTORY

EMPIRE: HOW BRITAIN MADE THE MODERN WORLD
NIALL FERGUSON

Once, vast swathes of the globe were coloured imperial red and Britannia ruled not just the waves, but the prairies of America, the plains of Asia, the jungles of Africa and the deserts of Arabia. Just how did a small, rainy island in the North Atlantic achieve all this? And why did the empire on which the sun literally never set finally decline and fall? Niall Ferguson's acclaimed *Empire* brilliantly unfolds the imperial story in all its splendours and its miseries, showing how a gang of buccaneers and gold-diggers planted the seed of the biggest empire in history – and set the world on the road to modernity.

'The most brilliant British historian of his generation … Ferguson examines the roles of "pirates, planters, missionaries, mandarins, bankers and bankrupts" in the creation of history's largest empire … he writes with splendid panache … and a seemingly effortless, debonair wit' Andrew Roberts, *The Times*

'Thrilling … an extraordinary story' *Daily Mail*

'A brilliant book … full of energy, imagination and curiosity' *Evening Standard*

'A remarkably readable précis of the whole British imperial story – triumphs, deceits, decencies, kindnesses, cruelties and all' Jan Morris

'Dazzling … wonderfully readable' *New York Review of Books*

'An enormous saga … crammed with the kind of anecdotes that leave the reader wanting more' *Sunday Herald*

PENGUIN PHILOSOPHY

THE ARGUMENTATIVE INDIAN
AMARTYA SEN

'Sen is unquestionably one of the most distinguished minds of our time … The product of a great mind at the peak of its power, this is one of the most stimulating books about India to be written for years, and deserves the widest possible readership' William Dalrymple, *Sunday Times*

India is a country with many distinct pursuits, vastly different convictions, widely divergent customs and viewpoints. *The Argumentative Indian* brings together an illuminating selection of writings from Nobel prize-winning economist Amartya Sen that outline the need to understand contemporary India in the light of its long argumentative tradition.

Sen argues for the success of India's democracy, the defence of its secular politics, the removal of inequalities related to class, caste, gender and community, and the pursuit of sub-continental peace.

He just wanted a decent book to read ...

Not too much to ask, is it? It was in 1935 when Allen Lane, Managing Director of Bodley Head Publishers, stood on a platform at Exeter railway station looking for something good to read on his journey back to London. His choice was limited to popular magazines and poor-quality paperbacks – the same choice faced every day by the vast majority of readers, few of whom could afford hardbacks. Lane's disappointment and subsequent anger at the range of books generally available led him to found a company – and change the world.

'We believed in the existence in this country of a vast reading public for intelligent books at a low price, and staked everything on it'
Sir Allen Lane, 1902–1970, founder of Penguin Books

The quality paperback had arrived – and not just in bookshops. Lane was adamant that his Penguins should appear in chain stores and tobacconists, and should cost no more than a packet of cigarettes.

Reading habits (and cigarette prices) have changed since 1935, but Penguin still believes in publishing the best books for everybody to enjoy. We still believe that good design costs no more than bad design, and we still believe that quality books published passionately and responsibly make the world a better place.

So wherever you see the little bird – whether it's on a piece of prize-winning literary fiction or a celebrity autobiography, political tour de force or historical masterpiece, a serial-killer thriller, reference book, world classic or a piece of pure escapism – you can bet that it represents the very best that the genre has to offer.

Whatever you like to read – trust Penguin.

read more
www.penguin.co.uk